CORRESPONDENCE OF WILLIAM SHIRLEY

PRO · REGE · ET · REPUBLICA ·

1. SHIRLEY.	5. BREWSE of Wenham.	9. VALERS.	13. BASSET of Chaddesford.
2. WALDESHEF.	6. BREWSE of Fressingfield.	10. BAVENT.	14. RYDELL.
3. BASSET of Blore.	7. MILO.	11. WISTOWE.	15. BRAYLESFORD.
4. RYDELL.	8. NEWMARCH.	12.	16. TWYFORD.

THE COAT OF ARMS OF THE SHIRLEY FAMILY

CORRESPONDENCE OF WILLIAM SHIRLEY

GOVERNOR OF MASSACHUSETTS

AND

MILITARY COMMANDER IN AMERICA

1731–1760

EDITED UNDER THE AUSPICES OF

THE NATIONAL SOCIETY OF THE COLONIAL DAMES OF AMERICA

BY

CHARLES HENRY LINCOLN, Ph.D.

TWO VOLUMES

Vol. II

New York

THE MACMILLAN COMPANY

1912

A Facsimile Reprint
Published 2003 by

HERITAGE BOOKS, INC.
1540E Pointer Ridge Place
Bowie, Maryland 20716
1-800-398-7709
www.heritagebooks.com

ISBN 0-7884-2340-1

A Complete Catalog Listing Hundreds of Titles
On History, Genealogy, and Americana
Available Free Upon Request

CONTENTS

CONTENTS

CONTENTS

CONTENTS

CONTENTS

CONTENTS

CONTENTS

xi

CONTENTS

CONTENTS

CONTENTS

CONTENTS

CONTENTS

xvi

CONTENTS

CONTENTS

ILLUSTRATIONS

CORRESPONDENCE OF WILLIAM SHIRLEY

WILLIAM SHIRLEY TO THE DUKE OF NEWCASTLE [1]

St. James's Street, Novr. 23, 1752.

My Lord Duke,

Having lately taken the liberty to beg of your Grace to favour my application for the government of the Leeward Islands, and inclos'd a letter from Mr. Western to your Grace upon that subject; That I may trespass, as little as may be, upon your Grace's time, I beg leave to lay before you a state of the grounds of my request, before I have the honour of waiting upon your Grace again.

Before I had any pretensions of publick service to recommend me to your Grace's protection, your Grace was pleas'd in mere Goodness to me to procure me the government of the Massachusetts Bay in New England. The Factious Temper of the people there towards their former Governours, and the Distracted state of the Affairs of the province, when I had the honour of being appointed to the government, with the happy Alteration in both, since my Administration of it, are well known to your Grace.

I improv'd the Opportunities, which this post gave me of doing several National Services; I sav'd Nova Scotia with the English cod fishery more than once from falling into the

[1] *B. M., Additional Manuscript 32730, 281.* A transcript is in the Library of Congress.

hands of the French during the late Warr; and form'd, set on foot, and conducted an Expedition, the immediate Consequences of which were, that Cape Breton was taken, the French lost their Codfishery, and about £800,000 Sterl in prizes, as they were sailing into the Harbour of Louisbourg, before they knew that it was surrender'd to the English.

As the benefits, which accru'd to the Nation from these Services, happen'd under your Grace's Administration, I won't presume to observe to your Grace of what Importance they were to the Kingdom, or what Effect it might have had upon the State of publick Affairs, if instead of preserving Nova Scotia, and taking Cape Breton, his Majesty had lost the former to the French, and they had kept the latter; which would have been the case, if it had not been prevented by my vigilance.

Soon after the taking of Cape Breton I was oblig'd to make a voyage to Louisbourg and reside there as Governour of it, about seven Months, to retain the American forces which were frequently upon the point of a General Mutiny for being kept (from their farms and families) in Garrison there, untill the Arrival of the Regimts. from England, to take possession of it for his Majesty, and to hinder a Distribution of the Island from being made among the Captors, as was propos'd by Sir Peter Warren.

At my return from Louisbourg besides the care I had in common with the other Governours in North America to raise Levies for the intended Expedition against Canada, I receiv'd your Grace's Commands to take several preparatory steps for the execution of the plan; the settling of which was committed to me in conjunction with Genl St. Clair, and Sir Peter Warren; and I went thro' a considerable Duty on that acct., tho' the Expedition happen'd not to take Effect.

The principal part of the care of the whole Governmt of Nova Scotia was likewise committed to me; and I took the Burthen of it upon me untill Mr. Cornwallis's Arrival in America: The Orders sent me from time to time for that purpose were of great latitude, and contain'd high marks of his Majesty's Confidence in me; and I had the honour of receiving his Approbation of my Conduct in the Execution of them. And my Accts will shew how inconsiderable an Expence I put the Nation to in clearing that province of the Enemy, and preserving it during the whole Warr; tho' it was the principal Object of their Attempts in North America, as well from Old France, as from Canada.

The last Orders, I receiv'd from your Grace on acct of that province were to form plans for the Civil Governmt and fortification of it, both which I did, and transmitted them to your Grace's Office.

Upon the Expedition against Canada's being laid aside, I had your Grace's orders to discharge, in concert with Admiral Knowles, the American forces, upon such Terms, as we thought would be most adviseable for his Majesty's Service, and to collect, liquidate and adjust the Accompts of all the Governours concern'd in that Expedition, and to transmit them to be lay'd before his Majesty.

I will not trouble your Grace with an acct of the Execution of these Orders (which rested wholly in myself) either in America or here, further than to observe that I lessen'd the publick Expence by it to the amount of at least £40, or £50,000.

The Execution of this trust chiefly employ'd my whole time after my Arrival in England, untill my going to Paris in another Branch of his Majesty's service; and for my behaviour in that I may appeal to his Majesty's Ministers, with whom I corresponded, who, I believe would do me the honour to express their perfect Approbation of my Conduct in it.

After these services, at the End of eight Years, which I have spent in them, I find myself, my Lord, in a worse situation than I was in before I engag'd in them; my Regiment, the only mark, which I receiv'd of his Majesty's favour for them, is reduc'd; That was a profitable one, the short time, it lasted; But the Extraordinary Expences I was put to in the whole Course of my services will over ballance the profits of it.

I am without even half pay, which every other Officer of

my Regiment enjoys upon the reduction of it; and my Governmt of the Massachusetts Bay hath been within these three Years, dismember'd of the only Valuable perquisite in it, the Naval Office.

What compleats my Disappointments is, that my private fortune is not sufficient to enable me to make a provision for my Family without some mark of his Majesty's favour.

The Vacancy of the Governmt of the Leeward Islands, which I flatter myself, I might obtain, if your Grace shall be pleas'd to favour my pretensions, seems now to afford an opportunity for my doing this; and I am encourag'd to hope from the first instance of your Grace's goodness to me in patronizing me, and the kind Intentions, your Grace hath been pleas'd at several times to declare to me of supporting me with farther marks of his Majesty's favour in recompence of my services, that your Grace will favour me with your protection in this instance.

I am with the highest respect,

My Lord,

Your Grace's most Oblig'd, and

most Dutifull Servant,

W. SHIRLEY.

His Grace the Duke of Newcastle.

Endorsed:

    St. James's Street.

      Novr. 23. 1752.

        GOVR. SHIRLEY.

WILLIAM SHIRLEY TO THE DUKE OF NEWCASTLE [1]

St. James's Street, Jany. 23, 1753.

MY LORD,

Having been inform'd by one of your Grace's servants at Newcastle House, that your Grace saw no Company this

---

[1] *B. M., Additional Manuscript 32731, 100.* A transcript is in the Library of Congress.

4

morning, I beg leave to express in a few lines the extreme anxiety, which the Attempts, that I understand from your Grace, some Person, or Persons are making to wound my character with your Grace, give me.

My Case is the more cruel, as the Offence, I have given these persons, was incurr'd in a Service, which I had your Grace's and Mr. Pelham's express Commands to execute and therefore was not to be declin'd by me, tho' it was an extraordinary Duty lay'd upon me.

I foresaw from the beginning how Invidious, as well as difficult, and uneasy a Task it would be to me; But I had no way to avoid the Envy which was likely to attend it, without betraying my Trust to the Publick, which I hope I shall never be capable of doing.

Your Grace hath already inform'd me, that my Lord Halifax hath been pleas'd to declare to your Grace his Approbation of my Conduct in this Service.

Mr. Pelham, I was told in the time of the Execution of it, mention'd my name (with honour to me), to the House Commons upon that Occasion: and I dare say, that he, the Paymaster General, Secretary at Warr, and the whole Board of Trade, who were privy to my liquidating of every Article of the Accompts, which it seems, hath drawn upon me the Ill will of some New York Merchant, or Merchants, would do me the honour to declare their full Satisfaction in my Impartiality between the Crown, and the other Parties concern'd: and that I us'd my best Endeavours to do Justice to every particular person, as well as right to the publick.

It is true, my Lord, I made a very considerable saving to the Crown by detecting, and cutting off many extravagant impositions, which were attempted to be made upon it, both at home, and in America; but I flatter'd myelf, that tho' that might draw some Ill will upon me from some particular Merchants, or even Colonies in general, it would have added to my merit with his Majesty's Ministers.

But, my Lord, if instead of that, the Objections which have been suggested to your Grace against me, shall be thought sufficient to disqualify me for that Mark of his

Majesty's Favour, which was propos'd to your Grace for me in the recommendation of me to him for the Governmt of New York;[1] Like Objections from New England Merchts may be as strong an Argumt for removing me from his Majesty's service in the Governmt of the Massachusetts Bay: For they have just the same reason to object against me to your Grace, as the Merchts of New York have: I am sure, the Massachusetts Assembly have much more.

I would therefore intreat your Grace to indulge me with a short Audience, and that you will be pleas'd to let me know, who he or they are, which are thus wounding my Character in the Dark; that I may have an Opportunity of vindicating it against their Objections, and clearing my services of every Imputation of Demerit, which may sully them.

As I am conscious, my Lord, that I have behav'd myself in every Trust, which his Majesty hath been pleas'd to honour me with in his service, with the strictest fidelity, and unblameably in every respect, I think it a Duty, which I owe my self, to inquire after the Author, or Authors of these reproaches of my Character to your Grace; and hope your Grace will be pleas'd therefore to excuse it.

I am with the Highest Respect,
My Lord Duke,
Your Grace's most Oblig'd, and
most Dutifull Servant,
W. Shirley.

His Grace the Duke of Newcastle.

Endorsed:
St. James's Street.
Janry 23d. 1753.
Govr. Shirley.

[1] See Shirley to Newcastle, September 1, 1750 (I, 508), requesting an appointment as governor of New York.

WILLIAM SHIRLEY TO THE DUKE OF NEWCASTLE [1]

St. James's Street, March 29, 1753.

My Lord Duke,

My Intention in endeavouring to speak to your Grace yesterday at Kensington was only to have the honour of taking my leave of your Grace, before I return'd to my Governmt in New England; to thank your Grace for all your favours; and to beg the continuance of your protection.

I am now upon the point of going to Portsmouth, and as your Grace's Hurry would not permit me to have the honour, I design'd my self yesterday, I beg leave to wait upon your Grace in these few lines, which is the only way left me, of doing it now.

I wish your Grace Success, and Happiness in all your Undertakings, and am with the most Gratefull sense of all your Grace's favours,

My Lord,
Your Grace's most Obliged,
and most Dutifull Servant,
W. Shirley.

His Grace the Duke of Newcastle.

Endorsed:
St. James's Street.
Mar. 29th. 1753.
Govr. Shirley.

WILLIAM SHIRLEY TO JOSIAH WILLARD [2]

St James's Street, April 27, 1753.

Some days ago I obtained an order from Lt. Anson to Capt. Montague of his Majesty's Ship Port Mahon which is

[1] *B. M., Additional Manuscript 32731, 518.* A transcript is in the Library of Congress.
[2] Original, Mass. Arch., Col. Ser. 54, 232.

appointed for the Newfoundland Station this year, to set me down at Boston before he proceeds upon his Station. His ship will, I believe, sail in 14 or 15 days.

I have petitioned the King in Council for 11 cannon of 24 lb. ball which number will compleat the Royal Battery at Castle William with suitable Guns, and for two Mortars with a proportion of ball, shells and all other stores except powder, which last it is a settled rule not to grant. Upon my apprizing Mr Sharpe Clerk of the Council of my Petition, I had the Discouragemt to hear that a fortnight before Mr Pelham had absolutely rejected a petition from the Province of Maryland to have 300 Musquets replac'd which they had furnished the Soldiers rais'd for the Canada Expedition with, out of the Province stores, but upon my delivering it to my Lord President his Lordship was pleased to receive it very graciously and tell me it should be granted, and in order to give it the greatest Dispatch, he has referr'd it to the Board of Ordnance for an Estimate of the Ordnance stores prayed for, to be directly made out without making any report of their opinion upon the substance or fitness of the Petition as is the usual manner of those References and which frequently occasions delay and difficulties.

Upon getting this Reference from the Council of the Board of Ordnance, I delivered it myself to Sir John Legonier begging the favour of him to order it to be dispatch'd. The Easter Holydays have delayed it, but I am promis'd by the Secry. of the Board, that the Estimate shall be finish'd this day and be signed by Sir John and the Principal Officers of the Board in time to be returned into the Council Office on Tuesday next. I have taken Care to get the Freight of these stores included in the Board of Ordnance's Estimate which is not usual and I flatter myself with the Hopes of obtaining an absolute order for the delivery of them before I imbark, and for their being forthwith transported to Castle William at the Expence of the Crown. I thought it was most adviseable to postpone an application for the Pictures of the Royal Family in the Room of those which were burnt in the Council Chamber untill the Ordnance stores were secured for the Province, being unwilling to run the least risque of that Application's interfering with the other more essential one, but as soon as an absolute order is passed for the stores I will apply to Mr Pelham for the Pictures.[1]

The Application for a reimbursement of the remainder of the stores bought by the Province for the New England Soldiers in the Expedition against Cape Breton, and made use of by Mr Knowles, stands still for the arrival of some evidence from Boston which Mr Bollan hath sent for to ascertain the value of them as does the Affair of the Townships controverted between the Province and Colony of Connecticutt and of the new Line claimed by the Colony of Rhode Island for Evidence from the Records of the two Colonies, which in my opinion is absolutely necessary to be procur'd if possible before those Matters are brot to a Decision before the King in Council, or at least to have a denial from the Assemblies of those Colonies to let the Massa. Agent in New England search and take copies of their Records in order to intitle the Province's agent here to produce copies of its own Records which cant be regularly admitted as Evidence in its own Case untill the Province is denied Copies of the Rhode Island and Connecticutt records upon the point in question. Mr. Bollan was in hopes of receiving those papers by the last ships. When he is furnished with 'em I am persuaded no Pains nor good Conduct will be wanting to establish the Province's just rights in these disputes which to me appear clear and evident and that the pretentions of both the Colonies are unreasonable and vexatious.

As to the Province's demands against that of New Hampshire on account of their maintaining Fort Dummer during the War Mr Bollan had obtained, before he brought over the money granted the Province by Parliament for the reimbursement of their Expences in the Expedition against Cape Breton, a Report from the Board of Trade in favour of it, but soon after Mr Bollan was imbarked for Boston the

---

[1] Shirley's petition for additional levy money for his late regiment beyond that allowed in 1750 had been refused by Fox on April 25 (War Office, Class 4, 49, p. 157).

Agent of the Province of New Hampshire prepared a Petition to the King in Council to be heard against the Report, and an Order of Council was thereupon made that the Matter should stay untill the Lords or Council should call the Agents of both Provinces before them. It is necessary to stay a decent Time out of Respect to that Order, without moving by a Petition on the Part of the Province to have the hearing brought on. When that is done Mr Bollan will move it, and I hope there can be no danger of having the Report of the Lords Commissioners of Trade confirmed.

There is an appearance that the Settlement of a Line between the Province and N. York may soon be brought on. The finishing Memorial upon the Limits of Nova Scotia as claimed by his Majesty to extend as far as the Southern Bank of the River St. Lawrence hath been some months transmitted by Lord Holderness to the Court of France. I flatter myself that in the opinion of all His Majesty's Ministers the English right to the Limits which they claim (particularly with Respect to the Ancient Limits of the Province) is asserted in the clearest and most convincing Manner, even upon the Foot of the French Records and Histories which themselves have produc'd to maintain their Pretensions in their Answer to our first Memorial and that there is not the least Colour or Shadow of Argument or rather Sophistry which they have advanced left unanswered and unconfuted.

I can't conclude without observing that when the Supply for the Maintenance of Nova Scotia came on in the House of Commons to be debated it was not only unanimously voted, but with the most visible Satisfaction on the Countenance of every Member that was ever known there upon any such occasion, most explicit strong declarations were made by the Minister in favour of its Support and of the Importance of it to the Nation and the Parliamentary Faith was plighted for it as much as could be done by his Declaration. . . . I am Sir
Your most humble Servant
W. SHIRLEY.

WILLIAM SHIRLEY TO JOSIAH WILLARD [1]

St. James's Street, May 16, 1753.

SIR,

About a Month ago I wrote you word that I believed I should embark on board his Majesty's ship the Port Mahon, Capt. Montague, who has Orders to carry me to Boston, within 14 or 15 days; But the Ship I find, will not sail before the beginning of the Week after next; when the Captain hath given me an Assurance, he will be ready the day after my arrival at Portsmouth.

Last night I obtained a report of the Lords of the Committee of Council, in favour of my Petition for the Ordnance Stores, for Castle William, together with the Freight of them, at the Charge of the Crown, which Article, it is computed, will amount to about £300; so that the Province will receive them free of all Charges, except fees of Office and Clerk's Perquisites; Nothing remains to perfect the Affair but the reports being approved by his Majesty, which is esteem'd a thing of Course; If he appoints a Council before I go, I shall get the Order for the Immediate delivery of the Stores, which are all ready, and indent for them myself : If there should be no Council before my Departure, that must be left for Mr. Bollan to do : I will however endeavour to get the Board of Ordnance to fix upon a good Vessell here for the transportation of the Stores, before I go, that a Ship may be ready to receive them, as soon as they can be deliver'd.

I have also to add, that a strong Attempt being made to continue the act for laying the present Duty upon foreign Molasses &c which expires the Session after next, to a further long Period Mr Bollan hath petition'd against it, and succeeded so well in his Opposition, that it seems to me, he hath pretty nearly given that Act its Death wound; I shall refer you to him for a particular acct of the matter, But he is at present so busy in attending the House to oppose another Attempt making by the Sugar bakers here to put down all

[1] Original, Mass. Arch., Col. Ser. 54, 303.

Sugar houses in the Colonies, that you will scarcely hear from him by this Ship.

I hope to have a good sight soon of Boston and am

Sir

Your Humble Servant

W. SHIRLEY.

Secretary Willard.

THE EARL OF HOLDERNESS TO WILLIAM SHIRLEY [1]

Whitehall. 28. August 1753.

SIR,

His Majesty having received Information of the March of a considerable number of Indians not in alliance with the King, supported by some regular European Troops, intending as it is apprehended, to commit some hostilities on parts of his Majesty's dominions in America, I have the King's commands to send you this intelligence, and to direct you to use your utmost diligence, to learn, how far the same may be well grounded, and to put you upon your guard, that you may, at all events, be in a condition to resist any hostile attempts that may be made upon any parts of His Majesty's Dominions within your Government; and to direct you in the King's Name, that in case the subjects of any Foreign Prince or State, should presume to make any incroachment on the limits of His Majty's dominions, or to erect Forts on His Majesty's Land, or commit any other act of hostility, you are immediately, to represent the injustice of such proceed-

[1] P. R. O., C. O. 211, Entry Book. Printed: Docts. rel. Col. Hist. N. Y. 6, 795. See Shirley's reply of Jan. 7, 1754, *post*, p. 18. The letter is a circular to the various governors in North America, and from it the Massachusetts Governor took the cue for his letter of January, 1754, to the Lords Commissioners of Trade, *post*, p. 26, in which he declares that a union of the Colonies is necessary for defense, and that the quota of men and money to be furnished by each colony should be fixed by the king. Holderness had succeeded Bedford as a Secretary of State in June, 1751, serving until March, 1761.

ing, and to require them forthwith to desist from any such unlawful undertaking; but if notwithstanding your requisition, they should still persist, you are then to draw forth the armed Force of the Province, and to use your best endeavours, to repell force by force.[1] But as it is His Majesty's determination not to be the agressor, I have the King's commands, most strictly to enjoin you, not to make use of the armed force under your direction, excepting within the undoubted limits of his Majesty's dominions.

And whereas it may be greatly conducive to His Majesty's service, that all his Provinces in America should be aiding and assisting each other, in case of any invasion, I have it particularly in charge from his Majesty, to acquaint you, that it is his Royal will and pleasure, that you should keep up an exact correspondence with all His Majesty's Governors on the Continent;[2] and in case you shall be informed by any of them, of any hostile attempts, you are immediately to assemble the general assembly within your Government, and lay before them, the necessity of a mutual assistance, and engage them to grant such supplies as the exigency of affairs may require. I have wrote by this conveyance to all his Majesty's Govrs to the same purpose. I am ettc.

HOLDERNESS.

LORDS OF TRADE TO WILLIAM SHIRLEY [3]

To William Shirley Esquire Governour of Massachusetts
Bay.
SIR,

His Majesty having been pleased to order a sum of money to be issued for presents to the Six Nations of Indians and

[1] Two months earlier Holderness had written Shirley as to furnishing 500 muskets for the use of foreign Protestants in Nova Scotia. The letter is in P. R. O., C. O. 5, 886.

[2] See Shirley to Horatio Sharpe, Nov. 26, 1753, *post*, p. 14.

[3] This is a circular letter to the Governors in America, and is Printed: Docts. rel. Col. Hist. N. Y. 6, 802. A like letter was sent to the Governors of Virginia, New Jersey, New Hampshire, Maryland, and Pennsylvania.

to direct his Governor of New York to hold an interview with them, for delivering those presents, for burying the hatchet, and for renewing the Covenant Chain with them; we think it our duty to acquaint you therewith, and as we find it has been usual upon former occasions when an interview has been held with those Indians, for all His Majesty's Colonies whose interest and security is connected with and depends upon them, to join in such interview, and as the present disposition of those Indians and the attempts which have been made to withdraw them from the British interest, appears to us to make such a general interview more particularly necessary at this time; we desire you will lay this matter before the Council and General Assembly of the Province under your government and recommend to them forthwith to make a proper provision for appointing Commissioners, to be joined with those of the other Governments, for renewing the Covenant Chain with the Six Nations, and for making such presents to them as has been usual upon the like occasions. And we desire that in the Choice and nomination of the Commissioners, you will take care that they are men of Character ability and integrity, and well acquainted with Indian Affairs.

As to the time and place of meeting it is left to the Governor of New York to fix it, and he has orders to give you early notice of it. We are, Sir

Your very loving friends
and humble Servants
Dunk Halifax

Whitehall   Jam: Grenville.

Septemb: 18 1753   Dupplin.

WILLIAM SHIRLEY TO HORATIO SHARPE [1]

Sir,   Boston November 26th 1753.

I received by the last post a Letter from the Earle of Holdernesse dated 28 August past (a Circular one as it ap-

[1] Original in the Maryland Historical Society. Printed: Arch. of Md. 6, 11; 31, 25.

pears to be to all his Majestys Governments in North America) acquainting me that his Majesty had received Information of the March of a Considerable Number of Indians not in Alliance with him Supported by some regular European Troops intending as it is apprehended to commit some Hostilities on parts of his Majestys Dominions in America, and directing me to use my utmost diligence to learn how far the same may be well grounded Acquainting me also that his Lordship had it particularly in Charge to let me know that it was his Majestys Royal will and Pleasure, that I should keep up an exact Correspondence with all his Majestys Governors on the Continent and in Case I should be informed by any of them of any Hostile Attempts, that I should immediately Assemble the General Assembly within my Government and lay before them the necessity of a mutual Assistance and engage them to grant such Supplies as the Exigency of Affairs may require.

In obedience to these Instructions I trouble you with this Letter to let you know that in case any Hostile Attempts shall be comitted upon his Majestys Territories within the Limits of your Honours Government, for repelling of which that may Stand in need of the Assistance of his Majestys other Colonies upon the Continent, I shall be ready upon my being informed of it by your honour to do my duty within my own Government for procuring their due Proportion of Supplies upon the Emergency; and for this Purpose I shall be very glad to maintain a Strict Correspondence with your honour, pursuant to his Majestys Commands Signified to me in the Earl of Holdernesses before mentioned Letter. I am with great Esteem Sr.

Your honours most humble and most Obedient Servt
W. Shirley.

Honourable Horatio Sharpe Esqr.

WILLIAM PEPPERRELL TO WILLIAM SHIRLEY AND THE MASSACHUSETTS GENERAL COURT[1]

[*Memorial regarding compensation for expenditures.*]

To His Excellency William Shirley
> Governour and Commander in Chief of the Province of the Massachusets Bay; The Honble. His Majesty's Council, and Honble. House of Representatives, in General Court Assembled, at Boston December 1753

The Memorial of Sir William Pepperrell Baronet, Sheweth,

That your Memorialist, being called upon by this Government, to take upon him the Chief Command, of all the Forces raised for the Expedition against Cape Breton, did accept of that difficult and hazardous Service, in duty to God, His King and his Country; and on the 31st. January. 1744. received a Commission appointing him Lieutenant General and Commander in Chief, by Land and Sea, of all the Forces raised and to be raised for the Said Service.

That your Memorialist, after the Reduction of Louisbourg, at the Command of this Government "chearfully Submitted to the difficultys and inconveniences of continuing on the Place for the quiet and Sattisfaction of the officers and Soldiers and the preservation of that important Acquisition" as this Honourable Court were pleased to express themselves, in their Letter to their Memorialist: And the inconveniencies, of his being absent from his Family and private affairs for so long a time; were farr from being Small to him.

Furthermore, that your Memorialist, soon after his return home was obliged to take a Journy to Boston, to attend the Committee of Warr to Sign the Accounts to be sent to the Court of Great Britain, of the Charges, This Province had been at in carrying on Said Expedition.

And besides all this, that your Memorialist was under a necessity to take a Voyage to London, to get the Accounts,

---

[1] Massachusetts Manuscripts, Vol. I. Library of Congress.

of what was expended at Louisbourg during his tarry there, Passed.

By the aforesaid means, Your Memorialist, has been exposed to an expence exceeding all the advantages he has received in consequence of his Services : and in as much as nothing has been yet given him by this Government as a reward herefor, though they were pleased to say,

"his important Trust was bravely, and Successfully executed :"

Prays that your Excellency and Honours would be pleased to make such a Grant of money to him, as you in your Wisdom shall think proper, all which is Humbly Submitd by

Your Excellency and Honrs,

Faithfull Humble Servant

WM. PEPPERRELL.

On the third day of January 1754 the Great and General Court made a Grant to yor. Memorialist of one hundred and forty four pounds in full for his pay and Service at Cape Breton which was about Eighteen months before he could return to His Family as he was desired not to Leave Cape Breton untill the Provential Troops was releaved in obedience to which I complyd with tho' at a Great charge and preventing me being with an agreable Family. Your Memorialist being informd Since sd. Grant was made that the reason sd. Grant was made so Small was that he had Several Sums of money given him before by this Governmt which was Groundless for he never did directly or indirectly receive one penny but what he paid agreable to the order of the General Court and Accounted with the Committee of Warr for the same, except one hundred and fifty pounds of the then Paper Currency which was given him to Provide for a General Table no other then having any thing Else given for that End and he has never as yet received any part of the sd. Grant of one hundred and forty foure pounds.

Endorsed :

A Copy of Sir Wm. Pepperrells
Memorial to the Great and Gl. Court.

WILLIAM SHIRLEY TO THE EARL OF HOLDERNESS [1]

Boston, January 7, 1754.

My Lord,

I have the honour of Your Lordship's letter dated 28th August last,[2] signifying to me, "that His Majesty had received information of the march of a considerable Number of Indians, not in his alliance, supported by some Regular European Troops, intending, as was apprehended, to commit some hostilities on parts of His Majesty's dominions in America, and directing me to use my utmost diligence to learn how far the same may be well grounded, and to put me upon my guard, that I may at all events be in a condition to resist any hostile attempts, that may be made upon any parts of His Majesty's dominions within my Government" signifying likewise "that it is the King's Royal will and pleasure that I should keep up an exact correspondence with all His Majesty's Governors on the Continent; and in case I should be informed by any of them of any hostile attempts; that I should immediately assemble the General Assembly within my Government, and lay before them the necessity of a mutual assistance, and engage them to grant such supplies as the exigency of affairs may require" —

In obedience to His Majesty's pleasure I have used my utmost diligence to learn how far the information of the March of the Indians and Troops mentioned in your Lordship's letter may be well grounded, together with their designs and destination: and the result of my inquiry is contained in the inclosed paper No 1. to which I beg leave to referr Your Lordp.

I have taken the necessary measures for putting the Militia of the province into a readiness for His Majesty's service, in

[1] Original, P. R. O., C. O. 5, 14. Printed: Docts. rel. Col. Hist. N. Y. 6, 822. A transcript from the original in the Public Record Office is in the Parkman Papers in the Mass. Hist. Society.

[2] See *ante*, p. 12.

case of any sudden exigency; and have recommended to the Assembly to make provision for putting several Forts and Garrisons into a proper posture of defence, and communicated to them His Majesty's Royal pleasure concerning his Colonies upon this Continent, giving mutual assistance to each other, in case of any hostile attempts against any of them.

In answer to this they have sent me a Message; a copy of which marked No 2. I have taken the liberty of inclosing to Your Lordship in order to be layd before His Majesty according to the Assembly's request, provided your Lordship shall judge that proper to be done.

I likewise take upon this occasion, the liberty to observe to your Lordship that tho' I am fully persuaded, that this Province (as the Assembly undertakes for it in their Message) will at all times with great cheerfulness furnish their just and reasonable quota of Men or money towards the assistance of any other of His Majesty's Colonies upon this continent, in case of an invasion or hostile attempt; and can't but hope, from the necessity of an union among all the Colonies for their mutual defence against the common Enemy, that the others may be likewise disposed to do the same; yet, unless it shall be determined by His Majesty, what is each Colony's just quota of Men or Money which it shall raise or contribute in the common cause, when any one or more of them shall be invaded, or harras'd by the French or Indians, whether in a time of open declared Warr or not, and they shall be obliged in some effectual manner (as his Majesty shall think most proper) to conform to that determination upon every emergency; yet, I say, My Lord, there seems just reason to apprehend from past experience, that the want of such a settlement, and a method to enforce its taking effect, will be an obstacle to the carrying into execution any general plan for cementing an Union among His Majesty's subjects upon this continent, for the defence of His Majestys territories committed to their trust.

What greatly incourages me to take the liberty of submitting this observation to your Lordship's consideration, is, that it was thought necessary by the Government in King William's Reign to settle the Quota of Men and Money, which every one of the Colonies should be alloted to raise for the defence of New York; and that I find the like settlement continued in Sir Danvers Osborne's, late Govr. of New York's 95th and 96th instructions; a copy of which No 3. to save your Lordship trouble, I likewise inclose.

The carrying of this settlement into execution, Your Lordship will be pleased to observe, stands solely upon the King's recommendation of it, and I can't learn upon the best inquiry, I have been able to make hitherto, that it ever took effect, yet, I must likewise remark this fact to Your Lordship, that since the time of making that settlement, the abilities and circumstances of several Colonies are much altered, so that, that would be a very unequal rule for settling the just proportion of their Quota's in Men or money at this day. For instance: Your Lordship will find the Quota of Men allotted to this Province to raise for the assistance of New York is 350, and that allotted to Pennsylvania is 80. Now, such a proportion between the two governments at this time would be extreamly unequal; the Number of Inhabitants in Pensylvania having since King William the 3rd's Reign been so much increased by the great number of Foreigners, who have annually transplanted themselves and their families thither, from the Palatinate, Swiss Cantons and Northern Parts of Germany, and by the natural increase of the people, that some have computed them at 500,000 persons; whereas the increase of the numbers of Inhabitants in the Massachusets Bay within that time (not to mention their having had but a very inconsiderable number of Foreigners transplanted among them) hath been greatly hindered by having many of their valuable Townships lately lopped off by the new Settlement of the boundaries between them and the Province of New Hampshire in 1737 as also by the settlement of the boundaries between them and the Colony of Rhode Island in 1741; and the province hath been further reduced by the great loss it sustained of its inhabitants by sea and Land in the expedition against Cape Breton, and the preservation of Nova Scotia, both, before and during the whole course of the late Warr; so that there is no reason to doubt but that at this day the Inhabitants of Pensylvania tho' they should be computed only 400,000, are about double the number of those of this Province.

The like remark may be made upon the proportion of the Quota of men and Money settled between the Colony of Connecticut and this Province, which is about 1 to 3, that Colony being alloted to raise 120 Men, and the Province 350, whereas the Colony, by means of the beforementioned reduction of the ancient, reputed limits of this Province, and its being exhausted of its Inhabitants in the late expeditions, and Warr, hath since making the aforesaid settlement so far got the start of the Province in the increase of its Inhabitants, that the just proportion at this day between them is (according to the computation of good Judges) no more than as 2 to 3. There are other circumstances besides to be considered in adjusting the proportion of the Quota between the Colony and the Province; viz: the Colony is entirely covered by this Province, so that it hath no frontier of its own, to defend in time of war, and consequently is at no expence in the maintenance of marching Companies, Forts and garrisons for that purpose; whereas the Province hath a very extensive frontier, which is constantly harras'd by the Indians and French, upon every rupture, and at a very considerable charge in maintaining marching Companies, Forts and Garrisons; and in time of peace the Colony's Taxes for the support of His Majty's Government among them, is very trifling in comparison of that of the Province's.

I submit these observations to your Lordship's consideration as specimens of the alteration of the circumstances of the Colonies with regard to the proportion, which they bore to each other in respect of their number of Inhabitants and ability in King William's Reign, and their present state, and to shew, how unequal a rule the settlement made at that time for adjusting their respective Quotas of Men and Money, would be for adjusting them at this day.

I must further add upon this head, that nothing would

contribute more effectually to secure His Majesty's subjects and territories upon this continent, against the rapid progress, which the French seem to be making in perfecting a strong line of Forts upon our backs from Bay Verté Easterly, to the utmost extent of His Majesty's Dominions Westward, and to bring the Indians to a dependance upon the English, than a well concerted scheme, for uniting all His Majesty's Colonies upon it, in a mutual defence of each other, duely carried into execution.

I have the utmost reason, My Lord, to think that the People of this Province are most readily disposed to do their part in promoting so necessary an Union, and to exert the same spirit, which they have hitherto in His Majty's service, to the utmost of their abilities, in concurrence with his other Colonies for their mutual defence; but I think it my duty to mention to your Lordp that the thoughts of bearing the burthen of defending the wide frontier, upon which Fort Dummer stands, and was in the year 1737 adjudged to belong to the Province of New Hampshire, as they did the last War, seem so grievous to them, that I much question whether in case of another rupture with France, they could be induced to do it; and whether, unless some especial provision is made for the protection of it by his Majesty, it would not then be greatly exposed to be ravaged by the Enemy.

The daily intelligence that is received here from the Indians which frequent our Truck houses, our Traders to the Bay of Fundy, and even the Officers of Fort Lawrence in Schiegnecto, of the great Diligence of the French in strengthening their Forts and Block Houses in that District, and that on the Isthmus near Bay Vert, together with their having possessed themselves of St John's River, and the commerce they carry on in the Bay of Fundy, hath greatly alarmed the Assembly; and they extreamly dread bad consequences to the Province from such a neighbourhood; in case it shall continue until another rupture: as they do also from the French encroachments at Crown Point, unless something is done to curb them; towards the expence of doing which, and maintaining a Fort and garrison, if it should be His Majesty's pleasure to have one erected for that service; I have reason to hope that the Province would contribute their just Quota of Men and money, in proportion to the protection which their western frontier would receive from it, in common with the Provinces of New York, Pensylvania, New Jersey, Connecticut, Rhode Island and New Hampshire, as His Majesty shall be pleased to allot each Colony to do the same.

I shall carefully observe, His Majesty's commands not to make use of the armed force, under my direction, excepting within the undoubted limits of His Majesty's Dominions.

As I have the honour to be accuainted with the sentiments of the Right Honble the Lords Commissioners for Trade and Plantations concerning the Isthmus of the Peninsula of Nova Scotia, where the French have erected their Forts, and the River of St John's in the Bay of Funda, founded upon the vouchers and evidences produced by the Commissarys of both Crowns in the negociation at Paris; vizt : that they are clearly within the limits of His Majesty's Province of Nova Scotia, I suppose we may deem them to be so, notwithstanding the claim of the French in their memorials, which extend as far as the River Kennebeck to the Westward, and to the City of Annapolis Royal, as also part of the lands lying between that and the Sea coast of Nova Scotia, from Cape Sable to Cape Canseau to the Eastward.

I have the honor to be with the highest respect
My Lord
Your Lordships most Humble
and most Obedient Servant
W. SHIRLEY.

WILLIAM SHIRLEY TO WILLIAM GREENE [1]

Boston, January 13, 1754.

SIR,

Some weeks ago, I had the honor of a letter from the Earl of Holdernesse, one of His Majesty's principal secretaries of

[1] Col. Rec. of R. I. 5, 380.

state, directing me to send a quantity of muskets out of those which had been saved out of the late intended expedition against Canada, to Halifax, in Nova Scotia, for His Majesty's service there; and signifying to me, that he had written to the Governors of New Hampshire, Connecticut and Rhode Island, directing them to transmit to me what arms and military stores had been saved out of their aforesaid expedition, within their respective governments, to be lodged in Castle William, for His Majesty's further orders.

As I cannot collect the quantity of good, serviceable muskets, which I am directed to send to Halifax, within this Province, out of those which were saved out of that expedition,I desire Your Honor would be pleased to let me know by the first post, whether I am to expect any muskets from your government, according to the Earl of Holdernesse's orders.

I am, with great regard, sir,
Your Honor's most obedient servant,
W. Shirley.

To the Hon. Governor Greene.

MASSACHUSETTS GENERAL COURT TO THE BRITISH CROWN[1]

To the King's most excellent Majesty —
The humble Address of the Council and House of Representatives of the Province of the Massachusets Bay in New England —
We your Majesty's most loyal and most dutiful Subjects the Council and House of Representatives of your Province of the Massachusets Bay beg leave to return your Majesty our humble thanks for your paternal Goodness to your Subjects in this Province, and among other Instances thereof for your late royal Bounty in causing to be replaced at Castle William eleven Cannon in lieu of those which were taken thence for the Service of the Expedition against Cape Breton, together with an Addition of other Ordnance Stores for the further strengthning of that important Fortress.

[1] Mass. Arch. 21, 138.

May Almighty God long preserve the precious Life of your Majesty during whose auspicious Reign we have enjoyed so many invaluable Blessings, in the grateful Sense whereof we humbly beg leave to assure your Majesty that we shall make it our constant endeavour to approve Ourselves,

May it please your Majesty
Your Majestys most loyal
and most dutiful Subjects.

In Council January 21 1754 Read and Accepted and Ordered that the Secretary be directed to Subscribe in behalf of the Council

Sent down for Concurrence
Thos. Clarke, Depty. Secry

In the House of Representatives Janry 21 1754.
Read and Concurred and Ordered thaᴜ the Speaker Subscribe in Behalf of the House

Sent up for Concurrence
T. Hubbard   Spkr.

In Council Jan. 21. 1754.   Read and Concurred
J Willard   Secry [1]

[1] In the records of the Privy Council (15, 171) there is the following note of the reception of this address on June 21, 1754:

"Whereas the Lords Commissioners for Trade and Plantations have laid before His Majesty at this Board, an humble Address of the Council and House of Representatives of His Majestys Province of the Massachusets Bay in New England, returning their humble thanks to His Majesty for His Paternal Goodness to His Subjects in that Province, and among other instances thereof, for His late Royal bounty, in Causing a supply of Ordnance and Ordnance Stores to be sent thither. His Majesty was this day pleased to receive the said Address very graciously. It is therefore hereby Ordered, that the Lords Commissioners for Trade and Plantations, do signify the same, to His Majestys Governor of the Said Province of the Massachusets Bay."

This is an unique entry: No other record of an American Colony giving such thanks for stores received from the home government is found in the Privy Council records. It is here given as

WILLIAM SHIRLEY TO ISRAEL WILLIAMS[1]

SIR, Boston Jany 24. 1754.

You are hereby directed to send out your Orders to the several Captains and Commanding Officers of the Companies of Militia in the Regimt under your Command, requiring them to take exact Lists of the Officers and private Men in their respective Companies by Law obliged to appear under Arms at the usual times of Appearance; And after you have receiv'd such Lists, you must make out one general List from them all, setting forth the Town where the Company is, the Name of the Captain, the Number of Officers, vizt Lieut Ensign, Clerk, Sergeants, Corporals and Drummers, and the Number of Centinels in each Company, and transmit the same to me as soon as possible; Or if this has been already done in Compliance of the Lieutenant Governour's Order, dated the 20th of Decemr 1752, and your general List has miscarried, send it now without delay.

I am, Sir,
Your humble Servant

Colonel Israel Williams. W. SHIRLEY.

WILLIAM SHIRLEY TO THE LORDS COMMISSIONERS[2]

MY LORDS, Boston New England Jany 1754.

Six Weeks ago I had the Honour of a Letter from the Earl of Holdernesse dated 28th of August last,[3] signifying to me

an illustration of the pleasant relations existing between Crown and Colony at this time, and to which Shirley refers in his letter to the Lords Commissioners of January, when stating the willingness of Massachusetts to enter into a scheme for mutual defense among the colonies.

[1] Original, D. S. Mass. Hist. Society, Col. Israel Williams Manuscripts, 71 D, 68.
[2] P. R. O., C. O. 5, 887.   [3] *Ante*, p. 12.

that "His Majesty had receiv'd Information of the March
"of a considerable Number of Indians, not in his Alliance,
"supported by some Regular European Troops, intending
"as was apprehended, to commit some Hostilities on parts
"of His Majesty's Dominions in America;" and directing
me "to use my utmost Diligence to learn how far the same
"may be well grounded, and to put me upon my Guard,
"that at all Events I may be in a Condition to resist any
"hostile Attempts that may be made upon any parts of His
"Majesty's Dominions within my Government;" but
strictly enjoining me "not to make use of the arm'd force
"under my direction except within the undoubted Limits
"of His Majesty's Dominions;" signifying likewise "that it
"is the King's Royal Will and Pleasure that I should keep up
"an exact Correspondence with all His Majesty's Govern-
"ours on the Continent; and in case I should be inform'd
"by any of them of any hostile Attempts, that I should im-
"mediately assemble the General Assembly within my
"Government and lay before them the Necessity of a mutual
"Assistance, and engage them to grant such Supplies as the
"Exigency of Affairs may require."

And as I think it my Duty to communicate the several
Matters contain'd in my Answer, to your Lordships, I shall
now lay them before You.

In Obedience to His Majesty's Pleasure I us'd my utmost
Diligence to learn how far the Information of the March of
the Indians and Troops mention'd in His Lordship's Letter,
may be well grounded, together with their Designs and Destination: and the Result of my Inquiry is contain'd in the
inclos'd Papers No 1, to which I beg Leave to referr Your
Lordships.

I took the necessary Measures for putting the Militia of
the Province into a Readiness for His Majesty's Service in
case of any sudden Exigency; and have recommended to the
Assembly to make Provision for putting the several forts and
Garrisons into a proper Posture of Defence; and communicated to them His Majesty's Royal Pleasure concerning
his Colonies upon this Continent's giving mutual Assistance

to each other, in Case of any Hostile Attempts against any of them.

In Answer to this they sent me a Message, a Copy of which mark'd No 2, is inclos'd.

I took the Liberty to observe to His Lordship, that though I am fully perswaded, that this Province (as the Assembly undertakes for it in their Message) will at all times with great Chearfulness furnish their just Quota of Men or Money towards the Assistance of any other of His Majesty's Colonies upon this Continent, in case of an Invasion or hostile Attempt, and can't but hope, from the Necessity of an Union among all the Colonies for their mutual Defence against the Common Enemy, that the others may be likewise dispos'd to do the same; yet unless it shall be determin'd by His Majesty, what is each Colony's just Quota of Men or Money, which it shall raise or contribute in the common Cause, when any one or more of them shall be invaded or harrass'd by the French or Indians, whether in a time of open declar'd Warr or not; and they shall be oblig'd in some effectual Manner (as His Majesty shall think most proper) to conform to that Determination; yet, I observ'd to his Lordship, there seems just reason to apprehend from past Experience, that the Want of such a Settlement, and a Method to enforce it's taking Effect, will be an Obstacle to the carrying into Execution any general Plan for cementing an Union among his Majesty's Subjects upon this Continent, for the Defence of His Majesty's Territories committed to their Trust.

What greatly encourag'd me to take the Liberty of submitting that Observation to his Lordship's Consideration, is that it was thought necessary by the Government in King William's time to settle the Quota of Men and Money, which every one of the Colonies should be allotted to raise for the Defence of New York; and that I find a like Settlement of it continu'd in Sir Danvers Osborne, late Governour of New York's 95th and 96th Instructions.

I observ'd to his Lordship that the Carrying of that Settlement into Execution stands solely upon the King's Recommendation, and that I could not learn upon the best Inquiry

I have been able to make hitherto, that it ever took Effect yet: And I likewise remark'd this fact to his Lordship, that since the time of making that Settlement, the Abilities and Circumstances of the several Colonies are much alter'd; so that that would be a very unequal Rule for settling the just Proportion of their Quotas in Men and Money at this day; For Instance the Quota of men allotted to this Province, to raise for the Assistance of New York, is 350, and that allotted to Pensilvania is 80: Now such a Proportion between the two Governments at this time would be extremely unequal; The Number of Inhabitants in Pensilvania having since King William's Reign been so much increas'd by the great number of Foreigners, who have annually transplanted themselves and their families thither, from the Palatinate, Swiss Cantons and Northern parts of Germany, and by the natural Increase of the People, that some have computed them at 500,000 Persons; Whereas the Increase of the Number of Inhabitants in the Massachusetts Bay within that time (not to mention their having had but a very inconsiderable number of Foreigners transplanted among them) hath been greatly hinder'd by having many of their valuable Townships lately lopp'd off by the new Settlement of the Boundaries between them and the Province of New Hampshire in 1737; as also by the Settlement of the Boundaries between them and the Colony of Rhode Island in 1741: And the Province hath been further reduc'd by the great losses it sustain'd of it's Inhabitants by Sea and Land in the Expedition against Cape Breton, and the Preservation of Nova Scotia, both before, and during the whole Course of the late Warr: so that there is no reason to doubt but that at this day the Inhabitants of Pensilvania, though they should be computed at only 400,000 are . . . about double the Number of those of this Province.

The like Remark may be made upon the Proportion of the Quota of Men or Money settled between the Colony of Connecticutt and this Province, which is about 1 to 3; that Colony being allotted to raise 120 men, and the Province 350; Whereas the Colony, by means of the before mentioned Reduction of the ancient, reputed Limits of this Province, and it's being exhausted of it's Inhabitants in the late Expeditions, and Warr, hath since making the aforesaid Settlement, so far got the start of the Province in the Increase of it's Inhabitants, that the just Proportion at this day between them is (according to the Computation of good Judges) no more than as 2 to 3 : There are other Circumstances besides to be considered in adjusting the Proportion of the Quota between the Colony and the Province; vizt the Colony is intirely cover'd by this Province, so that it hath no Frontier of it's own to defend in time of Warr; and consequently is at no Expence in the Maintenance of marching Companies, forts and Garrisons for that Purpose; whereas the Province hath a very extensive Frontier, which is constantly harrass'd by the Indians and French upon every Rupture, and at a very considerable charge in maintaining Marching Companies, forts and Garrisons: And in time of Peace the Colony's Taxes for the Support of His Majesty's Government among them, is very trifling in Comparison of those of this Province.

I submitted these Observations to his Lordship's Consideration, as Specimens of the Alteration of the Circumstances of the Colonies with regard to the Proportion, which they bore to each other in respect of their Numbers and Abilities in King William the 3d's Reign, and their present State; and to shew how unequal a Rule the Settlement made at that time for adjusting their respective Quotas of Men and Money would be for adjusting them at this day.

I further added upon this head, that Nothing would contribute more effectually to secure His Majesty's Subjects and Territories upon this Continent, against the rapid Progress which the French seem to be making in perfecting a strong Line of Forts upon our backs from Bay Verte easterly, to the utmost Extent of His Majesty's Dominions westward, and to bring the Indians to a Dependence upon the English, than a well concerted Scheme for uniting all His Majesty's Colonies upon it in a mutual Defence of each other, duely carry'd into Execution.

I observ'd to his Lordship that I had the utmost Reason to think, that the People of this Province are most readily dispos'd to do their part in promoting so necessary an Union; and to exert the same Spirit which they have hitherto done in His Majesty's Service, to the utmost of their Abilities, in Concurrence with His other Colonies for their mutual Defence: But I thought it my Duty to mention to his Lordship, that the Thoughts of bearing the Burthen of defending the wide Frontier, upon which fort Dummer stands, and which was in the year 1741 adjudg'd to belong to the Province of New Hampshire, as they did the last Warr, seems so grievous to them, that I much question whether, in case of another Rupture with France, they could be induc'd to do it; and whether unless some special Provision is made for the Protection of it by His Majesty, it would not then be greatly expos'd to be ravag'd by the Enemy.

I observ'd to his Lordship that the daily Intelligence which is receiv'd from the Indians, who resort to our truck-Houses, our Traders to the Bay of Funda, and even the Officers of fort Lawrence in Schiegnecto, of the great Diligence of the French in strengthening their fort and Block House in that District, and that on the Isthmus near Bay Verte, together with their having possess'd themselves of St John's River, and the Commerce they carry on in the Bay of Funda, hath greatly alarm'd the Assembly, and they extremely dread bad Consequences to the Province from such a Neighbourhood, in case it shall continue untill another Rupture; as they also do from the French Incroachments at Crown-point, unless something is done to curb them: towards the Expence of doing which and maintaining a fort and Garrison, if it should be His Majesty's Pleasure to have one erected for that Service, I observ'd to his Lordship, that I had Reason to hope that the Province would contribute their just Quota of Men or Money in proportion to the Protection, which their western Frontier would receive from it, in common with the Provinces of New York, New Jerseys, Pensilvania, Connecticutt, Rhode Island and New Hampshire, as His Majesty shall be pleas'd to allot each Colony to do the same.

I assur'd his Lordship I should carefully observe His Majesty's Commands not to make use of the arm'd force under my Direction, excepting within the undoubted Limits of His Majesty's Territories.

And I added that as I had the Honour to be acquainted with your Lordships's Sentiments concerning the Isthmus of the Peninsula of Nova Scotia, where the French have erected their forts, and the River of St. John's in the Bay of Funda, founded upon the Vouchers and Evidences produc'd by the Commissaries of both Crowns in the Negotiation at Paris, vizt that they are clearly within the Limits of His Majesty's Province of Nova Scotia, I suppos'd we might deem them to be so, notwithstanding the Claims of the French in their Memorials, which extend as far as the River Kennebeck to the Westward, and to the City of Annapolis Royal, as also part of the Lands lying between that and the Sea Coast of Nova Scotia from Cape Sable to Cape Canseau, to the eastward.

I have the Honour to be with the highest Respect
>My Lords
>>your Lordships' most Humble
>>and most Obedient Servant
>>>W. Shirley.

P.S. I inclose likewise to your Lordships a Copy of M. Du Quesne, the Governour of Canada's Letter in Answer to my Letter to him dated 22d of last October upon the Detention of some English Children as Slaves in Canada, a Copy of which last Letter, and of the Assembly's Message to me thereupon, I have before transmitted to your Lordships.

Rt Honble the Lords Commissioners ⎱
for Trade and Plantations. ⎰

Endorsed:
>Massachusets

Lr̃e from Wm Shirley Esqr Govr of the Massachusets Bay, to the Board, dated Janry.   1754 acquainting their Lordships with his having recd the King's Commands, in case of any hostile Attempt on His Majesty's Dominions.

>Recd Febry 21 ⎱ 1754
>Read April 5 ⎰

WILLIAM SHIRLEY TO THE GENERAL COURT OF MASSACHUSETTS [1]

Gentlemen of the Council and House of Representatives:

Having received, in the Recess of the Court, some Dispatches, which nearly concern the Welfare of the Province, I thought it necessary to require a general Attendance of the Members of both Houses at this Meeting of the Assembly, that the Matters, contain'd in them, may have as full and speedy a Consideration as the Importance of them seems to demand.

By Accounts sent from Richmond Fort and Declarations made before Me and His Majesty's Council by two of the Settlers at Frankfort upon the River Kennebeck, I am informed that in the Summer before last, a considerable Number of French settled themselves on a noted carrying Place, made Use of by the several Indian Tribes inhabiting that part of the Country in their Passage to and from Canada, being about 10 or 12 Miles wide which separates the head of the aforesd: River from that of the River Chaudiere, which last falls into the great River St: Lawrence at 4 Miles, and an half above the City of Quebec: and, from a Canada Indian, who quitted that City about 3 Years ago, on Accot. of his having incurr'd the Displeasure of the late Governour, and hath since resided in the Eastern parts of this Province for Protection.

I have receiv'd further Intelligence that the French are settled very thick for 12 Miles on each Side of the said River Chaudiere at about 30 Miles Distance above the Mouth of it, and in the Midway between the River St. Lawrence and the beforementioned carrying Place, and the Captain of Richmond Fort in his Letter dated 23d. of last Janry informs me that the Norridgewalk Indians have declared to him " [2] That they had given the New French Settlers, upon the

[1] *B.M.*, *Additional Manuscript 32735, 119.* A transcript is in the Library of Congress.
[2] There is but one quotation mark in the original.

Carrying place Liberty to hunt any where in that Country, as a Recompence for the great Service they will be of to them in a time of War with the English by supplying them with Provisions and Military Stores.

The same Officer further acquaints in another Letter datd Feby 11th., that several Indians of the Arrassangunticook[1] and some of Penobscot Tribe amounting together with the Norridgwalk Indians to 60 effective Men, besides Boys, capable of using Arms, were then lately arrived in the Neighbourhood of the Fort under his Command; and that tho' They assembled there on Pretence of Writing a joint Letter to me, as They have done, yet he had reason to expect, from their haughty insolent Behaviour, the repeated open Threats of some of them, and private Warning from others, That as soon as the Rivers should be free from Ice, They would commit Hostilities against the English, upon That, and the Neighbouring Rivers; in which they intimate They are to be assisted by a Number of French from Canada disguised like Indians; and in another Letter, dated the 10th. March he acquaints me, that the French Priest, Missionary to the Indians, of the River Kennebeck appear'd to him to be continually using Artifices to excite the Indians to prevent our Settlements from being extended higher up it; to set Them at Variance with the English, and dispose them to a War with Them this Spring.

Most of these Accounts are confirmed by the Declarations of the before mentioned Settlers at Frankfort with these additional Circumstances, that the French Priest hath been very inquisitive after Roman Catholick Families in that Settlement, and used Endeavours to draw off some of the Inhabitants into the Service of the French, particularly for building a Chapel, and a Dwelling House for himself upon that River about 3 or 4 Miles above Cushana, and at the Distance of 24 from Frankfort, and been very industrious to

---

[1] This name is spelled in various ways by Shirley. Among the spellings Arsegunticook and Arreregunticook are used. They are more commonly known as the St. Francis or St. François tribe.

persuade Them, that it was within the French Territories: and the Indians have further declared that they have been instigated by the Govr: of Canada to hinder the English from settling upon any part of the River, which is strongly confirmed by a Deposition of Capt: Lithgow, made in August last.

Upon this Occasion, Gentlemen, I sent, as soon as might be, with the Advice of his Majesty's Council, the necessary Reinforcements of Men and Stores to all the Eastern Forts, issued Commissions for raising Six Independent Companies in the Township and Districts next adjacent to Them, with Orders for the Officers and Soldiers to hold themselves in constant Readiness to march upon any Alarm, to the Succour of any Neighbouring Fort or Settlement which may be attacked, to cut off the Enemy in their Retreat, and, in case they shall find that the Norridgewalk Indians have committed Hostilities, to break up their Villages and Settlements upon Kennebeck, and to kill or captivate all they can meet with of their Tribe. I likewise ordered an Officer, commissioned by me for that purpose, to proceed, by the first Opportunity, to the suppos'd place of the new French Settlement, in order to discover the Certainty and Circumstances of it, and to require the French Commandant to retire, and withdraw the People under his Command from that Spot, as being under His Majesty's Dominion and within the Limits of this Government.

And I doubt not Gentlemen from your Distinguished Zeal for the Defence of His Majesty's Territories, and the Protection of his Subjects within this Government, upon all Occasions, but that, upon a Refusal of the French, to comply with that Requisition, you will make sufficient Provision for enabling me to compel Them with the armed Force of the Province to free it from their Incroachments.

The Concern Gentlemen, which you expressed in your Message to me at Our Meeting in December last, upon Your Apprehensions of the imminent Danger which the Province was in from the French's having fortified Themselves upon the River of St. John's, close to our Borders, leaves me no room to doubt of your being sensible of the fatal Consequences, in general, that must attend the Incroachments, which, it seems plain, they are now pushing into the Heart of the Province (as the General Court in a Vote passed the 16th. of January 1749, justly calls the River Kennebeck) unless they are timely removed.

But it may not be improper for me to observe to you in particular that it appears from an Extract which I have lately caused to be made of some original Letters, taken among Father Ralle's Papers at breaking up the Indian Settlement at Norridgewalk in 1724, and which passed between him, Father Lauverjat Priest of the Penobscot Tribe, and Father La Chasse Superiour of the Jesuits of Quebec, during the Indian War, in the Years 1723 and 1724; That the Head of Kennebeck River near which the Indians have declared the French have made a new Settlement, was the Centre of most of the Tribes then at War with us, and the general Rendezvous of all that came to the Eastern parts: The Hurons, the Iroquois of the Falls of St. Lewis, the Tribe of St. Francis (or Arrassangunticooks) and the Indians of the Seigneurie (as the French call them) of Becancour on the one hand, used to assemble with the Norridgewalks here, from their several Settlements, and the Penobscots from their River on the other; here They held their Consultations, and from hence issued out in Parties united or separate, as best suited them, against the English, hither They retired after Action, and brought their wounded for Relief, and here, if they met with Provisions they fared well, if not, They suffer'd greatly for want of Them.

It appears further from these Letters, that the several French Missionaries chiefly conducted and managed this War, That they had the Care of supplying the Indians with the necessary Provisions and Stores for carrying it on; were employed to make Them persevere in it, and to push Them on to their boldest Enterprizes; That they transmitted Accots: of their Proceedings to the Government of Canada, thro' the Hands of the Superiour of the Jesuits at Quebec, thro' whom likewise, they received their Directions from thence; as the Govr. of Canada seems to have done his upon this Occasion from the Court of France.

And I would further observe that this Route affords the French a shorter Passage for making Descents, from Quebec, upon this Province, and destroying the whole Province of Main, with the King's Woods there, and in the Government of New Hampshire, than any other whatever from Canada.

These Advantages, which the Possession of this River would give the French over this Province, make it easy to account for their constant Endeavours, ever since the Treaty of Breda, at which it was determined, in the most solemn manner, between the two Crowns that the River Pentagoet or Penobscot was the Boundary between New England and Accadia or Nova Scotia, to extend their Limits by Claim upon all Occasions, (as in fact they have done) to the Eastern Side of the River Kennebeck tho' they never attempted, until within these few Years, to pass over the River St. Lawrence within the Extent of this Province.

I am satisfied it is needless for me Gentlemen to urge any Thing more to shew, how necessary, for the Safety of this Government, it is, that We should secure to ourselves the Possession of this important River, against the Incroachments of the French, without Delay; and I think the present Situation of Affairs in that Country must convince you, how vain a Scheme it would now be, to have your sole Dependance for gaining this Point upon making Annual Presents to Indians, who appear to have enter'd into an Offensive Alliance with the French against you, and have shewn evident Marks of a Disposition to put the River into their Power.

How different are such Proceedings from those of the French? Whilst we have been suing in vain to a few Indians for their Permission to settle Lands within the undoubted Limits of this Province, and which Themselves can't deny to have been purchased of their Ancestors; and have in effect promis'd them a yearly Tribute, to restrain Them from committing Acts of Hostility against us; the French have marched Armies into distant Countrys of numerous and powerfull Tribes, which without any Colour of Right, They have invaded. They have forbid Them to make further Grants of any of Their Lands to the English, and have built, and are still building Strong Forts with an avow'd Intent to drive Them off from the Lands already granted to Them, and to exclude Them from all Commerce with those Indians, whom They have threatned with Destruction, if they shall presume to interfere in their favour.

It is time, Gentlemen, for you to desist from having your chief Dependance upon Temporary Expedients, which seem rather to have exposed the Government to the Contempt of these Indians than to have conciliated their Friendship to it, and to take Counsel in part from the Policy of our Neighbours.

Vigourous Measures against the French, in case they shall refuse to quit his Majesty's Territories within this Government, without being compell'd to it by Force, building a strong Fort near the Head of the River Kennebeck, above the Settlements of the Norridgewalk Indians, and pushing on our own Settlements upon it in a defensible Manner, would effectually rid the Province of the Incroachments of the former, and either hold the latter in a due Dependance upon us or oblige Them to abandon the River.

And further by making ourselves, thro' this means Masters of the Pass, which was the general Place of Rendezvous during the Indian War in 1723 and 1724 of all the Tribes engaged in it, both in their Incursions and Retreats, We should have it in our power to curb all those Indians for the future, and, in a great Measure, prevent them from attempting to make Depredations in our exposed Settlements.

I must further observe to you, upon this Occasion, Gentlemen, how dangerous Delays to make suitable Preparations for removing the French would be.

How practicable was it, at first, to have put a Stop to their Proceedings in building their Fort at Crown Point ? and you can't but remember, what mischievous Effects of the neglect to do that in the Beginning, were felt by This, and the Province of New York, in the Ravages which they suffer'd from thence during the late War.

A Short Delay to dislodge Them from their Incroachments

near the River Kennebeck, might give Them an Opportunity of making Themselves Masters of that River likewise in the End, and in that case we may expect soon to see another Fort built by Them near the Mouth of it, and the French in Possession of all the Sea Coast between that and River St. Johns.

GENTLEMEN,

I have other Matters of Importance to lay before You, But as Those I have already mentioned, require a most speedy and mature Consideration, and I would not, in the least, divert your Attention from providing for what is immediately necessary to be done for the Safety of the Province; I shall defer communicating them to you for a few Days.

But must not omit to apprize you that tho' I have sent Orders to Capt. Lithgow for putting Fort Richmond into as good a Posture of Defence, as the ruinous State of it would admit, which the imminent Danger it may be in from a sudden Attack made necessary for me to do, yet I can't but think that all Money expended upon the Repairs of it above what the present Emergency makes absolutely necessary, will be an useless Expence to the Province, it being so far decayed, as not to be capable of being made strong by any Repairs whatsoever.

Gentlemen of the Council and House of Representatives:
I hope you will proceed in the Consideration of these Matters, with that Unanimity and Dispatch, which His Majesty's Service, and the Safety of the Province requires, and that you, Gentlemen, of the House of Representatives will make the necessary Supplies.   W. SHIRLEY.

Council Chamber, March 28th. 1754.

Endorsed:
    Copy of Govr. Shirley's
    Speech to the Council and
    House of Representatives
    of the Massachusets Bay.
    March 28th. 1754. No: 1. in
    Govr. Shirley's Letter of April 19th: 1754.

WILLIAM SHIRLEY TO THE GENERAL COURT OF MASSACHUSETTS [1]

Gentlemen of the Council and House of Representatives:
The Occasion of my speaking to you now is to acquaint
You that I received a Letter from the Rt: Hble: the Lords
Commrs: for Trade and the Plantations, signifying to me,
that His Majesty had been pleased to order a Sum of Money
to be issued for Presents to the Six Nations of Indians, and
to direct the Govrs: of New York to hold an Interview with
them for delivering those Presents at such Place and Time
as he shall appoint; and I am directed to lay this Matter
before You and to recommend to You to make a proper
Provision for appointing Commissioners from this Government to meet Commissioners of Virginia, Maryland, Pensylvania, New Jerseys, and New Hampshire (to the respective
Govrs: of which Colonies their Lordships have wrote to the
same Effect) as also for making such Presents as hath been
usual upon the like Occasions.

I have likewise to acquaint You that I find by a Paragraph
of Their Lordships' Letter upon this Occasion to the Govr:
of New York, which His Honour Lt: Govr: DeLancey Commandr: in Chief of that Province, hath communicated to
me, that he is therein directed to take Care that all the Provinces be (if practicable) comprized in one general Treaty to
be made in His Majesty's Name, and that Mr: DeLancey
hath given me Notice, that he hath appointed the said Interview to be held at the City of Albany on the 14th: of June
next.

I am persuaded, Gentlemen, I need not use Arguments to
convince You that it is of very great Consequence to the

---

[1] *B. M.*, *Additional Manuscript 32735, 129.* A transcript is in
the Library of Congress. As will be seen from the endorsement
this most forcible presentation of the position and needs of the
American Colonies was forwarded to the London government on
April 19, giving the ministry a clear presentation of Shirley's plans
for America.

Interest of his Majesty's Colonies upon this Continent at all Times, that as many of the Tribes of Indians inhabiting it as may be (those of the Six Nations more especially) should be kept in Friendship with the English, and a Dependance upon the Crown of Great Britain, and that as free a Commerce and Intercourse should be maintained with them as is possible; But I think it my Duty at this Time to enter into a particular Detail of these Matters.

At the Treaty of Utrecht, which is confirmed by That of Aix la Chapelle, "These were looked upon to be points of that Importance to the British Interest in North America, that Care was taken in that Treaty to have the Indians of the Six Nations acknowledged by France to be subject to the Dominion of Great Britain, and it is therein expressly stipulated that the French shall give no Hindrance or Molestation either to them, or the other Natives of America, who were Friends to the English; it is also stipulated that the Subjects of both Crowns should enjoy full Liberty of going or coming upon this Continent on Account of Trade, and that the Natives of the Countries upon it should with the same Liberty, resort as they please, to the British and French Colonies, for promoting Trade on the one Side, and the other without any Molestation or Hindrance, either on the Part of the British Subjects, or of the French.

With regard to the Indians of the Six Nations in particular, I would observe to You, that according to an Account given by them in an open Council at Turpehawkie at their Return from the Indian Treaty at Philadelphia in 1742, of the several Indian Nations which have been conquered by them and are now in their Alliance, and trade with the English (which Account seems to be the best we have of that Matter) the Warriours belonging to those Tribes may be computed to amount to 16,000 at least; and the French Indian whom I have retained in His Majesty's Service, who must be a good Judge of the Strength of the Five Nations themselves, upon being interrogated by me concerning the Number of their fighting Men, made Answer "That he did not know their Number, but well knew that they are a numerous People, a terrible Body of Men, and able to burn all the Indians in Canada."

You must be sensible Gentlemen, what frequent Attempts the French have made from Time to Time to draw off the Six Nations from the English Interest into their own; and from the repeated Advices We have received from His Majesty's Southern Colonies on this Continent, what Efforts they have lately exerted to win over their Allies, together with the other numerous Tribes inhabiting the vast Country lying along the great Lakes and Rivers, and to the Westward of the Apalachean Mountains, (all which may be reckoned to exceed double the Number of the Indians of the Six Nations and those in their Alliance,) as also what Measures the French are taking to exclude the English from all Trade and Commerce with those Indians.

To compass this, they have in manifest Violation of the aforesaid Treaties, entered the Country of these Indians upon the Back of His Majesty's Southern Colonies, and within the Limits of his Territories, with large Bodies of Troops, seized the Effects, and captivated the Persons of the English whom they have found trading there, absolutely denied their Right to Traffick with those Nations, and erected a Line of Forts upon the Lakes and Rivers from Canada to Mississippi, to cut off all Commerce and Intercourse between them; They have committed Hostilities against some of the Tribes in Friendship with the English, engaged others to take up the Hatchet against them, and threatened those with Destruction who shall interfere in their avowed Design to drive the English out of that Country.

Should the Indians of the Six Nations at this critical Conjuncture desert Our Alliance, and go over to the French, how fatal an Influence must such an Event have upon the British Interest? On the other Hand, should proper Measures be taken to attach them firmly to it, how greatly would it disappoint and check the present Scheme and Enterprizes of our dangerous Neighbours.

It is well known how wavering the Disposition of these Indians hath of late been; and how visibly they have abated their former Enmity to the French, and we can't be at a Loss to discover the real Causes of it; Nothing could at this Time so effectually reclaim them to their old Alliance with Us, as the Measures directed by Their Lordships of the Board of Trade, one general League of Friendship, comprising all His Majesty's Colonies, to be made with them in His Majesty's Name, with Stipulations to build such Forts in their Country as they shall choose, and may be judged necessary for their Shelter and Protection against the French.

Such a Coalition of the Colonies for their Defence would be a convincing Proof to them, that they might safely depend upon His Maty for Protection, and confirm them in their ancient Alliance with the English; and how necessary such a Confederacy of the Colonies for their Safeguard is, may appear to You from the following Account given by an Indian Trader, who, for more than 20 Years had carried on a Trade among the different Nations of Indians some Hundred Miles West of Philadelphia, the Truth of which I've great Reason to depend upon, Viz: "That in Novr: 1750, he with sundry other Traders of the English, was taken Prisoner by some Frenchmen belonging to a Fort upon the River Ohio, and from thence was transported from Fort to Fort to Quebeck, by Means of which Forts and the Lakes, the French, he says have a Communication open from Quebec to Mississippi; that they have Forts there within 20 or 30 miles Distance of each other, with a Command of from 10 to 20 Men in each; in which he says they put the Squaws and Papooses of the Indians in Alliance with them for Protection, whilst the Men go out to War, and there keep them untill the Men return; and he observes, that by means of these Forts, they bid fair in a little Time to seduce the Indians in Alliance with the English, as the English do not afford the same Protection to their Women and Children, whilst the Men are gone to War, as the French do."

I would therefore earnestly recommend to You, Gentlemen of the House of Representatives, to make suitable Provision for sending Commissioners on the Part of this Government, to join in the approaching Interview at Albany duly authorized to concert such Measures in Conjunction with the Government of New York, and Commissioners of the beforementioned Governments, as shall be judged proper to be entered into, for cementing a firm League of Friendship with the Indians of the Six Nations, and retaining them in the British Interest, and to give those Commissioners full Powers to agree with the other Governments upon the Quota of Money and Men to be furnished by the Province for this Service.

I have taken the Liberty to propose the same Thing to be done by the other Governments concerned in this Interview in my Letters to His Majesty's governors, and have Reason to hope they will promote so salutary a Measure.

Such an Union of Councils besides the happy Effect it will probably have upon the Indians of the Six Nations may lay a Foundation for a general one among all His Majesty's Colonies, for the mutual Support and Defence against the present dangerous Enterprizes of the French on every Side of them.

I have already let You know, Gentlemen, His Majesty's Orders to me and his other Governors upon this Point, signified to Us in the Earl of Holdernesse's Letter of the 28th : of last August, and how necessary it is that such an Union should be immediately formed in the Common Cause, whoever takes a Survey of the whole Extent of the Invasions and Encroachments which the French are surrounding His Majesty's Territories upon this Continent with, from their Most Eastern to their Most Western Limits must soon be convinced.

Close on the Back of the Settlements of His Majesty's Southern Colonies, they are joining Canada to the Mississippi by a Line of Forts and Settlements along the great Lakes and Rivers, and cutting off all Commerce and Intercourse between the English and the numerous powerfull Tribes of Indians inhabiting that Country, whom they are attempting to engage in their Interest by all Manner of Hostilities and Artifices : and at the same Time they are pushing on their Encroachments with equal Vigour quite round His Majesty's

Eastern Colonies, where they have secured all the Indians in those Parts to join them against the English.

Should the French prevail in the former Part of their Scheme, and gain a general Influence and Dominion over the Indians behind the Apalachean Mountains, which they must in the ordinary Course of human Events do in a short Time, if they are not timely prevented by an Union of His Majesty's Colonies, they will have in a very few Years a most formidable Army of those Indians at their Command, maintained without any Expence to themselves, but on the other Hand, with great Profit, arising from an immense Fur Trade carried on with them; And what fatal Consequences such an Army of Warriours (a few of which have been found sufficient to keep a large Frontier in continual Alarm) must have upon all His Majesty's Southern Colonies, by continually harrassing them at the Direction of the French, and supported by them from Canada on one Side, and Mississippi on the other, and covered in their Retreat behind the Mountains by a strong Line of Forts commanding the Navigation of all the Lakes and Rivers, is easy to conceive, especially if the Indians of the Six Nations should desert our Alliance, and join the French, which must in such Case, be a decisive Blow to the British Interest in that Part of the Continent.

At the same Time if they are not prevented by a Coalition of the Colonies from finishing the Scheme, which it is most manifest they are forming against the Eastern Provinces, and already far advanced in, they must soon have it in their power equally to distress them likewise; and all the English Colonies will be involved together in one general Flame.

It is true, those Colonies are far superiour to the French in their Numbers and Strength, but if that strength, Gentlemen, is not properly exerted by an Union among themselves, how little will it avail?

It is not difficult to imagine that such a Body of Troops as the French may soon collect, together with the Assistance of all the Indians scattered throughout this Continent, on the Back of the English Colonies (as the French Settlements likewise are) when under the Command of the Govr. Genl.

of New France, who upon all Emergencies can direct their Force as he pleases, may reduce a Number of disunited Provinces, many of them very remote from each other, tho' much superiour in Point of the Number of Inhabitants.

For forming this general Union, Gentlemen, there is no Time to be lost, the French seem to have advanced further towards making themselves Masters of this Continent within these last five or six Years, than they have done ever since the first Beginning of their Settlements upon it; and how determined they are to accomplish their Scheme as soon as possible, appears from their breaking thro' the most recent solemn Treaties and Agreements made between the two Crowns in order to effect it.

Gentlemen:

His Majesty hath on all Occasions given the strongest Proof of His paternal Care of His Colonies, and constant Attention to their Safety, particularly at this Time, in directing his Govrs: to promote this Union within their respective Governmts:; and I hope You will not be wanting on your parts to contribute all in your Power towards effecting it, by improving the Opportunity which the approaching Interview with the Indians of the Six Nations at Albany, happily presents for that Purpose; And I doubt not but that You may depend on all reasonable Support and Protection on the Part of His Majesty against all present and future Enterprizes and Attempts of the French against You.

W. SHIRLEY.

Council Chamber, April 2, 1754.

Endorsed:

> Copy of Govr. Shirley's
> Speech to the Council and House
> of Representatives of the Province
> Massachusets Bay 2d: April 1754.
> No. 4. in Govr. Shirley's Lre of 19th: April 1754.

GENERAL COURT OF MASSACHUSETTS TO WILLIAM SHIRLEY [1]

May it please your Excellency,

The Council and House of Representatives of this His Majesty's Province have given very great Attention to the two Speeches which you have been pleased to make from the Chair on the 28th March and the 2d of April. We are Sensible they contain Matters of the last Importance, not only to the Inhabitants of this Government but to every other of His Majesty's Subjects in America, to the British Interest in General, and to the Interest of all Europe.

It now evidently appears that the French are far advanced in the Execution of a Plan, projected more than fifty Years Since, for the extending their Possessions from the Mouth of the Mississippi on the South, to Hudsons Bay on the North for Securing the vast Body of Indians in that inland Country, and for Subjecting this whole Continent to the Crown of France. This Plan agreeable to the Genius and Policy of the French Nation was laid for a future Age, the Operation of it has been gradual and almost insensible, whilst the British Governments in the Plantations, have been consulting temporary Expedients, and they are in Danger of continuing to do so untill it be too late to defeat it. And however improbable it may seem that this scheme should succeed, since the French Inhabitants on the Continent, at present, bear but a small proportion to the English, yet there are many other Circumstances which give them a great Advantage over us, and which if not attended to will soon over balance our superiority in Numbers. The French pay no Regard to the most Solemn Engagements but immediately after a Peace take and keep Possession of a Country which by Treaty they had just before expressly ceded, whilst the English, in the Plantations afraid of incurring Displeasure and of being instrumental of bringing on a War in Europe

[1] *B. M., Additional Manuscript 32735, 123.* A transcript is in the Library of Congress.

suffer these Incroachments to be made and continu'd. The French in time of Peace are continually exciting the Indians settled among them to come upon our Frontiers, to kill and captivate Our People and to carry their Scalps and Prisoners to Canada, where, as We have full Evidence, a reward is given for them, and by this Means we are prevented from extending our Settlements in Our Own Country, whilst the English from the Principle just now mentioned Scruple to avenge themselves by carrying the War into the Indian Settlements, least they Should annoy His Majesty's Allies amongst whom our most barbarous Enemies are Settled, and by whom they are cherished and encouraged. The French have under their Influence by far the greatest Part of the Indians on the Continent, whilst the English by the different Measures of the several Governments, are in danger of losing the small Proportion which at present are attached to them. The French have but one Interest and keep one Point in view, the English Governments have different Interests, are disunited, some of them have their Frontier covered by their Neighbouring Governments and not being immediately effected seem unconcerned.

The French are Supported by the Crown and Treasure of France which seems now more than ever to have made the Plantations the Object of it's Attention, the English Governmts. are obliged to carry on any Schemes at their own Expence and are not able long to Support any great Undertaking.

These are some of the disadvantages which the English at present labour under and they are not likely to be removed without His Majesty's gracious Interposition. We therefore desire your Excellency to represent to His Majesty the exposed, hazardous State of these his Governments, and humbly to pray, that he would be pleased to cause the most effectual Measures to be taken for the removal of any French Forts or Settlements that are or may be made in any part of his Territories on this Continent; and in particular, that the Subjects of the French King may be compelled to quit the Province of Nova Scotia, where, in direct violation of the most express Agreement to the Contrary they are daily increasing and fortifying themselves; that His Majesty would allow and order that whensoever the Indians who are Settled among the French or are under their Direction and control shall captivate and destroy his English Subjects, his respective Governments shall suffer and encourage the Indians who are in the English Interest to make reprisals upon the French, there being no other way of putting a Stop to the Incursions of the French Indians, or of forwarding the Settlement of Our Frontiers, That Affairs which relate to the Indians of the Six Nations and their Allies under some general Direction as His Majesty shall think proper may be constantly regarded, and that the Interests or Measures of particular Governments or Persons may not be Suffered to interfere with such Direction; that the several Governments may be obliged to bear their proportion of the Charge of defending His Majesty's Territories against the Encroachments of the French and the Ravages and Incursions of the Indians, and that in Case of any great and heavy Charge His Majesty would be graciously pleased to Relieve Us.

In the mean time We assure Your Excellency that we are ready to do every Thing that can be expected from Us on the present Emergency. We think Ourselves happy that we have a Gentleman at the head of the Province who is so perfectly acquainted with His Majesty's just Title to the Country encroached upon by the French, who has given such distinguished Proofs of his Zeal for His Majesty's Service, whose Endeavours to defend his Territories and enlarge his Dominions in time of War have been attended with such happy Success, and whose abhorrence of such perfidious Invasions in Time of Peace we are so well acquainted with.

We take great Pleasure and Satisfaction in Measures taken by Your Excellency with the Advice of His Majesty's Council in the Recess of the Court and will chearfully Support the Execution of them.

We look upon it to be of absolute Necessity that the French should at all Events be prevented from making any Settlement whatsoever on the River Kennebeck or the carrying

Place at the Head of it. As Richmond Fort on that River is in a decayed State we desire your Excellency to order a New Fort to be erected of about 120 Feet Square as far up the River above Richmond Fort, as your Excellency shall think fit, and to cause the Garrison, Artillery and Stores at Richmond to be removed to the new Fort and the old one to be demolished.

We pray Your Excellency likewise to order a Sufficient Force up to the Carrying Place to remove any French that may be Settling there, But, as We apprehend that our Success under Providence, will depend very much on your taking this Affair into your immediate Care and Direction, we therefore pray your Excellency to Submit to the inconveniences of a Voyage to the Eastern Parts of the Province and there to give Such Orders for the Purposes aforesaid as you shall find necessary.

And that Your Excellency's Person may be Secure against any Attempts of French or Indians and that you may be enabled to effect the building the Fort aforesaid and to destroy any French Settlements that may be carrying on we will make Provision for the Pay and Subsistence of 500 Men which number, including the Six independent Companies already ordered we desire you to cause to be enlisted as soon as you shall think proper. We will also make ample Provision for your Excellency's Voyage and for an interview with the Indians if you shall find it expedient. We hope by your Excellency's prudent Management these Indians will be convinced that it is their Interest to continue at Peace with Us, and as We are Sincerely desirous that every thing may be done which may tend to perpetuate the same we will readily defray the Charge of Supporting and educating a considerable Number of the principal Indian Children if your Excellency can prevail on their Friends to agree to it.

We are Situated remote from the Six Nations and have never had the benefit of a Trade with them, yet we have frequently joined in the Treaties with them and have contributed largely towards Presents and other Expences attending Such Treaties, and are Still ready to do all that can be reasonably desired from Us for securing their **Attachment** to his Majesty's Interest.

Your Excellency must be Sensible that an Union of the Several Governments for their mutual Defense and for the Annoyance of the Enemy, has long been desired by this Province and Proposals made for this Purpose. We are Still in the same Sentiments and shall use our Endeavours to effect it. An heavy charge must necessarily attend the Several Measures proposed and we shall forthwith apply ourselves to the making Provision for defraying the same.

J. Osborne P Order.

In the House of Representatives April 9th 1754. Read and Accepted and Ordered that Colo. Richards, Capt. Chandler, and Mr. Greenleaf with Such as the Honble. Board shall join be a Committee to wait upon His Excellency the Governor with the foregoing Message.

Sent up for Concurrence

T. Hubbard Spkr.

In Council April 10th 1754. Read and Concurred and Benjamin Lynde and John Cushing Esqrs. are joined with the Committee of the House in the Affair aforementioned.

J. Willard. Secretary.

A True Copy Examined

Thos. Clarke Deputy Secretary.

Endorsed:

Copy of a Message from the
Council and Representatives of the
Province of the Massachusets Bay to
Govr. Shirley in Answer to his two
Speeches.

WILLIAM SHIRLEY TO THE EARL OF HOLDERNESS [1]

Boston New England April 19th, 1754.

My Lord,

Since I had the Honour of writing to your Lordship, I have receiv'd Intelligence, that in the Summer before last, the French made a Settlement upon a Tract of Land, which lies wholly to the Westward of the River Kennebeck and Separates a Branch of it from the Source of the River Chaudiere, being reckoned to be ten or twelve Miles over. The former of these Rivers after a Computed Course of about 150 Miles discharges itself into the Atlantic Ocean in the Latitude of about 44 Degrees North, and the latter after running about 70 Miles, falls into the River St. Lawrence in about 46 Degrees 50 Min. of the same Latitude, about one French League and a half above the City of Quebec.

This is the principal Carrying Place made use of by the Indians in their passage between this Province and Canada, and lies near the Place of Rendez-vous, from whence the several Tribes at War with this Government in the Years 1723 and 1724 made their Incursions.

This Intelligence I have communicated to the General Assembly at their late Session, and recommended to them upon the Motives set forth in my inclosed Speech, to make Provision for enabling me to Act with regard to the Supposed Settlement of the French, as the present Emergency might require, and to build a Fort higher up the River Kennebeck for securing the Possession of it against the French, and curbing the Indians in any future hostile Attempts.

Upon these Advices, My Lord, the General Assembly hav-

---

[1] *B. M.*, *Additional Manuscript 32735, 110.* A transcript is in the Library of Congress. Substantially the same letter to the Lords of Trade of the same date is in C. O. 5, 887. This letter was intended by Shirley to bring his views specifically before the Ministry, and his speeches to the Massachusetts Assembly and its reply were therefore inclosed in it. See also the map drawn by Shirley's order at the close of this volume.

ing experienced the great Ravages, which were made in the Country from the Neighbourhood of this Carrying Place during the before mentioned Indian War (which could not be extinguished without destroying the Indian Settlements upon this River and driving them off it,) are extremely Apprehensive of much more Mischievous Consequences from that, which it is evident, the French are now kindling between us and the Indians, if the Indians shall be supported by a French Settlement near the Head of Kennebeck, as they will also be from another Settlement of the French, made as I understand, within the last thirty years, upon the River Chaudiere, neither of which was in being during the before mentioned War, and they have upon this Occasion desired me in their Inclosed Message to remove the French from their Settlement at the Carrying Place.

It seems certain, My Lord, that if both these French Settlements are suffered to remain, there may be Danger of their soon becoming Masters of the whole River Kennebeck; which Event would prove very destructive to His Majesty's Subjects within this Province, and greatly Affect the Security of his Territories within the other Colonies of New England: But as I am strictly enjoyned by your Lordship, in the Letter, which I had the honour to receive from You, dated the 28th of August 1753, not to make use of the Armed Force under my Direction "excepting within the undoubted Limits of His Majesty's Dominions"; I have before I determined to use any Force to remove the French, examined His Majesty's Right to the Country in Question, as thoroughly as I am able, and beg leave to lay the Result of that Inquiry before your Lordship.

According to Letters Patent under the Great Seal of England, from King James 1st in the eighteenth Year of his Reign, to the Council established at Plymouth in the County of Devon, for the planting, ruling, Ordering and Governing of New England; and to others from King Charles 2d bearing date in the Sixteenth Year of his Reign to the then Duke of York, his Brother, and to the Charter granted by King William and Queen Mary in the third Year of their Reign to this Province, (Extracts from all which I have inclosed) both the River Kennebeck and Chaudiere with the Adjacent Country, from the Atlantic Sea to the River of St. Lawrence, appear to be undoubtedly within the Limits of His Majesty's Dominions; And what seems greatly to confirm the Ancient Claim of the Crown to this Country is, that in the Year 1613, which is five years prior to the date of the Eldest of these Patents, and but eight after the Epocha fixed by the French for their first Attempt to make Settlements in North America; Sir Samuel Argall, who then guarded the New England Coast by Sea, received Orders from England to displant them, and accordingly in that Year, upon receiving Intelligence of the Arrival of a Company of French under the Command of one Captain Saussaye at Pentagoet, destroyed the Fortification, they had begun there, with the Cross they had erected, setting up in its Place, the English Standard, and removed the French with their Effects from thence; after which he proceeded to the River St. Croix in the Bay of Funda; where he demolish'd the French Works, which the Sieur de Monts left standing, in the first Expedition of the French into North America; and then going to Port Royal (now Annapolis Royal) which he likewise found deserted, demolished all the Buildings there, and reduced the Place to a Solitude: and it doth not appear that the Court of France made any Complaints against Sr. Samuel Argall to the Government of England, for these proceedings, which were made in a time of Peace, between the two Crowns; But thereupon confined their Settlements, upon this part of the Continent, to the North Side of the River St. Lawrence; which Acquiescence in their Expulsion out of that Country, seems not to be accounted for otherwise than that they were satisfied at that time, that their Attempts to make Settlements to the Southward of the River St. Lawrence, were Encroachments upon the Right of the English; and that they had no just Cause of Complaint, for Sir Samuel Argall's breaking up their Settlements there and driving the French out of that part of the Country.

I would further Observe to your Lordship that it appears

from the Execution of the Treaty of Breda in 1667, by which Accadia was yielded to France, that at that time, it was determined between the two Crowns, after great Deliberation, that the Eastern Limits of New England extended to the River Pentagoet or Penobscot, which lies about twenty Leagues to the Eastward of the River Kennebeck.

And though the French took all Opportunities soon after to extend their Limits by Claim, as far as the River Kennebeck; yet it appears in every instance of their making that Claim, and particularly by their Declaration concerning the Ancient Limits of Accadia during the Negotiation of the Treaty of Utrecht; (as is plain by the Transactions of that Treaty,) that it was wholly founded upon this pretence, vizt that the Country lying between Kennebeck and Pentagoet was part of Accadia; which, if it had been true, yet as the whole of that Province is in express terms ceded by that Treaty to the Crown of Great Britain, must even by Virtue of that appertain to the English.

And as to the Northern and Eastern Limits of Accadia; that they were originally deemed to extend as far as the Southern Bank of the River St Lawrence, seems clear from the Testimony of Monsr. Champlain, who in his Voyages de la Nouvelle France, upon the Authority of which the French Commissaries greatly rely, to prove what were the Ancient Limits of Accadia, speaking of that part of the Continent, thro' which the River Pentagoet runs, expressly says, that the River of St. Lawrence washes the Coast of Accadia in these words "la grande Riviere St. Laurent costoye la coste d'Acadie;" from whence it necessarily follows, that the Limits of Accadia must extend as far as the Southern Bank of the River.

To shew the Weight of this Authority, it is necessary to Observe, that the Sieur Champlain was, as the French call him, "the Father and Founder of Quebec," and must consequently know in what Country the Southern Bank of the River St. Lawrence lay, better than any other Frenchman whatever, and that the time, he speaks of in the passage referred to, was about the Year 1604 and 1605, whilst he was with the Sieur De Monts upon the first Expedition of the French into North America.

And upon these Grounds His Majesty's Commissaries at Paris, according to the Instructions given them by the Rt. Honble. the Lords Commissioners for Trade and Plantations, in their Memorial dated in January 1750/1751, and by them delivered to the French Commissaries, claimed the Territory lying between the Rivers Kennebeck and Pentagoet bounded Northerly by the River St. Lawrence, to belong to the Crown of Great Britain, as well by original ancient Right, as by Virtue of the Treaty of Utrecht.

I shall now proceed to Observe to your Lordship, how the Actual Possession of the Rivers Kennebeck and Chaudiere hath gone and what Settlemts. have been made upon them by the English or French.

It appears from Purchas's Pilgrim, to which the French Commissaries have in this Dispute appealed, that the English had in the Year 1602, made Plantations in North America, between the 43d. and 45th. Degrees of North Latitude, of which part of the Country, then called by the Indians *Mawooshen*, he gives a particular Description, and therein takes Notice of the Rivers Pemaquid and Sagadehock, and the Towns of *Penobscot*, *Kennebeck* and *Narragooc;* as lying within that part of the Country, which the English were then Settling.

And Monsr. St. Denis, one of the French governors of part of Accadia, about the Year 1654, in his [1] Description Geographique and Historique des Costes de l'Amerique Septentrionale, which is frequently cited by the French Commissionaries in their Memorial dated in October 1751 and delivered by them to the English Commissaries, expressly says, that the River Pentagoet, which is before observed to lie about twenty Leagues to the Eastward of Kennebeck River, was the dividing Line between the English and French Limits, and that the English had many Settlements on the Western side of it.

[1] Note by Shirley: " *Vide* the Passage among the inclosed Citations."

It appears further, that the American Colony of New Plymouth, did soon after the Year [   ][1] by Virtue of a Patent from the beforementioned Council established by King James 1st at Plymouth in the County of Devon (whereby they granted the Colony a Tract of Land extending fifteen Miles on each side the River Kennebeck, together with the River itself,) built a Trading House, and made Settlements as high up the River, as a Place called *Cussenac* above forty Miles from the Mouth of it, where they exercised likewise a Government and Jurisdiction; and the English have many Years had Townships well Settled, and Forts built on that River and its principal Branches.

And that in the Year 1649, the Indians sold to the Colony their native Right to that River from Cussenac aforesaid to a Branch of the River called Wesserunkick, which is ninety Miles up it; and during the War in 1724, the English by breaking up the Settlemts. of the Indians there, and driving them off the River, acquired a Right to the whole of it, against the Indians themselves by Conquest; and accordingly built Richmond Fort there, in that, or the Year following to preserve it.

As to the French; they, as hath been Observed, never extended their Claim as far as this River, untill after the Treaty of Breda; and then it was done in contravention to the Treaty; and only the [2] Eastern Bank of it was claimed, as being the Western limits of Accadia, leaving the Stream common to both Nations; But they were never made nor Attempted to make any upon the Carrying-Place, the whole of which lies to the *Westd:* of it, untill the Summer before last.

As to the River Chaudiere; I can't find that the English ever had Settlements upon it; But I understand the French have made one on both sides of it; beginning at thirty Miles distance from the River St. Lawrence, and extending about Twelve Miles; But that hath been made within the last

[1] The date is omitted in the Ms.
[2] Note by Shirley: " *Vide* the Passage of Mr. Villebon's Letter among the Inclosed Citations."

Thirty Years; and owes its Rise and Growth to its lying out of the Observation of the English.

Upon this State of the Evidence I should not hesitate to determine that both the Kennebeck and Chaudiere were within his Majesty's Territories; But as an Attempt to disturb the French upon the last mentioned River, where they had settled before the late War; and extending His Majesty's Claim, at this Conjuncture, so near to Quebec itself might give extreme Umbrage to them, and tend to beget a National Misunderstanding; I shall not do it, without receiving His Majesty's Commands for that Purpose.

As to their supposed Settlement upon the Carrying Place between the two Rivers; if it is Advanced beyond the Middle of it, and so near to the Head of Kennebeck as to endanger the loss of that, and of the Adjacent Country, to His Majesty's Subjects, within the Province under my Government, I purpose, if the French will not remove from it, after a requisition made by me in His Majesty's Name to the Commandant for that purpose; (pursuant to the Directions in your Lordship's Letter) to use my best Endeavours to compel them to quit it with the Armed Force of the Province.

It seems clear, My Lord, that the French must, at all Events, be deemed Aggressors in this Case, since if it could be Admitted to be doubtfull whether that half at least of the Carrying Place, which lies next to the River Kennebeck, was within His Majesty's Territories or the French King's yet these proceedings of the French are a plain Breach of the Agreement entered into between the two Crowns, sometime before the Nomination of Commissaries on both sides; whereby it was Stipulated that neither party should make Settlements upon any controverted Tract in America, untill it should be determined by the Commissaries, within the Dominions of which Prince the Tract lay; and consequently the English seem to have an undoubted Right to remove the Settlement in Question, by Virtue of *that* Agreement. I shall strictly Observe this Agreement on the part of His Majesty, and hope there can be no Colour for charging what is done in Opposition to any Breach of it committed by the French, (when necessary for the Protection of his Subjects) as any Violation of the Amity, which ought to Subsist between the two Nations.

I have further to Acquaint your Lordship, that pursuant to the Directions signified to me, by the Rt. Honble. the Lords Commissioners for Trade and Plantations in their Letter, dated Septr. 18th 1753,[1] I Recommended in my Speech to the General Assembly, (a copy of which I inclose) to make provision for sending Commissioners from this Government to joyn with the Governmt. of New York, and the Commissioners which should come from Virginia, Maryland, the New Jerseys and New Hampshire in the Interview to be held with the Indians of the five Nations at Albany in June next; and for making them Presents: And I took Occasion therein further to recommend to them, to Impower their Commissioners to concert Measures with those, who shall be sent from the other Governmts. concerned, for cementing a General League of Friendship between those Indians and the English, and to agree on the behalf of this Government, with the others, upon the reasonable Quota of Men and Money to be found by them for this Service; as also to lay a foundation at that Meeting, for a general Union between all his Majesty's Colonies upon this Continent for their mutual Defence and Protection against an Enemy.

The Assembly, My Lord, have readily complied with every thing I have proposed to them upon this Occasion, and if the other Governments concerned in the Interview at Albany shall be equally disposed to promote His Majesty's Service, and unite in the Support of the common Cause at that Meeting, there is reason to hope it may have a considerable Effect towards beginning the General Union, which it is His Majesty's Pleasure that all his Colonies should Enter into.

I have the Honour to be etca.

W. SHIRLEY.

P.S. I should have Observed to Your Lordship, that the River Kennebeck remarkably abounds with white Pine

[1] *Ante*, p. 13.

Trees fit for the Service of the Royal Navy; and with fine large Oaks.

Colonel Westbroke, who for many Years furnished the Masts etca. for Messrs. Gulstons, Contractors with the Government for supplying the Masts etca. for the King's Yards, made an Observation upon this River, that it had a sufficient Quantity of white Pines to Supply the Royal Navy for more than fifty Years.

Rt. Honble. Earl of Holderness.

Endorsed:

Boston 19th: April 1754.
Govr. Shirley.

WILLIAM SHIRLEY TO MASSACHUSETTS COMMISSIONERS [1]

[LS.]
⎰William Shirley Esqr., Captain General and Governour in Chief in and over his Majesty's Province of the Massachusetts Bay in New England.

To Samuel Welles, John Chandler, Thomas Hutchinson, Oliver Partridge and John Worthington, Esqr., Greeting:⎱

Whereas, in Pursuance of Letters from the Right Honourable the Lords Commissioners for Trade and the Plantations, dated the 28th of August and 19th of September, 1753, to the Governors of several of his Majesties Plantations in North America, a General Convention of Commissioners for their respective Governments is appointed to be held at the City of Albany in the Month of June next for holding an Interview with the Indians of the five nations, and making them Presents on the Part of the said Governments, usual upon such occasions in order to confirm and Establish their

---

[1] Printed: 1 Penna. Arch. 2, 137. The Proceedings of the Indian Conference at Albany, June 19 – July 11, 1754, are in the Sir William Johnson Mss., N. Y. State Library, 1, 127.

ancient attachments to his Majesty and their constant Friendship to his Majesty's Subjects on this Continent: and Whereas the Great and General Court or Assembly of the Province of the Massachusetts Bay aforesaid, have elected and appointed you to represent and appear for the said Province at the Convention aforesd, for the Purposes abovementioned: as also for entring into articles of Union and Confederation with the aforesaid Governments for the General Defence of his Majesty's Subjects and Interests in North America as well in time of Peace as of War.

Now I do by these Presents impower and Commissionate you the said Samuel Welles, John Chandler, Thomas Hutchinson, Oliver Partridge and John Worthington as Commissioners (or any three of you) to appear for and represent the Province of the Massachusetts Bay aforesaid, at the proposed Convention of Commissioners, to be held at the City of Albany in the Month of June Next, then and there to Concert, with the Commissioners (from all or any of his Majesty's British Governments) that may be there Convened, Such Measures as may be judged proper for the Purposes aforesd, and to agree upon the same; and herein you must observe Such Instructions as are herewith delivered you, or may from time to time be given you by the Great and General Court or Assembly of this Province.

Given under my hand and the Publick Seal of the Province of the Massachusetts Bay aforesaid the nineteenth Day of April, 1754, in the twenty-seventh year of his Majesty's Reign.

W. SHIRLEY.

By his Excellency's Command,
J. WILLARD, Secry.
A true Copy Att:

SAMUEL WELLES,
JOHN CHANDLER,
OLR. PARTRIDGE,
JOHN WORTHINGTON.

WILLIAM SHIRLEY TO SIR THOMAS ROBINSON
[Extract] [1]

Boston, New England, May 8th, 1754.

SIR,   *   *   *   *   *   *

I have not dwelt, my Lord, so long upon the State of the French Incroachments, and English Settlements in Nova Scotia, in order to convince your Lordship of the Necessity of removing the former before a Rupture shall happen with France; That would be needless: Your Lordship did me the honor to inform me at Horton fully of your Sentiments upon that point; But my intent is to submit it to your Lordship's consideration, whether it is not high time, that it should be done, as soon as may be. It seems certain that it will grow more and more difficult, if not soon done.

It would have been much more practicable to have dislodg'd the French from St. John's River, before they had fortified themselves upon it, and gain'd such an Influence over the Indians there, as they now have; and to have drove them off the Isthmus, before they had any Cannon or Fortress upon it.

However, tho' at present it might be no easy matter for His Majesty's Troops, with their present strength in Nova Scotia, to reduce the French Fort at Beau Sejour by assault, as they have three Bomb-Proofs within it, yet I am assured by the Commandant of Fort Lawrence, as well as other Officers of it, that it is practicable for them, with the assistance of 1000 Men from New England, (if that should be rather approved of than transporting the like Number of Troops from Europe,) to distress their Garrison so much, by cutting them off from all Supplies of Provisions and Water, (which last they are oblig'd to fetch half a Mile from their Fort, not being able after many attempts to find any within it) that they could not hold out long.

[1] *B. M.*, *Additional Manuscript 32736, 259.* A transcript is in the Library of Congress.

It seems not to be doubted but that the Force I have before mention'd, might enable the Kings Troops to make themselves very easily Masters of the small Fort at Gaspero, and the Town of Bay Vert, and hinder Provisions or other Stores from being landed there, or transported to Beau Sejour; as also of the small French Fort on the point of Land between the Rivers Amrancook, and Petcoject [sic] the Village of Westcough, and the point of Wood near it, with all the French Settlements along the Coast of the Gulf of St. Lawrence between Bay Vert and the Gut of Canseau, where Provisions, stores, or Troops may be landed.

The Reduction of the French Settlements upon the River St. Johns seems still easier; Besides the practicableness of cutting them off from all Supplies of Stores and Provisions, (it being agreed on all hands to be impracticable for them to receive any from Canada down the River, on account of the many falls and Carrying-Places near the head of it) the two small Forts near the mouth of it, supposing both of them to be garrison'd, and mounted with Cannon, which I believe is not the case, may be soon reduc'd by Ships; They are not more than two miles and an half up the River, where they stand opposite almost to each other in water deep enough for large Ships of War to ride in, and where the River is not much more than a Musquet Shot over. The Fort or Forts here in Oliver Cromwell's time were taken by Ships.

When the French were drove off the Isthmus, and out of the River St. Johns, it would be very easy to secure the whole Peninsula and Bay of Funda.

As to the former, the Revolt of the Inhabitants of Chignecto to the French might in such case be made a favorable Circumstance, as it hath left a large Tract of rich Lands capable of maintaining 1000 Families, which if settled with Protestants from New England, who would make the best Settlers there, or from the North of Ireland, who would be the next best, or from old England, with a strong large Fort and Garrison behind them, between Bay Vert and Beau Basin in the Bay of Chignecto, with one or more Block-houses on each side, would not only be a good Barrier against the French of Canada, but by cutting off all Communication between them and the Indians of the Peninsula, make the latter wholly dependent upon our own Truck-houses for all necessary supplies, and soon beget in them an attachment to the English. This propos'd Settlement in Chignecto, and Fort upon the Isthmus would likewise very much conduce towards reclaiming the Inhabitants of Minas and Annapolis River to a due sense of their Allegiance to his Majesty, and proper disposition towards his Government, by a constant inspection of their behavior, promoting Traffick and all manner of Intercourse between them and the English, gradually introduce the English manners, customs, and language among them; which, with the help of some French Protestant Minister residing there, capable of teaching the English Tongue, and some Privileges or Exemptions allowed to those, who should send their Children to learn English, and be instructed in the Protestant Religion, or at least to do one of them; prohibiting French Missionary Priests to reside amongst them, and allowing them in their stead one or more Romish Priests in each district, of another nation, for the publick Exercise of their Religion, at least for some years, might in a few Generations make them good Subjects; which they would naturally incline to be, when they found the English would remain Masters of the Province and they could depend upon his Majesty's Government for protection both against the French and Indians; In such case Intermarriages would naturally be introduced, and they would in the end become wholly English.

The continuance of the Inhabitants of Chignecto in that district ever seem'd so dangerous to me, that upon being order'd by the Duke of Newcastle to form a Plan of a Civil Governmt for the Colony, and to transmit my sentiments to him of what was necessary to be done for the security of it, I propos'd in my letters to his Grace, and to the Duke of Bedford his Successor, the removal of the Accadians from Chignecto, and placing them near the Fort of Annapolis Royal, where they might be properly look'd after, planting the district of Chignecto, with Inhabitants, whose fidelity to the English Government might be depended upon, and erecting a strong Fort upon the Isthmus.

I am sensible, my Lord, what additional Strength the loss of these Rebel Subjects will give to the French; But considering their extreme ill behavior, and the hazard of suffering them to return to their Possessions again upon their former Terms, I would submit it to Your Lordship's Consideration whether above one half at most should be permitted to return to their Lands; and even those upon the Terms of taking the Oath of Allegiance to his Majesty without any exemption from bearing arms in defence of his Government; and the other half of their Lands planted with English Settlers to be interspers'd among them.

The good Consequences of ridding the Isthmus and St. John's River of the French would, my Lord, soon extend to the Settlements at Halifax and Lunenburgh; the former of which would in a short time draw a settled Fishery to it (one of the most essential Sources of it's wealth) as well as other Settlers from the neighbouring Colonies, with little or no expence to the Nation.

For securing the possession of the Bay of Funda it seems necessary, my Lord, to fortify the Rivers of St. John's and Pentagoet. The French, whilst they held Accadie, before Oliver Cromwell dispossess'd them in 1652, maintain'd Forts upon these Rivers, as well as at Annapolis Royal, and the English afterwards kept Garrisons in them, until the Province was restor'd to the French by King Charles the 2d in 1667.

The necessity that the English should make themselves intire Masters of these Rivers is evident; The French have a communication thro' them with the Bay of Funda, and as they are grown stronger in Canada, than they were in Oliver Cromwell's and King Charles the 2d's time, it seems more necessary to secure the possession of these Rivers now, than it was then.

If the French have erected a new fort 60 miles up St. Johns River, it seems likewise necessary for excluding them from every part of it, that besides maintaining one Fort near the mouth of the River, where the two old French Forts were built, either the new French Fort, when they are dislodg'd, should be kept garrison'd, or another strong one erected there, or else higher up, The French Settlers be turned off (to prevent the same dangerous consequences of their being suffer'd to remain there, as have been experienc'd from the Accadians upon the Peninsula) and English Settlements encouraged upon the River.

If the general Assertion is well founded, that it is impracticable to transport military stores or Provisions down this River, the reduction of the new French Fort would be an easy Conquest.

These Proceedings, my Lord, besides contributing greatly towards the security of the Bay of Funda, and regaining a rich Furr trade, would make the St. John's Indians dependant upon us, and be a great Curb to Canada.

I can't learn that the French now have or ever had any settlement high up the River Pentagoet; the maintaining therefore one Fort at the mouth of it, as was done formerly, seems to be sufficient; And this, besides contributing to the security of the Bay, would keep the Penobscot Indians inhabiting that River in an absolute dependance upon us.

The next great River, my Lord, which it is of the utmost importance to secure the possession of is Kennebeck, within the limits of my own government; and for doing this, Your Lordship will perceive by the Message of the General Assembly to me in answer to my Speech to them upon this head, that I have prevail'd upon them to enable me to build a new Fort, higher up the River, where I shall think proper, and to raise 500 Men (which I have done) for removing any French Fort, which may be found upon it, or upon the carrying place between that and the River Chaudiere; which, after a course of about 70 miles, falls into the River St. Lawrence, at about a league and an half above the city of Quebec; I purpose accordingly to go to the Eastern Parts with this party in about a month; and to use my best endeavours to effect what they have requested of me.

But my chief aim is, after having caus'd the Fort to be erected, which I purpose at present, about 60 miles up the River to get another very strong one built at or near the head of it, capable of containing upon occasion 1000 or 1500 Men, from whence a large Body of Troops might be march'd, and Artillery transported within 6 or 7 days to the River St. Lawrence, within the before-mention'd distance of Quebec; which there seems reason to think, my Lord, would go farther towards keeping Canada in a proper Respect, than the most solemn treaties have hitherto done; especially if this River shall be strengthen'd with the Settlement of 7 or 800 Families upon it, which I am not without hopes may be soon accomplish'd.

To complete this Scheme for forming a Barrier to his Majesty's Eastern Colonies upon this Continent, from Nova Scotia inclusive to Pensylvania, which I am laying a rough sketch of before your Lordship, it is necessary to build another Fort of equal Strength with that propos'd for the River Kennebeck upon an eminence near Lake Champlain, and at the distance of less than point-blank Shot from Fort St. Frederick, erected by the French at Crown Point, which I mention'd once to your Lordship, when I had the honour to wait upon you in Grosvenor Square, as necessary to be done before a Rupture with France, in case they could not be brought to consent to the demolition of Fort St. Frederick. This Fort, from whence a Body of Troops might be march'd or transported with Artillery Stores to Montreal in about 7 days time, would be as great a curb upon the motions of the French in that Quarter as the last before-mention'd Fort would be upon them in Quebec; and in conjunction with the other propos'd Forts would not only be a good Barrier to the Eastern Colonies, and confine the French within their just bounds that way, but by keeping them upon their Guard, leave them less at liberty to fit out distant expeditions against his Majesty's Southern Colonies.

Another good Effect of building the propos'd Fort would be that it would have a great tendency to confirm the Indians of the Six Nations in a dependence upon us; from which it seems they have in part been discourag'd by Fort St. Frederick's being suffer'd to remain. And it seems a strong argument for doing it, that the French being apprehensive that Fort St. Frederick may be commanded from the Eminence propos'd for the Place of the English Fort, will probably forestall us by their building one there themselves, if it is not soon done, as appears from the inclos'd deposition of one Peter Frank.

I cant take upon me, my Lord, to form a certain judgement of what Sea Force may be necessary for effecting the Business propos'd to be done in the Bay of Funda, and at Bay Vert, but think it must require at least two sixty Gun Ships, two of his Majesty's Troops, and four small arm'd Tenders.

I have other Matters to propose for Your Lordship's consideration upon the present state of North America. But, as this Letter is grown to such a length, as must I fear tire out your Lordship's patience in the perusal of it, I shall reserve them for another Opportunity. And since Your Lordship allows me that honour, I shall write frequently to you, whenever I have any thing to communicate worthy of your Lordship's notice; but must not omit mentioning here, that in case any Men shall be order'd from Home to be rais'd here for his Majesty's Service in any Expedition, it will be absolutely necessary to send over a sufficient number of Stands of Arms for the occasion, good ones not being to be found in New England for such service.

*　　*　　*　　*　　*　　*　　*

I am with the greatest Respect
Sir,
Your most humble and
most Obedient Servant,
W. SHIRLEY.
Rt. Honble. Sir Thomas Robinson Knt. of the Bath.

Endorsed:
Extract of a letter
from Govr. Shirley.

WILLIAM SHIRLEY TO THE LORDS COMMISSIONERS [1]

Boston, New England, May 23d, 1754.

My Lords,

The inclos'd Papers contain an Authentick Account of the taking of an English Fort upon the Ohio, by the French: which I thought it my Duty to transmit to your Lordships by this Opportunity, as I believe it may be the first of conveying it to your Lordships directly by the way of London.[2]

I purpose to set out for the Eastern parts of this Province in about 17 Days with a party of 500 men, which is to proceed up the River Kennebeck in quest of a French Fort or Settlement said to be erected or made there in the Summer before last, of which I had the honour to acquaint your Lordships in a former Letter, and to cause a Fort to be built about 60 Miles up the River, and to have an Interview with the Norridgwalk, Penobscot, and Arrassangunticook Indians at Falmouth in Casco Bay; But if the Advices are well founded, which I have this morning received from Halifax and Annapolis Royal, that some of the Rebel Inhabitants of Chignecto, together with the Indians of the peninsula and St. John's River, are thro' the Influence of the French Garrison at Beau Sejour engaged in an Enterprize to break up all the Eastern Settlements of this Province, as far as the River Kennebeck, where it is suspected they are gone; the Force, which is rais'd to proceed with me, will not be sufficient to execute the Design, I go upon.

If these Advices are true, they will afford your Lordships one instance of the many mischievous Consequences, to the Colonies of New England, as well as to His Majesty's Province of Nova Scotia, which must proceed from the French of Canada's having possessed themselves of the Isthmus of the

[1] P.R.O., C. O. 5, 887.
[2] The fort begun by William Trent in February, 1754, and taken by the French on April 17. On this site Fort Duquesne was at once erected by the captors.

Peninsula, and St. John's River in the Bay of Funda, and continuing their Incroachments within his Majesty's Territories. I have the Honour to be with the greatest Respect,
My Lords,
Your Lordships's most humble
and most Obedient Servant
W. Shirley.

The Rt Honble Lords Commissioners for Trade and the Plantations.

Endorsed:

Massachusets Bay

Letter from Willm Shirley Esqr Govr of the Massachusets-Bay to the Board, dated at Boston the 23d of May 1754, transmitting four Papers containg an authentick Account of the taking of an English Fort upon the Ohio, by the French.

Recd July the 2d } 1754
Read —Do

SIR THOMAS ROBINSON TO WILLIAM SHIRLEY [1]

Whitehall, une 21, 1754.

Sir,

Having received your Dispatches of the 19th of April and 1st of May last, with their several enclosures, and having laid the same before the King, I am to acquaint you, that His Majesty extremely approves the resolution which has been taken by the Assembly of your Province, in consequence of the proposal recommended by you, to use their best endeavors to drive the French from the river Kennebeck.

[1] Mass. Col. Ser. Letters, 54, 306–308. A copy is in P. R. O., C. O. 5, 211. Sir Thomas Robinson was born in 1695 and served as a diplomatist at the court of Maria Theresa. On the death of Pelham in 1754 Robinson was made Secretary of State for the Southern Department, and gave way to Fox in November, 1755.

And I am at the same time to inform you, that His Majesty is graciously pleased to authorize and direct you to proceed upon the plan, and to pursue the measures which appear, by your speeches to the Assembly, and their answer thereto, to have been so well calculated for that purpose.

I am likewise to assure you, as a mark of His Majesty's particular attention to the welfare of his loyal subjects in New England, that everything recommended by the said Assembly, will be fully considered: and that immediate directions will be given for promoting the plan of a general concert between His Majesty's Colonies, in order to prevent or remove any encroachments upon the dominions of the crown of Great Britain.

It is with the greatest pleasure, that I take this early opportunity of giving you the satisfaction to know the very favorable manner in which the account of your prudent and vigorous conduct, as well of the zeal and activity of those under your government, have been received by the King, which cannot fail to excite and encourage them in taking such farther steps as will, most effectually, provide for their own security, and will give a proper example to His Majesty's neighbouring Colonies.

I am Sir

Your most obedient humble Servant

T. ROBINSON.

To Governor William Shirley.

WILLIAM SHIRLEY TO JOSIAH WILLARD [1]

Falmouth, Casco Bay, July 8th, 1754.

SIR,

The Speaker to whom I am much obliged for his Assistance in the Publick business here, and the Pleasure of his Company, both which I shall miss upon his leaving us, doth me the favor to be the bearer of this.

As he is able to give you a perfect Acct. of the Issue of the Conference with the Indians, I refer you to him for it; It hath been, I think favorable, beyond even our Expectation;

[1] Mass. Col. Ser. Letters, 54, 309.

and may I hope have good Consequences for the tranquility of the Province, and the general service : It certainly will, if Indian Faith may be in the least depended upon.

Mr. Danforth, Mr. Oliver and Colonel Brown are to imbark this day with the Speaker, and some other Gentlemen of the House for Boston, and Mr. Fox is extremely ill, so that there will be wanting four Gentlemen of the Council to make up a Quorum upon any Emergency of Publick business. I must therefore desire you to let Mr. Wheelwright, Mr. Cheever, Colonel Minot, and Colonel Lincoln know that their attendance upon it here will be requisite, and that I hope they will not fail of letting me see them here, as soon as may be; They will have an Opportunity of coming in the Ship, which I have ordered to wait upon the Gentlemen of the Council and Mr. Speaker and the Gentlemen of the House, who go to Boston, and to attend upon Mr. Wheelwright and the other three Gentlemen to bring them hither.

I desire you will transmit to me what Publick Letters, or accounts of Publick Affairs, you shall judge proper to be communicated to me here; It will be a great pleasure to me to hear from time to time, how matters go on, and to receive your letters upon any subject.

I am with truth,

Sir,

Your faithful Friend and

Humble Servant

W. Shirley.

The Honble Mr. Secretary Willard.

WILLIAM SHIRLEY TO SIR THOMAS ROBINSON [1]

Falmouth, in Casco Bay, August 19th, 1754.

Sir,

In a former Packet,[2] which I had the Honour to transmit to the Earl of Holderness, I acquainted his Lordship that

---

[1] *B. M.*, *Additional Manuscript 32736, 314.* A transcript is in the Library of Congress.

[2] See letter of April 19, *ante*, p. 52.

upon my having receiv'd Advice from the Commander at Fort Richmond, upon the River Kennebeck within the limits of this Government that some of the Norridgwalks, a Tribe of Indians inhabiting that River, had given him Intelligence that the French had the summer before last made a considerable Settlement upon a Carrying place near the head of it, that this was done with the Allowance of those Indians, in consideration that the French had agreed to supply them with Arms, Ammunition, and other Stores in time of War with the English, and that that Tribe and another called the Arrassangunticooks or St. Francois Indians, assisted by other Indians from Canada, and a great Number of French in Indian Disguise (a practice not uncommon with the French) would fall upon the New England Settlements this Summer, which last circumstance seem'd confirm'd by the insolent behaviour of the two beforementioned Tribes, who appear'd to be upon the brink of committing Hostilities. I lay'd these Accots before the Assembly and urg'd them to make Provision for raising Forces to remove the French from this Incroachment on his Majesty's Territories, in case they should refuse to quit it upon a peaceable Summons, as also for building a new fort as high up Kennebeck River, as should be found upon a Survey of it to be practicable at present, in order to prevent the French from taking Possession of any part of it, and either keep the Indians Inhabiting it in a due Subjection for the future or oblige them wholly to abandon it.

I further acquainted his Lordship, that the Assembly in answer to what I recommended to them, sent me a Message of both Houses, wherein, they desir'd me to take measures as soon as might be for removing the French from their beforemention'd Settlement, and building a new fort as high up the River as I should think proper, praying me to take those matters under my immediate direction, and for that purpose to make a voyage to the Eastern parts of the Province, promising that for the safe guard of my person in effecting the Service they would make Provision for raising 500 men (which they soon afterwards augmented to one for

800) and desiring me, in case I should judge that proper, to have an Interview and Conference with the Indians upon my Arrival in those parts.

In consequence of this Message, Sir, I rais'd 800 men and having sent orders to the Commanders of the Eastern Forts to notify the two beforemention'd Tribes of Indians and another call'd the Penobscots to meet me here, the middle of June last, I embark'd with the forces as soon as the other Business of my Government would permit for this place, where I arriv'd the 26th of June accompany'd by Colonel Mascarene, who had been appointed by Governour Hopson a Commissioner on the part of Nova Scotia, to join with this Government on an Interview with the Eastern Indians; and upon my Arrival I was met by three Commissioners from the Government of New Hampshire, which I had notified of my intended Interview with the Indians, for the same purpose.

As it could not be doubted but that the building a new fort, and making the propos'd march to the head of the River and extending the English Settlements upon it would be very disagreeable to the Indians, I determin'd to get an Interview with them, if possible, before I proceeded in the intended Service; that appearing to be the only chance, there was to prevent an Impending War with them. On the other hand the two Priests of the Norridgwalk and Penobscot Tribes, both French Jesuits, who notwithstanding the Indians had all Accepted Presents from this Province, and ratify'd former Treaties of Peace with it the last fall, and press'd me by letters to have a Personal Conference with them in the Spring, had so wrought upon their Dispositions in the Winter, that the Norridgwalks and Arssegunticooks seem'd, as I before observ'd to be upon the point of breaking out into Hostilities before we had taken resolution to erect the fort and reconnoitre the river and carrying place at the head of it, now redoubled their Efforts to prevent the Indians from coming to a Conference with us and they had so far succeeded, that the Penobscot Tribe, which was the only one of the three I had hopes of gaining an Interview with let me know in a letter from them before I left Boston, that they would not meet me at this place, and the Norridgwalk and Arssegunticook Indians had shew'd such signs of their making a sudden Stroke upon our most expos'd Eastern Settlements, that the Settlers upon Kennebeck River had betaken themselves to their Garrisons, and those upon St. George's were preparing to do the same.

However, contrary to my expectations I found upon my arrival at this place, that several of the Norridgwalks had been assembled here some days to meet me; which was principally owing to the accident of their Priest's having left them about 20 days before to go to Canada, and the miscarriage of a letter from the Penobscot Priest to their Priest, which the Commander of St. George's fort had found means to intercept and send me.

As to the Arssegunticook Indians, who have their head quarters near the Southern Bank of the River Canada, and are generally reckon'd among the French Indians the Commander of fort Richmond and the Norridgwalks themselves inform'd me that a part of them now lurking in the Neighbourhood of Fort Richmond had declar'd in Answer to my letter of Notifica- [sic] to them to meet me, that they would have no Interview with the English until they had (to speak in Indian Phrase) wip'd away the Blood of two Indians belonging to their Tribe, who had been unfortunately kill'd within the Government of New Hampshire above a Year ago; and the New Hampshire Commissioners acquainted me, that some of that Tribe had about three weeks before carry'd off a whole Family Captive, and Pillag'd and burnt two houses within that Province; so that there was not the least Expectation of their sending any of their Tribe to the Interview.

As to the Penobscot Indians I was inform'd by a letter, which I found at my Arrival here, that they had receiv'd messages inviting them to join with the French Indians in taking up the Hatchet against the English; which matter they had under consideration; and by another letter which I found here from the Commanding Officer of Fort St. George, that they were soon to hold a Grand Council upon what I had order'd him to tell them in answer to their letter of refusal to meet me here, but that he was almost sure they would persist in their former Resolution.

In this Letter Sir, I found inclos'd the beforementioned letter from the Penobscot missionary to the Jesuit of the Norridgwalks a Copy of which I send you at full length as I think it may give a just notion of the Principles and Intrigues of the Jesuit Missionaries here, what lengths they will go for the sake of saving one of their missions which is in danger of being lost to them, even such as would embroil all Parties in War and which they are affraid should be discover'd by the Indians, or even the French Government.

As the Penobscots are esteem'd the most powerfull of the Eastern Indians, and have ever appear'd the best affected of those Tribes towards the English, I determin'd to use my utmost efforts to draw them hither from their Priest, and have a conference with them. Accordingly I dispatch'd a Vessell to St. George's River to bring them to Falmouth, with a letter acquainting them that upon their own request made to me in the last Winter that I would have an Interview and Conference with them in person this Summer, I was come so far to brighten the Covenant Chain with them, and was surpriz'd at not finding them here upon my Arrival as I did the Norridgwalks.

That I expected them to attend me at Falmouth without delay and should look upon their refusal as a renouncing of all amity with the English.

At the same time, as the Norridgwalk Indians were the Original Proprietors of the Lands upon Kennebeck River, and the only Indians now Interested in them, and I had reason to expect that the presence of the Penobscots would embarrass our Conference concerning the intended march, fort, and further settlements up the river, I determin'd to have a separate Conference with the Norridgwalks, and dispatch them from hence before the arrival of the Penobscot Indians here.

I shall not trouble, You, Sir, with the particulars of my Conference with the Norridgwalk Indians, but mention only so much, as will shew what were the principal points and result of it.

Upon acquainting them with our intended proceedings and the true motive of them, which I told them was to secure the River Kennebeck against the French who had of late built several forts within his Majestys territories upon this Continent, and not with the least view of incroaching upon their Lands, They at first told me in a peremptory manner, that they would not Consent to it, that they lik'd well the Treaty which Lt. Govr. Dummer had made with them and the other Eastern Tribes in 1725 and 1726, and they would stand by it : they acknowledg'd that Richmond fort was King George's, and said, all below it belonged to the English but all above it to them.

In answer to this I told them I did not ask their Consent to the building the new fort, or extending the English Settlements upon the River Kennebeck, but only appriz'd them of our intentions, that they might not conceive false Alarm at our proceedings ; That all Princes had a right to build forts for the protection of their Subjects within their own Territories as they pleas'd ; they well knew the French King did so ; that the building of this fort would not affect their properties in any lands upon the River ; That by Govr. Dummer's Treaty, which they just now express'd their satisfaction in they had acknowledg'd their "Subjection to King George, Submitted to be Governed by his Laws, and desir'd to have the advantage of them" whereby, the English and they were become Brethren, and King George their Common father, and that he had no other view in building this fort than the protection of his children, Indians as well as English against the French ; and they might have the Benefit of it as well as we, if they pleas'd. I reminded them of the Calamities, which going to War with the English had brought upon them. That in the Year 1724 the English broke up their Settlement at Norridgwalk destroy'd near half their Tribe, and drove them intirely off the River Kennebeck, whereby according to the Rules of War, receivd and practic'd by all Indians the English gain'd from them by right of Conquest all their Lands upon the River; and that it was wholly owing to their Kindness for them that they were suffer'd afterwards by Govr. Dummer's Treaty to return to their Possessions there.

I shew'd them that above 100 Years ago the English had purchas'd all the Lands of their forefathers as high up that River as a branch called Wesserunskik, being near 100 miles, by Deeds which themselves had at the Treaty last Year acknowledg'd to be genuine, and that by Virtue of those purchases the English had made Settlements at Cushenoc[1] and Taconnett, being about forty miles above Richmond, the Ruins of which were still visible and particularly at Taconnett they had built a Truck house above 100 Years ago where a greater Trade was carried on by them with the Indians for Beaver and Furrs than is now at all the Truckhouses in this Province, as themselves well knew by Tradition from their Forefathers and have likewise acknowledg'd; and I shew'd them that by Lt. Govr. Dummer's Treaty, under which they hold all their Lands upon the River, it was Stipulated by the Indians that the English should quietly enter upon and hold all their former Possessions and Lands, which they had purchas'd of the Indians without any molestation from them; so that the English had full as good right to extend their Settlements as far as their ancient possessions and purchases reach'd, as the Indians had to hold the Lands, which were upon that River beyond them; and I demanded of them, if they would now ratify Lt. Govr. Dummers Treaty, which they had just before told me they would stand by, and the Treaty of Peace concluded between them and the English in 1749; To this they readily answer'd me, that they were willing and desirous; whereupon I acquainted them at our meeting the next morning, that the Instruments of Ratification were prepar'd, but advis'd them to consider well before we proceeded to execute them whether they were absolutely determin'd to observe them; That they had

[1] This settlement is elsewhere spelled Cussenac. It was a small town about forty miles from the mouth of the Kennebec River where Fort Richmond was located.

better not sign them than do it, and break faith with us; For if after concluding this Treaty they should be guilty of another breach of their faith, we should never trust them again: I told them we had now fully open'd our hearts to them, and hop'd they would hide nothing which was in theirs from us; and if their hearts were as right towards us as ours were towards them, we would interchangeably sign the ratifications.

Their Speaker then stood up and declar'd in the Name of them all, that the English should be welcome to build their intended forts upon the River Kennebeck and to extend Settlements there as far as their ancient possessions and purchases reach'd and only desir'd, I wou'd let them know how high up the River I design'd to erect the fort; which I told them: they made professions in the most solemn manner, that what they had last said was spoke in the Sincerity of their hearts; and let me know that the Arssegunticooks had sent messages to the Penobscots, inviting them to join them in taking the Hatchet up against the English.

We then sign'd the Ratifications; after which I let them know that as a Testimony of the good Disposition of the English towards them, if they would send any of their Children to Boston to be instructed in the English Language, the Government there would be at the Expence of maintaining and Educating them in a proper manner, and would send them back to their Parents whenever it should be requir'd and that I propos'd this to them as the means of cementing still a closer Friendship and perpetuating Peace between them and the English.

Upon this proposal three of their young men of about 16 years of age immediately offer'd themselves to me in the presence of the rest to go to Boston; and one of their noted Captains, who had before accepted a Commission from the French, desir'd leave to send two of his sons to be educated in Boston which I readily promised, and sent the three young men there two days after: the day following I dispatch'd all the Norridgwalk Indians back to Kennebeck River and caus'd the forces to embark and proceed upon the intended service; and I hear the Indians shew'd signs of satisfaction at their arrival in particular that they discover'd and have brought back to the Commander of the forces two deserters who were going to Canada.

The next day the Vessell, which I had sent to St. George's River to bring hither such of the Penobscot Chiefs, as that Tribe should delegate to come to the Conference, return'd with fourteen of them: And the next morning I open'd the Conference with them.

I acquainted them with what We design'd to do upon the River Kennebeck, and what had pass'd between me and the Norridgwalks upon that subject, telling them that though I was sensible they had no property in that River, yet I thought fit, as they were our Friends to apprize them of what we intended to do there with the motives of our proceedings. They did not discover the least uneasiness at what I said, and in their answer only desir'd, I would build no fort higher up St. George's River than the present fort, assuring me that they would not suffer the French to make any Settlement, or set up any fort upon their Lands, and profest in the strongest Terms a sincere Disposition to cultivate a perfect harmony with us.

They shew'd themselves very ready and desirous to ratify the former Treaties of Peace; which was done; and in four days after their Arrival here, I sent them back to St. George's in perfect good humour, having first made them the same Offer of maintaining and Educating any of their Children at the Charge of the Province, that I had to the Norridgwalk Indians. Whereupon two of their young men desir'd leave of me to go to Boston to learn the English Language, and one of their Chiefs offer'd to bring his Son there the next Spring, and leave him to be educated.

The Arssegunticooks still stand out; and the only expedient, which occurr'd to me for putting a Stop to their Hostilities, was to observe to the Norridgwalks and Penobscots, that by Lt. Governour Dummer's Treaty with them the Arssegunticooks and other Eastern Tribes, to which Treaty the Government of New Hampshire was a Party it is Stipulated between the English and Indians "That if any Controversy or Difference at any time thereafter should happen to arise between any of the English and Indians for any real or suppos'd Wrong or injury done on either side, no private Revenge should be taken for the same, but a proper application made to his majestys Government upon the place for Remedy or Redress thereof in a due Course of Justice" and that by the Treaty of Peace made in 1749 between the same English Governments and Indians those Tribes Engag'd "That if any Indians should at any time thereafter Committ any acts of Hostility against the English they would join their Young men with the English in reducing such Indians to Reason."

I then observ'd to them that three Commissioners from the Government of New Hampshire were, in Conformity to those Treaties, now come to meet the Arssegunticooks, in order to give and receive satisfaction for mischiefs done on either side; but that the Arssegunticooks have absolutely refus'd to Appear here, and insist upon taking their own Revenge on the English, have actually carried off one Family captive, pillag'd and burnt two houses, and are watching for opportunities to commit further Hostilities.

Wherefore, as the English had on their part observ'd the before mention'd Treaties and the Arssegunticook Indians had broke them, and absolutely refus'd to submit to them, We had, I told them, a right by virtue of those Treaties to call upon them "to join their Young men with ours to reduce the Arssegunticooks to reason" which I now demanded of them.

This was a very serious Affair with them, and seem'd to Embarrass them. The Norridgwalk Indians in their Conference Assur'd me they had already put a Stop to the Hostilities of the Arssegunticooks until their Return to Norridgwalk, that they were sure they would commit none before they called upon them there; and that then they would use their best endeavours to restrain them from committing any further; and undertook, if they should fail of success, to give the English notice before they did more mischief; The

Speaker of the Penobscots in their Conference with me, assur'd me, that himself would at their return to Penobscot go to the head Quarters of the Arssegunticooks and make them call their Indians in from committing Hostilities against the English.

I let both these Tribes know, that we should depend upon their effecting this, and if they did not, that we must insist upon their joining with us to reduce the Arssegunticooks to reason.

This is the issue, Sir, of the Conferences held here; and I hope the effect of them may be to divert the Indians from further thoughts of War at present, and make them acquiesce in our new forts and settlements upon the River Kennebeck which, it seems clear to me with regard to the Indians, we have a just right to carry on; and let their Disposition be what it will, that it is necessary to be done for securing the possession of this most essential River against the incroachments of the French, whether present or future, of which there appears to be no end upon this Continent.

As to the progress, which is made by our forces upon the River Kennebeck, I shall defer, Sir, giving you an account of it 'till their Return to Taconnett.

I dont apprehend much danger that the French will Attempt to give them any Interruption in their march, or to molest us in carrying on the two forts upon the River. However, as the Governour of Canada's receiving frequent accounts at Quebec of our Number and motions could not be avoided, and the French may possibly be elated with their late Success upon the Ohio against Colo. Washington, whose Forces consisting of about 4 or 500 men, I hear, they have defeated;[1] I am determined to remain here until their return, and our works upon the River shall be either compleated, or so far advanc'd, as to be out of danger, that I may be ready, in case of any unforeseen Emergency, to support the 800 men we have now upon the River with 500 more, which I should not much doubt in such case to be able to raise forthwith in these parts, where I have taken care to have a Corps

[1] Fort Necessity surrendered on July 4, 1754.

de Reserve left for that purpose, and to keep a quorum of his Majesty's Council with me as their advice to me for taking any extraordinary measures, which the present Service may require, will be agreeable to the Assembly. And as expresses by whale boats are continually passing and repassing between me, the forts, and forces now on their march, I hope sufficient precautions are taken to prevent surprizes, and secure the success of the service I am engag'd in.

I am with the Highest Respect,
Sir,
Your most humble and
most Obedient Servant,

W. SHIRLEY.

Rt. Honble. Sir Thomas Robinson
Knt. of the Bath.

Endorsed:
Augt. 19, 1754.
GOVR. SHIRLEY
Octr. 7th.

WILLIAM SHIRLEY TO ISRAEL WILLIAMS [1]

Falmouth, Casco Bay, Septr. 3d, 1754.

SIR,
Herewith you will receive my Orders to you in form; the Execution of which I with great Satisfaction intrust you with, being persuaded of your abilities, and zeal for his majesty's service, and that of the province at this critical conjuncture.

I must not detain the express longer than to assure you that I am
Sir,
Your real Friend and
Servant,

W. SHIRLEY.

Colonel Israel Williams.

[1] Original, A. L. S., Mass. Hist. Society, Col. Israel Williams Manuscripts, 71 D, 75.

JOSIAH WILLARD TO ISRAEL WILLIAMS [1]

Boston, Septr. 7, 1754.

SIR,

Late last night, I received a Packet from his Excellency, by the Express I sent on Lords Day Evening with your Letters, advising of the Mischief done by the Indians in the Western Parts. In these Dispatches I have his Excy's Warrant to you for doing what is necessary for the Protection of the Frontiers in the Western Parts; but it being thro' Haste much altered, interlined and obliterated, His Excellency orders me to have it transcribed fairly, and that I should sign it in his Name, and send it to you by Express. He also ordered me to call the Council together, and have their Advice upon these Matters, Leaving it to them to make any Alterations as to these Instructions which they should judge needful; But upon Consideration thereof they thought them full and sufficient; And have only directed me to put you in mind of sending to the Government of Connecticut (which is covered by our Frontier Towns) for Assistance upon the next Emergency.

I am
Sir,
Your very humble Servant,
J. WILLARD.

P.S. I have sent you by this Express twenty blank Commissions which are all that can be spared at present; the Govrs. Return is expected within a few days.

I have this Minute received Advice of the Assault of the Enemy at Stockbridge and of Connecticuts sending Succours. The Council have no doubt of your doing every thing in your Power for the Safety of the Frontiers.

Colo. Israel Williams.

[1] Original, L. S., Mass. Hist. Society, Col. Israel Williams Manuscripts, 71 D, 76.

WILLIAM SHIRLEY TO ISRAEL WILLIAMS [1]

Boston, September 11th, 1754.

SIR,

Your two last Letters to the Secretary, dated the 8th and 9th of September Current, with an other from Colo. Worthington, giving a more full Account of the Incursions of the Enemy upon the Frontiers, and what he has done for the Relief of the Places in his own Regiment, have been laid before me: And as you particularly mention in your first Letters to the Secretary the Advantage of keeping the Inhabitants of the outmost Frontiers upon their Lands, for the Security of the Places within them, I had immediate Regard to that Matter in my special Power to you, sent by the Secretary, and intended that you order a Number of Soldiers to be posted in the exposed Towns, if you should think it needful, and there to remain 'till my further Order; And now perceive by Colo. Worthingtons Letter that many Difficulties may arise, unless I give him the Power contained in the inclosed, which is a Copy of the Orders I have sent him, and which I apprehend to be consistent with the Command with which I have invested you by my former Orders to you: And I would have you accordingly act in concert with him, pursuant to my aforesaid Orders to him.

And you are hereby especially directed to post such a Number of Soldiers in the expos'd Towns within the Limits of the Command which I have given you, as you shall think their Safety and his Majesty's Service may require, there to remain untill farther Orders from me.

I am,
Sir,
Your Faithfull Friend,
and Servant,

W. SHIRLEY.

[1] Original, L. S., Mass. Hist. Society, Col. Israel Williams Manuscripts, 71 D, 77.

P.S. The inclosed to Colo. Worthington, after you have perused, seal up and send to him.

Colo. Israel Williams.

ISRAEL WILLIAMS TO WILLIAM SHIRLEY [1]

Hatfield, Sepr. 12th, 1754.

SIR,

I conclude by this time you are fully inform'd of the hostile attacks of the Indians, and the mischief done by them in our own Frontiers and the neighbouring Governments in one of which they have made terrible waste burning and destroying all before 'em.

It is now open war with us, and a dark distressing scene opening. A merciless miscreant Enemy invading us in every quarter, push'd on by our inveterate Enemy (as if their savage nature and blood thirsty temper needed excitement to cruelty and barbarity) with views and designs to prevent our settling any further to the Northward, the Northern Governments sending any assistance to Ohio, impoverishing them as much as possible, preventing their Indians trading to Albany, preparing the way for the reduction of that City; the securing the Six Nations of Indians the more easily in their Interest, which when effected, farewell Peace and Prosperity to New England, yea, to North America.

It gives me no small satisfaction that, under God, we have your Excellency still to apply to for relief in our distress, whose Enterprizes against our constant enemy have been attended with success, and of whose Resolution, Wisdom, Care and Compassion, we have had large Experience. In full assurance of your readiness to grant us succour and relief under our pressures we shall as to our common Father make application.

My situation and circumstances makes the Western Frontiers the more immediate object of my attention, and the

[1] Original, A. L. S., Mass. Col. Ser. Letters, 54, 329.

violent attacks of the Enemy in this quarter calls for the publick more than any other part of the Province. I beg leave therefore to represent the state of this Frontier and to lay before your Excellency what I think would most conduce to the safety and security of his Majesty's here and the Neighbouring Governments. Herewith I send a plan of the Western Parts of this Province by which your Excellency will be able to form a judgment of our situation and whether what I am about to propose will serve the general Interest of the whole Which is, — That there be a Garrison at Fall Town, another at Morrisons in Colrain, two at Charlemont, Massachusetts Fort and a garrison at Pontoosook. The People are preparing for their defence, as I suppose, and the charge of making those places sufficient will not as I apprehend be very great to the Government.

I propose that there be at least fifty men at Fort Massachusetts, thirty at Pontoosook, they to maintain a constant scout from Stockbridge thro the Western part of Framingham township, and the West Township at Hooseck to the said Fort and from thence to the top of Hooseck Mountain. That there be 14 men at Fall Town, 20 at Morrisons and 12 at each garrison at Charlemont, these to perform a constant scout from Connecticut River against Northfield to the top of Hooseck Mountain. These scouts thus performed will cross all the roads the Enemy ever travel to come within the aforesaid Line of Forts. There will doubtless be more wanted for the Protection of some Places within the Line. However if the scouting be faithfully performed there will not, I apprehend, any considerable body of the enemy get within the Line aforesaid undiscovered and there will be a great restraint upon small parties who will be afear'd of being ensnar'd. I propose that some of the men posted at Massachusetts be employ'd to waylay the roads from Crown Point south of which places I conclude has not been ceded to the French. The Enemy generally when they leave that place come to the South side of the Lake or drowned lands, leave their canoes and come down to Hooseck, or they may turn off to the East; let which will be the case that Fort is best situated to send parties from for the purpose aforesaid to gain advantages.

The reasons why I would neglect Shirley and Pelham Fort is because the Indians were scarce ever known the last war to come down Deerfield River, and that road is very bad and almost impassable. Shirley is rotten and if maintained must be rebuilt. That at Morrisons will answer as well and can be much easier supply'd. After all if our Government would build a Fort upon the top of Hooseck Mountain between Pelham and Fort Massachusetts it would shorten the scouting and answer as well the first proposed line thro Charlemont.

I would further propose that two Forts be built between Massachusetts Fort and Hudsons River, as laid down in the plan, between which places there is a large opening where the Enemy can (now Hooseck is destroyed) come down to the Dutch Settlements, Stockbridge and Sheffield, *and where they are gone to Connecticut without difficulty, nay I apprehend the Westerly towns of Connecticut are exposed now to such bold fellows as were at Stockbridge;* that one Fort be built and garrisoned *by Connecticut,* the other *by New York.* This line of Forts will shut up all between Connecticut and Hudson's Rivers and be the cheapest and best defence and security to all within, if well supplyd with men, of anything I can at present think of, and if your Excellency approves of it and should press it upon those Govts. it is so reasonable and also necessary for their safety I cant but hope they would at once comply with it.

As to the Forts above the line, if the Govt. of New Hampshire would support them it might be well, but the Advantages that would arise to this Govt. by doing it, would not countervail the expence, nor lessen the charge we might be at in defending our Frontiers in the Left Sides of the River where they can be much easier and Cheaper Supply'd with Provisions. Notwithstanding the Garrison at No. 4. the Enemy can and will come down Black River, Williams River, or West River, go over East or turn down South, without hazard, and return with like Security the same ways or go above.

The grand design Colo. Stoddard had in Garrisoning No. 4, was that Parties might be sent out from thence to waylay the roads from Crown Point and said there ought to be 100 men, posted there, well supply'd, fifty to be out at a Time. But he liv'd to see himself disappointed, the Govt. never did afford a sufficient Number of men for that Purpose, and it was with the utmost difficulty Provisions were obtained for those that were there, many were lost there and in going without doing any great good. That Fort might divert the Enemy Sometimes, but 'till the French join openly with the Indians, they will not fight Forts much, but in Small Parties carry on a Scalping War, and the more Compact the better it will be for us.

The Attempt to settle those distant places in the Wilderness in the manner it has been carried on, I never tho't prudent and to protect them will be extremely difficult and chargeable.

I Submit the whole, who am your Excelcys.
most obedt. Humble Sert.
ISR. WILLIAMS.

His Excelcy. Wm Shirley Esqr.

WILLIAM SHIRLEY TO ISRAEL WILLIAMS [1]

Boston, September 26, 1754.

SIR,

I have received a Packet from you by Major Williams, containing a Plan of the Western Parts of the Province, a List of the Officers and Centinells in your Regiment, and three Letters, one dated the 12th and two the 17th of September Instant.

I am extremely well satisfied with the great care and vigilance you have already shew'd for the protection and safety of the people upon the Western Frontier, and have great Confidence in your abilities and fidelity in the discharge of

[1] Original, L. S., Mass. Hist. Society, Col. Israel Williams Manuscripts, 71 D, 87.

your military trust, upon any future emergency, at this dangerous conjuncture.

As to the difficulty, you mention in your letter of the 12th Instant to arise from the appearance, which my second Orders to you have of abridging the Power given you in my first Orders, and confining it to the Limits of your own Regiment, I think my remarks upon the inclos'd copys of the Orders, I sent to Colo. Worthington, and my second Orders to your self, will best clear that up, and explain both of them, so as to make them consistent with each other.

I am glad, you found your Regiment and the towns within the limits of it, so well provided with arms and ammunition, as they appear to be by your return upon those articles. Exact care should be taken that all failures and deficiencies be fully and speedily made up: The refusal of the Selectmen of the Town of Northampton to give any Account of their Town Stock shall be inquired into.

It is necessary, that the limits of your's and Colonel Worthington's respective Regiments should be settled, I don't apprehend any better rule for doing that than the former settlement under Colo. Stoddard, vizt. the Northern Line of Springfield, which is the Southern Line of Northampton and Hadley to be the dividing Line; and so I state it, at least for the present; if there should be any good reason for altering it, that may be done hereafter.

Major Williams will accept of a new commission for Fort Massachusetts, which I design shall be enlarged by a superior command over the soldiers posted at Pontoosuck in special cases; I should be sorry to do anything, which may look like a slight upon the present Commander Captn. Chapin, of whose courage I have a good opinion; but as the command which the King's service now requires the Captain of that fort to have given him, must be enlarged, and Major Williams, besides being an officer whom I look upon to be well qualified for it, hath those further pretensions to it, that it was upon his resignation of the command of the Fort, that Captn. Chapin was commission'd for it, I hope he will not think it a slight upon him, if when I add another charge to the Captain's Commission for that Fort, I give it [to] Major Williams; I shall be very glad if he will serve as Lieutenant under Major Williams, and will give him the first proper promotion, which shall happen in my power; You will be pleased to let Captn. Chapin know this; and I leave it to your discretion to act in the manner, you shall think proper, with the inclos'd *blank* commissions concerning the Captain and Lieutt. of Fort Massachusetts as well as the others.

I inclose a Major's commission for Captn. Elijah Williams, dated the day after Major Hawley's commission; Be pleased to let him know that it is my clear opinion, he may accept it quite consistently with his honour, considering the circumstances of Major Hawley's appointment, notwithstanding Major Hawley is a Junior Captain to him: I shall likewise appoint Captn. Williams Commissary, as desired in your letter.

I approve very well of the command, you propose for Lieutent. Hawkes, whom I have a good knowledge and opinion of, and inclose a blank commission for him, to be filled up by yourself accordingly.

The plan you sent hath been of great service for my information in the state of the Western Frontier, and I much approve of the Line of Forts propos'd by you for the defence and protection of it, by marching parties or scouts.

So far as I could go in the execution of it before the meeting of the General Court, I have gone, and propos'd to his Majesty's Council the augmentation of the garrison of Fort assachusetts with 25 men, and 30 men to be posted and employed in scouting as you shall think most for the protection of the frontier under your care, which you will find they have advis'd to, and you will raise the men accordingly.

When the General Court meets I shall endeavour to carry the remainder of your scheme into execution, and shall make the protection and defence of that part of the Province, in the most effectual manner in every respect, one of the principal objects of my attention.

Major Williams put me in mind of a special commission which I gave the late Colo. Stoddard, appointg him to a military command, which he held during the late war, for the defence of the Western Parts of the Province: I should be glad if you or Major Williams could by any means recover a copy of that commission for me.

I shall be glad to give you a mark of the regard, I have for you, in that way, or any other which may happen in my power; and am,

Sir,
Your most assur'd Friend
and Servant.

W. SHIRLEY.

Colonel Israel Williams.

STATE OF THE REGIMENTS OF WILLIAM SHIRLEY AND SIR WILLIAM PEPPERRELL [1]

Mr. Shirleys and Mr. Pepperels Regts. were raised out of the men who went to take Cape Breton.

The Estabt. was made to commence from 24th Septr. 1745. and the first Estabt was for 92 days to 25 Decr. 1745.

18 Septr. 1754. The Paymt. Genl., by letter from Mr. Scrope, was directed to advance 3 months subsistence for the Officers and Companies of those Regts. to enable them to proceed there and to raise Men for forming the Regts.

In 1750 [Apr. 10] Sr. Wm. Pepperel demanded £6292. 16: for Levy money Contingencies for 832 men at 7. 11. 3 ℔ man. He was allowed 3733. 7. 0. for 758 men only, and it was paid out of monies in the hands of the Paymat. by mustering the Regt. compleat to 24 Decr. 1745, and by savings by Respits on the Muster Rolls.

Mr. Shirley also demanded £8364. 8. 0 for 1103 men at £7. 12. 1 a man which was reduced to £6691. 13. 4 which was for 880 men and paid in like manner.

The first Establishment of Shirleys and Pepperels Regiments was for 92 days from 24 Septr: 1745 to 24 Decr. fol-

[1] *B. M.*, *Additional Manuscript 33046, 293-315.* A transcript is in the Library of Congress.

lowing, and amounted each to £5054. 12s. 8d, which together makes £10109. 5s. 4d. for 3 Months.

The Saving on each of these Establishmts. for this time only, amounted to £2714. which the Colonels received in part of money allowed to them by the Kings Warrt. of 10. April 1750 for recruit money and Contingent Charges. Vizt: To Sr. Wm. Pepperel for 758 men at £7. 11s. 3d each . . . £5733. 7s. 0d.

To Mr. Shirley . . . $\frac{880}{1638}$ at 7: 12: 1. each . . . 6691. 13. 4.

The rest was paid out of Savings by Respits on Muster Rolls.

It may be six months or more before any men can be raised and should Establishments be now formed, those Establishments will amount to £20218: 10s: 8d for both Regiments, for six months out of which, only the Officers Subsistance *and Cloaths* will be wanted; And it is presumed the Field Officers Pay, and the Pay of the Officers to be appointed abroad, will not commence till they receive their Commissions.

Supposing 2000 men to be raised at £7: 12s: 0d a man it will amount to £15200.

But if only 1638 men as above which was the Case formerly, then no more will be wanted than £12448: 16s: 0d, at those Rates. But Mr. Kilby said the Recruit money would be more or less according to the humour of the people from 40s. to 14 or 15£ a head.

Endorsed:

> State of Shirley and Pepperels
> Regts.   Whether best to be raised
> by an immediate Establishmt.
> or otherwise.[1]

[1] At the time of the difficulty over the union of Provincial and English soldiers in 1756 (*post*, p. 495 ff.) the cost of the provision for such regiments as these became a matter of considerable interest.

CORRESPONDENCE OF WILLIAM SHIRLEY

PAPER DELIVERED TO SIR THOMAS ROBINSON, BY COLONEL NAPIER

Septr. 29th, 1754.

The List of the Officers for Shirley's and Pepperell's Regiments is not yet made out, but as soon as it is, Sir Thomas Robinson shall have it; and be acquainted what Number of Blank Commissions are to be sent over.

In Nova Scotia, Victualling was allowed. It must be considered, upon what Footing (with regard to that) the Government will put these Regiments.

Whatever Questions Sir Thomas Robinson would have mentioned to His Royal Highness, upon any Part of the Scheme, Colonel Napier will have the Honor of Sending to His Royal Highness; and has Orders to let Him know what Steps are taken, or what Orders given, in relation to it.

'Tis proposed to give Two Musters Subsistance for the Levy. And Mr. Mann is to provide a plain Cloathing for them. Accoutrements are likewise to be ordered here.

The Colonels are to appoint their own Agents.

WARRANTS ISSUED REGARDING THE REGIMENTS

Orders for Raising the Two Regiments in America.

Orders for Augmenting the Two Irish Regts. to English Numbers.

Warrants for Bas Horses. Forrage and Baggage Money for the Four Regiments.

Warrant appointing an Agent to the Two Regts. to be raised in America, untill Agents are appointed by the Colonels.[1]

Endorsed:
List of Warrants etc.

[1] Directions are given for Chests of Medicines, Cloathings and Accoutrements for the New raised Regiments, and for the Additional Men to the Irish Regiment, and Camp Necessaries, so as to be ready to go with the Transports.

ESTIMATE OF THE CHARGE OF TWO REGIMENTS OF FOOT

	Numbers	Pay 365 daies		
		£	s	d
Colonel Shirley's Regt: of Foot	1,145	20,175	7	6
Sr: Willm: Pepperell's Regt: of Foot	1,145	20,175	7	6
	2,290	40,350	15	

Endorsed:

Estimate of the Charge of Two Regiments of Foot to be Raised for his Majesty's Service in North America for the year 1755.

WILLIAM SHIRLEY TO ROBERT HUNTER MORRIS [1]

Boston, October 21st, 1754.

DEAR SIR,

Mr. Franklin hath deliver'd me the favour of your Letter [2] together with one from Sir Thomas Robinson, for your care of which, and the pleasure your own gave me, I am much oblig'd to you; and finding by last Week's Prints that you was arriv'd within your Governmt, I take the first Opportunity of congratulating you upon it, and wishing you an Easy and Happy Administration. If it is not a successful one for the Publick, I am satisfy'd it will be the People's fault.

I experienc'd too much, whilst I was in Europe last, the Spirit which you observe still prevails at home. But the letter I received from Sir Thomas Robinson was a very encouraging one, and I have the pleasure at least to flatter myself with hopes of better things from them.

I have no leaf in my book for managing a Quaker Assembly. If I had, it should be at your Service. Your predecessor, Mr. Hamilton, to whom I would beg the favour of you to

---

[1] 1 Penna. Arch. 2, 181.

[2] The letter of Morris to which Shirley refers was of Oct. 13 and gave notice of his entrance upon the government of Pennsylvania.

make my Complimts, will give you a better insight into the Light within them, than I can pretend to do.

The Best Advice I can give you, is to lose no time for promoting the Plan of an Union of the Colonies for their mutual Defence to be concerted at home, and establish'd by Act of Parliamt, as soon as is possible. The proceedings of the Commrs at Albany, from the general Governmts, will shew you the necessity of it. I am labouring this point, totis viribus. It would ease you of a great part of the burthen, your Governmt may probably bring upon you otherwise, in the managemt of Military and Indian Affairs.

I have one thing to mention to you, which I own gives me some surprize; I had, at the desire of the Council, wrote to Mr. De Lancey to know, whether there was any foundation for the report that the Commissioners for Indian Affairs, at Albany, had made a Treaty of Neutrality for the Governmt of New York with the Cagnawaga Indians, and I find by his answer to me that it is so; but he intimates that it is made for all the Colonies. I am to have Copies from him of all Papers relating to it. If a neutrality is concluded for this Governmt with those Indians, it is what was a Dead Secret to us before, I believe it would have been more satisfactory to this Governmt if the Treaty had been transacted by the Commissioners from the Colonies, when at Albany. I am perswaded we shall never intrust the care of any of Our Interests with the Commrs of Indian Affairs at Albany.

I shall take a great Pleasure in maintaining a strict Correspondence with you, both Publick and Private; am obliged to you for the Expressions of your friendship to my family, and there is no person who more sincerely desires to have it in his Power to give you proofs of a real Esteem and friendship for you, then,

    Dear Sir,
      Your most faithful,
      Humble Servant,

           W. Shirley.

P.S. Be pleas'd to make my Complimts to Govr. Tinker. I will send you a copy of my Conference with the Eastern

Indians by Mr. Franklin, with whom I shall have the Pleasure of drinking your health to day at the Province House.

Endorsed:
GOVR. SHIRLEY—That Delancey, in his letter, Had Owned that a treaty of Neutrality was concluded with the Cagnawaga's by the Governmt of N. York and recommending to me to press the Union of the Colonies.
Octor. 21, 1754.

SIR THOMAS ROBINSON TO WILLIAM SHIRLEY [1]

GOVR. SHIRLEY.   Whitehall, Octr. 26th, 1754.
SIR,
   The King having taken into consideration the State of His Colonies, and the Encroachments made by the French, in several parts of North America You will see by my Letter of this date to you [2] and to the respective Governours of the several Colonies and Provinces in No. America, the Orders, which His Majesty has thought proper to give for the Defence of His just Rights and Dominions, and as the King has, upon former occasions, experienced your Activity and Fidelity in His Service, He has been graciously pleased to appoint you to be Colonel of a Regiment of Foot, consisting of one Thousand men, to be raised by you, and to rendezvous at Boston, when raised, and you will accordingly receive, in a short time, a proper Commission for that purpose. The King having likewise nominated a certain number of Field Officers, Captains, Lieutenants, Ensigns, an Adjutant, and a Quarter Master, and having been pleased to sign Blank Commissions, for the remaining Complement of Officers, the same will be transmitted to you, together, with a List of the whole Number with all possible dispatch.

[1] P. R. O., C. O. 5, 211, 201. A similar letter was sent to Sir William Pepperell, and see also general letter of the same date *post*, p. 98.
[2] The wording to William Pepperell varies slightly at this point.

His Majesty having appointed Sir William Pepperell to be Colonel of a Regt to be raised in the same manner, and to consist of the same number with that, whereof you are now appointed Colonel, I have acquainted him therewith by this Conveyance, and I have likewise informed him, that it is the King's Pleasure, that the said Regiment when raised, shall rendez-vous at New York and Philadelphia, in like manner, as that under your Command will rendez-vous at Boston.

You will carefully correspond with the Commander in Chief when He arrives, and Sir Wm. Pepperell, and will communicate to them, from time to time, the Progress you shall have made in the Execution of these His Majesty's Orders; and you will likewise correspond with the several Govrs. of His Majesty's Colonies, as often as the service shall require it.

I am etc.

T. ROBINSON.

Endorsed:

> Octr. 26th 1754.
> To Govr. Shirley
> and
> Sir Wm. Pepperell.

> by Mr. Pitcher; and Duptes.
> by Sir J. St. Clair.

SIR THOMAS ROBINSON TO WILLIAM SHIRLEY [1]

Whitehall, Octr. 26th, 1754.

SIR,

Having informed you in my letter of July 5th that the King had under his Royal consideration the State of affairs in North America; I am now to acquaint you, that, amongst

---

[1] P. R. O., C. O. 5, 211. This letter with minor variations was sent to each of the British governors in North America. See the letter of Dep. Gov. Gardner of Rhode Island to Shirley of Jan. 4, 1755, reciting the measures taken by that colony in response. R. I. Col. Rec. 5, 405.

other measures, that are thought proper for the defence of His Majesty's just rights and dominions, in those parts, the King has not only been pleased to order two Regiments of Foot, consisting of 500 Men each, besides Commissioned and non Commissioned Officers, commanded by Sir Peter Halkett [1] and Col. Dunbar [2] to repair to Virginia, and to be there augmented to the number of 700, each; but, likewise, to send orders to Sir William Pepperell, and yourself to raise two Regiments, whereof you are respectively appointed Colonels, of 1000 Men each; and, also to sign Commissions for a number of Officers to serve in the said two Regiments, and who will forthwith repair to North America, for that purpose.

Whereas there will be wanting a considerable number of Men to make up the designed complement of the said four Regiments, it is His Majesty's pleasure, that you should be taking the previous steps, towards contributing, as far as you can, to have about 3000 Men in readiness to be enlisted; and it is His Majesty's intention, that a General Officer, of

---

[1] Sir Peter Halkett, of Pitferran, Fifeshire, a baronet of Nova Scotia, was the son of Sir Peter Wedderburne, of Gosford, who assumed his wife's name. In 1734 he sat in the House of Commons, for Dunferline; and was Lieutenant Colonel of the 44th at Sir John Copes' defeat, in 1745. Being released on his parole, by Charles Edward, he was ordered by Cumberland to rejoin his regiment and serve again against the Jacobites. With great propriety, he refused such a dishonorable duty, saying that "his Royal Highness was master of his commission, but not of his honor." The king approved of Sir Peter's course, and he retained his rank. On the 26th of February, 1751, he succeeded to the Colonelcy of his regiment. He was killed, at the head of his regiment, in the battle of Monongahela, on the 9th of July, 1755. *Sargent's Expedition against Fort Duquesne*, 274, 294.

[2] Colonel Thomas Dunbar, had been Lieutenant Colonel of the 18th or Royal Irish regiment, and on the 29th of April, 1752, was promoted to the Colonelcy of the 48th regiment of Foot. In November, 1755, he was superseded in the command of this regiment, and honorably retired as Lieutenant Governor of Gibraltar, in consequence of his retreat, after General Braddock's defeat. He became Major General on the 18th of January, 1758, and a Lieutenant General on December 18th, 1760, but was never again employed in active service. *Ibid.* 267.

Rank and Capacity, to be appointed to command in Chief all the King's forces in North America, a Deputy Quarter Master General, and a Commissary of the Musters, shall set out, as soon as conveniently may be, in order to prepare every thing for the arrival of the Forces abovementioned from Europe, and for the raising of the others in America.

You will receive from that General, and the other Officers just mentioned, a full and exact account of the Arms, Cloathing, and other necessaries, to be sent, upon this important occasion, as likewise of the Ordnance Stores, and of the Officers, and attendants, belonging thereto. All which being ordered for this service, are such proofs of His Majesty's regard for the security and welfare of his subjects in those parts, as cannot fail to excite you to exert yourself, and those under your care, to take the most vigorous steps to repel your common danger, and to shew, that the Kings orders, which were sent you last year, by the Earle of Holdernesse, and were renewed to you in my letter of the 5th July,[1] have, at last, roused that emulation, and spirit, which every Man owes at this time, to His Majesty, the publick and himself. The King will not therefore imagine, that either you, or the rest of his Govrs., will suffer the least neglect or delay, in the performance of the present service, now strongly recommended to you; particularly with regard to the following points: vizt: That you should carefully provide a sufficient quantity of fresh victuals, at the expence of your Governt, to be ready for the use of the Troops at their arrival.—That you should likewise, furnish the Officers, who may have occasion to go from place to place, with all necessaries for traveling by land, in case there are no means of going by sea; and: That you should use your utmost diligence, and authority, in procuring an exact observance of such orders, as shall be issued from time to time by the Commander in chief, for

[1] Robinson's letter of July 5 to Shirley is in P. R. O., C. O. 5, 211. It is of about three hundred words, and directs him as to formation of plans for the Kennebec campaign and coöperation with other officers in Nova Scotia. See Shirley to Robinson, Dec. 14, *post*, p. 107.

quartering the Troops, impressing carriages, and providing all necessaries for such forces, as shall arrive, or be raised within your Government.

As the Articles above-mentioned are of a local and peculiar nature, and arising entirely within your Govert, it is almost needless for me to acquaint you, that His Majesty will expect, that the charge thereof be defrayed by His subjects belonging to the same. But, with regard to such other articles, which are of a more general concern, it is the King's pleasure, that the same should be supplied by a common fund, to be established for the benefit of all the Colonies collectively in North America; for which purpose, you will use your utmost endeavours to induce the assembly of your province, to raise forthwith as large a sum as can be afforded, as their contribution to this common fund, to be employed, provisionally, for the General service of North America, (particularly for paying the charge of levying the Troops, to make up the complements of the Regiments abovementioned) until such time, as a plan of general union of His Majesty's Northern Colonies, for their common defence, can be perfected.

You will carefully conferr, or correspond as you shall have opportunities upon every thing relative to the present service, with the said Genl., Sir William Pepperell, and as it is the King's intention to give all proper encouragement to such persons, who shall engage to serve upon this occasion, you will acquaint all such persons, in the King's name that they will receive arms and cloathing from hence, and that they shall be sent back if desired to their respective habitations, when the service in America shall be over.

As the several Governors, in all the King's provinces and Colonies in North America, will receive by this conveyance a letter to the same effect with this, which I now send you, they will be prepared at the same time, to obey His Majesty's commands; and I am to direct you to correspond with all, or either of them, occasionally, as you shall find it expedient for the General service.

I am ettc.

T. ROBINSON.

WILLIAM SHIRLEY TO ISRAEL WILLIAMS [1]

Boston, Novemr. 7, 1754.

Sir,

I have received Advice of a Party of Indians setting upon a small Detachmt sent out from the Garrison at Teconick, killing and scalping one, and taking four of them Prisoners, as you will see by an Extract from Captain Lane's Letter to me, dated the 30th of October last,[2] By which and an Extract of another Letter from Lieutt. Howard, you will find Grounds strongly to suspect that the Norridgewock Indians were Privy to this Design, if not actually concerned in the Execution of it. And by these Extracts you have also Information of further Mischief forming among the Canada and other Indians against our Frontiers; Therefore you will send Advice thereof to the exposed Places in your Parts of their Danger, that so they may be upon their Guard to prevent a Surprize.

I am,
Sir,
Your Assur'd Friend and
Servant,   W. Shirley.
Colo. Israel Williams.

[1] Original, Mass. Hist. Society, Col. Israel Williams Manuscripts, 71 D, 92.

[2] The following is the extract mentioned (Col. Israel Williams Manuscripts, 71 D, 92):

Fort Hallifax, Octor. 30, 1754.

May it please your Excellency,

I beg leave to acquaint your Excy. that this Morning I ordered a Detachment of ten Men to go with the Team to fetch a Load of Logs, and they went and loaded the Team (not above two Gun Shott from the Block House upon the Hill) and as they were coming back the Indians fired upon them, and kill'd one man and scalp'd him, carried off four of the Men, and shott two of the Oxen. I immediately issued out with all that was able to go, and pursued them as far as we thought convenient, but they went off with all the Expedition that was possible.

Copy Attest, J. Willard, Secry.

BENJAMIN FRANKLIN TO WILLIAM SHIRLEY [1]

SIR, Boston. December 4, 1754.

I mentiond it Yesterday to your Excellency as my Opinion, that Excluding the People of the Colonies from all Share in the Choice of the Grand Council would probably give extreme Dissatisfaction, as well as the Taxing them by Act of Parliament where they have no Representative. In Matters of General Concern to the People, and especially where Burthens are to be laid upon them, it is of Use to consider as well what they will *be apt* to think and say, as what they *ought* to think. I shall therefore, as your Excellency requires it of me, briefly mention what of either Kind occurs at present, on this Occasion.

First, they will say, and perhaps with Justice, that the Body of the People in the Colonies are as loyal, and as firmly attach'd to the present Constitution and reigning Family, as any Subjects in the King's Dominions; that there is no Reason to doubt the Readiness and Willingness of their Representatives to grant, from Time to Time, such Supplies, for the Defence of the Country, as shall be judg'd necessary, so far as their Abilities will allow; That the People in the Colonies, who are to feel the immediate Mischiefs of Invasion and Conquest by an Enemy, in the Loss of their Estates, Lives and Liberties, are likely to be better Judges of the Quantity of Forces necessary to be raised and maintain'd, Forts to be built and supported, and of their own Abilities to bear the Expence, than the Parliament of England at so great a Distance. That Governors often come to the Colonies merely to make Fortunes, with which they intend to return to Britain, are not always Men of the best Abilities and Integrity, have no Estates here, nor any natural Connections with us that should make them heartily concern'd

---

[1] *B. M., Additional Manuscript 35911, 60.* A transcript is in the Library of Congress. Shirley could hardly have found a better representative of the colonies at large than Benjamin Franklin, and the governor's caution is shown in this request for his opinion.

for our Welfare; and might possibly be sometimes fond of raising and keeping up more Forces than necessary, from the Profits accruing to themselves and to make Provision for their Friends and Dependants. That the Councellors in most of the Colonies, being appointed by the Crown, on the Recommendation of Governors, are often of small Estates, frequently dependant on the Governor for Offices, and therefore too much under Influence. That there is therefore great Reason to be jealous of a Power in such Governors and Councils, to raise such Sums as they shall judge necessary, by Draft on the Lords of the Treasury, to be afterwards laid on the Colonies by Act of Parliament, and paid by the People here; since they might abuse it, by projecting useless Expeditions, harrassing the People, and taking them from their Labour to execute such Projects, and merely to create Offices and Employments, gratify their Dependants, and divide Profits. That the Parliament of England is at a great Distance, subject to be misinform'd by such Governors and Councils, whose united Interests might probably secure them against the Effect of any Complaints from hence. That it is suppos'd an undoubted Right of Englishmen not to be taxed but by their own Consent given thro' their Representatives. That the Colonies have no Representatives in Parliament. That to propose taxing them by Parliament, and refusing them the Liberty of chusing a Representative Council, to meet in the Colonies, and consider and judge of the Necessity of any General Tax and the Quantum, shews a Suspicion of their Loyalty to the Crown, or Regard for their Country, or of their Common Sense and Understanding, which they have not deserv'd. That compelling the Colonies to pay Money without their Consent would be rather like raising Contributions in an Enemy's Country, than taxing of Englishmen for their own publick Benefit. That it would be treating them as a conquer'd People, and not as true British Subjects. That a Tax laid by the Representatives of the Colonies might easily be lessened as the Occasions should lessen, but being once laid by Parliament, under the Influence of the Representations made by Governors, would probably be kept up and continued, for the Benefit of Governors, to the grievous Burthen and Discouragement of the Colonies, and preventing their Growth and Increase. That a Power in Governors to march the Inhabitants from one End of the British and French Colonies to the other, being a Country of at least 1500 Miles square, without the Approbation or Consent of their Representatives first obtain'd to such Expeditions, might be grievous and ruinous to the People, and would put them on a Footing with the Subjects of France in Canada, that now groan under such Oppression from their Governor, who for two Years past has harrass'd them with long and destructive Marches to the Ohio. That if the Colonies in a Body may be well governed by Governors and Councils, appointed by the Crown, without Representatives, particular Colonies may as well or better be so governed; a Tax may be laid on them all by Act of Parliament; for Support of Government, and their Assemblies be dismiss'd, as a useless Part of their Constitution. That the Powers propos'd, by the Albany Plan of Union, to be vested in a Grand Council representative of the People, even with Regard to Military Matters, are not so great as those the Colonies of Rhode-Island and Connecticut are intrusted with, and have never abused; for by this Plan the President General is appointed by the Crown and controlls all by his Negative; but in those Governments the People chuse the Governor, and yet allow him no Negative. That the British Colonies, bordering on the French are properly Frontiers of the British Empire; and that the Frontiers of an Empire are properly defended at the joint Expence of the Body of People in such Empire. It would now be thought hard, by Act of Parliament, to oblige the Cinque Ports or Sea Coasts of Britain to maintain the whole Navy, because they are more immediately defended by it, not allowing them, at the same Time, a Vote in chusing Members of Parliament: And if the Frontiers in America must bear the Expence of their own Defence, it seems hard to allow them no Share in Voting the Money, judging of the Necessity and Sum, or advising the Measures. That besides the Taxes necessary for the Defence of the Frontiers, the Colonies pay yearly great Sums to the Mother Country unnotic'd. For taxes, paid in Britain by the Land holder or Artificer, must enter into and increase the Price of the Produce of Land, and of Manufactures made of it; and a great part of this is paid by Consumers in the Colonies, who thereby pay a considerable Part of the British Taxes. We are restrain'd in our Trade with Foreign Nations, and where we could be supplied with any Manufactures cheaper from them, but must buy the same dearer from Britain, the Difference of Price is a clear Tax to Britain. We are oblig'd to carry a great part of our Produce directly to Britain, and where the Duties there laid upon it lessens its Price to the Planter, or it sells for less than it would in Foreign Markets, the Difference is a Tax paid to Britain. Some Manufactures we could make, but are forbid, and must take them of British Merchants; the whole Price of these is a Tax paid to Britain. By our greatly increasing the *Consumption* and *Demand* of British Manufactures, their Price is considerably rais'd of late Years; the Advance is clear Profit to Britain, and enables its People better to pay great Taxes; and much of it being paid by us is clear Tax to Britain. In short, as we are not suffer'd to regulate our Trade, and restrain the Importation and Consumption of British Superfluities, (as Britain can the Consumption of Foreign Superfluities) our whole Wealth centers finally among the Merchants and Inhabitants of Britain, and if we make them richer, and enable them better to pay their Taxes, it is nearly the same as being taxed ourselves, and equally beneficial to the Crown. These Kind of Secondary Taxes, however, we do not complain of, tho' we have no Share in the Laying or Disposing of them; but to pay immediate heavy Taxes, in the Laying, Appropriation or Disposition of which, we have no Part, and which perhaps we may know to be as unnecessary as grievous, must seem hard Measure to Englishmen, who cannot conceive, that by hazarding their Lives and Fortunes in subduing and settling new Countries, extending the Dominion and encreasing the Commerce of their Mother Nation, they have forfeited the native Rights of Britons, which they think ought rather to have been given them, as due to such Merit, if they had been before in a State of Slavery.

These, and such Kind of Things as these, I apprehend will be thought and said by the People, if the propos'd Alteration of the Albany Plan should take Place. Then, the Administration of the Board of Governors and Council so appointed, not having any Representative Body of the People to approve and unite in its Measures, and conciliate the Minds of the People to them, will probably become suspected and odious. Animosities and dangerous Feuds will arise between the Governors and Governed, and every Thing go into Confusion. Perhaps I am too apprehensive in this Matter, but having freely given my Opinion and Reasons, your Excellency can better judge whether there be any Weight in them. — And the Shortness of the Time allow'd me will I hope, in some Degree, excuse the Imperfections of this Scrawl.

With the greatest Respect and Fidelity,
I am,
Your Excellency's most obedient
and most humble Servant
B. FRANKLIN.

Addressed
To Pr. Collinson

Endorsed:
Copy of a Letter to Govr. Shirley on the Proposal of excluding the American Assemblies from the Choice of the Grand Council, and taxing the People in America by Parliament.

WILLIAM SHIRLEY TO SIR THOMAS ROBINSON [1]

SIR, Boston, New Engld. Decr. 14th, 1754.

In my last I acknowledg'd the honour, I had, of receiving three letters from you, two of them dated the 26th of October

[1] P. R. O., C. O. 5, 46. A transcript is in the Library of Congress. See Robinson to Shirley, *ante*, pp. 97 and 98.

last, and the other on the 25th, and I shall punctually conform to his Majesty's Orders signify'd in the two former of them to me concerning the raising of the Regiment, of which his Majesty hath done me the honour to appoint me Colonel, to the utmost of my power, particularly in procuring the Assembly within my own Governmt to contribute their proportion towards the Expence of Levy money etc. for the Troops sent over from Ireland, and to be rais'd here.

In the mean time as Sir William Pepperell's and my delay to begin raising our respective Regimts untill Levy money can be obtain'd from the several Colonies, (a point which I am apprehensive may prove difficult to be carry'd) would disappoint his Majesty's Service very much, We shall be under the necessity of raising Money at present by drawing upon our Agent; which may be reimburs'd to the Crown, upon the Colonies complying with his Majesty's pleasure; for inducing my own Assembly to do which I shall use my best Endeavours, as also that our beginning to raise the two Regimts at present shall be of no Disadvantage to my Application to them to be at their part of the Charge for the requisite Levy Money.

I now beg leave, Sir, to mention to you that my Lieutent Colonel and Mr. Pitcher, the Commissary General of the Musters of all his Majesty's forces rais'd and to be rais'd in North America, have both assur'd me that my Regimt was to rendezvous at Boston, and Sir William Pepperell's in New York and Philadelphia, and the latter of those Gentlemen tells me that he is certain that the place assign'd for the Rendezvous of my Regiment in your letter which is New York and Philadelphia, and that for Sir William Pepperell's, which is Boston, must be an Error of the Clerk in filling up the Blanks left for the names of those places : If it is not, I would beg leave, Sir, to submit to your Consideration whether in all cases it might not be for his Majesty's Service that the General plan of Rendezvous for my Regimt should be Boston rather than New York and Pensilvania, as in the former case I might have it more under my eye and immediate command, than I could have in the latter, since by his

Majesty's Instructions to me as Governour of the province of the Massachusetts Bay, I am forbid to stir out of it without his express leave; whereas Sir William Pepperell may attend and Inspect his Regiment any where. At this time particularly I am concerting Measures with Colonel Lawrence to drive the French out of Nova Scotia next Spring, in Obedience to his Majesty's Orders signify'd to me in your Letter, Sir, dated the 5th of July last, and propose that my Regimt should assist in the Service, unless I am forbid by different Orders; in which first case their being rendezvous'd, as they are rais'd, in New York and Pensilvania instead of Boston would be an hindrance to the Service.

Upon these considerations, and the Assurance of the Commissary General of the Musters, that it was design'd by you, Sir, that my Regiment should be rendezvous'd at Boston, and that it must be owing to the Error of the Clerk in copying the letter, that it is there otherwise express'd which seems very probable, I shall assemble my Regimt at Boston, as fast as I can raise them, and continue to do so, untill I have the honour to receive your further Orders upon this head.

> I am with the greatest respect,
> > Sir,
> > > Your most Humble, and
> > > most Obedient Servant,
> > > > W. Shirley.

P.S. I shall observe your Directions, Sir, concerning giving Mr. Pitcher all Assistance in my power; and am oblig'd to you for the honour of your Message to me by him.

I am affraid there was a mistake in my last, viz, that the 1st of April was the time, by which the 20,00 (*sic*) stands of Arms should be shipp'd and Dispatches sent in Answer to that letter, whereas it should have been the 1st day of February.

Rt. Honble Sir Thomas Robinson
One of his Majesty's principal Secretaries
of State.

WILLIAM SHIRLEY TO ROBERT HUNTER MORRIS [1]

Boston, Decr. 17th, 1754.

Dear Sir,

Many thanks to you for all your kindness to Jack. He soon returns to you, like a bad penny. I shall be extremely oblig'd to you for your favour in encouraging Enlistmts into my Regimt, by your Countenancing him in the shape of a Recruiting Officer. I flatter myself it may be for the publick Service, as well as my own and Jack's in particular, as his success in recruiting may facilitate my Obtaining a Company for him in my Regimt, in the first step.

I find by your late Message and Speech to the Assembly within your Governmt, that the French are as much in Motion upon the Ohio as we are at Boston. I hope that will instill a little into them, and more into Maryland and Virginia. I can't but think the Maryland Commander in Chief makes a poor figure with his single Company rais'd in his own Government.

I detain'd the ship which sailed from hence for London on Monday, till I could get the Message and an Extract of your Speech copy'd out for Lord Halifax, as I imagine that Vessell might be the first Opportunity of conveying them to England.

Surely these Commotions will drive the Spirit of Quietism out of your Assembly; and I hope they may turn to the advantage of the publick, and your own in the End.

I would beg the favour of you to give my Complimts to Govr. Tinker and your predecessor, Mr. Hamilton. I will do myself the honour to write to the former by next post.

[1] 1 Penna. Arch. 2, 215.

My hands are full at present, as you will easily imagine, with different matters, which inevitably throw me into a hurry, which I hope will be a sufficient Apology for the Abruptness of this Letter.

Be assur'd, Dear Sir, that I wish you all possible success for your own sake, as well as that of the publick; and that I shall, with great pleasure, receive and execute any Commands from you in my power, being with great truth and Esteem,

> Dear Sir,
> Your Honour's most faithfull
> and Obedient Servant,
>
> W. SHIRLEY.

P.S. I refer you to Jack for all particulars of our movements here.

Endorsed:

GOVR. SHIRLEY — By his son John, who he sent to recruit for his regiment, recd. Jany. 20.

WILLIAM SHIRLEY TO SIR THOMAS ROBINSON [1]

Boston, New England, December 24th, 1754.

SIR,

I suppose Gov. Delancey may have sent you a copy of the proceedings of the Commissioners of several of His Majesty's Governments upon this Continent lately assembled at Albany in the Province of New York; least that, by any accident should have miscarry'd, I inclose you one here.

That meeting, Sir, gave the Colonies concern'd a fair opportunity of agreeing by their respective Commissioners in a conclusive manner upon Articles of Union and Confederation

---

[1] P. R. O., C. O. 5, 15. Printed: Docts. rel. Col. Hist. New York, 6, 930. The Minutes of the Proceedings of the Albany Congress are in Johnson Mss., N. Y. State Library, 1, 127, and printed in Doc. Hist. N. Y. (Q.) 2, 317 ff.

for the general defence of His Majesty's subjects and interests in North America as well in time of peace as of war; and it is most evident that their present state requires such an Union to be form'd as soon as is possible, in order to put an immediate stop to the encroachments with which the French have, ever since the conclusion of the late treaty at Aix la Chapelle, been and still are surrounding them and to prevent the total defection of all the Indians, not already gain'd over by that nation from the British interest.

The Commissioners of the Massachusetts Province were accordingly furnished with plenary powers for agreeing conclusively on the part of that government with the Commissioners of all or any of the other governments who should be convened at the Congress upon the Articles of such an Union; but the powers produced by all the other Commissioners there, being defective, (as may appear to you Sir by the copies of them which are made part of the record of their proceedings) nothing binding upon their respective governments either for building forts for the defence of the country of the Five Nations or cementing a general Union of the Colonies, could be concluded and agreed upon by them.

As to the plan of the proposed Union agreed upon by the Commissioners in order to be layd before their respective constituents for their consideration, a copy of which is contain'd in their proceedings; they had no expectation that it will have any effect, nor could any proper plan be form'd, as I apprehend, in which the several Govts would unite; their different constitutions, situations, circumstances and tempers, will ever be found an invincible obstacle to their agreement upon any one plan in very article, or (if they ever should happen to agree upon one) to their duly carrying it into execution.

It appears from that part of the proposed plan fram'd at Albany, which provides that it shall be established by Act of Parliament, that the opinion of the Commissioners there present was that nothing under the force of that would effect such an Union, and what seems to give weight to their opinion is, that the Crown's recommendation of the Union proposed in King William's reign among several of the Colonies for their mutual defence, and the quotas of men and money allotted to each government to pay, never had the least effect as I can learn.

However tho' the Commissioners have fail'd for want of sufficient powers to perfect an Union among the Colonies at their Congress, yet they have made a great progress in concerting the proper measures for effecting one, and discovering the absolute necessity of it's being done without delay; and their several determinations upon this point seem to have pav'd the way clearly for His Majesty's ordering a plan of an Union to be form'd at home, and the execution of it inforc'd here by Act of Parliament, if that shall be agreeable to his royal pleasure.

These gentlemen, Sir, having been chosen Commissioners by the General Assemblies of the several colonies which they represented at the Congress, tho' commission'd by the Govrs. of them, must be consider'd as the most intelligent persons of their respective governments in the general state of the Colonies, and as having a just attention to the interest of their own Colonies in particular, in all their consultations, so that their determinations of these points (in all which they were as I am assured by the Massachusetts' Commissioners very near unanimous) vizt 1st That a General Union of their Forces and Councils are necessary at this conjuncture for saving them from the incroachmts of the French. 2. That an effectual scheme for such an Union can't be carry'd into execution but by authority of the Parliament of Great Britain. 3. What may serve as a present rule for fixing the several proportions which each Colony should be allotted to bear of the charges of supporting the government propos'd to be erected in the Plan, there estimated by the number of members allotted for each government to send to the General Council: I say, Sir, that their determination of these points ought to be look'd upon as the declared sense of all the Colonies; and this together with their representation of the state of the Colonies seems to have laid a good foundation for immediately proceeding at home to the forming of a proper plan in all points for a General Union of the Colonies, settling the quotas of men and money for each Colony to find towards the charge of it as stated in the plan of the Commissioners to be establish'd by authority of Parliamt and carry'd into execution in the Colonies without further consulting them upon any points whatever.

As to the plan of Union form'd at Albany, I would beg leave, Sir, to submit the following remarks upon it to your consideration, vizt[1]

1. That the reason of committing to the several Houses of Representatives *solely* the choice of the members which each Colony is allowed to send to the Grand Council seems to be because it is propos'd that the Council should have power to levy taxes upon the People, which it is thought could not be exercis'd by any Council whatsoever in the Colonies which should not be wholly chosen by the People, or at least by their Representatives, without raising a general dissatisfaction.

2. That on the other hand it is clear that as such Council can be consider'd no otherwise than as the General Representative body of all the people of the Colonies compriz'd in the Union, the giving to them a share in making peace and war with the Indians and concluding treaties with them, in the disposal of military commissions, in the power of raising troops and erecting Forts, would be a great strain upon the prerogative of the Crown and contrary to the English Constitution.

3. That the command over the Militia, power of raising them by warrant of impress, marching them upon any service at least within the limits of the several Colonies, appointing all military Officers, erecting and demolishing of Forts, declaring war against the Indians and making treaties of peace with them; are vested solely in the respective Governours of all of them, proprietary and charter, as well as those whose government is founded on His Majesty's commission, except in the two Colonies of Connecticutt and Rhode Island, whose governmts stand upon their old char-

[1] Compare Shirley's remarks with Franklin to Shirley, Dec. 4, 1754, *ante*, p. 103.

ters, by which the Crown hath divested itself almost of the whole prerogative, and transferr'd it to the populace, in whom the several above mention'd powers are lodg'd, the Governours not having so much as a negative in any election of officers or Act of Legislature.

4. That the institution of these old Charter Governments in the Colonies during the state of their infancy, tho' well accommodated to draw together numbers of settlers in the beginning of the English Plantations and for the regulation of each settlement whilst it consisted of but an handfull of people, yet seems by no means well calculated for the government of them when the inhabitants considerably increas'd in numbers and wealth. The present state of the government of Rhode Island is an instance of this. The Colony is computed to have upwards of   [1] inhabitants and a proportionable share of property; the reins of their government prove now so loose that a spirit of mobbism prevails in every part of it; they pay no regard to the Kings instruction, and very little or none to Acts of Parliament, particularly to Acts of Trade, in which they seem to look upon themselves as freebooters, as their government was not originally calculated for preserving their dependency upon Great Britain, they have little or no appearance of it among them now, and their example hath by degrees infected His Majesty's neighbouring governments with irregularities which they might not otherwise have gone into. I would be understood to speak this only of the natural tendency of their government. Their Assembly have given proofs of a public spirit for promoting the general welfare of His Majestys Colonies against the encroachmts of the French, and extending his dominions in America; they have a strong attachment to His Majesty's person and the Protestant Succession in his family, and likewise to the English government so far as it is consistent with the spirit of riot which reigns among them, and may be call'd rather the fault of the form of their Colony government then of the people, the most considerate of which are said to be much tir'd of it.

[1] No estimate of the population is given.

5. That the unfitness of these old Charter Governments for the Colonies when they are grown up and come out of their infancy, was I suppose the reason why in the beginning of King William and Queen Mary's reign the government at home refus'd to the old Massachusett's Colony to renew their Charter which had been vacated by a judgment in the Court of Chancery in Westminster Hall in a late reign, tho' their principles and loyalty to the Crown at that time greatly recommended them to its favour; but instead of that it was thought good policy to put an end likewise to the Charter Colony of New Plymouth and to erect and incorporate the old colonies of the Massachusetts Bay and New Plymouth, together with the Provinces of Main and Nova Scotia into one Province, which is now the present Province of the Massachusetts Bay, saving that the Crown hath disannex'd Nova Scotia from it, and to grant them a new Charter, wherein the Crown hath resum'd its prerogative; and this form of government was as readily accepted by the People of the old Charter Colonies, who were in a great measure surfeited of their government and former popular privileges, then become disproportion'd to the state of the inhabitants.

The result from these observations, Sir, which I would submit to your consideration is, that if the old charter form of government, such as that is which is proposed in the Albany plan of Union, is unfitt for ruling a particular Colony, it seems much more improper for establishing a General Government and *Imperium* over all the Colonies to be comprized in the Union.

The only material difference between an old charter government and the Albany Plan appears to be, that by the latter it is propos'd that the Governour General shall be appointed and supported by His Majesty and have a negative in every Act of the Grand Council (as it is there called) whereas in the former the Governour is annually elected by the People, dependent upon them for his support and hath no negative in the Acts of Assembly.

This is relied upon as a most favourable circumstance on the part of the Crown in the following remarks, drawn up by a gentleman who had a principle hand in forming the Albany Plan, vizt "That the Government or Constitution propos'd to be form'd by the plan consists " of two branc[h]es, a Presi-"dent General appointed by the Crown and a Council chosen by the People or by the People's Representative which is the same thing.

"That by a subsequent article the Council chosen by the "People can effect nothing without the consent of the Presi-"dent General appointed by the Crown; the Crown possesses "therefore full one half of the power of this Constitution."

"That in the British Constitution the Crown is suppos'd "to possess but one third, the Lords having their share.

"That the Constitution therefore seem'd rather more "favourable for the Crown."

But it seems an obvious answer to say that the power of the President General which in the remarks is called *one half of the Power of the Constitution*, is only a *Negative* one, stripped of every branch of the prerogative, and is at best only a preventative power in a small degree. It may controll the other half of the constitution from doing mischief by any act of theirs, but it can't prevent mischiefs arising from their inactivity, neglect or obstinacy.

As to the remark "that in the British Constitution the "Crown is supposed to possess but one third of the power, the "Lords having *their* share;" with the consequences drawn from it in favour of the Albany Plan; it seems a palpable error to suppose that the Peers of the Realm who are created by the Crown, weaken its influence and power in the state by their being one of the three branches of it.

It may be further observ'd that the prerogative is so much relaxed in the Albany Plan, that it doth not appear well calculated to strengthen the dependency of the Colonies upon the Crown; which seems a very important article in the consideration of this affair.

I have I am affraid, Sir, been too diffuse in my remarks upon the Albany Plan, and it may perhaps be expected that I should offer some other plan in lieu of it.

I have turn'd my thoughts upon one, Sir, and form'd a

rough sketch of it; but as I understood the Lords Commissioners for Trade and Plantations were forming a plan themselves, I did not think it proper for me to transmit my crude sentiments to you upon so difficult and delicate a work. I am, with the highest respect,

Sir,
Your most Humble and
most Obedient Servant,

W. SHIRLEY.

The Right Honble Sir Thomas Robinson.

WILLIAM SHIRLEY TO ISRAEL WILLIAMS [1]

Boston, Jany. 4th, 1755.

SIR,

Having lately receiv'd orders from his majesty to raise forthwith a Regiment of foot for the Defence of his majesty's Colonies in North America of which I am appointed Colonel, I would desire the favour of you to promote the Inlistment of the said men in the Regimt of Militia whereof you are Colonel. If you should be able to procure me any on the Terms herein inclos'd you will very much oblige me.[2]

---

[1] L. S. without address, Mass. Hist. Society, Col. Israel Williams Manuscripts, 71 D, 107. See Robinson to Shirley, Oct. 26, 1754, Shirley to Robinson, Dec. 14, 1754, and Williams to Shirley, Feb. 1, 1755, pp. 98, 107, and 121.

[2] The orders referred to by Shirley appear to have been transmitted by Secy. Fox to Shirley in his letter of Nov. 4, 1754 (War Office, Class 4, v. 50, p. 58), and are as follows:

George R.:

Whereas We have thought fit to raise a Regiment of Foot under your Command, for the Service and Defence of our Provinces in America, which is to consist of Ten Companies, of four Serjeants, four Corporals, two Drummers, and one hundred Effective Private Men in each Company, besides Commission Officers; These are to Authorize you by Beat of Drum or otherwise, to raise so many Voluntiers, in any of our Provinces in America, as shall be wanting to compleat the said Regiment to the above-mentioned numbers. And all Magistrates, Justices of the Peace, Constables, and other

I would not ask this if I had not a moral assurance that my Regiment will be employ'd in the Defence of this Province, and of Nova Scotia in case they should be wanted there to help to drive the French out of that province, and perhaps for the Demolition of the French fort at Crown Point, or driving the French from all their Settlements on this side St. Lawrence's River, and not for the Southward, and I am perfectly assur'd that the place of it's Rendezvous will be at Boston.

I can't therefore suppose that this Request will be disagreeable to you.

I am,

Sir,

Your humble Servant,

W. SHIRLEY.

SIR THOMAS ROBINSON TO WILLIAM SHIRLEY [1]

Whitehall, Jan. 23, 1755.

SIR,

The King, being determined that nothing shall be wanting, towards the support of his Colonies and Subjects in North America, has commanded me to signify to you, his Majesty's

our Officers whom it may concern, are hereby required to be Assisting unto you in providing Quarters, in pressing Carriages, and otherwise, as there shall be Occasion. And we do hereby further direct, that this our Order, shall remain in force for twelve months from the date hereof, and no longer.

Given at our Court, at Kensington, this 7th day of Octor, 1754, in the twenty-eighth year of our Reign.

By His Majesty's Command.

H. Fox.

To our Trusty and well-beloved William Shirley, Esqr. Colonel of one of our Regimts of foot to be forthwith rais'd for the Service and defence of our Provinces in America, or to the Officer or Officers appointed by you to raise Volunteers for our said Regiment.

[1] This is a circular letter and a copy was sent to all the governors in British America. The original is in P. R. O., C. O. 5, 211. It is printed in 2 Penna. Arch. 6, 218 and N. Y. Col. Docts. 6, 934.

intention to augment the Regiments in British pay (vizt not only Sir Peter Halkets, and Col. Dunbar's, but, likewise those which are now employed in Nova Scotia) to the number of 1000 Men each, to which end, you will correspond with Major General Braddock, or the commander of the King's forces for the time being, from whom you will receive directions for the sending such contributions of Men, as shall be wanting, and to such places where the same shall be quartered or employed under his command.

As there is probably, a considerable number of persons, as well among the Natives of America, as among such Foreigners, who may be arrived there from different Parts, particularly from Germany, who will be capable and willing to bear arms upon this occasion; the King does not doubt, but that you will be able by care and diligence to effect this intended augmentation and to defray the charge of levying the same from the common fund, to be established for the benefit of all the Colonies collectively in North America, pursuant to His Majesty's directions, signified to you, by my letter of the 26th of October last, for that purpose[1]; and as an encouragement to all such persons who, shall engage in this service, it is the King's intention (which you will assure them in his Majesty's name) that they shall receive arms and cloathing, at the King's expence, and that they shall not only be sent back, (if desired) to their respective habitations when the service in America shall be compleated and ended, but shall be entitled in every respect, to the same advantages with those Troops which may be already raised in consequence of your former orders.

I am etc.

T. ROBINSON.

[1] See Robinson to Shirley, Oct. 26, 1754, *ante*, p. 98.

ISRAEL WILLIAMS TO WILLIAM SHIRLEY[1]

Hatfield, Feb: 1, 1755.

SIR,

I recd. your favour of the 4th Ulto, and agreeable to your directions have Enlisted into your Excelnys. Regiment four likely men, for three years each, and directed them, to be ready at a minutes warning to attend your orders, in the meantime to Support themselves — have given my Word that they Shall have your Excys. promise to be dischargd at the end of the Term, and be possess'd of it before they march, without which they would not Enlist. I find a backwardness for want of the Security, none was Enclosed and but one blank Enlistment. — Its probable more will be Inclined to Enlist.[2]

I heartily wish Success to all Enterprizes against the common Enemy, and that the Expectations from our Mother Country may not be disappointed. What measures may be devised and Settled at home for our good, dont pretend to know, hope for the best, make no doubt their Eye is chiefly upon the Fishery to Save that and Nova Scotia, and that the Revenue from Virginia been't lost, what further am left to guess; and cannot but fear poor New England will be left to Struggle with Canada, and all the force they can Muster against our Frontiers; which may be easily Attackd in all Parts, and by a few, the whole Country kept in an Alarm all the Summer, and so be Impoverish'd, and yet not defend our Borders.[3]

[1] Original, Massachusetts Manuscripts, Vol. 1, Library of Congress. See Shirley to Williams, Jan. 4, *ante*, p. 118.

[2] On Dec. 29, 1754, Gov. Morris of Pennsylvania had promised Shirley his aid for the war, 1 Penna. Arch. 2, 231, and on Jan. 4, Dep. Gov. Gardner notified him that Rhode Island had provided for raising 100 men. R. I. Col. Rec. 5, 405. In his reply of Jan. 13, Shirley complimented Rhode Island for her zeal in regard to the Colonial welfare, Corres. Col. Govr. of R. I. 2, 147, and on Feb. 5, Shirley outlined his proposals more at length.

[3] On Jan. 9, William Lithgow had written Shirley as to the distress of the soldiers at Fort Halifax and the urgent need of relief. The letter is in Mass. Arch. Col. Ser. 54, 360. At the same time

I have always tho't it much the best to Strike at the Root, which once destroy'd the Branches fall of Course. For Such an Enterprize there is a Wonderful Spirit in People, and multitudes would heartily engage — yea even in an Attempt to Demolish Fort Frederick, in which also we may Expect the assistance of the Indians, and should it prove Successful, would Secure them and open the best way in my opinion for a Land Army to go further, and the Indians then (and not Ye) would be easily perswaded to go into Canada in Small parties, and would look upon their retreat Secure, and by them the Country might be distress'd and Impoverish'd, and the People be universally drove into their Strongholds, where they must soon starve, if a good Number of Ships were sent up the river, to prevent Supplys that way. In this Way the march of an army would be greatly facilitated and the Enemy fill'd with Terror and distress, and bro't to yield without the Effusion of much Blood, or loss of time. This may appear at first too Romantick, but it is what I verily beleive would be the Case. If such an Enterprize, should be undertaken, now is the time to prepare but if our Strength and Treasure must be Spent elsewhere, I desire to acquiese, and at present content myself with wishing, for what I have only some feint glimmering hopes. Let the plan of operation be what it will as soon as the French know it they will doubtless send their Indians upon the Frontiers press very hard and bring us into the utmost distress, therefore begg your Excy. would give Effectual orders that the proposed Forts be built without delay and Supply'd with Men, and that a Considerable number of the forces now raising or some others may be destin'd to the Frontiers Relying upon your Ex. Goodness to excuse all defects in this feeble uncalled for Attempt.

I am with great Submission

Your most Obt, Huml. Sev.

I. W.

(Jan. 14) Gov. Dinwiddie of Virginia was requesting supplies for the troops at the South. Dinwiddie Papers, 1, 458.

Endorsed:
An Important letter
from Colo. Williams
to the Governor Feby. 1755.

WILLIAM SHIRLEY TO SIR THOMAS ROBINSON [1]

Boston, New England, Feb. 4, 1755.

SIR,

I beg leave to take notice of a chart which Mr. Pownall hath transmitted to the Earl of Halifax one part of the design of which is to give a specimen of the disposition of an Indian Colony in such a manner as to make the Indians inhabiting it, a good barrier against the French, and at the same time dependent upon the English.

The Indians in general are certainly uneasy at any incroachments upon their lands whether by French or English: could we but perswade them by such plans of settlements in their country as the inclosed Chart exhibits a specimen of, that the real design of the English was to protect them in the possession of their country, not to take it away, it would be carrying all points with them. This seems to me an object well worth attention.

I find Sir by the Western prints that the Assembly of Pennsilvania after an absurd obstinate dispute with Govr Morris, about instructions, have adjourn'd themselves, whilst the enemy is at their doors, to the beginning of May, without doing any thing for the preservation of their country. The Assembly of Maryland hath likewise risen without doing any thing further than having rais'd a Company of 50 men, which was done before. I can't find any appearance of South Carolina's being active in the common cause; and whether the populous rich country of Virginia will pursue proper measures for retrieving the bad consequences of the defeat they have suffer'd from an invading enemy, thro' their

[1] P. R. O., C. O. 5, 15. Printed: Docts. rel. Col. Hist. N. Y. 6, 939; 2 Penna. Arch. 6, 219.

former weak measures, I mean whether they will now act with suitable vigour, is not yet known. Every ninth fighting man went out of the Province of the Massachusetts Bay upon the expedition against Cape Breton and for the defence of Nova Scotia in 1745. Why should not every twelfth fighting man at least in Virginia be rais'd there to repel the enemy out of their country, which would make a body of between 4 and 5000 men. You well know Sir what part New Jersey hath acted, and the conduct of New York.

This behaviour seems to shew the necessity not only of a Parliamentary Union, but taxation, for the preservation of His Majesty's dominions upon this Continent, which the several Assemblies have in so great a measure abandon'd the defence of, and thereby lay'd His Majesty's Governmt at home under a necessity of taking care of it for the State, by suitable assessmts upon the Colonies.

> I am with the Highest Respect,
> Sir,
> Your most Humble and
> most Obedient Servant,
> W. SHIRLEY.

P.S.   I perceive by a letter from Colonel Lawrence that he is in expectation of a visit from Mr. Galissonière, in the spring; at least preparing for his reception.

Rt Honble Sir Thomas Robinson
one of His Majesty's Principal Secretaries of State.

WILLIAM SHIRLEY TO WILLIAM GREENE [1]

Boston, February 5th, 1755.

SIR,
A month ago, I received a letter from the Honorable John Gardner, Esq., Deputy Governor of your colony, acquainting me, that the Assembly there "had passed an act to raise a

[1] Printed: R. I. Col. Rec. 5, 412.

company of an hundred men, including officers, and made suitable provision for all other necessaries, agreeably to the directions of the Right Honorable Sir Thomas Robinson's letter, of the 26th October last; and that the Assembly only waited for the arrival of blank commissions, to be filled by Your Honour."

I had the honour of a letter from Sir Thomas Robinson, of the same tenor and date with that above mentioned, as Governor Gardner observes he imagines I had. It is a circular one, written to the Governors of the several colonies concerned.

I acknowledged the receipt of Mr. Gardner's letter, by Mr. Chace, a few days after I received it, in one to himself, and am now to answer it more fully to Your Honour.

The purport of His Majesty's orders, signified to the several Governors, by Sir Thomas Robinson's letter, is (among other things) that they should recommend it to their respective Assemblies to furnish fresh provisions for the troops that should arrive in their colonies; and to raise among them three thousand men, and a sum of money towards paying their respective quotas of the levy money.

Those three thousand men are (as it seems clear to me) intended to complete mine, and Sir William Pepperell's regiments, now raising in America, which are to consist of one thousand privates each, besides non-commissioned officers, sergeants, corporals and drums, which will amount to one hundred more, for each regiment; and that the remaining eight hundred men are to complete the two Irish regiments, designed for Virginia, from five hundred to seven hundred and fifty privates each; as also to fill up the number of those which may be lost in the passage.

As to the two Irish regiments, they being old corps, were both full officered before they left Europe; and Your Honour must have observed from the public prints, that five of the captaincies both in mine and Sir William Pepperell's regiments, besides the three field officers' companies in each, were filled up by His Majesty, soon after the revival of the regiments; as were all the lieutenancies, except four; and ensigncies, except four or five; so that it seems to be most evident, that it was not His Majesty's intent that the Governors should have the appointment of the officers [of the force] raised within their respective colonies.

Neither Sir William Pepperell nor myself can be certain what commissions will be sent blank, to be filled up by ourselves, until the arrival of our lieutenant colonels; we can't possibly have but a very few; and Your Honour is sensible that it may be expected some at least of those should be distributed among the half-pay officers of our late regiments, now here and unprovided for.

I should be extremely glad, if it was in my power, to oblige Your Honour's Assembly with blank commissions, for a set of officers, to be filled up by Your Honour, for the company to be raised by them in your colony; and as that is not in my power, if it would be acceptable to the Assembly, that I should be their captain, I will take them for my own company, and will fill up a lieutenant's and ensign's commissions for it, upon my receiving my blanks, with such persons as Your Honour shall be pleased to appoint; and I shall moreover esteem the company's being raised by the Assembly of the colony of Rhode Island under these terms, to be a great honor done me, which I shall acknowledge upon any occasion in my power, of serving them.

If what I propose, is not agreeable, Your Honour and the Assembly may have the men drafted either into Sir William Pepperell's and mine, or the two Virginia regiments, as the King's service may require, which ever is chosen. The ready compliance which the Assembly has paid to His Majesty's orders contained in Sir Thomas Robinson's letter, according to their act, will be, doubtless, extremely acceptable to His Majesty.

If what I propose to Your Honour, is agreeable, I should be glad if the Assembly would increase the number of the men to one hundred and ten, exclusive of commissioned officers; out of which, four may be enlisted as sergeants, four for corporals, and two for drums, as Your Honour shall order. I have likewise sent one hundred and ten blank enlistments, and one hundred and ten certificates, the form of beating orders, some articles of war, and instructions for the officers, whether commissioned or non-commissioned, whom Your Honour shall think fit to choose to proceed to enlisting the men.

I am, with very great Respect, Sir,
Your Honour's most humble
and most Obedient Servant,

W. SHIRLEY.

To the Hon. William Greene, Esq., Governor of the colony of Rhode Island.

P.S. I have ordered the bearer to wait for Your Honour's answer.[1]

WILLIAM SHIRLEY TO THE GENERAL COURT OF MASSACHUSETTS [2]

GENTLEMEN OF THE COUNCIL AND HOUSE OF REPRESEN-
TATIVES,

Since making my Speech to you at the beginning of this Session, upon considering the happy Effects which through the Divine Blessing upon his Majestys Arms, we may Prom-

---

[1] In reply to this letter Dep. Gov. Gardner, to whom it was delivered, assured Shirley of the Assembly's "utmost alacrity to perform every thing His Majesty hath been pleased to command," stating that they "will have their men ready for such time and in such manner as you shall direct" (Feb. 8, 1755). Nine days later Shirley writes of the measures taken in Massachusetts for confining all French subjects lest they aid the French, and concludes: Therefore, at the desire of the Assembly of this Province, I would earnestly desire Your Honour to use your utmost endeavour that the like precaution be immediately taken in your government, to prevent the mischief which probably will otherwise ensue.

[2] Mass. Arch., Journals of the House. An attested Copy is in the Historical Society of Pennsylvania Collections, and another in the Collections of the American Antiquarian Society. See also the Resolutions of the Mass. Assembly, Feb. 18, in reply to this appeal, Journals of House of Representatives, and N. H. Prov. Papers, 6, 359. A contemporary Copy attested by Thomas Clarke is in the Collections of the American Antiquarian Society.

ise ourselves for this Government, from the Expedition now fitting out for dislodging the French from their forts upon the Isthmus and St. Johns River in Nova Scotia and driving them out of that Province: It hath occur'd to me as a Very Considerable one that it affords us a most favourable Opportunity for building a Fort upon the rockey Eminence near Crown Point, within the limits of his Majesty's Territories, which may command the French fort there and put it into our Power, in case of a rupture with France, to march an Army in a few days to the Gates of the City of Montreal itself, and Pour our Troops into the heart of their Country.

How Greatly such an Event is to be wished for; How much blood and Treasure it would Save to his Majestys Subjects of New England and New York in a time of War, I need not Observe Gentlemen, to you; The depredations Committed upon us in the late War by the French and their Indians from Fort St. Frederic, are still fresh in our Memories; and Providence seems to Point out the Present Conjuncture as the most Proper opportunity for securing ourselves against them for the future.

The Chief Force and Attention of the French is now employed upon the Ohio in Extending their Incroachments upon his Majestys Territories in those Parts; and in a Short time, upon the first alarm, which the Enterprize for removing the French out of Nova Scotia will give them in Canada, they will naturally draw from thence what force they can spare for the support of their Incroachments upon the Isthmus and St. Johns River; and in this divided State of their Force and Counsels, it is most evident, that the Country about Montreal must be very unprepard to repel the attempt, I am now speaking of; Especially if to the surprize; which they must then be in at the Appearance of a Considerable Body of Troops so near one of their two Capitol Cities a feint should be made at the head of Kenebeck or the river Chaudiere, to cause a diversion of their Forces in Canada for the defence of their Metropolis at Quebec.[1]

[1] On this same day (Feb. 13) Thomas Fletcher was writing of the trouble with the Penobscot Indians in Maine. Mass. Arch.,

How Greatly the Operations, I propose, if carried on this year must Contribute towards ridding his Majestys Colonies upon this Continent of the French Incroachments with which they are now hemm'd in from Nova Scotia as far as North Carolina; to the reclaiming of the whole Body of Indians to the English Interest; Establishing a Barrier line of Forts against the French settlements on the north side of the river St. Lawrence and making ourselves Masters of the Principal passes into Canada; for driving the French off this Continent whenever it shall be his Majestys Pleasure to Order that to be done, I am Perswaded Gentlemen, you so fully Concieve, that it is needless for me to dilate upon it.

You will know how much the success of the Expedition against Louisbourg was owing to its being *well timd;* had it been deferrd to the year following, it seems doubtfull what might have been the Event of it.

Let us avail ourselves of the Present Conjuncture with the same prudence and activity, that we did of that against Cape Breton and we may hope for equal Success; and this Province will have the honour to be the first mover in the Operations for restoring the General Tranquility of North America, as it had of being in those of 1745 which contributed so Greatly towards the restoration of a General Peace to his Majestys Dominions.

It will require no small force Gentlemen to Execute with success the Enterprize I Propose; and so far as it depends upon me you may rely upon the assistance at least of my regiment to do it.

This is an Object Gentlemen, well worthey of your Closest Attention; and I should have been greatly Wanting in my Vigilance for the Security and Welfare of his Majestys good People within this Province, if I had not warn'd you of it: what I Propose to you for your Consideration may Possibly prevent a long Expensive War which seems nearly Approaching us.

If you will make Provision for enabling me to pursue the

Col. Ser. 54, 370. The few troops which Shirley planned to send into that region would therefore serve a double purpose.

measures proper for the Occasion, you may be assured Gentlemen that I shall exert my best endeavours to Carry them into Execution.

W. SHIRLEY.

Council Chamber Febry: 13th: 1755.

WILLIAM SHIRLEY TO ROBERT HUNTER MORRIS [1]

SIR,   Boston, February 17, 1755.

The Designs of the French (in which they have so far already succeeded) for invading His Majesty's just Rights in these Northern Parts of America, contrary to the most Solemn Treaties, require these Governments, as well for their own Safety, as in Faithfulness to his Majesty, without Delay to use all Means in their Power to frustrate these perfidious and pernicious Practices.

Among other Measures necessary to be taken especially at this critical Conjuncture, (the present Aspect of Affairs threatning a speedy Rupture) Nothing we can do seems likely to tend more by the Blessing of God, to defeat the Schemes of the French to swallow up all his Majesty's Dominions on the Continent of America, than that the Governments should agree in the most effectual Means for stopping all Supplies of Provision and Warlike Stores being sent out of any of these Colonies, without the inclosed Precaution against their being carried to the French.

The General Assembly of this Province have pass'd, an Order for that End (a Copy of which I now inclose [2]) and

---

[1] Original, Massachusetts Papers, Library of Congress. A similar letter to Gov. Greene of Rhode Island is in R. I. Col. Rec. 5, 413–414. That Shirley expected hostilities at any time is shown by his letter to James Johnson in Mass. Arch., Col. Ser. 54, 370.

[2] The reply of Morris of March 4, acknowledging the receipt of this letter and the enclosed order of the Mass. Assembly is printed: 1 Penna. Arch. 2, 262. In it Morris thanks Shirley for appointing the former's nephew to command of a company in Shirley's own regiment.

have desired me to solicit the Governours of the rest of His Majesty's Colonies, to joyn with us in this necessary Expedient for our common Safety. Your Honour will observe that the time for the Continuance of this Prohibition is restrained to three Months. But if the other Governments should join with us; I make no Doubt of bringing my Assembly to extend it further.

It would give me great Pleasure to have your Honour's Concurrence with me in Sentiments, concerning what appears to me so salutary a Measure, at this Conjuncture for the general Good of all His Majesty's Colonies in North America.

I have the Honour to be with the greatest Respect
   Sir,
     Your Honour's most Humble
      and most Obedient Servant
        W. SHIRLEY.

Captn. Morris sets out
to morrow with my answer
to those I have been favour'd
with from you.
The Honble. Robert Hunter Morris Esqr.

Endorsed:
 Febry: 17th: 1755
  GOVR. SHIRLEY
   Enterd in Council Minute of 10th March, 1755.

WILLIAM SHIRLEY TO ROBERT HALE [1]

By his Excellency WILLIAM SHIRLEY ESQ. Captain General and Governour in Chief in and over his Majesty's Province of the Massachusetts Bay in New England.

INSTRUCTIONS to Robert Hale Esqr. for Soliciting the Government of New Hampshire to unite with this Government

---

[1] Original, with autograph postscript of later date, in Amer. Antiq. Society.

and the other two Governments of New England etc. in an Expedition proposed for preventing the further encroachments of the French.

You are hereby directed to proceed to Portsmouth with my dispatches to His Excellency Benning Wentworth Esqr. Governor of that Province.

Upon your arrival there and appearance either before the Governor and Council or the General Assembly of that Province or before the Governor alone (as you may have opportunity) you are strongly to solicit the joining of that Government with this and the other two Governments of New England and in a vigorous and speedy prosecution of the Expedition proposed in my Speech [1] to the Assembly of this Province and to contribute towards the Execution of it that Governmts Quota of Men and Provisions set forth in the said Assembly's Resolves a Copy of which as also of my said speech will be delivered to you. And you are in a particular manner among such reasons and arguments as shall occurr to you for inducing them to join in the said Expedition, to urge those which are contained in my aforesaid Speech and in my letters to the respective Governors Copy of which last shall likewise be delivered to you.

In case you shall not be able to induce the said Governments to join in the prosecution of the aforesaid Expedition upon the terms proposed in the before mentioned Resolves of the Great and General Assembly of this Province, you are to desire of them to let you know whether they will join it upon any and what other terms together with the reasons of their noncompliance with those proposed by this Government.

Lastly you are from time to time to transmit to me accounts of your proceedings herein and the progress you make in the discharge of this Commission either by the Post or Express as the Occasion may require and upon finishing your Negotiations with that Government you are to return to

[1] See Shirley to the General Court of Massachusetts, Feb. 13, 1755, *ante*, p. 127. The Resolves of the Mass. Court are printed in N. H. Prov. Papers, 6, 359.

Boston and lay an account of your whole proceedings therein with the final answer of the said Government before me.

GIVEN under my hand in Boston the twenty second day of February, 1755; In the twenty-eighth year of his Majesty's Reign.

W. SHIRLEY.

P.S. You are to make use or not of the inclosed Vote of the Assembly dated the 27th of February according to your own discretion. You are to Endeavour to induce the Governmt of New Hampshire to raise a greater number of men than what is mention'd as their Quota in the Resolves of the Assembly dated February provisionally, viz in case the Governmt of New York shall not raise the Eight hundred men alloted to them to raise.

W. SHIRLEY.

WILLIAM SHIRLEY TO JAMES DELANCEY [1]

Boston, New England, Feby. 24th, 1755.

[SIR,]

It would be needless for me to observe to you, how His Majesty's Colonies upon this Continent are surrounded with the encroachments of the French, they have long since marked out for themselves a large Empire upon the back of it, extending from Cape Breton, to the Gulf of Mexico, and Comprehending the Country between the Apalachian Mountains and Pacific Ocean, with the numerous powerful Tribes of Indians inhabitting it, and they are now finishing the extreme parts by a communication between Louisbourg and Quebec, across the Isthmus of Nova Scotia and Bay of

[1] New York State Library, Sir William Johnson Papers, 1, 144. Copy in Ms. of Johnson. See also Shirley to William Greene, R. I. Col. Rec. 5, 414; to Robert Hunter Morris, Penna. Col. Rec. 6, 310, and substantially the same letter to Benning Wentworth of New Hampshire in Amer. Antiq. Society under date of Feb. 25. Words within brackets were burned from the original or otherwise lost.

Fonda, at one End, and a Junction of Canada with the Mississippi by a Line of Forts, upon the great Lakes and Rivers, at the other.

It is fallen to the Lott of the most Eastern Colonies to be Hemmed in by that part of their encroachments, which begin in Nova Scotia, and End at Crown Point, among which the fort of Beau Sejour upon the Isthmus of the Peninsula, that on St. John's River, and Fort St. Frederic near Crown Point, are the Principall.

His Majesty out of his Paternal Care for the Welfare, and security of his good Subjects of these Colonies, in September, 1753 Signified his Royal pleasure, by the Rt. Honble. Earl of Holderness's letter, dated the 21st of that Month to his Governours there, that they should, with the armed Force of the Militia under their respective Commands (if need be), remove all encroachments upon his Territories within the limits of their Severall Governments, and use their best endeavours for promoting a general Union among them for their Common defence against an Invader.

In July last, by a letter from the Rt. Honble. Sr. Thomas Robinson, dated the 5th of that Month, His Majesty Signified his Orders to me and Colo. Lawrence, Lieut. Govr. and Commandr. in Chief of Nova Scotia, that we should concert measures for attacking the French Forts in that Province, And in Decembr last, I had the honour to receive another letter from Sr. Thos. Robinson dated the 26th of October, wherein he acquainted me, that His Majesty, upon taking the State of His Colonies in North America, into his Royal consideration was graciously pleased, ordering two Regiments of Foot from Ireland, under the command of Sr. Peter Halket and Colo. Dunbar, to be sent to Virginia, to order Me and Sir William Pepperell, to raise each of us a Regiment of Foot, consisting of 1000 men, under our respective Commands, for the defence of his Colonies here.

In obedience to the first mentioned Orders, Colo. Lawrence and I have concerted measures for dislodging the French from their Forts in Nova Scotia, and driving them out of that Province, and, among other preparations for that purpose, I am now raising a reinforcement of 2000 Men, for His Majesty's Regular Troops there, to be imbarked in time to be landed in the Bay of Funda by the first week of April, which I have reason to think, I can depend upon accomplishing.

In consequence of the latter I have made a great progress in raising my Regiment, and believe there is no great doubt of its being compleated by the latter End of March.

Mr. Dinwiddie, Govr. of Virginia, in his letter to me, dated Janry. [the 14th, acquaints] me that his government had great dependance upon a strong Diversion's being made by Sr. Wm. Pepperell's and my Regiments this Summer, at some part of Canada [in favour] of the Attempts of the Western Colonies, to repel the French upon the Ohio, and [such a] Diversion of the French Forces, must likewise greatly facilitate the Enterprise [for] driveing the French from their incroachments in Nova Scotia; It is most evident, [that] at the same time, the expedition in Nova Scotia, and the Schemes which principally employ the attention of the French, and a great part of their Forces upon the [Ohio,] afford a most favorable opportunity for the four Colonies of New England, and [those] of New York, and the New Jerseys, with their united Strength to Erect such a Fort near [Crown] Point, as may command the French Fort there, and curb the City of Montreal [itself.]

These were the motives which induced me to make the proposal [of] such an Attempt to the Assembly within my own Government, which is particularly set [forth] in my speech to them upon this occasion; a Coppy of which, together with a Coppy of the Resolves of the Assembly consequent upon it, I enclose to Your Honour.

In these Resolves Sir you will find what Number of Troops this Government thinks necessary to be raised in the whole for the Execution of this Attempt, with [the] Quotas they propose, for the consideration of the Severall Colonies concerned, and I [hope] it will not be thought they have under rated their own Quota, when it is considered that out of the 2200 Men, which are raising for Sir Wm. Pepperrell's and my

Regiments, and 2000 now raising for the expedition to Nova Scotia, upwards of 3000 of them will be taken out of this Province; which with the 1200 proposed to be raised in it for Crown point, will amount to considerably More than one Eighth part of its fighting Men, and that they were at an heavy charge last year in carrying on an Expedition upon the river Kennebeck, and erecting Fort Hallifax there, which as it is a great advance towards securing the principal pass into the heart of Canada over against their Metropolis of Quebec, and through which River, the French have the shortest passage into the Atlantick Ocean of any River in North America, must be deemed an advantage to all the Eastern Colonies in general.

Your Honour will observe, that the Assembly hath desired me to appoint an officer for the Chief Command of the proposed Expedition. It is essential to the Service, that such an one should be appointed, and as it seemed necessary that He should be proposed at the beginning, and this government is the first Mover in this expedition (as it was likewise in that against Cape Breton, of which also I appointed the Commander in Chief) it is hoped the other colonies will have no objection to it. The Gentleman whom I shall nominate for that Command, will, I am persuaded, show Your Honour that the only motive which will sway me in this appointment, is a strict regard to His Majesty's Service, and the Interest of the Common Cause, without the least partiality to any one of the governments concerned.

The Gentleman I have thought of on this important Occasion, is Colonel William Johnson, of Mount Johnson, in the Mohawk Country, whose distinguished Character for the great Influence He hath for Severall Years mantained over the Indians of the Six Nations, is the circumstance which determines me in my Choice, preferably to any gentleman in my own government tho there are not wanting there Officers of Rank and Experience out of Whom I could have nominated one.

Your Honour is sensible that one of the Principall things we have in View in this Expedition, is to retain such of those [castles as] are not yet gone over to the French, in the English interest, and to reclaim [those which] are; and it would be of Unspeakable advantage to Us at this Conjuncture, if we could [engage any] of them in the proposed Service. Colonel Johnson raised and Commanded a [Regiment of Indians in the late intended Expedition against Canada; and with regard [to his] power to engage them now, No Gentleman can stand in Competition with him; [besid]es, his Military qualifications for this particular Service, and knowledge of [the] Country and place, against which this Expedition is destined, are very [con]spicuous.

The Fort intended to be built in this Expedition [is pr]oposed to be so situated as to command Fort St Frederick at Crown point, to be made defensible against the strength which the French can suddenly bring against it from Montreal, to be erected by the army employed, and as to the Support, garrisoning and command of it, that must depend upon His Majesty's pleasure, which will be soon known concerning it.

It must be fresh in Your Honour's memory, that the reduction of the French Fort, at Crown point, was looked upon as a necessary Step in the late intended Expedition against Canada, And how far and advanced the preparations of the Colonies concerned in that Scheme were, till I know not by what fatal Disunion of our Counsels, a most unhappy Stop was put to it.

One remarkable Circumstance occurs to me upon this Occasion. When the late Sr Peter Warren and myself were endeavouring to engage one Monsieur Vaudreuil, then at Boston, a very intelligent Frenchman, as a Pilot to our Forces up the river St Lawrence, in the aforesaid late expedition, He smiled, and told Us He should not be convinced that the English did in good earnest design an expedition against Canada from these colonies, Untill he should hear that Fort St Frederick was attacked.

But I am perswaded nothing more need be urged, to Your Honour, concerning the great importance of the proposed expedition, [except] that besides secureing our Selves against future depredations of the French [from] their Fort at Crown

Point in a time of War; We shall Wipe off the reproach of the Colonies for Suffering that dangerous Encroachment upon His Majesty's Territories, to be at first erected. I should have mentioned to Your Honour, that the two Houses of the Assembly in this Province, have bound themselves [by oath] to secrecy, both with respect to the expedition now preparing against the [French] Encroachments in Nova Scotia, and that proposed against those at Crown Point; [which I] thought proper to observe, that Your Honor may use your discretion in that [point,] with regard to the Assembly within your own Government.

The same [union of] Sentiments, and like Spirit with which the four sister Colonies of New England acted in the late expeditions against Cape Breton and Canada, will I hope prevail in their Counsels at this most Critical conjuncture, and particularly that the depredations which the County of Albany [suffers ?] from the French and their Indians at Crown Point, not only in time of War, but [as well] in time of peace, together with its present exposed State, will move the Government of New York to an Hearty concurrence with the Massachusets Bay in the proposed Expedition.

Your Honour is Sensible that, in order to avail our selves of the favourable opportunity for such an Enterprise, a Speedy determination upon it and the greatest dispatch in our preparations for it is Necessary.

I have Commissionated Thomas Pownall, Esqr' to wait on Your Honour upon this occasion and to solicit your government to Join with my own, in this necessary piece of Service for the protection of His Majestys Colonies under Our care against the dangerous encroachments of the French, and hope he will Succeed in the Execution of his Commission.

I am with the greatest Regard, Sir
Your Honours Most Humble and
Most Obedient Servant,

W. SHIRLEY.

To Governour De Lancey of New York.
Copia Vera Verbatim.

WILLIAM SHIRLEY TO ELIJAH WILLIAMS AND OTHERS [1]

Boston, Feby. 27, 1755.

GENTLEMEN,

At the motion and desire of the Council and House of Representatives I do hereby direct you forthwith to desist from Building and Repairing the Line of Block Houses (you were directed to build and repair) until my further orders. And in particular you must desist from building the Fort you were ordered to build at a Place west of Massachusetts Fort until I receive an answer to a Letter I shall send to the Honble James DeLancey Esq. Lieut. Governr of New York by the next Conveyance.

I am Sir

Your assured Friend

W. SHIRLEY.

To Elijah Williams Esqr. and the Comee for building and repairing Forts and Block Houses West of Connectt. River.

WILLIAM SHIRLEY TO ROBERT HALE [2]

Boston, March 4th, 1755.

SIR,

I thought it might be of use to you to have a copy of Governour Wentworth's letter to me and of my answer to it, I have therefore inclos'd them.[3]

[1] Original, Mass. Arch., Col. Ser. 54, 382. A letter from Joseph Dwight to Shirley of Feb. 25, giving an account of conditions at Stockbridge and the movements of Indians toward the Ohio, is in Mass. Arch., Col. Ser. 54, 380. The needs of Fort Halifax are given in a letter of Feb. 20-21 from William Lithgow, *ibid.* pp. 371-379. Shirley's reply to Lithgow is in the same volume, p. 383, and Williams to Shirley, stating conditions west of the Connecticut, with map inclosed (Feb. 10), is on p. 367.

[2] Original, Amer. Antiq. Society.

[3] Shirley wrote the New Hampshire governor as to Crown Point on Feb. 21. Wentworth replied a week later, and the second Shirley

I hope the inclos'd papers will be sufficient, with what other Arguments may occurr to you, for making your negotiations succeed, which I heartily wish it may. I have taken care of your friend Captn Bagley,[1] whom I like much. I hope you will be at Portsmouth in time and am with great truth,

Sir,

Your very assur'd Friend and Servant,

W. SHIRLEY.

P.S. Mr Hutchinson set out yesterday for Rhode Island, as did the Commissioners for New York, New Jersey and Pensilvania.[2] I dare say Mr Wentworth will be ready for you by the time you can get to Portsmouth.
Colonel Hale.

WILLIAM SHIRLEY TO BENNING WENTWORTH[3]

Boston, March 4, 1755.

SIR,

I have the Honour of your Excellency's Letter in Answer to mine of the 21st of Feby and am glad that what is therein propos'd hath your Approbation; I doubt not, when your Excy. shall consider it with a clear Attention in full Council, as you propose, but that the point under Consideration will appear to be the most interesting one in its Consequences at this Conjuncture, for the general service of his Majesty's Colonies upon this Continent, as well as for the particular security of the Colonies propos'd to be concern'd in the Ex-

letter accompanied this letter to Hale. See Shirley to Wentworth, following, for outline of plans and note to same on p. 142 for Wentworth's reply to Shirley of Feb. 28. A contemporary copy of each of the last two letters is in the Amer. Antiq. Society.

[1] Jonathan Bagley.
[2] Thomas Pownall and Josiah Quincy. See Shirley to Morris, I Penna. Arch. 2, 260.
[3] Cont. Copy in Amer. Antiq. Society. See Transactions and Collections Amer. Antiq. Soc. 11, 10.

cution of it, that ever was depending before your Excellency and Council.

I agree with your Excellency that Coos should be fortify'd; I look upon a Fort there to be an essential one in the line of Forts we ought to have, as a very strong one likewise at or near the head of Kennebeck River to curb the French Settlemts at Quebec and upon the Chaudiere and a Fort also at Penobscot another perhaps at Woodcreek, not to mention any other Interior Forts; But I doubt not if the grand point under Consideration is Embarrass'd with the Settlement of any others, before we enter upon the Execution of it, that the favourable Opportunity of doing it, which will be about the same time with the landing of the Troops destin'd for Nova Scotia, will be lost. That seems to be at present the sole Object of our united Counsels and that against which our united Forces should be bent. Your Excellency sees by my speech that I purpose making a feint at the head of the River Chaudiere to alarm the French at Quebec and cause a Diversion of their Forces from Montreal, and if our united Forces should be strong enough to spare a sufficient party to go after the Indians above St. Francois River, and even to fortify Coos immediately, I shall be very glad; But I think, if that or any other point of Inferiour Consideration can't be instantly settled among all the Colonies concern'd, it ought not to interfere with the carrying of the Grand point into Execution at the proper time for doing it. The fortifying of Coos and other places will follow of course and I will join heartily with your Excy. in a Representation to his Majesty that a Fort ought to be supported there at the joint Expence of the Colonies, among other Forts necessary for the Common defence of the whole.

It gives me great satisfaction that your Excellency intirely approves of my Nomination of Colo. Johnson for the Chief Command in the propos'd Expedition. As to the manner of his appointment, which your Excy. mentions as a matter to be considered of, it is a point of so small Consideration in my Apprehension, that I am not sollicitous how it is settled. Besides the reasons mentiond in my Letter to your Excellency I think others might be mentioned to shew that there was no Impropriety in what I have done; I would only beg leave to assure your Excellency that no desire of preference or precedence mov'd me to do it. Provided his Majestys Service in so essential a point as the present one is consulted, I care not who takes the Lead in any Punctilios attending it.

I have desir'd Colonel Hale to wait on your Excellency in the manner propos'd in your Letter, and I am sure he will be glad of your Advice for working the Miracle so greatly to be wished for upon the Exeter men.[1]

As to the Difficulty of your Exys. Government's raising their Quota of Money to defray the Charge of the propos'd service I should think it might be done one of these three ways; either by borrowing it for a short time and payment of Interest as my own Govt. does when the Treasury is empty; or by an Emission of Paper Bills, to be sunk within five years, according to the liberty given by the late Act of Parliament upon such sudden Emergencies for his Majesty's Service as this which is the method used a few days ago by the Govt of New York for raising £15000 of their Currency or by Appropriating the Sterling Money, your Excellency's Government hath now in England. Your Excellency is the best judge which of these Methods is the preferable one, but certainly it may be done in one or other of them.

I omitted mentioning in my last Letter that I design to

---

[1] Governor Wentworth considered the delegation from Exeter in the N. H. Assembly as the center of the opposition to Shirley's plans for the Crown Point expedition. In his letter of Feb. 28, of which Shirley had given Hale a copy and to which this is a reply, Wentworth had written of Hale: "if he can convert the Exeter members he will gain a great point if not a miraculous one." Wentworth had feared also the difficulty of raising money and had asked Shirley's advice as to the best means to be employed for this purpose. Hale's letters to Shirley relating his experiences in New Hampshire and the measure of success obtained are of Mar. 14, 15, 18, and 21, and are in Amer. Antiq. Society. For summaries of them see Lincoln, Manuscript Records of the French and Indian War, A. A. S. Trans. and Coll. 11, 139 ff.

apply to General Braddock to assist with an Engineer or two for building the propos'd Fort and other parts of the Service. I cant but hope that all the Colonies concern'd will readily join in this Expedition. It would be a matter of great concern that it should stick with any one of the New England Govts. and that too a Government which from its being more immediately under his Majesty's Direction may be reasonably expected to be an Example to the Charter ones in all great Emergencies for his Service.

I am Sir
Your most humble Servt.
W. Shirley.

Gov. Wentworth.

WILLIAM SHIRLEY TO EPHRAIM WILLIAMS [1]

Boston, March 10th, 1755.

Sir,

I am sorry you meet with the Difficulties, in raising Men for my Regiment, which you mention in your letter of the 7th Instant by Express: I am perswaded that my Regiment will be continually imploy'd to the Northward and Eastward of Philadelphia; But such Conditional Inlistments, as you mention, in your letter, are not allowed in his Majesty's Service. [2]

As there is this Obstacle in the way of your coming into my Regiment, I shall think no more of it; But you may depend upon my providing for you in the other Service to the Northward, which you hint at in your letter (if it goes on as I hope it will) in the best manner I can. I was very much dispos'd to have given you the Captain-Lieutenancy in my Regiment, as I told Colonel Partridge, I design'd to

---

[1] Original, Mass. Hist. Soc., Col. Israel Williams Manuscripts, 71 D, 118.

[2] Men were in such demand that there was a tendency to accept enlistment on any terms. A good example of the calls upon Shirley is the letter of James Howard at Fort Western, Mar. 5, Mass. Col. Ser. 54, 383.

do: But a letter, I have receiv'd since that from England, hath put it out of my power: it would have given me pleasure to have done you that piece of service, if it would have been very agreeable to you: and as things have happen'd, I am glad, you are not over-anxious about it.

You will greatly oblige me, if you can raise me some Men for my own Regiment, and to make it more practicable I will allow fifteen pounds Old Tenour per Man for three Years, Twenty for five, Thirty for seven, and thirty five for such, as shall enlist at large: The more you shall inlist the better; But I desire, there may be none, but right good Men enlisted, and not under five feet five Inches without their shoes, unless they are young enough to grow to that Height; and none above forty years old.

I desire you would pay the Express and charge it to me:
> I am,
> > Sir,
> > Your most Assur'd Friend and Servant,
> > > W. SHIRLEY.

Major Ephraim Williams.

WILLIAM SHIRLEY TO SIR THOMAS ROBINSON [1]

> Boston, New England, March 24th, 1755.

SIR,

On the 18th Instant in the evening I had the honour of your letter dated the 26th of November last,[2] transmitted to me by Major Genl Braddock, and have, pursuant to your directions appointed to meet him at Annapolis in Maryland, (the place nam'd by himself) about the fourth of April, which I apprehend will be as early as he can come from Williamsburgh to Annapolis, after he shall have received my letter to him by the return of his express.

[1] P. R. O., C. O. 5, 15.   Printed: Docts. rel. Col. Hist. of N. Y. 6, 941.
[2] See letter of Nov. 26, C. O. 5, 211 ; Belcher to Shirley, Mar. 19, Mass. Arch., Col. Ser. 54, 390; and Johnson to Shirley, Mar. 17, Johnson Manuscripts, 1, 146; Docts. rel. Col. Hist. of N. Y. 6, 946.

I intend to set out upon my journey for this purpose Thursday the 28th instant, before which time I can't possibly leave Boston without infinite prejudice to His Majesty's service in the enterprize I am engaged in with Lt Governor Lawrence for dislodging the French from their incroachments in Nova Scotia, and the scheme I have set on foot among the Colonies of New England and the neighbouring ones for dislodging them from their incroachments near Crown Point at the same time [1]: the great importance of both which, to His Majesty's service upon the Continent of North America at this conjuncture, and the progress I have made in them are fully mentioned to you Sir in my other letters, that it is needless for me to repeat them here.

You will easily conceive Sir from the part I have in both these expeditions, how essential to the timely execution of them, my presence is here, until I can finish all the necessary dispatches and orders for the fitting out and imbarcation of the 2000 men, which I have reason to think are near being completed for that in Nova Scotia, and to the adjusting of the very many points necessary to be settled among the Colonies concern'd in that destin'd for Crown Point, and putting it in motion before I set out for Annapolis; neither of which can be done before I meet my Assembly, which stands prorogu'd to the 25th Instant, when I shall endeavour to put these affairs into the best train I can, for going on during my absence, and I propose if possible to return from the interview with General Braddock in time to finish every thing requisite for carrying both the expeditions into execution and to put my own regiment, which I hope will be compleated in three weeks, into the best order the short time will allow, for receiving General Braddock's orders.

The General, in a letter I had the honour to receive from him, acquaints me that the plan of operations he proposes is to begin with the attack of the French Forts upon the Ohio, and at the same time to attempt the reduction of those at the Falls of Niagara; that for the first of these purposes he

[1] See Shirley to De Lancey, Feb. 24, and to Wentworth, Mar. 4, *ante*, pp. 133 and 139.

intends as soon as the transports arrive with the two Irish Regiments, to march himself with the forces he shall have with him, amounting as he expects in the whole to about 2300 British and Provincial troops, and to pass Allegheny Mountains the latter end of April. The other part of the services he proposes to put under my direction and to appoint me to march as early as possible with the corps of the two American regiments to the attack of the Forts at Niagara, in order to cut off their communication with the French to the Northward by intercepting their reinforcements and to prevent their retreat.

Nothing in my opinion Sir, can be better projected than this scheme, or coincide more with the enterprizes set on foot in the Colonies of New England before the General's arrival in America.[1] If all them are successfully executed it will settle every point with the French this year; the demolition of their Forts upon the Isthmus, St John's River, at Crown Point, the Falls of Niagara, and upon the Ohio, and erecting defensible ones at those places and near the head of Kennebeck for His Majesty, would most effectually rid his Colonies of all incroachments, establish a barrier for them against all attempts either directly from Europe upon their sea coasts or thro' the River St Lawrence, the Great Lakes and the River Ohio on the back of them; and by putting His Majesty into possession of the principal passes into Canada, go half way towards the reduction of that whole country.

It would have been very practicable to have executed in this spring and the succeeding summer every part of the

---

[1] The plan of campaign proposed for Shirley and Braddock was not new. It was outlined by Shirley in his letters of Jan. and May 8, 1754, *ante*, pp. 26 and 62, and again is mentioned in his letters to Sir Thomas Robinson of Aug. 12 and 15, *post*, pp. 221 and 238. It was adopted by Pitt at the close of 1757 and outlined in his letters to the governors of the Northern Colonies and to Abercromby, Dec. 30, 1757, C. O. 5, 212. The greatest difference between the campaigns of 1754–1756 and those of the three years following was the difference between the officials in control at London during the two periods and the relative attention paid to America.

before mentioned general scheme if the five most Western Colonies had exerted themselves for their own defence, as much as the Province of the Massachusets Bay and other Colonies of New England have done for the general service. Including the 800 men rais'd last fall for the expedition up Kennebeck River and building a Fort there, and the men that are already and will be rais'd towards compleating the two American regiments and those for the protection of Nova Scotia and His Majesty's lands at Crown Point, upwards of 4500 men will have been raised within the Massachusetts Bay, 2000 of them at the expence of that government, and the three other New England Governments have voted 2100 men besides, for the service at Crown Point at *their* charge. The five most Western Colonies after being harrass'd by a dangerous and increasing enemy at their doors, after suffering two defeats from them, and tho' more populous and much richer than those of New England, have not as far as I can learn, raised above 1100 men for their own defence, nor a man towards augmenting the two British regiments to 700 men a piece, as was proposed by the Crown. The effect of this backwardness in them may be to make it questionable whether the General will be strong enough in conjunction with the Provincial troops in Virginia and the corps of the two American regiments supposing the former to amount to 1300, and the latter, which are all raw troops almost wholly undisciplin'd, to 1700 (which will make up his whole force of 4000 men) to attack the French Forts upon the Ohio, and at the same time attempt the reduction of those near the Falls of Niagara.

However if the General should finally judge it not adviseable to make both attempts with his forces divided, but proceed first with the main body of his forces to attack the French Forts near the Falls of Niagara, sending only such a detachment to the Ohio as might amuse the French Forts there with the expectation of a speedy visit from him, the reduction of the first mentioned forts would penetrate into the heart of their incroachments upon the Great Lakes and the Ohio, and by cutting off all communication between

Canada and their forces upon that river, leave them an easy prey to famine, if no other stroke should be given them (which yet might be done soon after the reduction of the Forts at Niagara was effected) and make them in a short time be glad to accept of a safe passage back to Montreal, if that should be permitted to them. The dislodging of the French from these Forts Sir, and building a defensible fort some where on the Streight between Lake Erie and Lake Ontario with one or two vessells of force upon each Lake to command the navigation of them, and a few small fortify'd places of Shelter upon the River Ohio, would in all appearance most effectually put an end to the encroachments of the French there from Montreal; and as to those which may be expected from the Mississippi, after their support from Canada is cut off, it seems probable that they would scarce attempt any, or if they should, that a most easy conquest might be made of them.[1]

Having observed to you, Sir, of what importance I conceive the reduction of the French Forts at the Falls of Niagara would be to His Majesty's Western Colonies in particular, I shall now proceed to state the advantages which I apprehend would arise to all his Colonies in General upon this Continent from the operations proposed to be carry'd on at the same time in the eastern part of them.

The importance of the Province of Nova Scotia to Great Britain consists in the following particulars vizt whilst the English remain in the *Intire* possession of it, the French will not be able either to assemble or subsist for any long time a large body of regular troops in the Eastern parts of this Continent, without great difficulty; the Island of Cape Breton and country of Canada can't produce provisions sufficient to support their present inhabitants, without foreign

---

[1] It is interesting to compare these words of Shirley with those of Amherst to Pitt, June 19, 1759 (Amer. and West Indies, V, 90), and even with those of Perry to the U. S. Government in 1813. All recognize the great importance of holding Niagara and the adjacent lakes if an invasion of Canada is intended by the south or if one from the north is to be defeated.

supplies. The French have now but one harbour in North America upon the Atlantick Ocean, and their navigation from thence to Canada which lies thro' the Gulf and River of St Lawrence, is difficult at all times, and practicable but a few months in the year, so that they frequently lose a large ship in it.

And in these disadvantages of the French, very much lies the security of the English Northern Colonies against the power of France.

But if the French should make themselves masters of that Province which is the key of all the Eastern Colonies upon the Northern Continent on this side of Newfoundland, abounds with more safe and commodious harbours capable of entertaining large squadrons than the same extent of Sea coast in any other part of the world, and hath a fertile soil for provisions of all kinds; they would then have it in their power to introduce into North America directly from old France, and to support a very considerable number of land forces.

The loss of this Province would most probably be attended with a further *immediate* loss of the most Eastern parts of New England and the whole Province of New Hampshire; within which tract of territory is contained that part of the King's woods from whence the Royal Navy is almost wholly supply'd with masts yards and bowsprits, and a sea coast of fifty leagues upon the Ocean, besides that round the Bay of Funda.[1]

The acquisition of it by the French would give them the Cod fishery of New England, Nova Scotia and the whole of that in the Gulf of St Lawrence, which together with that which they already have upon the coast of Cape Breton and Banks of New Foundland would maintain an immense nursery of seamen to man their Navy, and this advantage 'with the great extent of Sea Coast it would give them upon the Atlantick Ocean and the numerous harbours there,

---

[1] Shirley knew by experience the aid furnished by the Navy to British operations in America and appears to have lost few opportunities to impress upon the home government the assistance the Colonies were in maintaining that side of the British armament.

situated well to intercept all the trade which passes thro' the Western seas in their return to Europe from the East and West Indies and South Sea, might go far in time towards putting it into their power to dispute the mastery of this part of the Atlantick Sea with the navy of Great Britain.

Another advantage which the French would gain by this acquisition, and would crown the whole, is, that the Province of Nova Scotia lies contiguous to Canada and but two or three leagues from the Island of Cape Breton, and all these held together would give them so strong an hold upon this Continent, as might enable them in the end thro' the many other advantages they have over the English Colonies in time of war from the form of their government, their influence over the Indians and compactness of their territories, to accomplish the reduction of every one of them.

It would at least, as I have taken the liberty to observe to you Sir in another letter, be the business of a long and successfull war, to recover the Province from them.

The negotiations preceding the treaty of Utrecht shew with how great reluctance France was brought at the close of a war which had much enfeebled her, to consent to yield up this Province to Great Britain.

The artifices which she hath used to elude the Treaty ever since the making of that cession the hazard she ran in losing above half her Naval force in the armament fitted out during the late war, under the Duke d'Anville for the harbour of Chebucto (now Halifax) at a time when His Majesty had a squadron of seven ships of the line in the harbour of Louisbourg and there was the utmost reason to apprehend that a much larger squadron would soon arrive there from England; the immoderate claims the French Ministers have made since the treaty of Aix la Chapelle for extending the limits of Canada from the Southern bank of the River St Lawrence as far as Annapolis Royal upon the Peninsula on one side of the Bay of Funda and to the River Kennebeck on the other side of it, claiming even the Islands of Canso, and leaving no part of the Province to Great Britain except the spot upon which the City and garrison of Annapolis stand, and a narrow slip upon the Sea Coast from Cape Sable to the Islands of Canso exclusive; as also the manifest incroachments she hath made in contempt of the faith of treaties upon the lands concerning which a negociation was then actually depending: I say, Sir, these circumstances shew how great an object the Province of Nova Scotia is with the Court of France and how much it hath the reduction of it at heart.

The observations I have made Sir in my former letters upon the progress which the French have already made therein, make it needless for me to trouble you with the repetition of them in this, and Governour Lawrence's letters fully shew the great danger there is that the French will very soon extend their incroachments upon the Peninsula, unless they are prevented by our striking the first blow as early as may be this spring.

And this Sir seems clearly to evince the necessity of carrying into execution, without delay, the measures which Mr Lawrence and I have concerted in consequence of His Majesty's orders signify'd to us in your letter of the 5th of July,[1] and repeated in a duplicate of it transmitted to me in October last, for taking all advantages to attack the French Forts in that Province.

As to the other enterprizes set on foot in the Colonies of New England, before the arrival of General Braddock, it seems most evident Sir that the attempt against Crown Point, besides the effect it may have for facilitating the execution of the intended one in Nova Scotia and reclaiming the Indians of the Six Nations and their Allies, as is set forth in the inclos'd extract of a letter from Colonel Johnson to me,[2] who is the best judge in America of their dispositions, must greatly facilitate the reduction of the French Forts near the Falls of Niagara and securing that pass, by the very great diversion it must necessarily make of their forces at Montreal, (from whence their Forts at Niagara must expect their whole sup-

---

[1] The letter of July 5 is in C. O. 5, 211. Its duplicate of Oct. 26 is printed *ante*, p. 98, together with a personal letter from Robinson of the same date.

[2] For Johnson to Shirley, see note on p. 152.

port) for the protection of that part of the country; especially if another should be made at the same time at Quebec, by a feint on the River Chaudiere, as I propos'd in my speech to the Assembly, and the expediency of securing the two most important passes into Canada, by erecting two Forts, one at or near the head of the river Kennebeck within a few days march of the City of Quebec, and an other at Crown Point within near the same distance from their other capital city of Montreal; from both which sudden descents might be made into the heart of Canada at the same time; is so apparent that I need not observe upon them.

> I am, with the Highest Respect
>> Sir
>>> Your most humble and
>>> most Obedient Servant

W. Shirley.[1]

The Rt Honble Sir Thomas Robinson Knt of the Bath, one of His Majesty's Principal Secretaries of the State.

WILLIAM SHIRLEY TO WILLIAM JOHNSON [2]

Boston, March 26, 1755.

Sir,

I am now to acknowledge the receipt of your letter from New York of the 17th instant.[3] I am very glad to find that

---

[1] See: Shirley to Mass. Gen'l Court of Mar. 25, and action thereon in Mass. Archives; Shirley to Gov. Wentworth of Mar. 26 and 27, N. H. Prov. Papers, 6, 363, 365; Shirley to Gov. Greene of Mar. 26, Corres. Col. Govs. of R. I. 2, 149, and Shirley to Gov. Morris of Mar. 24 and 31, 1 Penna. Arch. 2, 278, 282.

[2] Auto. Draft, Mass. Arch., Col. Ser. 54, 398.

[3] Johnson's letter to Shirley is in Johnson Manuscripts, N. Y. State Library, 1, 146. An extract from that letter was forwarded by Shirley to Sir Thomas Robinson. It is in C. O. 5, 15, and is here given:

The Six Nations consider the lands on which Fort St. Frederick [Crown Point] is built and considerably further to the Northward as belonging to them, and when this encroachment was first made, were not only ready to join but sollicited the English to drive off the French from thence, and afterwards when in the late war it

there is no exception to your engaging in the Service, for you have mentioned none to me that ought to have any weight, and I hope that you left New York at the time you proposed

was proposed to reduce that fortress engag'd heartily in it, but to no purpose, it being laid aside, and if the being so often trifled with and the want of places of security for their women and children and themselves in case of need to retire to (which they have frequently complain'd of) does not deter them, I think I can, upon proper encouragement, engage the assistance of two or three hundred, which I think a sufficient number,.and if we succeed it will not only reclaim those who are lately gone over to the French but probably the Cagnawagas too, and attach the whole body of the Six Nations and their allies so firmly to the British interest, that we might depend on their assistance at all times if not wanting to our selves in a due management of their affairs. This and the success of your Excellency's plan of operations to the Eastward, which we have little reason to doubt of, would revive their spirits and convince them we mean in earnest to oppose the French vigorously. For while they observe the French so active and enterprizing, and we on the contrary intirely inattentive to our interests they will be averse to the taking any step that may draw on them the resentment of the French.

Your Excellency's letter to Govr. De Lancey of the 24th Ulto. [*ante*, p. 133] hath determin'd him to call the Assembly who are to meet here the 25th of this month, and in the mean time the Gentlemen of the Council and six of the Members of the Assembly now in town are to confer with Mr Pownall on the proposals from your Governmt which I heartily wish may be attended with the desir'd success. The Council as far as I can ,observe will come into the scheme. I can say nothing as to the Lower House, and until I know the result of this Governmt or your Excellency points out to me in what manner I may be of service either in engaging the Indians or otherwise, should the expedition go on, I cannot be very explicit. It may be necessary however to mention that a great number of battoes will be wanting to transport the provisions, stores, &c none of those being left which were provided for the late expedition intended to Canada, and should your Excellency determine to proceed, I apprehend workmen should be employed to make them as soon as possible; as many as can should be made here, for building a great number at Albany or Schenectady may be the means of apprizing the French of our design, and put them on their guard.

I have been detained here since the first notice of Commissioners setting out from your Governmt and as my staying can be of no

and that you are now disposing your Private affairs so as that you may be able to take upon you the Command of the Forces of the several Governments as soon as they shall be raised. I have this day ordered a Proclamation to be issued for encouraging the enlistment on the part of this Province, and I shall immediately cause advice thereof to be communicated to the Governments of New Hampshire, Connecticut and Rhode Island, and as soon as they receive it they will respectively begin their enlistments also, so that I hope in three or four weeks the proposed number from each Government may be raised.

I have very unexpectedly received such letters from the Ministry by General Braddock, as well as from the General himself, that I cannot avoid leaving my Government, for a short time, in order to meet him at Annapolis in Maryland, and I intend to begin my journey next day after to morrow. I cannot expect to see you at New York, in going out, but I hope to do it on my return. I may probably be at that city in my way home by the 14th of April and any parts of your letter which the hurry I am in now prevents a particular answer to, I shall then have an opportunity of conferring

service to further the scheme on foot, I propose to leave this place on Tuesday or Wednesday next, imagining I shall know by that time the opinion of the Gentlemen who confer with Mr Pownall, and on my arrival at home can be taking the proper measure to prepare the Indians in case their assistance should be wanted, which is very necessary, and may be done without even raising in them a suspicion of our real intentions.

Your Excellency's zeal for His Majesty's service and the welfare and security of his Colonies, is not more conspicuous in any thing than the measures you are at present taking; and if all the Colonies propos'd to be engag'd in the operations this way, act with equal spirit with your own, I think at this favourable juncture we have well grounded hopes of a happy issue. It is my own and the opinion of every one I converse with that should the General begin the attack at Niagara (leaving a few men towards the Ohio to keep the French in expectation of a visit there) it would be the speediest method to deprive them of their incroachments on the Ohio, which they would soon find themselves under a necessity even to abandon, if we take and keep possession of that important pass,

with you upon. I shall not be unmindful, when I see the General of what you mention relating to Niagara; for such a further division as this proposal will cause in the French forces may as greatly serve our proposed Expedition as it may the success of any other operation we propose for his Majestys Service on the other parts of the Continent.

But what I have greatly at heart and that which is the principal reason for my hastening away this Express to you, is the engaging every warriour of the Six Nations that you can by any means bring into the Expedition. The manner of doing it whether by an advance as a present, to each man, or to any or all of their Chiefs, or by promising wages or rewards for their services I must leave to you who are so well acquainted with their dispositions, but let them be secured at all events. I have by recommendation obtained a Vote of the Assembly of this Province, copy of which I shall inclose to you, engaging for their part of the expense you may find necessary in this affair, and you need not doubt their complyance; and I shall also send a Copy to each of the other Governments who I am satisfied will make no difficulty of their Parts also, for no one branch of the Charges that must attend this Expedition can be more necessary. At all events I cant think it possible that the Ministry will not esteem this important service of yours at a very high rate, and not only defray all necessary expence, if there was a possibility of any difficulty in the Colony Government doing it, which I can't conceive there will, but make you a suitable recompence over and above what the Govts. concerned may do, or what they will come more readily into.

I shall leave such directions for prosecuting the affair during my absence as that it may be as little retarded as possible and I expect to return to give the necessary Orders before the time when it shall be requisite to begin the march.

I am,

Sir Yours

WILLIAM SHIRLEY.

Col. William Johnson.

WILLIAM SHIRLEY TO ISRAEL WILLIAMS [1]

Boston, March 29th, 1755.

SIR,

I am now Setting out on my Journey to meet with General Braddock and must intreat your favour and assistance in settling the Officers for a Regiment to go against Crown point, the Regiment to Consist of 500 Men with ten Captains ten Lieutenants and ten Ensigns including field Officers : it will be a great pleasure to me to have Majr. Ephraim Williams to engage as one, I can't be content without having the Officers of one Regiment from your parts ; Major Hawley is coming up to settle the Affair with you, who will bring all Necessary Papers with him.

I am with Truth and Esteem,
Sir,
Your most Assur'd
Friend and Servant,

W. SHIRLEY.

Col : Israel Williams, Hatfield.

WILLIAM SHIRLEY TO JOSIAH WILLARD [2]

Philadelphia, April 9th, 1755.

SIR,

The inclos'd copy of the Vote of the Assembly of this Province will inform you how far they have acceded to the intended Expedition to Crown point and I have the pleasure further to inform you that the Assembly of New York have passed a Vote for the raising of 800 men for the same service provided General Braddock shall approve of the Expedition.

[1] Original, Mass. Hist. Society, Col. Israel Williams Manuscripts, 71 D, 121.

[2] Original, Mass. Arch., Col. Ser. 54, 405. On April 6 Shirley had written directing that the General Court remain in session until his return, *ibid.* 54, 403.

As I think there is not the least room to doubt of that, I look upon the general concurrence of all the Colonies propos'd to be concerned in this important Enterprize, except that of the New Jersies (the result of whose determination is not yet known but may be hoped will be favourable to the general cause) to be a most encouraging Circumstance: Nothing is now wanting but that the several governments should proceed with the utmost Vigour and Dispatch in their respective preparations to carry the Expedition into Execution which I cant doubt of in the Gentlemen of the Committee of War of my town during my absence.

I thought proper to apprize you of the proceedings [of] the Govts. of New York and Pensilvania and am in some hopes that the Express may bring you an acct. of the determination of the Govt. of the New Jersies from Mr. Oliver as he passes thro it.

Mr. Partridge I am informed by Mr. Franklin of this place, hath sent him a letter dated 4th February at London in which he says they had a certain Acct. there that six French Men of Warr were sailed from Brest, with 9000 Troops, destin'd as is suppos'd for some port of North America. If this article of News is well founded, it should quicken our proceedings. The Advices say that the British Squadron designed to watch their motions would be fitted out by the 22d of February.

As I cant possibly find time to write to Colonel Monckton, I must desire you will communicate this last paragraph to him and beg of him to take the first opportunity of acquainting Govr. Lawrence with it.

You will be pleased to communicate the whole letter to the Council and forward a copy of it to Govr. Wentworth and Govr. Greene as soon as possible. I have transmitted one myself to Govr. Fitch.

        I am,
          Sir,
            Your most assur'd Friend
            and Servant,

                  W. SHIRLEY.

Honble Josiah Willard Esqr.

P.S. Upon considering the circumstance of New York's making the raising of their 800 men depend upon General Braddock's approbation more attentively, I don't think we can absolutely depend upon having the benefit of them, tho I doubt not of this approbation of the Expedition to Crown point so that the Govts. of New England should not in the least slacken as to the augmentation of their respective quotas.

Mr. Franklin hath desir'd me to give directions concerning the species of provisions and would have the 10,000 Pensilvania currency, voted for the use of the Expedition, layed out in and where I would have them sent etc. I therefore desire you to transmit to me the desire of the Committee of Warr upon these heads without the least delay, that I may give the orders at my return to this place as is expected.[1]

WILLIAM SHIRLEY TO WILLIAM JOHNSON

[*Commission*][2]

By His Excellency William Shirley Esqr. Captain General and Commander in Chief in and over his Majesty's Province of the Massachusets Bay in New England, and the Lands and Territories thereon depending; Vice Admiral of same, and Colonel in his Majesty's Army.

To WILLIAM JOHNSON Esqr. Greeting.

Whereas by my Messages on the thirteenth and fifteenth Days of last February to his Majestys Council and the House

---

[1] The Governor incloses in this letter a copy of the resolve of the Pennsylvania Assembly, Apr. 2, 1755, appropriating 15,000 pounds for the king's use, 5000 of which is to repay expense incurred in victualing the troops in Virginia, the remainder to be expended under direction of a committee named in the resolution for purchasing and forwarding provisions requested by the Government of Massachusetts Bay. As to the expenditure of this appropriation, see Franklin to Shirley of May 22, *post*, p. 171.

[2] Johnson Manuscripts, New York State Library, I, 153.

of Representatives for the aforesaid Province in Great and General Court assembled, recommending to them to make Provision for carrying on an Attempt, in conjunction with some of his Majesty's other Neighbouring Governments to erect a Strong Fortress upon an Eminence near to the French Fort at Crown point, and other Services in the said Messages express'd; In answer to which the said two Houses of the aforesaid Assembly by their Message to me on the eighteenth of the same February among other things therein contained desir'd me forthwith to make the necessary preparations for such an Expedition; to appoint and Commissionate a General Officer to command the same, to advise his Majestys other Governments therein after mention'd of the said Design, and in such Manner as I should think most effectual to urge them to join therein, and to raise their Respective Proportions of Men as follows vizt. New Hampshire Six Hundred, Connecticutt One Thousand, Rhode Island four hundred, New York Eight Hundred, or such larger Proportions as each of the said Governments should think proper, and to cause twelve Hundred Men to be inlisted for the Service of the said Expedition, as the proportion of the Province of the Massachusets Bay, as soon as it should appear that the Three Thousand Men propos'd to be rais'd by the before mention'd Colonies of New Hampshire, Connecticutt, Rhode Island and New York, should be agreed to be rais'd;

And Whereas in Consequence of my aforesaid Messages recommending the said Expedition, and of the Resolves of the Assembly of the Province of the Massachusets Bay thereupon, (Copies of both which I transmitted to the before mention'd four Neighbouring Governments together with a Letter to each of them, urging them to join in the same, as propos'd by the Assembly of the Massachusets Bay), and nominating you to be the Commander in chief of the Provincial Forces to be employ'd in the said Expedition, The Governments of New York, New Hampshire, Connecticutt and Rhode Island have agreed to raise in the whole Two Thousand Nine hundred Men for his Majesty's Service in the aforesaid Expedition, which with Fifteen hundred Men since agreed to be rais'd for the aforesaid Service by the Province of the Massachusets Bay, will make up Four Thousand four hundred Men, and acquiesc'd in my Nomination of you to be Commander in Chief of the said Forces;[1] And Whereas his Excellency Major General Braddock Commander in Chief of all his Majesty's Forces in North America, hath since approv'd of my Appointmt. of you to the said Command. Now reposing especial Trust and Confidence in your Fidelity, Courage and good Conduct I do by Virtue of the Authority to me granted in and by his Majesty's Royal Commission under the Great Seal of Great Britain, and in consequence of the several proceedings of the Governments of the aforesaid Colonies of New England and New York, and of the Approbation of Major General Braddock, Appoint you to be Major General and Commander in Chief of the Forces rais'd and to be rais'd by the aforesaid Five Governments or any of them, for the Service of the aforesaid Expedition; as also of such Indians as shall assist his Majesty in the same:

You are therefore to take upon you the Command of the said Forces, and diligently to execute the Duty and Office of Commander in Chief of the said Expedition, according to such Instructions as you shall receive from me bearing even date with these Presents: and to follow such further Orders as you shall from time to time receive from me or any your Superior Officer herein: Hereby also requiring all Officers and Soldiers employ'd or to be employ'd by the aforesaid five Governments in the said Expedition to obey you as their Commander in Chief.

> Given under my Hand and Seal at Arms the Sixteenth Day of April in the Twenty eighth Year of the Reign of our Sovereign Lord, George the Second, by the Grace of

[1] Lieutenant Governor De Lancey's Commission to Johnson is in Sir William Johnson's Manuscripts, 1, 154, and is printed in Doct. Hist. of New York, 2, 281. For approval of Governor Wentworth, see Johnson Manuscripts, 1, 182.

God of Great Britain France and Ireland King, Defender of the Faith, &ca and in the Year of our Lord Christ One Thousand Seven Hundred and Fifty-five.

W. SHIRLEY.

By his Excellency's Command
WILLIAM ALEXANDER, Sec'ry.

Endorsed by Johnson:
April the 16, 1755.
Coppy of my Commissn.

WILLIAM SHIRLEY TO WILLIAM JOHNSON

[Instructions][1]

By his Excellency William Shirley Esqr. Captain General and Commander in Chief in and over the Province of the Massachusets Bay in New England and of the Lands and Territories thereon depending Vice Admiral of the same and Colonel in His Majesty's Army.

To WILLIAM JOHNSON, Esqr. Greeting:
Whereas by my Commission dated this day under my Seal at Arms, I have appointed you to be Major General and Commander in Chief of the Forces now raising by the said Governments of the Massachusets Bay, New York, New Hampshire, Connecticut and Rhode Island for an Expedition against the French Incroachments at Crown Point, and upon the Lake Champlain, as also of such Indians as shall assist in the Service of the said Expedition, I do hereby give you the following Instructions and Orders for the Regulation of your Conduct.

1st You are to engage as soon as possible as many Indians of the Six Nations as you can in the aforesaid Service upon

---

[1] Johnson Manuscripts, New York State Library, I, 152.

the Encouragements proposed to be given them by the aforesaid Colonies, as also those Ordered by his Excellency Major General Braddock to be given them in His Majesty's Name, and you are to appoint such officers to lead and Conduct the said Indians as you shall Judge for His Majesty's Service.

2dly When you shall have finished your aforesaid Business with the Indians, you are to repair to the City of Albany, and there wait the Arrival of the forces to be Employed in the aforesaid Expedition; and as soon as such a Number of them shall arrive there as you shall judge sufficient for that Service, you are to proceed with the Train of Artillery and Ordnance Stores Provided for the Expedition, under their Convoy to Crown Point, clearing as you pass along a practical Road for the transportation of them and the other stores, and to cause such strong Houses and places of Security to be ordered as shall be requisite to serve Magazines of Stores, Places of Shelter for the Men in their March, and return to and from the said City of Albany; and you are to leave the necessary Orders for such of the said Forces, as shall not be arrived at the time of your Departure from Albany, to follow you to Crown point as soon as may be.

3dly Upon your arrival at Crown point you are to cause one or more Batteries to be ordered upon the rocky Eminence nigh Fort St Frederick or as near as may be to the said Fort upon the Most advantageous Ground for Commanding the same, and to point the said Battery or Batteries against the said Fort; and in case you shall meet with any resistance in the Erecting of the said Battery or Batteries from the Garrison of Fort Frederick you are to attack the same; and use your utmost Efforts to dislodge the French Garrison and to take possession thereof.

4thly In case you shall not be interrupt'd or annoy'd by the French in erecting the said Batteries, then as soon as you shall have finished the same; you are to send a Summons to the Commandant of Fort St Frederick requiring him forthwith to retire with the Garrison under his Command, from the same, as being an Encroachment upon His Majesty's Territories within the Country belonging to the Indians of the

Six Nations, and erected contrary to the Treaty of Utrecht, made between the Crowns of Great Britain and France whereby the Indians of the then Six [Five] Nations are expressly declared to be subject to the Crown of Great Britain; and in case the said Commandant shall upon such Summons refuse or neglect to evacuate the same, you are to Compel him to do it by force of Arms, and to break up all the French settlements which you shall find near the said Fort or upon the Lake Champlain.

5thly If you should succeed in your Attempt against Fort St Frederick, you are immediately upon your becoming Master of it to strengthen yourself therein, and erect such Works as with the advice of a Council of War, which you shall Summon for that purpose, you shall think necessary to preserve that important post; and you are to put into it such a Garrison as you shall judge sufficient to maintain the same. But as the said Fort may not be situated in the most convenient or advantageous place for securing the possession of that Country to the English, you are by yourself and your Officers to Survey and Examine the several places upon the Lake Champlain and to find out such other place as you and a Council of War shall judge best to Answer that purpose, of which you are to give me immediate Notice with your and the Council's Reasons for making Choice of the place you shall agree upon, that I may be enabled to give the necessary Orders for fortifying the same.

6thly You are to give me a regular and constant Account from time to time of what you do in discharge of the Trust reposed in you, which you are to transmit by express to me wherever I shall happen to be.

7thly You are by means of the Indians, or by any other means, to procure the best intelligence you can of the designs and motions of the French, the number of any Body of Troops they may Employ to oppose you or any other of the King's Forces; all which you are to Communicate to me from time to time.

8thly You are to acquaint the Indians of the Six Nations, if you shall judge it from the Temper you find them in, proper so to do, with his Majesty's design to recover their Lands at Niagara and upon the River Ohio out of the Hands of the French, and to protect them against future Encroachments for the benefit of their Tribes; and to engage some of them to meet me at Oswego in order to assist me therein, upon such Services as I shall Order them to Go upon, assuring them of my good disposition toward their several Castles, and that they shall be generously entertained by me.

LASTLY you are to use your discretion in acting for the Good of his Majesty's Service, consistent with the Instructions before given you, in the Business Committed to your Charge, in any matters concerning which you have no particular Instructions Given you; acquainting me constantly with your doing therein as soon as possible.

GIVEN under my Hand the sixteenth day of April, One thousand seven hundred and fifty five.

W. SHIRLEY.

WILLIAM SHIRLEY TO HORATIO SHARPE [1]

April 24, 1755.

SIR,

In consequence of His Majesty's Royal Orders to his Several Govrs. upon this Continent to Maintain a Strict Correspondence upon Matters relative to his Service at this Critical Conjuncture I think it my Duty to Observe to you, that some weeks agoe undoubted accounts arrived that the French were fitting out at Brest a Strong Squadron, and Transports for a very considerable number of Troops, the destination of which was Suspected by the Government at home to be for North America : that since then we have received accounts from England of Six large Ships of war being Sailed from Brest with some Transports, and very lately we have had advices of that Number of Large Ships

[1] Original, L. S., Hist. Soc. of Penna. See Shirley to Robert H. Morris, 1 Penna. Arch. 2, 292.

of Warr together with some Transport Vessells being seen to go into the Harbour of Louisbourg.

If this should be the Case, and the French receive a reinforcement of Troops from Europe this Spring, they may doubtless in conjunction with their Militia of Canada soon have a Superior force upon this Continent to that of his Majesty's regular and provincial Troops; and what fatal Effects all the Colonies, the most Western of them, more especially, may experience from it in the Course of this Year, is easy to Conceive.

The two Last Articles of the before mentioned Intelligence, tho' not absolutely certain, seem not improbable, and it highly imports the several Colonies, to do their respective parts for guarding even against the possibility of such an Event.

His Majesty hath been graciously pleased to furnish his Colonies with upwards of Six thousand Troops (including the 2000 which I have lately raised in New England at the Expence of the Crown for the protection of Nova Scotia,[1] in which all the others are deeply interested) for their preservation at this crisis of their affairs; He hath assisted his Colony of Virginia with Arms and money besides. The four Colonies of New England with those of New York and the New Jersies are raising 5000 men for an Attack of the French fort at Crown point, and their other Incroachments upon Lake Champlain, and have determined to be at the necessary expence of engaging the Indians of the Six Nations in this important Enterprise: As to the Exact Number of Troops raised by the Governments of Pensylvania, Maryland, Virginia and the two Carolina's I dont certainly know it; But I may Venture to say that it is most reasonable it should be at least equal to the Number of Troops raised in the Six most Eastern Colonies, especially if it is consider'd that the driving of the Enemy from their Doors is what has occasion'd the present motions of the English upon the Ohio and Great Lakes: and brought every part of his Majesty's

---

[1] Plans for a fort at Halifax had been sent to Shirley on Apr. 19. See William Lithgow to Shirley, Mass. Arch., Col. Ser. 54, 412.

Territories upon this Continent into its present dangerous scituation.

Your Excellency knows so well what your own Governmt. among the rest owes to their King and Country upon this Extraordinary Occasion for Troops to rid the English Colonies of the dangerous Encroachments which the French have already made, and protect them against the further Attempts they are now meditating, that I am perswaded you will press it upon your Assembly in the Strongest Manner; and Can't but hope that they will think themselves so much interested in the Common Cause as to execute what your Excellency Shall recommend to them as their Duty for promoting it.

> I am with great Regard
> Sir
> Your Excellencys Most Humble
> and Most Obedient Servt.
> W. SHIRLEY.

The Honble. Horatio Sharpe Esq.

WILLIAM SHIRLEY TO WILLIAM JOHNSON [1]

Stratford, Connecticutt Colony,
SIR,
May 7, 1755.

I am favored with your's of the 4th Inst. wherein You observe that the Officers to be appointed for the Indians have no Assurance of Pay and that you think there was room for those officers to doubt of pay; They shall certainly receive the same which the Officers of the Provincial Troops have given them; If that will not satisfy 'em, it must depend upon yourself to ascertain it; I will be answerable to you for my own Government's making good your agreements as to its proportion, and can't doubt the same as to the other Governments doing the same; If you mean by those Officers having more than a bare Assurance, that they should receive

---

[1] Original, L. S., Johnson Manuscripts, New York State Library, I, 164.

some advance Pay, I will endeavour to get some. I can't think they will be scrupulous to insist upon any thing further; If you mean any thing more be pleas'd to let me know it.

As there is no Estimate of what it will cost to engage the Indians, and the Number that will be engag'd is uncertain, the Assembly of the Massachusetts Bay left the doing of what is necessary for that purpose to your discretion, and passed a general Vote for paying their share of whatever that should amount to; and I will answer for their punctually performing it; In the meantime I think a sum ought to be advanced to you for that service, that you may not be under the necessity of advancing your own; But if that should not be effected, I can't see the least room for you to scruple making use of the £800 lodg'd in your hands by General Braddock; the whole end of it's being lodg'd there is to engage the Indians at this juncture, and if that is lost by your not making that use of it, in case you shall have no other money in your hands for that service it will certainly be thought an ill-judg'd Parsimony.

*   *   *   *   *   *   *

In the meantime, I must apprize you that upon my pressing the Assembly of New York (in a Letter to Mr. DeLancey) to make provision on their part for engaging the Indians, as also in particular for defraying the Expence of a row galley for Lake Champlain, he observed as to the first to me, that Genl. Braddock had order'd £2000 into your Hands for the Indians, which I have insisted upon is a mistake, and must desire you to let me know how that matter is; and as to the latter, he told me there would be a Vote of his Assembly to pay their share of your expenses; which is by no means satisfactory to me, and I now let him know it again.

You may depend upon my exerting my best endeavours with all the other Assemblies to make provision for the special Expence of building a row galley, as also a proper one for engaging the Indians; and in particular for Ordnance Stores; and if it is possible for me to get you an Engineer, I will. The only Engineers we had at Cape Breton (I mean of any real service) was the late gunner of our Castle,[1] and a scholar of his, Captn. Gridley; I must make as bad a shift in this respect at Niagara.

I must desire you to send me as soon as may be, a copy of the General's Power to you to draw on me for the exigencies of the service you are engag'd in. Your drafts will be answer'd, but I desire you would particularize the Articles on acct. of which you draw; and I would have you in my absence draw on Mr. John Erving Junr. of Boston whom I will order to honour your bills. You may in the whole depend that nothing in my power shall be wanting in any regard to render the execution of your command easy and successfull and to represent in a just light, the merit of your service to His Majesty and his Ministers according to the high opinion I have of it.

I am with much Truth Sir, Your Faithfull Humble Servant.

W. SHIRLEY.

Major General Johnson.

Endorsed by Johnson:

Govr. Shirleys letter concerning the officers pay and the Indians.

Some things material.

Sent Extracts of this to the Genl. [Braddock] May 18th, 1755.

WILLIAM JOHNSON TO WILLIAM SHIRLEY

[Extracts][2]

SIR,   Mount Johnson, May 16, 1755.

Your favor of the 7th Inst came last night to my hand. The Indian officers will doubtless and with reason request

[1] John H. Bastide here noticed was made a lieutenant general in the British army in 1770 because of his services at Louisbourg and later; Richard Gridley, who also served at Louisbourg, was prominent at Bunker Hill and throughout the American war. He died in 1796.

[2] Auto. copy signed, Johnson Manuscripts, New York State Library, 1, 171. Words in brackets are erased in the draft.

more pay than those of the Provincial Troops: The service will be severe and much more fatiguing and by the wear and tear of their cloaths be more expe[n]sive to them. In the last Expedition their pay was equal to that of the British Foot, and as I propose to employ the same persons again, they will [undoubtedly] naturally and reasonably insist upon their former pay.

I am fully satisfied that mere verbal assurances for their pay will not [suffice] be sufficient, that they will demand a more solid satisfaction and this ought to have been already done that they might expect to be put upon a certain footing with regard thereto. It is impossible for me with any tollerable exactness to make an estimate of the expences which may arise from my attempts to engage and maintain the Six Nations and their Allies in the British Interest.

* * * * * * *

As to the £2000 which Mr DeLancey told you Genl. Braddock had put into my hands, or rather, which is the case, had given me orders to draw for on Mr O. DeLancey, £800 or upwards out of that sum is already laid out in a present for the Six Nations when they meet me here, and from the remainder I am now daily expending in previous measures and shall continue to make use of it as occasion may [require] call for, but this sum will fall very short of the services agreed upon and required, and a further provision from the Colonies will be absolutely necessary and that put upon a determinate footing [with the utmost despatch ?] as soon as possible. Herewith agreeable to your Excellency's desire I send you a copy of General Braddock's powers to me in relation to drawing on you.

* * * * * * *

I am extreamly obliged to Your Excellency for Your assurances of giving me Your friendly influence and support in the command you have honoured me with, and my dependance thereon has been and will be one of my chief [supports] resources and animates me with hopes and alacrity in an undertaking for which I confess and feel myself not so equal as I could wish [myself] to be. Upon this head I must beg leave to mention to you as my friend that hitherto the Colonies have made no provision to support me in that distinguishing character to which your favour and friendship have been pleased to promote me. As I assure you I neither seek nor desire any emolument to my private fortune thereby, so I hope you and they will judge it not unreasonable [*sic*] for me to be left without a necessary and proper establishment.

I am with the utmost respect and with unfeigned Gratitude, Sir,

Your Excellency's Most Obedt. and obliged Humb. Servt.

W. JOHNSON.

Upon second thought it appears to me that it will be more proper and effectual for your Excelly to acquaint the several Govrs with such of this letter as you think necessary [and so add your sentiments in order to render them effectual], and therefore I shall decline writing to them except to Mr. DeLancey.

WILLIAM SHIRLEY TO ISRAEL WILLIAMS AND OTHERS [1]

Boston, May 17, 1755.

GENTLEMEN,

There being divers Persons belonging to the Colony of New York apprehended and committed to his Majesty's Gaol in

[1] L. S., Mass. Hist. Society, Col. Israel Williams Manuscripts, 71 D, 129. There was much trouble in connection with raising troops and other aids for Shirley in New York. See: Shirley-Johnson correspondence in Johnson Manuscripts, 3, 8; 1, 160, 163, 169; Shirley to Governor Morris of May 2, 1 Penna. Arch. 2, 297; William Alexander to Shirley of May 10 and 18, *ibid.* pp. 348–350; and William Alexander and Lewis Morris to Shirley of May 17, *ibid.* p. 314. In a letter of May 24 (*post*, p. 174) Shirley pledges his coöperation and influence to Johnson, and in letters of May 26 to Lieutenant Governor DeLancey and May 28 to Governor Morris he writes about the efforts made in Connecticut to raise a portion of New York's contribution in that colony, 1 Penna. Arch. 2, 326, 330. See also Shirley to DeLancey, June 1, *post*, p. 182.

Springfield for some Riotous Actions perpetrated on the borders of this Province where one of his Majesty's subjects was Murthered in the said Riot.

I do therefore with the Advice of his Majesty's Council direct you or any two of you forthwith to make Inquiry into the Circumstances of the Commitment of divers Persons taken at Mr. Livingston's Iron Works or any other Persons committed on Account of the late riotous Disorders near the Line and that you cause the said Persons to be admitted to Bail upon their recognizg with Sureties for their Appearance and taking their Trial according to the Nature of their Offence Provided they are not charged with the *Actual* Murther of William Race, and that you represent the State of this Affair as soon as may be.

I am

Gentlemen,

Your Assured Friend

and Servant

W. SHIRLEY.

Israel Williams, Josiah Dwight and John Worthington Esqrs.

BENJAMIN FRANKLIN TO WILLIAM SHIRLEY [1]

Philada., May 22, 1755.

SIR,

Mr. Norris [2] not being in Town, your Excelly's Letter of the 14th Instant pr Express, was delivered to me. I immediately conven'd the Committee, and communicated the Contents. In answer, they desire me to acquaint your Excelly with the State of the Provisions they have procured which is as follows —

They have purchased but 500 barrels of Pork. It is all of the best Burlington Pork, and not one Barrel among it of any other sort. There is no more of the kind to be bought;

[1] Original, Mass. Arch., Col. Ser. 54, 438.
[2] Isaac Norris.

so that this Article will fall short 700 Barrels of the Quantity required by your Committee.

They have bought 250 barrels of Beef, and can get no more that they would chuse to send. This is all choice Stall-fed Beef, exceeding good, most of it kill'd in this Town and put up on purpose, and the rest carefully examin'd and repack'd here. The Gentlemen of the Committee who purchase the Provisions are Messrs. John Mifflin, Saml Smith and Reese Meredith, all long practis'd in the Provi-sion-Way, and esteemed thorough Judges; they are of Opinion that no better Beef will or can be brought to the Army from any Country; and as your Excelly's Request that it may be sold again, and not sent, seems founded on a mistaken Supposition of your Committee, that good Beef is not to be expected from Pensilvania, these Gentlemen will venture their own Credit and that of their Country on this Beef, that it shall prove as good as any from Boston; and they suppose that in such Case, neither your Excelly. nor your Committee would desire to have it omitted. They therefore propose to send the said 250 Barrels, and no more. All the Casks, both of the Pork and Beef, are full trimm'd, and in the best Order.

Rum was one of the Articles directed in your Excelly's Orders given to the Committee here. They had accordingly bought and shipt 50 Hogsheads before they received your Committe's Letter of the 14th April, in which there is no mention of Rum. They have Advice that the Rum is ar-riv'd in York; so much less therefore need be sent from Boston; and the Committee conceive that the Army will not be discontented at finding it good Barbadoes, instead of New England.

A Thousand Pounds worth of Pease are also purchased in Albany by Order of the Committee; and they have shipt and sent forward 140 Barrels of Meal and Flour. 600 Barrels more of Flour are purchased and actually in Store ready to send; to which they will add 50 Tierces of Rice, and the Remainder of the Sum in Bread of the kind required. If your Committee should think that Quantity of Bread too great (for it will become greater by the Diminution of the Pork) they may accomodate the New York Forces with some of it in Exchange for Pork: Connecticut Pork being plenty at New York and Bread wanting.[1]

The Committee will send all to the Persons recommended; but doubt they shall not be able to get the whole delivered at Albany in time, without re-shipping some at New York; our Vessels of any Burthen drawing too much Water for that River. They will however comply with this Direction as far as they can.

This being the exact State of the Provisions sent and to be sent from hence, your Committee can now regulate their remaining Purchases accordingly.

I did not reach home 'till the 12th Instant, from the Journey, in which I had the Honr. to accompany your Excy. as far as Annapolis. In my way I have had the good Fortune to do an acceptable Piece of Service to the Forces under General Braddock. I found them stuck fast, and unable to move for want of Horses and Carriages; all their Dependencies for those Articles having failed. They are now supply'd with both as well as with 6000 Bushels of Oats and Indian Corn, which were much wanted but scarce expected. Your Excy, I find by the Papers, got well home about the same time. I do not expect more Pleasure from any News, till I hear of your safe Return after a successful Campaign at Niagara.

With the greatest Respect and Esteem, I have the Honr. to be,

Your Excy's most obedient
and most humble Servant,
B. FRANKLIN.

---

[1] For other aid to Shirley in securing provisions see William Alexander and Lewis Morris to Shirley, May 24, 1 Penna. Arch. 2, 315. On the following day Shirley wrote Lieutenant Governor De Lancey to keep French Indians from having any intercourse with Albany, thus guarding provisions collecting at that place. Johnson Manuscripts, 1, 188.

WILLIAM SHIRLEY TO THE GENERAL COURT OF MASSACHUSETTS [1]

GENTLEMEN,   Boston, May 23, 1755.

This Morning I received by Express from Major General Johnson [2] dated at Mount Johnson in the Mohawks Country, among other things of Importance, the inclosed Articles of what he proposes as necessary to be done without delay, and which I shall press the other Govts. concerned to comply with likewise. Besides what is included in this Extract he computes 800 barrells of Gun powder, and the like proportion of Ball to be necessary for the service of the Expedition; As I shall want 5 or 600 barrells for Niagara, will it not be adviseable for us both to lay in for some at New York and Philadelphia least both of us should not be supply'd at Boston.

It is proper you should secure forthwith a competent number of small arms to supply all deficiencies that may happen among the soldiers, who may want arms. The News I have from Albany, and Intelligence from Crown point require your utmost dispatch in the Execution of the Trust repos'd on you upon which I know I may depend.

I am, Gentlemen,
Your most Assured Friend,
and Servant
W. SHIRLEY.

WILLIAM SHIRLEY TO WILLIAM JOHNSON [3]

SIR,   Boston, May 24th, 1755.

Yesterday I received your Packet dated at Mount Johnson the 16th Instant by Express.

[1] Original, A. L. S., Mass. Arch., Col. Ser. 54, 442.
[2] A letter from Johnson dated May 16 is in *ibid.* 428. For other memoranda of same date see Johnson papers in New York State Library, and Johnson to Shirley, *ante,* p. 168.
[3] Original, L. S., Johnson Manuscripts, New York State Library, I, 184.

I am intirely of your Opinion with regard to the Indian Officers, and will lose no time in pressing the several Governments concern'd forthwith to make the needfull Provision for their Pay in the manner propos'd by you; as also for defraying the Expence of engaging and Maintaining the Indians in the English Interest, by fix'd Funds, and giving you an absolute Power to draw upon them for that Service according to their respective proportions; which is doubtless necessary to be done.

The Assembly of my own Province was dissolv'd before my Arrival here, and a new one can't meet by the Charter before the 28th Instant; I will then obtain a positive and explicit Answer from them in the particular you desire; I have no reason to doubt of it's being satisfactory to you. I will also let the other Governments concern'd except that of New York (which Mr DeLancey will do) know the absolute Necessity there is of their coming to an immediate Determination in these Points, and making a certain Provision by some fix'd Fund accordingly; and I think with you, this may be best done by communicating to them the proper paragraphs of your Letter to me, and enforcing them with Arguments drawn from the reasonableness and Necessity of the Thing.

The £800 must, as you observe, be apply'd to making a present to the Indians; and I am sensible the Remainder of the £2000 will soon be exhausted in the articles mention'd in your Letter. I have already let you know that I shall answer your Drafts for what may be necessary over and above the money advanc'd to you by General Braddock for carrying on and supporting the Alliance with the Six Nations, pursuant to the General's Order to me for that Purpose.

I know the Difficulties you must be under in reclaiming the almost lost affections of the Six Nations to the English and engaging them in the present Service against the thousand Artifices of the French; But I can't but be perswaded, from the Knowledge I have of your Influence over them, and the Talents you have for effecting this most important business, that you will surmount them and do your King and

Country the desir'd Service. The Progress you have already made, and the scheme for satisfying their Minds with regard to the fortifying of Oswego which is a most necessary thing,. give me great satisfaction; You will not forget to engage some good Indians to meet me at Oswego.

I doubt not but that the carriages and everything belonging to the Artillery design'd for the Service under your command, are rotten and unfit for Service; and shall accordingly take care to have new ones made. A large Number of Workmen are on their way to Albany from Boston, to make this Government's Battoes. I shall press the other Governments to take the same care; and will use the like Endeavours for having all the Military Stores provided in time; and that the Companies shall be sent to Albany as they are compleated.

*　　*　　*　　*　　*　　*　　*

I shall not lose a day for pushing on all preparations, and the marching of the Forces to Albany; and shall write to you again in a few days; when I hope I shall be able to mention the time of my coming to Albany. You will make the utmost dispatch on your part with regard to your business with the Indians, and giving the necessary orders concerning the Provincial Forces as they shall arrive at Albany.

The fixing of a proper Allowance by the several Colonies, I shall particularly have at heart. The intelligence contain'd in your inclos'd papers is of great service. You will have, if New York raises their 800 men, and the Colony of Connecticut their designed augmentation as I hope they will both, 4,700 men besides the Indians for the Expedition against Crown Point.

I am with much Truth and Esteem, Sir,
Your faithfull Humble Servant,
W. SHIRLEY.[1]

[1] Ten "Suggestions for a Commanding Officer" follow this letter. Among them are the following: If you lose, don't despair. Distinguish a brave man and reward a gallant action upon the spot. Be careful of your sick men, and visit them sometimes yourself. Make sure of a safe retreat in case of accidents.

WILLIAM ALEXANDER TO WILLIAM SHIRLEY [1]

Albany, May 27th, 1755.

SIR,

Your Excellency's Letter of the 20th, by Joseph Glidden, I received yesterday afternoon. He and the other five Ship Carpenters set out this Morning for Schenectady, where they are to embark to-morrow Morning for Oswego, in Company with 12 Battoes, which I send there with Provisions, each of these Battoes have two Men in them, who in General are provided with Fire Arms. This is all the Guard it is possible to get for the Carpenters (for there are no Troops left here) and I am in hopes it will be sufficient, for the People of this Country are daily passing betwixt this and Osweego, without any apprehension of danger that way.

The Stores sent us by Commodore Keppel, and most of the other Necessaries, for the two Vessels, are already in proper Store-houses at Schenectady, also the greatest part of the Provisions, which Your Excellency ordered to be provided for your own and Sir William's Regiments, and stores are there provided to receive all the other Necessaries, which shall be sent there as fast as they arrive here.[2]

I have viewed all the Grounds about Schenectady fit for Encampments, and three places which I think the most convenient I shall have Plans of, ready to lay before Your Excellency at New York. Col. Glen's House, which is the most convenient about Schenectady, will be proposed for Your Excellency's own quarters. I have also engaged for you a convenient House in this Town. A Number of People are at Work in the Wood Creek, and on the Carrying Place, to mend the Passage there which was the most needful to

---

[1] Printed: 1 Penna. Arch. 2, 351.

[2] On May 20 Shirley had written Keppel that he would endeavor to make up the complement of men for two vessels to be built on Lake Ontario and would furnish a model for them. The letter is in P. R. O., Admiralty Section, Insular Letters, 480, and is in reply to Keppel's letter of April 15.

Oswego. Others are employed in making Passages thro' the most shallow Rifts in the Mohawk's River. I have directed two Store-houses to be built, one on each end of the Carrying place, of Strong Logs, covered and floor'd with bark, 35 feet long and 20 feet broad. These will be sufficient, and the cost of them trifling, but it will be of great use that some Men encamp at each of the said Houses, until all the Stores are carried over. The Battoes are in great forwardness, the whole Number of them which Your Excellency Ordered will be ready at Schenectady within twenty days from this time, and every thing else which you have Ordered, I think may be there before that time, And I must take the Liberty of saying that I heartily wish Your Excellency with the Troops could be there about that time, many things make it necessary that no time be lost. The Water in the Mohawk's River and Wood Creek grows shallow about the middle and latter end of the Summer, which makes the Passage tedious. The French in Canada are not in the least apprized or apprehensive of any Attack from the English, but on the Ohio, and to the Eastward. The Troops going to Oswego are looked upon only as a Reinforcement of that Garrison, and Col. Johnson's Enterprise will be looked upon as only a design of building a strong Fort on the Carrying place, a Report of which they have had some time. The Govr. of Canada has acquainted the Caghnawagas that he has nothing against it, if they don't come over the middle of the Carrying place, so far he allows the English to have right, but if they do he is determined to oppose with Force. This is what all the Caghnawagas lately here, and the French Gentleman mentioned in my last, agree in.

I have obtained an actual Survey of Oswego and the Fort there, also an actual Survey of the greatest part of the way between that place and this, the Maps and Plans of which I shall have ready at New York. Several of the principal Indian Traders have promised me, that if Your Excellency Chuses it, they will attend You to Oswego, or wherever else you please. Some of them may be of great use.

There are no Sailors to be had here, and I believe but few

at New York; if You can get about 20 good ones from Boston We may, I believe, make up the remainder at about 50s sterl. per Month. By a Sloop just arrived from New York, I have an account of the Arrival of a Vessel there in 28 days from London, and brings advice that a War is speedily expected. If the Wind be fair I shall set out for New York this afternoon.

I am Sir,

WM. ALEXANDER.

To Govr. Shirley at Boston.

WILLIAM SHIRLEY TO WILLIAM JOHNSON [1]

> *State of the Case of the Expedition against Niagara with regard to the Number of Troops Sufficient for the Service.*

When the Expedition to Crown point was first determined upon by the Colonies concern'd in it, there was no thought of making any Attempt for the Reduction of the French Forts at Niagara at the same time, and it was Expected that the Forces employ'd against Crown point, would have the whole Strength of the Country about Montreal to encounter. The Provincial Forces which were then depended upon, being rais'd as Sufficient for that Service, were 4000 Men, as to New Jersey's sending any, tho' that Government was desir'd in General to send some, Yet it was Scarcely expected from them, and therefore, no Quota was alloted to them; And in the Resolves of the Massachusetts Assembly, it was determined to begin to raise their Quota of Men as Soon as it should be certainly known, that the Colonies of New York, Connecticutt, New Hampshire, and Rhode Island should raise their respective Proportions, without staying to know the Success of the Application to the Govr. of New Jerseys, or whether they could have the Assistance of one of the Kings American Regim'ts or not, which tho'

---

[1] N. Y. State Library, Johnson Manuscripts, 1, 196.

desir'd was very precarious. This alteration of the General Plan of Operations, is a very material one, as it will Occasion a Considerable Diversion of the French Forces, which would otherwise be employ'd in the defence of Crown point.

It is well known that the Value of Canada to the French consists chiefly in its convenient Situation for Carrying on the Great Furr Trade they have with all the Indians inhabiting the Country behind the Appalachian[1] Mountains, and for making them Masters of that Country, and of those Nations, the former of which they have openly invaded, and begun to force the latter into their Interest. This Acquisition would of itself be a very large and Valuable Dominion to the French, Especially as it would be Contiguous to their Settlements upon the Mississippi, and must if they should gain it, contribute greatly towards their Reduction of all the English Colonies in North America. It is as well known likewise, that in Order to make this Acquisition, it is necessary for the French to hold possession of the Lakes Ontario, and Erie, the Strait of Niagara, and the River Ohio, since it is only by means of them, that they can maintain an usefull Communication between Canada and the Mississippi; Their former Route from Montreal thro' the River Outouwoais,[2] and by way of [Lake] Mischelimakenak, is practicable only for light birch Canoes, as it abounds with Falls, and hath Thirty Six portages or Carrying places.

The Cutting the French off therefore from the Navigation of the Lakes Ontario and Erie, and the pass at Niagara, must prevent them from effecting a Junction of Canada with the Mississippi, disconcert their Schemes upon the Ohio, and put an End to their Views of Compassing that Empire, which they have long mark'd out for themselves upon the Back of the English Colonies, and of late made a progress towards Obtaining. Consequently it is to be expected, that they will exert their utmost Efforts to defend their Possession of these Lakes, and the pass at Niagara, which must of course, occasion a great Diversion of the Forces in Canada,

---

[1] Apalactrian in the manuscript.
[2] Ottawa River.

they would otherwise employ at Crown point, and of Course facilitate the Reduction of the French Fort there.

The forces now raising for the Expedition to Crown point, are 800 by the Govt. of New York, 1000 by the Colony of Connecticutt, 1500 by the Massachusetts Bay, 500 by the Province of New Hampshire, and 400 by that of Rhode Island, in all 4200 Men, which with the Indians that General [William] Johnson may be expected to raise will amount in the whole to 4400 Men at least, and if even 1000 Men were to be spar'd from them, for the Service at Niagara, the remainder would be a much more Sufficient force to attempt the Reduction of Crown point with now, than 5000 would have been, if no Diversion had been made by the Expedition to Niagara.

It ought to be Considered in this case, if the French are Obliged to run the Risque of loosing either their Fort at Crown point, or all the Southern Country, which Risque they would Sooner run, the former or latter. If they should lose Crown point, they might easily Strengthen themselves upon Lake Champlain, if they should lose the latter, Canada itself would not be worth holding, nor Could they well maintain the Expence of it without the Fur Trade.

Further it seems very likely that upon the arrival of General Braddock's Forces at the French Forts upon the Ohio in good Order, they will Quit them, and Come in their Battoes across Lake Erie to Niagara, in which case with the Forces which they would send from Montreal across Lake Ontario on the other hand, supposing them to be only 1000, and what they could soon Muster from among the Indians, they might easily make up double the Number of what would be employed in the attempt at Niagara, even with the addition of the 500 Men proposed by the Province of the Massachusetts Bay.

There is another very Material thing, likewise in the Case, which is, That the Forces employ'd in the Expedition to Niagara, will intercept the French now upon the Ohio, if they should attempt to cross Lake Ontario to come to the relief of Crown point, which is another Circumstance that would Greatly facilitate the Reduction of Crown point, and is much in favour of the Expedition to Niagara being Supported. Another thing to be Considered is, that a Defeat at Niagara, would forever fix all the Indians in the Interest of the French, on the other hand succeeding there, would bring 'em all over to the English Interest.

It should be further Observed that as Govr. Shirley hath full power to employ the Forces under his Command in any part of the Kings Service, after that at Niagara is Effected, he may possibly be able especially in case there should be but little Opposition there, to Strengthen the Forces at Crown point, with those under his own Command, at all Events if the Service at Crown point should Labour for want of a larger Number of Troops, it would be very practicable for it to be Strengh'd in time from the Colonies, as Those Troops may intrench or otherwise Secure themselves against a Stronger Force, untill they should receive such Succours, but that would not be the Case with the Forces at Niagara, under like Circumstances.

W. SHIRLEY.

Boston, May 31st, 1755.

Endorsed by Johnson: Govr. Shirley's Reasons for reinforcing the troops designed against Niagara &c. with Volunteers from the troops destined for Crown Point.

WILLIAM SHIRLEY TO JAMES DE LANCEY [1]

Boston, June 1st, 1755.

SIR,

I have received Your Honours Letter dated the 20th May, with the Opinion of his Majesty's Council for your Province upon the subject of the Cannon I desired the Loan of; I am sorry that I have given yourself or the Council so much Trouble about this Affair. Had I thought that your sparing two more of your Brass twelve Pounders for the King's service at Niagara would have exposed your Fort to any

[1] 1 Penna. Arch. 2, 338.

danger, I should not have urg'd my request so far as I have done; which I have continued to importune you for in my last, I would trouble your Honour no more about it.

As to my proposing to your Honour the lending of the ten eighteen Pounders for his Majesty's Service now carrying on in Nova Scotia with the Carriages, &c. Mr. Clinton having lent them to the King's service in the Expedition against Cape Breton in a time of actual War, I apprehended they might as well be spar'd now with safety to the City of New York, for his Majesty's Service in Nova Scotia; and as there were no Cannon in this Province so fit for Battering pieces in that Service, I proposed to your Honour the Loan of them, which I should not have troubled you with if they had been to be found here. The same Service required that 2000 Men should be rais'd in the Colonies, as my own Government abounded with Men, I rais'd at least 1700 of them there, without proposing it to your Honour to raise any in your own; I thought this Province might spare them better than New York; as I now believe that your Honour's Government can much better spare the ten 18 Pounders in question than my own can the six pieces of Ordnance which I have sent to Nova Scotia out of Castle William. It must at least be allowed that the Province is considerably weak by sparing so many Men as also these Cannon out of the principal Battery of a Fortress, which is its Key, and only considerable Defence against any Attack by Sea.

As to the six 18 Pounders and 4 small brass field pieces, which your Honour hath spared for the Service of the Expedition against Crown point, as Mr. Clinton had done before, for the like service in 1746: I understand they were sent out of Albany, where they have laid these last ten years, and I dont well see how the Loan of them now can have weakened the City of New York.

However, Sir, to put this matter out of Question, upon the advice which I received in a Letter from Mr. Alexander concerning the difficulties under which my request to Your Honour for the two last brass twelve Pounders labour'd; I had caus'd before I received your last Letter, two of your ten Eighteen Pounders, together with two 24 Pounders out of Castle William, with Carriages and Implements to be put on board a Sloop, which is to sail to-day for New York, and have Ordered the two last mentioned Cannon to be delivered to your Honour with the two 18 Pounders, which I hope will be satisfactory to you and the Gentlemen of his Majesty's Council. I dont suppose it adviseable for your Honour to part with any Cannon without their advice; at the same time I am persuaded that your Honour's sentiments have great weight with them, upon such, and indeed every other occasion.[1]

I shall trouble your Honour no further upon this point than to observe, that in 1745 and 1746 all these Cannon were lent by the Government of New York to his Majesty's service for the Expedition against Cape Breton, and the then intended one against Crown point, without any demand of their being replaced from this Government, and indeed they were most readily for the present Service in which they are employed without any hesitation by your Honour until I requested of you to spare me the six 12 Pounders for his Majesty's Service in which I am engaged at Niagara. I am sorry that that hath occasioned any difficulty, and upon the whole would beg the favour of your Honour, if any should still remain, to acquaint me with it, that I may certainly know what I have to depend upon, and provide as well as I can for the service in case of any disappointment as to the six 12 Pounders, and I would further desire if I am to have them, that your Honour would be pleased to give Orders for the immediate delivery of them to Mr. Alexander and Lewis Morris, that they may be transported to Oswego before the Waters are too low.

*   *   *   *   *   *   *

Your Honour observes, that I must be sensible from Mr. Stoddard's Letter which you put into my hands, that the Fort which the French have at Niagara is a weak triffling thing, and incapable of Defence, and that you are of opinion

[1] See William Alexander to Shirley, June 5 and 7, 1 Penna. Arch. 2, 353–354.

five hundred would easily reduce it, *unless the French have time to throw up some new Works about it, and reinforce it with a Body of Troops.* I agree with your Honour in this; but that is not the point under Consideration. The Question is, Whether the French will not probably have thrown up new Works, and reinforced it with a Body of Troops, before the Forces destined for the reduction of that Fort can arrive at Niagara, especially as the French have had an Opportunity of gaining Intelligence of our designs against that Fort by the way of Albany. Every Person who is allowed to be a good Judge in this matter here that I have Conversed with, is fully of that Opinion, as is the General Assembly of this Province, who have informed themselves very critically in the Affair from Mr. Lydius of your Government and Capt. Kellogg of this Province, who are both remarkably well acquainted with the Country and matters in Question. Your Honour acknowledges in Your Letter, that the reduction of the French Fort and the gaining possession of the Pass at Niagara, are of the importance to the British interests in general which I represent it to be of. Upon what then does Your Honour ground your opinion; that the French will give it up to the English without exerting their utmost Efforts, and mustering a strong Body of Troops in the Defence of it, before it is possible for the English Forces to arrive at Niagara, since there can be no reasonable doubt but that our designs against it must be violently suspected by them, if not known with absolute certainty.

If that should not be Your Opinion, then why does Your Honour think that no part of the forces originally designed for the Expedition against Crown point can be spared from that Service to strengthen those which are designed for Niagara. You expressly acknowledge in your Letter that, "I certainly look upon the attempt against Niagara in a "true light, and that if the French muster a Strong Force at "that place, *it must weaken their Forces at Crown point.*"

Your Honour says in your Letter, "That if, the other "Governments take no Umbrage at the present destination "of the New Jersey Forces, — you shall acquiesce, and you

" hope they will not." I beg leave to acquaint your Honour that I fully laid this matter before the Government of Connecticut, when I was at Hartford, and they took not the least umbrage at it; and you will see by the Vote of my own Government, that they are far from doing it, and you are sensible that these two Governments, with that of New York, will raise 3300 of the 4200 men which are to be raised for the Expedition against Crown point, so that I have reason to hope that neither New Hampshire nor Rhode Island Government will.

I beg leave to add, that General Braddock originally intended that the whole corps of mine and Sir William Pepperrells Regiments, should proceed to Niagara. But that, as your Honour advised him to post two Companies of the latter Regiment at Oswego, for the defence of that Fort, (within the Government of New York), which your honour says in your Letter, was the reason of his doing it, and consequently occasioned the lessening of the Forces, that would otherwise have gone in that Expedition; I hope you may think that a reason, why neither your Honour nor your Government should take Exception to those forces being further strengthened out of those raised for the Service at Crown Point, if the other Governments agree to it.[1] . . .

[1] The proposals made by Braddock at the Alexandria Council of Apr. 14 were as follows:

1st That a fund should be established conformable to his Instructions and to Sir Thomas Robinson's Letter to the several Governors dated Octobr 26, 1754.

2d It being of the utmost importance that the five Nations of Indians and their Allies should be gained and secured to the British Interest, that a proper person should be sent with full powers from him to treat with them, and that Colonel Johnston, appearing to his Excellency the fittest person for that purpose, should be employed in it.

And in order to promote the success of the Treaty, the General proposed that presents should be made to the said Indians in which he desired the opinion of the Council as to the value to which the said presents should be made, and the manner of their being Supplied.

3d His Excellency acquainted the Council that he proposed to attack the French Forts at Crown point and Niagara and desired

Your Honour says in Your Letter "you should be glad to understand my reasoning, how Your applying at the request of the Assembly to the Government of Connecticut, for leave to raise Men in that Colony, can with any Propriety, be said to weaken the forces for Crown point." I hope my last letter to You hath fully explained it. The Governor of Connecticut told me at Hartford, that if the Assembly should give your Government leave to raise 500 men within their Colony, pursuant to your Honours request, they would lay aside all thoughts of making an Augmentation to their own Troops, which they had before thought of doing, to the amount of 500 Men. I presume Your Honour will allow, that in such Case, your raising the 500 Men desired, in Connecticut, instead of your own Government, and by that means, preventing the Government of Connecticut from making their designed addition of 500 Men to their own Troops, might with propriety, be said to weaken the forces "raised for Crown point."

Your Honour concludes Your Letter with telling me, that you mentioned it as Your Opinion to General Braddock, at Alexandria, "that 1300 Men of the two Regiments, should go to reduce Niagara, and that having secured that Pass, and

their Opinion whether it was advisable that the Reduction of Crown point should be undertaken with the forces agreed to be Supplyed by the Several Colonies concerned in it amounting in the whole to 4400 Men and whether it was their opinion that Colonel Johnston was a proper person to Command in Chief the said service.

4th His Excellency considering the Fort at Oswego as a Post of the greatest importance for facilitating the proposed attack of Niagara, and securing the retreat of the Troops to be employed in that service, and having been informed of Its present Defenceless condition and of the weakness of its Garrison acquainted the Council that he should order it to be reinforced by the two Independent Companies of New York and two Companies of Sir William Pepperels Regiment, and desired to have their opinion whether it would not be proper to build one or more Vessels upon the Lake Ontario for asserting His Majesty's right to that Lake as well as for a Security to the Forces to be employed in the attack of Niagara, and of what burthen or Force the said Vessels should be. P. R. O., C. O. 5, 15.

left there a Garrison of 300 Men, the remaining thousand should proceed to the Peninsula, on the Lake Erie, and secure that Post, by which means the General would with more ease, penetrate through that Country from the Ohio, and so return by the way of Niagara, and that the General seem'd to approve of the Plan." And you advise me to pursue it. The General communicated to me the Plan he proposed, with regard to the Operations upon the Ohio, and the reduction of Niagara, at first by Letter from Williamsburg, afterwards the *whole* Plan was settled the first day of my Meeting him at Alexandria, between him, Commodore Keppel, and myself, and I beg leave to assure Your Honour, however the General might seem to approve of your Plan of my passing over to the Presque Isle and Riviere au Boeuff, (as You elsewhere in Your Letter propose,) to assist him, he did not let one Word drop to me, either in his Letter, or at the settlement of the Plan, or in Conversation afterwards concerning it; and my Orders for employing the Forces under my Command, after securing the Pass at Niagara, are discretionary. I thank Your Honour for Your advice to myself, which will have great weight with me. But I am informed I shall meet with an insuperable difficulty in executing Your Scheme, as without Horses, which are not to be had at Niagara, I shall not be so able to transport the Battoes and Train of Artillery, over the Strait to Lake Erie, which, I presume, Your Honour thinks necessary to be done; I beg Leave, upon the whole, to assure you, that I will use my utmost endeavours to execute my Command, in the best manner I can for his Majesty's Service, and that any Obstacles, which may be thrown in my way, will allow.

I am, with great Regard, Sir,
Your Honours most Humble,
and most Obedient Servant,
W. SHIRLEY.

WILLIAM SHIRLEY TO THE GENERAL COURT OF MASSACHUSETTS[1]

Friday, June 6, 1755.

*   *   *   *   *   *   *

GENTLEMEN OF THE COUNCIL AND HOUSE OF REPRESENTATIVES,

I send you the Extract of a Letter, which I received last Night by Express from the Governor of Conecticut:

I must desire you will forthwith take the Proposal of that Government concerning the Pensylvania Provisions, under Consideration and let me know your Determination thereupon, that I may send an answer by the Return of the Express. I should be glad if by the same Express, I could send them an Account of your Resolutions upon the Several Matters which I have laid before you, out of Major General Johnson's Letter. It is of absolute necessity that you should forthwith determine upon them, and make the necessary provision, and that he and the Colonies may know it.

The Season is so far advanced, and the Forces destined to Crown Point should keep Pace with those designed for Niagara, in order to secure as much as may be the Success of both Expeditions. The first Division of the latter of these Forces will march on Monday next for Providence, in the Colony of Rhode Island where Transports are waiting for them, and they will be all imbarked in seven days from that Time, and sail for Albany, and from there proceed directly for Oswego, their battoes for transporting them and their stores being in such Forwardness as to be ready to receive them upon their Arrival at Schenectady.

I would not mention to you how much General Johnson's success in ingaging the Indians depends upon your making Provision for that Purpose.

W. SHIRLEY.

In the House of Representatives: Read and Ordered that Colo. Lawrence, Colo. Williams, Capt. Livermore, Mr. Tyng

[1] Mass. Arch., Records of General Court, 20. See Message of May 23, *ante*, p. 174.

and Mr. Taylour with such as the Honble. Board shall join, be a Committee to take the foregoing Message from His Excellency under Consideration, together with the Extracts from Governour Wentworths and Governour Fitch's Letters, and report thereon; and that the Committee be directed to sit forthwith;—In Council; Read and Concur'd, and John Otis, Thomas Hutchinson, Eleazer Porter and William Brattle Esqr. are joined in the Affair.[1]

MASSACHUSETTS GENERAL COURT ACTION ON WILLIAM SHIRLEY'S MESSAGE OF JUNE 6[2]

At a Great and General Court or Assembly for his Majesty's Province of the Massachusetts Bay in New England,

[1] See Action of General Court, following.

[2] Mass. Arch., Records of General Court, 20.

On the receipt of these resolutions by the New York Assembly the following action was taken in July (Doct. Hist. N. Y. 2, 389):

Resolved, that in case the Army destined for Crown Point shall stand in need of Reinforcements, This House will provide ways and means for Supplying the Quota of this Colony of such Reinforcements, and *Ordered*, That Capt. Walton and Capt. Winne wait on his Honour the Lieutenant Governor and desire that he will be pleased to acquaint Major General Johnson that on this Colony's having furnished and Supplyed the Sum of nine hundred and forty four pounds — towards the Train of Artillery for the Expedition to Crown Point, over and above the sum of Two thousand pounds the proper Quota of this Colony and the sum of One thousand pounds advanced on the security of Part of the provisions allowed by the Colony of Pensilvania, His Excellency Govr. Shirley has engaged to furnish and Supply the sum of £1652, New York Currency or thereabouts for the said Train over and above the sum of £3500 Lawfull money already provided by the Colony of the Massachusetts Bay for that Service which Sums Compleat the whole Estimate of the Train of Artillery, and that Major General Johnson is to Apply to his Excellency Govr. Shirley for the aforesaid Sum of one thousand six hundred and fifty two pounds.

By order of the General Assembly

ABRM. LOTT, junr. Clk.

The action of the assembly of Massachusetts on June 12 and June 13 is of equal interest in this connection. Notes of this action

begun and held at Boston upon Wednesday the 28th day of May 1755, being convened by His Majesty's Writts.

The Committee appointed to take under consideration his Excellency's Message to both Houses of the 6th Instant, have so far attended the Service as to consider the Extract from Major General Johnson's Letter, referr'd to in his Excellency's said Message, and report as their humble Opinion.

That a Sum not exceeding Six hundred Pounds be granted

were inclosed by Shirley in his letter of June 20 to Robinson, *post*, p. 195. The original papers are in Records of the General Court, 20, 482–484, and are as follows:

June 12. "A Memorial of the Committee of War for the Expedition to Crown Point, shewing that they have not been able to purchase any Gun Powder, nor have any Prospect of doing it soon (all at the Markett having been bought up for the Expedition to Nova Scotia,) and New Hampshire and Connecticut Governments depending in a great Measure upon this Province to be furnished here; Therefore, Praying that the Memorialists may be allowed to take One hundred Barrells out of the publick Magazines. . . . In the House of Representatives; Read and Voted that his Excellency the Captain General be desired to give Orders that Two hundred Barrells of Powder be delivered out of the Magazines of this Province to the Committee of War in order to their being transported to Albany for the use of the Forces employed on the Expedition to Crown Point.

"In Council; Read and Concur'd; . . . Consented to by the Governour."

"In the House of Representatives; June 13, 1755: The House taking into Serious Consideration his Excellency's Message of this Day, to both Houses passed the following Vote; Viz. Resolved that Three hundred of the 1500 Men raised by this Province for the Expedition to Crown Point, be allowed if they voluntarily enlist, to proceed with the Forces destined to Niagara, Provided the Enlistment of the other Twelve hundred Men, to be raised by this Province be compleated, Provided also that the said Three hundred Men be transported and subsisted without any Expense to this Province, and shall be dismissed at the End of Eight Months from their Enlistment; Provided also that the full number of Three Thousand seven hundred, agreed upon to be raised by the several Governments appear upon the Muster at Albany for the Expedition to Crown Point, and are ordered to that service.

"In Council; Read and Concur'd; . . . Consented to by the Governour."

and allowed to be paid out of the Treasury of this Province, for the Service of the Expedition against Crown Point, to be applied towards engaging the Indians of the Six Nations, and supporting them and their Families during the Continuance of the said Expedition; and that the Treasurer be directed to reserve the aforesaid Sum to be always ready to answer any Draughts that may be made on him by Major General Johnson, for the purpose aforesaid, Provided that the said Major General be accountable therefor, and that he draw on the Treasurer for so much only of the whole Charge, as shall be in Proportion to the Number of Troops in the Pay of this Province, compared with the whole Forces of the several Colonies concerned in the Expedition.

That for every Company of Indians, consisting of One hundred Men there be allowed Wages to a Captain at the Rate of Nine Pounds Sterling per Month; To a Lieutenant at the Rate of Six Pounds Sterling per Month, and, to an Ensign at the Rate of Four Pounds Sterling per Month; their Pay to commence at the Time when they shall receive their Commissions.

That the Wages of the General or Commander in Chief of the Forces in the aforesaid Expedition be at the Rate of Twenty five Pounds Sterling per Month, to commence at the Date of his Commission.

That this Province do pay towards the Wages of the General and also towards the Wages of the Officers over the Indian Forces in the same Proportion as is before proposed in this Report it should pay towards the Charge of securing and supporting the said Indians.

Which is humbly submitted,
Per Order
JOHN OTIS.

In Council, June 7, 1755, Read and sent down,
In the House of Represves, June 7. 1755. Read and Ordered that this Report be accepted.

Sent up for Concurrence
T. HUBBARD Spkr.

In Council, June 7. 1755, Read and Concur'd.
Consented to
THOS CLARKE Depty. Secry.
W. SHIRLEY.

WILLIAM JOHNSON TO WILLIAM SHIRLEY

[Extracts][1]

June 19, 1755.

With your Excellency's favour of the 9th Inst. I received a Specification of the Sundrys which your Province have provided and are providing. Herewith I send you a list of those things which are yet wanting or of which there is not a sufficient quantity in the said specification relating to the Artillery, and which I must earnestly recommend to your Excellency may be furnished without loss of time. The Report of the Committee of both Houses, in which they have concurred, and your Excellency consented, I have read and considered and beg leave to observe thereupon,

That the £600 therein mentioned for the Indian Service, is not specified to be Sterling or what Currency. I make no doubt it is the former and that the word Sterling is an omission. In this you will make me positive.

To establish the Indians into Companys of 100 men each with Captains, Lieutenants and Ensigns, is impossible, that sort of regularity cannot be obtained amongst those People their officers must be Interpreters and take care of them in all respects, besides doing their Duty as officers. Ensigns will be needless. You may depend I will employ no more officers than what are absolutely necessary for the service. Herein I expect the Governments will confide in me and they shall have no just cause for reproach.

The Pay set down for me, their Proportion of which your Province is to be answerable for, I submit to, but surely your Government doth not intend or suppose these Wages (as they term it) is to supply me with Equipage, with necessarys, charge of servants and the various other Expences which the Command will subject me to. I am far from intending or desiring a support for a vain or useless Ostentation, but

---

[1] Original, Johnson Manuscripts, 2, 24; printed: Doct. Hist. of New York (Quarto), 2, 386.

they will I presume think it necessary that I sustain the honour conferred upon me with a Decent Dignity; the troops will naturally expect to see it, the officers to feel it, neither my policy nor my spirit will allow me to disgrace the Character I am placed in. The Province of New Jersey have agreed to give Collo. Peter Schuyler who commands but 500 men £300. Currency for his Table &ca. Is not a Secretary, are not Aid de Camps necessary about me, is there to be no Establishment for them; must they be always of my Table?

I supposed these matters would naturally occur to the Gentlemen of your Legislature, and I thought it would with more propriety come from them then be proposed by me. Perhaps thro hurry it may have been omitted in the Report you send me — for the Wages allowed me are I suppose considered only as a compensation for my Time and Fatigue. Tho I make no objection on that head, yet I must on this occasion say, that no pay which even a lavish Generosity might have given me would be adequate to the loss and prejudice I shall sustain in my own private affairs, and if publick spirit had not prevailed with me above all other motives, I should have declined the honour which was offered me. I have already declared to you Sir and permit me to repeat it, that I disavow the least Intentions or desire of increasing my private fortune by this Command. I laid it to account in the best light, that I should be a considerable looser. I am contented to be so as far as I can prudently bear. I am fully sensible and Gratefull for the honour done me, I am ambitious, and if the Plan agreed upon at Alexandria is put into Effect, I hope with the Divine assistance to do honour to my Country, and Contribute to her future Tranquility.

Your Excellency must pardon me for giving you so much interruption on this subject, but I thought myself obliged to be thus explicit.

If the Indians should agree to assist us in our enterprizes, they will throw themselves immediately upon me for their maintainance, which will be daily a very great Expence. If the measures agreed upon against the French,[1] of which in my principal Speech I shall give them some general Notices, should be laid aside, depend upon it, we shall loose them for ever, nay I fear if we are not successful their opinion of us will be very fatal for our Interest. If on the Contrary we should chastize the Insolence of the French, drive them from their Encroachments and maintain our Conquests, I dare prophecy with common prudence on our side, the French will not rule a Nation of Indians on the Continent, and the Inhabitants of these Colonies will reap a thousand fold for their present Expences, and enjoy their possessions in uninterrupted security. . . .

WILLIAM SHIRLEY TO SIR THOMAS ROBINSON [2]

Boston, New England, June 20, 1755.

SIR,

I had the honour to acquaint you in my last [3] that Major General Braddock had inform'd me by letter from Williamsburg soon after his arrival in America, of the plan of operations he propos'd this year, vizt the attack of the French Forts upon the Ohio with the two British regiments, two of the New York Independent Companies and the Provincial troops of Virginia, Maryland and North Carolina, amounting all of them to about 2400 men, under his own command; and the reduction of the French Forts at the Strait of Niagara with the two American new rais'd regiments, which service he

[1] In a letter of June 15, Shirley had written Peter Schuyler that Lt. Col. Thomas Ellison, Johnson, John Henry Lydius and Schuyler were to confer upon the proper measures to be taken to convey the troops destined for Niagara in the expedition under Shirley's command. Manuscripts in N. Y. State Library (1909).

[2] P. R. O., C. O. 5, 15. Printed: Docts. rel. Col. Hist. of New York, 6, 953; 2 Penna. Arch. 6, 245. With this letter Shirley forwarded copies of the Minute of the Council of Alexandria of April 14, Braddock's instructions and letter of April 16, his own message to the Massachusetts Assembly of June 13, and the answer of the General Court to that message, *ante*, p. 190, note.

[3] See Shirley to Robinson, Mar. 24, *ante*, p. 144.

purposed to put under my command. The measures for removing the French from their incroachments upon the Isthmus of Nova Scotia and St John's River were as I had before acquainted you Sir, concerted, and the expedition against the French incroachments at Crown point form'd, before the General's arrival. The business of my own Government (the General Court being sitting when I received His Excellency's letter) and in particular the disposition and orders relative to the two last mention'd expeditions, which were requisite to be settled before I left the Province in order to keep all the preparations going on in my absence, for carrying them into execution in case the General should approve of them at my interview with him, necessarily detained me from setting out from Boston untill the 30th of March. On the twelfth day of April I arrived at the Camp at Alexandria in Virginia, about 565 miles distance from this place, where I had the honour of meeting the General and the same day, after consulting with Commodore Keppell and myself, His Excellency determin'd upon the whole plan which consisted of the before mention'd operations upon the Ohio, at Niagara, in Nova Scotia, and Crown Point, to be executed as near as might be about the same time. The first part of the plan indeed, was in effect concluded upon, and several steps taken in it (the whole corps of the British Regiments, except two Companies, being march'd with their baggage and greatest part of the train of artillery for Winchester in their way to Wills Creek) before my arrival.

The attempt to remove the French from their incroachments in Nova Scotia and at Crown Point were, upon my communicating the propos'd schemes for effecting them, to the General, both intirely approv'd of by him; and an express was thereupon sent the same day, with his directions for Colonel Lawrence [1] immediately to proceed in the former

---

[1] Charles Lawrence was a member of His Majesty's Council in Nova Scotia in 1749. He became Administrator of the government, November 1, 1753; Lieutenant Governor, October 21, 1754, and Governor of the Province July 23, 1756. Major of the Royal

according to the plans concerted between him and me, without staying till the regiments in Nova Scotia should be compleated to 1000 men each for which he had lately received orders. The attempt of the reduction of the French Forts at Niagara with mine and Sir Wililam Pepperrell's regiments (as His Excellency had propos'd in his letter) was at the same time determin'd upon by him, and in order to secure the important pass there in the most effectual manner, it was agreed to have some vessells forthwith built to command the navigation of the Lake Ontario; the care of doing which the Commodore hath committed to me.[1]

According to this plan, the French will be attack'd almost at the same time in all their incroachments in North America; and if it should be successfully executed in every part, it seems highly probable that all points in dispute there with them may be adjusted this year, and in case of a sudden rupture between the two Crowns the way pav'd for the reduction of Canada, whenever it shall be His Majesty's pleasure to order it.

After I parted with the General, I found from the deficiency of Sir William Pepperell's levies, that there was no prospect of his raising more than 600 men by the time that the troops destin'd for Niagara must begin their march, and as two of the Companies of his regiment were order'd to be posted at Oswego upon an expectation that the French would attack it which will reduce them to 1400 men, and that force would in the general opinion as well as my own be too weak an one to secure the pass at Niagara; in my return thro' the Government of New Jerseys, I apply'd to the Assembly which was then sitting there, to permit the Regiment of 500 men, which they had lately voted to raise for the expedition against Crown Point, to join their forces under my command in the reduction of Niagara, and prevail'd with

American Regiment in 1750, he was advanced to the post of Colonel on Sept. 28, 1757, and became Brigadier General in America on Dec. 31 of the same year. He died Oct. 19, 1759.

[1] Braddock's instructions to Shirley for the Niagara campaign are in A. H. Hoyt, Pepperrell Papers (1874), p. 20.

them and Govr Belcher to pass an Act for that purpose, by which means my troops were augmented to 1900.

As the diversion which must be occasioned to the French Forces in Canada by the attack of Niagara, must make a less force sufficient for the reduction of the French Fort at Crown Point than was at first determin'd to have been employ'd in it; before the attempt on Niagara was projected, I thought this regiment might be spar'd from the service at Crown Point; and the General hath since approv'd of this augmentation of the Niagara forces.[1]

It being generally apprehended that the troops under my command would be still too weak for the service at Niagara, as with that pass the French must lose the only *practicable* communication they have be[twe]en Canada and the Missisippi (that lying across the Lake Ontario from thence over the Strait of Niagara to Lake Erie, and over that into the River Ohio which falls into the Missisippi), and consequently all hopes of establishing themselves in the rich country behind the Apalachian Mountains, or of maintaining their extensive furr trade there, without both which Canada can be of but small value to them; so that it must be expected they will use their utmost efforts to defend it: this I say, Sir, being the general apprehension, at my return to Boston, the Assembly of my own Government pass'd a vote enabling me to employ as many of the troops rais'd within this Province for the service at Crown Point, as I should think proper in that against Niagara; leaving 3700 in the whole for Crown Point, and provided the men were willing to go with me and the other governments concern'd consented to it. Since which I have obtain'd the consent of all the other governments, but one.

With this reinforcement I shall not have an opportunity of acquainting the General in time to receive his approbation, before I set out for Niagara. But as 3700 men, in conjunction with 300 Indians which we have reason to depend

[1] See note, Johnson to Shirley of June 19, *ante*, p. 195, and Shirley's letter to Johnson giving news from Braddock and other details, Johnson Manuscripts, 2, 3.

upon being engag'd in the expedition against Crown Point, is doubtless a much more adequate force now for the reduction of the French Fort there, than 5000 the utmost that was proposed before would have been when the whole strength that is left in Canada would have been muster'd at Crown Point to defend it against our attack; and are certainly a much more sufficient force for that service than 2400 (the whole of my troops, if they should be increased with 500 more) will be for gaining and securing the pass at Niagara, upon which depends the Southern Dominion now in dispute between us and the French, which is of infinitely more value than the Fort at Crown Point; I think there can be no doubt of his approving it.

In addition to these reinforcements I am in hopes of procuring a number of Indians to join with me at Schenectady and Oswego, which are necessary in the service for scouts, outguards in marches thro' narrow defiles, and to guard the battoes in their passage thro' the narrow parts of rivers and creeks, and gaining intelligence; and as the General could nŏt spare me any part of his train of artillery, I have, with the pieces I have taken from Castle William in this Province, others which I have borrow'd of Governor De Lancey from New York, and some pieces of ordnance which I have caused to be cast within my own Government, collected a proper train for the service.

In my passage back to Boston thro' the several Governments concern'd in the expedition against Crown Point, I had an opportunity of settling several points among them which retarded their movements in it; and I hope the troops destin'd for that service will be fitted out in proper time; they are most or all of them upon their march for Albany the place of rendezvous, and many of them arrived there and on the point of proceeding from thence towards Lake Champlain.

My own regiment began 13 days ago to march in divisions from hence to Providence in Rhode Island government where they were all imbark'd and sail'd five days since with a fair wind for Albany, thro' which they will directly march for Schenectady, without making any halt; and I hope by this time their transports may have enter'd Hudson's River. The New Jersey regiment arriv'd at Schenectady some days ago, as I have reason to hope all the heavy pieces of artillery did, which I have order'd to be immediately put on board the battoes prepar'd there for them, and transported with other military stores and part of the provisions to Oswego with that Regiment before the waters grow low. The two Companies of Sir William Pepperrell's regiment and one of the Independent Companies of New York have been some weeks at that Fort and employ'd in strengthening it and making it as defensible as the very weak state of it will admit in so short a time. Two other Companies of Pepperrell's have been several days detach'd to the Great Carrying Place near the Wood Creek in the way to Oswego, with orders to clear it of any French Indians which may be sent to obstruct the passage of the Creek by falling great trees across it, to guard the battoes as they pass thro' it, mend the roads for the more easy conveyance of the artillery, stores, and battoes over the Carrying Place, and making the passage of the battoes thro' the narrow parts of the Creek more practicable in the difficult places.

The battoes for transporting the forces have been all made and ready at Schenectady some time, together with the stores procur'd at New York and those purchas'd here, and the builders and workmen whom I have hir'd for building the vessells and boats to be employ'd on the Lake Ontario, which must be built at Oswego, have been sent there several weeks ago, and at work upon them; so that I hope to get them upon the Lake before I leave Oswego, which I look upon to be a point of great importance. I have procured seamen to navigate them, and the Officers appointed by the Commodore to command them are arriv'd from Virginia, and are gone with the stores for Oswego to have them rigg'd and fitted out with the utmost expedition. Part of my regiment is order'd to proceed with their baggage in battoes as soon as may be from Schenectady to Oswego, and having now set the forces for Crown Point in motion and settled the affairs of my government as much as I can before I go, I shall set out the 24th Instant for Providence and imbark on board the Province Sloop for New York, from whence I shall proceed in 24 hours after my arrival for Albany up Hudson's River with the remainder of Sir William Pepperrell's regiment now at New York and some levies of my own, which are to join me there; and having settled every thing which remains to be determin'd between me and Colonel Johnson concerning the expedition to Crown Point under his command, and the forces to be employ'd in it, I shall pass on to Schenectady and proceed directly from thence to Oswego, with the remainder of the forces destin'd for that service; and having seen the vessells and boats to be employ'd on the Lake Ontario or at least some of them fitted out, or very near it, and gain'd what intelligence I can and the time will allow, of the situation of the French at Niagara, I shall proceed with all the forces artillery and stores there, as soon as may be.

The New England troops rais'd for the service at Nova Scotia were order'd, before I left Boston to repair thither on the 7th of April, in order to sail for the Bay of Funda, and about 2000 of them accordingly appeared there, and were imbark'd by the 22d of that month, and waited for the arms from England, which did not arrive at Boston until the 17th of May, being the day before my return thither from Virginia; the vessell in which they were sent happening to have a long passage of about ten weeks, so that the troops did not sail untill the 23d of May. Their stay the last month gave me uneasiness. Had I been upon the spot as there were 1000 stands of arms at Annapolis Royal and 800 might have been had here, tho' not so good as those sent from England, I should have chosen to have sent them away before; but I have reason to hope that they will succeed as it is. I have receiv'd an account, dated 15th instant from Col. Lawrence, of their arrival at Scheignecto on the 2d and that he concluded from not having received any news from thence, that they were by that time masters of the Isthmus, and was of opinion the reduction of the French Fort at St. Johns River would after that be an easy task, if the two French

34 Gun Frigates, which he had intelligence were in the Bay of Funda, for the protection as he supposed of that River, should not be too hard for our sea force there, which consisted of three twenty gun ships only, and a sloop of war.

The news I received here four days ago of a French squadron being spoken with off Bank Vert near Newfoundland, full of soldiers standing for Louisbourg, gave me no small concern for the success of the expedition to Nova Scotia; but it was reliev'd in two hours by an account of Admirals Boscawen and Mostyn with eleven sail of the line being spoken with off St. Johns River at Newfoundland nine days ago, close at the heels of the French, and having sent a letter to Capt. Aldrich the Commandant there, acquainting him that they were going to cruize off Louisbourg; otherwise the stay of the New England troops here the last month, might have ruin'd the attempt for recovering the Isthmus, if not occasion'd the loss of the whole Province.

The Acts pass'd lately in the several Colonies to prevent the exportation of provisions to Louisbourg, together with the embargo in Ireland, have greatly distress'd the French at Louisbourg and the effects must be soon felt in all their settlements in North America.[1]

A few days ago I had a letter from the General dated 20th of May from Fort Cumberland at Wills Creek in which he complains that the inexpressible disappointmts he hath met with, hath retarded his march a month beyond the time he at first intended; but by the advices I have since received from Govr. Morris and Govr. Dinwiddie, I hear he hath surmounted his difficulties, and it was judg'd would proceed the beginning of this month from Fort Cumberland for the French Fort called Fort Du Quesne upon the Ohio, which is computed to be from 90 to 110 miles distance from Wills's Creek, where very possibly he may be arriv'd by this time and begun his attack, in which I have little or no doubt in my own opinion of his succeeding, tho' it is pretty certain the French have sent a reinforcement of 900 men (100 of

---

[1] See Act of Massachusetts General Court, June 14, 1755, in Mass. Arch., and printed: N. H. Prov. Papers, 6, 401.

them regular troops) and stores, very lately either to the Ohio or Niagara, and many of their battoes have pass'd by in sight of Oswego.

When I had the honour of conferring with His Excellency at Alexandria, he purpos'd to build some vessells at Presque Isle for securing the navigation of the Lake Erie; which if effected must, together with those designed for the Lake Ontario, make us masters of the Great Lakes and Ohio and the country there, until the French can get a superior force upon those Lakes, which it seems very difficult if not impracticable for 'em to do, when our vessells shall be cruizing upon them. I hear from Govr. Morris that at the General's request he hath establish'd a magazine of Provisions in the back parts of Pennsylvania, from whence he will be easily supply'd by a new road, which he, Mr Morris, is making thro' the mountains to the waters of the Ohio, and which the General proposes to him to extend to Veningo and Niagara; all which, if executed, must be of infinite use for marching the troops to and subsisting them upon the Ohio and at Niagara from a Colony more abounding with provisions than any at present in North America.

The General's presence and activity hath infus'd spirit into the Colonies concern'd in the attempt against Crown Poent, and by the Commission which he hath given to Colonel Johnson for taking upon him the management of the Indian Affairs, and the ready money he hath most opportunely advanc'd to him for engaging 'em in the English Intrest, he has greatly promoted that service. The expedition to Niagara this year is wholly owing to His Excellency's proposal of it.

I am now to acknowledge, Sir, the receipt of your letters dated the 23d and 24th of Jany, and 10th of February the contents of which are answer'd in the foregoing part of this letter, except that I beg leave to observe that in the last mentioned you seem to think that the soldiers in New England are enlisted for His Majesty's service in general terms, whereas it is at present impracticable to raise any number of them without acquainting them with the place of their immediate destination, nor will any born in these Colonies inlist to go to the Southward of Niagara, at furthest. The command under which they are to act, is likewise another very material point with them.

I beg leave further to observe Sir, that the common fund, which you seem to suppose to be provided by the several Governmts in the Colonies for the support of His Majesty's service will never be agreed upon by the Assemblies among themselves, tho' acknowledg'd to be necessary to all; that, and a plan of Union must be establish'd by an authority from home or neither of them will be effected; and this you will perceive by the inclos'd extract of the minutes of Council at Alexandria, is the opinion of the other Governors who were present there as well as my own. And if I might presume, Sir, to suggest my opinion further in this matter, nothing would be a firmer cement of His Majesty's colonies, or go further towards consolidating them in the support of his service and government there, and the defence of their common interests against a foreign power, than the establishment of such a fund and a plan of Union among 'em; nor do I think they would be difficultly recd by them from the Parliament.

You will perceive, Sir, by the inclosed copies of my message to the Assembly of my own government and their message in answer to it, upon the subject of their finding provisions for mine and Sir William Pepperrell's regiments, according to the directions of Genl Braddock's inclos'd letter, and paying their Quota of the levy money for the raising of them, that they refuse to do it.[1]

---

[1] Shirley's letter to the Committee of War as to Supplies for the Crown Point Expedition is in Mass. Arch., Col. Ser. 54, 467. Whether or not Shirley approved a threefold attack upon the French is not clear. It is probable that he would have preferred that the resources placed at Johnson's disposal should have been used for the Niagara expedition. At all events, he makes plain that the expedition was supported by Braddock's authority if not by British troops or money, with which he considers himself poorly supplied. If the Crown will not advance the funds, it must unite the colonies that they may support him.

I beg leave to assure you Sir that I shall consult economy as much as may be consistent with His Majesty's service in the expence of the expedition under my command. I omitted to observe to you before that the reason of my being the Colonel of the two New England Regiments gone to Nova Scotia was principally for the sake of encouraging the inlistmts and saving the expence of the pay of two Colonels, having no expectation of any allowance or pay to myself in it.

I hope Sir, consideration will be had of an allowance for my necessary suite in the expedition under my command, and as the execution of the command will be attended with an extraordinary charge to myself, especially in the rank to which I have lately had the honour to be promoted in His Majesty's army, I hope His Majesty will be pleas'd to order me a proper support in it during the time of the service. The expence of my travelling charges out of my own pockett in my journey to Alexandria and back (being about 1250 miles) tho' I made use of my own horses half the way and my servants the whole, and had some horses found for me in two of the governments, exceeded £200 sterling, which is near double the income of my government to me for the time I was absent from Boston.

The inclos'd copy of the General's instructions will show you Sir, the extent of my command.

My desire of laying before you a particular state of the Colonies with regard to the operations carrying on there against the French, and the very little appearance there is of their forming a plan of Union among themselves, as recommended by His Majesty, in one view, hath drawn this letter into a greater length than I design'd, which I hope you will be pleas'd to excuse on that account.

I am with the greatest Regard
Sir Your most humble
and most Obedient Servant W. SHIRLEY.

The Right Honorable Sir Thomas
Robinson one of His Majesty's
Principal Secretaries of State.

WILLIAM SHIRLEY TO SIR THOMAS ROBINSON [1]

Sir,   Boston, New England, June 25, 1755.

I have the pleasure to inclose you a copy of the letter which I received Yesterday from Lt. Colonel Monckton Commander in Chief of the forces employed in the Expedition for removing the French from their Incroachment in Nova Scotia, giving me Advice of the Surrender of the French forts upon the Isthmus on the 16th Instant, with Copies of the Articles of Capitulation proposed on the part of the French, as also of those granted them by Colonel Monckton.

I hope those Troops will soon be Masters of the French Forts upon the River St. Johns in the Bay of Funda; and that like Success will attend the other parts of the general plan of operations now carrying on for the recovery of all his Majesty's just rights in North America.

I beg leave to recommend Lt. Loring [2] who will have the Honour to deliver my dispatch to you and whom I employed in the Expedition against Cape Breton. he is a Lieutenant upon half pay in the King's Navy, and was made a Lieutenant for his good Services in that Expedition, and has a thorough knowledge of the Sea Coasts in these parts.

I am Sir with the highest Respect
Your most humble
and most Obedient Servant

Endorsed: W. SHIRLEY.
Governor Shirley
    Boston, June 25 1755
Received July 27.

[1] *B. M., Additional Manuscript 32856, 195.* A transcript is in the Library of Congress.

[2] Joshua Loring was born in Boston in 1716 and served as a captain in the provincial service during the Louisburg expedition of 1745. As a result of that service he became a lieutenant in the Royal Navy. He was advanced to the grade of Captain in 1757, and in 1759 commanded on Lake George and Lake Champlain. Captain Loring stood by his king in 1776 and went to England, where he died in 1781, after seeing his estates in America confiscated by the new government.

WILLIAM SHIRLEY TO WILLIAM JOHNSON [1]

Albany, July 16th, 1755.

SIR,

Yesterday I received the Engineer's Report of the State of the Powder in your Stores, with his Opinion that it is not safe to proceed in the Expedition under your Command without an Addition of 64 Barrells, as also your Representation to me thereupon. As I have greatly at Heart the Success of his Majesty's Arms, and particularly of the Command, which I have intrusted you with, I have examin'd into the Stores of the Niagara Expedition; and as I find I may spare you 52 Barrells of Powder out of 'em, which is the utmost I think I can safely do; that the Expedition to Crown point may by no means be retarded, I have now given Directions to Lt Winder who hath at present the Care of my Stores, to deliver immediately that Number of Barrells to your Order, taking a Receipt for the same.

I am, Sir,
Your most Humble Servant.
W. SHIRLEY.

Major General Johnson.

ROBERT ORME TO WILLIAM SHIRLEY [2]

Fort Cumberland, July 18th, 1755.

DEAR SIR,

As so much Business of great Importance was transacted between you and the General, I thought it my Duty to give you the most early Intelligence of his Death, and the Occasion of it.

On the 8th Instant we encamp'd about ten Miles from the French Fort, and upon calling all the Guides, the General, from the Intelligence he could collect, determin'd to pass the

---

[1] Doct. Hist. New York, 2, 391.

[2] P. R. O., C. O. 5, 46. Inclosed in Shirley to Robinson, Aug. 11. A transcript is in the Library of Congress.

Monongahela twice in order to avoid a very bad and dangerous defile call'd the Narrows. To secure our Passage, Lieut. Col. Gage was order'd, about an hour before Day break, to march with a Detachment of 300 Men to make the two Crossings, and to take Post upon Advantageous Ground after the last Crossing.

Sir John St. Clair with a working Party follow'd at Day break, and the whole march'd at six o'clock. Lt. Col. Gage and Sir John St. Clair's Detachments having made the two Passages, the General pass'd with the Column of Artillery, Ammunition, Provision and Baggage, and the main Body of the Troops about one o'clock. When the whole had march'd about half a mile, the advanc'd Party found some French and Indians posted on a very advantageous Heighth, some of whom fir'd upon one of their flank Parties, which immediately alarm'd the whole, and brought on a very severe Firing without any Order or Execution.

The General immediately sent forward his van guard under the Command of Lieut. Col. Burton[1] to sustain the two Detachments, and instantly form'd the Column in such a manner as to secure it, and to be able to bring more men to Act in case of Necessity.

The two Advanc'd Parties gave way, and fell back upon our Van, which very much disconcerted the Men, and that, added to a manner of fighting they were quite unacquainted with, struck such a Pannick that all the Intreaties, Perswasions, and Examples of the General and Officers could avail nothing, nor could order be ever regain'd; after firing away all their Ammunition they gave ground and left the Artillery, Baggage, etc. in the hands of the Enemy.

The General was with great Difficulty brought out of the Field, he had five Horses Shot under him, and was at last mortally wounded, of which he died the 13th Instant.

---

[1] Lt. Col. Ralph Burton was wounded in this engagement, but recovered in time to command a brigade in the Louisburg campaign of 1758 and to become lieutenant governor of Quebec after its capture by Wolfe. He was advanced to a major generalship in 1762 and died in 1768.

I should be extremely happy to have your Directions as soon as possible in relation to the papers of the General, which should go with the Command. As Col. Dunbar seems to think that he has an Independent Command,[1] and as it was always imagin'd that in case of any Accident the whole Command on the Continent devolv'd to you, I shall not part with any Papers 'till I receive your Instructions; I heartily wish you Success, and am with the greatest Sincerity.

Dear Sir,

Your most Obedient, and

most Humble Servant.

ROBT. ORME.

I am so extremely ill in Bed with the Wound I have receiv'd, and Capt. Morris likewise wounded that I have been oblig'd to beg the favour of Capt. Dobson to write this Letter; I propose to remove to Philadelphia as soon as I'm able; from thence to Boston, where, if you should be anyways near; will do myself the pleasure to wait upon you. Col. Dunbar is returning to this Place with the remainder of the Troops and Convoy. As the whole Baggage fell into the Enemy's hands, the Papers the General had with him are all lost.

A true Copy

Examd. WM. ALEXANDER Secy.

Endorsed: Copy letter from Robert Orme Esqr. to Major General Shirley dated Fort Cumberland July 18th, 1755, in Majr. Genl. Shirleys letter of Augt. 11th, 1755.

WILLIAM SHIRLEY TO RICHARD PETERS[2]

Albany, July 23, 1755.

SIR,

At 11 o'Clock at Night on the 27th Inst. I receiv'd your Advice and Letter dated 18th dispatch'd to me by Order of

---

[1] That Governor Shirley had no intention of acquiescing in this claim of Dunbar is seen from his orders of Aug. 6 and 12, *post*, pp. 215 and 231.   [2] Original, Historical Society of Pennsylvania.

the Council of your Government. If Colonel Innes's account is right, it is fatal News indeed; but I think there is room to hope from the account of the Disposition of General Braddock's Army given in the Letter contain'd in Governor Sharpe's; and one from the General himself to me dated from Bear camp the 22d of June, wherein he tells me, that he was advanc'd with 1100 pick'd Men; that at the worst it is only part of the General's Army that is defeated, and that Col. Dunbar had not join'd him, and very possibly, Sir John Sinclair was not with him. In Short, I hope for a better account by the next Advices, as Col. Innes seems to have wrote in an Hurry, and does not mention by whom he recd. his Intelligence: It is nevertheless prudent to act with the same Circumspection, as if the News were true.

I shall set out from hence to morrow for Schenectady, and march with the last Division but one of my Forces the Day following, for Oswego, where I expect to be detain'd some little time: Advices sent by Express directed to Mr. Stephenson of this Place Merchant, will be dispatch'd after me to Oswego or Niagara; and as sending any important Intelligence from the General's Camp with the utmost Speed may be of Consequence to his Majesty's Service. I hope your Govt. will be pleas'd to order what they may receive from them to be transmitted to me.

Be pleas'd to make my Compliments to Govr. Morris, upon his Return to Philadelphia, and let his Honour know I ask the same Favour of him.

> I am,
> > Sir,
> > > Your most Humble Servant
> > > > > W. SHIRLEY.[1]

[To Richard Peters.]

P.S. Excuse my detaining your Express so long; I could not avoid it.

[1] Shirley sent a second letter on July 24 to the same effect. It is in the Archives of the Historical Society of Pennsylvania, and is as follows : —

ROBERT DINWIDDIE TO WILLIAM SHIRLEY[1]

Williamsburg, Virginia, July 29th, 1755.

Sir,

I doubt not before this you have heard of the unexpected Defeat of our Forces on the Banks of Monongahela under the Command of General Braddock, of his death and many more brave Officers etc.

I send you also a Copy of Mr. Orme's and Col. Washington's Letter on that unlucky Affair; as also a List of the Officers kill'd and Wounded: This News gave me a most sensible Concern as I never doubted of the Success of our Arms on the Ohio, as I think we were more numerous than the Enemy, besides having so large a Train of Artillery. But the Battle we may observe is not to the strong, nor the Race to the Swift.

On this misfortune I considered we had four Months of the best Weather in the Year to retrieve our Loss (we have very little Winter here before Xmas) I therefore wrote my thoughts and Opinion to Col. Dunbar; Copy thereof you have here inclosed; on the Death of the General the su-

Dear Sir,

I receiv'd your second Letter late last night for which I am much oblig'd to You. I am just now setting off for Schenectady and can only observe that as I never imagin'd but that the first account you sent me of the General's Engagement had been much exaggerated by Mr. Innes's hurry and Surprize so I can't but hope the next account will be more favourable still and that the General may recover his Artillery with the force Col. Dunbar had behind. Your first Express did infinite Mischief by spreading the Report as he came along. I could wish Caution might be given to these People not to prate. I am

Sir,

Albany   Your most Humble Servt.
July 24, 1755.   W. Shirley.

Richd. Peters Esqr.

[1] P. R. O., C. O. 5, 46. Inclosed in Shirley to Robinson of Aug. 11. See also Colonial Records of North Carolina, 5, 429, and the Pennsylvania Magazine of History, 20, 409; 23, 310; 26, 499.

preme Command devolves upon you, I therefore thought it necessary to send you a Copy of that Letter, believing Col. Dunbar would do nothing without your Orders. Our Assembly meets next Tuesday when I have no doubt of their qualifying me to reinforce him with 4 or 500 Men if you approve of my Plan.

It's very probable that the French will sit down easy and expect no further Attempts this Year, and it's likely that many of them will go to Canada, if so, I hope the Vessels on Lake Ontario will give a good Account of them. If you should not approve of my Proposal, I hope you will Order Col. Dunbar and the Forces to remain on our Frontiers to defend His Majesty's Colonies from the Insults and Devastation of the Enemy; for if he should leave our Frontiers, it's more than probable they will come over the mountains and rob and murder our People. There has already been many flying Parties of French and Indians, that have murdered forty of our People, rob'd them of what they had and burn'd their Houses; I immediately Ordered three Companies of Rangers to go on our Frontiers to resist their Insults, with Orders to kill all the French Indians they met with.

I do not doubt but you will be of Opinion with me, that Something should be immediately done, and that the Forces remaining are not to sit down quietly after the Loss we have sustained but if the Panic that seized the private Soldiers should be removed, after a Month's Refreshment and recovery of their Spirits they may be able to retrieve our Loss, but this I leave to Your superior Judgment.

I think if we remain easy under this Loss it will give great Spirits to the Enemy, and therefore am of Opinion that something should be done while they remain in Security thinking no more will be attempted this Year, they may be the sooner vanquish'd. I send this Express on purpose for your Orders and Instructions on this emergent Occasion and hope you will give him quick dispatch and no doubt your Orders will be complyed with.

I hope this will find you in possession of the Fort at Niagara and shall be glad to hear General Johnson prevailed with the Six Nations to take up the Hatchet against the French, and that he is on his march to Crown Point. We cannot expect to be fortunate in all our Plans of Operations, but the Success of his Majesties Arms in Nova Scotia gives us great pleasure and in some measure eleviates [*sic*] the great loss at Monongahela.

The loss of our Artillery is monstrous, as no doubt the Enemy will turn them against us, I know not how much of them are lost but I think if Col. Dunbar had made a Stand at the Meadows, the Enemy wou'd not have attack'd us in an open Field; But I hear he destroyed every thing that was there, Provisions and all, and marched into Fort Cumberland. As he is esteemed a good Officer, no doubt he had good reasons for so doing; but I am fully convinced, they would not have attacked him there. The People in this Dominion are greatly alarmed and I have good reason to think they will do every thing in their power to forward a second Attempt against the Enemy.

I shall wait with great Impatience for the return of this Express, as the future designation of the Forces is entirely with You, I therefore hope you will give the Messenger all possible dispatch.

Wishing you Health and Success in all Your Operations, I remain with great Esteem, and due Respect.

Your Excellency's

Most Obedt. humble Servt

ROBT DINWIDDIE.

A true Copy Exam'd by
WM ALEXANDER Secy.

Endorsed:

Copy of a Letter from the Honble Robert Dinwiddie Esqr to His Excellency Major General Shirley dated the 29th July 1755. in Majr Genl. Shirley's Letter of Augt. 11th, 1755.

PROCEEDINGS OF A COUNCIL HELD IN THE CITY OF NEW YORK

[Extract] [1]

PRESENT

The Honble James De Lancey Esqr Lieut Govr. etc.

Mr Alexander	Mr Holland
Mr Kennedy	Mr Chambers
Mr Murray	Mr Smith

The Board also took this Opportunity to represent to his Honour the great Concern they were under to hear that the Army was going into Quarters, for that it will probably give the French Army at Fort Duquesne or the greatest part of them an Opportunity to march with the Artillery they have taken from General Braddocks Army, to reinforce the Garrison at Niagara, and thereby endanger the Success of the Expedition intended against that Fortress, and perhaps risque the Fort of Oswego, a post of the last Importance on the Lake Ontario: and as the Season is not yet so far spent, but a great part of the Army late under the Command of General Braddock, may as yet march into this Province, in order to reinforce or sustain his Majesty's Troops under the Command of Major General Shirley at Oswego, or the Provincial Forces under Major General Johnson at Crown Point, they humbly Conceive they may be of much more use in this way than in Quarters. And the Board are the rather of this Opinion because from the situation of places they apprehend the French may be attacked and driven from all the Incroachments, with the greatest advantage by the way of Oswego or Crown Point. And therefore it should seem that not only the Kings Forces to the Southward, but also

[1] P. R. O., C. O. 5, 46. Inclosed in Shirley to Robinson, Aug. II.

those that can be spared from Nova Scotia should Quarter near Albany to be ready for any future Operations.

A true Copy Examined by
GEO : BANYAR D : Cl. Conl.

A true Copy Exd by
WM. ALEXANDER Secy.

Endorsed:
Extract of a Council held at New York on Friday
    the 1st day of Augt 1755.
        in Majr. Genl. Shirley's Letter
            of Augt. 11th, 1755.

WILLIAM SHIRLEY TO THOMAS DUNBAR [1]

[Orders to Col. Thomas Dunbar]

From the Camp on the Mohawk
River 36 Miles distant from the Oneida
Carrying Place, August 6th, 1755. —

SIR,

I am now upon my March to Oswego in order to proceed to the Strait of Niagara in the Expedition under my own immediate Command; and an Express from Govr. Morris having overtaken me here with a Letter, Inclosing a Copy of one from yourself to him, dated July 16th in which you inform him that you are on your March with the Forces late under the Command of Major Generall Braddock, to Philadelphia in order to go into Winter Quarters there with about 1200 Men and Officers, I am to acquaint you that two Expeditions of very great Consequence to his Majesty's Service, are now carrying on, One Against the French Forts at Niagara, and on the Lake Ontario, and the other against their Forts at Crown Point, and on the Lake Champlain; and

---

[1] P. R. O., C. O. 5, 46, and Massachusetts Manuscripts, Vol. 1, Library of Congress. See also Shirley to Dunbar of Aug. 12, *post*, p. 231.

that the French with their Indians are so much strengthen'd, at both places, by the Generals Defeat, and the retreat of the Forces to Pensilvania, that the Troops employ'd in both the said Expeditions stand in need of being reinforc'd.

Wherefore, as the Chief Command of all his Majesty's Forces in North America is now devolv'd upon me by the Death of General Braddock, I think it my Duty to employ the Troops belonging to your own, and the late Sir Peter Halkett's Regiments, in such parts of his Majesty's Service to the Northward, as shall most require their Assistance; for which purpose I have sent you the Inclos'd Orders. I desire you will be pleasd to make me a Return of the State and Condition of His Majesty's two British Regiments, and the three Independent Companies under your own Command, as Also of Fort Cumberland at Wills's Creek, which I doubt not, you will take the best Care you can to have put into a proper posture of Defence.

I am

Sir

Your Most Obedt. Humble Servt.

W. SHIRLEY.[1]

A true Copy Examd.

WM. ALEXANDER Secy.

Endorsed:

Copy

Major General Shirley's Letter to Colo: Dunbar dated Camp on Mohawks River Aug. 6th: 1755.

---

[1] Shirley has been censured for ordering Dunbar to New York, but this disposal of the British forces seems to have been the first effort to offset Dunbar's resolution to go into winter quarters in August. On hearing more definitely of conditions in Western Maryland and Virginia, Shirley at once determined that the frontiers should not be abandoned. See Shirley to Robinson, Aug. 11, following and to Dunbar, Aug. 12, p. 231. No change of view came to Lt. Gov. De Lancey, who would have agreed with Dunbar that nothing more should be attempted in the west.

WILLIAM SHIRLEY TO SIR THOMAS ROBINSON [1]

Camp at the Carrying place of Oneida
near the head of the Mohawks River
Augt. 11th, 1755.

SIR,

It is with great Concern, that I transmit you the inclos'd Accounts of the Defeat of the Southern Forces under the immediate Command of the late Major General Braddock, and of the Retreat, which ensu'd upon it under the Command of Colonel Dunbar, contain'd in the Copies of two Letters from Capt. Orme his first Aid de Camp, one to myself, the other to Govr. Dinwiddie, another from Major Washington to Govr. Dinwiddie, a Letter from Colonel Dunbar to Govr. Morris, one from Govr. Dinwiddie to myself, and another from him to Colonel Dunbar; two of which I received on my March upon the Mohawk's River within these six days, and four by Express from Virginia last night, and beg leave to refer to for the particulars both of the Action, and the Retreat.

From these Accounts it appears to me, that the first of these unfortunate Events is very much to be imputed to the Advantage, which the Enemy had of his Majesty's Forces from the Situation of the Ground, they were posted upon during the Engagement, and their Covert way of fighting in the Indian Manner from behind Trees and Logs; which occasion'd that Panick and Confusion in the Troops, that expos'd them not only to be shot down at Pleasure by the Enemy, but to be destroy'd by each other.

---

[1] P. R. O., C. O., 5, 46. A transcript is in the Library of Congress. Inclosed in this letter are Robert Orme to Shirley of July 18 (*ante*, p. 207); George Washington to Robert Dinwiddie of same date (Ford, Writings of Washington, I, 173); Robert Dinwiddie to Shirley of July 29 (*ante*, p. 211); and Extract of Proceedings of Council of War at New York, Aug. 1 (*ante*, p. 214). For a French account of the battle see 2 Penna. Arch. 6, 256. See also Winthrop Sargent, History of Braddock's Expedition, Philadelphia, 1855, and Shirley to Robinson, Nov. 5, *post*, p. 315. Other letters mentioned as inclosed are here omitted.

The Subsequent Retreat must, I suppose, be attributed to the Continuance of the Panick which had seiz'd the Men. This Blow must Operate very much to the Prejudice of the English Interest among the Indians, and disadvantage of the other two Expeditions now carrying on against Niagara and Crown point, if not immediately retriev'd by a second Attempt against Fort Duquesne; without which the Retreat of the Forces, and the Loss of our Ordnance and Artillery Stores to the Enemy must leave them intirely at Liberty to employ the whole Force, they have upon the Ohio, and possibly the very Artillery, they have taken from General Braddock, in defence of their Forts at the former of those Places, so that the Reduction of it will in such Case doubtless require double the Strength, it would do, if the French still remain in Expectation of being soon attack'd upon that River; for doing which this Season, I am of Opinion, for the Reasons urg'd by Govr. Dinwiddie in his Letters to Col. Dunbar and myself, and those set forth in mine to Col. Dunbar, a Copy of which is Inclos'd, there is time enough left; and I can't but hope that the Reduction of Fort Duquesne may still be attempted with Success this Year, which I think is of the last Importance to be done, if possible, for recovering this dangerous Wound given to his Majesty's Service at Monongahela, and retrieving the Honour of the British Arms upon this Continent.

As therefore I conceive the Chief Command of his Majesty's Forces upon this Continent is, by the Death of Major General Braddock, devolv'd upon myself, I have thought it my Duty to Send Colonel Dunbar the inclos'd Letter, with Orders to march back the Forces under his Command to Fort Duquesne, as soon as may be.

From the accounts I had receiv'd of these unfortunate events before Govr. Dinwiddie's packet arriv'd here, it appear'd to me most adviseable for his Majesty's Service to send Col. Dunbar Orders to march the Forces under his Command forthwith to Albany, there to remain untill he should receive further Orders from me (which I propos'd to send him immediately after my Arrival at Oswego) for proceeding from thence either to assist or sustain me in the Expedition against Niagara, or the Forces employ'd in that against Crown point, as I sho'd find his Majesty's Service would most require, according to the Inclos'd Copy of my Letter to him dated the Sixth Instant, and you will perceive, Sir, from the Extract of the Inclos'd Minute of Council, that the Governor of New York likewise saw this matter in the same light with myself. These Orders were likewise sent before I had any account whether the Colonies of Pensilvania, Maryland, and Virginia would raise any Reinforcements for Col. Dunbar, or could furnish him with another Train of Artillery and Stores in time to make a second Attempt this Year for the Reduction of Fort Duquesne; which I have reason now to depend upon, so that he may go with a Stronger Force than the General had with him at first, if those Colonies don't fail in their Promises.

I have besides, the satisfaction to hear from the Governor of New York that his Govt hath, since the General's Defeat, voted 400 Men to be rais'd for the Reinforcement of the Expedition against Crown point, and I am in hopes to prevail with the Colony of Connecticutt, and my own Govt to reinforce it further with 1000 Men: The Govt of New Jerseys, I hear, hath likewise voted £30,000 of their Currency, of the Value of about £17,600 Sterling, but for the Support of which Expedition I don't yet hear.

As to the Forces proceeding with me upon the Expedition under my immediate Command which consists of about 1200 Regulars of my own and Sir William Pepperrell's Regts, exclusive of about 350 of them which I must leave at Schenectady to escort Provisions and Stores up the Mohawk's River to this Place from time to time; to guard this Carrying place, and to garrison Asswego [sic]; 400 New Jersey Irregulars, 50 Albany Scouts, whom I have been oblig'd to hire, and 100 Indians, which I already have, and may further pick up in my passage thro' the country of the Six Nations, amounting in the whole to 1750 Men, whether I say, Sir, they are now sufficient for the Reduction of Virginia, will depend upon the Intelligence, I shall receive on my Arrival at Oswego (where I hope to be by the 16th or 17th Instant) of the Strength of the French at that place.

I beg leave to assure you, Sir, that I most ardently wish the Intelligence may be such, as to render it adviseable for me to make an immediate Attempt for the Reduction of it; and nothing will give me an higher pleasure than to be instrumental in retrieving the Loss which his Majesty's Service hath sustain'd in the late unhappy Action near the Banks of the Monongahela.

For gaining Intelligence of the Strength and Circumstances of the French at Niagara, I have employ'd two trusty intelligent Indians, and two Albany Traders who are to accompany them in Indian Disguise, all extremely well qualify'd for the Purpose, and who yesterday morning set out for that Place, and may, I hope, meet me at Oswego in fifteen days at furthest from this Date, with a discovery of the Situation and designs of the French both there and upon the Ohio.

At all Events, if thro' Col. Dunbar's being by any Accident prevented from marching the Forces under his Command to Fort Duquesne, according to the Orders sent him, and my Intelligence of the Strength of the French at Niagara, it should appear to be a rash Proceeding for me to attempt the Reduction of the Fort there this Season with the Forces I have with me; and it would hazard not only the loss of the Troops, but of Oswego itself to the French which must be the Consequence of the other, and an irretrievable Misfortune to his Majesty's Service, yet I have the Satisfaction to be perswaded, that I shall be able with the Naval Force, I have upon the Lake Ontario to cut off the Return of the French from their Forts on the Ohio as well as at Niagara this year as also from being supply'd with Provisions from Montreal, and so Starving their Garrisons there this Winter, of Strengthening Oswego in such manner as to make it defensible against the Attempt of the Enemy, and wholly cutting off the French from the Navigation of the Lake Ontario, all which if effected this Year, will lay a foundation for such early Operations the next Spring, as must irresistibly secure the Dominon of the whole Southern Country to his Majesty in a few months.

The Business, which [is] the Dispatches I am indispensably oblig'd to finish for the several Governments, both to the Westward and Northward before I leave this Place, which must be tomorrow Morning, will not permit me to enlarge on this Letter, so much as I could wish to do, But I shall have the Honour of writing further to you, Sir, upon my next Halt, which will be at Oswego in a few days.

I am with the greatest Respect
Sir,
Your most Humble, and
most Obedient Servant

W. SHIRLEY.

Rt. Honble Sir Thomas Robinson Knt of the Bath⎫
one of his Majesty's principal Secretaries of State.⎰

Endorsed:
> Camp at the Carrying Place
> of Oneida, near the Head
> of the Mohawk's River.
> Augt. 11th 1755.
> R. Octr. 3d.   MAJR. GENL. SHIRLEY.

WILLIAM SHIRLEY TO SIR THOMAS ROBINSON [1]

Camp on the Great Carrying Place of Oneida near the Head of the Mohawk's River, August 12th, 1755.

SIR,

In my Letter of the 11th Instant I informed you of the Defeat of the Forces under the immediate Command of the late Major General Braddock; and as the advanced Season of the Year, and the long March I am upon, make it uncertain whether I shall have another Opportunity, after leaving

[1] P. R. O., C. O. 5, 46.   A transcript is in the Library of Congress.

this place, of writing in time for me to receive an Answer so soon as His Majesty's Service may require, I thought it better to make use of this Opportunity to lay before you the present State of His Majesty's Forces in these Colonies, and what Plan of Operations I humbly apprehend may best Suit His Service this Year, and the ensuing Spring, than to stay until my Arrival at Oswego, as I mentioned in my Letter of Yesterday's Date I should do.[1]

[1] The letters of Shirley to Robinson of Aug. 11 and 12 were summarized (for the use of the Government at London ?) and are preserved in that form among the Additional Manuscripts in the British Museum. Few letters from Shirley present more adequately his views as to the needs for a vigorous American Campaign, and his plan of operations may be profitably compared with the lines along which success was obtained four years later. Because of their importance and to illustrate the method of condensed despatches the summary is here given. It is from *B.M. Additional Manuscript 33,029, 198.* See also the later letter to Robinson of Sep. 28, *post*, p. 289.

Account of Braddocks Defeat — has taken the Command in America — Sent Orders, at first to Dunbar to come with the Forces to Albany, and waite there till he heard farther; But, on receiving Letters from Virginia, representing the defenceless State of that Colony, and promising great Assistance from thence and the neighbouring Governments had ordered Dunbar to make another Attempt against Fort Du Quesne, but if he should find that Step impracticable, to obey the former Orders to come to Albany.

New York has voted 400 Men for Crown Point — hopes Connecticut and Massachusets Bay will vote 1000. more. New Jersey has voted £30,000. Currency, about £17,000. Sterling, but uncertain for which Expedition.

Shirley's own Force is 1200. Regulars of his own and Pepperell's, exclusive of 350, left at Shenectady to escort Provisions etc. — 400. Irregulars from New Jersey — 50 Albany Scouts, and 100 Indians, of whom he hopes to pick up more Doubtful, whether they are sufficient for Niagara; — has sent some proper Persons to procure Intelligence.

M. G.
Shirley
Aug. 12th.
Oneida.
Recites Orders, already received for raising Men, Vizt. to Compleat the Several Regts. to 1000, and to raise 2000, over and above in the Massachusets, by Sir Thomas Robinson's Letter of Febry 10th. — Which 2000. Men, Mr. Shirley understands, exclusively of the like Number, raised under Colonel Monckton for Nova Scotia, who were inlisted for one Year, which expires in

CORRESPONDENCE OF WILLIAM SHIRLEY

As to the former Article, In the Letter I had the Honour to receive from you dated the 10th February last you acquainted me, it was His Majesty's Pleasure "that I should raise 2000 Men exclusive of the Number requisite for my

Febry or March, — the present State of the Forces is. Regular 1300 wanted for the Regimts. in Nova Scotia; — 1000. Forces. for Dunbar and Halkets; — 450. for Shirley's and Pepperell's — Hopes to raise all these Men in the Winter, including the 2000. ordered as above.

Regular Forces.
1300.
1000.
450.
2,750.

The Provincial Troops consist of 9. Regimts. making about 4000. Men, — those from New Jersey Provincials. 450. are with Shirley, — the Rest gone to Crown Point, They are only inlisted for Six Months. — Don't know the State of the North Carolina, Virginia and Maryland Troops; — Thinks they do not exceed 1000, raised for a Short time.

Nova Scotia being Secured; the principal Business is Plan of to reduce the Forts on the Great Lakes Erie and Huron, Operations. and Missilimackinack, which would secure the Western Colonies, reduce the Country behind the Apalackean Mountains, and make Canada of little Use, by cutting off the French Trade with the Indians, and preventing the Junction of Canada with the Mississippi.

This may be done by cutting off the Communication, by the Lakes Erie and Ontario. The French would have another Route by the River Outawaies and Missilimackinack, but it being a difficult Passage of 6 Months and only for light Canoes, would be of little or no Use.

A Naval Force on the Lakes being necessary for Naval this Purpose, Mr. Shirley has built two Schooners of 60. Force on Tons each, and 2 Row Gallies of 20. Tons as Tenders, the Lakes with some Whale Boats for Lake Ontario; Had already Braddock succeeded, he would have built one, or ordered. more Vessels at Presqu' Isle, for Lake Erie.

The French can never carry on their Communication without a Superior Naval Force on Ontario, even tho' they keep Niagara and Frontenac, while the English keep Oswego. If the French lose Niagara and Frontenac, they will have no Fort on Lake Ontario; Mr. Shirley don't think it would be adviseable to keep a Garrison at Frontenac, being so near Montreal; but a strong Fort at Niagara will be necessary, and also to secure the Navigation of Lake Erie, and take the French

own and Sir William Pepperrell's Regiments, and for the Augmentation of the five Regiments mentioned in your Letter of the 23d past, to one thousand Men each" and "that I should make no other use or Disposition of these additional two thousand Men, nor of those ordered in your former Letters, than such as should be particularly directed by Major General Braddock."

In Consequence of your Letters to myself and Colonel

Fort at Detroit, between that Lake and Lake St. Clair and to open a Passage into Lake Huron, after which the Forts on the Ohio, and Oubasch would easily be reduced, and also Missilimackenack (if necessary) which would cut off all Communication between Canada and Mississippi.

Importance of Oswego. The Length and Difficulties of the March to Oswego, will not admit the Execution of the Plan this Year, especially as Oswego must be put in a State of Defence against any Attempt from Frontenac, which is only 50. Miles distant. The Security of Oswego is of the greatest Importance, It being the only Opening the English have on the Lake, and should the French take it, It would make them entire Masters of the Trade and Navigation, and greatly endanger New York.

6000. Men for the Execution of Shirley's Plan. Mr. Shirley thinks, He shall have the Start of the French in the Naval Force, and provided the Operations are begun early in the Spring, that the whole Plan may be executed, and that Six Regimts. of 1000. each will be sufficient against any Force the French can bring.

Manner of Providing the 6000. Men. For this purpose, Shirley's and Pepperell's Regimts. to winter at Oswego; — Dunbar's and Halket's to proceed as early as may be next Year to Albany and Oswego. These Regimts. when compleated will be 4000., and the 2000., Ordered to be raised, over and above other Services, will make the 6000.

Additional Vessels for the Lakes. There will be also wanted one or more Vessels of 80. Tons for Ontario; — and a Sloop of 60., a Row Galley of 20., and a few Whale Boats for Lake Erie. The above Force, Mr. Shirley thinks will be sufficient.

Endorsed:

M. G. Shirley Augst. 11, and 12. The 1st. contains the Orders sent to Dunbar, on Braddock's Defeat. The 2d. Plan of Operations for destroying the French Settlements on the Lakes.

Lawrence, Lieutt. Govr. of Nova Scotia dated 5th July, containing His Majesty's Instruction to us "forthwith to concert Measures for attacking the French Forts in Nova Scotia." I had, before I went from Boston to meet the General, rais'd 2000 Men for that special Service, and given Orders that the Officers and Men should hold themselves in readiness to proceed to Nova Scotia in the beginning of April; and upon my laying these Measures before General Braddock at Alexandria for his directions thereupon, he immediately gave Orders for carrying every part of the Plan into Execution in the manner concerted by me and Mr. Lawrence. The 2000 Troops accordingly proceeded to Nova Scotia, and you are already acquainted Sir, with the Success they and His Majesty's Regular Forces, which join'd them, had in their Attack of the French Fort upon the Isthmus and St. John's River.

It was proposed on the part of Govr. Lawrence to me to raise the 2000 New England Men for no longer than four or six months, as the only possible means for raising them in time for the Service; But as I then apprehended, his Majesty's Service might, on several Accounts, require the continuance of them in Nova Scotia some time after striking the intended Blow, and that they might be inlisted for a Year, upon the same Bounty, that would engage them for six months, I advised to the inlisting of them for that Term, so that Govr. Lawrence might have it in his Power to retain them until the Expiration of it; which will be in February or March; or discharge them sooner, as the Circumstances of the Service should require.

I have not yet received Returns of the State of the three Regiments of Nova Scotia, or of those under the Command of Colonel Dunbar and the late Sir Peter Halket; but it requires 1300 Men to compleat those of Nova Scotia from their former Complement to their respective Augmentation's ordered by His Majesty, 1000 to Compleat those of Col. Dunbar's and the late Sir Peter Halket's, and upwards of 450 to compleat mine and Sir William Pepperrell's to 1000 privates each, their original Complement; so that I believe the present Deficiency of the seven Regiments exceeds the 2000 New England Men rais'd in his Majesty's Pay, and sent to Nova Scotia, 750, And as I did not receive your Letter, Sir, of the 10th of Feby. till the 25th April, when I was upon my Return from Alexandria to Boston, where I did not arrive before the 17th May ; and 4500 Men were then raising within the Governments of New England, New York and New Jersey in the Provincial Pay for the Expedition against Crown Point, it was impracticable for me to raise the 2000 Men ordered by His Majesty, over and above the Number sufficient to compleat the other seven Regiments in North America, before I set out upon the Expedition under my Command : But I hope to be able to do it this Winter, in time for the Operations of the next Spring, at which time his Majesty's Service will require that additional number of Troops, if the present State of Hostilities with the French continues.

As to the Troops rais'd by the Colonies and in their Pay, those to the Northward consist of nine Regiments, which may amount to 4000 Men in the whole, one of which, vizt. the New Jersey Regiment, consisting of 450 Men, hath joined me in the Expedition under my Command ; the remainder are employed in that against Crown Point, and none of 'em are rais'd for a longer Term than six Months from the dates of their Inlistments.

I have not a perfect Knowledge of the Provincial Troops of North Carolina, Virginia and Maryland but I don't think they at present exceed 1000 Men, and they are all I suppose, rais'd for a short Term.

I come now, Sir, to the Plan of Operations, which I would propose for His Majesty's Service in North America this Fall and the coming Spring.

The French Incroachments being entirely removed from the Peninsula of Nova Scotia, and the Mouth of St. John's River (the Indians of which have made their Submission) and the Sea Coast there being under the protection of his Majesty's Ships, every thing seems at present so far secured to the Northward, as to Make it the principal Business of all His Majesty's Forces in North America, at least on this side of Nova Scotia, to attempt a Reduction of the French Forts upon the Great Lakes, on the Ohio, and the strait of Niagara, Fort Detroit between the Lakes Erie and Huron, and that at Missilimackinack, the effecting of which would not only secure the back parts of his Majesty's Western Colonies from future Incroachments, but reduce the whole Southern Country behind the Appalachian or Alleghenny Mountains to the Crown of Great Britain, and have a further effect, to render Canada itself, of little or no value to the French, as the Cost of maintaining it, after the loss of their Trade with the Indians, of all hopes of making a Junction of their Territories there with those upon the Missisippi by establishing a Line of Forts and Settlements between them, would greatly exceed any Advantages, which the French can reap from the possession of a Country so barren, and of so difficult a Navigation.

All this might be effectually done by cutting off that Communication between Canada and the Mississippi which is carried on from Montreal over the Lake Ontario, and thro' the Strait of Niagara into Lake Erie, and from thence into the River Ohio, which falls into the Missisippi.

There will still remain another Route for them from Montreal thro' the River Outawaias round by Missilimackinac; but as that is practicable only for light Bark Canoes, and a Passage to the Missisippi this way takes up near six Month's, it would be of little or no use.

It is evident, Sir, that for securing the Command of the Lakes Ontario and Erie, and cutting off the French of Canada from their present Communication with the Missisippi thro' them, a naval Force is necessary: towards providing this, I have taken care to have two Schooners of 60 Ton each, and two Row Gallies of 20 Ton for Tenders to them, with some Whale Boats, built for the Lake Ontario; and General Braddock, if he succeeded in his Attempt upon the Ohio; design'd, as I have reason to believe, to have caus'd one or more Vessels to be built at Presque Isle for navigating the Lake Erie.[1]

[1] The thorough familiarity shown by Shirley with the geography of the battle ground of the French and Indian War was one of

The latter part of this Scheme hath for the present fail'd, but if the Navigation of the Lake Erie is secured this Year, it must effectually cut off the only useful Communication, which the French have between Canada and the Lake Erie and River Ohio, at least until they can get a superior naval Force upon the Lake Ontario: This it will be difficult for them to gain, whilst the English keep Oswego, even tho' the French should remain in possession of their Fort at Niagara, and of Fort Frontenac, at the North East End of Ontario; and would be altogether impracticable, if they should lose those Forts, as they would then be without one Fort upon the Lake Ontario, under the protection of which any Vessels of Force could be built.

I can't at present take upon me to say, Sir, that it would be adviseable to keep an English Garrison where Fort Frontenac now stands (that might be difficult against the Strength of Montreal) but only to demolish it; But the securing of the Pass at Niagara by a strong Fort, as also the Navigation of Lake Erie by one or more Vessels of Force, and removing the French from their Settlements at Fort Detroit between that Lake and Lake St Clair, and so opening a Communication with Lake Huron, seem requisite for gaining the Dominion of the whole Country, rooting out the French Settlements, and securing the Indians and their Trade to the English. As to the French Forts upon the Rivers Ohio, and Oubasche, when they are thus cut off from all support from Canada, if they should not fall of themselves, they might be easily reduc'd by Force, as might their Fort at Missilimackinac too (if found necessary) which would obstruct their Passage to the Missisippi; even thro' the River Outouaias, and absolutely cut off all communication by water between Canada, and those settlements.

his strongest qualifications for command. In 1749 he had had a map of the territory from the Great Lakes to the Gulf of St. Lawrence prepared for him (reproduced, *post*, p. 622) and certainly no provincial leader had a more adequate idea of the difficulties of distance and the advantages of controlling the water routes in America than did the Governor of Massachusetts.

The late Arrival of the Deputy Pay Master of the Forces for the Northern District at Boston made it impracticable to march the Soldiers of my Regiment from thence, until the twenty first of May; their March to the place of Embarkation for Albany with their Voyage thither, and their March and the Transportation of the Artillery, Military Stores, Provisions and Baggage from thence to Skenectady took up twenty two days, and their Transportation from thence with the Artillery etc. in Battoes up the Mohawk's River, thro' the Wood Creek, across the Lake Oneida, and thro' the Rivers Onondaga and Oswego, all which being for the greatest part against strong Currents, and abounding with Hills, Rifts and Shoals, makes a difficult Navigation of about 215 Miles, and together with the delays occasioned by three Carrying Places (at two of which the Battoes are obliged to be unloaded, and with the Ladings transported in Slay's by Horses and afterwards reloaded at their Entrance again into the Water): and the necessity of making this March in eight Division's, on Account of the Want of Battoe Men, and Horses to perform it in fewer: All this, I say, Sir, will make it impracticable for all the Forces to arrive at Oswego, before it will be too late to accomplish this Year, the several Operations propos'd in the before mentioned Plan; especially as it will be necessary, before the Troops leave that place, to put it into a defensible State against any Attempts, which may be made upon it, in their Absence, from Fort Frontenac, which is within 50 Miles of it.

It is proper here to observe to You, Sir, that the securing of Oswego is of the last Importance, as it affords the only opening, the English have to any of the great Lakes, the only Trading House they have with the Western Indians, and the only Fort and Harbour, which his Majesty hath upon the Lakes for the Protection of his Vessels, so that it is as much the Key of these Lakes and the Southern and Western Country lying round them, to the English, as Nova Scotia is of the Sea Coast and Eastern parts of North America; and the loss of it to the French (from whom it would be extremely difficult to retake it) must not only make them absolute

Masters of the Navigation of all these Lakes, and Trade upon them, together with the Country to the Southward of them, but let them into the Heart of the Country inhabited by the Six Nations, and consequently be attended with the immediate Defection of all those Castles to the French Interest: and in such Case we have the greatest reason to expect, the French will very speedily have a strong Fort upon the Great Carrying Place at the Head of the Mohawk's River which would be soon followed by the loss of Albany and Hudson's River; the Consequence of which must in a short time prove fatal to the whole Province of New York.

Oswego being secur'd, a sure Foundation will be lay'd for finishing, the next Summer, such parts of the before mentioned Plan, as can't be accomplish'd this Fall, provided the Operations are begun early in the Spring with a proper Force: and I think, as we shall or may have the Start of the French in our Naval Force upon the Lake Ontario, that six Regiments of 1000 Men each would be a sufficient Strength to accomplish every thing against any Force, the French will probably be able to bring upon the Lake Ontario from Canada; or muster up in any of their Garrisons upon those Lakes or the Ohio to oppose us.

For furnishing this force in time next Spring, I propose, Sir, to leave my own and Sir William Pepperrell's Regiments, in Winter Quarters at Oswego, which will save the Fatigue and Expence of their going back to Boston, New York and Philadelphia this Year, and returning here in a few Months; and to order the two Regiments under the Command of Col. Dunbar, and the late Sir Peter Halket to March as early as may be the next Year to Albany and from thence proceed to Oswego, and join the other Forces as soon as possible. These four Regiments being recruited to their full Complement, as I hope they may be in the Winter, will produce 4000 Men, and the 2000 Ordered by His Majesty to be rais'd, exclusive of the Number requisite to compleat these and the three Regiments posted in Nova Scotia to 1000 each, will make 6000 Men, and together with one more Vessel of Eighty Ton upon the Lake Ontario, and a Sloop of 60, with a small Row

Galley of 20 Ton for the Lake Erie, and a few Whale Boats, will in my Opinion be a sufficient Force, if properly exerted early in the beginning of the Summer, to secure the Dominion of the Southern and Western Country, behind the Apalachian Mountains, at least as far as the Missisippi to the Crown of Great Britain by the end of the Year; and I might add that this would make it a very easy Task to break up the French Settlements upon that River the Year following, if that should be His Majesty's Pleasure.

I am with the greatest Respect,

Sir,

Your most Humble and

most Obedient Servant

W. SHIRLEY.

Rt: Honble: Sir Thos: Robinson Knt: of the Bath, } one of His Majesty's principal Secretaries of State. }

Endorsed:

  Camp at the Great carrying place
    at Oneida. 12 Augt. 1755.
    M G SHIRLEY.
R: 20th: Novr 1755.

WILLIAM SHIRLEY TO THOMAS DUNBAR [1]

[Orders to Colonel Thomas Dunbar.]

Whereas by the Death of Major General Braddock the Command of all his Majesty's Forces in North America devolves upon me, and upon advices received from the Governors of Pensilvania and Dominion of Virginia, of the Defeat of part of his Majesty's Forces under the said late General's Command I think it for the good of his Majesty's service that an Attempt should be made as soon as possible for the Reduction of the Forts Duquesne and

[1] P. R. O., C. O. 5, 46. Massachusetts Manuscripts, Vol. 1, Library of Congress. See also Shirley to Dunbar of Aug. 6, p. 215.

Presque Isle with the Forces now under your Command and those which shall be raised by the Governments of Pensilvania Maryland and Virginia or either of them for the same Service —

Now I do hereby direct that upon the receipt of these my Orders (any thing before contain'd in my former Orders to you of the 6th instant to the contrary thereof in any wise notwithstanding) you collect as soon as may be such Provisions, Pieces of Ordnance, Ammunition and Stores as you may meet with at Winchester and Fort Cumberland or elsewhere in Virginia (reserving for the said Fort what you think necessary for the Defence thereof) as also such as you shall receive from the Lieut: Govr: of Pensilvania and Maryland (to whom as also the Lieut: Govr: of Virginia you will be pleased to make application for the same) and those you buried in your Retreat, and after making the proper Dispositions of his majesty's forces under your Command and the Provincial Troops you shall receive, you are immediately to march with the said Troops to Fort Duquesne at which place I don't in the least doubt from your Experience and good Conduct of your safe arrival: and you are to send me as soon as may be a return of the strength you march off with as well as the Artillery Ammunition Stores Provisions etc.[1]

[1] The retreat of Dunbar after the battle of Fort Duquesne was considered a great reflection on the character of the British soldiers. As John Shirley wrote Governor Morris of Pennsylvania on the same date as this letter: (1 Penna. Arch. 2, 387.)

DEAR SIR,

*　　　*　　　*　　　*　　　*　　　*　　　*

I have little of News to add since my father's last letter to You, inclosing Copies of his Orders to Col. Dunbarr, whose Retreat is tho't by many here to be a greater Misfortune than the late Genl Braddock's unhappy Defeat. What Dishonour is thereby reflected upon the British Army! Mr. Dunbarr has ever been esteem'd an exceeding good Officer, but nobody here can yet guess at the Reason of his Retreat in the Circumstances he was in, and some severe Reflections are thrown out upon his Conduct; Some would have him sent with 500 Men to bring back what he bury'd

Upon your arrival with the Forces under your Command before Fort Duquesne you are to beseige it in the manner you shall judge most proper for the reduction thereof and upon your succeeding in it, you are to leave a Garrison there sufficient for the Defence of it, and to proceed with the Forces under your Command to the French Fort at Presque Isle,

with 1500. As for my own part I think one can't be too cautious how they blame on these Occasions, and let the appearances be what they will time shd be allow'd for a fair and impartial inquiry. In the mean time it is a most mortifying and shocking Consideration that so fine an Army shd be beat and intirely drove out of not only the field, but so far ·from it, by abt 500 Indians and French, which indeed is enough to provoke any People to speak what they think. How do you approve of my father's Disposal of the forces remaining with Col. Dunbarr ? I could not write to You 'till that was over, and don't know what to say now. Upon the whole I think it will turn out to be the best Disposition that could be made of 'em : We may want some of 'em to secure this Place and the Wood Creek 'till our Return, and Johnson may now want to be supported; besides which the Mohawks who go with us and Johnson must have their Women and Children and old Men well defended against any Insults from the French and their Indians by my father, and the N. Y. Indep. Compy are at Fort Cumberland. Add to this that they will be so much the nearer the Seat of Action for the next Campaigne.

We left Albany the 24th of July and with great Difficulty got here not till the 8th Instant, the Water being excessively low and our 84 Battoes (for my father wd see all the Powder and Shot up with him) being as deep again as any which went before us : but these were not the only Difficulties we had to surmount; we were oblig'd to stop to confer with the Indians which cost us three days, and we found that instead of Mr. Johnson's securing for our Expedition a Number of men and having them ready, he had lay'd every Obstacle in our way, and had forbid 'em going with us, telling 'em by Hendrick that there was nothing to be done at Niagara, and that such of 'em who prefered going with us rather than to Crown Point wo'd be look'd upon as Cowards. However, by means of Lydius and Mr. Fisher we have got 26 of 'em here ; we had thirty, but Hendrick took away four of 'em, and for a time confin'd Fisher, and we have, and shall have when Col. Mercer brings up the Rear, abot the same Number of Stockbridge Indians, and I look upon abot thirty young fellows from Albany and it's Environs to be as good as Indians. We have likewise engag'd 40 Irregulars to re-

and attempt the Reduction thereof and in Case of success against it to leave a Garrison in it sufficient for it's Defence, both which Garrisons are to remain there untill further Orders.

And in case of your failure in both these Attempts (which God forbid) you are to make the most proper Disposition of his Majesty's Forces to Cover the Frontiers of the provinces particularly at the Towns of Shippenburgh and Carlisle at or near a place called McDowell's Mill where the new Road to the Alleghany Mountains begins in Pensilvania from the Incursions of the Enemy untill you shall receive further Orders.

You will carry Mr. McMullengh and Mr. Orde officers of the Train of Artillery and Matrosses, as also such of his Majesty's Independent Companies now posted at Fort Cumberland as you shall think proper with you to Fort Duquesne.

Lastly if thro' any unforeseen Accident it shall become absolutely Impracticable for you to put these Orders in Execution which yet I hope can't be the case, then you are forthwith to follow my former Orders of the 6th instant.

W. SHIRLEY.

A true Copy Examd.
WM. ALEXANDER Secy.

Endorsed:
Majr. General Shirley's
Orders to Colonel Dunbar
Dated August 12 : 1755.

main on this Place well arm'd to help keep this and the Creek 'till we Return. We go from hence to-morrow, and expect to be at Oswego in 4 days afterwards. Col. Mercer will be six days behind us, and we can't have less than six more to fit out from Oswego after he joins us, so that we shan't be before Niagara 'till the 1st Week in the next month.

WILLIAM SHIRLEY TO WILLIAM WILLIAMS [1]

[Instructions for Captain Williams]

The Great Carrying Place
August 12, 1755.

You are as soon as Capt. Marcus Petri arrives here with his Company, to Collect the Detachment that Came under your Command from New York at the East end of this Carrying place and there remain encamp'd till further orders.

You are to use your best endeavours to protect the Stores and provisions going over this Carrying place from any attempts of the French or their Indians, and to forward what Stores and provisions may come here for the forces on Lake Ontario, to Oswego with the utmost dispatch,

You are to keep twenty Battoes with a proper Number of Battoe men constantly employed in bringing provisions and stores from Johan Jost Herkimer to this place and also 30 Battoes in Carrying the same from Wood Creek to Oswego, you shall be furnished with a power to Impress men if Necessary for this Service, and you are to keep the Slay men employed in Carrying the same from hence to the other end of the Carrying place, and to keep exact accounts of what provisions and Stores come here, what you send to Oswego, and of the Service of the Battoe men and Slay men, employed in the Same, and as none are to be paid for the future without your Certificate of their work, you are from time to time to give them proper Certificates of the same, and you are to give such Certificates to none who quit their work without your leave.

And lastly you are from time to time to send me exact returns of the State of your Command and of what provisions and Stores are with you.

W. SHIRLEY.

Endorsed:
Genl. Shirley's orders
Augt. 12, 1755 —

By his Exys. Command
WM. ALEXANDER Secy.

[1] P. R. O., C. O. 5, 46. A transcript is in the Library of Congress.

WILLIAM SHIRLEY TO HORATIO SHARPE [1]

> Camp on the Great Carrying Place
> between the Mohawk River and the
> Wood Creek

> August 13th, 1755.

SIR,

I have but a few Minutes time before I proceed on my March, to write and inclose you a Copy of the Letter and Orders sent to Col. Dunbar.

The Successful Execution of them will be of the last Importance to his Majesty's Service.

It will now, Sir, depend upon your own Government and those of Pensilvania and Virginia, to assist him with Reinforcements, — Provisions, Ammunition, Artillery, Ordnance Stores, Carriages, Horses and all other things, necessary to fit him out for his March, and the Service he is ordered upon. And I have wrote to the same Effect to Govr. Dinwiddie and Morris, whose Assistance with your own I must entirely rely upon at this Extraordinary Crisis.

As to the Expence of the necessary Supplies your Honour I know and his Majesty's two other Governors will do the Crown all the Justice you can, in getting your respective Assembly's to bear the whole, or as great a part of it as is possible; the remainder of it I must for the good of his Majesty's Service which is now at Stake, submit to draw upon the Deputy Pay Master for, which you may depend upon it I will, trusting that the Government at Home will take proper Measures for reimbursing the Crown from the Colonies.

I am with great regard and Esteem,
> Sir,
> Your Honour's most Humble
> and most Obedt. Servt.

> W. SHIRLEY.

The Honble. Horatio Sharpe Esqr.

[1] Original, Historical Society of Pennsylvania.

WILLIAM SHIRLEY TO THOMAS DUNBAR [1]

Camp at Canada Creek, August 14, 1755.

SIR,

It appearing to me from several Lists which have been transmitted me of the Officers of his Majesty's two Regiments of foot under the respective Command of yourself and the late Sir Peter Halket who were kill'd in the late Action near the Banks of the Monongahela under the Command of the late Major General Braddock that it is necessary for the good of his Majesty's present Service that the great number of Vacancies occasion'd by the Death of those Officers should be fill'd up as soon as may be by Appointmts to take place until his Majesty's pleasure shall be further known which cannot be done in the most regular and effectual manner until you shall make me a return of the officers of the afore-sd Regimts distinguishing those who were kill'd in the Said late Action or are dead of the wounds receiv'd in it, you are hereby directed to make me such Return with the several Ranks of those Officers, and seniority of their respective Commissions in such Ranks, and in the mean time the eldest Lieutenant or Lieutenants in each of the sd Regiments are ordered to do Duty as Captains therein in the room of such Captains as are Killed, and the eldest Ensign or Ensigns to do Duty as Lieutents in their Room until further order.

I am,
Sir,
Your most humble Servant
W. SHIRLEY.

A true Copy examin'd
by
WM. ALEXANDER Secy.

Endorsed: Copy Major General Shirley's letter to Col Dunbar dated Camp at Canada creek, Augst. 14. 1755.

[1] P. R. O., C. O. 5, 46. A transcript is in the Library of Congress.

WILLIAM SHIRLEY TO SIR THOMAS ROBINSON[1]

[Abstract, Plan for the reduction of Canada]

M. G. Shirley August 15th, from Oneida. Plan for the Reduction of Canada.

This Plan is founded on One, laid during the last War; but Mr. Shirley thinks it would bear some Alterations, and therefore proposes,

That the King should Allot the Number of Men to be raised by each Province:

Virginia	2500.
Maryland	1000.
Pensylvania	2000.
New Jersey	1000.
New York	1200.
Connecticut	1200.
Massachusets	2000.
Rhode Island	500.
New Hampshire	300.
	11,700.

This would probably bring into the Field . . .	11,000.
The 4 Regiments of Halket, Dunbar, Shirley and Pepperell	4,000.
Last Number Order'd to be raised	2,000.
Four Independt. Companies at New York . . .	400.
Total	17,400.

[1] *B. M., Additional Manuscript 33029, 202.* A transcript is in the Library of Congress. The original letter of which this is an abstract is of 3200 words and is in P. R. O., C. O. 5, 46. This plan proposed by Shirley loses nothing when compared with that adopted by William Pitt in 1759, and carried out by Amherst, Prideaux, and Wolfe supported by an ample naval force. Pitt, indeed, worked along the very lines here proposed. Particularly noticeable is Shirley's argument that with the French driven from Canada the English Colonies could defend themselves. Twenty years later, with a population corresponding to the governor's estimate, they did so.

The Governors to be Nominal Colonels of the Provincial Troops, which would be a Saving and also encourage the Inlisting.

Arms, Powder, Artillery, Ordnance Stores, and Cloathing, or Materials for it, to be sent over early in the Spring.

Each Captain to be chargeable for the Return of the Arms of his Company to the Kings Magazines at Williamsburg, Boston, and New York.

A squadron, with five or six regiments from England to rendezvous at Halifax, early in the Spring, and proceed up the River St. Lawrence to Quebec.

3000 New England Men to go up the Kennebeck, and down the Chaudiere; destroy the French Settlements there; cross the River St. Lawrence, and join the English Regiments before Quebec.

3000 more to go from Oswego, cross the Lake Ontario, and thro' the River Iroquois, (which falls into the River St. Lawrence) to the Island of Montreal. And the remaining 11,400 to go thither by Lake Champlain, in which March the strongest Opposition is to be expected. Upon carrying Montreal, a Reinforcement may be sent to Quebec.

Embargoes in all the Colonies to prevent the Exportation of Provisions.[1]

Mr. Shirley, in this Letter, enters into long Reasonings on the many Advantages of taking Canada, and driving the French entirely out of No. America; and as to the Expence of Maintaining such a large Acquisition, He thinks a less Force will be Sufficient, than what is now necessary to defend the Frontiers against the Encroachments of the French, and the Depredations of their Indians; and Mr. Shirley imagines that a Body of 3000 Men, including the

---

[1] The manner in which provisions and indeed supplies of all kinds were exported from the English colonies to the French West Indies had been noticed in earlier wars. It was to be notorious before the conclusion of the war on which Great Britain was entering. Could this practice have been prevented by Shirley's plan or by any other it might have been unnecessary for England to have conquered America in Germany. See Stephen Hopkins to William Pitt in Kimball, Correspondence of William Pitt, 2, 373.

four Companies at New York, and that at So. Carolina will be sufficient; — And the increase of the Fur Trade, and the Provinces being eased from any Apprehensions on their Frontiers, will enable them to contribute largely to the Expence of these Troops.

Mr. Shirley mentions a Calculation of the Growth of the People in the Northern Colonies, which He has found right in the Massachuset's Bay; He says they double in twenty Years, and may be now set at 1,200,000.

Endorsed:
M. G. SHIRLEY August 15th.
Plan for the Reduction of Canada.

JOHN BRADSTREET TO WILLIAM SHIRLEY [1]

Oswego, Aug. 17, 1755.

SIR,
I am to acquaint your Excellency, I have just receiv'd Intelligence from Cadaraqui of about 600 Troops being got there from Canada, which came from France this Year, besides a large Number of Irregulars, and that they are now in two different Encampments; The Person, who brought me this Information further adds, that he was assur'd by the Commandant of Fort Frontenac that a large Body of Troops was arriv'd at Canada from France, who, with the General that came with them, were to be in a small time at

---

[1] P. R. O., C. O. 5, 46.   Inclosed in Shirley to Robinson, Sept. 19, 1755.   A transcript is in the Library of Congress.   John Bradstreet served as Lieutenant Colonel in the Louisbourg Expedition of 1745.   After receiving a captain's commission in the Regulars, he was appointed Lieutenant Governor of St. Johns, Newfoundland in 1746.   He served in the campaigns of 1755 and 1756 and was advanced to a Lieutenant Colonelship of Regulars in December, 1757.   Bradstreet served as Deputy-Quarter-Master-General under Shirley, and Fort Frontenac surrendered to him in August, 1758.   Successively promoted to a Colonelship in 1762 and to be Major General ten years later, Bradstreet died at New York in 1774.

Cadaraqui, and that as soon as they were arriv'd, with a considerable Body of Indians, which was certainly expected, an Express was to be immediately sent from thence to Niagara to inform the Officer, who commanded the 500 Men, who had been disappointed in the Surprize of this Place in July last, of their being there, and of the Day they were to set out to attack this Place, that they might, with all the Indians, they could collect from that Quarter set out at the same time, and join the French General here.

I have the Honour to be with great Respect,
Your Excellency's most Obedient
and most humble Servant.

JNO: BRADSTREET.

His Excellency General Shirley, etc. etc.
Examd. by WM. ALEXANDER Secy.

Endorsed:
Copy
Letter from Captain
Bradstreet to Major
General Shirley dated
Oswego Augst. 17th 1755.
in Majr. Genl. Shirley's
Letter of Sepr. 19th 1755.

SIR THOMAS ROBINSON TO WILLIAM SHIRLEY[1]

Whitehall, 28th August, 1755.

SIR,

Major General Braddock having been unfortunately killed in the late defeat of His Majesty's forces under his command on the Monongahela on the 9th of last month, and the Lords Justices being well satisfied with your diligence and activity in the several operations wherein you have been hitherto employed, they are pleased to order you to take for the

[1] P. R. O., C. O. 5, 211. A transcript is in the Library of Congress.

present, and till His Majesty's farther pleasure shall be signified, the Command in Chief of all His Majesty's Forces in North America, in the same manner, and with the same Powers as the late Major Genl. Braddock had the said command and a proper Commission will be sent to you by this conveyance. Altho' you are, in many respects, already acquainted with the several Orders, Letters, and Instructions, which have been given, at different times, to the late Mr. Braddock, for his guidance and direction in the King's Service, yet, for your more certain information, I send you inclosed copies of the same; and likewise copies of all his letters to me.

The Lords Justices are pleased particularly to direct you, to make all possible enquiry into the causes and circumstances of the late bad behaviour of the King's Troops upon the Monongahela, and to make as many examples of the most notorious delinquents as shall be found requisite and expedient to restore the Discipline of His Majesty's Forces in America. And it is the Intention of the Lords Justices, that those private men only who shall bring certificates of their good behavior on the late occasion, shall be entitled to the King's Bounty at Chelsea Hospital, of which you will give the proper notice to the Officers.

You will see, by the inclosed copy of my Circular Letter, of this date, to the several Governors of His Majesty's Colonies, that your being now appointed Commander in Chief in North America, for the time being, is properly notified to them, and the inclosed copy of my Letter to Colonel Dunbar will acquaint you with the special orders sent to him for recruiting his own, and the late Sir Peter Halket's regiment, and that he is particularly commanded, and all other Officers bearing the King's Commission in North America, to act in due subordination to you.

I am &c^a.

T. ROBINSON.

Endorsed:

    To Major General Shirley, 28th August, 1755.

SIR THOMAS ROBINSON TO THE GOVERNORS IN NORTH AMERICA [1]

Sir, Whitehall, 28th August, 1755.

The Lords Justices having thought it necessary to appoint without Loss of Time, a Commander in Chief of his Majesty's Forces in North America, in the room of the late Major General Braddock, who was killed in the unfortunate affair of the 9th of last month on the Monongehla; I am to acquaint you that Major General Shirley is ordered to take upon him, till His Majesty's farther Pleasure shall be signifyed, that Command, with like Powers, with which Major General Braddock held the same, and as Mr. Shirley is furnished with Copies of every order, Letter and Instruction that has been sent from hence, at any Time, to, or received from his Predecessor; you may correspond with him, and apply to him upon every occasion, and upon all points, in such manner as you was empowered to do, to Major General Braddock, and you will not only regularly observe such Directions as you shall receive from him thereupon, But will also transmit to Him forthwith Copies of your whole Correspondence with the late Major General Braddock since his first arrival in North America.

I am, Sir,
Your most obedient,
humble servant,
T. Robinson.

WILLIAM JOHNSON TO THE LORDS OF TRADE

[*Extract*] [2]

My Lords, Lake George, Sept. 3d, 1755.

As I left all those papers which were not necessary to the Military undertaking I am now engaged in behind me I can-

[1] P. R. O., C. O. 5, 211. Inclosed in the preceding letter and printed: 1 Penna. Arch. 2, 764, with date 1756.

[2] Johnson Manuscripts, 2, 199. Printed: Docts. rel. Col. Hist. of N. Y. 6, 993.

not be exact as to the date when I had the honour to write your Lordships with a Copy of my Proceedings at the late meeting with our Indians. I think it was about the middle of July.

* * * * * * *

Governor Shirley soon after his arrival at Albany on his Way to Oswego, grew dissatisfied with my proceedings — Employed one Lydius of that place, a man whom he knew and I told him was extreamly obnoxious to me, and the very man whom the Indians had [at] their public meeting, so warmly complained of, to oppose my Interest and management with them. Under this man several others were employed. These persons went to the Indian Castles, and by bribes, keeping them constantly feasting and drunk, calumniating my character, depreciating my commission, authority and management, in short by the most Licentious and abandoned proceedings, raised such a confusion amongst the Indians particularly the Two Mohock Castles, that their Sachems were under the utmost consternation, sent Deputies down to me to know what was the occasion of all these surprising Proceedings, that I had told them I was appointed Sole Superintendent of their affairs which had given an universal satisfaction thro' all their Nations, but that now every Fellow pretended to be vested with Commissions and authority &c. I sent several Messages and the Interpreters up to quiet their minds, for my military department would not suffer me to leave Albany, as I was marching with the troops under my command, or I would have gone up and should have soon overset all these violent measures. I have at Albany a great number of Letters and Papers which give particular relations of the Behavior and villainous Conduct of these Agents of Govr. Shirley, but if I had them here I would not trouble your Lordships with a Detail which tho' very shocking would be extreamly tedious.[1]

[1] These complaints are based in part on information from Daniel Claus to Johnson as to movements of Lydius and Fisher, the agents of Shirley, among the Indians. Johnson Manuscripts, 3, 17.

I shall only say in general, that a complication of more Scurrilous Falsehoods, more Base and Insolent Behaviour, more corrupt, more Destructive measures to overset that Plan of general Harmony which I had with infinite Pains and at a great expense to the public so lately established, could not have taken place than did in the conduct of these Agents of Govr. Shirley's. I spoke of it to Govr. Shirley, I wrote to him of it, but without Remedy. They pleaded his authority for all they did, and said they had his Commissions, and I can't but presume it must have been done with his knowledge and consent, in which I am confirmed by his letters to me.

The reason or the pretended reason which Govr. Shirley gives for his opposing my Indian management and employing these Persons, is, that I would not get some Indians to escort him from Schenectady to Oswego. I had indeed mentioned it to some of their Sachems, who told me that, as his way to Oswego lay through their severall countries and Oswego itself is in the Senecas Country, they could not conceive there was any occasion for their escorting him, and that when he came to Oswego there was no fear but many of the Six Nations would according to my desire meet him there and assist him. Numbers of the Troops had gone up without any molestation not the least Interruption had been given to any one, the Traders to Oswego were daily going and returning with single Battoes, those who are acquainted with Indian Affairs well know that it would have been the worst of policy for the French at that time to violate the tranquility of the country of the Six Nations. Tis true some small parties of enemy Indians had been discovered between Schenectady and my house, but they are looked upon as a set of free Booters and Govr. Shirley's Body Guard

Johnson was very fearful lest in some way his supremacy with the Indians should be interrupted. An indication of his increasing jealousy of Shirley is his neglect to report to him in full regarding the battle of Lake George or Fort William Henry. See Shirley's rebuke of this lack of discipline in his letter to Johnson of Sept. 19, *post*, p. 270.

would have been a full security to him against any such — even his primier Lydius when I talked to him on this head told me he saw no want of Indians to escort him and that he would endeavour to dissuade him from it.

It is with Reluctance I trouble your Lordships with these matters, but as I have been honoured with a station of great Importance and entrusted with monies belonging to the Crown, it behooves me on every acct not to be wholly silent, and I have said as little as I possibly could to give your Lordships some Idea of affairs for which I apprehend myself accountable to your Board.

Govr. Shirleys conduct not only shook the system of Indian affairs, gave me fresh vexation and perplexity but occasioned considerable and additional Expenses which would otherwise have been saved; the profuse offers which his agents made to the Indians in order to debauch them from joining me, tho' it did not succeed but with very few, yet gave to all such self-importance, that when I urged to any of them who made demands upon me the unreasonableness of them &c. they reproached me that they had refused Govr. Shirley's great offers from whom they would have had every thing they wanted. Under these circumstances and the acct. coming at that time of our unhappy defeat on the Ohio, I was forced to make compliances which otherwise they would neither have expected nor I have submitted to.

My Lords, I will hasten to a conclusion. From Govr. Shirley's late Behaviour and his Letters to me I am under no doubt that he is become my inveterate enemy and that the whole weight of his Power and abilities will be exerted to blast if he can my Character — here and here only am I anxious. Gross Falsehoods (such he has already asserted in his letters to me,) artful misrepresentations, Deliberate malice, Resentment worked up by People in his confidence, whose Interest, nay whose very livelihood depends upon their inflaming him — these my Lords are circumstances which I own disturb me. I am sensible Govr. Shirley has in many respects been an active and a useful servt to the Crown — his rank in public Life will natturally give him consequence and gain him Influence. Were I to lay open in a particular manner the whole scene of my Conduct with regard to the public and him, and from the Papers and Letters in my possession to contrast his conduct with regard to the Disputes between us. I say were I to do this and any one should think it worth their while calmly to peruse and impartially to examine the full state of the Affair between us, I would rest Character, Fortune, and Life upon the Decision; but I apprehend, unless I am properly called upon to do this, such a voluminous appeal would not find either leisure or Patience from those Persons to read it and consider it whose opinions would be of the greatest Consequence, they would rather I believe think me Impertinent and too full of my own Importance. Therefore my present address on this Subject to your Lordships is to entreat you will at least receive those accusations against me which I suspect already are or will be transmitted by Govr. Shirley, with a suspension of your Judgment. If your Lordships are disposed to have the whole amply laid before you, and I live to receive your commands, they shall be obeyed with all possible dispatch.

* * * * * * *

From Govr. Shirleys ill grounded resentment, from the imperious stile he writes to me since Genl. Braddock's death, from his threatning intimations and his temper, I am confirmed in this lesson, that a subordinate power here with regard to Indian Affairs, and a fund dependant upon the will and pleasure of His Majesty's Governours in these Colonies, will be incompatible with my abilities and inclinations to conduct them; and as I have no private or mercenary views to serve, I must humbly beg leave to decline the charge, unless I am put upon the footing [of independence] as above intimated.

I shall always be disposed to take advice from any of his Majesty's servants here, and to be accountable for my conduct to any Judicature his Majesty thinks proper to appoint; but to be subjected to the caprice or political views of governours, I cannot think will ever harmonize with that uniform direction of Indian Affairs which in my humble opinion is the only judicious plan which can be pursued.

Persuaded I am that if the management of Indian Affairs (those of the Six Nations I mean) are branched out into various channels of Power, the British interest relative to them will be unstable, perplexed and in the end, totally lost — this, past experience teaches.

* * * * * * *

I am with the utmost respect My Lords.
Your Lordships most obedient humble servant.

WM. JOHNSON.

WILLIAM SHIRLEY TO JOSIAH WILLARD [1]

Camp at Oswego, September 9th, 1755.

SIR,

I have receiv'd his Honour the Lieut. Governor's pacquet dated 8th of August last, and your own letter dated August the 4th wrote by the Order of the Council, both which give me great Satisfaction.

As I think it would be acceptable to the General Court to know the Situation of the Service, which is under my immediate care; I transmit you the following account of it, which, together with this whole letter, you will lay before them.

The last Division of the Forces under my Command were twenty-six Days upon their march from Schenectady to this Place, where they did not arrive untill the 2d Instant. The Troops are so much reduc'd by Desertion and Sickness, and Absence of Detachments upon Parties and Command, that

---

[1] Original, Mass. Arch., Col. Ser. Letters, 54, 111. Somewhat similar but less complete letters were sent to Horatio Sharpe of Maryland (Printed: Arch. of Md. 6, 280; 31, 76), to Robert Hunter Morris of Pennsylvania (1 Penna. Arch. 2, 405), and to Benning Wentworth of New Hampshire (N. H. Prov. Papers, 6, 432). See also Willard to Shirley, Sept. 15, Mass. Arch., Col. Ser. 54, 132.

by a field Return, which I order'd to be taken yesterday, it appears that the number of men in the three Regiments and Independent Company fit for Duty upon this Spot don't amount to 1400, out of which we are oblig'd to keep 100 at work upon a new Fort, and if the Body of the Forces moves from this Place, must leave 300 at least for the Defence of it, so that not 1000 men will remain for other Service, and of these 60 must be employed as Matrosses, and a number as Pioneers. To this I am to add, that we have suffer'd greatly by Desertion of Battoe men, after being impress'd and even proceeding part of the way with us; by which means we are in want of provisions for any service that will require ten Days in the Execution.

However, if I am not disappointed of Supplies of Provisions, which I hourly expect, I am encourag'd, upon the Intelligence I have gained since my arrival here, that with our Naval Force, and the Assistance of the Indians whom I have pick'd up in my passage thro' the Country of the five nations, and the Albany men, whom I hir'd to go with me as a scouting party of guards (both which may amount to 140 men) I say, I am encourag'd, Sir, to hope that we may proceed upon Action in a very few Days, and that a foundation will be lay'd this year for such a Campaign the next, as I flatter myself (provided the Colonies shall then exert a proper Spirit) may secure all points in dispute between us and the French.[1]

[1] On Sept. 8–11, John Shirley in behalf of his father wrote to Governor Morris of Pennsylvania that he thought both Frontenac (Caderaqui) and Niagara could be taken but not held: "If we take or destroy their two Vessells at Frontenac and ruin their Harbour there and destroy the two forts of that and Niagara, I shall think we have done great things; which together with the making this Place defensible, which it was not before against a very small force, will lay a good foundation for a glorious campaign next Year, when we must take Care to be early enough. As to floating Batteries if You was to see what a rough piece of Water this Lake is with a common Breeze, You would soon be convinc'd there is no possibility of having 'em unless You were to build 'em under the Walls of Niagara, or in the Harbour of Frontenac. I should have mention'd before that it will be thought necessary to

The thought of having a meeting with Commissioners from the Colonies in order to consult upon the most proper measures to be taken for the general Interest of the common cause the next Spring was suggested to me by the inclos'd

leave at least 200 of our 1500 Men here, who may go on with the Works on the Hill and the Barracks on this Side.

The Conference is just ended and the Indians have declar'd in a seeming hearty Manner, that they will be true to him, my father, and follow him where ever he goes. They are certainly a most necessary and useful set of People to have with us, but then they are by far the most troublesome in the World. You can't conceive the difficulties we have had to struggle with in getting up here, and here I must acknowledge the Services of the Albany People, who have given us all the Assistance in their Power, notwithstanding their former bad character, and I esteem a company of about 80 of their young Men which we have with us, to be by much the best Company we have. Indeed the Battoe-Men have deserted us, but a whole County is not answerable for the faults of their lowest Set of Men, tho' most of the English Officers blame Albany without Distinction for the faults of these People. . . . Nobody holds it out better than my father and myself. We shall all of us relish a good House over our heads, being all incampt except the General and some few field Officers, who have what are call'd at Oswego, houses, but they would in other Countries be call'd only Sheds, except the fort where my father is. Adieu, Dear Sir, I hope my next will be directed from Frontenac.

I am ever with a most sincere Regard,
Yours most Affectionately,
JOHN SHIRLEY.

Oswego, 10 o'Clock at Night,
  in a Wet Tent, Sepr. 8th, 1755.

P.S. We sent out two Indians with two of our Albany Men eight days ago, who were within less than half a Mile of the fort at Frontenac, and opposite to the Harbour, where they stay'd half an hour just at noon, when the French were suppos'd to be all at Dinner, as they did not see a Person stirr either in the Camp or fort: They saw the two Vessells very plain and say they are about as large as our two large ones, one of 'em quite new and unrigg'd. As to the Situation of the fort, if they are not much mistaken in the Description they give of the Ground round about it, it is such that I think it must be an easy Conquest. Septr 9th. Two of our Indians have just return'd from Niagara, where they have been scouting and treating with the Ottawa Indians who were returning

Acct given to Govr. DeLancey by Mr. Alexander a member of his Majesty's Council for the Provinces of New York and New Jersey; and as it seems to me a very adviseable proceeding, I desire his Honour would take the first Opportunity of proposing it to the General Assembly for their Consideration; and shall myself mention it to the Govrs. of all the other Colonies as far westward as Virginia inclusive for the Consideration of their respective Assemblies.[1] The

discontented from the Ohio, from whose Accots we have the greatest Reason to believe that they will stand neuter, in Case we attack Niagara. God send us Success that we may get in Time from Frontenac, to go to the other Place where we shall have little to do, and I verily believe fix those Indians who have so lately acted against us firmly in our Interest. We have likewise sent Belts and Presents to the far Nations.

Ten o'Clock at Night, Septr 11th.

We have just receiv'd fresh Intelligence from Frontenac, by which it appears that the French have about 1200 Men there, and they told the Indian who brings the Accot that they were coming here. I suppose they wait for us to go to Niagara first. Our Battoemen desert us in large Numbers, as do the Soldiers who are dissatisfy'd at our being oblig'd to allow 'em no more than half a pound of bread and no Rum. We lost 21 of the latter last Night, 15 of 'em are Schuyler's. Had we but Provisions we might, I am satisfy'd, with our fleet and Train, save the French the Trouble of coming hither, and give You a good Accot of Frontenac fort and their two Vessells.

I am Your most Affectionate,
faithfull Hum. Servt,

JOHN SHIRLEY.
(Penna. Arch. 2, 403.)

[1] The following is the account to which Shirley refers:

Extract of an account of the proceedings of the New Jersey Assembly drawn up, at the request of the Governor De Lancey by Mr Alexander a Member of his Majestys Council for the Provinces of New York and New Jersey and communicated to Major General Shirley by the Governor.

Sundrys of the Assembly heartily wish that a Congress of Commissioners should meet with Major General Shirley at Albany or where else he would be pleased to appoint in October or November next, to Agree on the further necessary Supplies and Forces for next year, that should be provided in the Winter, so that all might

place of meeting which first occurr'd to my mind, for the sake of my own conveniency, as well as on account of the satisfaction it would otherwise have given me, was Boston; But when I consider'd, that in such case we should have had no chance for the Attendance of Commissioners from the Western Governments at a Winter Congress so distant from their respective Colonies, and by that means lose the Benefit of their joining with us, at least in the expence of the measures which should be concerted for the Common Cause, I determin'd to propose the meeting to be at New York, on the 15th of November, at which time I shall be there in my return to Boston, where I purpose to be by the second week in December.

As I think a very early campaign the next year necessary, I have sent orders to Col. Dunbar [1] the Commanding Officer of his Majesty's two British Regiments and two Independent Companies of New York to march directly to Albany where I design their winter quarters shall be, and to leave at this place as many of the Troops now with me as can be supported here during the Winter; that they may be assembled ready to act either separately or in conjunction with such provincial Troops as the Colonies shall think fit to raise against French settlements either upon the Lakes and Ohio which last place is very accessible thro' that Route, or against any part of Canada, as his Majesty's Service, and the General Interest of the Colonies may most require.

I have given orders likewise to have these four Regiments and the four independent Companies of New York compleated to 4400 men by the Spring.

It is a great Satisfaction to me to hear of the Reinforce-

be at the Place of Rendezvous by the first of the Spring, that the Commissioners should be appointed by Acts of the Several Legislatures, but as they are one of the Smallest Colonies they durst not take upon them to begin a proportion for that purpose but will most readilly follow the Example of the other Greater Colonies as far as their Abilities can go.

[1] For the opinion in which Dunbar was held by Governor Morris of Pennsylvania, see Morris to Shirley Sept. 5, 1 Penna. Arch. 2, 400.

ment lately sent to Crown point[1] for strengthening the Expedition against that Place, which I hope may succeed; But whatever the Success may be there or upon the Lake Ontario this year, I can't but hope, if the same Spirit shall be exerted in all the Colonies the next Spring, that hath prevail'd in some of the Eastern Colonies this Summer, that we may then irresistably carry all points, which shall be then attempted against the French.

I am with much truth and Esteem
Your most assured Friend and
Humble Servant

W. SHIRLEY.

Honble. Josiah Willard Esq.

WILLIAM JOHNSON TO WILLIAM SHIRLEY[2]

Camp at Lake George, Septr. 9, 1755.

SIR,

Sunday evening the 7th instant I received intelligence from some Indian scouts I had sent out, that they had discovered three large roads about the South Bay, and were confident a very considerable number of the enemy were marched, or on their march towards our encampment at the Carrying-place, where were posted about 250 of the New

---

[1] See Action of Massachusetts on June 26 (N. H. Prov. Papers 6, 407, and Mass. Arch.), for Connecticut, Letter of Fitch to Wentworth, Aug. 29 (N. H. Prov. Papers 6, 426), for Rhode Island, Sept. 8 (R. I. Col. Rec. 5, 448–455), and for New York, Spencer Phips to Wentworth, Aug. 14 (N. H. Prov. Papers 6, 424). The action taken by Virginia in response to Shirley's letter of Sept. 9 is given in Dinwiddie to Shirley, Oct. 18, 1755 (Dinwiddie Papers, 2, 244).

[2] Johnson Manuscripts, N. Y. State Library, 23, 190. P. R. O., C. O. 5, 46. Inclosed in Shirley to Robinson, Oct. 5, 1755. Printed: Doct. Hist. of New York, 2, 402, where a sketch of the country about Lake George, taken from the Gentleman's Magazine, is given. See reply of Shirley of Sept. 19, *post*, p. 261, where the governor states that it was practically by chance that a copy of this letter, sent in duplicate to other governors, reached him.

Hampshire troops, and five companies of the New York regiment. I got one Adams, a waggoner, who voluntarily and bravely consented to ride express with my orders to Colonel Blanchard of the New Hampshire regiment, commanding officer there. I acquainted him with my intelligence, and directed him to withdraw all the troops there within the works thrown up. About half an hour, or near an hour after this, I got two Indians and two soldiers to go on foot with another letter to the same purpose.

About twelve o'clock that night the Indians and soldiers returned with a waggoner who had stole from the camp, with about eight others their waggoners and forces without orders. This waggoner says they heard and saw the enemy about four miles from this side the Carrying-place. They heard a gun fire, and a man call upon heaven for mercy, which he judged to be Adams. The next morning I called a council of war, who gave it as their opinion, and in which the Indians were extremely urgent that 1000 men should be detached, and a number of their people would go with them, in order to catch the enemy in their retreat from the other camp, either as victors, or defeated in their design. The 1000 men were detached under the command of Colonel Williams, of one of the Boston regiments, with upwards of 200 Indians. They marched between eight and nine o'clock. In about an hour and half afterwards we heard a heavy firing, and all the marks of a warm engagement, which we judged was about three or four miles from us; we beat to arms, and got our men all in readiness. The fire approached nearer, upon which I judged our people were retreating, and detached Lieutenant Colonel Cole, with about 300 men to cover their retreat. About ten o'clock some of our men in the rear, and some Indians of the said party, came running into camp, and acquainted us, that our men were retreating, that the enemy were too strong for them. The whole party that escaped returned to us in large bodies.

As we had thrown up a breastwork of trees round our encampment, and planted some field-pieces to defend the same, we immediately hauled some heavy cannon up there to strengthen our front, took possession of some eminences on our left flank, and got one field-piece there in a very advantageous situation: The breastwork was manned throughout by our people, and the best disposition made through our whole encampment, which time and circumstances would permit. About half an hour after eleven, the enemy appeared in sight, and marched along the road in very regular order directly upon our center: They made a small halt about 150 yards from our breast-work, when the regular troops (whom we judged to be such by their bright and fixed bayonets) made the grand and center attack. The Canadians and Indians squatted and dispersed on our flanks. The enemy's fire we received first from their regulars in platoons, but it did no great execution, being at too great a distance, and our men defended by the breast-work. Our artillery then began to play on them, and was served, under the direction of Captain Eyre, during the whole engagement, in a manner very advantageous to his character, and those concerned in the management of it.[1] The engagement now became general on both sides. The French regulars kept their ground and order for some time with great resolution and good conduct, but the warm and constant fire from our artillery and troops put them into disorder; their fire became more scattered and unequal, and the enemy's fire on our left grew very faint. They moved then to the right of our encampment, and attacked Colonel Ruggles, Colonel Williams, and Colonel Titcomb's regiment, where they maintained a very warm fire for near an hour, still keeping up their fire in the other parts of our line, tho' not very strong. The three regiments on the right supported the attack very resolutely, and kept a constant and strong fire upon the enemy. This attack failing, and the artillery still playing along the line, we found their fire very weak, with considerable intervals. This was about four o'clock, when our men and the Indians jumped over the breast-work, pursued the enemy, slaughtered numbers, and took several prisoners, amongst whom was the Baron de

[1] See Eyre to Shirley, Sept. 10, *post*, p. 259.

Dieskau,[1] the French general of all the regular forces lately arrived from Europe, who was brought to my tent about six o'clock, just as a wound I had received was dressed. The whole engagement and pursuit ended about seven o'clock.

I do not know whether I can get the returns of the slain and wounded on our side to transmit herewith; but more of that by and by.

The greatest loss we have sustained was in the party commanded by Colonel Williams in the morning, who was attacked, and the men gave way, before Colonel Whiting, who brought up the rear, could come to his assistance. The enemy, who were more numerous, endeavoured to surround them; upon which the officers found they had no way to save the troops but by retreating; which they did as fast as they could. In this engagement we suffered our greatest loss; Colonel Williams, Major Ashley, Captain Ingersol, and Captain Puter, of the same regiment; Captain Ferrall, brother in-law to the general, who commanded a party of Indians, Captain Stoddert, Captain M'Ginnis, Captain Stevens, all Indian officers, and the Indians say near forty of their people, who fought like lions, were all slain. Old Hendrick, the great Mohawk Sachem, we fear is killed. We have abundant reason to think we killed a great number of the enemy; amongst whom is Mons. St. Pierre, who commanded all the Indians. The exact number on either side I cannot obtain; for tho' I sent a party to bury our dead this afternoon, it being a running scattered engagement, we can neither find all our dead, nor give an exact account. As fast as these troops joined us, they formed with the rest in the main battle of the day; so that the killed and wounded, in both engagements, officers excepted, must stand upon one return.

About eight o'clock last night, a party of 120 of the

[1] Although in the French service Dieskau was a German baron. Taken prisoner at the time of this attack upon Fort William Henry he was held at New York until February, 1757, when he was sent to England and at length exchanged.

New Hampshire regiment, and 90 of the New York regiment, who were detached to our assistance, under the command of Captain M'Ginnes, from the camp at the Carrying-place, to reinforce us, were attacked by a party of Indians and Canadians, at the place where Colonel Williams was attacked in the morning; their engagement began between four and five o'clock. This party who our people say were between 3 and 400, had fled from the engagement here, and gone to scalp our people killed in the morning. Our brave men fought them for near two hours, and made a considerable slaughter amongst them. Of this brave party two were killed and eleven wounded, and five missing. Captain M'Ginnes, who behaved with the utmost calmness and resolution, was brought on a horse here, and, I fear, his wounds will prove mortal. Ensign Falsam, of the New Hampshire regiment, was wounded thro' the shoulder.

I have this morning called a council of war, a copy of the minutes of which I send you herewith.

Monsieur le baron de Dieskau, the French general, is badly wounded in the leg, and thro' both his hips, and the surgeon very much fears his life. He is an elderly gentleman, an experienced officer, and a man of high consideration in France. From his papers, I find he brought under his command to Canada, in the men of war lately arrived at Quebec, 3171 regular troops, who were partly in garrison at Crown-Point, and encamped at Ticonderoga, and other advantageous passes, between this and Crown-Point. He tells me he had with him yesterday morning 200 grenadiers, 800 Canadians, and 700 Indians of different nations. His aid de camp says, (they being separately asked) their whole force was about 2000. Several of the prisoners say, about 2300. The baron says, his major-general was killed, and his aid-de-camp says, the greater part of the chief officers also. He thinks by the morning and afternoon actions they have lost near 1000 men, but I can get no regular accounts. Most of our people think from 5 to 600. We have about 30 prisoners, most of them badly wounded. The Indians scalped of their dead already near 70, and were employed after the battle last night, and all this afternoon, in bringing in scalps; and great numbers of French and Indians yet left unscalped. They carried off numbers of their dead, and secreted them. Our men have suffered so much fatigue for three days past, and are constantly standing upon their arms by day, half the whole upon guard every night, and the rest lay down armed and accoutred, that both officers and men are almost wore out. The enemy may rally, and we judge they have considerable reinforcements near at hand; so that I think it necessary we be upon our guard, and be watchful to maintain the advantages we have gained. For these reasons I do not think it either prudent or safe to be sending out parties in search of the dead.

I do not hear of any officers killed at our camp but Colonel Titcomb, and none wounded but myself, and Major Nichols of Colonel Titcomb's. I cannot yet get certain returns of our dead and wounded; but from the best accounts I can obtain, we have lost about 130 who are killed, about 60 wounded, and several missing from the morning and afternoon's engagement.

I think we may expect very shortly another and more formidable attack, and that the enemy will then come with artillery. The late Colonel Williams had the ground cleared for building a stockaded fort. Our men are so harassed, and obliged to be so constantly upon watchful duty, that I think it would be both unreasonable, and I fear in vain, to set them at work upon the designed fort.

I design to order the New Hampshire regiment up here to reinforce us, and I hope some of the designed reinforcements will be with us in a few days. When these fresh troops arrive, I shall immediately set about building a fort.

My wound is in my thigh and is very painful. The ball is lodged, and cannot be got out; by which means I am, to my mortification, confined to my tent.

This letter was begun, and should have been dispatched yesterday; but we had two alarms, and neither time or prudence would permit it. I hope, sir, you will place the incorrectness hereof to the account of our situation. I am, sir, most respectfully,

Your most obedient servant,

WILLIAM JOHNSON.[1]

WILLIAM EYRE TO WILLIAM SHIRLEY [2]

Lake George, September 10, 1755.

SIR,

As Major General Johnson is sending your Excellency an Express to inform your Excellency of our Affairs in these parts, I take the Opportunity to inform you, that by his Order I have built a Fort at the Carrying place, which will contain 300 Men; it's in the form of a Square with three Bastions, and takes in Col. Lydius's House. This Work is pallisaded quite round, which is its chief Security from a surprize or sudden Attack; as I was oblig'd to leave that place, and most of the Troops to come here, it was out of my power to make the Rampart and Parapet, of a sufficient height and thickness, to stand Cannon, or the Ditch wide and deep enough to make it's Passage very difficult; however I think 3 or 400 Men will be able to resist 1500, provided they do their Duty, if Cannon is not brought against it. I beg leave to inform your Excellency, that I am of Opinion, its very necessary that a strong and regular Work

---

[1] Parkman notes that Johnson does not mention Lyman in this account although admitting privately his aid in the battle.

[2] P. R. O., C. O. 5, 46. Inclosed, Johnson to Shirley, Sept. 9. Copy inclosed, Shirley to Robinson, Oct. 5, 1755. Captain William Eyre was serving as engineer under Johnson and seems to have considered it his duty to report directly to Shirley. He had been in the 44th regiment of foot under Braddock at Fort Duquesne, going thence to New York. Here he built Fort William Henry at the head of Lake George. Eyre became later Chief Engineer under Amherst and planned the fort at Ticonderoga, after the capture of the old fortress from the French. He was drowned in 1764.

is erected at this place, to keep possession, so far of this Country, and the more so, if it should be found not practicable to go any further this Campaign.

The Enemy by all Accounts are very formidable; and I think it not improbable, they will pay us another Visit soon : if they can seize, and take our Work at the Carrying Place, I fear it would be attended with bad Consequences, as it would cut off our retreat and Communication with Albany, and totally stop our Reinforcement and Provisions from joining us; if another Road could be not found; which I believe is not easy to be met with. I cannot help thinking, that what induced the French, or may induce them hereafter to attack us here, is fearing we would not attempt to go any further, so was resolved to cutt us off before we retired; for surely, if they are a match for us, and dare storm our Camp so far from Crown Point; and consequently from their own Strength, how much more advantage would they have over us, if they waited for our approaching them, and that with part of our force; whilst they could make use of all theirs, besides being posted advantageously; it's certain the Enemy behaved gallantly, and did much more than I thought they dare attempt: however they are repulsed, and their General taken, who I believe to be an excellent Officer, and who we are sure is a Man of resolution. These few thoughts I beg leave to throw before your Excellency : General Johnson was wounded soon after the Action began in encouraging the Troops, and making the necessary disposition to sustain the Attack, the Numbers of our killed, Wounded and missing I presume he acquaints you of, but the loss of the Enemy is very uncertain. I sincerely wish your Excellency Success.

And am
Your Excellency's most Obedient
humble Servant

WILL: EYRE.

His Excellency General Shirley,
a true Copy Exa. by
WM. ALEXANDER Secy.

Endorsed:
    Copy
    Letter from Capt. Eyre
    to Major General Shirley
        dated 10th Sepr. 1755:
            in Majr. Genl. Shirley's Letter
                of Octr. 5th 1755.

WILLIAM SHIRLEY TO SIR THOMAS ROBINSON [1]

Camp at Oswego, Septr. 19th, 1755.

Sir,
    I have the Honour to acquaint you that I arriv'd here the 18th of August.
    I had before receiv'd Accounts from the Commandant of this Fort, that upwards of 1600 French had at several times, this summer, pass'd by in Sight of it towards Niagara in their Way, (as was suppos'd) either to the Ohio, or else to strengthen that Pass; and that in the Month of July part of them, vizt: 300 French and 200 Indians had encamp'd within five Miles of this Fort, with a Design, as the Commandant thought, to attack it, but that finding the Garrison too strong for their Force, they pass'd on towards Niagara.
    The Night before my Arrival I receiv'd by Express from the Officer here an Account that an Onondaga Indian, who had arriv'd three Days before from Fort Frontenac, which is situated on the North East Edge of the Lake Ontario, (call'd also Cadaraqui) and about 50 Miles distant from this Place, had brought Intelligence, that the French design'd very suddenly to attack Oswego from thence; the Particu-

[1] P. R. O., C. O. 5, 46. A transcript is in the Library of Congress. See also Shirley to Col. Thomas Dunbar of equal date. Extract is in 1 Penna. Arch. 2, 417–418. A copy of Shirley's orders to Dunbar was sent by the former to Governor Dinwiddie of Virginia. In his reply of Sept. 20 Dinwiddie acknowledges its receipt and gives an account of Dunbar's conduct in disobedience of those orders. Dinwiddie Papers, 2, 208.

lars of which are contain'd in the inclos'd Copy of the Officer's Letter.[1]

Upon my Arrival at this Place, I found it, notwithstanding Captain Bradstreet, the Commandant, had done every thing, that an active, able Officer in his Situation could do, in a very defenceless Condition. The Strength of the Fort, which was mounted with seven Cannon of 3 lb Ball, and two of 4 lb, consists of a Stone Wall of about 600 feet in Circumference, and three and a half feet thick, so ill cemented, as not to be able to stand against a Cannon of 4 lb. Shot. It is situated upon the South Edge of Lake Ontario on a small Eminence, but which is commanded at 450 Yards distance, to the North East, by a Point of much higher Ground on the opposite Side of the River, which forms its' Harbour, and by another Eminence behind it, Westward, at the distance of 540 Yards. And in this expos'd State of it, the French might have landed cannon out of their Vessells upon the Lake, within five Miles of the before mention'd Point, and one Mile of the Eminence behind the Fort.

Upon a Survey taken of both these Eminences on the afternoon of my Arrival, the high Point on the opposite Side appear'd to be a most advantageous one, not only for commanding the Harbour, the Lake, and the Fort, but likewise for defence against the Approach of an Enemy; and the high Ground behind the Fort a very advantageous one, and necessary to be secur'd, tho' not equally so with the opposite point.

From the late General Braddock's Instructions, which he communicated to me at Alexandria,[2] I found he was restraind from building any Fort of great Expence, untill he should first transmit an Estimate of it for Approbation: But if that had not been the Case, the time, I had to erect any Work upon either of these two Eminences, would not have

[1] Bradstreet to Shirley, Aug. 17, *ante*, p. 240.
[2] The royal instructions of Nov. 25, 1754, to Braddock are printed 1 Penna Arch. 2, 203; and the secret instructions of same date in Docts. rel. Col. Hist. N. Y. 6, 920, also 2 Penna. Arch. 6, 211.

allow'd of the raising a Regular, strong Fortification this Year: I therefore determin'd to have a Logg palisadoed Fort built, according to the inclos'd Plan of one, I had erected upon the River Kennebeck the last Year, capable of mounting large Cannon upon the middle Block House, and containing Barracks for 300 Men; and which I apprehend will, with a Garrison of that Strength, and from the Dimensions of it's Loggs, be defensible against small Cannon: and if it should be judg'd requisite to have a Strong, regular Fortification built round it another Year, may be of Service, not only whilst the new work shall be erecting, but after it is finish'd.

The work, I have concluded to erect upon the other Eminence, as soon as that upon the Point is finish'd, is a small square Fort of Earth and Masonry, with four Bastions, a Rampart, Parapet, Ditch and Cover'd way according to the inclos'd plan, with Barracks to contain 200 Men.[1]

I have so fully observ'd in my Letter to you, Sir, of the 12th of August upon the Importance of this Place,[2] that I need add nothing to Shew the necessity of it's being secur'd, as soon as possible, against any Sudden Attempt of the French from Fort Frontenac, with which it hath been threaten'd.

I have acquainted you, Sir, in my Letter of the 11th of August,[3] that I had sent two trusty Indians with two Albany Traders from the Carrying Place at Oneida to Niagara, to gain Intelligence of the Strength and Designs of the French there, and to meet me at this Place; and soon after my Arrival here, I sent, at different times, two Parties of Indians and Albany Men to discover the Strength and Motions of the French at Fort Frontenac; the Party return'd from Niagara on the 4th Instant, and I beg leave to refer you to

[1] Shirley inclosed three plans with this letter. The first is of Oswego, the second is of Fort Oswego at Oswego, and a third is called the Fort of the Six Nations at Oswego. See Doct. Hist. of N. Y. 1, 315, and Winsor, N. C. H. 5, 511. All the forts were destroyed by Montcalm on his capture of the town.

[2] *Ante*, p. 221.

[3] *Ante*, p. 217.

the inclos'd Copy [1] of the Minutes of a Council of War for the Intelligence, they brought me. The Party, which I sent last to Fort Frontenac, return'd five Days after; and their Intelligence, together with that of an Indian, who arriv'd

[1] The Minutes inclosed follow:

At a Council of Warr, held at the Camp at Oswego, on Lake Ontario, September 18th, 1755.

His Excellency William Shirley, Esqr., Major General and Commander in Chief of all His Majesty's Forces in North America. [Names of Council members follow.]

His Excellency acquainted the Council, that through the great Desertion of Battoe-men, and Scarcity of Waggons on the Mohawk's River, and the Desertion of Slaymen on the Great Carrying Place at Oneida, the bringing up of Provisions and other Stores to this Place had been so much retarded, that there had not been, at any time since his Arrival, a sufficient Quantity of dry Provisions here to enable him to proceed upon the Expedition under his Command; That now as a Number of Battoes is hourly Expected, with a great Quantity of the Species of Provisions wanted, he has conven'd them in Council, to let them know his Intention of going immediately upon Action, and to ask their Opinions and Advice on several points relative to the Service, and in Order thereto, should inform them of the Intelligence, he had procur'd of the Situation and Strength of the Enemy.

His Excellency then acquainted the Council, that before he left the Great Carrying Place at Oneida, he employ'd two trusty intelligent Indians, and two Albany Traders to go to Niagara, and bring him from thence an Account of the Strength and Designs of the French; That they return'd about fourteen Days ago, with the following Account, vizt., the Indians, who went into the French Fort, and continu'd two Days there, report that their Works, which consisted part of Stone, but chiefly of Logs, are very weak and in ruinous Condition; That their Garrison then consisted of about sixty French, and that they had upwards of an hundred Indians about the Fort (chiefly Piarondacks;) That the French told them they had, for some time, expected 900 Indians from Canada, and a large Quantity of Stores, and were under some Concern least the Vessels that were to have brought them should be taken by one of the English Vessels, they having heard nothing of them for some Weeks; That they had frequent Letters from Fort du Quesne, and expected every Day the Arrival of Troops and

here in their Absence, having left Fort Frontenac nine Days before, is likewise contain'd in the inclos'd Copy of the Minutes of Council.

The last Division of Sir William Pepperrell's Regiment, with part of the Artillery and Ordnance Stores, did not arrive here untill the first Instant; Carriages were to be

Indians from thence; that they told them, they had never been in so sharp a Fight as the Engagement with the English, and that thirty of their Party were kill'd in it: The Indian Spies added, that the French Indians were much disgusted at the Treatment they had receiv'd from the French in the Division of the Spoils, and at their Behaviour during the Action, and were most of them returning to their Castles; that they saw there many English Scalps, and much Cloaths and Furniture in particular, one very rich Saddle, all which, they understood, had been taken from the English at Monongahela; and that the French had at Niagara seventy or eighty very large Battoes, with which they told them they intended to meet the English Vessels and board them, which last Circumstance, His Excellency observ'd to the Council, was confirm'd by another Indian who lately came from Niagara, and upon meeting one of our Row Gallies upon the Lake, caution'd Captain Ayscough, the Commander of it, against proceeding further, for that Reason.

His Excellency also inform'd the Council, that one of the Indian Spies, who, since his leaving Niagata, hath been with the Outawawa Indians, which had assisted the French in the Action at Mononga-hela, told him, that those Indians had declar'd their Readiness to him to lay down the Hatchet against the English, as were also others of the Western Indians; whereupon, His Excellency hath sent two Indians and two Albany Traders to them with Belts of Wampum, to invite them to enter into an Alliance with the English, or at least into a State of Neutrality between them and the French.

His Excellency further acquainted the Council, that upon his Arrival at this Place, he sent a Party of the Albany men and two Indians to Fort Frontenac, upon the North East Edge of Lake Ontario, to procure Intelligence of the Situation and Strength of that Fort, as also of what Number of Forces were encamp'd about it; that they return'd about ten days ago with the following Account, vizt., That they landed upon an Island about three quarters of a Mile distant from the Fort, from whence they had a full View of it, and of the Land behind it, which was clear'd of Trees, and rises with a gradual Ascent; That the Fort stands a little way up a Bay, at a few Yards distance from the Water, and appears to be something bigger than the Fort at Oswego, and is surrounded with a

new made for nine large pieces of Artillery (those prepar'd
for them before I arriv'd not being sufficiently secur'd) an
Hospital necessary to be built; and from the Intelligence,
we had receiv'd, it seem'd not adviseable for any considerable part of the Forces with me to leave this Place in the

Stone Wall; that they had likewise a distinct View of two Vessells
of about 40 Tons each, which lay moor'd in the Harbour near the
Fort, and appear'd to them to have Guns mounted, and to be unrigg'd; Also, that they had a distinct View of a Regular Encampment at the East End of the Fort, in which they counted six large
Marquis Tents; and that they judg'd from the Extent of it that it
might contain three or four hundred men; That upon the Side of
the Bay opposite the Fort there is a point of Land about half a
Mile's distance from it; That between this Point and the Island,
where they landed, there is a small Island (said to be inhabited by
about twenty Indian Families,) situated within about three quarters of a Mile's distance of the Fort; That they think there is deep
Water between these Islands and the main Land, and that on the
back of the two Islands and point of Land there are two others at
about a Mile and half distance, and others adjacent; and upon
being ask'd if they could discover a Number of Battoes near the
Fort, they answer'd they could discover none.

His Excellency also acquainted the Council, that an Indian, who
came here soon after his Arrival, and who had left Fort Frontenac
nine Days before, inform'd him that when he left it the French had
about 30 Men within the Fort, and 600 Soldiers in Tents without it;
That he saw a great Number of Barrels of Powder within it, and
that the Stone Wall which surrounds it was about six feet thick,
and that it was mounted with a great many Guns, large and small;
That an Onondaga Indian now in the Camp, call'd Red Head, who
says he left Fort Frontenac about five Weeks ago, has inform'd his
Excellency that the Walls of Fort Frontenac were built with Stone
and about six feet thick; that the Fort is a weak one, that it had
two Encampments about it, one of Canadians, which is in View of
the Island, on which the said Party had landed, and another of
Regular Troops from France, which is in a hollow on the other Side
of the Fort, and not in View of the Island; that the French told
him they expected soon from Canada a much larger Number of
Troops, with an Officer they call'd the General, which were lately
arrived from France, and that the Commandant of the Fort told
him that then they should make the English a Visit at Oswego and
attack it.

His Excellency further inform'd the Council, that Major General
Johnson, in a Letter dated 1st September from the Camp at the

expos'd State it was in, untill at least the new Fort at the Point was inclos'd and ready to receive it's Cannon : But if all other Circumstances had favour'd our proceeding to Niagara sooner; yet from the time of my Arrival here to this Day we have not had a Quantity of dry provisions for

Lake, lately call'd Lake Sacrament, now nam'd Lake George, says, that some of the Indians, whom he had sent for Intelligence to Canada, and were returned from thence, inform'd him that the French told them there were 300 Canoes gone to Cadaraqui [Frontenac].

That His Excellency, upon laying this Intelligence, and the Acct of the Arrival of Troops from France this Summer together, and upon considering these Circumstances in particular, that all Intercourse between Frontenac and Niagara seems to have been suspended for some time, and that the French have lay'd still so long at the former of those Places, it appears not improbable to him that their Design may be, in case the whole Forces here, or much the greater part of them should be employ'd in an Attempt against Niagara (which, from its Distance of 150 Miles, and the advanc'd Season of the year may possibly take up thirty Days, or perhaps more in the Execution) to make a Descent in the mean time upon Oswego from Fort Frontenac, which is computed at not above 50 Miles distance from it : That what makes this more probable is the great Importance of which Oswego is to the securing the back parts of his Majesty's Western Colonies on this Continent, and for maintaining the Dominion over the Great Lakes, and the Country behind the Appalachian Mountains against the French, and the present expos'd State this Place would be in, unless a Strong Garrison shall be left to protect it; That the Number of Effectives upon the Spot fit for immediate Duty, in the three Regiments and Independent Company, including Serjeants and Corporals, amount to 1376 men; That besides these Troops the Number of Irregulars, consisting of Albany Men and Indians, which attend the Army, amount to about 120 Men.

His Excellency also inform'd the Council, that for securing the Fort at this Place against any Sudden Attack from the Eminence which commands it upon the opposite point on the East side of the River, he had Ordered a Strong Wooden Fort, surrounded with Picketts and a Ditch, and to be mounted with Cannon, to be built there with all possible Speed, and that the same was begun, and the Ground on which it is to be erected will be soon picketted in, and the whole building finish'd in about four Weeks; and that he had caus'd a Sloop and a Schooner of 60 Tons each, and two Row Gallies of 20 Tons each, all equipp'd in a Warlike manner, together

ten Day Subsistence at any one time in our Store, occasion'd by several Accidents, but principally the lowness of the Waters, Desertion of Battoe Men and Waggons (it being their time of Harvest) and, above all, by the insufficient

with eight Whale Boats, capable of holding 12 or sixteen men each, to be built.

His Excellency then acquainted the Council, that he propos'd, as soon as a Sufficient Quantity of Provisions should arrive, to proceed upon the intended Attempt for the Reduction of the French Fort and Settlements at Niagara, with such a Number of the Troops now upon the Spot, such of the aforesaid Vessells and Whale Boats, and such a Train of Artillery, as can be spar'd for that Service, leaving a sufficient Force for the Protection of this Fort against any Sudden Attack, which may probably be made upon it by the French from Fort Frontenac in his Absence.

That His Excellency proposes to take with him on the aforesaid Attempt 600 Regulars, including Gunners and Matrosses, besides the Albany Men and Indians, and a Train of Artillery, consisting of one Cannon carrying an eighteen pound Shott, and four twelve pounders, one ten inch Mortar, one seven inch Hoyett, two Royals, and five small Swivel Hoyets, with the four Vessells before mention'd, the Whale Boats, and a suitable number of Battoes; and that then the Force remaining for the Defence of this Place will be about 700 Effective men, two Cannon of twelve pounders, four nine pounders, ten six pounders, six three pounders, and eight Cohorns.

His Excellency then desir'd the Opinion and Advice of the Members of this Council on the following points, vizt.

First. Whether they were of Opinion that the Force propos'd for the intended Attempt against Niagara was a sufficient one, or what other they judg'd to be so?

Secondly. Whether they judge the Force propos'd to be left here, together with the New Fort building on the opposite point, to be sufficient for the Defence of this Place against any probable Attempt from Fort Frontenac, during His Excellency's Absence on the above Service?

Thirdly. Whether they think it will not be expedient to make a Feint at the same time at Cadaraqui, or a Real attempt to burn the French Vessells there?

Fourthly. Whether they think it necessary to build another Fort or Redoubt on the West Side of this Fort, on the Rising Ground, which commands it?

Fifthly. Whether it will be not advisable for his Majesty's Service, to prepare materials here this Winter, and build, as soon as

Number of them to be found in the Country for transporting the Baggage, Provisions, Artillery, and Ordnance Stores of the Forces employ'd in this Expedition, and that against Crown point, at the same time; so that I have been inevitably prevented from leaving this Place untill now, when, from the Prospect I have of a speedy Supply of dry Provisions, and the Works of the new Fort being so far advanc'd as to be ready in a few Days to receive it's Artillery and Garrison, I am in hopes, notwithstanding the lateness of the Season, of being able to proceed to Niagara with part of the Forces, and a Train of Artillery sufficient, according to our late Intelligence of the Strength of the French Fort there, for the Reduction of it; leaving a Body of Troops here strong enough for the Protection of this Place, and upon this Occasion I yesterday took the Opinion of a Council of War, Copy of the Minutes of which is inclos'd.

I am with the highest Respect,
Sir,
Your most Humble and
most Obedient Servant.

W. SHIRLEY.

Rt. Honble. Sir Thomas Robinson Knt: of the Bath,}
one of His Majesty's principal Secretaries of State. }

Endorsed:
Camp at Oswego, Sepr. 19th, 1755.
Major Genl. Shirley.
R Decr. 18th.

may be, one or more Vessells of a larger Size than the largest of those already built, and capable of mounting ten six pounders, besides Swivels, and also two more Row Galleys, and 100 more good Whale Boats? (P. R. O., C. O. 5, 46.)

To the copy sent by him to Governor Morris of Pennsylvania (1 Penna. Arch. 2, 413), John Shirley adds:

"Everything herein propos'd was unanimously agreed to, except the feint at Cadaraqui, which was not agreed to."

WILLIAM SHIRLEY TO WILLIAM JOHNSON [1]

Camp at Oswego, Sept. 19th, 1755.

SIR,

Three days ago, I receiv'd a Letter from Mr. Stevenson, of Albany, inclosing a Copy of the General Letter, which you have sent to Lt. Govr. Phipps, and the governors of the other Colonies, which have rais'd Forces for the Expedition against Crown-point, giving an Account of two Actions, which happen'd on the 8th instant, between the Army under your command, and the French; in the first of which, a detachmt. of 1000 English, commanded by Col. Williams, and a party of 200 Indians of the Six Nations, were defeated, with a considerable loss on their side. In the second, the French, and their Indians attack'd the main body of your Army in their Camp at Lake George, and were repulsed with a more considerable one on theirs. [2]

Mr. Stevenson informs me, that upon finding I had no Letter directed to me among the packetts, which came from your Camp, and discovering the words upon the seal side of that directed to Governor Phipps, "Please to despatch a Copy of this Letter to General Shirley; my time and circumstances won't permit my writing to him immediately," he open'd it, and took a Copy of it, to be sent forthwith to me; and as the Events contain'd in it, so nearly concern His Majesty's service, under my immediate Command, as well as his other service upon this Continent, under my Direction, I can't avoid expressing my surprize at your omission to acquaint me with them directly from yourself; which,

---

[1] Johnson Manuscripts, 2, 229; Mass. Arch., Col. Ser. 54, 136. Extract inclosed in Shirley to Robinson, Oct. 5, *post*, p. 309. Printed with certain errors and omissions: R. I. Col. Rec. 5, 455.

[2] Two letters of Johnson to Phips, the first of Sept. 9–10, the second of Sept. 17, may be referred to here, although the first is more probably the one intended. Both are in the Johnson Manuscripts (23, 190 and 2, 225). The former is printed Doct. Hist. N. Y. 2, 691. The latter supplements and revises the first.

let your Hurry and Circumstances be what they would, you might at least have done by ordering your secretary or any clerk to transcribe a copy of your Letter to the Governours, to be sent me from Albany, instead of desiring Lieut. Governour Phipps to send me one from Boston.

What could be your Reason for postponing my being acquainted with these matters, which I ought to have known as soon as possible, to so distant a time, as my hearing from Mr. Phipps must have been, seems difficult to say.

However that may be, my Duty to His Majesty requires me to take the first opportunity of transmitting you my sentiments upon the present State of the Service, which I have put under your immediate Direction.

Upon the statement of your letter to the several governours, sir, it appears to me that the late defeat of the French forces and their Indians in the engagement at your camp, hath given you a favorable opportunity of proceeding, as soon as the expected reinforcements from New England shall join you, to Ticonderoge; which post, since you have taken the route to Crown Point, that you have done, it is of the utmost consequence to the success of the expedition under your command, to make yourself master of as soon as possible.

By the account given in the copy of the minutes of your council of war, enclosed to me in your letter of the 1st instant, of the strength of your army a few days before the late actions, and in your letter to the governours, of the loss you have sustained in both engagements, the number of your remaining troops must, upon the arrival of your reinforcement from New England, exceed four thousand; and that of your Indians, be upwards of two hundred.

From the account given you by the French general, your prisoner, of the strength of his army, in the beginning of the first action, it consisted of two hundred grenadiers, eight hundred Canadians and seven hundred Indians, of different nations; and from the account given you by his aid-de-camp of the loss of the French and the Indians, in both actions, and the pursuit which ensued, they lost in the whole one thousand men, and the major part of their chief officers, together with Monsieur St. Pierre,[1] the officer who had the chief command and greatest influence over the Indians; so that according to their accounts, which seem most to be depended upon, the French had not above seven hundred men left of their whole army, which attacked your camp.

In these actions, Sir, you have experienc'd the good Behaviour of your Officers and Troops, who must be now flushed with their late Victory: The French on the other hand must be greatly disconcerted by the late Defeat of their Army and loss of their general, and so many of their principal officers; and the French Indians, in particular (which consists of different Nations), by the loss of Monsr. St. Pierre, who seems to have been a necessary Officer for keeping them together.

You had before acquainted me, in your Letter of the 1st instant, from your camp, at Lake George, that "some Indians, you sent out on the scout, told you, they had discovered a Party of French and Indians at Ticonderoge, but that no works were thrown up then; and that you was impatient to get a number of batteaux up, and put in order; when you proposed to proceed with a part of the troops, and endeavor to take post at Ticonderoge."

I hope, sir, if that is not yet done, that you still propose doing it, as soon as possible; the necessity of driving the enemy from that pass, still continues; the longer time is given them to fortify it, the more difficult it will be to dislodge them, and the more you will lose the advantage, which their defeat, and your own victory have given you to effect it.

You say in your letter to the governors, "Your men have suffered so much fatigue for three days past, and are con-

---

[1] Legardeur St. Pierre was, as Shirley states, a most potent influence with the Indians, and his death at this time seemed to afford Johnson a good opportunity of winning many of the French allies over to the English or to a position of neutrality.

stantly standing upon the arms by day, half the whole upon guard every night, and the rest lay down armed and accoutred, that both officers and men are almost worn out; that the enemy may rally, and you judge they have considerable reinforcements near at hand; so that you think it necessary to be on your guard, and be watchful to maintain the advantage, you have gained."

To make the most of the advantage you have gained, it seems clear, sir, that you should make use of the opportunity it hath given you, of proceeding upon your expedition, whilst the spirits of your army are elated with success, and those of the enemy lowered by the loss of the greatest part of theirs.

As to your apprehensions, that the enemy might rally, and that they had considerable reinforcements near at hand; it is mentioned in your letter, that your men and Indians pursued the French soon after their repulse, slaughtered great numbers, and took several prisoners, among whom, was the French general, himself; so that their army was entirely routed, and yours master of the field; rallying the second day after so general a route as this, is, I believe, unknown in the case even of great armies; and that the small remains of the French army should return the next day to the attack of your camp, where they had so lately felt the effects of your cannon against their musketry, seems not much to be apprehended; it is more probable, that the slaughter they had suffered in the pursuit, with their loss of most of their chief officers, will in the end occasion, if not a total dissipation of the Indians, yet at least a great desertion among them, and of the Canadians, too.

Upon what Foundation you judge that the French Army had considerable Reinforcements near at hand, is not mentioned in your letter; it seems more likely, that they sent all the Forces they could spare, from Ticonderoge and Crownpoint (where you say so many of the Regular Troops are posted) to attack your Camp; especially as they were to do it only with musketry.

You say, further, in your letter to the governors "that from the papers of Monsieur Dieskau, the French General, you find, he brought under his Command to Canada in the Men of War lately arrived at Quebec, 3171 regular troops, who are partly in garrisons at Crown Point, and encamped at Ticonderoge, and other advantageous passes between your camp and Crown Point.

That you expect very shortly, another and more formiable attack; and that the enemy will then come with artillery; that Col. Williams had the ground cleared for building a stockaded fort; and that your men are so harrassed, and obliged to be so constantly upon watchful duty, that you think it would be both unreasonable, and, as you fear, in vain to set them at work upon the designed fort.

That you design to order the New Hampshire regiment up to your camp, to reinforce you; and that you hoped some of the designed reinforcements would be with you in a few days; and that when those fresh troops arrived, . . . you should immediately set about building a fort."

I hope you will, before now, have received my letter of the 12th instant, in which I sent you an account from Admiral Boscawen's letter to the late General Braddock, of the number of troops which were sent from France this summer, to North America, and what part of them arrived in Canada; which will show you that there must be some mistake in the above account extracted by you from Monsieur Dieskau's papers, of the number of those which arrived with him at Quebec.[1]

It is clear from this account, that the whole number sent from France, was, as M. Dieskau's papers make them to be, about three thousand; and by other undoubted accounts, as well as the admiral's, that of these, he took eight companies in the Alcide and Lys men of war; and that eleven hundred are in garrison at Louisbourg.

[1] Shirley's letter of September 12 is in Johnson Manuscripts, 2, 213. Besides the matters here mentioned it contained an account of the instructions given Col. Dunbar, emphasized the pressure of business incident to the chief command now resting upon its writer, and asked Johnson for a copy of his instructions and commission from Genl. Braddock.

Now supposing that the remainder arriv'd at Quebec without any loss in their passage (which is not very likely), the most that got to Quebec, must be 1671, 500 at least of which, I have intelligence from Indians, who came here from Cadaraqui, at different times within these five weeks, and a party of Indians and Albany men, whom I sent there since that time, are now encamp'd close to that fort; and a number of them were killed (according to your own account,) in the late attack upon your camp and the pursuit which ensued; so that the remainder, supposing them to be now, as you say, partly in garrison at Crown Point, and encamped at Ticonderoge, and other advantageous passes between your camp and Crown Point, can't amount to near the number which you seem to think are there.

I can't therefore but think you may spare from the fort at the Carrying Place, and from your camp at Lake George, a body of troops more than sufficient to drive the French from Ticonderoge, and possess yourself of that pass; and hope you will lose no time in doing it.

If Crown Point is inaccessible to the army now with you, through the route you have taken to it, it will probably be more so to double the number of troops the next year, and must be come at through another route; in which case, the fort you design to build at the end of the lake, will be of little or no utility for carrying on another expedition, and but of very little, even for the defence of the country between Lake George, late St. Sacrament, and Hudson's River, whilst two roads lie open for the French to make incursions into it, viz. : through Wood Creek and the South Bay; the latter of which, they have lately made use of, to come at both your camps.

As to your Expectation of a more formidable attack very shortly from the Enemy, and that they will then come with artillery; I suppose that artillery must be brought from Crown Point or Ticonderoge; and if the French should imagine that you design to attempt nothing further this Campaign than building the stockaded fort you propose, I think it probable enough that they make you a visit at your camp with cannon, in which case, I doubt your fort, when built would not stand long. But I believe the thoughts of the French are at present taken up in securing themselves against a visit from you at Crown Point, which I hope may be still made them this year, with success; and that to enable you the better to do it, the Colonies may send you a second reinforcement in time.

I am sorry to hear that you received a wound in the late engagement, and hope that the ball is by this time extracted from your thigh, and your wound is in a fair way of healing; I congratulate you upon your success hitherto, and wish it may be increased in the remaining operations of the Campaign; and am,

> Sir,
>> Your most humble servant,
>>> W. SHIRLEY.

To Major General Johnson.

FIELD OFFICERS TO WILLIAM SHIRLEY [1]

> The Memorial of the Field Officers of Major General Shirley, and Major General Sir William Pepperrell's Regiments of Foot.

Sheweth

That we think it our indispensible Duty to represent to your Excellency the Insufficiency of the Arms and Accoutrements of both Regiments. The Locks being wore out and the Hammers so soft, that notwithstanding repeated repairs they are almost unfit for Service, particularly Sir William Pepperrell's Regiment being old Dutch Arms.

The holes of the Pouches and Boxes are so small that they cannot receive the Cartridge, nor is there Substance of the

---

[1] P. R. O., C. O. 5, 46. This memorial is without date, but was received about Sept. 20 by Shirley and inclosed in his letter to Robinson of Sept. 28, 1755. A transcript is in the Library of Congress. These regiments were known also as the 50th and 51st,

Wood, to widen them sufficiently, The Leather Scanty and bad likewise.

Which is humbly submitted to your Consideration by Your Excellency's most Obedient and Humble Servants.

ROBT. ELLISON.
JAMES F. MERCER.
JOHN LITTLEHALES.

To His Excellency Major
General Shirley Commander
in Chief of all his Majesty's
Forces in North America etc. etc.

a True Copy,
WM. ALEXANDER Secy.

Endorsed:

Copy Memorial of the Field Officers
of General Shirley's and General Pepperrell's
Regiment, in Majr. Genl. Shirley's Letter
of Sepr. 28th, 1755.

PETER SCHUYLER TO WILLIAM SHIRLEY [1]

SIR,

I beg leave to Represent to your Excellency, that the Arms which You Procured for the Regiment under my Command from the Governour of Virginia, are so extreamly bad, as to be hardly fitt for Service: They appear to me to be Dutch Arms, and of the worst sort, the Locks daily breaking in the common Exercise, and many of the Hammers not Steel'd: As to the Cartridge Boxes, they are almost all useless, being Slightly cover'd; They drop from the Belts in marching.

I must likewise inform Your Excellency, that out of the

[1] Copy inclosed: Shirley to Robinson, Oct. 5, 1755, P. R. O., C. O. 5, 46. A transcript is in the Library of Congress. Schuyler commanded the New Jersey regiments in the field and was captured by the French when Oswego fell in 1756. He was exchanged later and served under Amherst in 1759–1760. He died at his home near Newark, N.J., in 1762. Schuyler, " Colonial New York," 2, 210 ff.

five hundred sent from Virginia, we have lost by Desertion, and other Accidents, including the Bad not fitt for Service, one hundred and five, which will be wanted early in the Spring, and where to gett proper Arms to replace them, I know not — And am

Your Excellency's Most Obedt. and most
Hble. Servant

WM. ALEXANDER, Secy.   PETER SCHUYLER.

Endorsed:
Copy Letter from Col: Schuyler
to Major General Shirley
dated 20th Septr. 1755.

JOHN RUTHERFORD TO WILLIAM SHIRLEY

[*Extract*][1]

[Albany, Sep. 22, 1755.]

There is such various Accounts of the late Engagement at Lake George, that I shall give Your Excellency in a few words, what I think I can trust most to in our own Officers accounts of the English, and Le Baron Dieskau's account of the French, who is a Marechal de Camp, and Commander in Chief of those Troops sent from Brest, and, as His Aid De Camp tells us, of all the Forces in Canada : He was wounded, and made Prisoner, with about 30 more, mostly wounded after the retreat of the French; His wounds are very dangerous, but the Surgeons have some hopes of His recovery. Coll: Johnson might have about 2500 Men at the Camp Including Indians, and 500, at the Carrying Place Fort.

---

[1] Copy inclosed : Shirley to Robinson, Oct. 5, 1755. P. R. O., C. O. 5, 46. A transcript is in the Library of Congress. The name of this officer is spelled Rutherfurd also, but so far as ascertained not by himself. He was at this time a captain of one of the New York Independent Companies and member of His Majesty's Council for that province. See his letter of Sept. 30, *post*, p. 301.

The Baron's account of Troops brought from Montreal, to Crown Point and Ticonderogue is as follows, with the detachment he carry'd from thence with Him to reconnoitre the Carrying Place, and endeavour to surprize our Fort, not being able to gett Satisfactory Intelligence from the Indian Parties he hath sent out.

Troops brought from Canada		The Detachment with the Baron at the Engagement on the Carrying Place, and attack upon the English Camp on Lake George.	
2 Battaillons	774		
Milices	1393		
Troupes de la Colonie	192		
Cannoniers	67	Troupes reglées . . .	200
Officiers des Sauvages	14	Canadiens	600
Sauvages	659	Sauvages	600
	3099		1400

The two Battallions of 774 men, were of those newly arrived from Brest, as were the 200, call'd regular Troops in the detachment: the Baron march'd towards our Fort with His detachment, but changed his mind on a Post being kill'd, and some Waggoners taken, by whose letters and Information he found General Johnson was encamp'd at the Lake, and finding 1000 Men, and the Indians were comeing to assist those at the Fort from the Camp, He march'd towards the Camp, and made a very pretty disposition to surprize and cutt them off, vizt. : the 1000 Men, but the Caghnawaga's, who the Baron insists were Traitors to Him all along, discover'd themselves before the Time; however as Genl. Johnson's party retreated in confusion, after a few fires, the Baron follow'd them close in hopes of entering with them into the Camp; but He mett with such a Warm Reception from the Cannon, and Deserted by His Indians, and most of the Canadeans, That His Regulars were mostly all kill'd, and Himself wounded and made Prisoner.

       I am etc —

A true Copy
  WM. ALEXANDER Secy.

Endorsed:
  Extract of a Letter from
    Captain Rutherford to
      Major General Shirley
        dated Albany Septr. 22d 1755.
          in Majr. Genl. Shirley's
            Letter of Octr. 5th 1755.

WILLIAM SHIRLEY TO WILLIAM JOHNSON [1]

Camp at Oswego, September 24th, 1755.

SIR,

Yesterday afternoon, I received your Letter, dated 9th instant, being a copy of that to the several governors of the several colonies concerned in the expedition under your command; and the same with what Mr. Stevenson transcribed from your letter to Governor Phips, and sent me seven days ago, as you will perceive by mine to you of the 19th instant.

In your last, I received enclosed, a copy of the orders and instructions for the regular troops sent to Cadaraqui, which are a confirmation of the intelligence I sent you in my last, viz.: that five hundred of the regular troops which came from France, with Mr. Dieskau, are encamped at the fort there. It appears, also, by those instructions, that there were at least one hundred and sixty-six Canadians sent with them on the 1st and 2d of August last; and that a number of Indians are there, likewise.

By the express, which delivered me your letter, I received one dated the 10th instant, from Capt. Ayre,[2] your engineer, informing me of the strength of the fort built at the Carrying Place; . . . "that with a garrison of three or four hundred men, would be able to resist an attack of fifteen hundred, if no cannon were brought against it; and that in his opinion, it

---

[1] Johnson Manuscripts, 3, 9; Mass. Arch., Col. Ser. 54, 149; extract inclosed: Shirley to Robinson, Oct. 5, 1755 (P. R. O., C. O. 5, 46). See also R. I. Col. Rec. 5, 459.

[2] More accurately Eyre. See letter referred to, *ante*, p. 259.

is very necessary that a strong and regular work should be erected at Lake George, to keep possession of that country, so far; that if the French can seize and take the before mentioned work at the Carrying Place, he fears it would be attended with bad consequences; as it would cut off your retreat and communication with Albany, and totally stop your reinforcements and provisions, from joining you, if another road cannot be found, which he believes is not easy to be met with; that he thinks what induced the French, or may induce them hereafter to attack you at Lake George, is fearing that you would not attempt to go any further, and so were resolved to call you off, before you returned; and seems to infer from thence that the enemy must be so formidable, as to make it unadvisable for you to proceed further; and concludes with extolling the gallantry and resolution of the French troops in their late attack of you."

I agree, sir, in sentiments with your engineer, concerning the bad consequences of the enemy's taking the fort at the Carrying Place, and am much concerned at the weakness of its works; especially, as both yourself and he, are apprehensive of another attack at Lake George, with cannon.[1]

If I was in your situation, my chief apprehensions would be, that the French would make an attempt upon that fort with cannon, which they might transport thither as easily as to Lake George; and I think you judged extremely right in sending a detachment of one thousand men to its support, upon the first alarm of the enemy's being upon their march towards it; and for my own part, I must own, I should have thought it a better piece of conduct, in M. Dieskau, if, after defeating the party under Col. Williams's command, he had attacked the fort at the Carrying Place, instead of your camp; which, according to your engineer's account of it, might have been more easily won, with the force he had with him, than had your camp been stormed.

---

[1] Shirley thought Johnson had not made the most of his repulse of the French at Lake George. See John Shirley (for his father) to Governor R. H. Morris, Sept. 22–25, 1755, 1 Penna. Arch. 2, 423, and Shirley to Johnson, Sept. 19, *ante*, p. 270.

I can by no means adopt your engineer's opinion of the urgent necessity of immediately erecting a strong regular fort at Lake George, for maintaining possession of the country so far. In my opinion, the most material place for erecting the strongest works, is at the other end of the Carrying Place (at or near where the fort lately built, stands), which is about seventeen miles distant from it. It seems to me that a regular strong fort there, would be a much more essential one for covering the country against the attacks of the French, from the river Champlain, through the three several routes that lead from thence to it, than one at Lake George, which would leave it uncovered in two of those routes; besides, how could a fort at Lake George, be supported, when its communication with Albany was cut off, which, as your engineer rightly observes, would most probably be the case, if the French should take our fort at the Carrying Place.

I would therefore recommend it to you in the strongest manner, as an object which deserves your attention, to have the . . . fort at the Carrying Place strengthened as much as the circumstances of your army will admit, consistent with your proceeding directly to Ticonderoge.[1]

As to the formidable strength of the enemy, you will have to encounter in your march thither, I have told you my

---

[1] Letters of Shirley showing the importance of Crown Point and Fort Lyman are numerous. See Shirley to Governor Hopkins of Rhode Island, R. I. Col. Rec. 5, 461, for one in print. More important is Shirley's letter of Sept. 25, 1755 (Johnson Manuscripts, 3, 11; Mass. Arch., Col. Ser. 54, 153), in reply to Johnson's of Sept. 22 (Johnson Manuscripts, 2, 237; Mass. Arch., Col. Ser. 54, 142). The latter had spoken of lack of zeal in the army, other obstacles to advance, and brought up the matter of his commission and instructions from Braddock. Shirley urged advance, and suggests to Johnson that General Lyman and Colonel Ruggles were worthy commanders if the former did not care to lead because of his wound. He was not convinced by Johnson's statement of the superiority of the French, and was eager for an aggressive movement. Moreover, as early as Sept. 1 Johnson had spoken of his impaired health, and his delay in reporting to Shirley led the latter to mistrust that Johnson was not willing to contribute to another's success. See note, *ante*, p. 259.

sentiments at large in my last letter; and with regard to the gallant behaviour of their troops in the late actions, I must own, I differ widely in opinion from your engineer; their retreat was a very bad one, without conduct or resolution; they could not otherwise have suffered so great a slaughter as you say they did, in the short pursuit made of them by your troops and Indians, which jumped over the barricade of your camp after them.

The more I think of your situation, the more advisable I think it will be for you to proceed to Ticonderoge; as the honor of His Majesty's arms and the interest of the colonies seem to require it. The consequences, I fear, will be bad, if you do not; and I can't but hope that you will see these matters in the same light which I view them in.

The weak condition which I found this place in, and our want of dry provisions, have hitherto inevitably hindered me from proceeding in the expedition under my command; but both these obstacles will, I hope, be so far surmounted in three days, as to permit me to do it.

I wish you a speedy recovery of your wound, and much success; and am,

Sir, your most humble servant,

W. SHIRLEY.

To Major General Johnson.

MASSACHUSETTS GENERAL COURT TO WILLIAM BOLLAN [1]

> A Representation of the Case of his Majesty's Province of Massachusetts Bay, contain'd in a Letter from the General Assembly to their Agent dated Boston, Septemr. 26th, 1755.

We herewith transmit you an Address of the General Assembly to his Majesty upon occasion of the late Success

[1] *B. M., Additional Manuscript 33029, 206.* A transcript is in the Library of Congress.

obtain'd by his Majesty's Colony's Forces near Lake George, in which Address we represent the present State of our Affairs, and humbly crave that relief and Assistance which his Majesty in his great Wisdom and Paternal Goodness shall be pleased to afford us : We desire this Address may be immediately presented, but as we have not sett the Importance of the late Success in the fullest Light, neither have so largely represented the present Situation of Affairs, together with our particular Services as might be necessary in order to obtain what we hope for, it is needfull that we should add something further on these Heads. The proportion of Men this Province were by Contract to employ [for the Crown Point Expedition] in conjunction with the other Colony Troops was 1200, but so much had we the Design at heart that we made an Establishment for 1500, those Troops we apprehended might be sufficient to carry our Scheme into Effect, while we concluded that the Grand Expedition on the Ohio would have drawn the chief of their Attention and Strength that way, but the unhappy Defeat of that Army gave us so great an Alarm that we Voted a reinforcement of 2800 Men; it was while these Troops were raising that the late Action happen'd. The Enemy flush'd with their Success march'd about 2000 Men with Design to attack Fort Lyman not 50 Miles from Albany, but having made their Appearance turn'd off to follow General Johnson, who they learn'd had march'd but a little before to Lake George.

In their way they came up with a party of our men, detach'd by General Johnson, who being overpower'd with Numbers retreated to the Camp, which the Enemy attack'd but were defeated and pursued, the particulars of which are set forth in the General's Letter inclosed; but had not Providence turn'd the Victory in our favour, we tremble to think of the Consequence: New York and these Provinces would have laid open to their ravages, the Six Nations and other Indians lost to the English Interest, Albany could not have made a Stand, and by proceeding from thence up Mohawk river, they might possibly have cut off his Majesty's Regiments under General Shirley, then at Oswego, join'd their other

Forces station'd at Cattarocky[1] river, and had it in their power this Season so to have secured the great Lakes, and that part of the Country, as would have put his Majesty, or those Provinces to an Immense Charge in removing their Encroachments. But altho' the Enemy have received a very great Check by this seasonable Defeat, and the Ardour of our people is greatly heightened, we are not for all this quite out of pain as to the Success of the present Enterprize, and have much to apprehend from their future Attempts; this would not indeed be the Case had we only to deal with the Canadians and their Indian Allies, but for some time past, and at present the Treasure, and great Numbers of the regular Troops of Old France are employed against us, and this Province, upon whose Loyalty Zeal and Resolution his Majesty may place as great a Dependance as upon any other of his Provinces, have already exerted themselves in the common Cause so much beyond their Ability, that in our own Strength we can proceed but little further.

Not to mention the Number of Men employed the last Year in the Kennebeck and other Services we have near 8000 Men now employed against the Enemy, which Number will appear by the following Computation, about 1500 Men of the 2000 are gone to Nova Scotia, about 1000 were encouraged to enlist in Governor Shirley's and Sir William Pepperrell's Regiments, and it was supposed that one or both of those regiments would have gone in the Service General Johnson's Army is now engaged in, 4300 are now in and raised for the Army under General Johnson, upwards of 500 are stationed at our Forts and Garrison Houses on the Frontiers, about 600 are employed in scouting parties and other Military Services. Above 5400 of these Troops are in the actual pay of this Government, and we must soon have a larger Number, as all the Indians on our Borders have now commenced Hostilities against us.

The fortresses we have lately built and are now building for

[1] Otherwise the St. Lawrence River, known also by its French names as the Iroquois or Cadaracoui at the point of outlet for Lake Ontario.

our security have already consumed large sums and require further, and we have this Year, as well as formerly been at no little charge in order to engage the Six Nations to enter heartily into his Majesty's Service; but in this representation we do not design a retrospect upon former Services, it may be sufficient to declare that our late Exertions have so exhausted us that all our public Funds and Incomes are now mortgaged and anticipated, and we have been obliged to raise a Sum of Money by private Subscription for the purchase of Bread for our Forces, and to defray the Charge of transporting Provisions, Stores, etc. otherwise our Men must have been greatly distress'd, or forced to disband, but such is the present Scarcity of Specie that we should not have been able to have procured even the Sum necessary for that end, if Bills of Exchange on London had not answer'd as well in New York where Cash is plenty, as to have sent the Money for the above Uses: We think it proper to observe to You that no Expedition can be carried on by this Province but what must subject it to greater Inconveniences and Charges than it would the southern Governments, for we being no Provision Country, it is they that receive a benefit by the rise of Provisions, which such Expeditions always occasion, and our Cash must be remitted unto them for all we have Occasion for, and in the present Expedition we are under this disadvantage that all our Supplies must go by the Way of Albany, and be transported from thence to our Camp at a very great Expence, which nothing but Cash or sterling Bills will defray; but notwithstanding these very great Expences, this Province is much more distress'd by the loss or absence of so great a Part of our labouring Inhabitants, by reason of which our Trade languishes, and Lands lye uncultivated.

We have supplied for the general Good many more Men than all the other Colonies together, especially for his Majesty's Regiments, when some of them exceed this in Numbers, but this has not prevented the Governor of Halifax from sending over to us this Week about 20 recruiting Officers, who are now beating up in this and other

Towns for recruits at a time when we have been obliged to impress substantial Householders for the defence of our Frontiers, and other Services, We have already sent that Province 1500 Men, but it seems 1700 more are wanted to fill up the Regiments there on that Establishment, and tho' we suppose the Order for raising the Men in America was well design'd, we are yet of Opinion, and would desire Your noticing it, that as we are a new Country, and have so much Land to be given away to Settlers, or disposed of for a trifling Consideration, the Means of Subsistence is easily come at, and every Young fellow who inclines may without one farthing venture upon a family and the Charges consequent, which in old Countries cannot be done, so that every Man gone from the Province has really carried a family with him; moreover tho' it must be acknowledged a present saving is made to the Crown of the Charge which the transporting Men would amount to, yet in the end the Nation are losers, for the Means of Subsistence lying so open to the Industrious in a new Country occasions great Multiplication of Inhabitants, and consequently so great an Increase of the Consumption of the Manufactures of Great Britain, that if this is taken into the Scale, it will certainly turn it in favour of sending over what Garrison Soldiers may be thought necessary to be kept up in America; besides our People are not calculated to be confined in Garrisons, or kept in any particular Service, they soon grow troublesome and uneasy by reflecting upon their Folly in bringing themselves into a State of Subjection, when they might have continued free and independent. We therefore depend upon Your representations that those Fortresses which may be erected for the Defence of his Majesty's Territories may be garrisoned by his Majesty's Regulars, rather than by American Troops, tho' in the Pay of the Crown.

We have no inclination to compare our services with that of any other Colonies further than is necessary to sett our own Merit in a just light, and if this Comparison carries any reflection upon particular Governments we are not the faulty Causes. New York was obliged by the original Contract to supply 800 Men in the present Expedition, 300 of which Connecticutt has furnished them, but tho' the other Governments have added above thrice their Proportions they have contented themselves with making a small Grant to one of the Colonies concern'd, notwithstanding they will be most benefitted by the reduction of Crown Point, as almost the whole of the Indian Trade has and will center with them.[1]

We have no disposition for stopping the Current of his Majesty's Favours, may they continue to be diffusive through the Provinces, but hope we may be excused in saying that we think no Government can lay a better Claim to his Majesty's Bounty and Favours than ourselves. We have from the Beginning defended our Country free of Charge to the Crown. We have always chearfully complyed with the Demand of his Majesty, and have more than once saved the Province of Nova Scotia, and for many Years past protected others to which we are the Frontier; and have once and again made considerable Conquests for the Crown. The Province of Virginia have [sic] been a great while almost entirely free from any military Charge, their Frontiers are not so exposed as ours, the Mountains being a Barrier; but notwithstanding since the late Encroachments of the Enemy on their Territory, his Majesty has graciously made them the Object of his paternal Care, and assisted them with his Troops and Treasure: We know not in what light their late Conduct may appear in to his Majesty, but we flatter ourselves that our Men must appear in a very advantageous one, and from former Experiences of his royal favour and bounty we are naturally lead to presume upon its being still afforded to us, and doubt not of Your making Use, etc.

[1] Shirley's plans for the future of America were broad, and the colony of Massachusetts had begun to realize their extent and their cost. So long as Shirley could obtain a reasonable proportion of the expense from London and was successful of himself or by deputy in the field, Massachusetts and all New England stood behind him. Failing these essentials, his popularity began to wane, and particularly so if the advantage of victory was to fall to New York while New England continued to pay a large share of the expense.

for procuring the present relief we stand in such absolute Need of.

Endorsed:
A Representation of the Case of
the Province of Massachusetts Bay.

WILLIAM SHIRLEY TO SIR THOMAS ROBINSON [1]

Camp at Oswego, Sepr. 28th, 1755.

SIR,

In my Letter of the 19th Instant I acquainted you, that I was in hopes of being in a Condition to proceed to Niagara in a few Days: I had accordingly made preparations for embarking, and Yesterday a Supply of dry Provisions arriv'd here, with certain Advices that it would be speedily follow'd by a further large Quantity: But the immoderate Rains, and tempestuous Weather upon the Lake, which had continu'd thirteen Days successively, have so much retarded our Works, and increas'd the Number of the Sick; and the Albany Men and Indians, who are best acquainted with the general Course of the Weather here, and State of the Lake, have made such strong Representations to me concerning the Winter's being too far advanc'd for the Men to go now to Niagara in Battoes, that I found there was a considerable Uneasiness among the Officers, who had compos'd the late Council of War, at my Intention to proceed thither; I therefore thought it proper to convene them again in Council for their further Opinion, and Advice; a Copy of which, Sir, I have inclos'd; [2] and acknowledge I

[1] P. R. O., C. O. 5, 46. A transcript is in the Library of Congress and another is among the Parkman Papers in the Mass. Hist. Society. See also Shirley to Sir William Johnson of equal date in Mass. Arch., Col. Ser. 54, 159.

[2] The Council referred to was held on Sept. 27. Shirley presided, and there were eight other members exclusive of William Alexander, secretary. Shirley presented a statement of existing conditions, and the Council determined against proceeding to at-

am, for the Reasons there given, as well as several others, in Sentiment with them, that it is more adviseable to employ our whole Strength here the Remainder of this Season in finishing the necessary Barracks for the Men, and Works

tack Niagara or Frontenac. The Minutes of the Council are printed (1 Penna. Arch. 2, 427). Its conclusions follow :—

The Council after fully debating what his Excellency laid before them, acquainted him that Several matters of Consequence had occurred to them, which they conceiv'd ought to be made a part of the State of our present situation, and desired his leave to have them entered on the Minutes of this Council, which his Excellency consented to, and are as follows, Vizt. : Major Bradstreet declared that from his own Observation, and the Intelligence he had received since his residence here, he is persuaded that about 1650 Canadeans, went at several times this summer from Cadaraqui to Niagara in order to proceed to the Ohio; a great part of which for want of Provisions, must as he judg'd now be on their return to Canada; that a great Number of French Traders every year go from Canada to trade with the Indians living near the French Settlements at Fort Detroit, and to the Westward of it, who at this Season of the Year generally return home to Canada; That their Passage home is by the way of Niagara, and that it is very probable that they and all the French Troops will stop as long as their Provisions will admit of at Niagara, to defend it against the Attempt intended upon it, of which they doubtless have intelligence.

That we have but few proper Battoe Men here, nor is it possible to have a sufficient Number of them to Conduct the Battoes to Niagara, as the People of the Country who understand the management of them are chiefly employed in bringing our Provisions to us from Skenectady, and in carrying Provisions to the Army at Lake George, so that very few of the Albany Men are now with us. That the Soldiers cannot conduct the Battoes to Niagara thro' so ruff Water, as is now generally five days in six upon the Lake.

The Council, after mature advisement upon the several before mentioned matters, declared that they were unanimously of opinion that tho' from our advices, there appears to be a great probability of a sufficient Quantity of Provisions arriving here in a short time, they ought not to be depended upon, until their actual arrival, especially as since the last Council, we have had frequent Alarms of Indians in scalping Parties being in this Neighbourhood, one of which had killed and scalped three of our Men who were at Work near the new Fort building on the opposite side of the River, and had carried off two Prisoners, who may find Opfor securing this Place against any sudden Attempt; and to take the Advantage of an early campaign the next Spring for acting upon these Lakes, than to proceed this Year to Niagara: I think I may without presumption say, I could

portunities of cutting off our Provision Battoes, in their Passage between the Oneida Carrying Place and Oswego, notwithstanding the precautions which have been hitherto or may be taken hereafter for their protection; the Consequences of which would be very fatal to the Troops who remain here, and to the Party that goes to Niagara; this is the more to be apprehended, as most of our Indians are going home, and the French Indians at Cadaraqui may take the advantage of their Absence for that purpose; Also, that it is not adviseable for so many of the Troops to be risqu'd in Battoes on the Lake at this Season of the Year.

That they are unanimously of Opinion, that for the preservation of the Men at this place, it is absolutely necessary that Barracks for the Number of Men proposed by his Excellency, be built without delay; That the Fort already begun on the Hill, on the opposite side of the River be finished as soon as possible, and Cannon mounted in it, to prevent the Enemy from making themselves masters of it; that it is likewise very expedient to erect a Work as soon as may be on the Eminence West of the old Fort and Cannon mounted there, to prevent the Enemy landing on that Side and gaining the Eminence; all which cannot possibly be effected before the Winter is too far set in, without employing the whole Strength now at this place.

That they are unanimously of opinion that nothing more can be done at Niagara this Fall than to dislodge the French and demolish their Works there, which from our intelligence, appears to be so weak as not to make it adviseable for his Excellency to leave a Garrison there without erecting new Works, which neither the lateness of the Season nor the present Circumstances of our Provisions will admit, so that no effectual possession can be taken of that Pass this Year.

That therefore, upon the whole, they are unanimously and clearly of opinion that it would be much more adviseable for his Excellency to defer making any Attempt, either against Niagara or Cadaraqui until the next Year, when there is great reason to expect he will be joined in any Attempt against the French by great Numbers of Indians of the five Nations, and draw off some of the far Nations of Indians now in Alliance with the French, most of which had taken up the Hatchet against the English, and been active against General Braddock on the Ohio; as also, that he may have the advantage of opening the campaign at least 15 days

be answerable that every part of his Majesty's Service requisite to be done for securing the whole Western and Southern Country, as far as the Missisippi, together with the Indian Trade, might with 6000 Men, as I have mention'd in my Letter of the 12th of August,[1] and which may I hope be assembled here by the first of May or sooner, be effected the next Year. If more Force should be wanting, there·remain the four Independent Companies posted at New York, and the New Jersey's Provincial Regiment of 500 Men, which that Government hath lately voted to be continu'd in his Majesty's Service with me untill May, and I shall endeavour to get continu'd in it, the whole Summer.

What I mean by every part of his Majesty's Service requisite to be done for securing this whole Country and the Indian Trade, is the Reduction of Fort Frontenac in the first Place (which must be the Work of but a few Days, if attack'd early in the Spring with 4 or 5000 Men, and a proper Train of Artillery) and securing the Harbour there and River Iroquois, the Reduction of the small Fort Toronto upon this Lake, the Fort at Niagara, that at Presque Isle upon Lake Erie, Fort Pourchartrain on the Strait between Lake Erie, and Lake St Clair, commonly call'd the Detroit, and the Fort at Missilimackinac on the Lake Huron, and securing the sev-

earlier than the Enemy can from Montreal, on account of the distance of that place from Lake Ontario, and the difficulty of the Navigation thither at that Season, occasion'd by the Rapidity of the Waters of the Great Lake emptying into the River Iroquois; Besides, that his Excellency may then have such a further Number of Forces as may be judged sufficient for the intended Operations upon these Lakes, and a sufficient Number of Whale Boats instead of Battoes, together with a stronger naval force, both which they think necessary to be provided against next Spring for his Majesty's Service upon the Lake Ontario; and they are unanimously of Opinion that in the meantime it is most adviseable for his Excellency to employ the whole Strength now here in providing Barracks for the Men, erecting Forts on the two Eminences which Commands this place, and finishing the other necessary Works. P. R. O., C. O. 5, 46. A copy is in the Library of Congress and another in the Parkman transcripts in the Mass. Hist. Society.

[1] See the letter mentioned, *ante*, p. 221.

eral Harbours and passes upon these Lakes and Straits; all which, I am fully perswaded, might with the Force propos'd, a small Train of Artillery, and 400 Whale Boats for transporting the Men, Provisions and Stores upon the several Lakes, and 200 Indians, which Number I doubt not, would join in the Service, together with some of the Indian Traders from Albany and Pensilvania for Pilots, be done in the next Year.

The Effect of this, Sir, will be to exclude the French from the Lakes Ontario, Erie, St Clair, Huron, and Michigan, and the River Ohio thro all their Routes to it, and break up all their Settlements upon them, and consequently their Trade with all the Western Nations of Indians on this Side of their Settlements upon the Missisippi, as may appear upon the Inspection of the inclos'd Sketch.

That the Expediency of this Scheme may be the better judg'd of, I would beg leave to observe, that the only Entrance, which the French have from Canada into the Lake Ontario with Vessells or any kind of Boats, is thro' the River Iroquois; so that Fort Frontenac is as much the Key of the Lake to the French, as Oswego is the Key of it to the English.

That as all the French Settlements upon this Lake, and the Strait of Niagara, Lake Erie, the Detroit, Lake Huron, Lake Michigan, and the River Ohio depend upon Canada for their Support, the most remote of them being at too immense a Distance from the Missisippi to receive it from thence, and none of them being able to subsist themselves at present, the Cutting the French off from their Passage into the Lake Ontario, thro' the River Iroquois must be the Destruction of all those Settlements.

That covering Oswego and the Country of the Six Nations, as well as breaking up the before-mention'd Settlements of the French, and securing the back parts of his Majesty's Western Colonies against their Attempts would be more expeditiously and effectually done, and with less Expence by the Reduction of Fort Frontenac, and cutting off their Entrance into the Lake Ontario from Montreal thro' the

River Iroquois, as is above propos'd, than by beginning to oppose the French with a strong Fort at Niagara, which, it must be expected, they will be continually annoying with a considerable Naval, as well as Land Force, whilst they continue in the Possession of Fort Frontenac with Harbours upon this Lake, and an Entrance into Lake Ontario thro' the beforemention'd River, unless they are prevented by a superior Naval Force of the English; which it will probably be more expensive and difficult to do, than to cutt them off from their Navigation upon the Lake by the other Method.

I beg leave further to observe, Sir, that as the Execution of this Scheme will open an Entrance for the English into the most distant parts of the Country of the Western or far Nations of Indians (as they are frequently call'd) it will put it into their Power to secure those two great, essential points, the carrying on an exclusive Trade with those Indians, and thereby fixing them absolutely in the Interest of the English; the latter of which is the natural Consequence of the former, as Great Britain can supply the Indians with all their Woolens, (of which there is now a very great Consumption among 'em, as well as among the Eastern Nations) at a cheaper Rate than France can.

As to the Expence of maintaining this Acquisition, 800 Men properly distributed in the Forts and Trading Houses necessary for securing all the Settlements and Harbours within it, (except the Fort and Harbour at Cadaraqui, where Fort Frontenac stands, and the River Iroquois) together with two arm'd Schooners or Sloops of about 60 Tonn each, four Arm'd Schooners or Row Gallies of about 25 Tonn, to be distributed on the several Lakes before mention'd, and a proper Number of Whale Boats to attend them, would be sufficient. The great Stress would lie at Cadaraqui and on the River Iroquois. It must be expected, that the French will push with all their Force from Montreal to remove the English from thence, and regain the Harbour there, and Communication with Lake Ontario; on the other hand, it must be consider'd under what Disadvantages they must effect it. Cadaraqui is 180 Miles distant from Montreal, and the Navigation to it thro' the River Iroquois is against the Stream and practicable, for much the greatest part of the Way by Boats only: It is not above 50 miles distant from Oswego; and the navigation of it over the Lake in shipping [is by ships?]. It seems besides, from the account given of this River, easy to cutt off their Transportation of Men, Provisions, and Stores of all kinds thro' it, from Montreal; in which Case the French would be oblig'd to march their Troops, and transport their Provisions and Stores by Land; so that, at all Events, it would be much more difficult for them to support a Siege against a Fort at Cadaraqui, than for the English to support a Garrison there from Oswego.

I can't therefore but think that the Works necessary to be erected at Cadaraqui, and on the River Iroquois might be defended by 1000 Men against all the Force that Canada could bring against it, especially as they might be supported from Oswego by speedy Reinforcements from the Colonies; and it is highly probable, the six Nations, which are near at hand, would most heartily join in the Defence of them. The charge of these 1800 Men, and the Naval Force propos'd would be the standing Expence of maintaining the Dominion of the great Lakes and Southern Country, as far as the Missisippi, and be greatly overpaid by the Increase of the English Furr Trade; The Works at Cadaraqui and on the River Iroquois may be something expensive; but they will make a Saving in the Naval Force upon the Lake Ontario, and Works at Oswego and Niagara, which must otherwise be larger than what will be requisite according to the Scheme propos'd; and this too would be much overpaid by the immediate Increase of the Furr Trade.

Another Advantage arising from this Scheme deserves a particular Remark, vizt, that I find from the Accounts, I have receiv'd since I came here, that Montreal is at present more accessible thro' the River Iroquois than in any other way; and I think it very practicable, if the Colonies will join to compass the Reduction of it the next Spring, besides that of the Southern and Western Country, which, if effected, must end in that of all Canada, whenever it shall be his Majesty's Pleasure.

The Opportunities I have had since my Arrival here of informing myself with more precision than ever of the Spot upon which Fort Frontenac[1] is situated, and the Command it hath of the only Entrance of the French into the Lake Ontario from Canada, have shewn me the Importance of the immediate Reduction of that Fort, and of cutting the French off from their Passage thro' the River Iroquois in a clearer light than I had view'd it in before, and this soon bent my thoughts upon attempting both before I went to Niagara; But as the Intelligence, I had receiv'd of the number of veteran Forces then lately arriv'd from Montreal at the French Fort, and the Commandant's Expectation of the Speedy Arrival of a larger Number made the Attempt appear to me too hazardous for the Number of Raw Troops, which I could spare from this Place; I turn'd them upon the immediate Reduction of Niagara; which seem'd the only practicable Attempt in my Power this Year.

As I have been prevented from doing that, I am determin'd to begin the Operations of the next Year with attempting the Reduction of Fort Frontenac.

The Success of that and the Succeeding Operations under my present immediate Command will depend upon as early a Campaign, as the Season will allow; for which Reason, among others, I concluded upon leaving the Body of my own and Sir William Pepperrell's Regiments in Winter Quarters here, and order'd the two Regiments under the Command of Col. Dunbar and the late Sir Peter Halkett into Winter Quarters at Albany and Schenectady, where they are daily expected: The New Jersey Regiment will likewise go into Winter Quarters at or near Schenectady, as will the two

[1] Fort Frontenac, known also as Cadaraqui (Cadaracoui), was a French post on the northern shore of Lake Ontario at the entrance to the St. Lawrence (Iroquois, Cadaracoui) River. As Shirley points out its capture by Bradstreet, in 1758, not only cut off Fort Duquesne from Canadian support, but opened the way for the advance upon Montreal and Quebec. See *post*, p. 345, and Shirley's statement on p. 350.

Independent Companies, which were Sent from New York last Year to the late Major General Braddock, in Albany and the City of New York.

I am now employing the whole Strength, I have with me upon building Barracks and erecting the two Forts, which I hope to see near finish'd, together with the Hospital greatly wanted for the Sick, before I leave this Place, where I purpose staying untill the 20th of next Month.

On my Return I am in hopes of meeting the Governors of Maryland and Pensilvania at New York, and having a Conference with them and Sir Charles Hardy upon the general plan of Service for both the Eastern and Western Colonies next Year, and shall endeavour in my passage thro' Connecticutt and Rhode Island to have an Interview with the Governors of those Colonies for the same purpose, and hope, by the latter End of November or beginning of December, to meet my own Assembly at Boston, where my presence will be then very necessary.

As I look upon the Success of his Majesty's Service upon this Lake in the ensuing Year to depend greatly upon an early Campaign, and having a sufficient Force to open it vigourously with; I purpose, if it is his Majesty's Pleasure, that I should continue in my present general Command the next Year, to return to Albany by the beginning of April, and embrace the first Opportunity the Season will allow for proceeding to Oswego, and shall, upon my Arrival at Boston, use my utmost Endeavours to raise the 2000 Men, for which I had his Majesty's Orders in the Letter, I had the Honour to receive from you of the 10th of last February, and which I conceive his Service stands even much more in need of now, as the French have this Summer landed 3000 Veteran Troops from Europe in North America; and Hostilities are greatly increas'd there.

The Difficulties I shall have to encounter this Winter will be raising the 2000 new Levies in time, His Majesty's three Regiments of Nova Scotia, and the two British ones last arriv'd and Sir William Pepperrell's being all compleating to 1000 Men each upon this Continent, and my own and the four Independent Companies of New York standing in need of a large Number of Recruits likewise, besides the great Number of Provincial Troops, which should be rais'd or inlisted de novo by the Spring, all which must amount to many thousands : Also the providing proper Magazines of Provisions and Stores between this Place and Schenectady for the Service here, so as to be secure of their Arrival in time, and the getting 400 Whale boats built for transporting them and the Men, over and above the Battoes, we already have.

I am in Hopes, that from the Experience, we have had of the Disappointments in the transportation of so great a Quantity of provisions, Stores, and Baggage, and Number of Soldiers this Year from Albany and Schenectady to this Place; (being a vastly larger Embarcation, than was ever yet made in this Country) much Expence may be sav'd, in proportion to what will be transported, the next Spring; especially by means of the Whale-Boats propos'd to be built, which would otherwise have been necessary for the Navigation of the great Lakes, and are a new Species of Boats, which I have made a trial of here, having experienc'd the Utility of them in the Bay of Funda, and in our Eastern Rivers in New England.

Arms and Cloathing for the 2000 Men, I am order'd by his Majesty to raise, over and above what will compleat his other Regiments in North America to 1000 Men each, should be sent from England in time; the 2000 Stands of Arms consign'd to me the last Spring were all distributed among the 2000 New England Men sent then to Nova Scotia ; the time for which they were inlisted for that Service will not expire before March or April next; and from Lieut. Govr. Lawrence's Letters I find, his Majesty's Service in Nova Scotia will not permit him to discharge them sooner. I have already and shall again desire those Arms to be sent me to Boston, but it seems too uncertain to depend wholly upon having them in time for the 2000 New Levies. Many Arms, I find, have been likewise lost by the Soldiers of Col. Dunbar's and the late Sir Peter Halket's Regiments in the Action at Monongahela. The Sending of what Arms and Cloathing shall be judg'd proper to North America, if sent to New York instead of Boston, would save a fortnight or three Weeks time, as the Men may receive them at Albany, where the Governor of New York may, upon their Arrival there, be directed to send them. A Number of Arms likewise lost by Desertions from my own and Sir William Pepperrell's Regimts in their passage to this Place, and Since their Encampment here, according to the inclos'd Copy of a Return of them, sign'd by the proper Officers [of both those Regiments], are wanted to replace them: and I am bound in Fidelity to His Majesty's Service to inclose to you, Sir, a Copy of a late Memorial[1] to me from the Field Officers of both those Regiments, representing the bad Condition of the Arms and Accoutrements of the Soldiers (many of which are unserviceable) and further to acquaint You that the Arms sent the last Year to the Govr. of Virginia, part of which he lent to the provincial Troops of New York and New Jerseys, are equally bad; insomuch, that the general bad Character, which at present prevails by this means in the Colonies, of his Majesty's Arms, will, besides the other ill Consequences, which may arise to his Troops in Action, prejudice his Service here, if not rectify'd.[2]

A Train of Artillery, such an one as shall be judg'd proper, and Ordnance Stores of all kinds are likewise wanting, Sir,

[1] For the memorial referred to, see p. 276.

[2] Up to the entrance of William Pitt into the control of England's policy, in 1757, the defense of her Continental Colonies in America had rarely been considered by Great Britain as a duty. To a far greater degree than France England had expected America to care for herself, and the colonies had done so, but despite this fact British officers had considered the colonial soldier as hardly worthy of notice. The feeling of Braddock is well known and Wolfe at the outset of his campaigns in 1758 referred to Americans as "in general the dirtiest, most contemptable, cowardly dogs that you can conceive. . . . Such rascals are rather an incumbrance than any real strength to an army." Shirley had at least one qualification for his command in America. His experience had taught him not to despise the French and to place reliance upon a well-armed colonial soldier, and Wolfe also learned the same lesson.

As the transportation of pieces of Ordnance either by Land thro' this Wilderness Country, or Water thro' the Rivers and Creeks, which abound with Reefs and Shoals, is very difficult; Brass Pieces would be very convenient; in particular six, twelve, and eighteen pounders, Mortars of nine inch Diameter, and Hoyetts for seven Inch Shells; a thousand barrells of pistol powder, and the same Quantity of cannon powder should be sent, and Matrosses are likewise greatly wanted here.

It is necessary, Sir, to mention to you here, that there is not the least Expectation, that the Colonies can be induc'd to furnish Levy Money for raising the New Levies order'd by his Majesty: And as the commanding Officers of all his Majesty's Regiments have apply'd to me, since the Death of General Braddock, for Order's and Directions upon that Article among others, being, as they say, without Directions from home, I have not been able to direct them to any practicable Method of providing the Money, except drawing upon their respective Regiments; nor will it be possible for myself to raise the 2000 new levies without drawing upon the Paymaster General or his Deputies here, as for a contingent charge; nor can the levies be rais'd without a previous Appointment of Officers, the Captains and Subalterns at least, and I much question whether without a nomination of Field Officers as high as Lieutt. Colonels. I suppose it is not design'd that the 2000 shall be made Independent Companies.

I have not yet mention'd any thing concerning Fort Frontenac's being an Incroachment upon the Country of the Iroquois, or five Nations of Indians. The fierce wars, which they made upon the French on account of Monsr. Frontenac's first building it, and in which it was once destroy'd by them, leave no room for doubting that: The French to this Day mark the Country in their Charts with the Name of "pais des Iroquois du Nord"; and their calling the River Iroquois St Lawrence's River is but a late Innovation.

The only pretence, they can make for calling the River Iroquois a part of St. Lawrence's River, is because it falls

into it; for the same Reason they might call the River Ou-
taiais St Lawrence's River, which they never yet pretended
to do; The River Iroquois hath it's Source from the Lake
Ontario, and after a Course of near 180 Miles falls into the
River St Lawrence and if that makes it a part of that River;
then all the Rivers, which fall into the Danube may be call'd
the Danube, and the great Rivers, which fall into the Ocean,
Arms of the Sea.

As the inclos'd Sketch which is design'd chiefly to point
out the Several Routes thro' the Lakes, Straites, and
Rivers, there delineated, may serve to do that in a more un-
perplex'd Manner than in the Maps, I have inclos'd it.[1]

I am with the highest Regard,
    Sir,
        Your most Humble, and
           most Obedient Servant.
                W. SHIRLEY.

Rt. Honble. Sir Thomas Robinson Knt. of the Bath,
one of his Majesty's principal Secretaries of State.

JOHN RUTHERFORD TO WILLIAM SHIRLEY [2]

Albany, September 30, 1755.

SIR,
I give your Excellency the trouble of this from some things
that pass'd in a Conversation I had yesterday with the Baron

---

[1] On Oct. 10 Shirley emphasized his views as to the necessity
of taking positive action on the Great Lakes by writing Sir Thomas
Robinson a letter of over 500 words (P. R. O., C. O. 5, 46) on the
movements of the French. In this letter the Governor states that
he has intelligence that the French are building a Vessel of one
hundred or one hundred and twenty tons burden at Frontenac.
He considers it necessary for the English to have, at least, one
vessel of equal force, and very adviseable to have two, as early in
the spring as may be, adding that in his opinion the enemy are
preparing for an attack upon Oswego, and that one was intended
for the season just past.

[2] The original of this letter is in Mass. Arch., Col. Ser. 54, 168,
at Boston. A copy was inclosed by Shirley in his letter to Secy.

Dieskau, and his Aid de Camp, The Baron seemed not only to think the French would easily maintain Crown Point against General Johnston's Army, but that from what he had seen and been informed of their Discipline that I might Depend upon it though Doubted, they would never Arrive there. In talking of General Braddock's defeat, he said none of their Officers was Surprized in the least at it, as 'twas a Constant Maxim with them Never to expose Regulars in Woods, without a Sufficient Number of Indians and Irregulars for any Attack that Might be expected. But what I thought of most Consequence, to inform your Excellency of as immediately Concerning the Expedition you are now engaged in, is that I find the Baron is perfectly well Acquainted with the Country round Lake Ontario, with the great consequence Oswego, is of to us, and does not doubt but that you may take Niagara, if you carry the Forces, Artillery etca. you have at Oswego, Safely there, but in that case they have half the Forces that Arrived with him from Brest, with a Sufficient Number of Canadians and Indians not only to take Oswego but likewise Effectually to cut off your Retreat lying Ready at Fort Frontenac with boats etca. to set out on the first Notice, and seems very Confident that the Six Nations will Continue Steady in their Neutrality except the Mohawks who have Already Joined us.[1] Your

Robinson, Dec. 19, 1755, and a transcript of this is among the British transcripts in the Library of Congress at Washington. Rutherford, in 1761, requested through Lord Amherst a grant of land near Niagara and received from that general a permit to settle upon the spot desired. Amherst to Pitt, May 4, 1761.

[1] In P. R. O., C. O. 5, 46, there is a copy of a paper sent by Johnson to Shirley, and by the latter forwarded to the British Government, which gives a list of the French forces. The information in this list appears to have been obtained from, if not written by, Baron Dieskau. See Dieskau to Commissary Doreil, Aug. 16, 1755, 2 Penna. Arch. 6, 223 ; Account of French Army in Johnson Papers, 2, 221, and Johnson's letter to Sir Charles Hardy of Sept. 16, Johnson Papers, 2, 222 ; Docts. rel. Col. Hist. N. Y. 6, 1013. See also Shirley to Robinson, Oct. 5, *post*, p. 309, and Rutherford to Shirley, Sept. 22, *ante*, p. 278, where the information as to the French troops is summarized.

Excellency will see how this Agrees with your Intelligence from Fort Frontenac and I hope the Forces under Col. Dunbar expected here every day may be of Service at Least to Secure the Communication twixt this and Oswego at all events,

I have the Honour to be with the greatest Respect,
Sir
    Your Excellency's
        Most Obedient and Most
        Humble Servant
                            JOHN RUTHERFORD.

AMERICAN INTELLIGENCE FROM MR. POWNALL [1]

[London, October 1, 1755.]

The following Particulars relating to the Situation of Affairs in America are taken from private Letters and from the Boston News Papers of the 14, 15, and 18. of August, brought by a Vessel which arrived yesterday from Boston, viz.

That Advice had been received at Annapolis in Maryland, that Colo. Dunbar with the Remainder of the two Regiments under his Command was to march from Fort Cumberland on the 29th of July for Ray's Town in Pensylvania.

That it appeared from the Accounts given by a Man, who was taken Prisoner upon the Frontiers of Pensylvania, and carried to Fort du Quesne, from whence he escaped after the Action upon the Monongahela, that the French Forces at that Fort consisted of 3000 Men.

That General Shirley with the Forces under his Command was upon the Mohawk River about 100 Miles from Oswego on the 6th of August, and that he had sent Orders to Colo.

---

[1] *B. M., Additional Manuscript 33,029, 212.* A transcript is in the Library of Congress. Mr. Pownall was probably John Pownall, Secretary of the Lords of Trade, and the information presented to the Commissioners appears to have been obtained in large part from Sir William Johnson. See Pownall to Johnson, acknowledging letters and papers, Oct. 9, 1755, Johnson Manuscripts, 3, 56, and Docts. rel. Col. Hist. N. Y. 6, 1017.

Dunbar to compleat his two Regiments to 1000 each, and join him as soon as possible; for which purpose he was to embark at Amboy in New Jersey, and proceed by way of Albany.[1]

That Colo. Johnson was still at Albany waiting for some warlike Stores he expected; and that he was disappointed of part of his Force by the New Hampshire Troops not joining him.

That upon Advice of the Arrival of the French Troops from Europe at Quebec, several of the Colonies had agreed to an augmentation of the forces destined for Crown Point, viz.

New York	400.
Rhode Island	150.
Massachusets	300.
Connecticut	500.

That Captain Bradstreet, who commands at Oswego, had launched one of the Vessels built there to be employed upon Lake Ontario, and had sunk several French Canoes.

That the News of General Braddock's Defeat had not had any bad Effect upon the Indians of the Five Nations, who only took notice of it as an Accident, from which they should learn to proceed in their Expedition with more Caution.

That Colo. Lawrence, Lieut. Governor of Nova Scotia, had resolved to remove the French Inhabitants of that Province, and to disperse them in the other Colonies upon the Continent; for which purpose he had prepared Vessels to transport them.

That the Fleet under Admiral Boscawen's Command had taken a Snow from France laden with Provisions for Louisbourg; also a Ship from Canada for France; also a French armed Snow; and sent them into Halifax.

Endorsed:
American Intelligence from Mr. Pownall Octr. 1st, 1755.

[1] See Shirley to Josiah Willard, Oct. 1, 1755, in Mass. Arch., Col. Ser. 54, 170.

WILLIAM SHIRLEY TO CHARLES HARDY [1]

Camp at Oswego, October 4, 1755.

SIR,

Yesterday I had the Honour of your Excellency's Letter of the 26th September. The instance you have given of your Attention to the public Service, in removing from New York to Albany before you could be well recover'd from the Fatigue of your Voyage, must have a very good Effect for expediting it.

I am much afraid it will be thought an extraordinary Expence to the Crown for his Majesty to be oblig'd to build Barracks for the Reception of the Troops of Colonel Dunbar's and the late Sir Peter Halket's Regiments at Albany and Schenectady this Winter, when perhaps he may not have Occasion for Barracks there again. But as it is absolutely necessary for the good of his Service in the Operation of the next year's Campaign that those Troops should be quartered there this Winter, and your Excellency informs me in your Letter that you are apprehensive of great Inconveniencies in disposing of those Troops at Albany by hiring houses for them there, and you mention, that "you could "wish you had my Instructions for the constructing of Bar-"racks there and at Schenectady, which you apprehend may "be done at any easy Rate, least your Assembly should not "care to be at such an Expense;" I desire your Excellency would take the Care upon you of providing such Barracks at the two before mentioned places, as you shall judge proper for the reception of the two aforesd Regiments which I believe at present don't exceed 1200 Men, but will, I hope, be recruited by the Spring to 1000 each, and that you

---

[1] Printed: 1 Penna. Arch. 2, 435. See also Shirley to Gov. Horatio Sharpe, Arch. of Md. 6, 288, and Shirley to Josiah Willard, Mass. Arch., Col. Ser. 54, 173, both of equal date. Sir Charles Hardy was governor of Newfoundland in 1744, and served as British Administrative Governor of New York, 1755–1757. He was grandson of Sir Thomas Hardy, the naval commander, and served as Rear Admiral at Louisbourg in 1758.

would give Orders accordingly to have them built as soon as possible, that the Troops may not, upon their Arrival in your Government, be destitute of Quarters to receive them.

In case your Excellency can't induce the Assembly of New York to be at the Charge of building those Barracks, I will give you one or more Warrants upon the Deputy Paymaster for the Southern District for such Sums of money as shall be requisite to defray the Expence of building them, and your Excellency will be pleas'd to look upon this as my Instruction to you for that purpose.

I can't, however, but hope that the Assembly of New York will think it reasonable that the Province should be at the Charge. It was very much at the motion of their Govt. that I determined to draw these Troops from the Southward this Year. The Province will in an especial manner have not only the Benefit of being covered by them this Winter, but of their Service at Oswego in the ensuing Spring, and the Inhabitants draw very large Sums of Money from the Residence of the Troops among them, as they will in general from the Expedition, in which they are employ'd, and I have to add that the Province of the Massachusetts Bay thought it reasonable upon the raising of the Regiments under my own Command to erect Barracks at the Charge of the Govt. for the Reception of upwards of 800 Troops.

As to Garrisoning Fort Edward [1] or the Fort building at Lake George with any part of the Troops of these two Regiments this Winter, it would disappoint that part of the Service for which His Majesty principally destin'd them, and which is of infinitely more Consequence to the publick than any Saving it could make by their being quarter'd in those Forts so that I have no thought of posting any of them there.

I have kept two Companies posted the whole Campaign upon the Oneida Carrying place, and purpose to leave one there this Winter, but must endeavour to prevent its giving

---

[1] Fort Edward was on the Hudson river about fifteen miles south of Lake George, at what was known as the Great Carrying Place. It had been known as Fort Lyman, *ante*, p. 282 n.

Umbrage to the Oneida Indians who have express'd some uneasiness at the Building we have already there.

I shall place Garrisons in Fort Hunter and the Fort at Conejahora this Winter. They have had a Garrison of twenty-five men, and an Officer at each of them the whole Summer.

I approve much of having small Forts erected in every one of the Six Nations of Indians, as what will have a great tendency to conciliate them to the English, and to fix them in a dependence upon his Majesty. For this reason I will send thirty men to the Onandaga Castle to build them one at their own Request to me, and shall propose the same thing to the Oneidas, and if they consent to it, will have a small one built upon their Carrying place, as I shall likewise think it right to do in the Country of the Tuscaroras, Cayugas and Senecas. Not that I am of opinion these Forts will secure the Indian Country to his Majesty against the French; nothing can effectually do that or cover the English Territories South-Eastward of this Lake, but holding Oswego. If that, which is the Key of the Country of the six Nations, should be lost to the French, they will soon be masters of that whole Country, and draw all those Indians intirely into their Interest; and when that shall happen your Excellency may look upon all the intermediate Country between this Lake and the City of New York to be gone too.

With regard to the little security and cover, which the Fort now building by General Johnson at Lake George, will afford to the Country between Albany and Crown Point, and the necessity of his Forces proceeding as far at least as Ticonderoge this year, I have so fully express'd my Sentiments in my Letters to General Johnson, Copies of which I have transmitted to your Excellency, that I need say nothing further, and I can't but hope from the accounts I have of reinforcements daily pouring in upon him from New England, that the Troops under his Command are gone on.

The three points in which the General Welfare of his Majesty's Northern Colonies, and Consequently his Majesty's Service in North America, are at present most essentially interested, are the Removal of the French from their Incroachments in Nova Scotia, from those upon the Great Lakes and Rivers in the Southern Country between Canada and the Mississippi, and from those at Crown Point and upon the Lake Iroquois, commonly called Lake Champlain. These therefore ought to be the great objects of their present Attention.[1] As to inferior Securities and Covers of small Portions of the Country, when the principal parts of the Service are compass'd, they will fall in of Course. The first of these points is happily effected; the second of them may be most effectually carry'd into Execution in the Course of the next year, with the united Strength of his Majesty's Regular Troops and the New Jersey Regt. against all the Force that the French will probably be able to draw together upon the great Lakes and Rivers, provided the Campaign is begun early and the same Spirit is then exerted by the colonies for the reduction of the French forts at Crown Point &c. as hath been by those of New England and New York the last summer, and is still continued by the former. With respect to the third great point I can not but hope that if the Reduction of Crown Point should not be found practicable this Year, yet General Johnson may be able at least to make himself Master of the pass at Ticonderoge, which will put into our power to secure the Reduction of that Fortress early the next summer, provided the Colonies act with the same Vigour then that those concern'd in it have hitherto done. But this, and the Success of his Majesty's Service in the other point, or even in proceeding to Montreal itself, if that should be judg'd expedient, will very much depend upon as general a Congress as may be of commissioners from the several governments this winter,[2] in order to fix upon a plan for the year ensuing, which if some sudden

[1] See Shirley to Gov. Horatio Sharpe of Maryland, Oct. 7 (Arch. of Md. 6, 291), where the Massachusetts governor requests a meeting with Hardy, Morris, and Sharpe at New York within thirty days, to discuss these objects of attention.

[2] For letter of Phips to Gov. Stephen Hopkins of Rhode Island as to convening such a Congress as this and the action of Rhode Island, see Col. Rec. R. I. 5, 463–467.

adjustment of the American points in dispute between the two Crowns don't put an End to the present Commotions in North America, must be a most critical one, either for securing the Interests of the English Colonies, and promoting his Majesty's Service in North America against the French or losing Ground there, according to our improvement or neglect of the opportunities it shall afford, and it is this Consideration, Sir, which hath induc'd me to lay my sentiments before your Excellency in so explicit a manner.

I am, &c.

W. SHIRLEY.

His Excellency Sir Charles Hardy, Knt.

WILLIAM SHIRLEY TO SIR THOMAS ROBINSON [1]

Camp at Oswego, October, 5th 1755.

SIR,

Inclos'd is a Copy, No 1, of a Letter dated 9th of Septr: from Major General Johnson to me, giving a particular Account of two Actions between him and the French at and near the Camp at Lake George, late Lake Sacrament, in his way to Crown point; a Copy, No. 2, of a Letter from Captain Eyre, Engineer in that Expedition to me upon the same Subject, dated Sepr: 10th from the Camp at Lake George; a Copy, No 3, of a Letter dated Sepr: 19th from me to General Johnson in Answer to his of the 9th of Sepr:; a Copy No. 4, of another Letter from me to General Johnson dated Sepr: 24th in Answer to Captain Eyre's; Extract, No. 5, of a Letter from Captain Rutherford to me dated Sepr: 22d, giving a succinct, and I believe, exact Account of the two beforemention'd Actions, a Copy, No 6, of a List of the forces, which the French General is suppos'd by General Johnson to have brought with him from Canada to Crown point and Ticonderoge, found among his Papers, and thought to be wrote in his own hand.[2]

[1] P. R. O., C. O. 5, 46. A transcript is in the Library of Congress.
[2] For letters inclosed see Johnson to Shirley, *ante*, p. 253; Eyre to Shirley, *ante*, p. 259; Shirley to Johnson, *ante*, pp. 270

Since those two Actions General Johnson hath received very great Reinforcements from New England, particularly from my own Government of the Massachusetts Bay, and the Colony of Connecti utt, the former of which hath in the whole voted 4300 for that Expedition, and Mr. Johnson must, according to Accounts transmitted to me from New England have had in the whole 8000 Men at least. What will be the Issue of that Expedition this Year, I don't certainly know yet, but have Reason to think it will be a dissatisfactory one to all the Colonies of New England, as well as to myself.

I would for the present, Sir, beg leave to referr You to the inclos'd Copies of No 3 and 4 of my Letters to General Johnson for my Sentiments of his Conduct, and Directions to him upon these Events, so far as it was proper for me to send them to him at the Distance I am from him.

I have the Honour to be with the highest Respect,
> Sir,
>> Your most Humble and most
>> Obedient Servant,

W. SHIRLEY.

Right Honble : Sir Thomas Robinson ⎱
Knight of the Bath etc.　　　　　⎰

Endorsed :
Camp at Oswego Octr. 5th, 1755.
Majr. Genl. Shirley.
R. Decr. 18th.

INFORMATION FROM PARIS [1]

Paris, October 20th. We are in daily Expectation of receiving an Account of an Action near Fort Frederick [Crown Point] in Canada. According to a Letter receiv'd

and 280 ; Rutherford to Shirley, *ante,* p. 278 ; and note of Rutherford to Shirley of Sept. 30, *ante,* p. 301.

[1] P. R. O., C. O. 5, 46. This extract of a letter gave the American Commander an idea as to the knowledge current in Paris. It was inclosed in Shirley to Robinson, Jan. 12, 1756.

from Quebeck, dated the 17th August last they had re-ceiv'd advice there, that a body of 3000 English was Arriv'd about thirty Leagues Distance of Fort Frederick, and that Another Courier arriv'd at Montreal, with an Account, that on the 12th of August they were within Ten Leagues of the Fort; that Baron Dieskau, who was march'd with the Troops sent from France, and 4500 men part Canadians and part Wild Indians, to form the Siege of Fort Chouaguen, had given over that Enterprize, and was March'd towards Fort Frederick with two Battalions, 1200 Canadians, and 600 Indians, which the Governour of Quebeck got together upon the first News of the March of the English.

Extract of an Article from Paris
dated Octr. 20th, 1755.
Examin'd by
Wm. Alexander, Secy.

Endorsed:
Extract of an Article from Paris dated Octr. 20th, 1755. in M. G. Shirley's, Janry 12th, 1756.

THOMAS DUNBAR AND THOMAS GAGE TO WILLIAM SHIRLEY

BEHAVIOUR OF THE TROOPS AT THE MONONGAHELA [1]

Albany, [October] 21, 1755.

By Order of His Excellency Major General Shirley Commander in Chief of his Majesty's Forces in North America, — The different Officers of the late Sir Peter Halket's and Coll Dunbar's Regiment and Others, who were in the Late Action under

[1] P. R. O., C. O. 46. Inclosed in Shirley to Robinson, Nov. 5, 1755. The inquiry is endorsed Nov. 21, probably an error for Oct. 21, and was undertaken at Shirley's direction (pp. 242 and

Major General Braddock on the Monongahela on the 9th of July 1755, being Called
to enquire into the Causes and Circumstances of the bad Behaviour of the King's
Troops in the said Action, —
It Appears that the Troops were on their March when the
first Alarm was given by a Fire on the Van Guard, Commanded by Coll Gage; That an Order was then given to the
Main Body to advance; that they Accordingly Marched
forward in good Order and with great Alacrity, but when they
had Advanced to a particular place, they were ordered to
halt with a design of forming into a Line of Battle, But when
that was Attempted, it Proved ineffectual, the Whole falling
into Confusion, and all the endeavours of the Officers could
not get them into any Regular Form, and being by this time
within Reach of the Enemy's Fire, they Appeared Struck
with a panick, and though some seemed Willing to Obey,
when Ordered to form, Others Crowded upon them, Broke
their order, and Prevented it; and in this Irregular Manner
they Expended a great part of their Ammunition. Notwithstanding this Confusion, there were several Parties advanced from the Main Body in order to Recover the cannon,
but were fired upon, from the Rear by our own people, by
which Many were killed, and a great Many of them Discharged their pieces even in the Air; This confusion having
now Continued upwards of three hours, an Order was given
to beat a Retreat to bring the Men to Cover the Waggons,
and Carry off as Much as Could be, they stood about the
Waggons for some Little time Without any fire, and then

316). A transcript is in the Library of Congress and another
is among the Parkman Papers in the Mass. Hist. Society.

Thomas Gage was Lt. Col. of the 44th regiment under Braddock. He is better known to Americans as Governor of Massachusetts at the opening of the American Revolution, serving from
1774 to October 1775. His military advancement dates from 1758
when he became Colonel of the 80th regiment. He was placed in
command of the Army in North America in 1763 and made a Lt.
Genrl. in 1770. Retiring to England at the close of his career in
Massachusetts, Gage died in 1787.

a Smart fire Coming from the Front and Left Flank, the Whole took to Flight; Several Attempts were made to halt the Men, in Order to Make a Regular Retreat, but to no purpose, they went off as fast as they Could, until they got about three Miles from the field of Action, where there were about a hundred Men, halted with much Difficulty untill several Small Bodies Join'd them from the Rear, and then Continued the Retreat.

The Question being Asked, if any of the Men Could be Named, who had behaved Remarkably ill, Answer was made they Could Not Name any in particular and that the Bad behaviour was general; however, that Courts Martial were held on the Armys Arrival at Fort Cumberland, and the men, who had come off unwounded without Arms or Accoutrements were punished.

The Bad behaviour of the Men is in some Measures Attributed to the following Reasons.

1st: They were greatly Harrass'd by dutys unequal to their Numbers, Dispirited by Want of Sufficient Provisions, and not being allowed time to dress the little they had, with nothing to Drink but Water, and that Often Scarce and Bad.

2d: The frequent Conversations of the Provincial Troops and Country people was, that if they engaged the Indians in their European Manner of fighting, they would be Beat, and this some of their Officers Declared as their Opinion, and one of them to Coll Dunbar on the Retreat, for which he Severely Reprimanded him.

3d: The Want of Indians or other irregulars to give timely Notice of the Enemy's Approach, having only three or four guides for out Scouts.

Lastly the Novelty of an invisible enemy and the Nature of the Country, which was entirely a Forest.

THOS. DUNBAR Colo.
THOS. GAGE Lieut. Colo.

A true Copy Examin'd by
WM: ALEXANDER Secy.

Endorsed:

Inquiry into the Behaviour of the Troops at the Monongahela dated Albany 21st Novr. 1755. in Govr. Shirley's Novr. 5, 1755.

WILLIAM SHIRLEY TO WILLIAM WILLIAMS [1]

INSTRUCTIONS FOR CAPT. WILLIAMS

Fort Williams,
October 29, 1755.

You are to employ as many of the Men of the Detachment under your Command as you possibly can, in finishing the Fort this day marked out at this place and called Fort Williams,[2] and Compleating Barracks therein sufficient to contain 150 men. You are also to build therein a Store house of about the same dimensions of that already built here, and as soon as the Barracks are fit to receive the Men of your Detachment you are to Quarter them therein.

When the Works above directed are Compleated, you are to employ as many of the Men under your Command as you judge can be safely spared from Fort Williams in mending and repairing the road from hence to Wood Creek, especially in making a good Bridge over the place called the Morass, by first laying good sizeable Logs lengthways, parrallel to the road, well pinned down and then by laying other Logs of a less Size across and well fastned to the former.

And as I have ordered Lieutt. Col. Mercer to send from Oswego an Officer and thirty Men, to reinforce your De-

---

[1] P. R. O., C. O. 5, 46. A second copy is in C. O. 5, 47, and there is a transcript in the Library of Congress.

[2] Fort Williams was at the eastern end of the Mohawk or "Great Carrying Place." Its importance lay in its commanding the trade between the English and the Six Nations and guarding the route to Oswego and Lake Ontario. The carry was between the Mohawk River and Wood's Creek. A map in Hurlbut, "Historic Highways," 7, 143, reproducing one in the British Museum, shows the various forts at the crossing.

tachment, you are to take them under your Command, and quarter them also in Fort Williams.

And Whereas I have ordered Capt. Marcus Petri with the Men under his Command to build a Fort at the upper Landing on the Wood Creek, to be called Wood Creek Fort, and when that is Compleated to detain 20 of the Men of his Company to be employed in cleaning the Wood Creek down to the Mouth thereof and when that is finished and Capt. Petri leaves that Fort it will be proper to have a Guard there, you are then to send an Officer with thirty Men to Garrison that Fort.

When the Works above directed are Compleated you are to build another Storehouse in Wood Creek Fort.

And Lastly you are to endeavour to get as much Provision as you can, carried over to Wood Creek Fort.

W. Shirley.

Endo·sed:
Instructions for Capt. Williams
Octr. 29, 1755.

WILLIAM SHIRLEY TO SIR THOMAS ROBINSON [1]

Albany, November 5, 1755.

[Duplicate]

Sir,

Yesterday I had the Honour to receive a Letter from You dated the 28th of August,[2] acquainting me that their Excellencies the Lords Justices were pleased to order me to take, for the present and until His Majesty's Pleasure shall be further signified, the Command in Chief of all his Maj-

---

[1] P. R. O., C. O. 5, 46. A transcript is in the Library of Congress and another is in the Parkman Papers in the Mass. Hist. Society.

[2] *Ante*, p. 242. In a circular letter of November 4 from the Lords of Trade to the Colonial Governors, the establishment of a packet boat service between America and Great Britain had been considered, thus securing a more regular means of communication. (1 N. J. Arch. 8, pt. 2, 146.)

esty's Forces in North America, in the same manner and with the same powers, as the late General Braddock had it; and by the same conveyance I had the Honour to receive their Commission for that purpose transmitted to me by Mr. Fox.

I am likewise to acknowledge the receipt of copies of the several Orders, Letters and Instructions, which had been given at different times to the late General for his Guidance and Direction in the King's Service, as also of his letters to you.

You had before, Sir, in your Letter of the 31st of July [1] acquainted me the Earl of Holderness had made particular mention in a Letter to you from Hanover, of the high Honour his Majesty had been pleased to do me in Expressing his approbation of my Conduct and Behaviour in his Service; which Mark of his Royal Favour, I have the deepest Sense of, and shall Exert my best Endeavours for promoting his Service upon this Continent in Execution of the great Trust, which I have the Honour to have reposed in me.

In your beforementioned Letter of the 28th August, you likewise signified, Sir, the Directions of the Lords Justices to me, "to make all possible Enquiry into the Causes and Circumstances of the late bad Behaviour of the King's Troops upon the Monongahela, and to make as many Examples of the most notorious Delinquents, as should be found requisite and expedient to restore the Discipline of his Majesty's Forces in America." In Obedience to these Orders I directed the Commanding Officer of each of the Regiments concerned in that Action to enquire in the most particular and effectual manner into the Causes and Circumstances of the late bad Behaviour of those Troops, and to Report their Opinion to me, as also to let me know whether any and what Courts Martial had been held upon, and Examples made of the most notorious Delinquents among them; and inclos'd is the Report of those Officers, to which I beg leave to referr you.[2]

[1] Robinson's letter of July 31 is in P. R. O., C. O. 5, 281. It is devoted more particularly to an account of the success of Lt. Col. Robert Monckton in his attack on Beauséjour, Acadia, in June, 1755.
[2] This report is on p. 311. It is dated Nov. 21, evidently an error.

From this Report, as well as other Inquiries, I have made, it appears to me that the bad Behaviour of the Troops was so General, that there seems no room to distinguish any particular Delinquents to make Examples of, more than what the Report informs me hath been already done.

As to the Causes and Circumstances of this ill Behaviour, the Account of which, as given in the Report, doth not seem so distinct and clear as might be; they appear to me, Sir, from the best Inquiries, I have been able to make as follows.

I begin with the Marches, the General made with about 1400 picked troops for twenty days successively before the Action, because the first reason assigned in the latter end of the Report for their bad Behaviour alludes in a great Measure to those Marches, whereby they are supposed to have been harrass'd and dispirited.

In order to set this Article in a just Light, it is proper to acquaint you, Sir, that these Marches were occasioned by Intelligence the General had received of the Garrison of Fort Duquesne's expecting to be very suddenly Strengthned with a Considerable Reinforcement; which the General endeavoured to prevent by investing the Fort before their arrival there; and the Effect of those Marches seems to have been so far from dispiriting the Troops, or laying them under any disadvantages that by this means they passed the most dangerous defiles before they met the Enemy; and the Soldiers thereupon expressed a General Satisfaction, and advanced to meet them with great alacrity, as is taken notice of in the Report itself, the Officers on their part Congratulated the General upon it, as a most fortunate Event; and it seems clear from the inclosed Plan No. 1, in which is Delineated the disposition of the Kings Troops, and that of the Enemy, at the time of the latter's being discovered, that they were then in one Compact Body, and not possessed themselves of the Eminence, from whence it is observed in the Plan, they did the greatest Execution on the Kings Troops, but that the advanced Party under Lieut. Col. Gage and the working Party under Sir John St. Clair had both pass'd the

Hill before they received the Enemy's first Fire, which was made upon them in Front.

I would further observe, Sir, that the General Disposition of the Troops, he took with him, as it appears in the said Plan, seems to have been extremely well formed for the March he was upon, and to prevent Surprize: And though it is said in the Report that the first Alarm of the Enemy was given by a Fire on the Van Guard, Commanded by Colonel Gage, yet it appears from the said Plan, that the Scouts and Guides, which preceded the Troops, had given them a few Minutes notice of the Enemy's approach before the Van Guard received that Fire.

As to the Confusion, which the whole Body of Troops was thrown into soon after, the Account given of it in the Report is "That the main body being, upon the first News of the beforementioned Alarm, ordered to advance, they accordingly march'd in good Order and with great Alacrity; but when they had advanced to a particular place, they were ordered to halt with a design of forming into a Line of Battle, but when that was attempted it proved ineffectual the *whole* falling into Confusion."

The Place, at which the main Body halted, is not here mentioned, nor how it happened that the attempt made to form those Troops into a Line of Battle proved ineffectual, and that the whole thereupon fell into Confusion; but an Inspection into the other inclosed Plan No. 2. in which is delineated the disposition of the Troops when they were engaged with the Enemy, and the Account given me by some Officers, who were Eye Witnesses, and good Judges, may serve to shew the latter Circumstances. By the plan it appears that the Van Guard and Working Party had left the two Advanced Cannon and Artillery Stores with the Enemy, and Retreated about 400 Yards: and I have been well informed that those Parties falling back upon the main body, which, it is said, was too close upon their Rear, whilst it was forming, put it into Disorder, and that threw the whole into Confusion, which was increased by their finding themselves surrounded and fir'd upon on all sides by the Enemy, who had by this time possessed themselves of that Eminence. The Effect of this Confusion was, the Men could not be brought to form, nor the whole Body to advance; but they continued about two Hours and a half without either advancing or Retreating, and spent their Ammunition without doing Execution except upon a few Parties of their own, which made some Attempt to recover the advanced Cannon from the Enemy, and to gain the Hill.

The Enemy in the meantime made no use of the advanced Artillery and Stores, which were abandoned to them, except to Fire with their small Arms from behind the Waggons and Carriages. This State of Confusion lasted until Orders were given to Retreat; soon after which the whole Body took to flight (as is set forth in the Report) without any pursuit from the Enemy, and could not be brought to halt before they had fled three Miles.

It seems morally certain, that if the Eminence mark'd out in the Plans had been occupied in time by part of the General's troops, which it is agreed might have been done, he must have with ease defeated the Enemy. Some attempts were made to take possession of it, but it was then too late.

It seems agreed however, that notwithstanding these disadvantages, if the whole Body of the Troops could have been prevailed on to have march'd forward, the Enemy would have been defeated, and that whilst the few Parties, which did advance, continued in Motion it was observed that the Enemy's Fire ceased; but it was not in the Power of the Officers, who behaved with the greatest Gallantry and Bravery upon this occasion, particularly the General, to rouse the Men out of that Consternation and Stupidity, which their Confus'd Order, and the Novelty of an Attack made upon them by an Invisible Enemy in a Wilderness Country had thrown them into.[1]

The Baron de Dieskau (the French General who was taken Prisoner at Lake George) in speaking of General Brad-

---

[1] See Shirley's letters to Robinson, Aug. 11 and Aug. 12, *ante*, pp. 217–221, for an account of Braddock's defeat and the means proposed for retrieving the loss resulting from that misfortune.

dock's defeat, said that none of their (the French) Officers were in the least Surprized at it, as it was a Maxim with them never to Expose Regulars in the Woods, without a sufficient Number of Indians and Irregulars for any Attack that might be Expected.

The inclosed Extract of a Paper dated at Montreal July 25th taken among others of the Baron de Dieskau's intitled "Orders and Instructions pour le Battailon," which was sent four days after to Fort Frontenac on the Lake Ontario, for the Regulation of them in their March thither, will further shew, Sir, what use the French make of Irregulars when join'd with Regulars in Marching through the Woods; Vizt for Scouts, Ranging Parties and Outguards upon their Flanks to prevent Ambuscade or Surprize, which Services, the French call "la petite Guerre." The proportion of Irregulars to the Regular Troops in those Orders is one third of the former to two of the latter; four Cannadeans and Eight Soldiers of the Regulars are there ordered to Embark on board each Battoe.

The System of the French for making this use of Irregulars, when join'd in Service with their Regulars, is doubtless right, but it is as clear that his Majesty must now depend upon Disciplined Regular Troops for the preservation of his American Rights and Territories against the French, who have of late, and it seems to be expected, will continue to pour into North America as many Regular Troops from France, as they can find Opportunities of doing.

The second reason assigned in the Report for the bad behaviour of the Troops, Vizt. "The frequent Conversation of the Provincial Troops, and Country People, that if they engaged the Indians in their European manner of fighting, they would be beat." seems a slight one. It is plain from the Report itself, that it made little or no Impression upon the Soldiers; it is there observed that upon receiving orders to advance to meet the Enemy, "they march'd forward in good Order and *great Alacrity.*"

The Credit, I give to the two inclosed Plans is founded in this, that they were drawn by Engineer Mackellar; who was in the rear of the working Party under Sir John St. Clair's command, and approv'd of by the principal Officers in the action.

As to the Consequences of the General's Defeat, after his Troops who were concerned in that Action, had join'd the Division, which was left under the Command of Col Dunbar, I find that *now* the immediate Destruction of great Quantities of the Artillery Stores and Provisions is Condemned by some of the Field Officers. The Copy of an Order from the late General, signed by Capt. Dobson his fourth Aid de Camp hath been produced to me by Col. Dunbar in his own Justification, yet it seems difficult to say how that Order, which was given out from the General at a time, when the Colonel looked upon him, as he says, as a dying Man, and consequently incapable of Command, came to be so readily Complied with, as it seems to have been, and without any Attempt to prevent it, by Application to the General, if that was the Colonels opinion when the Stores were destroyed. I am told by Lieutt. Col. Gage, that upon a Message being sent from Colonel Dunbar to the General, he immediately resigned the Command to him. I won't take upon me to say, Sir, what the Effect of the Panic, to which so much is imputed, might be in the Soldiers after they were all join'd at Colonel Dunbars Camp in Numbers treble to those of the Enemy; but there seems to have been no reason to dread a pursuit from them at that distance.

The reason, which Colonel Dunbar gives for marching the Troops so suddenly to Philadelphia, with design of going into Winter Quarters there in August, is because he says General Braddock designed to go into Winter Quarters there himself. If that was ever his design, I have abundant reason to think he had altered it; For in his Secretary's last Letter to me a few days before the Action at Monongahela he acquainted me that if the Business at Fort Du Quesne should not take up too much time, the General would endeavour, if that was practicable, to join me at Niagara; In which Case I am Confident he would not have Winter'd his Troops near so far to the Westward as Philadelphia; and from my knowledge of the General, it is very difficult for me to Conceive that he would have entertained a thought of going into Winter Quarters in the Month of August, when so great a part of this Continent was entering upon Action.[1]

In my first Letter to Colonel Dunbar, for preventing his going into Winter Quarters at Philadelphia, and directing him to march the Troops under his Command to Albany;

[1] The feeling of consternation and helplessness prevalent in Pennsylvania, Maryland, and Virginia as a result of Braddock's defeat are well known. The withdrawal of troops by Dunbar resulted in many letters to Shirley for aid. See Dinwiddie to Shirley, Sept. 20 and Oct. 31, 1755 (Dinwiddie Papers, 2, 208, 257), Morris to Shirley, Sept. 5, Oct. 31, and Nov. 6 (1 Penna. Arch. 2, 400; Penna. Col. Rec. 6, 665; and 1 Penna. Arch. 2, 469), and Shirley to Sharpe, Aug. 13, *ante*, p. 236. On Nov. 2, 1755, Gov. R. H. Morris wrote as follows from Philadelphia to Shirley : —
DEAR SIR,
Last night I despatched an express to you with sundry letters and papers, relating to the present circumstances of the Province and other matters, and I now send away another with the further Intelligence that I have received within this hour, by which you will see that the Enemy whose numbers are still uncertain, are got much nigher to us than they were, being on the 31st of last month encamped near the Susquehannah, some few miles to the northward of the great road leading from this city to Carlisle, about one hundred and twenty miles from this place. Their scheme seems by their motion to be to take Possession of the Susquehannah, which we shall not be able to pass without great difficulty, and they will be in that case perfectly at Liberty to destroy all the rich country beyond that River, where there are many thousands of familys seated, what they may do afterwards time must discover. The Inhabitants in general are in great consternation, but being undisciplined and mostly without arms, they can do very little good. . . . My assembly meets to-morrow, but by what I can learn nothing is to be expected from them. Governor Sharpe will be here tomorrow night, and I am extremely concern'd I can not go with Him to New York, I must beg you would give me your advice what is best for me to do, in Case my Assembly shall continue to act the same part they have hitherto done. (1 Penna. Arch., 2, 467.)
On Nov. 4, Governor Dinwiddie of Virginia wrote Shirley requesting a commission for Col. George Washington and expressing the hope that the Virginia Assembly might grant some military

as I heard he designed to leave the Independent Companies at Fort Cumberland, I directed they should remain there for that Service until further Orders, and particularly recommended to him the protection of that Fort; but in his next Letter to me, he let me know, that upon his finding that General Braddock did not intend to leave those Companies at Fort Cumberland, he had brought them with him to Philadelphia, which he accordingly did, and is the reason for their not going into Garrison at Fort Cumberland.

My motive for ordering Colonel Dunbar to march his Troops to Albany, as soon as he could was, that if he had arriv'd there in time (which I was in hopes he might have done) he might have assisted in the Attempt against Crown Point, or at least have made ready to Cover Albany, in case General Johnson had been beat : and indeed it was extremely happy that the French Forces, which attacked General Johnson's camp, were repulsed and intirely defeated by him; for if they had prevailed in their Attack, there is the utmost reason to believe, as Colonel Dunbar did not arrive till about five Weeks after the Action, that the French General would have made himself Master of Albany, and in that Case have cutt off all Communication between Oswego and that Place; the Consequences of which might have been fatal to the Troops under my immediate Command, and very probably ended in the Loss of Oswego itself.

I have the Honor to be with the highest respect.
Sir
Your most Humble and
most Obedient Servant
W. SHIRLEY.

Rt. Honble. Sir Thomas Robinson Knt of the Bath, one of his Majesty's principal Secretaries of State.

provision for the spring campaign if not earlier (Dinwiddie Papers, 2, 261). The year following the defeat of Braddock was as severe as any year of war to Pennsylvania, Maryland, and Virginia. Parkman, "Montcalm and Wolfe," Vol. 1, *passim*. Note especially the report of the French commander at Fort Duquesne, Capt. Dumas, in July, 1756, *ibid*. 1, 329.

WILLIAM SHIRLEY TO CHARLES HARDY

[Extract] [1]

Albany, November 8, 1755.

I acquainted your Excellency from Oswego, that I designed to Garrison the two Forts, in the Mohawk's Country with the King's Troops during the Winter, and had given orders Concerning it at Schenectady; it would have made a saving to the Publick in the Article of Pay, Provisions, and Barracks, and been a More Expeditious way of Covering the King's Troops intended for that Service, in this Severe Season of the Year.

Since my Arrival here, your Excellency hath Acquainted me, that you have received Messages from those Indians, desiring that the Garrisons now Posted at those Forts may be Continued there, and Not exchanged for Others, Consisting of the Regular Troops. I have the Honour to be of the same Sentiments with you, that the Indians should not be Disgusted; Especially at this Critical Conjuncture, by putting Troops into their Forts, built for their Protection, that would be Disagreable to them; But as it Appears to me most probable, that this Application of the Indians to your Excellency was made at the Instigation of the Officers, who at Present Command those Forts; I would Mention it for your Consideration, whether it Might be Adviseable to try the Indians further upon that Point, by a Message to them, in which I will join with you letting them know that if any Regular Troops are sent to their Castles their Officers and Soldiers shall Consist Chiefly of Americans, who shall have Strict Orders to treat them with all Kindness and Civility and to know their Answer upon it.[2]

[1] P. R. O., C. O. 5, 46. Inclosed in Shirley to Robinson, Dec. 20. A transcript is in the Library of Congress.

[2] This letter, the reply of Hardy of Nov. 9, and Shirley's letter to Robinson of Dec. 20, in which both are inclosed, illustrate well the difficulties surrounding the Colonial Commander in Chief of the

His Excellency Sir Charles Hardy.

A true Copy Examined by
WM. ALEXANDER Secy.
Endorsed:
Extract of a Letter from
Major General Shirley to Govr. Hardy dated
Novr. 8. 1755. in Govr. Shirley's of
Decr. 20th, 1755.

CHARLES HARDY TO WILLIAM SHIRLEY [1]

Albany, Novr. 9th, 1755.
SIR,
After what has Passed Between the Indians and me with
Respect to Garrisons : which I have already acquainted your
Excellency with, I Cannot think it advisable to Send the
message you Propose and as General Braddock has in Consequence of his Instructions from home with the unanimous
opinion of the Council at Alexandria given General Johnson
a Commission to Take upon him the management and Care

British forces in America when he attempted to obtain aid from
New York for national purposes. That province would not work
under Shirley's leadership, and in the end secured his dismissal from
office. To the jealousy existing between New York and Massachusetts and the constant friction between DeLancey and Hardy
of the former and Shirley of the latter colony was added the fear
of Sir William Johnson that in some way his position as Superintendent of Indian relations would be lost. The letter of Dec. 2,
1755, from Secretary John Pownall to Johnson (Docts. rel. Col.
Hist. N. Y. 6, 1622) encouraged the latter greatly. See Sir William
Johnson to Governor Hardy, Oct. 22, Oct. 24, Oct. 31 ; to Governor
Hopkins of Rhode Island, Nov. 1 ; Shirley to Johnson, Nov. 15, and
Johnson to Shirley, Nov. 17, 1755, in Johnson Manuscripts. The
principle of the supreme authority of the commander in chief des-
ignated by the Crown was acknowledged by Shirley in defeat (Speech
to the General Court of Massachusetts, Sept. 8, 1756, *post*, p. 548)
as well as in time of success.
[1] P. R. O., C. O. 5, 46. A transcript is in the Library of Congress.

of Indian affairs, I Cannot but offer it as my opinion to your Excellency, that he be advised with on this occasion, and if the Indians Should make any Application to him on his Return from the Lake for Garrisons for their Protection I shall acquaint your Excellency with it, and Concert with you the Proper measures.[1] For Should Regular Troops be sent to their Castle without such an application from them, I apprehend it may Cause Great uneasiness among them.

In answer to your Excellency's Letter of yesterday with Respect to Victualling the Independent Companies: There can be no Dependance on the Assemblys making Provision for it. Those of them that have been Posted at Oswego have been Victualled by the Province out of the Duties arising on goods sold there.

I am Sir,
Your Excellency's
most obedt. and
Humble Servt.
CHARLES HARDY.

His Excellency Genl. Shirley
 a true Copy Examin'd by
  WM. ALEXANDER Secy.

Endorsed:
  Copy
 Letter from Govr. Hardy
  to Major General Shirley
   dated Albany 9th Novr. 1755
 in Govr. Shirley's of Decr. 20th, 1755.

[1] Shirley already had issued his summons for a Congress of Governors (Shirley to Benning Wentworth, Nov. 7, N. H. Prov. Papers, 6, 445). On Nov. 11 he wrote Governor Morris of Pennsylvania (1 Penna. Arch. 2, 481), and on Nov. 26 he requested Johnson (Johnson Manuscripts, 3, 259) to meet him at New York. Governor Sharpe of Maryland was invited also (1 Penna. Arch. 2, 497), but had little hopes of aggressive action resulting from the conference. As he wrote Dinwiddie: "It is reported that Genl. Johnson will proceed no farther this season." (Oct. 28, Arch. of Md. 6, 304.)

WILLIAM SHIRLEY TO ROBERT HUNTER MORRIS[1]

Albany, November 15th, 1755.

SIR,

Yesterday afternoon I had the honour of receiving two packetts from you by express, the first dated Octr. 31st, and a subsequent one without date. In the former of these you represent to me the devastations now making by the French, and Indians in their Interest, upon his Majesty's Subjects in the back Settlements of your Government, and the designs which you apprehend the French have upon his Majesty's Territories there, particularly Shamokin; and acquaint me "That your Council have unanimously advised You to apply to me, to order such of his Majesty's Forces as the present Exigencies of the Province under your Command require; and his Majesty's Service in the other Colonies will permitt me to spare," and in the latter you inform me, you have received further Intelligence of the Mischiefs and Crueltys by the Indians. "That you are without Men, money, Arms or Ammunition at your disposal; can gett no Aid from the Assembly of your Province, and do not see how you can protect the People, or secure the province from being laid waste, unless I will supply you with troops and money for that purpose"; and desire me to furnish you with the latter upon the foundation of Sir Thomas Robinson's circular Letter dated June 19th to the several Govrs. upon this Continent, directing them to Apply to the Commander in Chief of his Majestys Forces for the time being in North America, for such Sums of money which may be necessary to discharge such Expences, as have been or may be incurr'd on account of the Services or operations to be perform'd by them, or in any respect under their directions, and which are not properly chargeable to the account of their respective Governments.

[1] Original, Hist. Society of Pennsylvania. Printed: 1 Penna. Arch. 2, 493.

I am extreamly concern'd Sir at the calamitous situation of his Majestys depress'd Subjects in the back Settlements of your Province without any prospect of immediate relief from your Government, and the cruel Depopulations daily made in his Territories there, which seem at present to be abandon'd to the Enemy. I do assure you if it was in my power to send You present succour from his Majestys Forces under my Command, I would do it with the greatest pleasure ; But the State of those Forces, and the Colonies where they are posted will not admit of my doing it. The three Regiments in Nova Scotia are but barely sufficient with the New England Auxiliaries now there to protect that Province against the Attempts, which may be suddenly made by the French ; Sir William Pepperell's and my own Regiments, except a very small Detachment, are posted at Oswego, upon the carrying place of Oneida, and at the German flatts for the protection of the first mention'd important place, and our necessary Magazine of Stores and provisions at the other two, upon the preservation of which all the operations of an early Campaign the next Spring absolutely depend. Of the two British regiments in this City the Effectives fit for duty do not exceed 1050, and 600 of those have held themselves in readiness these two days to March to the Assistance of the Army at Lake George which is alarm'd with Intelligence of a very large body of the Enemy being in Motion to attack it,[1] and it is necessary the remainder of them should continue here ; besides the sending of these regiments or any considerable part of them this Winter to the back parts of your province must inevitably ruin his Majestys Service, for the next Spring.[2]

[1] The critical situation in New York was holding the attention of Colonial governors as far south as Virginia. See Dinwiddie to Shirley, Nov. 12, approving the conduct of the latter, stating the writer's efforts to raise troops in Virginia, inquiring as to the movements of Johnson and the possibility of capturing Crown Point. (Dinwiddie Papers, 2, 262.)

[2] In a second letter to Morris of the same date, Shirley continues : —

"It gives me Pain to See the Distress of mind, which I know so

As to my furnishing you with the Kings money, Sir, for defraying Expences, which You take notice of in your Letter is chargeable to the account of your Government, the bare inspection of Sir Thomas Robinson's letter must shew it to be out of my Power, and I can't but hope that your rich populous Government will not continue insensible of the devastations daily made in their Country; but if it was possible that their duty to his Majesty and a sense of the miseries of the people in the exposed parts of the Government should not be sufficient motives to them to protect the people under their Care, yet their own Interest and even preservation as a Government must effectually prevail with them to do it.

As to the Provisions, which you mention in your letter to have been purchased by You for General Braddock and to be left in your hands, and which you purpose to use for the people in the back parts of your province, if you will take upon You to have them replaced in the City of New York generous an one as yours must be in upon the Calamitous Situation of the poor People in the back Settlements of your Government, and the daily Devastation and Incroachments made within and upon his Majesty's Territories under your Command, owing to the Obstinacy and perverseness of your Assembly, and to find myself incapable of giving you and the poor expos'd Sufferers the desir'd Assistance.

"The only Advice I can give you under these melancholly Circumstances, is to continue to do (as you have hitherto done) every thing in your Power to encourage the People to exert themselves in their own Defence, and to persevere in your Representations to the Assembly of the ruinous State of these People, and the imminent danger there is of great part of the Provinces being suddenly lost to the Enemy, and in your Applications to them [the Assembly] to do their Duty to their King and Country in putting an End to the Miseries and Pain of the poor expos'd Sufferers, and preventing the loss which the Crown is threaten'd with.

"This, my Dear Sir, is all you can do at present, and to wait with patience for the Success of your Endeavours, which you should not dispair of."

For a review of local conditions in Pennsylvania at this time, see Lincoln, "The Revolutionary Movement in Pennsylvania" (Phila., 1901), pp. 16–22. The need of the colony was seized upon by the people as an opportunity to obtain privileges, and grants of money were withheld.

by April next, in such case I shall have no objection to your using them upon the present occasion, otherwise I can't consent to have those provisions diverted from the use of the King's troops.

The powder and ordnance Stores in Fort Cumberland are lodged there for his Majesty's service in an Expedition against the French Settlements upon the Ohio, which I hope will be effectually carried on the next Year, so that I can't possibly order any part of them for the use of the Inhabitants of your Government, where I suppose a sufficient Quantity may be had for the present occasion of the exposed Inhabitants.[1]

I am Sir
Your most Obedient Huml. Servant
WILLM. SHIRLEY.

WILLIAM SHIRLEY TO ROBERT HUNTER MORRIS [2]

Albany, Novr 19th, 1755.

SIR,

Upon further Consideration of the expos'd State of his Majesty's Territories in the back Settlements of the Province,

---

[1] Shirley was reluctant at this time to send money, arms, or stores to Pennsylvania. On Nov. 17 the Council of Governors and Commissioners at Albany had recommended an advance by Johnson with his army, the action of the Council had been sent to Johnson, and on the 18th Shirley had written asking what aid he could give for this advance. On Nov. 22 Johnson informed Shirley of the Council at Lake George which opposed the movement against Ticonderoga, and of the reluctance of the soldiers to advance. Not until Dec. 2 did Johnson announce the close of the campaign and formally resign his command, thus justifying the report which Governor Sharpe of Maryland had mentioned to Governor Dinwiddie (Oct. 28) that Johnson would not advance (Johnson Manuscripts, 3, 226, 227, 229, 232, 248, 249, 253, 265). See, however, Shirley to Morris, Nov. 19, following.

[2] Printed: 1 Penna. Arch. 2, 502. On Nov. 16, 1755, Morris had written Shirley as follows: "I have the pleasure to acquaint

under your Government and present Incursions of the French and Indians into them, together with the distress'd Condition of his Majesty's Subjects Inhabiting there, whom you have represented to be in want of Ammunition requisite for

you that the Indians, after having laid waste a considerable extent of country, and drove about a thousand families from their habitations, have retired from our borders, but am afraid they have left us but for a little time and will return with greater numbers and penetrate much further into the Province, as they have hitherto met with no resistance nor do I expect the Assembly will enable me to oppose them in their future operations.

* * * * * * *

" You must be sensible Sir, how necessary it is for his Majesty's Service, and the safety of His Dominions, that the strength of the Colonys should be united against the French, and under such a direction, that it may be employed in the most effectuall manner, for while they remain in this Present disjoynted state, and the several Colonys not only at liberty whether they will act or not, but also in what manner and where they will employ their strength, this must in its consequence weaken any operations that depend in the least upon what they will do. The formation of a union may not therefore be unworthy your consideration, at this time; a war with France seems to be at hand, the scene of which may probably be in America.

"The Plan formed at Albany, was upon such Republican Principles, that I do not wonder it was not relished at home, as it seemed calculated to unite the Colonys in such a manner, as to give the Crown little or no influence in their Councils; any new plan must therefore be such as will meet with approbation at home, to which end it should be drawn so as to enable the Government to employ the united force of the Colonys, where and when they may think it necessary, and at the same time to keep them in that Constitutional dependence upon the mother nation, that is so necessary for their mutual Interest and safety.

"When these matters are under your consideration, you will turn your thoughts to this Province, situated in the midst of the British Empire, extensive in its bounds, temperate in its climate, and from its produce, trade and number of inhabitants, capable of contributing largely towards the support of the Common cause. But unfortunately, under the Government of a set of men who are or pretend to be principled against defending themselves or their Country. To oblige this Rich and flourishing Province, therefore, to bear its part of the common and necessary Expences of defend-

defending themselves and the King's Rights against the Enemy, as also of Provisions, and that you have no Expectation of the Assembly in your Government providing the necessary Supplies for them in time, in order to prevent the immediate Depopulations and Incroachments, which threaten his Majesty's said Territories, and relieve his distress'd Subjects there, untill the Assembly of your Province shall make effectual provision for the Defence and protection of both, I inclose you an Order for 50 Barrels of the King's Powder in the Magazine at Fort Cumberland, near Will's Creek, for those purposes, and hereby consent to your Distributing such Quantities of his Majesty's Provisions in your Hands, as shall be necessary for the Support of such of the Inhabitants in the back Settlements as are employ'd in Defence of the King's Lands there, in confidence that your Assembly will soon order the 50 Barrells of Powder and Provisions, which shall be expended in the aforesaid Services to be replac'd in his Majesty's Stores.

Mr. Leake, the Commissary General of Provisions here, the Waggon Master, General Scott and Lieut. Leslie, Assistant to the Deputy Quarter Master General, will attend you soon at Philadelphia, and bring two Letters with them to Messrs James Turnass and Richard Vernon, . . . to attend the Settlements of the Accompts of what is due to the Waggoners, &c.

* * * * * * *

I am,
Sir,
Your most Obedient Humble Servant,
W. SHIRLEY.

Honble Robert Hunter Morris, Esqr.

ing and securing the whole, seems an object worthy your attention, and I cannot doubt but the several governors that will meet you at New York, will readily joyn you in such representations as you may judge necessary to obtain a thing so just and reasonable in itself." (1 Penna. Arch. 2, 448.) On the 17th a second letter was written, giving an account of an Indian attack since the letter of Nov. 16 (*ibid.* p. 501).

ROBERT HUNTER MORRIS TO WILLIAM SHIRLEY [1]

[Philadelphia, Nov. 26, 1755.]

SIR,

I am to acknowledge the receipt of your Excellency's several favours of 11th and 15th instant. That relative to the things requested for the security of this Province, I shall do myself the honour to make a particular answer to, and hope when you consider the nature of this government and its consequence to the crown and nation, you will afford us some relief; especially, as without such relief it will be disabled from furnishing the necessary Carriages and Provisions towards an Expedition against fort Duquesne in the next summer, which you seem to think will be undertaken.

It would give me very great pleasure to meet you in the Congress you have summond at New York, not only to assist you in any thing within the reach of my abilities, but to congratulate you upon your safe return from so fateguing a campaign. But the daily accounts I have of the cruelties committed on the Borders, and the necessity I am under of trying every method for the relief of the Inhabitants, will hardly admit me to leave the Province: which, however, if there is a possibility of doing, I will try to be with you.

This morning an Express came to town with an account that the Indians had cut off a Moravian settlement not far from the River Delaware, where they destroyed all the Inhabitants but two, and I am in hourly Expectation of hearing of more mischief in that quarter.

The Proprietors have sent me over an order for five thousand pounds; this money which they give freely towards the

[1] Draft. Printed: 1 Penna. Arch. 2, 524. On Nov. 20 Gov. Jonathan Belcher of New Jersey, replying to Shirley's letter of Nov. 11, assured the Massachusetts Governor of his belief that the American colonies could unite and overthrow the French power, and on Dec. 4 he expressed to Shirley his pleasure with the results of the Councils at Oswego and his willingness to aid in the campaigns of the next year (1 N. J. Arch. 8, pt. 2, pp. 168, 182).

Expences that they thought would attend the defeat of Genl. Braddock, for it was immediately upon receiving the account of that affair that they dispatched this order. But you are sensible this sum will go but little way towards the defence of a Province circumstanced as this is, and whether the assembly will make any addition to it, I can't as yet say.

I am etc.

[ROBERT H. MORRIS.]

WILLIAM SHIRLEY TO JOHN BRADSTREET [1]

Albany, Novr. 28th, 1755.

Memorandum for Lieut. Colonel Bradstreet.

To grant Furlows in my name to such men as shall be inlisted here for my Regiment as he shall judge adviseable, and send the remainder to Schenectady; and to pay those, who remain in Schenectady such part of their Bounty Money, as he shall find proper.

All proceedings for the winter expedition and raising men for the new Regiments to be suspended untill Col. Bradstreet hears from me: As to the men which he or the officers at Lake George have already inlisted, in case the Inlistments don't proceed, he is desir'd to use his Discretion in preventing Expence, which may arise from it; and if any of those men or others in passing thro' Albany can be oblig'd to go either into Sir William Pepperrell's Regiment or my own I should be glad [if] he would promote it; for which service he will upon his application be supply'd with money by Mr. Stephenson.

He is likewise desir'd, in case more Barracks are wanting either at Schenectady or Albany, to give his advice and assistance in the manner of constructing them or fitting up Quarters. He is likewise desir'd to take under his Care the building of the Whale Boats, and give such orders therein as he shall judge for his Majesty's Service. And he is desir'd to transmit to me from time to time his Sentiments upon every point of his Majesty's Service.

[1] Original, Amer. Antiq. Society, Bradstreet Papers.

And Whereas I have advanc'd 500 Dollars to Major Hoar[1] for inlisting men at Lake George. Col. Bradstreet is desir'd to settle the accounts thereof with him, and the other officers amongst whom it was distributed, and receive what shall become due to me, unless he thinks it may be employ'd in inlisting men for my own Regiment.

W. SHIRLEY.

Endorsed:
Genl. Shirley's Memorandum 1756.

JAMES F. MERCER TO WILLIAM ALEXANDER[2]

Oswego, November 30th, 1755.

DEAR SIR,

I send these few lines after Capt. More to acquaint you I have seen a Seneca Indian, who the Interpreter Says is of good Character, who informs me he has seen the Messenger that was sent to the Messessagues, and who is to be here in a few days. He told him that not only the Messessagues, but the Whole Neighbouring Nations have gladly accepted of General Shirley's Invitation, and were it not for the Dangers on the Lake in the Winter they would have been here before this time, but that we may Expect them Early in the Spring. I give you this Information that the General may be Apprised of it, that he may Either Send me Instructions or some proper person to treat with them. Let me likewise observe to you, that there are very few Indian presents left in the Store and will be Insufficient if great Numbers Come.

I am Sir
Yor Most Obedt.
Humble Servt. JAMES F. MERCER.

MR. ALEXANDER
A true Copy Examin'd by
WM. ALEXANDER Secy.

[1] Maj. William Hoar is the officer here meant. To him Shirley had given charge of enlistments at Lake George.
[2] P. R. O., C. O. 5, 46. Inclosed in Shirley to Robinson, Dec. 20. A transcript is in the Library of Congress. Alexander was secretary to Shirley.

WILLIAM SHIRLEY TO WILLIAM JOHNSON [1]

SIR,   New York, Dec. 7th, 1755.

You already know I have the honor to be appointed Commander in Chief of all His Majesty's Forces in North America, with the same Powers as the late General Braddock had the command.

Inclosed is the 8th article of His Majesty's Instructions to me concerning Indian affairs, which is a copy of that, and the only Instruction which the late Genl. Braddock had relative to that matter, you will find it refers to some appointment of you to the service therein mentioned, supposed to be made by His Majesty before Genl. Braddock left England. If you have received such a commission you will act in pursuance of it, according to the Instructions you may have received with it, and such further Instructions as I do now or shall hereafter send you. In case you have received no such commission, you will then act in pursuance to the Commission which I send you herewith, by virtue of the Power given me by His Majesty and founded upon the words and intent of his Royal Instructions, looking upon the Indians called there the Northern Indians, to be intended as those of the Six Nations, and whatever allies they may have to the Northward.

Inclosed are general Instructions for your Guidance and Directions in the execution of your Trust and some calculated for this occasion to which I refer you, and to the enclosed papers containing an account of Governor Morris's Intelligence and Proceedings relative to the Shawanese, Delawares, and other Indians therein mentioned and of his Messages to several Tribes of the Six Nations, which last mentioned papers will throw light upon the Service, I propose now by directing you to proceed to these Castles.

You will let me know by the return of this express whether

[1] P. R. O., C. O. 5, 46. Inclosed in Shirley to Robinson, Dec. 20. A transcript is in the Library of Congress. Printed: Docts. rel. Col. Hist. N. Y. 6, 1024.

you have received any other Commission than that from the late General Braddock relative to the care of the Indians and how far I may depend upon your acting under the inclosed Commission and proceeding in the Service I now direct you to go upon, that in case you may decline it, I may otherwise provide against His Majesty's Service being disappointed by that means.

If the advanced Season of the year, or your state of Health will not suffer you to go as far as the Onondaga Castle you will then transmit the business by proper Messages to such of them as you cannot personally go to.

As the effectual execution of the trust reposed in you, will on many accounts require my having an interview with you as soon as the business I now direct you to do will admit, I must desire you to let me see you at Boston this Winter some time before the month of March at furthest.

> I am Sir
> Your most humble Servt
> W. SHIRLEY.

To Major General Johnson.

WILLIAM SHIRLEY TO WILLIAM JOHNSON [1]

[Commission]

By His Excellency William Shirley Esqre Major General and Commander in Chief of all His Majestys Forces in North America

To Major General William Johnson,

By virtue of the Power and Authority to me given and granted by His Majesty to appoint a proper Person or Persons agreeable to the Northern Indians to improve a good correspondence with them, and to engage them to take part, and Act with His Majestys Forces, in such operations as I

---

[1] Inclosed in Shirley to Robinson, Dec. 20. A copy is in the New York papers in the Library of Congress. Printed: Docts. rel. Col. Hist. N. Y. 6, 1025.

shall think most expedient; I do by these presents in the name and behalf of His Majesty, commit to your care and management the execution of the aforesaid Trust, hereby appointing and fully authorizing you to repair to the Indians of the Six Nations and their Northern allies, and to use your best endeavours to engage them to take part and act with His Majestys Forces in such operations as I shall think most expedient and according to such Instructions as you shall from time to time receive from me. And you are from time to time to make report to me of your proceedings herein and of all material occurrences which may effect His Majestys Interest with the said Indians.

> Given under my hand and Seal at New York this seventh day of December in the twenty ninth year of His Majestys Reign.

W. Shirley.

By His Excellency's Command
Wm. Alexander Secry.

WILLIAM SHIRLEY TO WILLIAM JOHNSON [1]

[Instructions]

1. You are on the receipt hereof to send Messengers to the principle Castles of the Indians of the Six Nations and endeavour if possible to have a general meeting of their Chief Sachems and Warriors at their antient Council Place at Onondaga as soon as may be after you shall receive these Instructions and the Commission therewith.

2. You are then to acquaint them that I succeed the late General Braddock in his Command and that I have thought fit for His Majesty's Service to commit to your care the cultivating a Friendship between them and the Northern Nations of Indians depending upon them and His Majesty's

---

[1] Johnson Manuscripts, 4, 2. Copy inclosed in Shirley to Robinson, Dec. 20. A copy is in the New York papers in the Library of Congress. Printed: Docts. rel. Col. Hist. N. Y. 6, 1026; 2 Penna. Arch. 6, 333.

Subjects and engageing them in a firm alliance with His Majesty against the French and the Indians in their Interest, in the present expedition for recovering His Majesty's just rights, and the country out of the hands of the French.

3. You are then to acquaint them that your calling them together at this time, is occasioned by the late behavior of the Shawanese and Delawares Indians in the Province of Pensilvania.

4. You are then to deliver them my speech delivered to you herewith which you are to enforce by all arguments in your power and with such presents as you shall judge necessary and you are to endeavor to prevail on them to send some of their Warriors to forbid the Delaware and Shawanese Indians to commit any hostilities against the English and in case these Indians shall not comply with such Orders to chastize them for their Behaviour as it bids defiance to that Authority which the Six Nations always maintained against those Indians and to make them sensible that unless they do that, they will not only infallibly loose that authority for ever, but with it the Character the Six Nations have always sustained of being Masters of those Indians.

5. You are also to assure them in the strongest Terms that I shall do all in my power to protect them and their Allies from any danger they may apprehend from the French, and particularly the Oneidas, that agreeable to my promise to them I have ordered Justice Petri to engage a sufficient number of men to build them a Fort of such size and in such place in their country as is most convenient to them and that I will if they chuse to have them this Winter send an officer with 30 men to reside among them as soon as their Barracks in their New Fort are ready to receive them.

6. You are to use every expedient in your power to cultivate and improve a good correspondence with the Indians of the Six Nations and their Allies and endeavour to prevail on them to declare themselves, and to take up the Hatchet against the French and their Indians as well as to act immediately against those who have lately invested the borders of Pensilvania, Maryland and Virginia, as to be ready to

take part and act with His Majesty's Forces in such operations as I shall think most expedient.

7. You are from time to time to inform me of your proceedings herein, and particularly to inform me as soon as may be, the answer of those Indians to my speech now sent and to inform me of the state of the new Fort now building for the Oneidas and when you judge the Barracks in it will be in a condition to receive a Garrison of His Majesty's Troops and whether it will be absolutely necessary to send Troops to Garrison it this Winter, or whether the Indians will not be content to be without that Garrison until the Spring.

8. And whereas I have great reason to expect that a number of the Sachems and Warriors of the Messessagues, Cheppewes, and Outawas will meet me next Spring at Oswego and as the Chief Sachems of the Oneidas and Cayougas also have promised to meet me then and there, and as it will be necessary that as general a meeting as possible be had there with the Indians of the Six Nations you are therefore to use your best endeavours to engage some of the Chief Sachems and Warriors of all the Six Nations to meet me at Oswego early in the Spring to concert such measures as may be for the mutual benefit of them and us.

> Given under my hand at New York this tenth day of December Annoq. 1755.

W. Shirley.

By His Excellencys Command
　Wm Alexander Secry.

JAMES F. MERCER TO WILLIAM ALEXANDER

[Extract]¹

Sir,

I have the pleasure to acquaint you with the Success and return of General Shirley's Messenger to the Messessagues

---

¹ P. R. O., C. O. 5, 46. Inclosed in Shirley to Robinson, Jan. 12, 1756. A transcript is in the Library of Congress.

and the other Foreign Indians, that they have Accepted of his Excellency's offers and Invitation and that they will be here in great Numbers early in the Spring being disgusted . with the French for the little care they took of their families in their absence, their breach of promise in regard to presents and their want of Necessarys to supply their wants. He is anxious least we should not perform the absolute promise he made them in the General's name, of considerable presents and a large quantity of goods for trade, and as their being disappointed might be Attended with bad consequences; I have Directed the Commissary of the Stores to transmitt you an Account of the Indian goods in his possession, which is greatly short for the Occasion we may probably have to dispose of them. I have Signified this to the General and Doubt not of his taking care that a proper supply be sent.

The Information I sent you the 15th of November concerning the Retreat of the Oswegatchi, and other Indians from Canada is false, they have since made proposals to a Council held at Onondago, desiring the five Nations to join the French and them against us and when the Council denied them that, they desired a Neutrality, which was Consented to on Condition that all the French Indians should likewise Remain Unactive and Neutral; However the Council is broke up and nothing Concluded. The peace agreed upon betwixt the foreign Indians and the five Nations, I find gives them Universal Satisfaction, I hope it will Turn the Scale in our favour, Oswego, in their Opinion will soon be a great Mart, where the wants of all the Indians in America may be Supply'd.

a true Copy Examd by
WM ALEXANDER Secy.

Endorsed:
Extract of a Letter from
Lieut. Colonel Mercer
To William Alexander Esqr.
dated December 11th, 1755.
in M. G. Shirley's of Janry. 12th, 1756.

WILLIAM JOHNSON TO WILLIAM SHIRLEY [1]

Fort Johnson, Dec. 16, 1755.

Sir,

Your Excellency's Paquet I received this instant together with a Commission or Warrant from you for the Management of Indian Affairs, also a Letter and other Papers from Govr. Morris of Philadelphia concerning the Hostilities committed and still committing by the Indians on the Frontiers of that and the Neighbouring Provinces, desiring I would use my utmost endeavors to put a stop to it.

On my return from Lake George I received an account of the cruel proceedings of the Indians in them parts by an express from Sir Charles Hardy and as soon as I got home, despatched Messages to all the six Nations, and also to the Susquehanna Indians, Delawares and Shawanese acquainting the former of the Behavior of those Indians and insisted on their immediate Interposition. To the latter who are the people concerned, I sent a very smart reprimand for their unnatural and unjustifiable Behaviour to their Brethren and Neighbours the English; giving them a strong and warm Invitation to join us, and turn their arms this way against the French and their allies. What effect it will now have upon them I can't pretend to say with any certainty, but this much I make bold to say, that if I had not been so much employed otherwise this Time past and for some other Reasons I shall defer mentioning now Indian affairs would be in a much more favorable and prosperous way, and this perhaps not have happened.

I have this long time been told there was a Commission from His Majesty for me, and that it was sent by the late General Braddock, but I never received any, nor pay for the one I had of him, alltho' I have neglected all my own business, on account of it and suffered much thereby. I shall soon write your Excellency more fully and let you know my inclinations regarding the Commission.

[1] New York papers in the Library of Congress. Printed: Docts. rel. Col. Hist. N. Y. 6, 1027.

I proposed ere I received yours to have a meeting of all the Nations I could assemble at this Season of the year, in order to settle matters with them in the best manner possible, and prepare them for service in the Spring. It will take some time to get them together, so that I may go to New York for a Fortnight and settle affairs, and be back ere they are assembled.

> I am Your Excellencys
> Most obedient and most humble Servant
> WM JOHNSON.

WILLIAM SHIRLEY TO SIR THOMAS ROBINSON[1]

New York, December 19th, 1755.

SIR,

The variety of business, I found at Albany arising from the Expedition against Crown point, Indian Affairs, the settlement of several matters relative to the two British Regiments, and some of the Troops of the two American Regiments there and at Schenectady, together with the Disposition of them into Barracks at those two places, and Fort Hunter near the Mohawk's Castle delay'd my Arrival at this place 'till the second Instant; And the difficulty of getting the members together, who form'd the Council of War, which I held here the 12th and 13th Instant, pursuant to his Majesty's seventh Instruction to me, an Extract from which is inclos'd, made it impracticable for me to Send my dispatches from hence untill this day.[2]

[1] P. R. O., C. O. 5, 46. A transcript is in the Library of Congress and another in the Parkman Papers in the Mass. Hist. Society.

[2] The following "extract from his Majesty's Seventh Instruction to the Late Major General Braddock" was inclosed by Shirley in this letter to Sir Thomas Robinson:—

And if any preparations should be necessary for the carrying on of our Service, which is not Contained in these our Instructions you shall with the Concurrence of the Governours, who are to assist in any such service, make any such preparations, Provided that the same shall Appear to you absolutely Necessary for the

I have now, Sir, the Honour to transmit to you a Copy of the Minute of that Council;[1] to which I beg leave to subjoin the following Remarks.

1st. It seems clear that the securing his Majesty's just Rights and Dominion upon the great Lakes and Rivers, and in the Country behind the Apalachian Mountains against the present Incroachments and future Attempts of the French, together with the Indians of the six Nations, and those of the Western or far Nations in a firm Alliance with the Crown of Great Britain, depends upon gaining the Mastery of the Lake Ontario.

2dly. That for effecting this Service it is necessary for his Majesty to have such a Naval Force the next Summer upon the Lake Ontario, as may be superior to that, which the

Defence of our Just Rights and Dominions. And you will in all such Emergencies and Occurences that may happen, Whether herein Mentioned or not provided for by these Instructions, not only use your best Circumspection, but shall Likewise Call to your Assistance a Council of War when Necessary, which we have thought fit to Appoint upon this Occasion, Consisting of your self, the Commander in Chief of our Ships in those parts, such Governours of our Colonies or Provinces, and such Colonels and other of our Field Officers, as shall happen to be at a Convenient Distance from our said General and Commander of our Forces. And you shall with the Advice of them or the Majority of them, Determine all Operations, to be performed by our said Forces under your Command and all other important points relating thereto, in a Manner that shall be Most Conducive to the ends, for which the said Forces are intended and for the faithfull Discharge of the Great trust hereby Committed to you,

A true Copy Examined By
WM. ALEXANDER Secy.

Endorsed:
Extract from his Majesty's
7th Instruction to the late Major General
Braddock in Govr. Shirley's of the
19th Decr. 1755.

[1] P. R. O., C. O. 5, 46. A transcript is in the Library of Congress. See Braddock's Instructions in full, Nov. 25, 1754 (1 Penna. Arch. 2, 203). The proceedings of the Council of War of Dec. 12–13 to which Shirley refers are printed, among other places, in New Hampshire Prov. Papers, 6, 463–467.

French shall then have there; and such a Land Force at Oswego, as shall be sufficient to dislodge them from their Forts at Cadaraqui,[1] Toronto, and Niagara upon the Lake, and Fort la Gallette situate upon the River Iroquois at the Entrance into an Harbour there call'd Oswegatchi; between which Place and the Lake the River is navigable for Vessells of Force, but there ceases to be so on Account of the Falls between it and Montreal: And as the most effectual Measure for cutting off the Communication between Montreal and the said Lake will be to barr the passage of the French from the former to the latter thro' the River Iroquois, it seems most expedient for his Majesty's Service, that besides building a Fort upon the Niagara to Secure that Pass, as is directed by his Majesty's Instructions, another should be built either upon the main, where Fort la Gallette now stands, or some Island conveniently situated for that Purpose in the River Iroquois near it, to secure that pass, from whence the Navigation of the River, near as far down as Montreal itself, might on Occasion be commanded by small Craft sent from thence, whilst the Fort would prevent the French from building any Vessells of Force at Oswegochi for the Navigation of the Lake.

3dly. The only Objection to erecting an English Fort, at or near where Fort la Gallette now Stands, seems to be the difficulty of supporting it against the strong Force,[2] with which it must be expected, the French would, upon all favourable Opportunities, attack it from Montreal; especially

[1] Fort Cadaraqui, later known as Frontenac, commanded the outlet of Lake Ontario and the entrance to the Iroquois or St. Lawrence River. It was on the northern shore of the lake, and remained a French stronghold until its capture by John Bradstreet in August, 1758, when it was leveled to the ground. See Docts. rel. Col. Hist. N. Y. 10, 825, and *ante*, p. 296.

[2] Fort La Gallette was known later as Fort Présentation (or Patterson), and as Oswegatchi (or Swegatchi) from the river on which it was located. It was situated at the junction of the Oswegatchi and St. Lawrence rivers about sixty miles above Montreal. It was accessible from Lake Ontario by the St. Lawrence (Iroquois) River and by an Indian trail of approximately forty-five miles.

if there is a practicable Road to it from thence by Land for transporting Artillery and Stores, as is said by Pere Charlevoix in his History of New France. On the other Hand it may be observ'd, that it would be more easy for the English to support a Fort at that Place from Oswego, which does not exceed 110 Miles distance from it, and from whence it might be supply'd with Reinforcements and Provisions more easily across the Lake Ontario, and from thence by Water Carriage down the River Iroquois, than the French could support a Siege against it at the same Distance from Montreal by Land; especially if a proper Magazine was Establish'd at Cadaraqui, as well as at Oswego: That the Expence of maintaining this Fort would lessen that of the naval Force, and the Garrisons at Oswego and Niagara, which must be stronger, and consequently more expensive, if a Fort is not kept up at Oswegatchi; and that the maintaining of such a Fort there would so effectually curb the Force of Canada on the Side of the Lakes and River Ohio, and deprive the French of their Commerce and Traffick with the Indians, as to render the Country of Canada of very little Value to the Crown of France; especially if it should lose Crown point, and be curb'd on the other Side of Montreal by a Fort and Naval Force upon Lake Champlain, and on the Side of Quebec by another Strong Fort upon the River Kennebeck, at or near the Head of it, at about 100 Miles distance from that Metropolis.

4thly. As to the Opinion and Advice of the Council, with regard to the Operations upon the Lake Ontario being begun by the Attack of the French Fort at Cadaraqui, in which the Members were not unanimous; the Difference of their Opinion consisted only in this, that one of them was of Opinion, it would be more adviseable to begin them by an Attack upon the French Forts at the Strait of Niagara.

5thly. The Opinion of the Council concerning the number of additional Regular Troops necessary for recovering and securing His Majestys Rights and Dominion upon this Continent, was proposed by them to make part of their Determinations without being previously mov'd by me, and is founded upon these Reasons: they think there ought to be 1500 Regulars at least employ'd with what Provincial Troops shall be rais'd by the Colonies for the Expedition against Crown point; that no Regulars can be spar'd out of the two American and two British Regiments for this Service; nor any from the three Regiments of Regulars posted at Nova Scotia consistent with the Safety of that Province.

I would further observe, Sir, upon this Head, that as to the four Regiments of Regulars destin'd for the Service upon the Lakes, the two American ones consist wholly of Raw Troops; that out of the 1000 Veteran Troops, of which the two British Regiments consisted at their Arrival in Virginia, not more than 600 of them are left; that the Rest are made up of Provincials drafted into them the last Summer, and their New Augmentation from 700 to 1000 Men each, must be made up (if they can be rais'd in time) with fresh Recruits.

I beg leave further to acquaint you, Sir, that upon finding from the Copy of your Letter to the late General Braddock dated the 10th of February last, compar'd with your Letter to me of the same Date, that the 2000 Men, which I was therein order'd by his Majesty to raise, " exclusive of the Number requisite for my own Regiment, and Sir William Pepperrell's, and of the Augmentation to the five Regiments mention'd in a former Letter to 1000 Men each," were intended by his Majesty to be rais'd for the particular Service of Nova Scotia, and for no other, I shall not without his Majesty's further Orders take upon me to raise the two new Regiments, which I mention'd in my Letter of the 12th of August to you, I propos'd doing. That if I had rais'd them I have no Certainty of being able to provide them either with Arms or Cloathing, to take the Field in time for his Majesty's Service in the ensuing Campaign; And that thereupon, Sir, I beg leave humbly to offer my own Opinion with that of the Council, that it would greatly serve his Majesty's Interest if he should be pleas'd to order three Regiments from England of 700 privates each to be transported, as soon as may be, to New York, where they might possibly arrive in time to act, part of them with the Forces to be employ'd in the Expedition against Crown-point, and part with those destin'd for his Majesty's Service upon the Lakes under my immediate command, and would contribute greatly to the Success of both, which it seems of the last Importance to the Colonies in North America to have effected, if possible, in the ensuing Year; especially the Service upon the Lakes, as the inclos'd Copy of a Letter from Major Rutherford to me[1] whilst I was at Oswego, and an Examination of a French Soldier confirming the Intelligence, I had before receiv'd, seems to put it out of doubt that the great Object of the French upon the Lakes is to make themselves Masters of Oswego.

I can't take upon me to say what Success the Governors will have with their respective Assemblies in prevailing upon them to raise their Quotas of Troops and Money for the general services of the next year. Very little hath been done by the Western Colonies towards it hitherto;[2] and tho' the Reduction of Crown point is a favourite Expedition with the Colonies of New England, yet the failure in it this year, partly owing in all Appearance, to the Neglect of the Officers to push it on as far as it seems possible it might have been, and partly to their Want of due Supplies of provisions from Albany will, together with the great Numbers of Men already rais'd in vain for this Service, at a very heavy Expence to those Colonies, I am afraid, make them very backward to raise the necessary Forces for the ensuing Spring. At all Events, whatever it shall be adviseable for me to attempt the next year for his Majesty's Service with the Forces I shall have, I will endeavour to carry into Execution with Vigilance and Activity. Indeed if a new Supply of Regular Troops from France shall get into Louisbourg or Quebec very early

---

[1] See Rutherford to Shirley, Sept. 30, *ante*, p. 301.
[2] The Colonial authorities preferred that their troops should be used within their respective boundaries. See Jonathan Belcher to Shirley, Dec. 17, 1755, 1 N. J. Arch. 8, pt. 2, 194.

in the Spring, unless the Colonies are reinforc'd at the Same time with Troops from England, little more can be expected to be done than to act upon the Defensive; especially if Nova Scotia should stand in need of being immediately succour'd.

In the mean time while I can't but conceive strong hopes, that at least the French Forts at Niagara may be reduc'd early in the Summer, provided we shall be able to get ready a Sufficient Naval Force upon the Lake Ontario by that time; and proper Magazines of Provisions are secur'd this Winter; both which I shall use my utmost Endeavours to accomplish in time.

If upon my Arrival at Oswego I find my Strength shall be sufficient, I am fully determin'd to begin the Operations upon Lake Ontario by an Attack of Fort Frontenac alias Cadaraqui; unless I shall receive his Majesty's Orders to the contrary; concerning which and every other part of my propos'd plan for his Service I hope I shall know his Royal Pleasure, if possible, before the Operations are begun.

I have only further to acquaint you, Sir, that a Map intitul'd "a General Map of the Middle British Colonies in America, etc.," having been lately publish'd here by one Lewis Evans, in which Fort Frontenac and the whole North Side of Lake Ontario are mark'd a part of New France, and the River Iroquois call'd St. Lawrence's River, and in the Introductory Essays to it are asserted to belong to the French by Virtue of the Treaty of Reswick; which peremptory Assertion had begun to make an Impression unfavourable to the present exigencies of his Majesty's Service, and his just Rights in some leading persons here; I have look'd into, and set forth his Majesty's Claim to this most important Place in the most accurate manner, I can at present do it, in the inclos'd State,[1] which, I take the liberty to say, appears to me to shew clearly that it appertains to the Crown of

---

[1] See Shirley's "Claim of the English and French to the Possession of Fort Frontenac," following. This map was made to accompany the text of "Geographical, historical, political and mechanical Essays." Philadelphia, Franklin and Hall, 1755.

Britain by Virtue of the Treaty of Utrecht, as part of the Country of the six Nations.

I am with the highest Respect,

Sir,

Your most Humble, and

most Obedient Servant.

W. SHIRLEY.

Rt: Honble: Sir Thomas Robinson Knt: of the Bath, one of his Majesty's principal Secretaries of State

P.S.   I have, within these three Days, receiv'd fresh Intelligence by an Officer lately arriv'd from Oswego, that the French are building three new Vessells in the Harbour near Fort Frontenac.

Endorsed:

New York 19th. Decr. 1755.

Govr. Shirley

R. 10th. Febry. 1756 by Capt. Morris.

WILLIAM SHIRLEY TO SIR THOMAS ROBINSON [1]

CLAIM OF THE ENGLISH AND FRENCH TO THE POSSESSION OF FORT FRONTENAC, STATED AND EXAMIN'D

Fort Frontenac is built upon the North East Edge of the Lake Ontario at the Distance of about 180 miles from Montreal, and Situated near the head of a River, which takes its rise from the said Lake, and discharges itself into the River St. Lawrence at the Island of Montreal. The country between this Fort and Montreal is mark'd upon the French Charts of the best Authority *pais des Iroquois du Nord*, or *les Iroquois du Nord* in contradistinction to the *Iroquois* (under which General Appellation The French comprehend

[1] P. R. O., C. O. 5, 46.   Inclosed in Shirley to Robinson, Dec. 19.   A transcript is in the Library of Congress.   See note on p. 296, preceding.

the several Cantons of Indians, call'd by the English the five Nations) who Inhabit the Country on the South Side of the Lakes Ontario, Oneida, and Mohawk's River; and the Said River is mark'd on the same Maps *le fleuve des Iroquois* and both of them have been Treated from the beginning as well by the French as English as belonging to the Indians of the five Nations, who for a few years past have had a Settlement at Oswegachi on the River Iroquois consisting mostly of Onondagos.

In 1672 Monsr. Courcelles[1] then Governour of Canada, by large presents to the Indians and under pretence of building a trading house for their conveniency, but with a design of converting it soon into a Fort in order to bridle them, and keep them from making incursions into Montreal, obtain'd leave of them to Erect a Magazine which they have since Fortify'd and is now call'd Cadarraqui [*sic*] or Fort Frontenac from the Name of Monsr. Frontenac, Monsr. Courcelles Successor in the Government of Canada, who carried this project into Execution in the same Year.

In 1689 the French After many Hostilities from the Indians and disputes between them (among other things) concerning the former's holding Possession of this Fort destroy'd it and abandon'd the Country on the North side of the Lake Ontario to the Indians.

In 1695 during the War, which preceded the treaty of Reswick the French took the said Country from the Indians, and rebuilt Fort Cadarraqui on the Edge of the Lake, and Continued in Possession of it at the time of Concluding the Treaty of Reswick.

The Author of the Map referr'd to in the Letter Inclosing this,[2] hath the following Remark in his Political Essays upon it page 14 Vizt: "The French being in Possession of Fort Frontenac at the peace of Reswick, which they Attain'd during their War with the Confederates, gives them an undoubted Title to the Acquisition of the North West side of

[1] Daniel de Rény, Sieur de Courcelle, appointed Lieutenant General of Canada Mar. 23, 1665.
[2] Lewis [Louis] Evans, *ante*, p. 349.

St. Lawrance River, from thence to their Settlement at Montreal; but the Confederates still preserv'd their Rights to the other side, fully to Lake St. Francis,[1] leaving the rest to Montreal as a Boundary."

By the 7th Article of the Treaty of Reswick in 1697, which seems the only Applicable one to the Matter under Consideration, it is Stipulated that the most Christian King shall restore to the said King of Great Britain all Countries Islands, Forts, and Colonies wheresoever situated, which the English did possess before the Declaration of this present War, and in like manner the King of Great Britain shall restore to the most Christian King all Countries, Islands, Forts, and Colonies wheresoever situated, which the French did possess before the said Declaration of War, and this restitution shall be made on both sides, within the space of Six Months, or sooner if it can be done."

The Operation of this Treaty therefore, if it is Applicable to Question, which Crown hath the right to the Possession of Fort Frontenac and the North side of the Lake Ontario, seems to be Expressly Contrary to what the Writer of the above Political Remarks Asserts; For if the French *Attained, during their War with the Confederates, that possession which they had at the Peace of Reswick*, as they in fact did, after having in 1679, Evacuated it and Abandon'd it [to] the Indians, they ought by Virtue of a Treaty to have restor'd it to the King of Great Brittain.

The negotiation between Lord Bellomont, Governour of New England and New York, and the Count Frontenac Governour of all New France which pass'd in 1689 soon after the Treaty of Reswick was concluded, May serve to shew the Construction, which both Nations then made of this Treaty with regard to the point in Question; and the Subsequent convention of both Crowns will determine which of them hath the just right to the Possession of Fort Frontenac and the Country on the North side of the Lake Ontario near as far as Montreal.

[1] A name given to the St. Lawrence where it widens above Montreal.

Lord Bellomont demands of Frontenac all the Indians of the five Nations, who were made Prisoners in New France during the then Late War; Monsr. Frontenac in his Answer to this demand, [refuses?] to deliver them up, Insisting that the Indians of the Six Nations were Subjects of the French King, as having had Sovereignty over them before the English were Masters of New York, and says in Effect, *that the Treaty of Reswick had no Relation to the point in Dispute.* Lord Bellomont in his Reply to Monsr. Frontenac insisting upon the Indians ought to be Releas'd, as being Subjects of the King of England, and compriz'd as such, within the said Treaty. In answer to this Monsr. Frontenac acquaints Lord Bellomont "that the Kings their Masters had determined to Name Commissaries on the part of each Crown *to Settle the Limits of the Countries, which belong'd to each of them,* and that he must wait the decision of those Commissaries."

It does not Appear that any Decision of this Affair was made untill the Treaty of Utrecht concluded in 1713 by the 15th Article of which the Indians of the five Nations are declar'd to be Subjects to the Dominion of Great Britain; consequently their Lands to be under the Protection of that Crown.

This being the highest Decision of the point that could be made, Settles it to the Year 1713, and seems to put the Immediate possession, which the French had of Fort Frontenac, and the Country in dispute from the time of the Treaty of Reswick to that of Utrecht out of the Question.

The French still continued in possession of the aforesaid Fort from the time of the last mention'd Treaty [to that?] of Aix la Chapelle in the Year [1748].[1] By that the Treaty of Utrecht is renewed and confirmed, and it is stipulated that the Dominions of the contracting parties shall be put in the same condition with regard to the Possession of them by the severall Princes and States concern'd, *which they ought of right to have been in* before the Late War immediately preceding that Treaty; and for this purpose Commissaries were Appointed by his Majesty and the French King to meet at

[1] The date of the treaty is omitted in the text of the original.

Paris in order to settle and adjust, on the part of each, the Limits of the Controverted Countries in North America. Those Commissaries accordingly met and Enter'd upon their Negotiation, which Continued until it was broke off by the French Kings Seizing upon Several parts of Nova Scotia or Accadie, the Limits of which were referr'd to the Decision of the Commissaries.

It seems plain that his Majesty's Right to the Possession of the North side of the Lake so far as the Limits of the Country of the five Nations extend is not precluded by the Continued possession of the French ever since the Treaty of Utrecht, at which it was first formerly settled for if that is a good plea for the French in this case they might plead their possession of the Several Incroachments they have made in Nova Scotia, at Crown point, and Niagara, which have all of them been of a Considerable Continuance, some ever since the Treaty of Utrecht and others before the Treaty of Aix la Chapelle.

Upon the whole his Majesty's right to remove the French from the North side of Lake Ontario and take the Lands there under his protection seems full as Clear and Indubitable as his right to remove them from their Incroachments at Niagara etca. and to take possession of that Country; his right both to the one and the other standing upon the same foundation, Vizt: the Treaty of Utrecht, and Especially as the Indians of the five Nations have a right to the Country about Niagara by Conquest only, but an aboriginal one to the Country on the North side of the Lake Ontario.

Endorsed:
   Claim of the English and
     French to the Possession
      of Fort Frontenac stated
       and examined.
in Govr. Shirley's of the 19th. Decr. 1755.

WILLIAM SHIRLEY TO SIR THOMAS ROBINSON [1]

[Duplicate]

New York, Decembr. 20th, **1755.**

Sir,

I am now to lay before you an Account of what I have done in obedience to his Majestys 8th Instruction Relative to the Indians, a Copy of which is Inclos'd.[2]

Upon my Arrival at Albany I engag'd the Chief Men of a Tribe of Indians call'd the Stockbridge or River Indians and about 30 of their Warriors to proceed with me to Oswego upon the Expedition against Niagara.

In my passage thro' the Mohawks Country I visited their two Castles, at both which I had a Conferrence with their Chief Sachems, particularly Hendrick [3] and all their Warriors and Young Men, who were not then gone to join Major General Johnson in his Majesty's Service against Crown point, and Engag'd about 18 of those in both the Castles,

---

[1] P. R. O., C. O. 5, 46. A transcript is in the Library of Congress.

[2] The following "copy of his Majesty's Eighth Instruction to the Late Major General Braddock" was inclosed by Shirley in this letter to Sir Thomas Robinson. It is attested by William Alexander.

You will not only Cultivate the Best Harmony and Friendship possible with the Several Governours of our Colonies and Provinces but likewise with the Chiefs of the Indian Tribes, and for the better improvement of our good Correspondence with the said Indian Tribes you will find out some fit and proper person agreable to the Southern Indians, to be sent to them for this purpose in like Manner as we have Ordered Colonel Johnson to repair to the Northern Indians as the person thought to be the Most Acceptable to them, endeavour to engage them to take part and Act with our Forces in such Operations as you shall think Most Expedient. P. R. O., C. O. 5, 46. A transcript is in the Library of Congress. Compare with Instructions to Braddock, Nov. 25, 1754.

[3] See Information from Daniel Claus to Johnson (Johnson Manuscripts, 3, 17), where Shirley's agents, John Henry Lydius and John Fisher, are represented as working against Johnson, and Hendrick acts to defeat their purpose.

who had not Engag'd to proceed with General Johnson, to go with me in the Service under my Command, and in my passage from thence to Oswego I sent Messages to the Sachems of the Oneida's Cayuga's, Onondago's and Seneca's to meet me there with some of the Warriors of their respective Nations.

Soon after my Arrival at Oswego Several of the Sachems and Warriors of the Oneida's met me, as did, a few days after, almost all the Onondago Sachems, and a Considerable Number of their Warriors; and I had reason to Expect a large Number of the Seneca's, untill two of their Chief Sachems came to me to apologize for their Staying so long and to let me know it was owing to an Albany Trader having brought in among their Young Men a great quantity of Rum, which kept them continually drunk; that part of their Errand was to acquaint me, that the party I had sent after the Albany Trader to take away his Rum pursuant to the Power given by a Province Law of New York to the Commandant at Oswego for the time being, could not Execute their orders, and to assure me it was not the fault of the Sachems, and to Complain of this practice, as what was the ruin of their Young Men; I had however the Satisfaction to hear soon after, that the Seneca's had oblig'd Mr. Jonquiere,[1] who had been at their Castles two or three Months Endeavouring to Engage their Warriors in the French Service, and he actually Engag'd 15 of them, to take away the French Colours from among them, that the 15 Young Men had refus'd to go with him and that those Castles had promis'd to take up the Hatchet for the English.

A few days after one of the Indians, whom I had sent to gain Intelligence of the State of the French Fort and Garrison at Niagara brought me a Message from the Outowaias

---

[1] Chaubert Joncaire, son of Jean François Joncaire, is probably the person to whom reference is here made. He was a great power among the Seneca Indians, being the son of a French officer and a Seneca squaw. His name is given also as Chabert Jancour and Jan Coeur. See Johnson Manuscripts. Parkman, "Montcalm and Wolfe," appears uncertain whether the father or the son was the influential factor among the Indians at this time.

Indians who had been concern'd in the Action at the Monongahela against General Braddock that if I should come against Niagara and would Inform them of it, they would be *out of the way* [not use the Hatchet against the English] and I understood by the same Indians, that they had Encourag'd the Seneka's whose Castle is more Inclin'd to the French than any other of the five Nations, to take up the Hatchet with their Brethren against them, which was a great motive for useing Jonquiere as they did.

At my Conferences with the Indians at Oswego, the Onondago's desir'd me to build them a Fort at their said Castle, which I promis'd to do next Spring; the Oneida's have desir'd the same with a Garrison, and some pieces of Artillery; and in return they have given me leave to Fortify the great Carrying Place in their Lands at Oneida, as I should think proper during the Expedition, for Securing our Magazines of Stores and Provisions at each end of it, and for keeping open the Communication between Oswego and Albany.

The Cayugas desir'd I could send them two or three Men to Plough their Lands, and all of them Gunsmiths, which I have promis'd.

At other Conferences I acquainted them, that I had sent Messages to the Messasagaes, Chippowees, Outowaias, and other Western Castles, to meet me and the Brethren of the five Nations at Oswego next Spring, there to Consult in a General Council upon the best Measures for Settling a mutual Friendship and alliance, opening a free Trade and Commerce between the Indians and English, at such Trading Houses upon the Lakes as they should Choose and which, I propos'd to build for them, and for Engaging all the Western Indians to lay down the Hatchet against the English, and by that means establish a General Peace among all their Castles and putting an End to the destructive War, which the French were perpetually Engaging them in against the English, and against each other.

For this purpose I propos'd to the five Nations to send some of their Sachems to meet me in the Spring at Oswego, at which place I told them, that as it is the Center of their

Country and it was more fit that the far Nations should resort to *their* home, and take Law from them, than that they should go out of their own Territories to meet those Nations; I design'd (in the Indian Phrase) to kindle a new fire there, for them to have General Councils and meetings Annually or at other set times in order to Cultivate a good understanding among themselves, and peace and trade with the English, and to Consult upon every thing that might promote their own Interests.

This the leading Castles among them promis'd me to do, and Yesterday I had the pleasure to receive the Inclos'd Letter from Lieutenant Colonel Mercer,[1] whom I left Commanding Officer at Oswego, acquainting me with the Success of my Messages to the Messasague's and other Indians on the North side of the Lake Ontario etc: and I can't but hope if every one of those Measures are closely pursu'd and discreetly manag'd, and the Trade put under proper Regulations, they will go far towards Compassing that great Object, the drawing over all the Indians in General except perhaps, what the French call les Sauvages Domicilies (those Inhabiting Villages within Canada) to the English Interest.

A beneficial Trade to them will certainly be the greatest and most Extensive Attraction, and of much more Effect than the Richest of presents; though presents and small pensions properly plac'd among them at right times must be made use of too; But when the Trade is Settled, those need be made use of much more sparingly than at present: The keeping up Forts within the Territories of every one of the five Nations must have a great Effect to keep them united in a firm dependence upon the Crown of Great Britain; And if an Annual meeting of the far Nations with those of Oswego can be establish'd, it will give the five Nations a great figure and increase their Influence among the Castles of the far Nations and both together must greatly Contribute towards restoring them to their Antient Power among all the Indians, and their former Close Connections with the English.

[1] See letters of Mercer to William Alexander, Shirley's secretary, Nov. 30 and Dec. 11, *ante*, pp. 335 and 340.

I am now oblig'd to acquaint you, Sir, that General Braddock, upon his Arrival at Alexandria, gave the then Colonel Johnson, whom I had before appointed Commander in Chief of the Provincial Troops Employ'd in the Expedition against Crown Point, a Commission [1] Constituting him Sole "Superintendant and Manager of the Affairs of the Indians of the Six Nations, and Strictly requiring and enjoining all Persons to whom the direction of the Affairs of the said Nations or their Allies have been heretofore Committed, and all others whatsoever, to cease and forbear Acting or Intermedling therein"; and by the said late General's 6th Instruction to him he is directed to use every Expedient to prevail upon the Six Nations to declare themselves, and to take up Arms as well to Act in Conjunction with himself at the Attack of Crown point, *to March with those Troops, which are destin'd for the Reduction of Niagara;* and also to prevail upon them to Engage their Allies to join the General to the Southward.

Soon after my Return from Alexandria to Boston I wrote a Letter to Colonel Johnson by an Officer, to whom I had given the Chief Command of the Indians, who should proceed with me to Niagara, desiring he would assist him in procuring me some Indians to go in that Service, and ordering the officer to Act under Colonel Johnson's Direction; This Letter was delivered to him, but had a Contrary effect to what I hop'd.

The Construction, which Colonel Johnson made of his Indian Commission, was that it Excluded me from Employing any Person whatever to Engage any Indians to go with me to Niagara: one Instance, among others, of this is that he forbids one Captain Staats, who told him he should carry some Stockbridge Indians to Niagara in the Expedition under

[1] On Sept. 12 Shirley had written Johnson, asking, among other matters, for a copy of the latter's instructions and commission received from General Braddock (Johnson Manuscripts, 2, 213). This letter was answered by Johnson Sept. 22, 24, but the copy desired does not appear to have been sent (*ibid.* 2, 237). See Johnson to Shirley, Dec. 16 (*ante*, p. 342), where receipt of commission is denied.

my Command, to presume to take one of them into it; and what makes this more Extraordinary is, that these Indians are no part of the Six Nations, but Chiefly Inhabit within my own Government, and are dependent upon it; and were rais'd at first by Captain Staats [1] at the request of Colonel Johnson, to proceed to Crown Point with him, but afterwards refus'd by him on Account, I suppose, of his not much wanting them; and I have very great reason to believe from what pass'd between me and some of the Indians, that he Secretly Endeavour'd to prejudice them against going with me; nor had I one with me Except those Stockbridge Indians whom I Engag'd at Albany, and a few from every Castle, which I pick'd up as I pass'd thro' the Mohawk's, Oneida's and Onondaga's Country in my March to Oswego.

Since my Return from Oswego, I have receiv'd Complaints from two Mohawk Indians of the lower Castle, who were with me at Oswego, that in their absence their Families were deny'd by Colonel Johnsons Agent the Provisions which he allow'd to the Families of those Indians of the same Castle, who were in the Expedition against Crown Point with him.

I have the further Mortification to find that I have great reason to be persuaded, that Colonel Johnson is Supported by the Governour of New York in the wrong Notions, he hath Entertain'd of the Effect of his Indian Commission from General Braddock, with respect to its Excluding me from any Superintendency of Indian affairs by Virtue of my Commission: The Inclos'd Extract of my Letter to the Governour and his Answer to me,[2] both dated since it was known that I had the Honour of the Lords Justices Commission to Succeed the late General Braddock in his Command, will

[1] Joachim Staats.
[2] See Shirley to Hardy, Nov. 8, and reply of Hardy, Nov. 9, *ante*, pp. 324–5. Lieutenant Governor DeLancey appears to have sided with Johnson against Shirley during their disagreement. In a letter of Johnson to the Lieutenant Governor of July 30, 1755, the former denounced Shirley's mischievous Indian measures, to which DeLancey replied sympathetically on Aug. 3. Encouraged by this reply, Johnson, in his letter of Aug. 8 to the Lieut. Governor,

shew this in a very material Instance : And I understand that Sir Charles Hardy assumes to himself a power of sending Colonel Johnson directions for the Execution of his Trust, with regard to the Indians ; which Colonel Johnson follows, and both of them without first communicating with me; and this they have done in a very essential Article Vizt. the Disposition of the French Prisoners, concerning which I have his Majesty's Express orders to send them to France. And I hear they have taken upon them to give one or more of them to one of the Castles of the five Nations, a proceeding in my opinion, far from being adviseable at this Conjuncture.

Sir Charles Hardy observes, in his Inclos'd Answer to me "that General Braddock had in Consequence of Instructions from home, and with the unanimous Opinion of the Council at Alexandria given General Johnson a Commission to take upon him the Management and care of Indian Affairs;" I can undertake to say that not one of the Council at Alexandria ever imagin'd that the Effect of that Commission was to exclude the King's General, who gave it, or his Successor from Executing the Trust Committed to them by the King, for Cultivating a Friendship with the Indians and Engaging them to take part and Act with his forces in such operations as either of them should think it Expedient for the Indians to take. If any one particular Member hath advis'd Sir Charles Hardy in this Affair, it proceeds, I have reason to believe, from that Member's fondness to bring back by this means in the End the Indian Affairs to the Management of the Commissioners for them at Albany, whose long misconduct in that Trust, and the pernicious Consequences of it to his Majesty's Service and the Interest of his Subjects in General with the Six Nations are too well known to need being particularly mention'd.[1]

spoke of the scandalous conduct of Shirley's Indian agents and censured the commander who succeeded Braddock most roundly. See also Johnson to the Lords of Trade, Sept. 3, *ante*, p. 243.

[1] Among others in opposition to Shirley and friendly to Johnson in this matter Goldsbrow Banyar may be mentioned. His letter

To remove the foundation of these obstacles to me in Executing his Majesty's orders relative to the Indians, I have revok'd General Braddock's Commission to General Johnson, and sent him one founded upon the intent of his Majesty's Inclos'd Instruction without the Words *Sole Superintendent*, which are mention'd in his former Commission and accompany'd with a Letter to him a Copy of which is Inclos'd.[1]

Whether he will Act under this Commission, or at least follow my Instructions (which last will satisfy me) I know not yet: if he will do either, as he hath press'd for an acceptance of the Surrender of his Military Commission with all the Governments concern'd in the Expedition against Crown Point, as Interfering too much with his Attention to his Indian Commission, he will not be under his former Temptation to prevent me from having a Suitable proportion of the Indians to proceed with me in the Service under my Immediate Command, and may duely Execute the trust repos'd in him. If he refuse to do either I shall be under a necessity, in order to Enable me to do my own Duty in this Article of Appointing another in his Stead, which will be the Noted Conrad Weiser, who besides being a Person of the most Universal Influence over, and knowledge of all the Indians of the five Nations, of any one upon this Continent, is an adopted Sachem among them, and Constituted a Member of their General Council at Onondago.[2]

With regard to my Execution of that part of his Majesty's Inclos'd Instructions, which relates to the Southern Indians,

of Aug. 6, 1755, was an encouragement to Johnson (Johnson Manuscripts, 2, 158). The Indian Superintendent had endeavored to win Robert Orme also to his side (Aug. 1, 1755, Johnson Manuscripts, 2, 141). See also Johnson to Thomas Pownall, July 31 and Aug. 25 (*ibid*. 2, 140, 189).

[1] See Letter and Commission, Shirley to Johnson Dec. 7, *ante*, pp. 336–7, and Instructions, Dec. 10 and 24, *ante*, p. 338, and *post*, p. 367.

[2] Conrad Weiser had represented Pennsylvania in practically all her Indian negotiations for the previous decade. No better substitute for Johnson could have been selected if a change was necessary.

I have to acquaint you, Sir, that upon Governour Morris's representing to me [1] the present Devastations made there by the Indians within the Province of Pensilvania, under his Government, (an Account of which I understand, Sir, he hath sent to yourself) and the present defenceless State of the Province, for want of some Regular Troops to Act in Conjunction with what Provincials the Governour shall raise in his own Colony a Copy of which last is Inclos'd, I have propos'd the Inclos'd Measures to be taken by the Several Western Governments from Pensilvania to South Carolina both Inclusive; [2] which I have Transmitted to the respective Governours, as also the Inclos'd Instructions to Colonel Johnson; [3] and have Determin'd to send him a Detachment of 90 of the Regular Troops now at this Place, which is all the Succour, I have it in my Power to send at present, and may I hope Infuse a Sense of Discipline into the Irregulars, Encourage the Province to make some Opposition to the Enemy, which they have not hitherto done, and be some Check to the Enemy in making their Incursions.

I can't but Attribute, Sir, the present Confusion and Distress of Pensilvania principally to the Government's being but just now Beginning to recover from its principles of Non-defence, and the People's being unacustom'd to Attacks from the Indians and making a stand against them.

The Comparison of the State of Pensilvania with that of the Province of the Massachusets Bay may serve in some measure to shew the Justness of this Remark; the latter Government hath a very extended Frontier, which was for many Years us'd to feel Cruel Effects from the Incursions of the Eastern Indians by their cutting off whole Townships in time of War; and Still feels bad Effects from them in their most Expos'd Settlements; but from being long us'd

---

[1] See Morris to Shirley, Nov. 26, *ante*, p. 333, and same to same, Nov. 6, 1 Penna. Arch. 2, 469.   See also Morris to Sir Thomas Robinson, Oct. 27 and Oct. 28, 1755, *ibid.* 439, 440.

[2] See *post*, p. 364.

[3] See *ante*, p. 338.

to defend themselves they have establish'd a very different System of treating the Indians from that of Pensilvania: before I left the Government War was Declar'd against all the Eastern Indians except the Penobscots, and since I left it, they sent to demand of the Penobscots to bring in their Old Men, Women and Children into the Province, there to remain, during the War with the Indians, as Hostages for their fidelity, and on their Refusal to do it, the Government hath Declar'd Warr against them: and then at a time when a fifth part of the Province's fighting Men were Engag'd in other parts of the Kings Service

I am with the highest respect

Sir

Your most Humble and

most Obedient Servant. W. Shirley.

Rt. Honble. Sir Thomas Robinson Knt. of the Bath, ⎱
one of his Majesty's principal Secretaries of State. ⎰
Endorsed:
New York Decr. 20. 1755.
  Govr. Shirley
    R. 22 Janry. 1756.

MEASURES PROPOSED BY WILLIAM SHIRLEY FOR THE WESTERN GOVERNMENTS [1]

[Dec. 1755.]

By His Excellency Major General William Shirley, General and Commander in Chief of his Majesty's Forces in North America, &c.

Upon taking into his Consideration the very Great importance of the numerous nations of Indians in Alliance with

[1] P. R. O., C. O. 5, 46. Inclosed in Shirley to Robinson, Dec. 20, 1755. Shirley appears to have sent a copy to Robert H. Morris. See Morris to Horatio Sharpe, Arch. of Md. 6, 321, and Shirley to Sharpe, Dec. 30, 1755, *post*, p. 370. The plan here outlined was to embrace the colonies from Pennsylvania to South Carolina.

his Majesty's Southern Colonies, the advantages that will accrue to the English in General from their Friendship and the Particular necessity there is at this time, to enter into a Solemn Treaty with them in order not only to secure them to the British Interest, so far as to Prevent them from joining in the Designs of the French, but to engage them to Assist his Majestys Subjects in Defending their frontiers and annoying their Enemies;

It is Proposed,

1st That a Treaty be held with the several Tribes of Indians in Alliance with his Majesty's Southern Colonies, at such time and Place, as shall be agreed on between the Governments of North and South Carolina and notified by them to the General and to the other Western Colonies as far north as Pensylvania.

2dly That one or more Commissioners should be Appointed by each of the Western Provinces from South Carolina to Pensylvania both inclusive to carry on that Treaty, in behalf of his Majesty, and of those Colony's to be particularly instructed by their respective Governments for that Purpose.

3dly That such Instructions be without Delay transmitted to the General and that he or the Commander in-Chief of the Kings Forces for the time being give such further instructions to the Commissioners collective or seperately as he shall think necessary for his Majesty's Service.

4thly That the Governments of Virginia and the two Carolina's as soon as Possible Dispatch the Messengers to those Southern Tribes inviting them to a General Treaty in his Majesty's name and in the names of all the said Western Provinces, and that the time and Place agreed on for such Treaty be particularly mentioned in such invitation.

5thly That at such appointed place, Provision be made for the Reception and entertainment of the Indians that may Attend the Treaty, by the Province wherein such place is, to be Afterwards Reinbursed in Proportion by the other Colony's.

6thly That money be Provided by the said Western

Provinces for defraying the Expense of the Treaty and for Providing a Proper Assortment of Goods to be given in Presents to the Indians that shall attend, and sent into their Country's to be distributed among those that cannot personally Assist at the Treaty.

7thly That the Commissioners be instructed to engage those Tribes to Assist the English in the Present Dispute and to take up the Hatchet against the French and their Indians and that they be enabled to Promise English Pay and Provisions, Arms, Ammunition and Indian Cloaths, to such of Warriors as shall Join his Majesty's Forces, or the Troops in the Service of any of the Western Provinces, and as to such of them as shall incline to Attack the French upon the Ohio, or any of the Indians in their Alliance, to Promise them certain Rewards for every Prisoner or Scalp they shall bring in, and to Appoint certain Places to which such Scalps or Prisoners shall be brought.

8thly. That Proper persons be Appointed by the Commissioners to Return with the Indians from the Treaty into their own Country, if Necessary to conduct the Warriors to such places as shall be appointed for their Rendezvous where stores of Provisions, Arms and Ammunition should be Provided for their use.

ROBERT HUNTER MORRIS TO WILLIAM SHIRLEY [1]

New York, Decr. 22nd, 1755.

Sir,

I did myself the Honour to send your Excellency some Accts : I received on Saturday night of the Continuance of the Ravages of the Indians in the Province of Pensilvania requesting some Military Force might be sent to the relief of his Majesties distressed Subjects there. I think it my Duty further to represent to you that they are without a

[1] P. R. O., C. O. 5, 46. A transcript is in the Library of Congress.

Militia or any Law Obliging them to bear Arms, for want whereof the Commander in Chief cannot enforce Obedience to his Military orders tho' he shou'd be enabled to raise and support Men on this present Exigency and that this Obstacle which may prove Fatal and even [cause] the Loss of the province can only be removed by the Junction of Regulars with the Provincial Forces. The King's Service therefore Absolutely Obliges me again to request that your Excellency wou'd be pleased immediately to order that some Troops which may best be spared may March into Pensilvania and that you would favour me with your Orders and directions respecting them which shall be punctually Obeyed by Sir

Your Most faithfull and Obedient
Humble Servant.

ROBT. H. MORRIS.

His Exy. Genl. Shirley
   A true Copy examd. by
    WM. ALEXANDER Secy.

WILLIAM SHIRLEY TO WILLIAM JOHNSON [1]

New York Dec. 24 1755.

Additional Instructions to Major Genll. William Johnson relative to the Indians of the Six Nations under his command

That a party of the Six Nations to consist of a few Sachems the rest to be Warriors be engaged by private applications and the offer of rewards to take up the Hatchett against the French and their Indians who have fallen upon the Provinces of Virginia, Maryland and Pensilvania.

That they be requested immediately to proceed to Pensilvania where the[y] will find a large force actually in readiness, and there concert the best measures for carrying on the War.

[1] P. R. O., C. O. 5, 52. Another copy undated is in C. O. 5, 46, also Sir William Johnson Manuscripts, 4, 9–10. Printed: Docts. rel. Col. Hist. N. Y. 7, 10.

That they should go by the way of Susquehanna and call upon all the Indians settled upon both the Branches of that River and engage as many Indians as they have any Influence with to [join and] accompany them.

That assurance be given them of their being supplied with Arms Accoutrements, Cloaths, Provisions and pay. That they shall have besides these, a reward for every prisoner or scalp taken from the enemy and every other reasonable encouragement, all which to be ascertained to their satisfaction by Treaty as soon as they arrive in Pensilvania.

That as in all Indian Towns, some may be for the French and some for the English, they should be advised to use prudence in their applications to particular Indians, lest the French be too soon informed of their Intentions.

That they be instructed to look out for fit and proper persons to get intelligence and engage them to go to the French Fort on the Ohio and to the Towns in that neighborhood, and when they have made themselves masters of their future designs, and operations then to proceed to the Governor of Pensilvania with their information for which they shall be well paid.

That if any of the Indians are afraid to leave their wives and children they be desired to bring them along with them and care shall be taken to assign them a strong and well fortified place to live in where they shall be supplied with necessarys.

W. Shirley.

By His Excellencys command

Wm. Alexander Secry.

WILLIAM SHIRLEY TO SIR THOMAS ROBINSON [1]

New York Decr. 25th 1755.

Sir,

I have, for more Safety of the Conveyance of my Dispatches, and of the Answer I may receive to them, Sent them

[1] P. R. O., C. O. 5, 46. A transcript is in the Library of Congress. This letter is printed to illustrate the importance placed

under the Care of Captain Morris,[1] one of my Aids de Camp, who will have the Honour of delivering them into your Hands, and hath my Instructions to return to Boston or New York by the first Opportunity after he shall receive from you his Majesty's pleasure upon the Parts of his Service, which I have lay'd before you.

Captain Morris is knowing to all the proceedings in every part of his Majesty's Service in the Expedition under my immediate Command from his personal Attendance upon it; and to all the other Matters contain'd in my Letters of the 19th and 20th Instant, and is able to give you a very particular Account of any Circumstances, which may be inquir'd into.

He is an Officer of Merit, and a young Gentleman of Worth and Honour, and as Such I beg leave to recommend him Sir to your Countenance and Favour. I have the Honour to be with the Highest Respect

Sir,
Your most Humble, and
most Obedient Servant.

W. Shirley.

Rt. Honble: Sir Thomas Robinson Knt. of the Bath, one of his Majesty's principal Secretaries of State.

Endorsed:

New York, 25th Decr. 1755. Govr. Shirley R. 10th Febry. 1756. by Capt. Morris.

by Shirley upon his communications of Dec. 19 and 20, with their inclosures, and as showing an increased dignity due to his office of military commander in America. It was also essential in the mind of Shirley that he have a representative in London to explain his plans for the coming year.

[1] Roger Morris was born in England, Jan. 28, 1727. He was commissioned as Captain in Francis Ligonier's regiment Sept. 13, 1745, and served as Aide de Camp to Braddock in the expedition against Fort Duquesne. He held the same position under Shirley, and appears to have been one of his most trusted assistants. Morris served later with Wolfe at Quebec, being promoted to his majority on Feb. 16, 1758, and commissioned Lieutenant Colonel May 19, 1760.

WILLIAM SHIRLEY TO HORATIO SHARPE [1]

New York December 30th 1755.

Sir,

Being ordered by his Majesty in his Instructions to me as Commander in Chief of the Forces in North America not only to Cultivate the best Harmony and Friendship possible with the several Governors of his Colonies upon this Continent but likewise with the Chiefs of the Indian Tribes and for the better Improvement of his Good Correspondence with the said Indian Tribes to find out some fit and Proper Person agreeable to the Southern Indians to be Sent to them for this Purpose, and to Endeavour to engage them to Act with his Forces in such operations as I shall think most Expedient: I think I can't better Answer his Royal Intention, especially at this time of General Incursions of the Indians into his Western Frontiers, than by recommending the Inclosed Plan [2] to your Honour which if unanimously Executed by the Several Governments concerned, I can't but Conceive Strong hopes may provide in the most effectual manner for their mutual Security against the Hostile Attempts of the Southern Indians upon them and creating a Dependency of those Nations upon his Majesty.

If your Honour can Suggest to me any Amendment of this Plan or other Measures for compassing this great Object, I shall very gladly do all the Service I can in promoting them.

I have at the same time likewise Endeavoured to Induce the Indians of the Six Nations to join with us in putting a Stop to the Devastations of the Shawanese, Delaware, Susquehana, and other Southern Nations within his Majestys Western Colonies either by their Good offices and Authority

---

[1] Printed: Arch. of Md. 6, 330; 31, 90. Sharpe's reply of Jan. 24, in which he promises to furnish supplies, but will send no troops north of Fort Duquesne, is in Arch. of Md. 6, 337. Substantially the same letter was sent by Shirley to Benning Wentworth of New Hampshire, N. H. Prov. Papers, 6, 460.

[2] A copy of the plan referred to was sent by Shirley to Robinson in his letter of Dec. 20, and is printed on p. 364, *ante.*

over them or if those should prove ineffectual by taking up the Hatchet against them.

Inclosed I send your Honour a Copy of the Minutes of a Council of War composed of Governors and Field officers according to his Majestys Instructions held at this Place the 12th and 13th Instant upon the operations of the next years Campaign, at which your Honour assisted,[1] I doubt not but you will recommend to the Assembly within your Government in the Strongest Terms to Contribute their Just Quota by Men and Money towards carrying so Salutary a Plan into Execution; which if done with Vigour and in its proper Season, they must be Sensible will lay the most lasting foundation for the future Safety and Tranquility of their Province and I can't but hope that the Outrages and Devastations lately committed by the Enemy more or less within all his Majestys Western Colonies will Convince the Assembly of Maryland how essential it is for the welfare of his Majestys Subjects within their Province that they should heartily join in the Execution of this Plan which your Honour will be Pleased to Communicate either in part or in the whole as your Honour shall judge Proper and how loudly their Duty to their King and Country calls upon them to do it.

Upon this occasion I cant but hope that the Province under your Honours Government will consider how deeply it is Interested in the event of the next years Campaign.

I will not omit returning your Honour my thanks for the Journey you took from Annapolis at so late a Season of the year, and long attendance at this Place upon his Majestys Service: and acknowledging my obligations to you for the great assistance I have had in my Consultations with you upon the most Essential and difficult points of it; which hath put it into my power to promote it further than

[1] The Minutes of this Council were sent to various governors in America, and a copy was inclosed to Sir Thomas Robinson in Shirley's letter of Dec. 19. They are printed in N. H. Prov. Papers, 6, 463–467, and Arch. of Md. 31, 92. See Jonathan Belcher to Shirley of Dec. 26 regarding the Council and in appreciation of Shirley's commendation of Col. Peter Schuyler, 1 N. J. Arch. 8, pt. 2, 203.

I am perswaded I should have been able to have done without it.

I beg leave to assure you, Sir, that I shall ever esteem it an happiness and Honour to me to maintain the Closest Correspondence with you in the future Course of his Majestys Service, and to give you proofs with what an unfeigned Esteem and regard. I am Sir

Your Honours Most Humble and Most Obedient Servant

W. Shirley[1]

P.S. Inclosed are the Proportions according to the Plan Settled by the Commissioners at Albany; which though not perfectly Equal, are the only ones that can be made use of untill more exact can be formed; which cant be done in time for the Present purpose. All inequalitys must be Equitably Adjusted, and afterwards Set right upon the first Opportunity of doing it.

Your Honour must be Sensible that the Success of the next years operations depends upon an early Campaign.

I must desire your Honour to prevail on your Assembly to raise their Inclosed Proportion of 1000 men towards the Expedition against Crown Point in the first place, before you recomend to them to Raise their proportion towards the Expedition against Du Quesne.

Proportions of the 10,000 Men proposed to be rais'd for the Crown Point Expedition according to the Plan Settled by the Commissioners at Albany.

Maryland	1,000
Virginia	1,750
Pensilvania	1,500

[1] Much the same letter was sent by Shirley to Governor Dinwiddie of Virginia, and the question of the rank of Capt. John Dagworthy was taken up with him. See Dinwiddie's reply of Jan. 24 (Dinwiddie Papers, 2, 328), and Sharpe to Dinwiddie therein referred to (Jan. 4, 1756, Arch. of Md. 6, 333). See also Shirley to Sharpe, Mar. 5, 1756 (Arch. of Md. 6, 347), the extract of Dinwiddie's letter of Jan. 23 (*ibid.* p. 348), and Shirley's order of Mar. 5, 1756, *post*, p. 412.

New Jerseys	750
New York	1,000
Rhode Island	500
Conecticutt	1,250
New Hampshire	500
Massachusetts	1,750
	10,000

WILLIAM SHIRLEY TO THE LORDS OF TRADE

SKETCH OF A SYSTEM FOR THE MANAGEMENT OF INDIAN AFFAIRS IN NORTH AMERICA UNDER ONE GENERAL DIRECTION [1]

[New York, January 5, 1756.]

For the more distinct treating of this matter it may be proper to consider the Indians, to be comprehended in the propos'd System, as divided into four Districts, Vizt the Indians at first called the Five Nations, now the Six Nations, which Inhabit along the South side of the Mohawk's River, the Oneida Lake, the River Onondago, and the Lake Ontario; the Indians which inhabit along the North side of the Lakes Ontario and Erie and on Lake Huron, &c.; the Indians, which Inhabit the Rivers Delaware, Susquehanna, Ohio &c as far as Georgia; and the Indians which Inhabit to the Eastward of New England, and in the Service of Nova Scotia as far as the Southern Bank of the River St Lawrence.

The principal Articles, in which the proper management of these Indians, in order to fix them in the English Interest

[1] P. R. O., C. O. 5, 887. This sketch is preceded by the following abstract of the letter in which it is inclosed: —

Letter from Govr. Shirley dated Jan. 5, 1756, in answer to the Secretary's Letter, signifying the Directions of the Board, that the Governor should send them his Opinion, what may be a proper System . . . for the Management of Indian Affairs under one general Direction.

Read, March 11 1756.

and a Dependence upon the Crown of Great Britain consists are, 1st the affording their Old Men, Women and Children protection against the French and their Indians, whilst their Warriors were absent from them; 2dly a due Regulation of the Trade with them; 3dly a Regulation of the Sale of their Lands, and preventing Incroachmnets being made upon their Hunting Grounds; 4thly The expelling French Missionaires from among them, and Introducing English Protestant Ministers in their Room; 5thly the Convening them in General Councils among themselves Annually or oftner; 6thly the Establishing General Interviews between the Indians and the Kings Governours or Commissioners appointed by them at certain times, and making them Publick and private presents.

As to the 1st Article the building and maintaining small Forts and Garrisons in their Countries, with their Consent, is necessary; Besides the protection, this will afford to their Families, it will give us a constant inspection over them, and, if discreet Officers are posted in the Forts, will greatly Increase their Attachment to the English.

Great progress hath been lately made in this point in the Country of the Six Nations : At the desire of the two Castles of the Mohawks, a Fort was built at each of them by the Government of New York the last Summer, and Garrisons posted there during the Campaigne; The Onondago Indians requested of me at Oswego to build them a Fort near their Castle the next Spring; the Oneida Indians upon my proposal of it to them requested me, at the great carrying Place, on my return to their Country, to do the same thing as soon as possible, and send them some Soldiers for their protection; and upon my Arrival at Albany the Tuscarora Indians sent me a Message to the same effect; all which I accordingly promised them, and it seems highly probable that the Cayuga and Seneca Indians will soon follow their Examples.

As to the Second Article For the due Regulation of the Indian Trade so as to make it more beneficial to them than the French can do, which (as it is the most Interesting point with them, and universally striking in all their Nations), is the most essential Article to be taken care of, I would recommend the Scheme establish'd in the Province of the Massachusets Bay : That Government hath erected Truck Houses within their several Forts near the head quarters of all the Neighbouring Tribes of Indians dependent upon it, which are supply'd at those Houses with such goods as they want, Arms, Ammunition and other Indian necessarys in exchange for their Furrs and Pelleterie ; these goods are purchas'd with the Publick money at the best hand, by the Commissary General of Stores for the Province, an Officer annually chosen by the Assembly with the consent and appointment of the Governour, and distributed in every Truck House by him, to be sold by the truck Master there (an Officer chosen and appointed in like manner) at the prime Cost, with the Addition of so much per Cent as well pay the Expence of transporting the trade from Boston to the Truck Houses ; and to prevent any Imposition upon the Indians in this Trade, the rates at which the Pelleterie is to be taken from them in truck for the English goods, are stated by the Government, and tables of the several prices, which the Indians are to pay for each species of goods sold to them, together with the Rates, which they are to be allowed for every species of their Pelleterie, distinguishing the several prices of their Spring and Fall Skins, and to be hung upon the truck House, and made known to the Indians ; The truck Master is sworn to the due Execution of his Trust ; allowed a Salary by the Government, and forbid to trade with them on his own or any other private account ; and all private Trade with the Indians, particularly the Sale of Rum is prohibited under a penalty by a Law of the Province.

This method for supplying the Indians, who may be properly said to be dependent upon the English, with goods, is not practiced as far as I can learn, in any other Government besides the Massachusets Bay : As to the Province of Nova Scotia, it is not to be expected, that it should have been done within that as yet : I believe it is not practiced in the Southern and Western Governments ; and I am sure it is not in the Government of New York, but the Introducing of this method into the English Governments which Trade with the Indians, seems not difficult to be effected.

The opening and Establishing a Trade with the numerous Nations of Northern and Southern Indians Inhabiting the North side of the Lake Ontario, and as far Westward, as the Lakes Erie, the Detroit, and Lake Huron and &c. which is now wholly Engrossed by the French, and is the Chief Connexion between them and the Indians, may be attended with greater difficulty, but is I hope very practicable.

This I apprehend is to be done, at least to be begun, only at Oswego, as that is the only trading House in his Majesty's Colonies, which by its Situation will admit of such a Trade being carried on as is with those Indians : It was with this view that Mr. Burnet in the Year [1727] being then Governour of New York upon finding the French wholly in possession of that Trade, and foreseeing the many Evils, which the English Colonies have long experienced from the Attachment of those Indians to them on that Account first built Fort Oswego : but as he did not remain long after in his Government, his good intent hath been since wholly defeated by the Government of New York's having Burthened the Trade carried on with the before mentioned Northern and Western Indians at Oswego, whilst a Free Trade with the French Indians hath been left open at Albany, who have been carriers and Factors for the French, and supplyed them thro' that Channel with English Strouds and other goods necessary to Indians; by which means the French have furnished those Nations with English Woolens at as Cheap or Cheaper rates, at *their* Trading Houses in Canada and upon the great Lakes and Rivers, than the Indians could purchase them at Oswego itself.

To this pernicious Trade, carried on from Albany, in which the French have chiefly made use of the Cagnawaga Indians, who have been considerable gainers by it, it is the opinion of the best Judges here, must be due the continuance of those Indians in their defection from the English to the French; several Grievances flowing from this trade to the Neighbouring Colonies in time of a General Warr with the

French might likewise be pointed out; but that is beside my present purpose: what I would at present observe is that a prohibition of the Trade with the French carried on from Albany; and opening a free trade at Oswego with the Indians of the far Nations, would remedy these mischiefs, and lay a foundation not only for establishing a Trade with them, and bringing them into an Alliance with the English, but likewise of reclaiming the Cagnawagas, the most powerfull Tribe of Indians in Canada, to their antient Friendship with them.

As I look upon the opening of this Trade at Oswego, to be an object of the greatest importance to his Majesty's Service and the welfare of the Colonies, I used my utmost endeavours during my stay there, to engage the Indians of the Northern and Western Nations by messages to them to meet me there next spring, in order to consult with me and their Brethren of the Six Nations (most of whom there promised to meet me) upon opening a trade and Establishing a Friendship between them and the English: The success of my messages will appear by the inclosed Extract of a Letter from Lieutenent Colonel Mercer the Commanding Officer at Oswego to my Secretary: and I shall desire Sir Charles Hardy to recommend it to his Assembly to provide a Quantity of Goods proper for Indian Trade to be sent to Oswego, in time for their meeting me there; and to be sold to them at the prime cost free of the present duty as also to furnish me with some presents for them.

If this proposed meeting of the Indians at Oswego should take effect, and measures can be concerted there to Establish a Trade with the Northern and Western Indians, and an Annual meeting and Council between them and the Six Nations, I cannot but hope that it will contribute much to unite and fix them all in the English Interest.

Endorsed:
Sketch of a System for the Management of Indian Affairs in North America under one general Direction

WILLIAM SHIRLEY TO THE LORDS OF TRADE [1]

New York Janry 11th 1756.

My Lords,

I am honour'd with your Lordships' Letter of the 16th of August.

The Approbation, which your Lordships are pleas'd to express therein of my proceedings upon the River Kennebeck in the summer before last, and the Notice there taken of my Recommendation of the Proprietors of the Kennebeck Grant, together with your Lordships's Approbation of what I took the liberty to submit to your consideration in Support of the Excise Act pass'd by the Assembly within my own Government in the year 1754, give me very great Pleasure and Satisfaction; as I am sure the Approbation of the Act will to the General Court.

The bad Effects, which your Lordships observe in the same Letter, the Disputes between the Borderers upon both sides of the Boundary Line between this Government and my own have of late produc'd, notwithstanding the Endeavours of both Governments to prevent them, require an effectual stop to be put to them, as soon as possible; which as your Lordships further observe can be done only by a Commission from the Crown: No Endeavours shall be wanting on my part, My Lords, to induce the Province of the Massachusetts Bay to concurr in that Measure upon my Arrival at Boston.

I am likewise to acknowledge the Receipt of Mr Pownall's Letter to me dated the 19th of September, signifying to me your Lordships's Directions to transmit to you "an exact "and particular Account of the present actual State and "Quantity of the Cannon, small Arms, Ammunition, and "other Ordnance and Military Stores belonging to the Prov-"ince under my Government, either in the publick Magazines "or in the Possession of the Militia or other private Persons, "together with a true state of all places either already for-"tify'd, or which I judge further necessary to be fortify'd, "with my Opinion at large, how his Majesty may further

[1] P. R. O., C. O. 5, 887. [Copy.]

"contribute to the Security and Defence of the Province, and "as exact an Account as I can obtain of the Real Number of "Whites and Blacks, how many of the former are able to bear "Arms; of what number the Militia is compos'd, and how "arm'd, muster'd, and train'd"; which Orders I shall most punctually observe and execute by the first Opportunity after my arrival in my Govt, before which time it is impracticable for me to do it.

> I am with the greatest Respect,
> My Lords,
> Your Lordships's most Humble,
> and most Obedient Servant.

The Rt Honble Lords Commissioners⎱ W. SHIRLEY.
for Trade and Plantations. ⎰

Endorsed:

<u>*Massachusets Bay*</u>

Letter from Mr Shirley, Govr of the Massachusets Bay, dated at New York the 11th of Janry 1756, acknowledging the Receipt of a Letter from the Board dated the 16th of August last, and of one from Mr Pownall, dated the 19th of Septbr, and will punctually observe and execute the Orders therein by the first Opportunity after his Arrival in his Government.

Recd March⎱ 1756
Read —11 ⎰

WILLIAM SHIRLEY TO SIR THOMAS ROBINSON [1]

New York January 12th 1755. [1756.]

[Duplicate]

SIR.

Since I had the Honour of sending you mine of the 20th of December upon the Subject of Indian Affaires,[2] I have had

[1] P. R. O., C. O. 5, 46. A transcript is in the Library of Congress.   [2] *Ante*, p. 355.

the Satisfaction to receive the inclos'd advices from Oswego, concerning the Disposition of the Northern and Western Indians to meet me there in the Spring, contain'd in an Extract of a Letter from Lieut. Colonel Mercer commanding Officer at Oswego, to my Secretary,[1] since that likewise Colonel Johnson hath given me an Assurance to my Satisfaction, that he will follow my Instructions in the Execution of his trust relative to the Indians, which I have already Settled and delivered to him, and I have now the Utmost reason to hope that Sir Charles Hardy is perfectly disposed to Act in the utmost harmony with me for carrying on his Majesty's Service; The Baron De Dieskau's Aid De Camp, he lets me know, will go to England in his Majesty's Ship Nightingale which I think much more adviseable than to send him at Present to France: The Baron himself is so ill still of his wound that he cant be remov'd out of his bed without danger: as to the other prisoners taken at Lake George in the whole about twenty they were most of them taken by Indians, who I understand from Colonel Johnson claimed the Disposal of them among themselves.[2]

The inclos'd Extract from a Publick print seems fully to Confirm every part of the Intelligence I had concerning the Design of the French to Attack Fort Oswego called in the print Fort Chonaguen the Last Summer, if such a Diversion had not been given them at Crown point as was then done.

[1] See Mercer to Alexander, Dec. 11, 1755, *ante*, p. 340.

[2] On July 21, 1755, Johnson wrote the Lords of Trade: —
"I went to Alexandria in Virginia to wait on his Excellency General Braddock. I received from and signed by him, a warrant for the sole superintendency and management of the affairs of the Six Confederate Nations of Indians their allies and dependants, also some Instructions relating to my conduct; I further received from him two thousand pounds sterling, part to be laid out in presents and the remainder for various other expences, which would arise from the part I was to act; besides this the General has given me an unlimited Credit upon Govr. Shirley for what further sums this service might call for.

"Immediately upon my return home I sent Messages with Belts of Wampum thro' the several Nations, to acquaint them with my appointment, and to desire they would come down to my house

The designs of the French against Oswego seems an Additional Argument in favour of Attempting the Reduction of Fort Cadaraqui or Frontenac (from whence the Attack was to be made as early as may be, and Another Strong Motive

with all possible dispatch; they came and herewith I transmit to your Lordships an authenticated copy of my proceedings at this meeting. Tho' I have not General Braddocks Instructions for doing this, yet I have wrote him I should take this honour upon me, and as he is at a great distance from any of our Sea Ports Towns, I doubt not but both your Lordships and the General will approve of this method.

"In the monies I have laid out, in those I shall be obliged to lay out, I have and shall be governed, by the most prudent frugality, which circumstances will admitt of; my accounts shall be kept with all possible regularity, and an undeviating integrity shall govern my whole conduct."

Since the time of this letter the question of the funds from which Johnson should draw money and the person to whom he should be responsible had been constantly in the foreground.

Earlier in the month (July 5) Lieutenant Governor De Lancey had written the New York treasurer that 4451 pounds had been assigned Johnson for service of the Indians and "toward supplying the train." (Doct. Hist. N. Y. 2, 391.) On Sept. 3 Johnson had complained to the Board of Trade that Shirley was interfering with his work (*ante*, p. 243), and on Jan. 3, 1756, he wrote the Massachusetts Governor that he preferred to continue that work under the Braddock commission if Shirley agreed. (Johnson Manuscripts, 4, 16; Docts. rel. Col. Hist. N. Y. 7, 11.) The following day Shirley expressed his doubts as to a formal commission for Johnson ever having been sent by Braddock, and favored, although he did not insist on, a new commission. Johnson's reply of Jan. 5 (*ibid.* 7, 13) continues the discussion as to the commission under which the writer shall act, and a compromise seems to have been effected satisfactory to the Governor, for on the 7th in his instructions to Johnson for the Indian conference and for his particular duties as Indian superintendent, Shirley refers to himself as Braddock's successor, and on the 10th he sends word to James Stevenson at Albany leading to the handing over of clothing contributed by Pennsylvania to Johnson for use at Forts Edward and William Henry. (Johnson Manuscripts, 23, 177, 203, and 4, 19.)

In this letter to Sir Thomas Robinson, however, Shirley brings up the Johnson question once more, and asks for a clear statement as to financial payments. See also *ante*, pp. 342 and 367.

for doing it is, that as the French Vessells of Force design'd for the Lake Ontario the next Summer are Building in the harbour of Cadaraqui if we could be masters of that before those Vessells are Launch[ed][1] it would be the Destruction of their whole Naval Force there.

I have been detain'd at this place many days longer than I design'd on Account of a Winter Expedition, which from the Intelligence I have receiv'd of the French having drawn off all their Troops but 5 or 600, from Crown point and their advanced Work, at Ticonderoga, to Montreal, and the advantage of Suddenly Transporting men, Artillery, and Stores, and in Slays over the Ice at this Season, I was incouraged to form against it, as also to have built a Vessell of Force there upon the Edge of the Lake Champlain ready to have launch'd into it, upon the breaking up of the Ice, and thereby made Ourselves Masters of the Navigation of it: this Scheme being founded upon a proposal to the several Colonies of New England, and New York to raise among them 950 Provincial Troops to have Acted with 200 Regulars and a part of a Company of Artillery, I communicated to Sir Charles Hardy who most Readily Lay'd it before his Assembly: But they have declin'd raising their Quota of men, unless I would consent to employ such a Number of pick'd men for the Service out of the two British Regiments, as in the unanimous Opinion of a Council of War, Compos'd of the Field officers here present I could not spare Consistant with the Operations to be carry'd into Execution for his Majesty's Service upon the Lake Ontario, for the next Campaign, determined upon by the Council of Warr, held here the 12th and 13th of December; Minutes of which I have already transmitted, Sir, to you, and now inclose another Copy of; so that I am obliged to drop all thoughts of it.[2]

---

[1] The binding of this manuscript in the volume has cut off the termination of the word "launched."

[2] See Shirley to Robinson, Dec. 19, 1755, *ante;* Shirley to Governor Hopkins of Rhode Island in Corres. of Col. Govs. of R. I. 2, 181, 184; and Governor Wentworth of New Hampshire to the N. H. Assembly, Jan. 14, N. H. Prov. Papers, 6, 459, 469.

I had for some time Concluded in my own mind that there must be a Very Expeditious and Commodious passage for an Armament in whale boats down the River Iroquois to that side of the Island of Montreal which lies next the River St. Lawrence, whereby the Obstacles which Crown point lays in the way to it, thro' Lake Champlain are Avoided; And I had Yesterday the Satisfaction to have that Route for Attacking Montreal proposed to me by a very faithfull French man who hath lived many Years in the Jerseys, and knows the River Iroquois very well: which Article in Case of an Attack upon Montreal may be of Singlar Advantage.

Mr. Johnson having several times mention'd to me that he hath no Allowance made him for the Execution of the trust of Cultivating the Friendship of the Indians and management of their Affairs for that purpose, which General Braddock Appointed him to by Commission in Consequence of his Majesty's Instructions: I take the Liberty to mention this Matter, Sir for his Majesty's Consideration: it is a trust of wide Extent as well as great Importance, which will take up Mr. Johnsons whole time and Attention and be Attended with Expence to him, and I should be glad to have his Majesty's pleasure Signify'd to me upon that head, if Mr. Johnson is to draw his pay here.

I am with the highest respect,
Sir,
Your most Humble and
Most Obedient Servant,
W. Shirley.

Rt. Honble. Sir Thomas Robinson Knt. of the Bath ⎰
one of His Majesty's principal Secretaries of State ⎱

Endorsed:
New York Janry 12th. 1756
Majr. Genl. Shirley.
R. March 10th.

ROBERT DINWIDDIE TO WILLIAM SHIRLEY

[*Extract*] [1]

Extract of a Letter from The Honble. Govr. Dinwiddie to His Excellency General Shirley Dated at Williamsburgh in Virginia the 23d January, 1756.

I am in hopes of prevailing with the Catawbas and Cherokees to assist us with some of their Warriors; the latter have already taken up the Hatchet, and I have no great doubt but the Catawbas will do the Same; having sent two Commissioners from this, who are to be join'd by two from North Carolina, to go to these two Nations with a very handsome Present.

One hundred and thirty Cherokees, with two hundred and fifty of our Rangers are under Orders to attack the Shawanese in their Towns; these People have been very troublesome, by robbing and murdering many of our back Settlers — If Success attends this Expedition, I conceive it will be of great Service in reclaiming many of our Friendly Indians from the French and will raise the Spirits of other Indians to join us when they see the Southern Indians have taken up the Hatchet.

    a true Copy

                Wm. Alexander Secy.

Endorsed:

Extract of Govr. Dinwiddie's Letter to his Excellency Genl. Shirley. dated 23d Janry. 1756.

---

[1] Inclosed in Shirley to Fox, March 8, 1756 (second letter). A copy is in the Library of Congress. On Jan. 19 Secry. Willard had written Governor Wentworth of New Hampshire, warning him of a probable Indian attack in the north (N. H. Prov. Papers, 6, 471). See also Robert Burton and John Bradstreet to Shirley, Jan. 23 (Docts. rel. Col. Hist. N. Y. 7, 39), for French preparations for an attack.

WILLIAM SHIRLEY TO STEPHEN HOPKINS[1]

Boston, February 2d, 1756.

SIR,

I am favored with Your Honor's letter of the 16th of January, informing me that you had laid before the Assembly within your government, the scheme I had communicated to you, when I had the pleasure of seeing Your Honor, at Albany, for making an attempt, this winter, for the reduction of Crown Point, and their great readiness to join in it upon the terms proposed to them by you.

In answer to this, I am to acquaint Your Honor, that since I left Albany, Sir Charles Hardy and Governor Fitch[2] have laid the scheme for prosecuting the above mentioned expedition upon the terms I last proposed before their respective Assemblies; and that though neither of those governments objected to their part of the expense, as proposed in the last mentioned terms but expressed great readiness to join in it; yet such difficulties in other respects have arisen from both, as renders the prosecution of it impracticable, so that I have been obliged to drop the thoughts of it.

I now enclose Your Honor a copy of some intelligence sent me by express from Albany, which I received yesterday, and seems to demand the attention of all the colonies concerned in the expedition against Crown Point, and to show the necessity of their preparing with the utmost despatch and unanimity for prosecuting it in the most effectual manner, the ensuing spring; which I can't but hope they will.

I can't determine upon the raising of the two American regiments I talked of at Albany, till I hear from England, which I hourly expect.

I am, with a most real esteem and regard, sir,

Your Honor's most humble and most obedient servant,

W. SHIRLEY

To the Hon. Stephen Hopkins, Esq.

[1] R. I. Col. Rec. 5, 473.
[2] Gov. Thomas Fitch of Connecticut.

HORATIO SHARPE TO WILLIAM SHIRLEY [1]

Sir,   Annapolis Febry. 2d, 1756.

Within these three or four Days I have receiv'd several Letters from the Magistrates in different parts of this Province informing me that those of his Majesty's Officers, who have been order'd hither to recruit have lately receiv'd your positive Instructions to inlist without Exception or Distinction all Apprentices and Servants that they can perswade to enter into the Service; that the Inhabitants having a great part of their Property vested in Servants oppose the Execution of such Instructions; that on such Opposition Violences have been committed, and that unless their Cause of Complaint be remov'd an Insurrection of the People is likely to ensue : The Magistrates as well as myself have and shall endeavour to prevent Mischief, but as the Officers are determin'd [2] to persist, I cannot promise that the People will be restrain'd from expressing their Resentment by Actions; I think it my Duty to make this Representation to your Excellency, and hope you will not be averse to countermanding such Orders, otherwise I shall find myself under a Necessity of exerting the Power, with which I am invested to preserve the Peace of the Province.

With great Regard,
I am,
Your Excellency's most
Humble and Obedient Servant,
HORO. SHARPE [3]

[1] P. R. O., C. O. 5, 46. Inclosed in Shirley to Fox, Mar. 8 (first letter).

[2] The copy of this letter in Arch. of Md. 6, 342, reads from this point : "to persevere unless they are countermanded I think it my Duty to acquaint your Excellency with this Affair and to intimate to you my Fears and that I shall find myself under a necessity, (if a Stop be not put to such Proceedings) of making a Representation home on this subject."

[3] In response to this letter, the following was issued : —

"To all Officers employed in raising of Recruits for any of his Majesty's Regiments in North America.

"It is his Excellency General Shirley's Orders if amongst the

His Excellency General Shirley.
a true Copy
WM. ALEXANDER Secy.

Endorsed:
Copy
Letter from Govr. Sharpe
to General Shirley dated Febry. 2d, 1756.
in Majr. Genl. Shirley's Letter of March 8th, 1756.

WILLIAM SHIRLEY TO THE GENERAL COURT OF MASSACHUSETTS [1]

GENTLEMEN OF THE COUNCIL AND HOUSE OF REPRESENTA-
TIVES :

I am obliged to put you in Mind of the State and Circumstances of the Garrisons at Fort William Henry and Fort Edward, left there when the rest of the Forces raised for the Expedition against Crown Point were disbanded.

At a Meeting of the Governors, then at Albany, with the Commissioners from the Governments of the Massachusetts and Connecticut, held there the 20th of November last, it is determined that Six Hundred Men (or such further Number as should be afterwards agreed on) should be left to defend those Forts, to be detained no longer than their respective Enlistments : The Proportion of the Massachusetts Troops to 750 Men (the Number afterwards stated,) was Two

indented Servants you may have enlisted any of them are willing to return to their Masters; that you are to destroy their Attestations, provided the Masters to whom such Servants belong do furnish an able Bodied Man fit for the Kings Service, in lieu of every Servant they get back:

ROGER MORRIS
Aid de Camp.

See Arch. of Md. 31, 106.
[1] In manuscript of Josiah Willard, French Collection, Massachusetts Historical Society.

hundred and thirty Six; which Number was accordingly left there and now continue in Garrison.

Gentlemen, As the Time for which our Soldiers were enlisted is near expiring, I apprehend it to be of great Importance that those Men should be relieved and that the like Number of Soldiers should be raised in this Provin[ce] and sent to the said Forts without Delay; In which Affair I can do Nothing without your Assistance, I must therefore desire you would take this Matter under your immediate Consideration and make proper Provision for raising these Soldiers, that so his Majesty's Service and the Reputation and Influence of this Government may suffer no Damage by Delay. Province House Feby 4, 1756. W. SHIRLEY.

ROBERT HUNTER MORRIS TO WILLIAM SHIRLEY [1]

Feby. 9th, 1756.

SIR,

I am at last returned to this Town from a fatiguing Journey upon the frontiers, where I have been putting things into as good a posture of defence as the nature of our government will admit, and find that without some Law for the establishment of Military Discipline among the troops in the pay of the Province, a great deal of money will be expended without doing the good it otherwise would.

For the Defence of our western frontiers, I have caused four forts to Be built beyond the Kitticktiny Hills, The one stands upon the new Road opend by this Province towards the Ohio, and about twenty miles from the settlements, and I have calld it Fort Lytellton, in Honour of my friend Sr George. This fort will not only Protect the inhabitants in that part of the Province, but being upon a road that within a few miles Joyns Genl Braddocks rout, it will prevent the march of any regulars that way into the Province, and at the same time serve as an advanced post or magazine, in case

---

[1] P. R. O., C. O. 5, 46. Extract inclosed in Shirley to Fox, Mar. 8 (second letter). See 1 Penna. Arch. 2, 569.

of an attempt to the westward. For these reasons I have Caused it to be built in a regular form, so that it may in little time and at a small expence be so strengthened as to hold out against cannon.

About twenty miles northward of Fort Lytellton, at a place calld Aughwick, another fort is Erected something larger than Fort Lytellton, which I have taken the Liberty to Honour with the name of Fort Shirley. This stands near the great Path used by the Indians and Indian Traders, to and from the Ohio, and consequently the easiest way of access for the Indians into the settlements of this Province.

Fifteen miles northeast of Fort Shirley, near the mouth of a Branch of the Juniata called Kishequokilis, a third fort is erected, which I have called Fort Granville. This Fort commands a narrow pass where the Juniata falls through the mountains which is so circumstanced that a few men can maintain it against a much greater number, as the rocks are very High on each side, not above a gun shot assunder, and thus extended for six miles, and leads to a considerable settlement upon the Juniata, between Fort Granville and where that River falls into the Susquehana.

From fort Granville towards Susquehana, at the distance of fifteen miles, and about twelve from the River, another Fort is Erected that commands that country, and is intended to prevent the Indians from penetrating into the Settlements from that quarter. This I have called Pomfret Castle, and in each of these forts I have posted a Company in the pay of the Province, consisting of seventy-five men, exclusive of officers who are from time to time to detach partys to Range and scour the woods Each way, from the several forts, by which means the Indians will be prevented from falling upon the inhabitants, and these Soldiers by the next summer will become expert woodsmen, and proper rangers, to attend an army in case it should be thought necessary to march one to the westward.

On the East side of the Susquehanna, between that and the Delaware, are three forts at three of the most important passes through the mountains, the Principal and only Regular one is at a pass calld Tolihiao, which I named Fort Henry, the others are called Fort Allen and Fort Lebanon, and between these and in the same Range, there are small Staccados erected at the distance of about ten miles from each other, and the whole are garrisond with companys and detachments from fifty to twenty men each, according as the places are situated, and are of more or less importance. The troops stationed here are to employ themselves in ranging the woods, in the same manner as those on the west side the Susquehana.

Were these troops under military Discipline, I should think our frontiers well guarded, but I have it not in my Power, tho' they are regularly inlisted, to Punish an of them for want of an order from the Crown to hold Court Martials, which I believe you can supply and I propose to write to you upon that head, in case my assembly now sitting Do not pass an act to put those troops under a proper Discipline.

Inclosed I send you what I have said to my assembly upon the plan of operations, which I laid before them, but am quite unable to form a Judgment of what they will do in it. If the more Northern government could undertake to Carry on the Crown Point Expedition, I have some reason to think this Province would in that case enter willingly into one against Fort Duquesne.

The Regulars you favoured me with are in very good order, and are posted at the two towns of Reading and Easton, where Both the officers and men are taken good Care of to their own satisfaction, and prove a great protection not only to the towns where they are placed but to the whole Country about them.

Some days ago I had a letter from Govr. Dinwiddie, informing me that in a treaty he had held with the Cherokee and Catawba nations of Indians, he had prevailed on them to take up the Hatchet against the French and their allies the Shawanese. That one hundred and thirty of them had Joynd some of the Virginia Troops, and were gone against one of the Shawanese towns upon the Ohio, and he had reason to believe they would Joyn him with a thousand warriors in the Spring. His success in this treaty will in great measure render the meeting you proposed with the Southern Indians unnecessary however, I have recomended it to my assembly to send 'em some thing on the part of this Province as you will observe in my message.

To Genl. Shirley.

ROBERT HUNTER MORRIS TO WILLIAM SHIRLEY[1]

Philada, 16 Feby, 1756.

Sir,

I have the Honor to enclose you an address from the Assembly of this Province to me, relating to the inlistment of Indentured servants, and my answer to it; you will observe by the former how disagreable that matter is to them, and the reasons they offer against it are certainly cogent and

[1] A draft of this letter is printed: 1 Penna. Arch. 2, 576. See also Shirley to Fox, Mar. 8, 1756 (first letter), and Shirley to Morris of Feb. 29, *post*, p. 405. On Feb. 17 Shirley wrote Morris from Boston that he had "given orders to the Commanding officer of the Detachment of His Majesty's Troops in Pensilvania to march from there so as to be at the City of New York by the 15th day of March next." He closed by saying that he relied on Morris for carriages, quarters and provisions.

For troubles over the question of enlisted servants, see Sharpe to Shirley, Feb. 2, 1756, *ante*, p. 386; and Shirley to Robinson, Sept. 19, 1755, for plans for the winter. The following letter relates to the same matter. It is from Shirley to Morris, and dated Boston, Feb. 20, 1756.

Sir,

I inclose your Honour an Extract of a Letter to me from the Major of my Regiment, which gives me extreme Concern; I doubt not but your Honour will take Care that Justice is done to his Majesty for the loss of the Sergeant, who Mr. Kinneer informs me was murther'd by the Mob in the Discharge of his Duty, and which I am sorry to find there is so much Reason to attribute to the Encouragement given them by the Magistrates, if what Mr. Kinneer informs me is true, that they take all Servants and Appren-

strong, and I am satisfied your great regard for the people of this country will induce you to put a stop to a practice so injurious to the propertys of many of them, if it can be done Consistent with his Majesty's service and the genl Interest of this continent. As to the Legality of inlisting servants, no one can Judge better of that matter than yourself, whose knowledge and abilities in the laws of England make you perfectly acquainted with the rights both of the King and people.

I shall only say, that I am fearfull this affair of the servts will throw my Assembly into such a temper as may hinder them from taking the part they otherwise would in the operations of the year.

To General Shirley

tices who inlist into his Majesty's Service out of it, and put them in Goal, and confine the recruiting Officers.

I have already given an Instance of my great Desire that the recruiting Service should be attended with as few Inconveniences as might be to the people, by restraining the Officers from enlisting Indented Servants, whilst I thought the King's Service would admit of it, tho' I did not conceive the least Doubt but that his Majesty had as good a Right to their Service as to that of any others, who should voluntarily inlist as Soldiers.

As the Officers have assur'd me that they cannot compleat their Regiments in time without entertaining Indented Servants, it is now become my indispensable Duty to permit them to entertain such Recruits.

If the Masters are injur'd by that, they may sue the Recruiting Officers, and the Law ought to decide the point, according to the final Judgment which shall be given in the Case; and the sooner the point is try'd and receives such a determination, the better. In the mean time I hope that all Outrages of the populace and abuse of Civil power in the Magistrate against the Recruiting Officers will cease. If they do not, it must produce the most disagreeable Consequences in the Province under your Command.

I am, with great Regard, Sir,
Your Honour's most Humble
and most Obedient Servant,

W. Shirley.

WILLIAM SHIRLEY TO ROBERT HUNTER MORRIS[1]

Boston, Febry. 20th, 1756.

Sir,

I inclose to your Honour, at the Request of the Assembly of this Government, a Copy of their Resolves concerning the part they will take in the plan of Operations propos'd by me to them and his Majesty's other Northern Colonies, as far Westward as Virginia inclusive, for removing the Incroachments of the French at Crown point, upon the Lakes Ontario, Erie, and etc., and the River Ohio; and am in hopes, the Provinces of New York, Rhode Island, Connecticutt, New Hampshire, and the Massachusetts Bay will raise Troops sufficient for the propos'd Expedition against Crown Point, the last mention'd Province having, as you will perceive by the inclos'd Resolves of the Assembly, . . . determin'd to raise 3000 as their Quota, and if the others do in proportion, it will produce a Body of 9000 men for that Service. But unless the Governments of Virginia, Maryland, and Pensilvania send some considerable assistance, I shall not have a number sufficient for the Service propos'd on Lakes Ontario, Erie &c, and as I shall have no Troops for that Service, but his Majesty's four Regular Regiments, and the Independent Companies of New York, all which are still very incompleat and together with the Jersey Regiment of 500, will, I am affraid, fall far short of 4000 Effective men.

The Reduction of the French Forts at Niagara, and getting the Mastery of the Lake Ontario, according to his Majesty's Instructions to the late General and myself; which expressly mention it as a more important Service than the Reduction

---

[1] 1 Penna. Arch. 2, 579. For similar letter to Governor Wentworth see N. H. Prov. Papers, 6, 480, and to Governor Hopkins, see Kimball, Corres. R. I. Gov. 2, 188. On Mar. 13, in reply to a similar letter, Governor Dinwiddie of Va. wrote: "Our people seem to be wrap'd up in a lethargic supineness and continue inactive in the time of most apparent danger." Dinwiddie Papers, 2, 369.

of Fort Duquesne, is doubtless the most effectual measure for securing the Southern Colonies from the Incursions of the French and Indians, and the breaking up the possessions of the former on the Ohio and Lake Erie, as those settlements principally, if not wholly, draw their support from Canada, from which they would be cutt off, if their passage over the Lake Ontario was barr'd; at the same time it is necessary that the western Colonies should raise a Body of men, strong enough not only to repel the Incursions of the French and their Indians, but to attempt the Reduction of Fort Duquesne; for which Services I believe you will think 4000 men a sufficient Force.

By the inclos'd List your Honour will find that if the Governments of Virginia, Maryland and Pensilvania, do furnish their Quota for the Operations of this year, in the same manner as the Northern Colonies seem dispos'd to do, according to the proportions settled by the Commissioners at Albany in 1754; which I don't doubt his Majesty expects, and I can't but hope they will do; they ought to raise 7284 men; and if 4000 of them will be sufficient to be employ'd on the Frontiers of those Colonies, there will remain a Body of 3284 men, which I think cannot be employ'd more to the advantage of those colonies, than on the Lake Ontario, and when join'd with the Troops, I intend to take with me there, will give me a sufficient Force effectually to secure that Lake, and by that one Stroke to give an irrecoverable wound to all the French Incroachments upon the Great Lakes and Rivers; after which Fort Duquesne may very easily be reduc'd in the Course of the Summer, if the French should not abandon it without waiting 'till they should be attack'd there. What an effect this would have at the same time in our favour upon all the Indians on the Continent, I need not observe.

It gives me great pleasure to find that the measures, which Govr. Dinwiddie hath taken with the Cherokee Indians, have had so good success; I . . . heartily wish these measures, together with those he is pursuing with the Catawba's may induce them to furnish the number of men, they propos'd, which certainly will be of great Service in the Operations of the next Campaigne; 1000 of these Indians joining with 4000 men of the Southern Colonies will doubtless be sufficient to do every thing necessary on that side, and nothing seems wanting to enable us to carry every point against the French this year, but the Southern Colonies exerting themselves in the same proportion with the Eastern ones, and sending 3000 men to join the Regular Troops, intended for the Operations on the Lake Ontario, &c.

I can't but hope that your Honour will see these matters in the same light with me, and do every thing in your power with the Assembly of your Government to induce them to enable you to furnish the Quota of that Dominion, for repelling the French of Canada at this most critical Conjuncture, and before they are strengthen'd with fresh Reinforcements from France, from their dangerous Incroachments upon his majesty's Territories, and for putting an End to the Ravages and Depredations of them and the Indians in their Interest within the Borders of his Majesty's western Colonies upon this Continent: with regard to myself, your Honour may depend on my doing every thing in my power for the protection of the Frontiers of Pensilvania in particular.

As it is necessary that an Officer of Rank in his Majesty's Army should be appointed to take upon him the command of all the Forces rais'd in the Colonies of Pensilvania, Maryland and Virginia, and South Carolina to be employ'd in an Expedition against Fort Duquesne; I have appointed for that purpose Govr. Sharpe, whom his Majesty was pleas'd before the arrival of the late General Braddock in North America, to appoint to the like but more extensive command.

I am with Esteem and Regard,
Sir,
Your Honour's most Humble
and most obedient Servant, W. SHIRLEY.

Honble Robert Hunter Morris, Esqr.

Endorsed:
Genl Shirley, about the operations of the summer, 1756, and the numbers necessary.

WILLIAM SHIRLEY TO HORATIO SHARPE[1]

Boston, Febry 23d. 1756.

SIR,

I receiv'd your Favour of the 24th Jany.[2] a few Days since and am very glad to find what good Effect the Steps already taken have had towards engaging the Cherokees to the British Interest, and I have great hopes that if you can prevail on the Gentlemen of your Assembly to enable you in behalf of the Province of Maryland to join in the Measures prepar'd, the Friendship of not only the Cherokees, but also the Catawba's may be secur'd to us, and that they may be induc'd to join us with a considerable number of their Warriors, which certainly will be of exceeding great Service in the Operations of this Year.

I now inclose to your Honour, at the Request of the Assembly of this Government, a Copy of their Resolves concerning the part they will take in the plan of Operations propos'd by me to them and his Majesty's other Northern Colonies as far Westward as Virginia inclusive, for removing the Incroachments of the French at Crown-point, upon the Lakes Ontario, Erie, &c, and the River Ohio; and am in hopes, the Provinces of New York, Rhode Island, Connecticutt, New Hampshire and the Massachusetts Bay will raise Troops sufficient for the propos'd Expedition against Crown point, the last mention'd Province having, as you will perceive by the inclos'd Resolves of the Assembly, determin'd to raise 3000 as their Quota, and if the others do in proportion, it will produce a Body of 9000 Men for that Service; But unless the Government of Virginia, Maryland, and Pensilvania send some considerable Assistance, I shall not have a number sufficient for the Service propos'd on Lakes Ontario, Erie, &c, as I shall not have any Troops for that Service but his Majestys four Regular Regiments and the Independent Companies of New York, all which are still very incompleat,

[1] Original, Historical Society of Pennsylvania.
[2] Sharpe's letter of Jan. 24 is in Arch. of Md. 6, 337.

and together with the Jersey Regiment of 500 will, I am affraid, fall far short of 4000 Effective Men.

The Reduction of the French Forts at Niagara, and getting the Mastery of the Lake Ontario, according to his Majesty's Instructions to the late General and myself; which expressly mention it as a more important Service than the Reduction of Fort Duquesne, is doubtless the most effectual Measure for securing the Southern Colonies from the Incursions of the French and Indians, and the breaking in the possessions of the former on the Ohio and Lake Erie, as those Settlements principally, if not wholly, draw their Support from Canada, from which they would be cutt off, if their passage over the Lake Ontario was barr'd; at the same time it is necessary that the Western Colonies should raise a Body of Men strong enough not only to repel the Incursions of the French and their Indians, but to attempt the Reduction of Fort du Quesne; for which Services I believe you will think 4000 Men a sufficient Force.

By the inclos'd List your Honour will find that if the Governments of Virginia, Maryland, and Pensilvania do furnish their Quota for the Operations of this Year, in the same manner as the Northern Colonies seem dispos'd to do, according to the proportions settled by the Commissioners at Albany in 1754; which I don't doubt his Majesty expects, and I can't but hope they will do; they ought to raise 7284 Men; and if 4000 of them will be sufficient to be employ'd on the Frontiers of those Colonies, there will remain a Body of 3284 Men which I think cannot be employ'd more to the Advantage of those Colonies, than on the Lake Ontario, and when join'd with the other Troops, I intend to take with me these will give me a sufficient Force effectually to secure that Lake, and by that one Stroke to give an irrecoverable Wound to all the French Incroachments upon the Great Lakes and Rivers; after which Fort Duquesne may very easily be reduc'd in the Course of the Summer, if the French should not abandon it without waiting till they should be attack'd there: what an Effect this would have at the same time in our Favour upon all the Indians on the Continent I need not observe : and if the Cherokees and Catawbas can be induc'd to furnish the 1000 Warriors they have promis'd to be join'd to the 4000 Men of the Southern Colonies, it will doubtless be sufficient to do every thing necessary on that Side, and nothing seems wanting to enable us to carry every point against the French this Year but the Southern Colonies exerting themselves in the same proportion with the Eastern ones and sending 3000 Men to join the Regular Troops, intended for the Operations on the Lake Ontario, &c.

I can't but hope that your Honour will see these Matters in the same light with me, and do every thing in your power with the Assembly of your Government to induce them to enable you to furnish the Quota of your Province for repelling the French of Canada at this most critical Conjuncture (and before they are strengthen'd with fresh Reinforcements from France) from their dangerous Incroachments upon his Majesty's Territories, and for putting an End to the Ravages and Depredations of them and the Indians in their Interest within the Borders of his Western Colonies upon this Continent : with regard to myself, Your Honour may depend on my doing every thing in my power for the protection of the Frontier of Maryland in particular.

As it is necessary that an Officer of Rank in his Majesty's Army should be appointed to take upon him the Command of all the Forces rais'd in the Colonies of Pensilvania, Maryland, and Virginia and South Carolina to be employ'd in an Expedition against Fort Duquesne, I have appointed you, Sir, to that Command, and now inclose your Commission.

In Answer to that part of your Letter relating to the payment of the Waggoners, &c. that attended General Braddock from Wills's Creek, I am to inform your Honour that Mr. Leake Commissary General of all his Majesty's Forces on this Continent has my Orders and instructions to Settle and pay off all unsettled Contracts made by the late Genl Braddock, and whatever may be due for Water Carriage on the Potowmack or for Waggons or Horse hire for the Forces late under his Command ; Mr Leake went from

Philadelphia on this Business about the time I left New York, and I hope will be able to finish it to the Satisfaction of all parties by 25th of March.

I am with great Esteem and Regard,
Sir,
Your Honour's most Obedt.
Humble Servant,

W. Shirley.

Honble Horatio Sharpe Esqr.

WILLIAM SHIRLEY TO ROBERT HUNTER MORRIS [1]

Boston, Feby 23, 1756.

Dear Sir,

I am sorry to give you the trouble of the Inclos'd; I must further beg the favour of you to give orders to some justi-

[1] 1 Penna. Arch. 2, 582. On Feb. 24 Morris wrote Shirley: —

Dear Sir,

I wrote you a few days ago, and since have the honour of yours in answer to one from the President of the Council about indented Servants, and tho' the Burthen will fall much heavier upon this Province than any of the others, as we have a much greater number of Servants of that kind than any of them, Yet as his Majestys service is at this Juncture so much concerned in having the regiments filled in time, and there was little reason to think they would soon be done by the ordinary method of recruiting, I must approve of the determination you have given as to that matter, having no doubts in my own mind as to the Legality of taking into his Majestys service any subject that offers himself; for that purpose, I immediately sent your letter to the Assembly in hopes it would satisfy them, but they adjourned upon it for a week without any reason assigned, or indeed giving me notice of it. I have taken some pains to come at their intentions as to the Crown Point expedition, but cannot learn what they mean to do, or whether they will do any thing.

Immediately upon my return from the frontier counties I appointed Commissioners, in Conjunction with Mr. Leake, to settle the demands upon the Crown, for the service done by order of Genl Braddock, pursuant to your former letter to me on that head, and

fiable person to assist the officers, who shall be molested in the service, both with respect to their defending themselves in actions, which may be brought against them, and prosecuting in such as it may be necessary to commence against others for Injuries done them. I am determin'd the point shall be brought to a peremptory, authoritative Decision from home, in some shape or other. Whatever Assistance or Advice you can give the officers, without involving yourself in any Disputes or Trouble whatever with your Assembly or People, I shall be obliged to you for, But would by no means desire you to run the least risque of doing that.

As it seem'd necessary for me to appoint some person to the Chief Command of the Western Forces, which should be employed in an Expedition against Fort du Quesne, &c., and the circumstances of Govr Sharpe having been appointed to a like Command before by the King, with a Brevet Commission of Lt Colonel in his Army for that purpose, I thought my self likewise under a necessity of pitching upon him for the Command, and sending a Commission to him.

I am greatly obliged to you, Dear Sir, for supplying my late son, Shirley, with the sums express'd in two notes, which Mr. Alexander hath shew'd me, and I have order'd payment of, together with the balance which you paid Captn Orme for him.

He will give directions concerning the list of things you have been so kind as to transmit to him inclos'd in your letter.

of your Instructions to Mr. Leake, and they sat ten days at Lancaster upon the accounts brought in by the People of this Province, which they have adjusted, and are now sitting in this town upon those of Virginia and Maryland, and in as little time as Possible, will complete and settle the whole. Mr. Leake and the other officers assure me that it would have been impossible to have settled these matters without the aid of men of weight here, and that the savings on the part of the Crown through their means will be very considerable, but as I shall send your Excellency their Report at large, when the whole is finished I will not trouble you further upon the subject at present.

A draft of this letter is printed in 1 Penna. Arch. 2, 583.

Wishing you all success and happiness in your Publick and Private Affairs, I am, most affectionately,
Dear Sir,
Your Friend and Servt,
W. SHIRLEY.
Honble R. H. Morris, Esqr.

Endorsed:
Genl Shirley — that I would favour the officers that may be distressed in the recruiting service.
Boston, Feby 23, 1756.

WILLIAM SHIRLEY TO HENRY FOX [1]

Boston in the Province of the
Massachusetts Bay, Febry. 24th, 1756.
SIR,
Seven Days ago I had the Honour to receive two Letters dated 11th of November from Sir Thomas Robinson one of them signifying to me his Majesty's Royal Approbation of the Zeal and Spirit, which this Province hath exerted in his Service for removing the French from their Incroachments at Crown point; and his Majesty's Orders that I should communicate the same to the Council and Assembly, and let them know that his Majesty would be graciously pleas'd to recommend to his parliament to grant them such Assistance in consideration of the Charges, they have born, as their Circumstances shall require, and will enable them vigourously to pursue the aforesaid great and necessary Work: The other acquainting me that his Majesty had been pleas'd to direct 10,000 Stands of Arms with the proper Accoutrements, and a sufficient Quantity of Ammunition to be sent forthwith to Boston to be deliver'd to such persons and for such Uses as the Commander in Chief of his Majesty's Forces in North America shall from time to time think most expedient for the King's Service.

[1] P. R. O., C. O. 5, 46. A transcript is in the Library of Congress.

Nothing could arrive more seasonably for promoting his Majesty's Service in the Colonies of New England at this most critical Conjuncture of it, than the former of these Letters, which being deliver'd to me when the Assembly had just enter'd upon the Consideration of that part of my late Speech, which recommended to them to raise their Quota of the 10,000 Men determin'd upon in the Council of War held at New York the 12th of December (Copies of which I have before transmitted) to be necessary for prosecuting the Expedition against Crown point, to effect this Year, I immediately lay'd before them, in obedience to his Majesty's Orders.

This Government's Quota of the 10,000 Men to be divided among all the Northern Colonies according to their Several proportions of it as settled by the Commissioners at Albany in 1753, amounts to about 1750; and from the exhausted Circumstances of the Government under the very heavy Debt it contracted the last Year by the Expences incurr'd in this Expedition, I had Reason to apprehend that a Vote for raising that Number of Men would have been difficultly obtain'd, tho' the House in general retains the same Zeal and Spirit it manifested last Year for the Defence of his Majesty's just Rights and Dominions upon this Continent : But the Effect, which the timely Encouragement given them by his Majesty's Declaration of his Royal Favour towards them hath produc'd, is a Determination to raise 3000 Men as their Quota of 9000 to be rais'd by the three other Governments of New England and New York over and above what the Southern and Western Colonies shall raise for the beforemention'd Service.

As the Massachusetts Bay ever hath the lead among the other Colonies as far as the New Jerseys, and their Determinations of what part they will take in the Operations of the ensuing Campaign will very much depend upon those of this Government, I hope they will proportion the Number of their Forces for the Expedition against Crown point, to that now raising in this Province : And I have accordingly wrote a pressing Letter to each of them for that purpose, as also to the Govr. of New York proposing an Augmentation of that Province's Forces from 1000 to 2000 Men.

I wish I could entertain the same hopes of the proceedings of the Colonies to the Southward and Westward of the New Jerseys for promoting his Majesty's Service, as I have of the others: I have wrote most pressing Letters to them all, founded upon the Example set them by the Massachusetts Bay, and the Necessity of his Majestys Service.[1]

As his Majesty's Sloop Hornet will Sail for England in a few Days, I Shall have the Honour, Sir, to write more at large to you by that Opportunity; and would only add here that Lt. Colonel Ellison, whom his Majesty was pleas'd to appoint Colonel of the late Sir Peter Halket's Regiment being dead, the Command of that Regiment is again vacant; and As this Appointment of his Majesty hath not taken Effect, I think it my Duty not to post to that Command, as my Commission allows me to do, but let it continue vacant untill the Arrival of his Majesty's Commission to fill it up; begging leave in the mean time to express the very great Opinion I have of Lt. Colonel Gage as an Officer, who would discharge his Duty in that Post, if such should be his Majesty's pleasure, with the greatest Honour and good Abilities.

I have the Honour to be with the Highest Respect,
Sir,
Your most Humble, and most
Obedient Servant.

W. SHIRLEY.

P.S.   Preparations of all Kinds are making in this Government with the utmost Vigour for opening the Campaign as early as possible in the Spring against Crown Point.

Rt. Honble. Henry Fox, — }
one of his Majesty's principal Secretaries of State }

Endorsed:
Boston Febry. 24th. 1756.
GOVR. SHIRLEY.
R. April 21st.

[1] See Shirley to Sharpe, Dec. 30 and Feb. 23, *ante*, pp. 370 and 396.

WILLIAM SHIRLEY TO WILLIAM PEPPERRELL [1]

Boston, Febry. 26th, 1756.

Sir,

Mr. Alexander waits upon you with the late General Braddock's Appointment of me to the Command of the Expedition against Niagara; By which you will find I have no Allowance made by him for my own Pay as Commander in Chief, or Staff Officers settled for me; that was done by H. R. H. the Duke at Home; I find likewise upon Perusal of General Braddock's Letters to me that a Major General can't take the Field with a less Command than that of two Regiments of Regulars; and that his taking a Command consisting of Provincial Regiments without two of the Kings Regiments join'd with them is irregular, and no Staff is ever granted for such a Command.

The parting with two of the Regiments of Regulars to you would reduce me to the same Force, I had with me at Oswego the last Year which was two weak for me to act with upon Lake Ontario at that Time; And as for that Reason, and likewise on Account of the Opinion and Advice of the Councils of War which I held at New York, that was given me upon this Article, And the Letters I have wrote to the Secretaries of State and War concerning the Force I would proceed with to Oswego this Year Which Letters had slipt my Memory when we talk'd together; Sparing two Regiments of Regulars would expose me to Censure, I don't think it in my Power to do it.

I never proposed your going without one Regular Regiment at least and that upon having a Provincial One given me in the Room of it which I find from yourself and Others, the Assembly will find Difficulty in doing: But their consenting to that would not make the Matter regular.

As these Matters turn out thus upon my Perusal this Morning of my Papers relative to them, I thought it neces-

[1] P. R. O., C. O. 5, 46. A transcript is in the Library of Congress.

sary to apprize you of them for your own Consideration: For it would expose and hurt both of us to do an improper Thing in so delicate an Affair.

I am with great Truth and Esteem
Sir
Your most Obedient, Humble Servant
W. SHIRLEY.

Sir William Pepperrell.　　　　　Copy

Endorsed:
Copy of a Letter from Majr. Genl. Shirley
to Sir Willm : Pepperrell,
Boston, Septr : [*sic*] 26th : 1756.
in Sir W : Pepperrell's Letter of April 19th : 1756.

WILLIAM SHIRLEY TO ROBERT HUNTER MORRIS [1]

Boston, 29th February, 1756.

SIR

Yesterday late in the Evening I received the Favour of your Letter dated the 16th Instant, inclosing a Copy of the Assembly's Address to you on the 11th containing a Remonstrance against the Practice used at present by the officers now recruiting within your Province of entertaining indented Servants.

Though I have very lately wrote to you Sir upon this Head, and might rest the point in dispute upon your very reasonable, just and clear Answer to the Address, yet at the Instance of your Assembly to lay the Matter complained of before me for my Consideration I have reconsidered it, and

---

[1] P. R. O., C. O. 5, 46.　Inclosed in Shirley to Fox, Mar. 8 (first letter).　See also 1 Penna. Arch. 2, 587, and Arch. of Md. 31, 106. A transcript is in the Library of Congress; and see Morris to Shirley of Feb. 16, *ante*, p. 391.　For the royal warrant of George II apportioning £115,000 among the Colonies and dated Mar. 3, 1755, see N. H. Prov. Papers, 6, 543.

now transmit to you my farther Sentiments and final Determination thereon:

The Restraint I lately laid the recruiting Officers under, by forbidding them to enlist indented Servants (which the Assembly themselves referr to in their Address), must convince them how tender I am of suffering his Majesty's Service under my Care to break unnecessarily into the Contracts of these Servants with their Masters or their Assigns and depriving the latter of any part of the Service they originally indented for, though it was my settled clear opinion that the King has a Right to the Service of indented servants as well as other Voluntiers; and it is evident that a Liberty to enlist them must make the recruiting Officers Duty easier, and fill his Majesty's Regiments much sooner and at a less Expence to them, yet whilst I flattered myself with Hopes that the Officers might be able to compleat their Regiments in time for the Kings Service without entertaining indented servants, I chose to put them under this Restraint, rather than subject the Masters to the ill Conveniencies, and Hardships, which I am very sensible they frequently suffer from their Servants being indiscriminately enlisted into his Majesty's Service, for this Reason, I never allowed the Officers either of my former or present Regiment to enlist such Servants, always disapproved of the Practice of it (when unnecessary) in others, and since being invested with my present Command have forbid it in all as long as the Circumstances of his Majesty's service would admit.

But this is not now the case. Sir, his Majesty's Orders to augment his Regiments to 1000 Men each are positive; the execution of them before the opening this Years Campaign is necessary for the Preservation of his just Rights and Dominions upon this Continent against the Incroachments and Invasions of the French and to secure his Subjects from the farther Devastations, which it must otherwise be expected they will soon make within these Colonies: the recruiting Officers have represented to me, that it will be impracticable to compleat their Regiments in time for the Service, if I continue my former Restraint upon them. The season is now far advanced and the Preparations of the Enemy to distress his Majesty's Colonies in every Part are pushing on very fast; of which the late Ravages committed at their Instigation within the Borders of Pensilvania by Indians some of which were before at peace with that Government, and others in Friendship with it should be a most alarming Proof to the Assembly.

The Assembly will not infer that because I judged it expedient to forego his Majesty's Right to the Service of indented Servants in favour of their Masters whilst I apprehended such an Indulgence would not disappoint the raising a sufficient force for repelling the Enemy from his Territories, and the protection of his Subjects in North America, it can therefore be my Judgment that it is either consistent with my Duty to the King or the safety of his subjects within these Colonies, to continue this Indulgence at a time when the great Interests of both are so apparently at Stake, and such ruinous consequences may ensue from it to all his Majesties Governments upon this Continent.

The illegality of enlisting indented Servants Sir, which is asserted throughout the Address, seems to be there ultimately founded in this Argument that every person must have the same absolute property in what he purchases, that he had in the Purchase Money: many Instances might be cited to shew that this Position is not universally true; and as to the Case of indented Servants, the supposition that the King is precluded by the Contracts between them and their Masters from the Right he before had to their Service for the Defence of his Dominions is not founded in the nature of Government, in general and is contrary to the Practice of it in the English Constitution.

A Discussion of these Points at large would lead into too wide a Field for the Compass of this Letter, it may suffice to shew what the Practice upon them is in these Colonies; and in doing this I shall confine myself to that within the province of the Massachusets Bay, the Constitution of which as it is a Charter Government, will I suppose be admitted to be decisive in this Case.

The Governor of this Province by virtue of the Power given him by the Charter for raising the Militia (of which I presume indented Servants will be allowed to be a Part in every Colony) constantly impresses such Servants to be employed in marching Companies or Garrison Duty for the protection of the Province as long as he thinks his Majesty's service shall require it, and in one or other of these Duties they are frequently kept two or three years and with the Consent of the great and general Assembly of this Province, the Governor hath Power to transport any Number of the Militia out of it either by Sea or Land to be employed against the Enemy.

When Forces were raised by the Province for the Expeditions against Cape Breton, upon the River Kennebeck, and against Crown Point, indented Servants enlisted into them in common with others; and to compleat the Reinforcements sent into the last mentioned Service many such Servants were impressed by the Government.

When others were raised within this Province in the Pay of the Crown for the Expeditions against Canada, and to remove the French from their Incroachments in Nova Scotia indented Servants inlisted into them.

These Instances I think Sir afford in the whole a clear Proof of the Kings Right to the Service of indented Servants, inhabiting the Province of the Massachusetts Bay for the defence of his Dominions, at least in North America; and that no Contract between them and the Masters can extinguish either this Governments Right to impress them into the before mentioned Service, or the Servants Right voluntarily to enlist into it: And it seems a just Conclusion to say, if this Power of taking indented Servants from their Masters for his Majesty's Service is consistent with the civil Rights of the Subject in a Charter Government, and the Property which Masters have in those servants there; it is at least equally so in Pensilvania, that the recruiting Officers in that Province should entertain such Servants when they voluntarily enlist into the Kings Regiments unless it can be show that the Pensilvania Masters have some *special property* in their Servants which the Massachusetts Masters have not and which destroys his Majesty's Right to their Service for the Defence of his American Dominions against the common Enemy ; but this I have before observed is not founded in the nature of Government in general and is contrary to the Practice of it in the English Constitution.

As to the enlisting of indented Servants into his Majestys Regiment upon the Establishment, whenever Officers of such Regiments have recruited within the Province of the Massachusetts Bay more or less of those Servants have ever inlisted into them particularly when recruiting Officers of the Forces employed in the Expedition against the Spanish Settlements in the West Indies, arrived there from Jamaica many indented Servants inlisted with them and were transported to Cuba.

I am not ignorant that Pensilvania hath afforded great Numbers of Recruits to the Kings forces, but am not of Opinion with the Assembly that they are equal to those which have been raised in the Province of the Massachusetts Bay, for my own and Sir William Pepperells Regiments, and the three Regiments of Nova Scotia within these fourteen Months, which may be computed at upwards of 1500 Men, besides which near 6000 have been raised within it the last year for the Expeditions against the French Encroachments in Nova Scotia and against Crown Point ; and the Number of Soldiers raised in it over and above all these for the Protection of its Frontier, exceeds I believe the Body of Men employed by the Government of Pensilvania for the defence of theirs.

The Assembly complain that their Province is extreamly drained of their Labourers.   I think Sir that Pensilvania hath not been near so much exhausted of them as the Massachusetts Bay hath been by his Majesty's Service : In the Expedition against Cape Breton that Province lost 2000 Men at least by Sea and Land and upwards of 500 the year following in the Protection of Nova Scotia, the employing of any considerable Body of Troops for the defence of the Frontier of Pensilvania is a new Service within that Government but hath ever taken up a great Number of Men in time of Peace as well as War within the Massachusetts Bay. The Province of the Massachusetts Bay hath as few Slaves within it as Pensilvania, the number of its Inhabitants constantly employed in its fisheries, Ship building, Lumber Trade, and navigation greatly diminish the number of its Hands for Agriculture and other Labour; and it hath not the Benefit of those Resources for augmenting its Inhabitants from the northern parts of Germany &c. which hath for many years so greatly increased the People of Pensilvania, yet thus exhausted as it is, the Government, raises no Obstacles to the recruiting of his Majesty's Forces within it, and hath besides chearfully voted to raise a Number of Troops, which amounts to a ninth Part of its fighting Men this Year towards the Defence of his just Rights and Dominions upon this Continent; an Example which I can't but hope the Assembly will think the Interest of the Province, as well as their Duty to the Crown call upon them to follow.

The Assembly observe by their Address how great a quantity of Provisions their Province supplies the King's Army with, this Sir seems to be an Advantage which should make them easier under the Inconveniencies which attend his Majesty's Service in other Respects; and when they consider that all the Men which are now drawing out of Pensilvania for recruiting the Kings Forces will be employed in that part of his Service, which more immediately concerns the Protection of the Inhabitants of that Province against the growing Incroachments of the French they should as readily acquiesce in parting with some of their indented Servants, as any Charter Colony doth.

It is not necessary to enter into a minute Examination of every Part of the Deduction made by the Assembly of the mischievous Consequences, which arise to the Community from enlisting indented Servants into his Majestys Service, some of them seem too remote : when a Country is in Danger of being lost to the Enemy it is not a time for the Government of it, to enter into critical dissertations whether the enlisting of indented Servants for the Defence of it may not have a Tendency to lessen the Importation of them into the Country for future Tillage of the Land, and to increase that of Slaves; It would certainly have been more happy for the Province of Pensilvania to have lost the Service of some of their bought Servants last year in defending their Frontiers against the Incursions of the Enemy than to have suffered the cruel Ravages and Depopulation committed by them within their Borders.

I have already acknowledged that ill Conveniencies and Hardships frequently arise to Individuals from their inlisting indented Servants into the Kings Regiments, I am as ready now as ever to do every thing in my Power consistent with his Majestys Service to remedy such as have happened or may hereafter happen in the Province of Pensilvania or elsewhere: His Majesty hath ordered his Regiments employed in North America for the Defence of his just Rights and Dominions and protection of his Subjects there to be forthwith augmented to 1000 Men each out of such of the Inhabitants of these Colonies as will inlist into his Service, he hath an undoubted Right to do this: If it can't be done without receiving indented Servants into the Regiments; to forbid the Entertainment of them or order them to be discharged without being replaced by other effective Men would very probably defeat the Service for which the Regiments were ordered by his Majesty to be augmented; which the Assembly I am perswaded will upon further Consideration think would be a most unwarrantable Proceeding in the Kings General: The only Orders I can justify sending the Officers upon this occasion which I shall take care to do, will be to release such indented Servants as are willing to return to their Masters upon having good effective Men offered in Exchange for them; As to receiving them at first into the Service in cases which shall appear extremely hard to the Officers, they are at liberty to refuse it, and will I doubt not act with discretion: the Intention of my last Orders was only to take off the Restraint I had before laid upon them against receiving any indented Servants which I should not have done if the Regiments had met with that success in their recruiting as might have been expected. It must rest with the Assembly to ease such Masters as may notwithstanding this, sustain any great Hardship by the Loss of one or more of their servants in his Majestys Service, and if in doing that any considerable Burthen should fall upon the whole Community; upon a Representation of it to his Majesty it will doubtless have a proper Consideration given it; And this I can't but hope Sir, the Assembly will upon a cooler Thought of this Affair judge to be a more elligible Method of Proceeding, than to incite the Populace to pursue the violent Measures which the Address seems to point out to them.

> I am Sir
> Your Honors most obedient
> humble Servant
>
> W. Shirley.

WILLIAM SHIRLEY. ORDER AS TO GEORGE WASHINGTON [1]

Boston, 5 March, 1756.

Governor Dinwiddie, at the instance of Colonel Washington, having referred to me concerning the right of command between him and Captain Dagworthy, and desiring that I should determine it, I do therefore give it as my opinion, that Captain Dagworthy, who now acts under a commission from the Governor of Maryland, and where there are no regular

---

[1] Ford, "Writings of Washington," 1, 231; Sparks, "Writings of Washington," 2, 133. See Washington, Address to his Troops, 1756 (Va. Mag. of Hist. and Biog. 2, 343–346). Notes respecting the Militia, April and May, 1756 (Ford, "Writings of Washington," 1, 269–276), and extracts from Mem. Book at Fort Winchester, 1756–1757 (Va. Mag. Hist. and Biog. 3, 200–203). On this same date Shirley inclosed to Sharpe an extract of Dinwiddie's letter as brought to Boston by Washington, asking Shirley to determine the relative powers of Dagworthy and himself. Shirley's letter is in Arch. of Md. 6, 347, printed from the original. On Mar. 7 Sharpe thanked Shirley for his letter of Feb. 23 and his intention to give the writer command of forces in the South. Arch. of Md. 6, 351.

troops joined, can only take rank as a provincial Captain, and of course is under the command of all provincial field-officers; and, in case it should happen, that Colonel Washington and Captain Dagworthy should join at Fort Cumberland, it is my order that Colonel Washington shall take the command.

W. SHIRLEY.

WILLIAM SHIRLEY TO HENRY FOX [1]

Boston, New England, March 8th, 1756.

SIR,

Since the last Letter which I had the Honour to write to you there hath been a Dispute in the Colonies of New York, New Jerseys, Pensilvania, and Maryland between the Recruiting Officers and Masters of Indented Servants, who have voluntarily inlisted into his Majesty's Service; The Officers have been arrested for entertaining these Servants, Violences us'd by the populace in the two last mention'd Colonies for recovering them from the Officers, and the Servants imprison'd for inlisting; and the Assembly of Pensilvania hath made a Remonstrance upon this Occasion in an Address to their Governor, a Copy of which I have inclos'd, with one of mine to his Letter [2] sent me with the Address, as these contain a Discussion at large of the point in dispute, and I should be glad to receive his Majesty's Directions upon it; In the mean time I shall think myself oblig'd to insist upon his Majesty's Right to the Service of Indented Servants in the Colonies for the Defence of his American Dominions, and to support the Officers in entertaining them: I have been inform'd that this Dispute between the Assembly of Pensilvania and their late Governor, Colonel Thomas now

---

[1] (First letter) P. R. O., C. O. 5, 46. A transcript is in the Library of Congress. Shirley's second letter to Fox of this date is on p. 415, following.

[2] See Morris to Shirley, Feb. 16, *ante*, p. 391, Feb. 24, p. 399, note; also replies of Shirley to Morris, Feb. 20, *ante*, p. 391, note, and Feb. 29, *ante*, p. 405.

Governor of the Leward Islands, ran very high in the time of inlisting Men for his Majesty's Service in the Expedition against the Spanish Settlements in the West Indies in 1739; that the Assembly transmitted Complaints to his Majesty's Ministers against Colonel Thomas for admitting Indented Servants to be inlisted for that Service; That Mr. Thomas's Conduct in it was not disapprov'd of at home; But no Authoritative Determination therein having been transmitted to the Colonies, the Dispute still remains, and grows higher in some of them; as you will see, Sir, by the inclos'd Copy of the Governor of Maryland's Letter as well as by the Pensilvania Address.

I restrain'd the Officers from inlisting these Servants as long as I thought his Majesty's Service would allow me to exercise that Indulgence to the Masters; But the Continuance of the Restraint at this Conjuncture would have greatly prejudiced it; If it should be his Majesty's pleasure to order his express Directions to be transmitted to me upon this Point, they would, I conceive, very much allay the present Disputes and Heart-burnings in the Colonies upon it, and I hope be acquiesc'd in by the several Governments.

I have the honour to be with the Highest Respect
Sir,
Your most Humble and most
Obedient Servant.

W. SHIRLEY.

Rt. Honble. Henry Fox, one of
his Majesty's principal Secretaries of State.

Endorsed:
Boston, March 8th. 1756 Majr. Genl. Shirley
R. May 5th.

CORRESPONDENCE OF WILLIAM SHIRLEY

WILLIAM SHIRLEY TO HENRY FOX[1]

Boston, New England, March 8th, 1756.

Sir,

I have the Satisfaction to acquaint you that the Frontiers of his Majesty's Western Colonies on this Continent seem now to be in so good a posture of Defence that there is room to hope a Check will be soon put to the Incursions of the Indians upon them : By the inclos'd Extract of a letter from Governor Morris[2] you will find, Sir, that the Province of Pensilvania have lately built and garrison'd a line of Forts and Block houses from their most Northerly Settlements on Delaware River to within a few Miles of Fort Cumberland : The Province of New Jersey hath carried on this Line to the most Northern Boundary of their Government ; and the Province of New York have taken it up there, and built some Block Houses further North ;[3] And on the other Side the Government of Virginia hath on the same Range built a number of Forts, which continue the line to very near the most Southern Boundary of that Province : The whole forms a line of about 500 Miles in extent ; and as these Forts have all Garrisons from 20 to 70 Men each, who are employ'd in Scouring the interjacent Woods, it is to be hop'd, that not only an effectual Stop will be put to the Inroads and Devastations of the Enemy, and the Inhabitants of those Provinces be soon recover'd from their late Distress and Confusion, but that a Body of Men may by this Means be train'd up on these Frontiers, able to deal with the Indian Warriors in their own way of fighting ;[4]

---

[1] (Second letter) P. R. O., C. O. 5, 46. A transcript is in the Library of Congress. See also, Shirley's first letter of this date, *ante*, p. 413.

[2] Morris to Shirley, Feb. 9, *ante*, p. 388.

[3] See Thomas Ord, commanding officer of the Royal Artillery, to Shirley, Mar. 7 (N. H. Prov. Papers, 6, 493–497), giving " Proportion of Artillery and Ordinary Stores for an Attack on Fort Frederick at Crown Point."

[4] See Shirley to Wentworth, Mar. 8, N. H. Prov. Papers, 6, 489–490.

than which nothing would more contribute to the Security of that Country against an Indian Enemy.

I have also the Satisfaction to inform you, Sir, that the Measures propos'd by me to the Governments of Pensilvania, Maryland, Virginia and Carolina for engaging the Southern Indians in our Alliance, a Copy of which I sent you with my Letter of the 20th December,[1] are in a great Measure carried into Execution, and with Such Success, that the Cherokees, the most formidable of those Nations, have already taken up the Hatchet against the French and their Allies, and sent 130 of their Warriors to join a Number of Virginia Rangers, who are now out on an Expedition against the Shawanese Villages; and they have promis'd to join a much larger Number in the Spring; Commissioners are likewise gone from Virginia and Carolina to the Cherokees and Catawabas, to finish a Treaty offensive and defensive with the former, and to Stipulate the Number of Warriors they are to join us with next Summer: And those Commissioners are likewise to endeavour to prevail on the Catawbas to take up the Hatchet; All which Governour Dinwiddie, in the inclos'd Extract[2] of his Letter to me, expresses great Hopes of their being induc'd to do.

As the inclos'd Rough Sketch may serve to Shew at one View the Situation of the whole Line of Forts upon the Western Frontier, from New York inclusive to the most Southern limits of Virginia, I have inclos'd it.

I have the honour to be with the Highest Respect
 Sir,
  Your most Humble
   and
  most Obedient Servant,

         W. SHIRLEY.

The Rt. Honble. Henry Fox,
one of his Majesty's principal Secretaries of State.

[1] *Ante*, p. 355, addressed to Sir Thomas Robinson.
[2] See the extract referred to, *ante*, p. 384.

Endorsed:
Boston March 8th. 1756.
Majr. Genl. Shirley.
R. May 5th.

STEPHEN HOPKINS TO WILLIAM SHIRLEY [1]

Newport, March 11, 1756.

SIR,

The General Assembly of this colony met the 23d of February past, and I laid before them the determinations of the general council of war, held at New York, by Your Excellency, I also then laid before them your letter of the 20th of February,[2] accompanied with the act of the Great and General Court of the Province of the Massachusetts Bay, for raising three thousand men for the Crown Point expedition, the ensuing campaign; a letter from Sir Charles Hardy, and the resolve of the General Assembly of the colony of New York, for raising one thousand men for the same service, was then also laid before them.

After full consideration of these matters, the Assembly here came to a resolution to raise and furnish five hundred men for the aforementioned expedition, and have made the necessary provisions for raising, subsisting and paying that number of men; being of opinion that five hundred is as large a proportion for this colony, considering their ability, and number of inhabitants, as three thousand is for the Province of the Massachusetts Bay, or one thousand for the colony of New York; and do not think themselves obliged by any means to follow the unequal proportions raised by the several colonies the last year, at the beginning of this enterprise; however, they seem to be willing, and I dare venture to pass my word for them, that they shall cheerfully under-

---

[1] Printed: R. I. Col. Rec. 5, 563.

[2] Printed: Kimball, Corres. Col. Govs. of R. I. 2, 188. The letter is on the same lines as Shirley's letter to Governor Morris of same date, *ante*, p. 393.

take to bear an equal share of the expense of reducing Fort St. Frederic, and the whole Lake Champlain, with its appendages, to the obedience of His Majesty, in proportion to their abilities, when truly compared with the other colonies concerned in that enterprise; but what methods may be come into for settling such proportions among the colonies concerned, seems yet to be very uncertain; and the less to be depended on, as the Massachusetts Court absolutely refused, when earnestly pressed thereto, by Your Excellency, to nominate and authorize any commissioners for such a purpose, the preceding year.

As to the conditional acts of Assembly, in the Province of the Massachusetts, and in the colony of Connecticut, for raising men, I am persuaded they can be of very little service to the common cause.

The instructions framed by your General Court, to be given to their committee, placed at and near at Albany, for carrying their resolutions into execution, and a copy of which Your Excellency has been kind enough to communicate to me, I have shown to the committee of war, for the colony, with whom powers are lodged for the like purposes, and are fully approved of by them; and full powers immediately will be given to some proper person or persons, in behalf of this colony, to repair directly to Albany, and to act there in concert with the gentlemen appointed by your Province, for carrying all the matters mentioned in those instructions into execution; and I shall be glad to be informed what number of troops will be sent by the Province of the Massachusetts, for transporting and guarding the provisions and stores in their passage from Albany, to Fort William Henry, and at what time they will be sent away, that I may order a proportionable number to join them in season, for that purpose, which I shall not fail to do.

The list of ordnance stores prepared by the commanding officer of the detachment of the royal regiment of artillery, and communicated to me by Your Excellency, as needful to be provided by the colonies, for the ensuing expedition, I have also laid before our committee of war, who agree that this colony ought to pay their proportion toward the expense of it; and will do it in such manner as may be proposed by Your Excellency, or others principally concerned in that matter; or otherwise, if their proportion can be set off to them, it shall be forthwith provided, and sent forward, as shall be ordered, — this colony and all employed by them for this expedition, being fully determined that whatever part this colony undertakes in it, shall be executed without any kind of delay.

The committee of war here have given me a list of sundry articles they would willingly furnish towards the train, if it be agreeable, with such others as might make up their full proportion, if those should fall short of it.

With the greatest respect,

I am Your Excellency's most humble
and most obedient servant,

STEPH. HOPKINS.

To His Excellency William Shirley, Esq.

WILLIAM SHIRLEY TO JOHN BRADSTREET [1]

INSTRUCTIONS FOR LIEUT: COLO. BRADSTREET

[Boston, March, 17, 1756.]

You are to proceed forthwith to the City of Albany and there take upon you the Command, of all the Battoemen engaged in His Majesty's Service, agreable to my Proclamation of the 19th of January Last. You are there to Muster them, and to Form them into Companies, and to such of the Captains and assistants as bring their Companies compleat,

[1] P. R. O., C. O. 5, 47. A transcript is in the Library of Congress. On Mar. 13 Fox had announced to the Colonial Governors the appointment of the Earl of Loudoun as Commander in Chief and the advance of Col. Daniel Webb to *ad interim* command. (Docts. rel. Col. Hist. N. Y. 7, 75.) This copy of Shirley's instructions to Bradstreet was forwarded by Loudoun Aug. 19, 1756. See also N. J. Arch. 8, pt. 2, pp. 209–212.

or who are deserving of the same, you are to fill up and deliver to them, the Warrants for their respective Posts, which shall be delivered Blank for that purpose. You are also to take upon you the direction of all the Whale boat Builders, and Battoe Builders, and all others Employed in building finishing or Supplying the same, both at Albany, and Schenectady, And all the Battoemen are hereby Strictly charged to observe and follow such Rules and directions as They shall receive from you, You are also to take upon you the direction and Command of all Such Waggons and Sleys employ'd at the Carrying places between Schenectady and Oswego, as may be necessary for the Transporting of the Battoes, Whale boats, Provisions etca. and all persons employ'd, or to be Employ'd in Transporting Provisions and Stores from Schenectady to Oswego, for His Majesty's Forces to be employ'd the ensuing Campaign on Lake Ontario. You are to get prepared and finished as many Whale boats and Battoes as Shall from time to time be necessary for Transporting Provisions and Stores for said Forces, and are with the utmost dispatch from time to time, to Transport the Provisions and Stores that Shall be Provided for said Forces at Schenectady, from thence to Oswego, You are to Appoint at Schenectady, and such other places as are necessary, proper persons for the Safe keeping of the Battoes and Whale boats and for keeping them in proper repair, and such other Officers, and Overseers as you find necessary for the well conducting the Business herein mention'd, And you are to constitute and make such Rules and Orders as you do from time to time find necessary for the well Conducting and good Management of the Same, informing me in Writing of them.

You are from time to time to make Application to me for what Money is necessary for the payment of the Wages of the Battoemen, and Waggoners aforesaid, and to pay them regularly, and you are to Employ proper persons to keep Regular accounts with the Capt. of each Company of Battoemen, and all others necessary in the business aforesaid, and all Commissaries, Deputy Commissaries, and all other Officers employ'd in keeping and Storing Provisions, or

Stores for the Service aforesaid, are hereby required to follow Your directions untill further Orders. And Whereas I have order'd James Fairservice with a Company of Carpenters, and Labourers to proceed to the Clearing and Mending the Passage between Schenectady and Oswego, and to mend the Falls, Rifts, Shoals, and carrying places between the Same; You are from time to time to give the said James Fourservice [*sic*] such further Instructions and directions as you shall find necessary for Carrying into Execution, the Instructions I have given him, a Copy of which is herewith, and the said James Fairservice and his Company are hereby required to Obey such Orders and directions, as they shall receive from you for doing the same, or any other further Service You shall think necessary, when that is compleated.

And Whereas I have propos'd to Johan Jost Petrie Esqr. to provide a Sufficient number of Waggons and Sleds, at the two carrying places at Conojohara Falls, and the Oneida Carrying place; a Copy of which proposals you have herewith, and if you find the said Petrie has not compleated a proper Supply of Waggons, and Sleds, you are to endeavour to get him to Supply the same, and if you find him deficient therein, you are to Employ or Contract with such persons to fullfill the Same in such manner that there may be no Insufficiency of Carriages, at those Carrying Places.

And in as much as there is not Store houses Sufficient at Oswego for containing the Provisions and Stores necessary for the Service there, nor any Boards there for erecting the same, you are therefore to order four Boards to be put into each Whale boat at Schenectady, And on your Arrival at Oswego, you are to Erect such Sheds, as will be necessary to receive the Same.

And Lastly as many unforeseen events may happen in the Execution of the Important extensive Work, hereby put under your direction, and altho' they may not be particularly mentioned herein, you are to use your best Judgment and discretion in every Point relating to the Service herein mention'd.

Nothing herein contain'd, to be Construed to Interfere with the Department of the Quarter Master General.
Given at Boston the 17th : day of March 1756.

WM. SHIRLEY.

By His Excellency's Command.
WM. ALEXANDER Secretary.

Endorsed:
Copy
General Shirley's Instructions To
 Lieut. Colonel Bradstreet.
  March 17th. 1756.
In the E. of Loudoun's Letter of
 Augt. 19th. 1756.

WILLIAM SHIRLEY TO ISRAEL WILLIAMS [1]

[SEAL]

WILLIAM SHIRLEY Esquire Captain Genll and Governour in Chief in and over his Majestys Province of the Massachusetts Bay in New England.

To ISRAEL WILLIAMS Esqr Greeting,
Whereas it is thought necessary that application should be made to the Colony of Connecticut for a Sufficient Number of Soldiers in their pay And Subsistance to be raised and Posted at Stockbridge and Pontoosuck for the Protection and Defence of those Places.
Reposing especial Trust and Confidence in your Loyalty ability and good Conduct I do by these presents constitute and appoint you the said Israel Williams to repair to Hartford in the Colony of Connecticut as soon as may be and on your Arrival there to Apply yourself to the Honble Thomas Fitch

---

[1] D. S., Mass. Hist. Society, Col. Israel Williams Manuscripts, 71 D, 207. See also Shirley's appeal to New Hampshire and Rhode Island for troops, N. H. Prov. Papers, 6, 498, and Kimball, Corres. R. I. Govs. 2, 201–203 (Mar. 16, 1756).

Esqr Governour and in his Absence to the Committee of War of that Colony for a Sufficient Number of Soldiers to be raised and sent by that Government to Stockbridge and Pontoosuck for the Protection and Defence of the Inhabitants of those Places in their Pay and Subsistance; and you are fully to represent the Necessity of this Measure as it will afford equal Protection to the Frontiers of that Colony as to those of this Province; you must urge their Complyance herewith in Consideration of the great Charge which Yearly arrises in this Province for its Defence; Return of your proceedings herein to be made into the Secretarys Office at Boston.

In testimony whereof I have Caused the public Seal of the Province of the Massachusetts Bay aforesaid to be hereunto Affixed; Dated at Boston the seventeenth day of March 1756: In the twenty ninth Year of his Majestys Reign.

W. SHIRLEY.

By his Excellencys Command.

WILLIAM SHIRLEY TO JOHN WINSLOW [1]

By His Excellency William Shirley Esqr. Capt. General Governor and Commander in Chief in and over the Province of the Massachusetts Bay in New England.

Instructions to John Winslow Esqr. Commander in Chief of all the Forces raised or to be raised within the Province

[1] Copy inclosed in Loudoun to Henry Fox, Aug. 19, 1756. P. R. O., C. O. 5, 47, 121. On Mar. 29, 1756, Governor Shirley had written from Boston to Chief Engineer James Montresor in reference to the expedition against Crown Point: —

"I now therefore desire Sir, that you will so dispose of the Brigade of Engineers, that I may have one or two for Crown Point, and a sufficient number for the Expeditions that may be carried on at and from Oswego." This letter to Winslow was written about the same time. See Wentworth to the Assembly of New Hampshire and its report as to troops for Crown Point, N. H. Prov. Papers, 6, 487, 502, 505.

of the Massachusetts Bay, Connecticut, New York, New Hampshire, New Jerseys, and Rhode Island, or other Provincial Troops from any of the Neighbouring Governments for the defence and Protection of His Majesty's Territories from any further encroachments of the French at Crown Point, and Upon Lake Iroquois commonly called by the French Lake Champlain, and for the removing the encroachments already made there.

You are hereby directed to take upon you the Command of the Forces raised and to be raised within the Province of the Massachusetts Bay and to take care that they be properly Armed and Accoutered, and cause them as soon as Possible to March for the City of Albany, where you will be Joined by the Forces of the other Governments above named, of which also you are to take the Command, and with them proceed to Lake George, and from thence to Crown Point, in the way you Judge most expedient, and to Oppose all persons by Force of Arms, either the Subjects of the French King, or Indians, or any other who shall appear to molest you on your way, and by every proper Method to reduce any Fortifications you shall find on the said Lake Iroquois or in your Passage thereto or places adjacent, more especially the Fort of Crown Point.

And Finally you are to use the utmost Dispatch in Executing these Orders, and such other or further Instructions as you shall at any time hereafter receive from me or the Commander in Chief for the time being of all His Majestys Forces raised and to be raised in North America. And as it is impossible to foresee all the accidents that may happen, and therefore proper instructions touching them cannot be given, I refer you to your Prudence, and good conduct with the advice of your Officers to take the most proper measures to repel or destroy all His Majesty's Enemies, and reduce their Fortifications to His Obedience, And Act as you apprehend will be for the good of His Majesty's Service either in an offensive or defensive manner.

W. Shirley.

Endorsed:
 Copy of Majr. Genl. Shirleys
  Instructions to Majr. Genl. Winslow,·
   to reduce Crown Point.
 in the E. of Loudoun's Letter of Augt. 19th. 1756.

HENRY FOX TO WILLIAM SHIRLEY [1]

Whitehall, March 31, 1756.

SIR,

 It having been represented to the King that your presence in England, may be very usefull and necessary to his Majesty's Service at this time, as you are able to give many lights and Information relative to the State of affairs in North America, I am to signify to you his Majestys pleasure, that as soon as you shall receive this Letter from Colonel Webb, who is appointed Commander-in-Chief in North America, you do repair to England with all possible Expedition, having first deliver'd to Col. Webb all such papers as relate to the King's Service.

I am with great Truth and Regard,

Sir,

Your most Obedient
Humble Servant,

H. Fox.

P.S. That there may not be the least Delay, H. M. has given Directions to the Lords of Admiralty, who have order'd a Frigate to receive you on board, and proceed with you directly to England.   H. F.

[1] P. R. O., C. O. 5, 212. Printed: 1 Penna. Arch. 2 ,606. In a letter of Mar. 13 to Shirley (C. O. 5, 212), Fox had stated that the expedition against Niagara was to be laid aside and that Col. Daniel Webb had been appointed Commander in Chief in North America. In this letter Shirley was informed of his probable appointment as Governor of Jamaica. A circular letter of the same date (Docts. rel. Col. Hist. N. Y. 7, 75) gave the information of Shirley's recall to other governors. Fox continued Secretary of State until October, 1756, having succeeded Robinson on Nov. 25, 1755.

JOHN BRADSTREET TO WILLIAM SHIRLEY[1]

SIR,

On my return to this place from Schenectady this day Captain Bradly shew'd me a letter he just received from Captain Laforay at Oswego giving him an account of the harbours being stopt and as I look upon it of the utmost importance that your Excellency should be made acquainted with it immediately I have advised him to send you a copy of it by express.

Should we have a dry spring its more than probable it will remain so all the year and certain it is that there is no snow to help it and too late to expect any, consequently the necessity of my proceeding to where your previous instructions commands me is become more necessary and [for] my hands to be strengthened with men and everything so as to make the Success pretty certain before the French get there. Your Excellency will forgive me saying that much will depend as matters are circumstanced on a sudden and quick push along shore.[2]

I have this day got off the remainder of the two hundred whaleboats and many battoes and shall get the rest off and myself gone in three days. Should your Exy have any orders to send me on this head it may meet me at the great Carrying place.

I have the honour

Albany 6 April 1756.

GENERAL SHIRLEY.

---

[1] Autograph draft, Amer. Antiq. Society.

[2] On Apr. 1, the New Hampshire Assembly had granted 30,000 pounds in bills of credit for the Crown Point expedition, and on Apr. 14, Governor Wentworth had agreed to the grant (N. H. Prov. Papers, 6, 506).

WILLIAM SHIRLEY TO HENRY FOX [1]

Boston, April 12th, 1756.

SIR,

A few days ago, His Majesty's Ships Woolwich and Lynn, arrived here, with part of the 10,000 Musquets, Ammunition etc., that were sent from the Office of Ordnance.

In Consequence of Sir Thomas Robinson's Letter to some of the Governors of the Provinces in North America, I have been applied to, to furnish them with Arms, Ammunition etc. for the Troops of their Several Provinces, that are now raising for the Service of the ensuing Campaign; And though I have made the most equal Distribution, in proportion to the numbers of Men each Government has consented to raise, I have not been able to comply with the full Demands of any one of them; And after having supplied His Majesty's Regular Troops, with their Deficiencies, amounting to 1200, including the four Independent Companies, whose Arms are returned by their respective Officers unfit for Service: I shall have remaining but 800, to supply the common Accidents of the Campaign, which I believe, Sir, you will think too small a number in proportion to the Troops that are to be employed.

I must therefore recommend, Sir, to your Consideration as a Measure absolutely necessary, and of the utmost Consequence to his Majesty's Service, the establishing of a public Magazine of small Arms and Ammunition in each Province; And I think, Sir, that 50,000 Stands of Arms at least, should be sent over for that purpose; as I believe that Number is scarce the fourth part of the fighting Men, in his Majesty's several Colonies in North America.

And that his Majesty might be assured of the Arms being properly taken care of, I would have, Sir, the several Governors Indent to the Crown for whatever number of Arms etc., they receive, and to be obliged to build Storehouses, in the most proper Places in each Province to lodge them in;

---

[1] P. R. O., C. O. 5, 46. A transcript is in the Library of Congress.

to make a Regular return of the State of them once a year, to His Majesty's Commander in Chief; to be liable to the inspection of the Comptroller of His Majesty's Ordnance, as often as shall be thought proper, and each Province to be obliged to keep up their Numbers compleat, and to have them in constant good Order and fit for Service.

Besides this, Sir, I would recommend the Establishment of a public Magazine of Artillery, Arms, Ammunition etc., for the use of his Majesty's Regular Troops; to be fix'd at New York, and to be in proportion to the number of Corps etc. His Majesty shall think proper to keep up in North America.

> I have the honour to be with the Highest Respect,
> Sir, Your most Humble and
> most Obedient Servant,
> W. SHIRLEY.

Rt. Honble. Henry Fox,
one of his Majesty's principal Secretaries of State.

Endorsed:
Boston April 12th. 1756. Majr. Genl. Shirley.
R June 8th.

WILLIAM SHIRLEY TO ROBERT HUNTER MORRIS [1]

Boston, Sunday, April 18, 1756.

DEAR SIR,

Two days ago I receiv'd letters from your Nephew, Staats, and Major Rutherford, informing me that Lord Loudon was appointed Commander in Chief of his Majestys Forces in North America, and that Colonels Abercromby and Webb, both made Lt. Generals upon this Occasion, are put upon the Staff; and that General Webb was to set out in the packet boat in ten days for North America, in order to take upon him the whole Command untill the Arrival of

---

[1] 1 Penna. Arch. 2, 630. See Morris to Shirley, Apr. 25, *post,* p. 431.

Lord Loudon; and I hear the Government of Jamaica is determin'd upon for me.

Upon this Occasion I think it my Indispensable Duty to push on all preparations for both Expeditions with as much Vigour as I was doing it before; and in case of any accidents befalling Genl. Webb in his passage, or not arriving here in time to begin the Operations when they ought to be, to begin them myself; For the News I have receiv'd, coming by private letters only, I can't take notice of it; However, as I am previously appriz'd of these Alterations, and that I may soon expect Orders in pursuance of them, It will be absolutely necessary for me to hold a Council of Warr at New York, consisting of Governours and Field Officers, (if to be had) according to his Maj'ys Instructions, before I enter upon any Operation.

In my way thro' Connecticutt I will engage Govr. Fitch, as I will Govr. Hopkins likewise, if I can, to be present at the Council; and as it is a matter of great Importance to his Majestys Service, as well of Consequence to my self, I must intreat the favour of you not to fail meeting me at New York, which would infinitely oblige,

My Dear, Sir,

Your most Affectionate,

Humble Servant,

W. SHIRLEY.

Staats hath acquitted himself in the business I sent him upon, with much honour to me, and to himself in the Opinion of the Ministry.

The Affair of Jamaica must be a dead Secret. I set out from hence for New York on Wednesday afternoon without fail, and shall be there by Monday night after.

If General Webb should be arriv'd before Monday, come se'n night at New York; there will not be the same necessity of your giving yourself the trouble to meet me.

Honble Robt. Hunter Morris, Esqr.

Endorsed:
April 18th, 1756, Genl. Shirley.

WILLIAM PEPPERRELL TO HENRY FOX [1]

Kittery, April 19, 1756.

Sir,

I had the Honour to receive your Excellencys Letter of November last in which you condescend to let me know that His Majesty had been pleased to declare His intentions of appointing you Secretary of State, I heartyly congratulate you Sir and Sincerely hope you will be continued for a long time to come a Great Blessing to His Majesty and all His Dominions.

As your Excellency in your Said Letter has done me the Honour of giving me Liberty of writing to you I take the fredom of leting you know that the first day of Last February Genl. Shirley told me that I must take the Command of the Expedition against Crown Point and that I Should have my own Regiment with me to joyn the Provential Troops, and that as I had the Honour to be president of His Majesty's Council of this Province of the Massachusets Bay that I would use my influence in making dispatch. I told him that although I was lame nothing that was in my power Should be wanting to promote His Majestys Service, I was Likewise desired by some of the most Leading men in the other Governments in New England to Head that Expedition and as I was preparing for it, I received a Letter from him datted the 26th. or 3d. February by his Secretary of which the inclosed is a copy by which you will see his determination, he has Since appointed Mr. Winslow General of Said Army and I heartyly hope this years Campaign will be more Successfull than the last was here but Should be glad they would make more dispatch.

My Son-in-Law Nathl. Sparkawk Esqr. tells me that he

[1] P. R. O., C. O. 5, 46. A transcript is in the Library of Congress. A letter of this date from Boston in the Johnson Manuscripts (4, 38a) mentions the appointment of Generals Loudoun, Abercromby, and Webb, and the consequent mortification of Shirley. It was forwarded to Johnson from New York by Goldsbrow Banyar with his letter of Apr. 25 as to new commissions and officers.

designs to address Your Excellency, if it Should be your pleasure to bestow any favours on him it will lay me under new obligations, with the Utmost Esteem I have the Honour to be

> Sir Your Excellencys
> Most and Obedient,
> Most Humble Servant,
> WM. PEPPERRELL.

His Excellency The Right Honourable Henry Fox etc. etc. etc.

Endorsed:

Kittery April 19th. 1756.
SIR WM. PEPPERRELL.
R. July 10th.

ROBERT HUNTER MORRIS TO WILLIAM SHIRLEY [1]

Philadelphia, 25th April 1756.

DEAR SIR,

It gives me pleasure to find by yours of the 18th Instant that your Dispatches by my Nephew were safe arrived, and that he had so well acquitted himself in the Business he was sent upon as to gain the good Opinion of the Ministry and your approbation.

Three Generals on the American staff make it probable that this Continent will be the Principal seat of the War, and that the views of the Ministry are very extensive, but whatever their measures may be, as they are taken Independent of the Plan of Operations agreed upon at New York, and as General Webb was to set out so soon after the Date of the Letters you have received that he may be expected to arrive every day, it appears to me that the Council of

---

[1] This letter illustrates the feeling felt for Shirley by Morris in this time of his humiliation. It is printed: 1 Penna. Arch. 2, 643. See also same to same of Apr. 22, *ibid.* p. 138, for service done by order of Genl. Braddock.

War will not incline to advise you to hasten the Execution of any Part of that Plan, but to wait his Arrival, and in the meantime to make the necessary Preparations with all profitable Vigour and Dispatch.

Probably Sir Charles Hardy and other Gentlemen may have received the Intelligence wrote you, and if so, they will not fail to publish all they know, and your Adversaries apprized of the alterations will take a Pride in impeding any Operations, tho' they will not venture to obstruct Preparations, and if you can put these into such forwardness as that the General may go upon action as soon as he arrives, You will render yourself extremely acceptable to His Majesty, the Ministry, and disappoint those who may take Occasion to put unfavourable constructions on any measures you shall devise and thence endeavour to set the Succeeding Commanders against you.

For my own part, my regards for you would prompt me at all adventures to wait on you, but I find myself so much embarassed by the perplexed Circumstances of this unhappy Province that it is not possible for me to follow the strong Inclinations I have to attend you. Your Dispatches found me preparing to set out for the Susquehanah, where the Provincial Forces are waiting for me, in order to proceed on an Expedition *for building a Fort at Shamokin*, and cannot on any Account be retarded, as the Season is already too far advanced, and I shall scarce be able to put them in motion before my Assembly will meet on my Summons to take into consideration how to prevent the total Desertion of the Counties on the Frontiers, of which I have reason to be very apprehensive.

I congratulate you on the King's Determination. I hope the Government intends you will be accompanied with the Command of the Regiment there, but sure I am that this change, tho' possibly more profitable to yourself, will not be agreeable to those who wish well to the Northern Colonies, as it must be universally acknowledged that you understand their Interests and Connections perfectly well and can give the best Information and Counsel in any matters respecting them.

Their grateful Acknowledgments will follow you wherever you go; to your well concerted Schemes and well conducted Operations they will attribute the Reduction of Cape Breton, the conquest of Nova Scotia and the lake; advantage gained over the French at Lake George, and indeed every thing that has given these Colonies so high a Reputation and placed them in so conspicuous a Light to his Majesty and the British Nation.

> I am, Dear Sir,
> Your most obliged and
> very obedient humble
> Servant,
> ROB. H. MORRIS.

I have been about a Letter to you some time but my Interruptions have hindred me from finishing it.

WILLIAM SHIRLEY TO HENRY FOX[1]

Albany, May 6th, 1756.

SIR,

I have now the Honour to acquaint you with my Arrival at this place, and the Progress made in the Preparations for the approaching Campaign.

Of the 10,000 Troops allotted by the Opinion of the Council of War held at New York the 12th and 13th of December for the Expedition against Crown point 1750 were propos'd by the Governors, then present, to be rais'd by the Province of the Massachusetts Bay, 1500 by Connecticutt, 1000 by New York, 300 by New Hampshire, 500 by Rhode Island, and the Remainder by the Colonies of New Jersey, Pensilvania, Maryland, and Virginia; But as I was under an Apprehension that little or no Dependance was to be had upon the New Jerseys and the three Western Governments raising their Quotas for this Service, which hath prov'd to be well

---

[1] P. R. O., C. O. 5, 46. A transcript is in the Library of Congress.

founded,[1] upon my Arrival at Boston soon after, I prevail'd upon the Massachusetts Assembly to make Provision for raising 3500 Men (Officers included) and upon their Example recommended it to the other three New England Governments, and that of New York to raise double their respective proportions; accordingly Connecticutt hath since voted 2500 Men, New York 1700, New Hampshire 500, and there is a prospect of Rhode Island's augmenting their first proportion of 500.

Before I left my own Government to come here I took Care, in order to expedite the Service, to have the 3500 Massachusetts Levies, which were then 1000 Short of Complement, compleated by an Impress, and to have several Companies of them immediately march'd to Albany; and finding in my Journey through Connecticutt, that 500 Rank and file Men remain'd to be rais'd of that Government's Quota, and observing it to the Governor, he promis'd me that at the Meeting of his Assembly, which will now be in two or three Days, he will procure their Levies likewise to be compleated by an Impress; and since my Arrival in New York, where not half the Levies of that Government were then raised, Sir Charles Hardy hath prevail'd upon his Assembly to have them also compleated in the same Manner; so that I am in hopes all the provincial Forces destin'd for Crown point may be soon assembled at Albany, the place of their general Rendezvous, and ready to open the Campaign by the 20th of this Month, provided the several Committees of War (as they are call'd in the New England Colonies), which, according to an invariable Rule observ'd among them upon these Occasions, are separately appointed by each Government to furnish their respective Quotas of provisions and Stores of all kinds for the Service, in such manner as they

[1] See Gov. Sharpe of Maryland to Shirley, Apr. 14 (Arch. of Md. 6, 389), and Governor Dinwiddie of Virginia to Shirley, Apr. 28 (Dinwiddie Papers, 2, 394). Both Maryland and Virginia placed more emphasis on the Fort Duquesne campaign. See Sharpe to the Earl of Albemarle, where the disapproval of drawing forces north is stated (Arch. of Md. 6, 406).

think proper, independently of each other, and of the Direction of the Commander in Chief, are as diligent and active as they ought, and have promis'd to be in pursuing the Measures, I have recommended to them.

To secure a timely Settlement and constant Supply of necessary Magazines of provisions and Stores at Fort Edward and Fort William Henry during the Campaign, for want of which his Majesty's Service suffer'd the last Year in the Expeditions both against Crown point and Niagara, occasion'd wholly by the failure of a sufficient Number of Waggons, Horses, and Battoe-men to be had within the Government of New York, or at least for Want of a sufficient Number of them being provided for the Service by the Commander in Chief of that Province, to whom Application was duely made for that purpose in pursuance of his Majesty's Orders signify'd to the several Governors in Sir Thomas Robinson's Circular Letter to them dated the 26th of October 1754, and with whom the sole power of impressing Men, Horses, and Carriages within that Province lay, I have taken Care that the Massachusetts Government shall buy or hire a sufficient Number of Oxen and Horses, and Waggons for the transportation of their Stores to Lake George.

For supplying them with a proper number of battoes and other small craft for transporting their Men, Provisions, Artillery and Military Stores over the Lake; I have order'd them to send several Companies of Carpenters and other Workmen to build a proper Number upon the Lake; which will save much time and trouble in transporting them 1400 Miles by Land over the Carrying place between Fort Edward and Fort William Henry; and I have recommended the same Measures to all the Governments concern'd, for the readier transportation of their respective Troops and Stores.

I have prevail'd likewise on the Assembly of the Massachusetts Bay to augment the Artillery of these Forces: to make Provision for a larger Number of Officers of the Train, and 200 Bombardiers and Matrosses for the Service at Crown point; and to extend the King's Articles of War to their Troops, when acting separately from the Regulars, (which

I am in hopes will induce the other Colonies concern'd to do the same with respect to their Forces) in order to inforce a proper Discipline among the Provincial Troops upon all Occasions, and take away all pretence of the Officers for exercising a Slack Command over the Soldiers, which I am inform'd, prevail'd among them at Lake George the last Year; but was unknown among the New England Troops during the Expedition against Cape Breton.

As I have found by Experience, that it is absolutely necessary for his Majesty's Service, that one Company at least of Rangers should be constantly employ'd in different Parties upon Lake George and Lake Iroquois, (alias Lake Champlain), and the Wood Creek and Lands adjacent, to make Discoveries of the proper Routes for our own Troops, procure Intelligence of the Enemy's Strength and Motions, destroy their out Magazines and Settlements, pick up small Parties of their Battoes upon the Lakes, and keep them under continual Alarms, I have rais'd one consisting of 60 pick'd Men under Officers, who have distinguish'd themselves by their Behaviour in this Branch of Service; from which I expect great Advantages may be reap'd in the Course of the Campaign.

And I have wrote to Sir William Johnson to engage a Party of Indians with their Officers to hold themselves in readiness to proceed with the Army from Lake George to Crown point in order to serve as Scouts, and in other parts of Indian Duty: so that I am in hopes every Step has been taken to get the Body of Troops, destin'd for that place, in a readiness to march upon the Arrival of the Vessell, which shall bring his Majesty's Royal pleasure upon the plan of Operations, which I had the Honour to transmit to you, Sir, in December last by Captain Morris and Major Rutherford, to be lay'd before his Majesty, whose Directions I am in hourly Expectation of reaching America; But if by any Accident they should miscarry, I shall proceed to carry that plan into Execution in the best manner I can, according to the Intelligence, I shall be able to procure of the Motions and Strength of the French.

I have only further to acquaint, you Sir, upon the Subject of the Expedition now preparing against Crown point, that on finding the Massachusetts Government so much exhausted of Money and Credit for borrowing it within the Province by the very great Expence, it was at in the last Years' Expedition against Crown point, that they were utterly disabled from paying the Arrears due to the Officers and Soldiers employ'd in that Service, and to advance the Sum necessary for inlisting their Forces in it this Year without being assisted with £30,000 Sterling ready Money for that Purpose, I agreed to lend them that Sum out of the Contingent Money, upon their securing by an Act of Assembly (as they have done) the Repayment of it out of the Money, which his Majesty was pleas'd, by Sir Thomas Robinson's Letter to me dated the 11th : Novr., to order me to declare to them, he would recommend to the Parliament to grant towards the Reimbursement of their Expences in the Last Year's Expedition against Crown point, or in failure of any such Grant, by a Tax upon the Polls and Estates of the Inhabitants to be levied in the Years 1757 and 1758, so that at all Events the Repayment of the £30,000 is absolutely secure to the Crown.

I have likewise, Sir, agreed to lend the Colony of Connecticutt £10,000, and the Province of New Hampshire £3000 out of the Contingent Money upon the like Security, in order to enable them to carry on their part of the same Expedition this Year; and as his Majesty's Royal Declaration in favour of these Colonies seems to be design'd to encourage them to prosecute the before mention'd Expedition to Effect this Year; it appear'd to me that the advancing these Sums of Money in the Manner, I have, to enable them to do it, answer'd the End of his Majesty's gracious Intentions in the most beneficial Manner for his Service; and will therefore I hope be approv'd of.

It is likewise necessary for me to observe, Sir, that in case a Grant should have been made by Parliament to the Colonies of a Sum of Money on Account of their Expences in the last Year's Expedition against Crown point, and that it is not already remitted to them in Specie, or paid to their Agents in England, the Several Sums of thirty thousand pounds, ten thousand pounds, and three thousand pounds, mention'd in this Letter to be advanc'd to the Governments of the Massachusetts Bay, Connecticutt, and New Hampshire, may be deducted out of their respective Shares in the parliamentary Grant, without being issu'd out of the Treasury.

I am with the highest Respect,
Sir,
Your most Humble, and
most Obedient Servant.

W. SHIRLEY.

The Rt. Honble. Henry Fox,
one of His Majesty's principal Secretaries of State.

Endorsed:
Albany May 6th, 1756.
Majr. Genl. Shirley.
R. June 7th.

RICHARD PETERS TO WILLIAM SHIRLEY[1]

Philadelphia, May 6th, 1756.

SIR,

In the absence of the Governor who went last Week to the Frontier Counties, the Council opened your Excellency's Letter of the 2d Instant, inclosing one of the 24th April, from Sir William Johnson to you finding great fault with Governor Morris for issuing his Proclamation[2] declaring the Delawares, tho' they were carrying on a most destructive and ruinous War against this Province, Enemies to his Majesty and offering a Reward for their Scalps — and on

---

[1] Johnson Manuscripts, N. Y. State Library, 23, 213; 1 Penna. Arch. 2, 651.   See Col. Rec. of Penna. 7, 210, also 1 Penna. Arch. 2, 654, Peters's Letter to Governor Morris.
[2] See Col. Rec. of Penna. 7, 88.

considering this Letter together with what your Excellency is pleased to say vizt. : that if there shoud appear any thing to governor Morris, "which upon a Reconsideration of this " matter may make it adviseable for him to suspend Hostili- " ties against the Indians affected by his Declaration until " the result of Sir William Johnson, Meeting the Indians at " Onondago is known, You did not doubt but he woud think " it a prudent Measure." And on likewise considering the Several Letters from Sir Charles Hardy Copys of some of which are inclosed, the Council have unanimously resolved to advise the Governor to Publish a Cessation of Hostilities against the Susquehannah Delawares, until further order, and have directed me to acquaint you with their having done so; and that they woud likewise have advised a general Cessation of Hostilities against the Delaware Tribe, was it not a matter of Fact that those from Ohio have but lately appeared in large Bodys on our Western Frontiers, and killed and carried away great Numbers of our Inhabitants over Susquehannah, and by the last post from Annapolis it is expressly wrote by the Post Master there that these Delaware Indians were then murdering twelve miles within Winchester, having destroy'd the settlements at Conegochege and the Conollaways and other places, as well in our Province as in Maryland and Virginia, and in several Depositions taken of Prisoners, who have from time to time made their Escape from these Delawares, it is positively declared that they were meditating a grand attack on the Inhabitants of this and the neighbouring Provinces and that we may expect them as soon as their Indian Corn is Planted to the number of two thousand Indians of different nations all embodied against us by the Influence of the French and these Delawares, the Council therefore cannot think it prudent, the Province being in such Circumstances, that these Indians shoud be included within the cessation of hostilities.

As Sir William Johnson has before this time received from Governor Morris one of the Printed Proclamations and his Letter accompanying it, sent by Mr. Claus, who had the charge of Conducting Scarroyday and his Company to Fort Johnson, and likewise heard the Accounts these Indians would give of the most miserable Condition of the Back Counties, it is hoped he sees the measure in another light than he did when he wrote his Letter, and will have considered the Reasons for it as set forth by the Governor in that Letter, a copy of which is here inclosed whereby it will appear that when that Declaration was published, the Enemy Indians were greatly encreased in their numbers, and appeared in more formidable Bodies upon every fresh descent. That the Frontier Counties were near being abandoned. That the Six Nation Indians to a Man who were Parties at the late Treaty thought the measure absolutely necessary, advised it, and assured us it would be agreeable to the Six Nations and even promised to engage some of their Warriors to assist us against them — that the formality of a Declaration tho' necessary to animate our own People coud make no manner of difference as to the Enemy, Delawares who had been for some time before and then were butchering the Kings Subjects like Beasts, appointed for Slaughter or driving them before them bound with Cords and Naked into a Shameful Captivity, the Council say when these matters come to be considered together with the Restrictions in the Proclamation and the Distinctions between those in Open war, and those who have not joined them no one can with Justice censure the Declaration but impute the Faults where it does in truth lye at the Door of the Delawares for they and they only not the Shawanese, who are included in the Declaration.

The Council desire further to inform your Excellency that the Governor by their Advice has sent four Indians, two of the Six Nations and two friendly Delawares to Wiomink the Principal place of Residence of the Susquehannah Delawares, to notify them and the neighbouring Indians of the Transactions between the Deputies of the Six Nations and the Chiefs and Warriors of these Susquehannah Indians at Otsaningo as Communicated to him by Sir Charles Hardy from Sir William Johnson, and that these messengers had further in Charge to assure those Indians that if the Treaty took full effect, and their future actions corresponded to the Professions made to the Deputies of the Six Nations, they shoud find a ready Disposition in this Government to return to their old Friendship, on their giving up the English Prisoners and acknowledging their Faults.

The Council requests of your Excellency that you will be pleased to make Sir William Johnson acquainted with these matters that they may be properly mentioned at the Treaty at Onondaga and if this be done they apprehend no ill consequences can attend the Declaration of war but that it will appear that this Government tho' reduced to the necessity of making it and offering rewards for such, as woud go out against such a Destructive Enemy, has paid a due regard to the Mediation of the Six Nations, and will still do it, nor do the council think that Sir William Johnson shoud blame, but rather justify this step, especially as during the time of the meeting at Otsaningo, the Delawares from the Ohio, were doing their greatest mischief both in this and the neighbouring Provinces, and do still vow not to leave an English Man alive, which shoud stir up these very Susquehannah Indians, in conjunction with the Six Nations to assist us in bringing them to terms of Peace, and to consider this Declaration as made against these implacable and obstinate Enemies and not against any that now are or hereafter may be disposed to hearken to the Six Nations mediating in our favour.

The Council doubts not but the Governor will concur with them in these Sentiments and supply what is wanting of his Authority in this letter, but in the mean time till he can signify this himself, as he is at a Distance they thought it their duty to lay these matters before your Excellency, and request they may be communicated to Sir William Johnson, with all possible dispatch to take off any prejudice that may arise in his mind or with the Indians, on occasion of this Declaration, and least any accident shoud have befallen Mr. Claus, and the Letters sent by him miscarry they further desire you will furnish Sir William Johnson, with one of the

Printed Proclamations and the Copy of the Governor's Letter to him, of the 24th April.

I am,

> Your Excellency's
> most obedient
> humble Servant,
>
> RICHARD PETERS, Sec.

By order of the Council.

WILLIAM SHIRLEY TO HENRY FOX [1]

Albany, May 7th, 1756.

SIR,

In this Letter I have the Honour to transmit you an Account of the Progress made in the Preparations for executing that part of the plan of Operations contain'd in the Council of War held at New York the 12th and 13th of December, which is there propos'd to be carry'd on this Year upon the Great Lakes and River Ohio.

In my Letter of the 6th Instant [2] I observ'd that his Majesty's Service both at Lake George, and Oswego had suffer'd the last Year for Want of a sufficient Number of Waggons, Horses, and Battoe-men's being furnish'd by the then Governor of New York, for transporting the Men, Provisions, Artillery and Military Stores necessary to be employ'd in those two Expeditions; and acquainted you with the Measures, I had taken for preventing his Majesty's Service from suffering in the same Manner this Year in the present Expedition against Crown-point; and am now to inform you, Sir, that to prevent it from suffering in this Article at Oswego, and to secure the transportation of a sufficient Quantity of Provisions and Stores to that place for 6000 Men during the whole Campaigne, I gave Orders for engaging 2000 Battoe-men to be dispos'd into Companies of 50 Men each under the Command

---

[1] P. R. O., C. O. 5, 46. A transcript is in the Library of Congress, and another among the Parkman Papers in the Mass. Hist. Society.
[2] *Ante*, p. 433.

of one Captain and an Assistant, and to be put under the General Direction of one Officer well Skill'd in the many Branches of this important Trust; the due Execution of which is absolutely necessary for supplying his Majesty's Service upon the Lake Ontario with Magazines of provisions and Stores, and will require not only the whole time and Attention of the Officer employ'd in it, but likewise his personal Attendance on every part of the Duty: and for this Reason, Sir, I have been oblig'd to constitute a New Officer (Lt. Colonel Bradstreet) to superintend this Busness, which together with the Care of overseeing the Construction of the Whale Boats propos'd to be employ'd on the same Lake, and clearing the Obstructions in the whole Water Carriage between Schenectada and Oswego could not possibly be executed by the Deputy Quarter Master General, consistently with the Business of his Department; especially if his Attendance should be necessary, any part of this Campaigne on Lake Champlain; which is most likely to be the case.

In Consequence of this Provision the 2000 Battoe-Men have been rais'd, and the Chief part of them been some time employ'd in transporting Provisions and Stores to Oswego, 600 Battoe Loads at least of which, and 200 Whale Boat Loads must be, as I am inform'd, at Oswego by this time.

The 44th, 48th, 50th, and 51st Regiments are now almost compleat.

The Recruits of the 50th and 51st, and the New Jersey Regiment are march'd for Oswego; the 44th and 48th, with the Detachment of Royal Artillery are under Orders to take the Field at 48 Hours warning; and two of the Independent Companies of New York are posted at the Magazine on the German Flatts, and the little Carrying place on this Side, for the Security of the Provisions there and keeping open the Communication between Schenectada and those places.

The greatest part of the Provisions necessary for the Troops destin'd for Oswego are at Albany and Schenectada, except that part of them, which, as I have before observ'd, are moving from thence to Oswego.

And as I can't find hitherto, that Sir William Johnson hath brought the Indians of the Six Nations to be of the least service in keeping the Road thro' their own Country to Oswego open, and free from Scalping parties of the French Indians, who have found means to surprize and cutt off a small Fort and Party of 25 Men at one End of the Great Carrying place, I have order'd three Companies of Rangers, consisting of one Captain, one Lieutenant, one Ensign, two Serjeants, two Corporals and 60 Men each to be rais'd as soon as may be, and constantly employ'd in Scouting the Country from the German Flatts to Oswego; which I am fully perswaded is absolutely necessary to be done for keeping open the Communication between that place and Oswego, and will effectually do it, besides making frequent Incursions into the Enemy's Country, and committing Ravages in it.[1]

I am likewise, Sir, to acquaint you that the Commanding Officer of the Vessells built on the Lake Ontario the last Year is gone to Oswego, with a sufficient Number of Sailors to fit them out as soon as possible; and 100 Carpenters are gone there to build three Vessells more, 30 of which have been at Work on them above five Weeks, and the Stores for them all are on their Way to Oswego.

I shall have the Honour of transmitting you an Account of the Situation of Indian Affairs by the next Opportunity;

[1] The following extract from a letter of Sir William Johnson to Shirley written May 10 shows the conditions on the route to Oswego: —

I wish the Companies of Rangers, your Excellency mentions, were ready to go upon Duty, when I would hope to be able to join Indians with them; and unless this Method takes place, I despair of the Communication to Oswego being secur'd.

a true Copy,
WM. ALEXANDER, Secy.

Endorsed:

Extract of Sir William
Johnson's Letter to
General Shirley dated
10th May 1756.

the time of this pacquets' Sailing not permitting me to do it now.

I am with the highest Respect,
Sir,
Your most Humble, and
most Obedient Servant.
W. SHIRLEY.

Rt. Honble. Henry Fox, one of his }
Majesty's principal Secretaries of State, }

Endorsed:
Albany, May 7th. 1756.
Majr. Genl. Shirley.
R. June 7th.

WILLIAM SHIRLEY TO STEPHEN HOPKINS[1]

Albany, 12th May, 1756.
SIR,

Before I left Boston, the Massachusetts government passed an act of Assembly, to subject the troops raised within this Province for the expedition against Crown Point, to the King's articles of war, a copy of which act, I have ordered the Province secretary to send Your Honour; and I look upon this point to be so essential an one for keeping up a proper command and discipline among the provincial troops, as well as regulars, that I must recommend it to Your Honour in the strongest terms, as I have to all the other governments concerned in this expedition, to pass a like act with regard to their troops.

The season of the year for opening the campaign, is now far advanced, and Your Honour is sensible how much the success of our operation against the enemy depends upon our entering early upon action.

[1] R. I. Col. Rec. 5, 526.   See *ibid.* 5, 492–494, for act of May 8 providing for the regulation and government of Rhode Island troops on the Crown Point Expedition.

I must therefore beg you would hasten the march of your troops to Albany, as fast as possible; and take every measure for immediately completing your magazines of provisions and stores, at Fort Edward and Fort William Henry, providing a sufficient number of oxen, horses and carriages for transporting them to the latter of these two forts, and of batteaux and other craft, for transporting them from Lake George to Ticonderoga, &c.; all which should be done without the least loss of time.

    I am, with great Regard and esteem, Sir,
        Your Honor's most humble and most Obedient Servant,

                    W. SHIRLEY.

To the Hon. Stephen Hopkins, Esq.

WILLIAM SHIRLEY TO HORATIO SHARPE [1]

Albany, May 16, 1756.

SIR,

    Three Days ago I was favour'd with your Letter dated the 10th of April inclosing one from Colonel Washington to me dated the 4th together with another from yourself dated the 14th of the same month.

    I am sorry to find from the Accounts given me in your Honour's Letters, and others from Govr Dinwiddie and Govr Morris, of the dangerous Situation of the three Provinces under your respective Governments, and the proceedings of the Assemblies within them, that there seems to be not the least Appearance of any provision's being made for prosecuting the propos'd Expedition under your Command against

[1] Original, Maryland Historical Society. Printed: Arch. of Md. 6, 415. On Apr. 10, Sharpe had written Shirley, requesting among other things the appointment of second in command for George Washington in case of a westward movement by Maryland and Virginia (Arch. of Md. 6, 389), as Shirley had given Sharpe the foremost post in such an expedition. (See Sharpe to Loudoun, May 31, 1756, Arch. of Md. 6, 432.) This letter is in reply to that of Sharpe.

the French Settlements on the Ohio, the succeeding in which it seems to me, would deliver you in the most effectual manner, from the Distresses, under which Virginia and Pensilvania now labour from the Ravages of the French and their Indians.

I can't find that the Assemblies of those two Provinces have any thing further in view than the bare protection of their own Frontiers against the growing Incursions of the Enemy; and as to your own Assembly, they are upon the point of disbanding the only Company they have at a time when his Majy's Fort Cumberland within the limits of the Province of Maryland, and several of his Majesty's Stores in it, is in danger of falling into the Enemy's Hands.

As to my taking upon me, Sir, to throw the whole Expence of supporting an Expedition from the Western Colonies to the Ohio upon the Crown, after his Majesty hath been at so great an one in the Regts he has already rais'd here, and sent, and is still sending over; and whilst the New England Colonies, and those of New York and New Jersey, whose Abilities don't exceed those of the Western Colonies, have besides raising Troops for the defence of their own Frontiers, rais'd upwards of 9000 Men for the asserting his Majestys just Rights and Dominions upon the Lake Champlain, and the Lake Ontario, &c., it is what I can't justify; especially now we are appriz'd from publick Accts in News-papers, and private Letters from England, that the Arrival of Lord Loudoun may be soon expected here with the Chief Command of his Majesty's Forces in North America.[1]

I am likewise in hourly Expectation of receiving his Majestys Commands by General Webb concerning the plan of Operations, he would have prosecuted this year, which is another Reason why I can't send you a peremptory Answer to the

---

[1] On Apr. 22, Shirley had written Dinwiddie of Loudoun's arrival. The Virginia Governor congratulated him in the words, "As we hear the Earl of Lowden is appointed to command-in-chief all the Forces on this Continent, it will ease you of the great trouble you have had and so carefully discharged." Dinwiddie Papers, 2, 428. Compare his letter to Fox on the same event, *ibid.* 2, 412.

points propos'd to me in your two letters, before I receive those orders : But your Honour may depend upon my sending it to you, as soon as they arrive.

In the mean time I beg you would be pleas'd to acquaint Col : Washington, that the Appointment of him to the second Command in the propos'd Expedition upon the Ohio, will give me great satisfaction and pleasure; that I know no Provincial Officer upon this Continent, to whom I would so readily give it as to himself; that I shall do it, if there is nothing in the King's Orders, which I am in continual Expectation of, that interferes with it; and that I will have the pleasure of answering his Letter immediately after my receiving them.

I have only to add, that upon Govr Dobb's[1] first acquainting me, about four months ago, with his Assembly's having raised three Companies to be employ'd in that part of his Majestys Service, which he should think best, and writing to me for directions concerning their Destination, I desir'd him to send them to act with the King's Troops upon Lake Ontario; But on my determining to recommend an Expedition upon the Ohio to the Western Colonies, I order'd them to be sent upon the service under your Command : You will perceive by the inclos'd Extract of his Letter to me dated 23d March, that he was then acquainted with those Orders thro' Mr Dinwiddie; But for the Reasons therein mentioned was determin'd to send his three Companies to join me, and not the Forces to be employ'd upon the Ohio; so that I am afraid you will be disappointed in your Expectation of them to Act with you.

> I am with great Regard and Esteem,
> Sir, Your Honour's most Humble
> and most Obedient Servant,
> W. Shirley.

[1] Arthur Dobbs was governor of North Carolina from 1753 to his death in 1765. See North Carolina Col. Rec. 5, Introduction.

HENRY FOX TO WILLIAM SHIRLEY [1]

Whitehall, May 17th, 1756.

Sir,

His Majesty having found it necessary to declare War against the French King, has been pleased, in a Council held this Day at Kensington for that purpose, to sign the inclosed Declaration, and to order that the same should be published to Morrow by the Heralds at Arms, in the usual Places, and with the accustomed Formalities; I am commanded to signify to you the King's Pleasure, that you should cause the said Declaration of War to be proclaimed in the Province under your Government, that His Majesty's Subjects having this Notice may take care to prevent any Mischief, which otherwise they might suffer from the Enemy, and do their Duty in their several Stations, to distress and annoy the Subjects of France; and His Majesty would have you be very rigorous and severe in preventing any Ammunition, or Stores of any kind, from being carried to them, and you are to use all proper Methods that may be most effectual for that purpose.

I am, Sir,
Your most obedient
humble servant;

H. Fox.

The Governor of Massachusetts Bay

P.S. His Majesty has been pleased to order Letters of Marque or Commissions to Privateers to be granted in the usual manner.

---

[1] A similar letter sent to the governor of Pennsylvania is in 1 Penna. Arch. 2, 659.

HIS MAJESTY'S DECLARATION OF WAR AGAINST THE FRENCH KING [1]

GEORGE R,

The unwarrantable Proceedings of the *French* in the *West Indies* and *North America*, since the Conclusion of the Treaty of *Aix la Chapelle* and the Usurpations and Encroachments made by them upon our Territories, and the Settlements of Our Subjects in those Parts, particularly in our Province of *Nova Scotia*, have been so notorious and so frequent, that they cannot but be looked upon as a sufficient Evidence of a formed Design and Resolution in that Court to pursue invariably such Measures as should most effectually promote their ambitious Views, without any Regard to the most solemn Treaties and Engagements. We have not been wanting on Our Part to make, from time to time, the most serious Representations to the *French* King upon these repeated Acts of Violence, and to endeavour to maintain Redress and Satisfaction for the Injuries done to Our Subjects, and to prevent the like Causes of Complaint for the future : But though frequent Assurances have been given that every thing should be settled agreeable to the Treaties subsisting between the Two Crowns, and particularly, that the Evacuation of the Four Neutral Islands in the *West Indies*, should be effected, (which was expressly promised to Our Ambassador in *France*) the Execution of these Assurances, and of the Treaties on which they were founded, has been evaded under the most frivolous Pretences ; and the unjustifiable Practices of the *French* Governors, and of the Officers acting under their Authority, were still carried on, till, at length, in the month of *April*, One thousand seven hundred and fifty-four, they broke out in open Acts of Hostility, when, in Time of profound Peace, without any Declaration of War, and without any previous Notice given or Applica-

[1] Printed : 1 Penna. Arch. 2, 735. This declaration was published at Easton, Pa., July 30, 1756, and at Philadelphia in August.

tion made, a Body of *French* Troops, under the Command of an Officer bearing the *French* King's Commission, attacked in a hostile Manner, and possessed themselves of the *English* Fort on the *Ohio*, in *North America*.

But notwithstanding this Act of Hostility, which could not but be looked upon as a Commencement of War, yet, from our earnest Desire of Peace, and in Hopes the Court of *France* would disavow this Violence and Injustice, We contented Ourselves with sending such a Force to *America*, as was indispensably necessary for the immediate Defence and Protection of Our Subjects against fresh Attacks and Insults.

In the mean Time great Naval Armaments were preparing in the Ports of *France*, and a considerable body of *French* Troops embarked for *North America;* and though the *French* Ambassador was sent back to *England* with specious Professions of a Desire to accommodate these Differences, yet it appeared that their real Design was only to gain Time for the Passage of those Troops to *America*, which they hoped would secure the Superiority of the *French* Forces in those Parts, and enable them to carry their ambitious and oppressive Projects into Execution.

In these Circumstances We could not but think it incumbent upon Us, to endeavour to prevent the Success of so dangerous a Design, and to oppose the Landing of the *French* Troops in *America;* and, in Consequence of the just and necessary Measures we had taken for that Purpose, the *French* Ambassador was immediately recalled from Our Court; the Fortifications at *Dunkirk*, which had been repairing for some Time, were enlarged; great Bodies of Troops marched down to the Coast, and Our Kingdoms were threatened with an Invasion.

In order to prevent the Execution of these Designs, and to provide for the Security of Our Kingdoms which were thus threatened, We could no longer forbear giving Orders for the seizing at Sea the Ships of the *French* King, and his Subjects. Notwithstanding which, as We were still unwilling to give up all Hopes that an Accommodation might be effected, We have contented Ourselves hitherto with detaining the said

Ships, and preserving them, and (as far as was possible) their Cargoes intire, without proceeding to the Confiscation of them; but it being now evident, by the hostile invasion actually made by the *French* King of Our Island of *Minorca*, that it is the determined Resolution of that Court to hearken to no Terms of Peace, but to carry on the War, which has been long begun on their Part with the utmost Violence, We can no longer remain, consistently with what We owe to Our own Honour, and to the Welfare of Our Subjects within those Bounds, which, from a Desire of Peace, We had hitherto observed.

We have therefore thought proper to declare War, and We do hereby Declare War against the *French* King, who hath so unjustly begun it, relying on the Help of Almighty God, in Our just undertaking, and being assured of the hearty Concurrence and Assistance of Our Subjects, in support of so good a Cause, hereby willing and requiring Our Captain General of Our Forces, Our Commissioners for executing the Office of Our High Admiral of *Great Britain*, Our Lieutenants of Our several Counties, Governors of our Forts and Garrisons, and all other Officers and Soldiers under them, by Sea and Land, to do and execute all Acts of Hostility, in the Prosecution of this War against the *French* King, his Vassals and Subjects, and to oppose their Attempts, Willing and requiring all Our Subjects to take Notice of the same, whom We henceforth strictly forbid to hold any Correspondence or Communication with the said *French* King, or his Subjects. And We do hereby command Our own Subjects, and advertise all other Persons, of what Nation soever, not to transport or carry any Soldiers, Arms, Powder, Ammunition, or other Contraband Goods, to any of the Territories, Lands, Plantations, or Countries of the said *French* King; Declaring, That whatsoever Ship or Vessel shall be met withal, transporting or carrying any Soldiers, Arms, Powder, Ammunition, or any other Contraband Goods, to any of the Territories, Lands, Plantation or Countries of the said *French* King, the same being taken, shall be condemned as good and lawful Prize.

And whereas there are remaining in Our Kingdom divers of the Subjects of the *French* King, We do hereby declare Our Royal Intention to be, That all the *French* Subjects who shall demean themselves dutifully towards Us, shall be safe in their Persons and Effects.

Given at Our Court at *Kensington*, the Seventeenth Day of *May*, 1756, in the Twenty ninth Year of our Reign.

God save the King.

MINUTES OF COUNCIL OF WAR HELD AT ALBANY [1]

At a Council of War held at the Camp at Albany May 25th 1756.

PRESENT

His Excellency William Shirley Esqr. General and Commander in Chief of all his Majesty's Forces in North America.

The Honble. Lieut. Col. Thomas Gage.

Lieut. Col. Ralph Burton.

Major [   ] [2] Chapman.

Major William Sparks.

Sir John St. Clair, Deputy Quarter Master General.

John Montresor Esqr. Chief Engineer.

His Excellency acquainted the Council, that he desir'd their Opinion and Advice upon several Matters relative to his Majesty's Service in this Campaigne.

That in order to set them in a proper light for their Consideration, it was necessary first to acquaint them with the plan of Operations, which was determined upon in a Council of War held at New York the 12th and 13th December last,

[1] P. R. O., C. O. 5, 46. Another copy is in C. O. 5, 47, and a transcript is in the Library of Congress. A copy was inclosed by Shirley in his letter of May 27 to Governor Hardy, and another in his letter to Fox of June 23.

[2] The name is omitted in the original.

453

consisting of Governors and Field Officers according to his Majesty's seventh Instruction to the late General Braddock and himself; which Plan was accordingly read.

His Excellency then inform'd the Council that he had transmitted the said Plan to England to the Right Honble: Sir Thomas Robinson, then one of his Majesty's principal Secretaries of State, to be lay'd before his Majesty, and that he acquainted Sir Thomas Robinson, that if he should not receive his Majesty's Commands upon it by the beginning of the Campaigne this Year, he should proceed to carry it into Execution.

His Excellency then acquainted the Council with the State and Strength of the Garrison at Oswego and of the Forces destin'd for the Expedition against Crown point, vizt:

That the Naval Force upon the Lake will consist this Year of two Vessells of ten Carriage Guns each and two Row Gallies of ten Swivels each, built last Year, and one Vessell of 18, one of 10, and another of eight Carriage Guns, for building and equipping of which preparations have been making at Oswego some time, and which were three Months ago order'd to be built and equipp'd, as soon as possible, this Year; and that there will be 250 Whale Boats for the Navigation of the Lake, capable of holding sixteen Men each.

That the Land Forces now at Oswego, and upon their March thither, and those which are design'd to be employ'd in keeping open the Communication between Albany, and Oswego, consist of the 50th and 51st Regiments, the New Jersey Regiment, and the four Independent Companies of New York, but for Want of exact Returns of the present Strength of the 50th and 51st Regiments on Account of their remote and scatter'd Situation, it can't be precisely determin'd what Number of Effectives fit for Service the whole will produce; That of these, 100 at least must be posted at the Conajohara Falls to guard the Magazine of Provisions and Stores there, and convoy them over that Carrying place, 100 at the German Flatts to guard the Magazine there, 200 more at the Oneida Carrying place to guard the Magazine there and convoy the Provisions and Stores over that Carrying place and thro' Wood Creek, and 50 at the Fort propos'd to be built at the Oswego Falls; That besides the before mention'd Regiments and Independent Companies, he propos'd to raise four ranging Companies of Irregulars consisting of 60 privates each to be employ'd in scouting parties for keeping open the Communication with Oswego, and harrassing the Enemy's Country between Fort Frontenac and Montreal.

That the Works at Oswego consist of the old Fort situated on the South Edge of the Lake Ontario, mounting five small Cannon towards the Lake and surrounded with a very weak Stone Wall, and that the Inside of this Fort is fit only to contain provisions and Stores; and the whole Fort would be of little or no Defence against an Enemy; Wherefore in order to protect it, together with the Harbour, a strong Log Fort mounting sixteen Cannon with Barracks for a Garrison of 300 Men was built last year on a high point opposite to the Fort on the East Side of the River, from whence it commands both that and the Harbour there at 450 yards distance, as also the Lake (which is at 100 yards distance from it) and the Country round it; And on the West Side of the old Fort, at the distance of about 450 yards from it, was built on an Eminence, which commands it, as also the Lake (which is 150 Yards from it) and the Country round it, a Regular Fort of a square Form with Bastions built of Earth and Masonry, and mounted with eight Cannon, with Barracks for a Garrison of 200 Men, and that Mr. Mackellar the Engineer en second, and one of the practitioner Engineers are sent to Oswego to add such Works, as shall be found necessary further to strengthen it.

His Excellency acquainted the Council, that as to the State of the Provisions and Stores in the several Magazines at the Conajohara Falls, German Flatts, Oneida Carrying place, and at Oswego itself, six Months provisions in the whole for 7000 Men were design'd to be lay'd in at these several places in proportion to the Number of Men to be posted in each of them; But what the present State of provisions at each of those places is does not yet appear, any further than that

200 Whale-Boat loads and about 500 Battoe loads have been sent from Schenectada to Oswego since the 1st of April last, where it is suppos'd the greatest part of it is arriv'd, and that the transportation of the Remainder of the Provisions propos'd to be sent to Oswego for the Support of the Forces to be employ'd there and the necessary Stores will take up untill the middle of July.

That the Provincial Troops voted for the Expedition against Crown point amount to 8800, Officers included, but from the Accounts, he hath lately receiv'd, he expects they will not produce more than 7000, inclusive of Officers; that part of those will be necessary for garrisoning Fort Edward and Fort William Henry, and escorting Provisions and Stores from Albany to those Forts; That he expects, they will be join'd by 100 or 200 Indians, and that he hath rais'd one Company of Rangers consisting of 70 privates, with proper Officers to harrass the Enemy upon Lake Champlain, and in scouting Parties by Land as far as Montreal, and to procure Intelligence; and is raising out of those Forces three more such Companies to be employ'd in the same Service.

That for an Account of the Strength of the French at Ticonderoge [1] and Crown point, he must referr them to the Intelligence, he receiv'd this Morning from Lake George, which from former Accounts he has receiv'd of their Numbers and Works appears to him to be depended upon.

His Excellency then proceeded to acquaint the Council, that as the Strength of the 50th and 51st Regiments and the four Independent Companies, with the Provincial Regiment of New Jersey will fall so far short of the Number of Troops judg'd requisite by the last Council of War to be employ'd on the Lake Ontario against the French Forts there this Year, and the Provincial Troops rais'd for the Expedition against Crown point fall so short likewise of the Number of Troops thought sufficient by the same Council for the Reduction of the French Forts at that place; it seems impracticable with these Troops even in Conjunction with his Majesty's 44th

---

[1] This fortress is occasionally referred to as Tionderoge as well as by the better-known name Ticonderoga.

and 48th Regiments to carry on the Expeditions upon the Lake Ontario and at Crown point, at the same time (as was propos'd to be done by the last Council of War) with a prospect of Success; and therefore desir'd the Opinion and Advice of the Council upon the Disposition of the two last mention'd Regiments, in giving which he desir'd they would consider.

1st. What Number of Troops they were of Opinion would be sufficient to put Oswego in a proper State of Defence, and to keep open the Communication between Albany and that place.

2dly. Whether if the 44th and 48th Regiments, which are judg'd to have about 1500 Men fit for Action, should be employ'd upon the Lake Ontario, together with what might be spar'd for that Service out of the 50th, 51st, and the New Jersey Regiments, and four Independent Companies of New York, with four Companies daily expected from North Carolina, would be a sufficient Force for attempting the Reduction of the French Forts at Niagara or on the Lake Ontario; and whether it would be adviseable to leave the securing of the Country Northward of the City of Albany, as also that City, to the Provincial Troops rais'd for the Expedition against Crown point.

3dly. Whether if the 44th and 48th Regiments should be employ'd in Conjunction with the before mention'd Provincial Forces, to attempt the Reduction of the French Forts at Ticonderoge and Crown point, they would be a sufficient Force for that Service.

His Excellency then proceeded to observe to the Council, that as from Sir William Johnson's success hitherto with the Indians of the Six Nations he found, he could have no Dependence on them for keeping out Parties to scout the Woods and keep the Communication with Oswego open thro' their Country; and it appear'd from one of Sir William's Letters, that he despair'd of keeping open the Communication without the Assistance of some Companies of Rangers fit for that Service, he was raising four such Companies of Rangers; part of which he design'd to employ in procuring

Intelligence and harrassing the Enemy in their own Country, and desir'd their Opinion and Advice upon the Utility of such Companies for his Majesty's Service in this Country.

His Excellency also propos'd to the Council to have a practicable Road made from the German Flatts to Oswego as soon as might be.

The Council having maturely consider'd and debated upon the several Points lay'd before them by his Excellency for their Opinion and Advice, were unanimously of Opinion.

1st. That 1300 Men would be necessary for putting Oswego into a proper State of Defence; and that for keeping open the Communication between Schenectada and Oswego, it was necessary to have 50 Men posted at the Oswego Falls, 200 at the Oneida Carrying place, 150 at the German Flatts, and 150 at the Conajohara Falls; which Troops together with the four Companies of Rangers propos'd to be employ'd by his Excellency in the manner, he hath mention'd, they judge would be sufficient for securing Oswego, and the Communication between that Place and Schenectada; And as they were of Opinion that the 50th and 51st and the New Jersey Regiments together with the four Independent Companies of New York, and four North Carolina Companies should not be depended upon for producing above 2000 Men fit for present Service, they advis'd his Excellency to employ the whole of these Regiments and Companies in the abovesaid Service.

2dly. That the 44th and 48th Regiments together with what could be spar'd out of the aforesaid Regiments and Companies for attempting the Reduction of the French Forts at Niagara or on the Lake Ontario, were not a sufficient Force for that Service, especially as it appears by the Minutes of the Council of War held at New York on the 12th and 13th of December last, which was compos'd of the principal Governors upon this Continent and his Majesty's Field Officers then present, that they were unanimously of Opinion that 6000 Troops at least were necessary for that purpose, and that it is not adviseable to leave the securing of the Country to the Northward of the City of Albany together with that City to the provincial Troops rais'd for the Expedition against Crown point.

3dly. That the 44th and 48th Regiments with the Provincial Troops appear to be, from the Intelligence of the Enemy's Strength, a sufficient Force to attempt the Reduction of the French Forts at Ticonderoge and Crown point; but that for the present those two Regiments do remain where they are now encamp'd, and that immediate Preparations be made for joining them with the Provincials in the Reduction of Crownpoint, that being the only Way at present, where they can be of use in annoying the Enemy.

4thly. That the Ranging Companies mention'd by his Excellency are necessary for his Majesty's Service, and they are of Opinion, that his Excellency should have as many more such Companies rais'd, as will make up the Number of them ten to be employ'd in keeping the Communication open between Schenectada and Oswego, and with our Advanc'd Forts, procuring Intelligence, surprizing and cutting off the Enemy's Convoys, and Stores, and harrassing them in Canada by scouting parties in every way they can.

5thly. They are unanimously of Opinion, that a practicable Road be made, as soon as conveniently may be, from the German Flatts to Oswego.

Lastly, That it appears to this Council very necessary further to strengthen Fort Edward, and to build a Fort at South Bay in the Way to Crown point; the former being a post of the utmost Consequence as a deposit for Stores and Provisions, and in the Center of all the different Routes to Crown point, the other commanding the Route, by which the Baron Dieskau came to attack Fort Edward, and by which all parties of the Enemy do come to invest our Northern Frontier, and which would cover our Convoys of Provisions for the Expedition against Crown point from the Insults of the Enemy.

a true Copy

WM. ALEXANDER Secy.

Endorsed:
Copy. Minutes of a Council of War held at Albany the 25th of May 1756. In Maj. Genl. Shirley's of June 23d, 1756.

WILLIAM SHIRLEY TO CHARLES HARDY [1]

Albany, May 27th, 1756.

SIR,

I inclose your Excellency a Copy of the Minutes of a Council of War held at Albany the 25th: Instant, which I have not done nor shall do to any other Governor, and now communicate it to your Excellency in confidence that you will not disclose it to your Council, or any other person whatever untill the 44th, and 48th Regiments shall actually Join the Provincial Troops in the Expedition against Crown Point, in case such a Junction shall ever take effect.

No person besides the Members of the Council of War and my Secretary, except my first Aid de Camp, my under Secretary, and the Captain of the Train of Artillery is privy to it. I believe it may be likewise necessary to communicate that part, which respects the Destination of the 44th: and 48th: Regimt: to General Winslow; and to induce an Expectation in all the Officers and others that those two Regiments are destin'd for Oswego; a Regulation of the Allottment of Battoes allow'd by the Crown for carrying the Officers Baggage, etca: will be given out in Publick orders, which may we hope keep their real Destination from Transpiring.

I promis'd your Excellency at New York to forward the making additional works at Fort Edward; And I shall accordingly give Instructions to General Winslow for that purpose, as also for building a Fort at South Bay; which will, I apprehend, be the most ready and effectual Way of having both done at the Joint expence of the Colonies; I only wait for the Opinion of Capt. Montresor as to the manner of doing it, which will be founded, with regard to

[1] P. R. O., C. O. 5, 47. A transcript is in the Library of Congress.

Fort Edward, upon a Report of Engineer Gordon, whom I have order'd to Survey it, as also Fort William Henry, and Expect him here in a day or two.

I also inclose your Excellency a Copy of the Examination of a French prisoner Taken by Capt. Rogers between Ticonderoge and the Enemy's advanced Guard; which will shew their Strength and motions; Likewise the Copy of Sir William Johnson's Conference with some Indians of the Six Nations at Fort Johnson on the 12th Instant; upon which I am to acquaint your Excellency, That Sir William is at last determin'd to go to Onondago, and I expect from thence after the meeting is ended, to Oswego.[1]

General Winslow, since his Arrival here, hath much alter'd the appearance of every part of the preparations making for the expedition, and I am now in hopes, things may be put under some Regulation, and in a proper Channel; I shall give him the utmost assistance in my power for extricating every thing out of the disorder, which he found them in.

I am to acknowledge the Receipt of your Excellencys Favour of the 16th: instant: Mr. Alexander has now the Account of the Balances due to the Several Waggoners for Waggon-hire etca:, and they have receiv'd Orders to come for their Money.

I am with Great Esteem
Sir
Your Excellencys most Humble
and most Obedient Servant W. SHIRLEY.

His Excellency Sir Charles Hardy.

WILLIAM SHIRLEY TO HENRY FOX [2]

Albany, June 13th, 1756.

SIR,

I have the Honour of your Letters dated the 13th and 31st of March; and shall in Obedience to his Majesty's

[1] See Johnson to the Lords of Trade, May 28, Doct. Hist. New York, 2, 418.

[2] P. R. O., C. O. 5, 46. Transcripts are in the Library of Congress and in the Parkman Papers in the Mass. Hist. Society.

Commands, signifi'd to me in the latter of them, repair to England with all possible Expedition, after delivering to Colonel Webb (whose Arrival at this Place from New York he informs me I may daily expect) all such Papers as relate to the King's Service, and having Notice of the Frigate, which the Lords of Admiralty have order'd to receive me on board, pursuant to the Directions, which you have inform'd me his Majesty hath been pleas'd to give them for that purpose.[1]

I am much oblig'd to you, Sir, for the high Pleasure you have given me in acquainting me with his Majesty's gracious Acceptance of my Services, and that he intends to give me a New Mark of his Royal Favour.

Upon Colonel Webb's communicating to me (as you are pleas'd to inform me he has Directions to do) his Orders and Instructions, and concerting with me in what manner it may be most adviseable to employ the King's Forces, now in America, untill the Earl of Loudown [*sic*] or Major General Abercromby shall arrive there with the Regular Troops, Artillery, and Stores, which his Majesty has order'd to be sent from England; I will give him, Sir, pursuant to your Directions all the lights, that are in my Power, to assist him in the Execution of the Commission, with which he is charg'd.

I have the honour to be with the Highest respect,

Sir,

Your most Humble

and most Obedient Servant,

W. SHIRLEY.

The Rt. Honble. Henry Fox one of his Majesty's principal Secretaries of State.

Endorsed:
  Albany June 13th. 1756.
    M. G. SHIRLEY.
R Augt. 6th.

[1] See letters Fox to Shirley, March 13 and 31, *ante*, p. 425 and note.

WILLIAM SHIRLEY TO HENRY FOX[1]

Albany, June 14th, 1756.

SIR,

With your Letter of the 13th of March, directed to me as Major General, I had the Honour to receive from you three others of the same Date, two of them (I suppose) Circular ones, number'd 1. 2., and the other a separate one, directed to the Governor of the Massachusetts Bay; The two former of these I have transmitted to Lieut. Governor Phipps by Express, that he may lose no time for convening the Massachusetts Assembly and Council, and acquainting them with the Grant of £115,000, which the parliament had, upon his Majesty's Recommendation, made to the Colonies concern'd for their past Services, and as an Encouragement for them to continue to act with the same Spirit and Vigour; As Also with his Majesty's Expectations of their complying with what was demanded of them for his Service in those Letters; and have us'd the best Endeavours, I can at this Distance, to induce them to pay the most dutifull Regard to what his Majesty requires.

Concerning these two Letters, Sir, I have nothing to observe in particular, except what regards the number of Provincial Troops, which it appears in that mark'd No. 1, his Majesty expects the New England Colonies and the Province of New York should raise for his Service this Year. I have acquainted you in my Letter of the 7th of May, that a much larger Number of Troops was voted by them to be rais'd this year than was the last; and that those Colonies, besides bearing that part of the Expence of the Troops, which his Majesty expects they shall, are by their Votes to find them with Provisions and Military Stores in proportion to their respective Quotas; so that his Majesty's signifying his Intentions to supply those provincial Troops with provisions and Stores out of his own Magazines ought to have the most powerfull Effect to make the Colonies comply with

[1] P. R. O., C. O. 5, 46. A transcript is in the Library of Congress.

what his Majesty expects from them, as should likewise the great Encouragements given to the Soldiers, have upon them to induce them to inlist into his Service.[1]

As to the separate Letter, Sir, which regards the 2000 New England Irregulars rais'd for his Majesty's Service in Nova Scotia in the Year 1755; the State of that Matter is as follows: Mr. Lawrence's proposal to me by Lieut. Colonel Monckton was to have them rais'd for six Months only, but as I judg'd it would be more adviseable to have them inlisted for a Year, I inlisted them for that time.

The Dispatch, with which these Troops were to be rais'd, that they might be compleated in time for effecting the Service, to which they were destin'd; the Necessity, there was at the same time that my own and Sir William Pepperrell's Regiments should likewise be rais'd soon enough to take the Field in the ensuing Campaigne, and the View, I had of bringing the four Colonies of New England, and the Province of New York into raising 4000 Men for an Attempt against Crown-point in the same Year (which likewise took place) made it impracticable to enlist the 2000 Men for Nova Scotia for a longer term than one year.

They were accordingly inlisted for that time, and had Certificates given them that they should be discharg'd at the End of it, or sooner if his Majesty's Service in Nova Scotia would Admit.

Soon after the Surrender of Beau Sejour, some small Animosities happen'd, as I have been inform'd, between the Commanding Officer of the Expedition and the principal Officers of the Irregulars, which were afterwards increas'd by an Order given in Nova Scotia, whilst the New England Regiment subsisted as a Corps, for inlisting such of the Soldiers of it into the King's Regiments, as could be got to do it; this was communicated to the Massachusetts Assembly in so unfavourable a light with regard to the Men's being,

---

[1] On June 9, Governor Hopkins of Rhode Island recommended that colony to raise more troops for Crown Point (Kimball, Corres. Col. Govs. of R. I. 2, 216), and on June 22, acts providing for troops and additional provisions were passed (R. I. Col. Rec. 5, 498–501).

as it was pretended, drove to it by Inconveniencies, which they suffer'd in the Service, beyond what the Regulars did, that it inflam'd the whole Province during my Absence, and produc'd a very warm Application of the Assembly to me upon my Return, desiring I would order all the New England Men, who had thus inlisted into the King's Regiments to be discharg'd from them, and forthwith to send Transport Vessells to bring the New England Battaillons back from Nova Scotia to Boston.

In my Answer to the Assembly's Message I moderated their Demands for having the New England Men, who had inlisted into the King's Regiments, immediately discharg'd, by confining it to such only as were born in New England or had Families or near Relations in it, and actually desir'd to be dismiss'd; and upon assuring them that the other Soldiers of the two Battaillons should be discharg'd and return'd home at the End of their Inlistments, if they requir'd it, and sending some Vessells to Halifax to lye ready there for the transportation of one of the Battaillons, I satisfy'd them, and hope all Heart-burnings on this Account are at an End.

When I sent the Vessels to Halifax I advis'd Governor Lawrence to endeavour to gain the Men of both the Battaillons Consent to continue in Nova Scotia under their own Officers, for such time as he thought his Majesty's Service might require it, by offering them a small Bounty; and wrote Letters to the Commanding Officers of both Battaillons, requiring them to exert their utmost Influence with the Men under their Command to induce them to consent to stay longer; which the Officers assur'd me they did; But Governor Lawrence informs me, that all Endeavours were in vain; that very few or none of the Soldiers could be prevail'd on to stay; and he thereupon order'd both Battaillons to be sent to Boston; which indeed could not be avoided without breaking faith with the Men, by holding them against their Consent beyond the terms of their Inlistments, and by that means producing bad Consequences to his Majesty's Service not only in Nova Scotia, but all over the Continent.

Neither of these Battaillons was return'd to Boston when I set out from thence for this place; But as several of the Officers, and a great part of the Men are very fit for the Duty of Rangers, and I found such Companies will be of great Utility in every part of the present Expedition, I left Orders for raising five such Companies out of them, to consist of 60 privates each; But have not yet Returns of the progress made in raising them, or whether they can be rais'd; but hope some of them at least will.

> I have the honour to be with the Highest respect,
> Sir,
> Your most Humble and
> most Obedient Servant
> W. SHIRLEY.

P. S. June 15. I have just now receiv'd an Acct. that two Companies of Rangers (I suppose of 100 privates each) are inlisted in Nova Scotia out of the best Men of the New England Battaillon, which was posted on the Isthmus, which I hope will be of considerable Service there.

> W. S.

The Rt. Honble. Henry Fox one of his ⎫
Majesty's principal Secretaries of State. ⎭

Endorsed:
Albany — June 14th, 1756. M. G. SHIRLEY.
R Augt. 6th.

WILLIAM SHIRLEY TO HENRY FOX[1]

Albany, June 23d, 1756.

SIR,

I have the Honour to transmit you a Copy of a Minute of Council of War held at this place the 25th of May;[2] and from the Progress made in the Preparations for the Expedi-

[1] P. R. O., C. O. 5, 46. A transcript is in the Library of Congress.
[2] Printed *ante*, p. 453.

tion against Crown Point since that time, have reason to think that the Provincial Troops will be ready in every Respect to take the Field in the first Week of July; as are now the 44th and 48th Regiments, which wait only for the Earl of Loudoun's arrival and determining the place of their Destination.

In my letter of the 7th May [1] to you, Sir, I mentioned that the 44th, 48th, 50th and 51st Regiments were near Compleated; I judg'd so from the Accounts given me of the Number of Recruits rais'd for each; but upon the last Returns made to me of their present Strength I find myself deceived; The four Regiments dont exceed 3100 Rank and File Men; This hath happened through very great Desertions in each of those Regiments, and the detention of Indented Servants (who had Inlisted) in Prison, and besides these Causes in the 50th and 51st Regiments, through Mortality in them, ever since their arrival at Oswego, particularly this Winter, and discharges of Men out of them, on Account of their being rendered unfit for Service by Sickness.

The New Jersey Regiment, which the Colony kept up in the Winter, in order to be ready to take the Field as soon as I should Call upon them, this Spring, and have with their Colonel been of great Service, is recruited to 450 Rank and File Men: I have indulg'd his Majesty's four Independent Companies of New York with every thing that Sir Charles Hardy the Govr. of that Province told me was necessary to be done, in order to put it into his Power to Recruit them, but I find from Reviews taken of them, that the four will not produce more than 150 Men fit for Duty; The four North Carolina Companies of the Complement of 50 Men each, who are now Upon their March for the Carrying Place at Connajoharia Falls, upon the Mohawk's River dont exceed 155 Rank and File Men.

I have this Morning heard from the Report of Masters of Sloops from New York that Otway's and the Highland Regiment are arrived there with Major General Abercromby;

[1] Printed *ante*, p. 442.

and am, as I have been many days, in hourly Expectation of Colonel Webb's arrival here.

I am with the Highest Respect
Sir, Your most Humble,
and most Obedient Servant,
W. SHIRLEY.

Rt. Honble. Henry Fox Esqr.
One of his Majesty's principal Secretaries of State. }

Endorsed:
Albany June 23d. 1756. M. G. SHIRLEY.
R Augt. 6th.

WILLIAM SHIRLEY TO JAMES ABERCROMBY[1]

Albany, June 27th, 1756.

SIR,

As you did me the Honour yesterday to Communicate to me his Majesty's Orders and Instructions to you for Carrying on his Service in North America in the ensuing Campaigne, I shall now, in Obedience to the King's Commands, give you all the Lights, that are in my power, to assist you in the Execution of the Commission, with which you are Charged.

The Inclosed Copy of the Minutes of a Council of War held in this City the 25th of last May,[2] with the Papers referred to in it, will shew you the unanimous Opinion of that Council concerning the most adviseable manner of employ-

---

[1] P. R. O., C. O. 5, 46. Another copy is in C. O. 5, 47. Transcripts are in the Library of Congress and in the Parkman Papers in the Mass. Hist. Society. Shirley inclosed a copy of this letter in his letter to Henry Fox of July 4, *post*, p. 478.

[2] See Minutes of Albany Council of May 25, *ante*, p. 453. The attention paid by Shirley in this letter to conditions at Oswego, means of communication thereto, and dangers from Indians thereabouts is to be borne in mind when reading Loudoun's statement in his letter of Aug. 29 (*post*, p. 521) that the defenseless condition of Oswego had been concealed from Abercromby by Shirley. See also *post*, pp. 538–539.

ing his Majesty's Troops in the 44th, 48th, 50th, 51st Regiments, and four Independent Companies of New York, and the Irregular Troops rais'd in the four Colonies of New England, and the Provinces of New York, New Jerseys, and North Carolina; Returns of the Strength of all which I have ordered to be lay'd before you, together with returns of the Brigade of Engineers and Train of Artillery now here, and Lists of the Ordnance and Military Stores now at Oswego, and at Forts Edward upon Hudson's River and William Henry at Lake George, and this place; as also of the addition of Artillery and Stores proposed to be provided for the Service upon the Lake Ontario and Lake George; likewise a State of the Magazines of Provisions now at Oswego and Lake George, with an Account of those daily carrying up there, and to Saratoga.

It is necessary, Sir, that I should acquaint you here, that the Provincial Troops rais'd by the four Governments of New England and New York are, by Acts of Assembly, destin'd and Confin'd to Act in his Majesty's Service in the Expedition against Crown Point; But those raised in New Jersey and North Carolina are to be employed in any part of the present Expedition in North America, where his Majesty's Commander in Chief shall think proper.

Besides the Regular and Irregular Troops mentioned in the Minute of the Council of War to be posted at Oswego and between that place and Schenectada, I have given Instructions to Sir William Johnson to use his best Endeavours to engage a large Body of Indians of the Six Nations to Stand ready to act this year with his Majesty's Forces in any Attempt, that may be made against the French Settlements upon the Lake Ontario, etc., which he hath given me Encouragement to hope he shall be able to do; and I have the greatest reason to hope, he will be able to effect it, as the Indians of those Nations, which came to me at Oswego the last Year, promised to join me there this Spring against the French in greater numbers: And Sir William Johnson hath further assured me, that he will use his best Endeavours to engage at least 100 more of them to join the English Forces in the Expedition against Crown Point; but he apprehends it will be difficult for him to do that. Since the holding of the Council of War at this place, I have rais'd a Company of the Stockbridge or River Indians, consisting of 45 Men, Commanded by Indian Officers, to be employed in gaining Intelligence and committing Hostilities against the French between Lake George and Montreal; and am in Expectation, that another Company of Indians, living on the East side of Hudson's River, below this place, will come in, to be employed in the same Service.

In Order to prevent his Majesty's Service from Suffering in this Campaigne the many Inconveniences and Disappointments, which happened to it the last Year, for want of a sufficient number of Battoemen to transport the necessary Provisions there, I caus'd to be inlisted early this Spring forty Companies of Battoemen, consisting of 50 Men each, a Captain and Assistant; the whole to be under the Command of a Director General of the Battoes, a Copy of whose Commission and Instructions you have inclos'd.

The raising of these Companies was the more necessary, as the Road between Schenectada and Oswego hath been greatly infested by the French Indians all this year, so that Small Parties of Battoes, which attempted to go thither, have been cutt off; and it would have been impracticable to have thrown in a sufficient Quantity of Provisions and Stores for the support of the Garrison at Oswego, and the Service on the Lake Ontario, without transporting them in large Squadrons of Battoes containing a strong Force towards securing their Passage upon the Water and over the Carrying Places: This body of Battoemen thus marshal'd might likewise be a considerable additional Strength to the Forces at Oswego, if employed in any Enterprize upon the Lake Ontario, etc.

In Order to clear the Obstructions as much as might be in the Navigation to Oswego through the Mohawk and other Rivers, and particularly the Wood Creek, and to shorten the Oneida Carrying Place (which hath, as has been represented to me, been accordingly reduc'd from eight to one Mile, besides Clearing the Wood Creek, etc. of some Obstructions)

I caused to be inlisted likewise early this Spring a Working Party, consisting of 80 Men, under the direction of one James Fairservice, a Copy of whose Instructions is inclosed.

It may not be improper to observe here, Sir, that it would be of very great Importance to his Majesty's Service if a successfull Attempt could be made this Campaigne against the French Fort at Niagara, for this reason in particular (among others) that the gaining or losing the Indians to the Interest of the English seems very much to depend upon the Activity and Success of the Operations this Year upon the Lake Ontario: And as it is possible that the Minutes of the two Councils of War, held at Oswego on the 18th, and 27th [1] Sepr. 1755, may give some lights into the adviseableness or impracticability of making such Attempt this Year, I have inclos'd Copies of them.

As it appears to me from the intelligence we have been able to gain hitherto, that the most adviseable Route for the English to take in order to attack Ticonderoge and Crown Point, is to march by Land on the West side of Lake George, to the Enemy's most advanced Works upon it, being five miles on this side of Ticonderoge, and to dislodge them from thence, which will secure the landing of our heavy Artillery and Stores at that place, from whence they may be transported by Land through a practicable Road either to Ticonderoge or Crown Point; I propos'd, in order to facilitate the taking of that Post, by attacking it with a Floating Battery, from the Lake at the same time that it is attack'd by Land, the Construction of such a Battery for this Service to his Majesty's Chief Engineer here, whose Report to me thereupon, together with his Report concerning the strengthning of Fort Edward upon Hudson's River and Fort William Henry at Lake George is Inclosed.

Upon the taking of Crown Point one or more Vessels of Force should be forthwith built upon Lake Champlain.

As to the Attempt propos'd and advis'd in the Council of War at New York to be made this Year with 3000 Men of the Western Colonies against Fort Duquesne, I recommended it

[1] For these Councils of War, see notes, *ante*, pp. 264 and 289.

to those Governments, and appointed Lieut. Colonel Sharpe, Govr. of Maryland to the Chief Command of the Expedition; But from the Accounts, I have received from him and the Govrs. of Virginia, and Pensilvania, nothing is at present likely to be effected in it.[1]

Govr. Dinwiddie, in his Letter of the 24th of May last, informs me "that he is endeavouring to Compleat their "Provincial Regiment to 1500 Men, with whom that Prov- "ince must remain on the defensive to protect their Frontiers, "having no great Guns or Engineers to make an Attack on "Fort Du Quesne; and that the two Proprietary Govern- "ments seem to remain unactive in not raising any Men to "their Assistance."

Governor Sharpe, in his Letter of the 14 April last,[2] acquaints me, that there was no appearance of his Assembly's raising any Men towards the Expedition; but that on the contrary they were upon the point of disbanding the Single Company which they had maintain'd the preceeding Year: And Govr. Morris hath informed me that the Assembly of Pensilvania have made Provision for the Support of 1500 Men for the protection of their own Frontiers, but for raising none towards an Expedition against Fort Du Quesne.

As to the State of his Majesty's Forces in Nova Scotia, the New England Irregulars, which were Sent there last Year, are all of them except two Companies of Rangers, which have been lately form'd out of them in Nova Scotia; and a few others which inlisted into the three Regiments of Regulars posted there, discharged and returned to New England; the Returns of his Majesty's three Regiments and old Company of Rangers, which I have order'd to be lay'd before you, will shew you their Strength; and Colonel Lawrence, the Commanding Officer and Governor of that Province, assures me, that they are but barely sufficient to do the Duty requisite at the Several Posts within that Province.

[1] See Shirley to Governor Sharpe, May 16, 1756, *ante*, p. 446, and Dinwiddie to Shirley, Apr. 28 and May 24 (Dinwiddie Papers, 2, 394 and 428).

[2] Arch. of Md. 6, 389; and see note, *ante*, p. 434.

As it seems necessary, Sir, that You should be informed of the present State and Disposition of the Indians with regard to the English, I shall give you a brief Account of it; During my Residence at Oswego, and upon my Return from thence, in my Conferences with the Deputies sent to me from the Seneca, Cayuga, Onondago, and Oneida Indians, who are part of the Six Nations, I propos'd to them to build and Garrison Forts near their Several Castles for the better protection of their old Men, Wives, and Children in time of War: The two latter of those Nations accepted the Proposal and desired the Forts might be mounted with Cannon; and the Tuscarora Indians, another Branch of the Six Nations, sent me a Message to Albany, desiring they might have the like Forts and Garrisons, which I accordingly promised them they Should.

Since this Sir William Johnson hath informed me that the three last mentioned Nations have desired that those Forts may be forthwith erected and that the Cayuga's and Seneca's have signify'd to him the Same Request for themselves; Whereupon I gave Sir William Johnson Orders to Cause the Forts to be built and Garrisoned, as soon as may be, and afterwards sent him a Plan of a Fort drawn upon this occasion by Capt. Montresor, his Majesty's Chief Engineer here, with Directions to Conform to it.

It was propos'd that each of these Forts should mount 8 Small Cannon, be made capable of entertaining 120 Men upon an Emergency, and of being defended by a Garrison of 40 Men; and that the Garrison might have it in their power to make the Forts defensible against small Cannon, in case any should suddenly be brought to attack them, a sufficient number of spare Stockadoes and Sand Baggs were to be lodged in the Forts.

But upon Sir William Johnson's acquainting me, that he could not get the Forts constructed according to Mr. Montresor's Model by the Workmen he had employ'd, and transmitting me a Plan, upon which one or more of the Forts have begun to be built, and finding that unless that Plan was prosecuted, a full Stop must be put to the Works for want of

Engineers to attend it; which would have had a bad Effect upon the Indians, I directed Mr. Montresor to make such Improvements upon Sir William Johnson's Plan, as could be executed by the Workmen employed by him, and ordered the Work to be prosecuted upon the improved Plan which is Inclosed.[1]

And as the building of defensible Forts in those several Quarters of the Country of the Six Nations and Garrisoning them with English, seems to be the most effectual means of securing them and their Country to his Majesty against the Attempts of the French; I have ordered the Work to be prosecuted with the utmost Expedition.

During my Residence at Oswego I likewise propos'd to such of the Indians of the Six Nations, as were present, to have a Meeting and Council there this Summer with the Indians inhabiting the North side of the Lake Ontario and round the Lake Erie, and adjacent parts, in order to their holding a general Consultation for promoting their common Interest, maintaining a constant good Correspondence at Oswego by annual Councils, and disengaging the latter from interfering in the Quarrells between us and the French; and for this purpose I propos'd the opening a free Trade with those Foreign Indians at Oswego, and letting them have English Goods there in Exchange for their Furs, not only upon a much more advantageous Foot than the French could supply them for with theirs, but even than they have of late been supplied by the English.

The Indians of the Six Nations then present, accordingly promised me at Oswego, that their Sachems should meet me there for this purpose in the Summer; and I sent Messages to the foreign Indians to invite them to the meeting; from whom I have received favourable Answers with Promises that they will come to Oswego for that purpose.

Concerning this point, and that of building Forts in the Country of the Six Nations and Garrisoning them with English, Sir William Johnson, to whom I had given Instruc-

[1] On Mar. 29, Shirley directed Montresor to furnish engineers for Crown Point and Oswego.

tions to Impress them upon those Indians as much as possible, says in his Letter to me, dated from Fort Johnson the 8th of March, "nothing could be more pleasing to the Six "Nations and their Allies, than the Promise he made them "concerning the Article of Trade, and thinks nothing deserves "our Attention more than that, and fortifying their Coun- "tries, and Garrisoning them; for that he is Convinced "were those two Articles Settled to their mind, every thing "else would go on successfully; Wherefore he doubts not, but "I would contribute all in my power towards accomplishing "those two Grand Points."

For compassing the former of those two Points it happens that the late Expiration of an Act of Assembly of New York, which had for Several years burthened the Indian Trade at Oswego with a considerable Duty, will greatly facilitate it, and I have accordingly directed Sir William Johnson, who is to be at Oswego in a short time, to meet the Foreign Indians there, and the Commanding Officer of the King's Forces at that place, to regulate the prices of the Indian Goods at Oswego; so that the Indians will now have them at a Rate much Cheaper than before; and to enable Sir William Johnson to provide proper Presents for those Indians and to Carry on the Forts now building in the Country of the Six Nations, Garrison them etc., I have supplyed him with £5,000 Sterling, (being the Sum he required) out of the Contingent Money; which with £5,000 more, advanced to him on Account of the Indians before by the late General Braddock and myself, in his life time, pursuant to the General's Orders, amounts to £10,000, *and* is to be accompted for.[1]

Sir William Johnson hath not been able yet to bring the Indians of the Six Nations to keep out Scouting Parties to range the Passes and places necessary to be kept clear, in order to Secure the Communication to Oswego through their own Country, for want of doing which, Mischief hath

---

[1] On Mar. 17, 1756, Shirley drew an order upon Abraham Mortier in favor of Johnson for £5000 sterling (Johnson **Manuscripts**, N. Y. State Library, 26, 1) as is here stated.

been done by the Enemy Indians upon the Oneida Carrying Place; and upon my pressing him to do it, he tells in his Letter of the 10th May last, "that he wish'd the Companies "of Rangers, I had mentioned to him in a former Letter were "ready to go upon Duty, when he hoped to be able to join "Indians with them, and that unless that Method takes place, "he *despair'd of the Communication to Oswego being secur'd.*" This is the State of the Northern Indians.

As to the State and Disposition of the Southern Indians, with regard to the English; By the Accounts, I have received from the Governor of Virginia it appears, that in the beginning of the Spring he had hopes of engaging 1000 of the Cherokee Indians to assist the English against the French, upon the Terms of building them a Fort in their own Country for the protection of their old Men, Wives, and Children against the Enemy; which Fort is I am Informed now building; and that he had fitted out an Expedition against one of the Towns of the Shawanese Indians, which hath miscarried; Since this the Colony of Virginia hath been so much Infested with Incursions of the Indians, that the Governor apprehended the Town of Winchester to be in such danger from them, that he determined to draft the Militia of ten Counties and send 4000 of them to oppose their Progress; But in his Letter of the 24th May he gives me the following Account Vizt., "that the Enemy had marched over the Alleghenney "Mountains for Fort Du Quesne, whether to return with "Stronger Force is uncertain, but that he think's it's proper "to be prepared for them."

By the Accounts I had from the Governor of Pensilvania, it appears that in last Summer the Susquehanah, Shawanese, and Delaware Indians, broke out into Hostilities against that Colony and lay'd many of their Settlements waste; that they have rais'd in the whole 1500 Men as was before observed, for the defence of their Frontier; and have built a Line of Forts on the West Side of the Kittatenny Mountains extending from New Jersey to Maryland; that on the [*sic* 1] the Governor with the advice of the Council,

¹ The date is not given by Shirley.

declared Warr against the Delaware Indians, and was upon the point of making an Attempt with 300 Men against one of the Shawanese Towns; But upon Sir William Johnson's representing to me that he had made up the Quarrell of those Indians against Pensilvania through the Interposition of the Six Nations; and that in Consequence of that, there was to be a Meeting of several of the Delaware and Susquehanah Indians with those of the Six Nations at the Castle of the Onondagoes, in order to make a final Settlement of that matter, and on his pressing me, in his Letter of the 24th of April, to interfere in the matter, and prevent the Commission of Hostilities on the part of the Pensilvanians until the Result of the Council at Onondago should be known; I did it; and the Governor and Council thereupon declared a Cessation of Hostilities for thirty days, and lay'd aside their intended Expedition against the Shawanese for the present.

Sir William Johnson is now gone up to the Council at Onondago; and what the Result of that will be is not yet known.

About two Months ago I received 10,000 Stand of Arms, with a proportion of military Stores from the Board of Ordnance with his Majesty's directions to issue them in such proportions to the Colonies, as I should judge most for his Service; and inclosed is an Account of those Issued and those remaining in his Majesty's Magazine at Boston from the Comptroller of the Ordnance there.

If any other Points should occur to you, in which you think I may give further light into the State of his Majesty's Service under your care, I shall be glad to receive your Commands upon them.

I have the Honour to be with the greatest Regard and Esteem,

Sir,

Your most Humble, and
most Obedient Servant

W. SHIRLEY.

Major General Abercromby
a true Copy
WM. ALEXANDER, Secy.

Endorsed:
  Copy
    Letter from General
      Shirley to General Abercromby
        dated Albany June 27th 1756.
  in Maj. Genl. Shirley's of July 4th 1756.

WILLIAM SHIRLEY TO HENRY FOX [1]

New York July 4th 1756.

SIR,

I have the Honour to acquaint you that I am just now arriv'd here, after a passage of four Days and a half from Albany, where Major General Abercromby arriv'd the 25th of June in the Evening and Colonel Webb the next Morning, with a great part of Otway's Regiment; And the Remainder of it with all the Highland Regiment were disembark'd in good Health before I left that place: Upon the General's Arrival I receiv'd a Letter by him from Commodore Holmes dated the 20th of June, letting me know that he design'd to sail that Night from New York for Halifax, from whence he would order one of his Majesty's Frigates for carrying me to England; but does not say whether he intended to send it to this port or Boston; But I suppose to the latter; It will be necessary for me to go there, as the Sterling Castle, which brings the Money granted by Parliament to the four Colonies of New England, and the Provinces of New York and New Jerseys is, I hear, to make that her first port, and I am desirous of seeing the £30,000, £10,000, and £3,000 Sterling, which I lent the Provinces of New York and New Hampshire and Colony of Connecticutt, in order to raise Men, and make preparations for this Campaigne paid out of their respective Quotas of that Grant, before I leave North America.[2]

[1] P. R. O., C. O. 5, 46. Transcripts are in the Library of Congress and in the Parkman Papers in the Mass. Hist. Society.
[2] On June 30, Great Britain had transmitted to the American Colonies copies of the Commissions and Instructions respecting

The inclos'd Copy of my Letter to General Abercromby, with the Minute of the Council of War held at Albany the 25th of May last, of which I some Days ago transmitted you a Copy, will shew you, Sir, the general State of his Majesty's Service with regard to the preparations in North America for this year's Campaigne, and the Situation of Indian Affairs there: It seems certain that in all this Week at furthest 7000 provincials will be ready to march from Lake George for Ticonderoge and Crown point; and Magazines of provisions are lay'd in at Sarahtoga for the British Troops, which by the Opinion of the Council of War at Albany were design'd to march to Fort Edward and Fort William Henry upon the provincials quitting them, in order to protect that and the adjacent Country in their Absence, and to be ready at hand to support them in their Attempt against Ticonderoge etc., if there should be occasion.

And I can't but hope, from the forwardness of the preparations made for the Campaigne at Oswego likewise, that it may be practicable with the Forces, which his Majesty now hath between Lake George and the Lake Ontario to make some Attempt against the French from that place this Year, as well as against their Forts at Ticonderoge and Crown point; provided Otway's and the Highland Regiments shall be ready to move in time; which will depend upon the Arrival of their Tents and Camp Utensils from England, or being immediately provided with others here, if that is possible.

I have the pleasure, Sir, to acquaint you, that the Provincials are in high Spirits, and perswaded of Success, which I flatter myself there is a good prospect of if they enter upon Action in time; And I had the Satisfaction to find at a Consultation between myself, General Abercromby, Colonel Webb, General Winslow, and the Commanding Officer of the provincial Artillery [1] held the Day I left Albany, at the

the issuance of Letters of Marque, so that from the date of their arrival in America the war with France was fully authorized, after having been carried on over a year. For the order mentioned, see 1 Penna. Arch. 2, 684.   [1] Richard Gridley.

desire of General Abercromby, that there is a very fair prospect of a Right Understanding, good Agreement and Harmony's being maintain'd between the Regulars and Provincials, upon which much will depend; as also that General Abercromby and Colonel Webb seem'd, so far as we then enter'd into the propos'd Measures for carrying the Attempt against Crown point into Execution, to approve of them.

As I find all final Determinations are to wait for the Arrival of Lord Loudoun and both General Abercromby and Colonel Webb, with whom I have had a very free Communication, have press'd me more than once in the Strongest Terms to stay at New York, 'till my Lord Loudoun arrives there, as they are perswaded that my acquainting his Lordship in a personal Conference with my Sentiments of what may be the most adviseable plan of Operations for his Majesty's Service this Year, in the most explicit manner, would be a great Satisfaction to his Lordship, and may promote the Service,[1] I shall stay here a very few Days for that purpose, and hope I shall have an Opportunity of seeing his Lordship, as he hath been hourly expected here above this fortnight.

Four or five Days before I left Albany I had Intelligence sent me that the French have lately abandon'd their most advanc'd Post on Lake George, and seem to muster their whole Strength at Ticonderoge, except a small party of Troops, which they have at Crown point, at the first of which places it is judg'd they have three thousand Men, and eighteen Cannon of different Natures, with some Mortars.

I have the honour to be with the Highest Respect,
Sir,
Your most Humble and
most Obedient Servant,
W. SHIRLEY.

[1] In like manner, Governor Dinwiddie wrote Shirley on July 1, relative to Lord Loudoun taking up the campaign against Fort Duquesne: "if he send proper officers and artillery it may be conducted to advantage," but he added that the Indians were on the point of making war. (Dinwiddie Papers, 2, 451.) Shirley's influence with Loudoun seems to have been overestimated.

Rt. Honble. Henry Fox, one of his   ⎫
Majesty's principal Secretaries of State. ⎭

Endorsed:
New York July 4th. 1756.
  Majr. G. Shirley
R Augt. 6th.

WILLIAM SHIRLEY TO ROBERT HUNTER MORRIS

[Extract][1]

New York, July 5th, 1756.

Dear Sir,

The Day I embark'd from Albany I had the pleasure of your Nephew, Capt. Staats's Arrival there, and as he was desirous of making you a Visit before he went to Oswego, I have brought him here with me for that Purpose.

---

[1] 1 Penna. Arch. 2, 693. The warm friendship existing between Shirley, Alexander, and Morris is shown here, and is emphasized by Shirley's letter of July 12. The consent of Morris to the departure of Alexander had been obtained. Shirley writes (*ibid.* 698) : —

The light in which you consider Mr. Alexander's going to England with me is I flatter myself a just one, and it will give me the highest pleasure to have that Voyage prove of real Service to him in the future course of his life.

We have followed your Advice in our application for his mothers leave; It was open'd with a letter from me to her, and followed the evening after with a Visit; we could not have desir'd better success with the Old Lady than we have met with, the whole affair was freely and fully talked over between her and me, her mind is perfectly settled to it, I think I might say she intirely approves of it; and it is Certainly a Circumstance of the greatest satisfaction to us in this Case, that Colonel Barton, and those of the best Sense, who are friends to us both, most earnestly press Mr. Alexander's going to England at this conjuncture, as indispensably necessary.

An happy meeting with you here for a few hours would Crown every thing, and I will not dispair of it.

After expressing the hope that Morris will find a pleasanter

He will acquaint you in what forwardness our Preparations are for opening the Campaign both upon Lake George and Lake Ontario; and I refer you to him for an Account of them, with only saying, that they exceed even my own Expectations; and that there is a very fair prospect of carrying our Points in a great Measure this year against the French at both places, if the carrying our preparations into Execution is not retarded beyond its just time.

   *   *   *   *   *   *   *

I am sorry to find that Mr. Alexander and I have miss'd of your Letter in answer to his and mine upon the Subject of his going with me to England; about which I am very anxious as I find his presence there may be absolutely necessary to clear up some Articles of the very large Accounts, which must be transmitted to England from him, your Nephew, Lewis Morris, and Mr. Ewing, and will be examin'd into at the Offices, &c at home; you are very sensible, my Dear Sir, how greatly any Difficulties in passing them would embarrass me as well as them; and how incapable I must be, without Mr. Alexander's Assistance in clearing them up; and consequently of what near Concern, and necessity to me, the Instance I ask of your Friendship is, that he may have your Consent to go with me; which I hope is contain'd in the Letters that are gone to Albany.

position than "the Chair of Government in Pensilvania" Shirley continues : —

Many thanks to you, Dear Sir, for the very affectionate instance of the kind regard you have shewn me in your endeavouring to procure a public Testimony, from Several of the Colonies in favor of my Services in North America, to attend my Exit. I shall ever retain a most gratefull sense of it, and the warmest Friendship my mind is capable of for you.

I hope the Revolution in your Nephew Staats affairs, during his stay in England, will, upon his explaining it to you, prove to your own approbation and promote his Happiness.

I am, with the most perfect Truth and Esteem,
      Sir,
         Your most Affectionate
         Friend and Servant,
               W. Shirley.

It would give me the greatest pleasure, was it possible for me to see you, before I go for England; many things might occurr to us, when together, which, might be proper to be talk'd over with the Ministry upon my Arrival there, which may otherwise slip me.

I am in the most affectionate manner,

Dear Sir,

Your most Obedient, and

faithfull Servant,

W. SHIRLEY.

Hon. Robert Hunter Morris, Esqr.

WILLIAM SHIRLEY TO STEPHEN HOPKINS[1]

New York, July 13th, 1756.

SIR,

Some days ago, I had the honor to receive at Albany, two letters from the Right Honorable Mr. Fox, one of His Maj-

---

[1] R. I. Col. Rec. 5, 531. Similar letters to Governor Sharpe of Maryland are printed, Arch. of Md. 6, 447–448.

The letter of Lord Loudoun to Governor Hopkins, announcing the writer's accession to command, follows (R. I. Col. Rec. 5, 531):

New York, 23d July, 1756.

SIR,

His Majesty having been graciously pleased to appoint me, by his commission, under the great seal, to be general and commander in chief of all his forces in North America, I take this first opportunity to acquaint you of my arrival this morning   As I have been unfortunately so long detained in my passage, I find it indispensably necessary that I go immediately to the army.   I must proceed accordingly.

I herewith send Your Honor the letters of Mr. Fox, His Majesty's secretary of state, and of the Earl of Halifax, His Majesty's first lord commissioner of the board of trade.   I do, from your zeal and attachment to His Majesty's service, and from the loyalty and good dispositions of your people, depend upon all assistance that the state and circumstances of your colony is able to give me.

I will beg Your Honor to assure the good people of your colony,

esty's principal secretaries of state, dated the 13th and 31st March last, acquainting me, in the former, with His Majesty's appointment of the Earl of Loudoun to be general and commander in chief of his forces in North America; and in the latter, signifying to me, that it having been represented to the King, that my presence in England may be very useful and necessary, to give many lights and informations relative to the state of affairs in North America, it was His Majesty's pleasure that I should repair to England with all possible expedition; and that, for this purpose, His Majesty had given directions to the lords of the admiralty, who have ordered a frigate to receive me on board, and to proceed with me directly to England.

And I have the pleasure of being acquainted in the former of these letters, "that the disposition His Majesty has thought proper to make of the command of his forces in North America, is not owing to any dissatisfaction with my services; but on the contrary, it is the King's intention to give me a new mark of his royal favor."

As I think it not improper for me to give Your Honor and the province under your government, notice of my departure for England, so I am desirous of taking this opportunity to

that they may depend upon my protection, and my utmost care to avoid and remove (as far as the circumstances of a country become the seat of war, will admit,) every thing that may any way burthen or hurt the interest of any individual.

I shall, on all occasions, and in every thing relative to the service and interest of the colonies, communicate with Your Honor; and beg at all times to be favored from you, with all matters of advice and intelligence, relative to the same; and shall impatiently expect the returns you are directed to send.

I beg you to be assured, that I am, with the highest esteem, sir,
Your Honor's most obedient and most humble servant,
LOUDOUN.

To the Hon. Stephen Hopkins, Esq.

P.S. I must beg Your Honor to send me, forthwith, copies of the acts or resolves of your Assemblies, by which the troops that are to act against Crown Point, have been raised, and of the instructions for their proceeding. L.

acknowledge their exertion of a most ready spirit for the defence of His Majesty's just rights and dominions, against the encroachments of the French, upon this continent, ever since I have had the honor to have any share in the command upon it; to assure them of my best wishes for their welfare, and that of His Majesty's other northern colonies; and that I shall think myself happy in being able, upon my arrival in England, to give such lights and informations relative to the state of affairs in North America, at this most critical conjuncture, as may best promote His Majesty's service, and the general interest of his subjects there.

I am, with great regard and esteem, sir,
Your Honor's most humble and most obedient servant,
W. SHIRLEY.
To the Hon. Stephen Hopkins, Esq.

JOHN BRADSTREET TO WILLIAM SHIRLEY

[Extract][1]

SIR,

I am to return to Oswego with Provisions and Stores, and only wait here for Money, the Battoe-Men not being willing to go without.

Colonel Webb and the 44th Regiment moves up there also; The 48th is gone from hence to day for Fort William Henry, and the New England Troops, etc., left the Half Moon Yesterday.

The French have had 1000 Men besides Indians out, for these two Months to cutt off the provisions and Stores, and their general Rendezvous has been at the Fort built 34 Miles from Oswego.

a true Copy
WM. ALEXANDER.

[1] P. R. O., C. O. 5, 46.   Inclosed in Shirley to Fox, Sept. 16, 1756. A transcript is in the Library of Congress.

Endorsed:
Extract of a Letter from Capt. Bradstreet to
Major General Shirley dated Albany, July 16th, 1756.
In Majr. Genl. Shirley's Letter of Septr. 16th, 1756.

ROBERT HUNTER MORRIS TO WILLIAM SHIRLEY [1]

July 22nd, 1756.

DEAR SIR,

I had not time to write you by the last post, and now acknowledge the receipt of your two letters, that by the former post I laid before the Assembly, and in several private conversations with some of the members have pointed out your services to the Continent, both before and since they had that letter, which I thought would have better effects than any thing I could say in a publick message, and what they do will have the more weight, coming unasked and of their own accord. I hear they intend to give you thanks for your services in some shape or other, but have not yet learnt the manner.

The Information I can give Lord Loudoun will in great measure be supplyd by Mr. F——, who waits at New York on purpose, and being connected with Pownall, will have all the credit he can desire. I know not what part Lord Loudoun may act, but to me it seems very impolitick to countenance, in any shape, a man that has in so remarkable a manner obstructed the Kings affairs, and gone such lengths to embody the Germans here against the Crown, by making them believe there was a fixd design to enslave and reduce them to

---

[1] 1 Penna. Arch. 2, 715. See Shirley to Morris, July 5 and 12, *ante*, p. 481 and note. The following words from Morris to Governor Dinwiddie are interesting in this connection. They are of July 20.

"General Shirley is hastening to England on the Invitation of the Ministry, who have paid him many just Complements, and express an hearty regard for him, and say they will stand in need of his Councils and Advice, and therefore think it necessary he shou'd hasten to England to be ready to assist them in their future Consultations on the affairs of America."

a state of vasselage, worse than what they fled from in their own Country. The Post office, I believe, have given him to understand that his conduct is disapproved of, which in my mind was paying him too high a Compliment, and I suppose he and P—— are to contrive some way of reinstating him in their favour, and possibly the Earl may be drawn into the measure.

I intended setting off at this day to pay my compliments to you, But some Messengers Employ'd by me to the Indians upon the Susquehana are returned, and have brought with them as far as Bethlehem the King of the Delawares, and a great number of his nation who are ready to enter into their former alliance with us, and I am under a necessity of going to meet them before I do any thing else, as so favourable a disposition in those people should not be neglected; from the treaty I shall proceed to New York, as Easton, the place of meeting, is about fifty mile on my way, and upon notice of Lord Loudouns arrival I intend to leave the treaty to Commissioners, and set off immediately. In about six hours I take Horse for Easton.

Endorsed:
Dft to General Shirley. July 22nd, 1756.

JOHN BRADSTREET TO WILLIAM SHIRLEY

[*Extract*][1]

Albany, July 24, 1756.

I should have set out some Days ago for Oswego with the #48th Regiment and Col. Webb, but no Care being taken to send Provisions for them to Schenectada, they cannot move 'till a large Quantity is sent there, which I fear will take some time for Want of Waggons.

[1] P. R. O., C. O. 5, 46. Inclosed Shirley to Fox, Sept. 16, 1756. A transcript is in the Library of Congress. The note is added by Shirley's secretary in the copy.

Notwithstanding every thing being so forward at Oswego for to proceed upon Action, by all Appearances nothing will be done that Way without the French make it a Visit, which by my Intelligence, is more than probable, if proper Care be not taken.

The French are certainly in great Numbers towards Crown point, and our Affairs that Way seem to wear a gloomy Aspect; this would not have happen'd had your Excellency continu'd here, and taken the Command upon you, as in that Case they would have consented to the Regulars joining them.

#N.B. he means the 44th Regiment instead of the 48th.
A true Copy.
WM. ALEXANDER Secy.

Endorsed:
Extract of a Letter from Captn. Bradstreet to Major General Shirley dated Albany July 24th, 1756. in Majr. Genl. Shirley's Letter of Septr. 16th, 1756.

WILLIAM SHIRLEY TO HENRY FOX [1]

New York, July 26th, 1756.

SIR,

I have the satisfaction to Acquaint you, that on the 3d of this Instant Captain Bradstreet Obtain'd an Advantage in an Engagement between a party of 250 of the Battoe-Men under his Command and one of the Enemy's, consisting of 400 Canadeans, 100 Regulars, and 100 Indians upon the River Onondago, at About 11 Miles distance from Oswego, which I hope will have a good effect for Checking their Incursions for the future, keeping open the Communication between that place and Schenectada, and deterring the In-

[1] P. R. O., C. O. 5, 46. A transcript is in the Library of Congress, and another in the Parkman Papers in the Mass. Hist. Society.

dians in the French Interest from being so forward to enter into their Quarrels with us.

It appears from the several Relations given of this Affair, that the Enemy, who had been in vain Waiting some time for an Opportunity to cutt Capt. Bradstreet off with his Convoy of Provisions in his passage to Oswego, fir'd upon about 100 of his Battoes in their Return from thence, which went before him in a scattering Manner, and kill'd Several of his Men; that he was Obliged himself to take to an Island near the place of the Attack with a party, which consisted of about Eight Men at first, and Never exceeded 20 during his stay upon the Island; that from thence he repuls'd them in three Attempts to ford the River in much superior Numbers to his own; that having collected about 250 of his Men on the South Side of the River Opposite to the Enemy, a large party of whom were now endeavouring to ford it about half a Mile above, he quitted the Island and Marched to meet them, and engaged about 400 of them in a Swamp; where, after Maintaining a Sharpe fight with them in the Indian Way upwards of an hour, he prevail'd on his Men to rush into the Swamp upon them, and drove them precipitately into the River, in which Many of them were kill'd; And from thence he proceeded higher up the River in pursuit of another party of the Enemy, which he had Intelligence were to cross it, a Mile about him, and soon fell in with some of the stragglers, upon which the rest betook themselves to flight.

In this Skirmish we had 20 kill'd and 24 Wounded, and it is judged from the Number of the Bodys of the Enemy; that were seen in the Water, besides those on Shoar, and of their Firelocks, Hatchets and Scalping knives, which were found that they lost at least, 100; Among which were several Indians; and in their flight they left behind them part of their Provisions and Many Blankets, which were found on the North side of the River, by our parties, which were sent out after the Engagement.

About an hour after the Action was over, the Grenadier Company of the 50th Regiment, which was upon their March to Oswego, in their return from Onondago, to which last place I had Ordered them to escort Sir William Johnson from the German Flatts, joined Capt. Bradstreet's party; and the next Morning a Detachment of 200 Men, was sent from the Garrison at Oswego to reinforce him, with which and the rest of his Battoe-Men, who were then all come up, he purposed to have gone in quest of the Main Body of the Enemy, which had been hovering several Weeks about Oswego and the 12 Mile falls, and it is judged Consisted of about 1200; But the heavy rains, which fell the whole day and Night following, prevented him.

It is agreed, that through the whole of this Action, Captain Bradstreet behaved with good Conduct as well as Gallantry, and I must in Justice to him Observe, that the transportation of the provisions and Stores this Spring to Oswego, (upon which the preservation of the place hath so much depended) is Chiefly owing to his indefatigable Activity, and Singular good Management in his Command.

I have further to Acquaint you, Sir, that Capt. Broadly Commanding Officer of his Majesty's Vessels upon the Lake Ontario hath met with four French ones upon it of Superior Force to the Schooner Oswego and Sloop Ontario, and two Small Row Gallies built there last Year (one of which last two is taken by the Enemy), And we have intelligence that the French have another Arm'd Vessell upon the Lake and a Ship of 20 Guns in Cadaraqui Harbour ready for the Water: It is therefore extremely fortunate, Sir, that his Majesty's Naval Force upon this Lake was ordered last Year to be Augmented with three more Vessells; the French must Otherwise have been absolute Masters of it, which would have greatly endanger'd Oswego.

Of the three New English Vessells, According to our Advices from Oswego, two were launched the 15th Instant, and the Snow which is to be Mounted with 18 Six pounders, was to be launched eight days after.

It may not be improper, Sir, to Observe here that as it is very Certain that the Depth of Water in the Harbour of Cadaracui [Frontenac], will admit of larger Vessells than that of Oswego, the French must have an Advantage over us in building Vessells of Force for the Lake, whilst they continue in possession of that Harbour; that on the other hand their Loss of that and Fort Frontenac would go far towards excluding them from the Navigation of it.

I have likewise Received an Account Since My last Letter to you, Sir, from Lake George that Capt. Rogers Commanding the Ranging Company of 70 Men, whom I sent five Weeks ago, with five Whale boats to try to intercept the Enemy's Convoy's of Provisions and Stores upon Lake Champlain and to make Discovery of their Strength and Motions, found means to pass the two Forts at Ticonderoge and Crown point undiscovered, and took two Boat Loads of French Provisions upon that Lake which he sunk and hath brought eight of their Crew prisoners (the remaining four of them being kill'd) to Fort William Henry; so that there is room to hope, that besides the Other good effects of this Success some seasonable intelligence may be got from the Prisoners of the Strength and Designs of the French before the March of our Troops for Ticonderoge, in case an Attempt shall be made for the Reduction of that Fort and Crown point this Campaign.[1]

In a late Letter I Acquainted you, Sir, that Sir William Johnson was gone to a Council of the Indians at Onondago, and was to go from thence to Oswego to be present at a Meeting of the Indians inhabiting the North side of the Lake Ontario, and the adjacent Country according to my invitation of them last fall when I was at Oswego, to come there to kindle a new fire, and settle a Trade at that place upon more advantageous Terms to them, than has been yet done: But I now hear, Sir William is return'd from Onondago, to his own house; having, as he informs me settled a peace with the Delawares and Shawanese Indians, who have agreed to cease all Hostilities against Pensilvania, and to take up the Hatchet for the English against the French.

The Earl of Loudoun arriv'd here the 23d Instant, and im-

[1] See Rogers, Robert, "Journal of a Scout." Johnson Manuscripts, 4, 80, and Doct. Hist. New York, 4, 285–287.

barked for Albany Yesterday in the afternoon; Tomorrow I purpose to embark for Boston, and upon the Arrival of the Frigate there which is appointed to carry me to England, I shall lose no time for going on board it, pursuant to his Majesty's Orders.

I have the honour to be with the Highest Respect
Sir,
Your most Humble and
most Obedient Servant,

W. SHIRLEY.

Rt. Honble: Henry Fox one of his ⎫
Majesty's principal Secretaries of State. ⎭

Endorsed:
New York July 26th, 1756.
  Majr. Genl. Shirley.
R Septr. 29th.

WILLIAM SHIRLEY TO JOHN WINSLOW

[Extract] [1]

[New York, July 26, 1756.]

Yesterday the Earl of Loudoun acquainted me that he had been informed, that you and other Officers of the Provincial Troops under your Command have declared that in case you should be joined by Regular Troops in your March to Ticonderoga for the Reduction of that Fort and Crown point, you would withdraw your Troops and return home, or to that Effect. I don't think it possible for yourself, or any Officer that has the least Sense of Honour and his Duty to make so mutinous a Declaration as this, or even to entertain so criminal a thought: I found this Representation had gained

---

[1] P. R. O., C. O. 5, 46; 5, 47. Inclosed in Shirley to Fox, Aug. 13, 1756. Transcripts are in the Library of Congress and in the Parkman Papers in the Mass. Hist. Society. See reply of Winslow on p. 495.

more Credit with his Lordship, than I could wish and I can assure you, it hath given me great Concern, both for the sakes of yourselves and the Governments which have raised the Troops; and I think it behooves you highly to lose no time for clearing up to Lord Loudoun this Imputation upon your Honour and Loyalty to the King: I must desire you will let me hear from you upon it by the return of the Express, which will deliver this to you; and I hope your answer will be such as to give me the satisfaction of being convinc'd that this Charge upon you and the other Provincial Officers is ill grounded.

Endorsed:
    Extract from Major
        General Shirley's Letter
            to Major General Winslow
                dated July 26th, 1756.
    in Majr. Genl. Shirley's
    Letter of Augt. 13th, 1756.

JOHN WINSLOW. ANSWER TO QUESTION OF THE COUNCIL[1]

[July, 1756.]

That His Majesty's Commission and Instructions to General Abercromby appointed him to be General and Commander "of all and Singular his Forces, employ'd or "to be employ'd in any or all of our Provinces in North " America."

And Whereas a Considerable Body of Provincials are on their March towards Crown-point, the Council Apply'd to General Abercromby, that he would be pleas'd to desire

[1] P. R. O., C. O. 5, 46.   Inclosed in Winslow to Shirley, Aug. 2, and by the latter forwarded to Henry Fox in his letter of Aug. 13, 1756.   A transcript is in the Library of Congress.   The question put to Winslow by Abercromby in behalf of the Council went to the bottom of the question whether or not provincials would serve with regulars, accepting the consequent loss in rank.

General Winslow would inform him what Effect the Junction of his Majesty's Forces would have with the Provincials, if order'd to join them on their intended Expedition.

The above Question being ask'd General Winslow said that he would be extremely well pleas'd such a Junction could be made; and that he look'd on himself to be under the Command of the Commander in Chief; But that he apprehended, that if his Majesty's Troops were order'd to join the Provincials, it would almost occasion an universal Desertion, because the Men were rais'd to serve solely under the Command of their own Officers, whose Commissions in the Massachusetts are worded in the following Manner; to be Colonel or Captain etc. in a Regiment or Company, to be employ'd on an Expedition against Crown point, whereof John Winslow Esqr. is Commander in Chief.

General Winslow further informs the Council, that he apprehended the four Provinces would not raise any More Men for any future Service, if his Majesty's Forces were to join the Provincials, and that as soon as he arrives in his Camp he will call a Council of his principal Officers, to know their Opinion on the above mention'd Question.

Copy Attest

Henry Leddel Secrety.

Endorsed:
Copy
General Winslow's Answer
to the Question propos'd to
him concerning a Junction
of the Regulars with the
Provincials.
in Majr. Genl. Shirley's
Letter of Augt: 13th: 1756.

THE EARL OF LOUDOUN TO WILLIAM SHIRLEY
[*Extract*] [1]

"As to the Provincial Troops, I am sorry to find so little appearance of their obeying his Majesty's Commands, for by a Council of War, I have seen of theirs, they not only refuse that Obedience, but take it upon them to direct the Motions of his Majesty's Troops, and from the best Information I have, the Gentlemen from Massachusetts are the principal Opposers, but I shall suspend my Belief of that, 'till I know with more Certainty."

Endorsed:
   Extract of a Letter from
      the Rt. Honble. Earl of
         Loudoun to Major General
            Shirley dated August 2d. 1756.
In Majr. Genl. Shirley's
   Letter of Augt. 13th: 1756

JOHN WINSLOW TO WILLIAM SHIRLEY
[*Extract*] [2]

Sir,

Your Excellency's favour from New York of 26th July [3] last I received the last Evening with an Account of the Information given Lord Loudoun in these words. Vizt. "That "you and other Officers of the Provincial Troops under your "Command, have declared that in case you should be Joined "by the Regular Troops in your March to Ticonderoga for

[1] P. R. O., C. O. 5, 46. Inclosed in Shirley to Fox, Aug. 13. A transcript is in the Library of Congress and in the Parkman Papers in the Mass. Hist. Society. Loudoun had been appointed Governor of Virginia Feb. 17, 1756, and on Mar. 20 Commander in Chief of the British forces in America. See Shirley's letters to Loudoun of Aug. 10, *post*, pp. 499 and 501.

[2] The extract printed is in P. R. O., C. O. 5, 47, where it is inclosed in the letter of the Earl of Loudoun of Aug. 19. A second extract duplicating this except for spelling, use of italics, etc., is in C. O. 5, 46, inclosed in Shirley's letter of Aug. 13, *post*, p. 515.

[3] See extract from letter mentioned *ante*, p. 492.

the Reduction of Crown point you would withdraw your Troops and return home or to that Effect;" and your Excellencys great surprize at so Mutinous a declaration and concern that it had gained Credit with his Lordship.

These facts were they true would have been Exceeding bad, but as all the Affairs that I have been concern'd in since I have seen your Excellency have been reduced to writing and nothing done on my part or I hope by the Gentlemen Concerned but what has been look'd on by General Abercromby, Sir Charles Hardy, Sir Willm Johnson, Colonel Webb, Governor Delancy and the Principal Officers of the Army so far from being Mutinous that it has met with their Approbation and with them I parted and from them receiv'd all tokens of Friendship when I left Albany on the 17th. July and have since pursued those plans that was then Agreed on without the least deviation and I am not sensible of any thing Criminal either in Debate or Otherwise but what Interpretation may be Maliciously made by far fetch'd Inferences of any thing urg'd in Argument before those Gentlemen by designing Persons I dont know but rest assured it is Impossible that thinking People can believe that they would Countenance any thing like Mutiny.

Your Excellency may remember that the day you left Albany when there was a Convention of Officers and I had the Honour to be present, the Plan was settled that the whole of the Provincials were to proceed forward and Endeavour the Removal of the Incroachments made by the French on his Majesty's Territories and that the Regulars should possess the Posts which we then Occup'd and have a Force at Fort William Henry to assist or sustain us as occasion should require which was then agreable to all concern'd and in the Situation we remain'd 'till the 14th. when we made our Grand March from Half Moon and being on my March I receiv'd by Mr. Adjutant General Glazier a verbal order from General Abercromby desiring my return to Albany which I immediately Obey'd and left Army on the March with our Train etca. under the Command of Genl. Lyman and when I arriv'd at that place was Informed by the General that it was agreed that one of the Regiments of the Regulars was to go on to Oswego and that Colonel Webb's was to take Possession of the Post at Half Moon, Still Water and Saratoga and also of Fort Edward when we should be able to Remove our Stores from thence and that the Provincials must Garrison Fort William Henry and that while we remain'd at the two last mentioned Forts we were to Supply what Workmen the Engineers had Occasion for which I made no Objection too although I much better lik'd the first Plan, after which the Inclosed Question was put me which after debating made the Answer to it Annex'd and found no one dissatisfied with it took my leave and the 17th. set out for the Army on the 19th. Overtook them at Saratoga and on the next'day pursued our March for Fort Edward and on that day arriv'd with the Front at the Fort last Mention'd and the Rear under General Lyman the next day as several of the Carriages of the Cannon were disabled which we were Oblig'd to repair but finally arrived all safe. On the 21st. Encamped, On the 22nd. Call'd all the Field Officers of that place together and according to my Promise made to Genl. Abercromby laid before them the Question mention'd which they had under debate and Consideration 'till the 24th. and on the 25th : reported to a part of which a Number Protested of all these matters I send your Excellency Copies. The whole Transactions as soon as ended with a Copy of my Commissions I forwarded by Colo. Fitch to the General and also to Sir Charles Hardy and other Governors concern'd in the Expedition. The Generals answer thereto I have not yet receiv'd nor Colonel Fitch return'd. The grand Debate with the Officers in regard to the Junction arises from the General and Field Officers losing their Rank and Command which they were Universally of Opinion they could not give up as the Army was a proper Organiz'd Body and that they by the Several Governments from whom these Troops were rais'd were Executors in Trust which was not in their power to resign, and, even should they do it, it would End in a DISSOLUTION OF THE ARMY as the Privates Universally hold it as one part of the Terms on which they Enlisted that they were to be Commanded by their own Officers and this is a Principle so strongly Imbib'd that it is not in the Power of Man to remove it.[1]

Your Excellency is full acquainted with the difficulty of Governing new rais'd Troops which on my hands is doubled by their Consisting of several different Governments and put under different Regulations by the Governments that rais'd them and must necessarily conclude my task is no easy one and you may be Assured that I have nothing at heart but the King's Service and the good of my Country which I certainly prefer to any private Advantage to myself or Applause and could the Business be carried on I should not look upon myself Disparag'd to serve under Men of more knowledge but on the other hand should I not freely open the difficulties which are so Obvious and plain to his Majesty's General I should look upon myself as deserving the Gallows as the fate of this Expensive Expedition depends on these matters and must be carried on by Numbers.

Thus have I endeavour'd to set the Fact in the true light and as no Aspersion that I know of lays on me by thos Gentlemen before resited before whom I have been heard and Concern'd with I hope your Excellency will be so far from blaming my Conduct in these Intricate Affairs that they will meet with your Approbation and I obtain the same favourable Opinion from your Excellency this Year as I have hitherto had.

Endorsed:
Extract from Majr. Genl. Winslow's
Letter to Major General Shirley.
dated 2d : August 1756.
 in the E. of Loudoun's Letter of
 Augt : 19th : 1756.

[1] In the copy forwarded by Shirley to Fox, Aug. 13, no words are underlined. This copy is used that the words considered offensive by Loudoun and quoted by Shirley, *post*, p. 503, may be the more marked. — EDITOR.

WILLIAM SHIRLEY TO THE EARL OF LOUDOUN[1]

Boston, Tuesday forenoon Augt. 10th, 1756.

My Lord,

On Sunday Evening I had the Honour of your Lordships Letter of the 2nd Instant as I was upon my Journey to this place and last Night your Lordships of the 5th Instant.

I am extreamly sorry to find that my Allowance of a Purchase in Major General Abercromby's Regiment is Irregular. It was represented otherwise to me by Officers upon whose Judgment in this point I thought I could depend and as I looked upon Capt. Hobson's retiring out of the Army on Accot. of his [age ?] and infirm state of Health, to be for his Majesty's Service and the filling up his Captaincy upon his Resignation came within the Letter of the King's Commission which allow'd me to fill up Vacancies made by Resignations, I did it without hesitation upon Lieutenant Colo. Gage's Memorial to [me ?] in favour of the Purchaser.

I have wrote to Mr. Alexander to send your Lordship Duplicates or Copies of such Contracts as remain in his hands with an Account of what advance and payments have been made upon each of them which I was in hopes had been given your Lordship at New York, and I have desired him to wait upon your Lordship directly at Albany in order to Clear up to your Lordship the Memorandums he left with Major Genl. Abercromby contained in a Quarto Book. But I must intreat your Lordship to dispatch him as soon as Possible as it is absolutely necessary for him to go to England with me on Accot. of my own Affairs and I am in daily Expectation of one of his Majestys Frigates arriving at Boston in order to carry me as soon as may be to England pursuant to his Majestys Commands.

In April last upon my leaving this place to go to Albany I ordered four Companies of Rangers consisting of 60 Privates each to be raised, and left it under the Care of Major Genl. Winslow. The service I designed them for was to be kept

[1] P. R. O., C. O. 5, 47. A transcript is in the Library of Congress.

Constantly Employed in Scouting Parties at the Oneida Carrying Place and other passes between the German Flatts and Oswego, in order to keep them clear of the Enemys Scalping parties which I find by the last Years Experience is not to be depended upon being done by the Indians of the Six Nations, though in their own Country. At my Arrival here I found two Companies compleated and shall order them to March to Albany as soon as possible there to receive your Lordships orders.

Inclosed is a set of the Resolves of the Assembly of this Province concerning the Forces raised by them for the Expedition against Crown Point.

I thank your Lordship for returning the Copies of the Instructions and the notice you will take of my Recommendations.

I have the Honour to be with the greatest Respect.

> My Lord
> > Your Lordships most humble:
> > and most Obedient Servant
> > > WILLIAM SHIRLEY.

P. S. I hear that his Majesty's Frigate which is appointed to carry me to England is just coming up the Bay.

Endorsed:
    Copy
        Major General Shirley's Letter
            to the Earl of Loudoun.
                Boston, in the forenoon, August 10th 1756.
    in the E. of Loudoun's Letter of
        Augt. 19th. 1756.

WILLIAM SHIRLEY TO THE EARL OF LOUDOUN[1]

Boston, Augst. 10th, 1756.

My Lord,

In my Letter dated in the Forenoon, I acknowledged my Receipt of the Honour of your Lordships of the 2d Instant, and answer'd every Part of it, except that, which refers to a Council of War held at Fort Edward on the 22d : of July by the Field Officers of the Provincial Troops, raised for the Expedition against Crown Point, upon the Question proposed to Mr. Winslow by Major General Abercromby, in a Council held by him at Albany a few Days before "concern-"ing the Effect, which a Junction of his "Majesty's Regular Troops wou'd have "with those Provincials, if the former "shou'd be order'd to join them in that "Expedition:" and in which Your Lordship mentions the little appearance, you find, from the Result of that Council of War, that the Provincial Troops will pay Obedience to his Majesty's Commands.[2]

In Order, my Lord, fully to answer this Part of Your Lordship's Letter (which gives me equal Surprize and Concern) so as to lay before You my

[1] P. R. O., C. O. 5, 47. Inclosed in Loudoun's letter to London of Aug. 19. A copy lacking the marginal notes is in C. O. 5, 46. Transcripts are in the Library of Congress and in the Parkman Papers in Mass. Hist. Society. The notes are added by Loudoun.

[2] See Loudoun to Shirley, Aug. 2, and John Winslow, Answer to the Council, *ante*, pp. 493 and 495. There is a transcript of the Minutes of the Council of Fort Edward in the Parkman Papers, Mass. Hist. Society.

Sentiments at large, upon the Whole of the Affair, it will be necessary for me to enter into the following Detail of it.

On the 30th: of June, after having some Days before, communicated to Major Gen: Abercromby, then General and Commander in Chief, the Minute of a Council of War held at Albany the 25th: of May, during the Continuance of my own Command; in which was set forth the Strength of his Majestys Forces, Regular and Irregular, then raised or arriv'd in America, for the Service of this Campaign, either upon the Lake Ontario or Lake George, together with the unanimous Opinion of that Council in Favor of making an Attempt for the Reduction of the French Forts at Ticonderoge and Crown Point, with the joint Forces of the Provincials raised for that Service, and his Majesty's 44th and 48th Regiments, I had, by the Desire of Major Genl. Abercromby, a Meeting at my own Lodgings of Mr. Winslow and Colo. Gridley, Commanding Officer of the Artillery of the Provincials and their Chief Engineer, with the General, Colo. Webb, and myself; At this Meeting General Abercromby, among other things, proposed to Mr. Winslow, that upon the Provincials leaving Fort Edward and Fort Willm. Henry and marching to Ticonderoge, the Regulars shou'd move to those Forts, and be ready there to support or assist them in their Attack of Ticonderoge, in Case they shou'd want assistance: and ask'd Mr. Winslow and Colo.

Mr. Winslow and Colonel Gridley, antecedent to the meeting of the 30: June, at Mr. Shirley's lodgings, declared that they Judged it impracticable to bring the Provincials, to Join with His Majesty's Troops, this they confirmed in presence of Mr. Shirley that very day; upon which M. G. Abercromby proposed *no more* than to take possession of the posts and Forts upon Hudsons river, and Fort William-Henry, with His Majestys Troops upon the Provincials evacuating the same.

As they were breaking up, Colonel Webb occasionally threw out to them, that if they were repulsed in their attempt upon Ticonderoge, whether or not in that event they would submit to a junction. — In that case, they replied, that they believed they would.

[1] For this I refer to Mr. Gl. Winslows Answer; transmitted to me in the same Cover with this Letter.[1]

Gridley how a Junction of the Regulars with the Provincials wou'd, in such Case, be liked by the latter; Upon this, My Lord, both those Officers repeatedly assured the General, in the strongest Terms, that a Junction wou'd, in such Case, be perfectly acceptable to the Provincial Troops in general, and that they cou'd be answerable, in this Re-

[2] The contrary of[2] this appears in the Council of War of 16th. July 1756, at which Mr. Winslow was called in herewith transmitted.[2]

spect, for every Officer among them; But no Mention was made of any Junction upon the March to Ticonderoge; And I find by Letters from Mr. Winslow to the New England Governments, wrote soon after this Meeting, that he calls what Passed in the Conference at it, the *Settlement of the Plan* for an Attempt against Crown Point, and mentions it as extremely acceptable to the Provincials.

Afterwards on the 25th of July at the last Meeting which I had the Honor to have with your Lordship at New York; upon your Lordship's acquainting me, that you had good Information that Mr. Winslow and others of the Provincial Officers had declared, that if the Regular Troops shou'd join the Pro-

[3] This is absolutely false, as to my having said it to him, but it stands in their own words; in debate as their opinion, that it would end in a desolution of the Provincial Troops.

vincials they wou'd withdraw With the Soldiers under their Command, or to that Effect; I express'd my Surprize at it, and let Your Lordship know what had passed at the Meeting at Albany on

[1] See John Winslow, Answer, *ante*, p. 493.

[2] The minutes of this Council of War are in P. R. O., C. O. 5, 46 and 47. They cover about 2700 words, and there is a transcript of the record in the Library of Congress. Shirley presided, and conditions at Oswego, as well as the Crown Point expedition, were discussed with other matters.

the 30th of June, between Major General Abercromby and Mr. Winslow; which had, I confess, given me Hopes, that there was a right Disposition in the Provincials to behave as their Duty shou'd require, and that an Harmony and Good Understanding wou'd be maintain'd between his Majesty's Regular Forces and them; and with Regard to the Sentiments of the New England Governments, which raised the latter, upon the Point of a Junction of the King's Regulars with the Provincial Forces, I inform'd Your Lordship, that the Assembly of the Massachusets Bay had made Application to me the last Year, upon the first raising their Troops, for this Expedition, to have my own and Sir Wm. Pepperell's Regiments, or at least one of them, employed in it. On July the 26th I acquainted Mr. Winslow, that Your Lordship had receiv'd Information, that he and other Officers of the Provincials had made such a Declaration as is before mentioned with Regard to a Junction of the Troops, in a Letter to him, which I now inclose Your Lordship a Copy of, together with one of his Answer to that Letter, and of the Opinion, he acquaints me he deliver'd to the Council held at Albany by Major General Abercromby upon the Effect of a Junction; to all which I beg leave to refer Your Lordship; as I must likewise do to the inclosed Copy of my Letter of this Day to Mr. Winslow for my Sentiments

[4] This application was prior to the King's Order settling the Rank of the Officers of the Provincial Troops, and prior to the arrival at Boston of the Act putting them under Military discipline when Join'd to the Kings Troops.

[5] This is only an Extract,[1] I wish it had been a Copy, it might have Clear'd more Points, but as it is, it contains several Material one's.

[1] *Ante*, p. 492.

upon his own Opinion,[1] and that of the before mentioned Council of War consisting of the Field Officers of the Provincials, held at Fort Edward on the 22d: of July; and shall content myself with observing here in general to Your Lordship: —

That Mr. Winslow, both in his Letter to me and Answer given to Major Genl. Abercromby, upon the Question proposed to him concerning the Junction of the Regulars and Provincials, appears to be fully sensible of his being under the Command of the King's General; and it appears from his Letter, that he readily submitted to the Alteration made in the first Plan, by ordering Fort Wm. Henry to be garrison'd by Provincials instead of Regulars; tho' he disliked it; that he is determined to pursue all the Plans, that were agreed upon in the Council held at Albany by Major General Abercromby, without the least Deviation; that he apprehended, the whole of his Proceedings to that Time had met with the Approbation of the Members of that Council; as also that when he gave in to Genl. Abercromby his Answer to the Question proposed to him concerning the Effect of a Junction of the Troops, and promised to lay it before the Field Officers of the Provincials in a Council of War, none of the Council at Albany

[2] I shall only observe on this long passage, that most of the things advanced in it, are false; and shall make no observations, on the Arguments made use of, either by Mr. Winslow or Mr. Shirley, to shew their Opinion of the King's Order, about the Rank of Provincial Officers; or Mr. Shirley's Notion, that it was referr'd to them to determine, and by such means to avail themselves, of settling the Letter of the King's Order, *and carrying their point;* as the passages are too glaring to need a Note: — But I hope the King has a better Opinion of Sir Charles Hardy, Mr. Abercromby and Mr. Webb, than to imagine that they could ever think they had a right to refer His Majesty's Commands, to be debated in a Provincial Council of War.

---

[1] See Shirley to Winslow, *post*, p. 510. The question of rank had caused some uneasiness in New York. See Goldsbrow Banyar to Sir William Johnson, June 8, 1756, Johnson Manuscripts, N. Y. State Library, 4, 62.

were dissatisfied with either; That most probably, before Mr. Winslow committed the Question to the Council held at Fort Edward for their Opinion, they were made acquainted with his own Answer to it before the Council at Albany, and the Reception it met with there: That it appears from Mr. Winslow's letter, that the *grand Debate* (as he calls it) among the Provincials in their Council *with Regard to the Junction, arose from their losing their Rank and Command by it:* And I may venture to add, My Lord, that an Apprehension of losing, by the proposed Junction, a great Part of the Honor of succeeding in the Reduction of Crown Point, which I have Reason to think, from the Declaration of some of their Principal Officers, they are persuaded they shou'd effect with their own Force, had very probably some Weight in their Debate; And lastly, that as the Plan first proposed was, that the Provincials shou'd Attempt the Reduction of the French Forts with their own Force, and a Body of the Regulars be posted at Fort Edward and Fort Wm. Henry in a Readiness to support or assist them, in Case they shou'd want Assistance; And Mr. Winslow's Opinion against a Junction of the Troops given in to the Council at Albany did not appear to be dissatisfactory to the Members of it; They look'd upon the Committing this Question to themselves convened in Council for their Opinion to be a referring of it to them, for a final Decision and endeavour'd to avail themselves of this Opportunity of Preserving their Rank and Command among the Provincial Troops, by making that a Condition of the proposed Junction; and that their Determination upon this Matter hath rather proceeded from a Notion of Carrying their Point by this Means, than a general Spirit of Disobedience to the King's Commands.

I took the Liberty, at my last Meeting with Your Lordship, to express my Sentiments concerning the Risque there wou'd be of the Provincials undertaking the Reduction of Crown Point without being supported with a Body of his Majesty's Regular Troops, as the French, according to the Intelligence we have gain'd, have a considerable Number of Regulars and strong Works at Ticonderoge; and in the Letter, which I had the Honor to write to your Lordship of the 26th of July, I acquainted Your Lordship, that I had so little Apprehension of the Provincial Officers starting any considerable Difficulties against a Junction of the Regular Forces with them, "that I had "determined before I left Boston, in "Case I shou'd not have been super-"ceded in my Command before the "Campaign had opened, to have join'd "the 44th and 48th Regiments with "the Provincials in their Attempt "against the French Forts at Crown "Point etc., and that Preparations "were accordingly begun to be made "for that Purpose."

[6] This, with the paragraph of M. G. Winslow's Letter transmitted to me, I leave as an answer to all that goes before, particularly where he mentions the grand debate, and their being Executors in Trust.

[7] Sir William Johnson, who Commanded the Provincials last year, is now by me, and declares, there never was one Man, of either of those two Regiments join'd with the Provincials — these two Regiments were Join'd at Oswego, by the New Jersey Regiment, and are this year Join'd again with them, having at all times been raised by the Collony, to be as much under the King's General's Command, as the regular Troops.

[8] He says "in his own mind"; — the Provincial Officers that were here, declared to me, in reading his Letter to Sir Charles Hardy, that they have a Letter from him, declaring in the strongest manner, that he will not Join any of the Regulars to them.

[9] This is to support what he is now insinuating in the Provinces, that I do not approve the place of the expedition against Crown Point; I am sure he knows no part of my plan, for I have not mentioned the one least word of it to him.

I will not pretend to say, My Lord, that I shou'd have been able to have compassed a Junction of the Troops, If I had continued in the Command, as I flatter'd myself, from the Application made to me the last Year by this Province for employing my own and Sir William Pepperell's Regiments with the Provincials in the expedition against Crown Point, and the Junction *there actually was of* those two Regiments the last Campaign, and is in the present Year, with the New Jersey Regiment of Irregulars at Oswego, I might have done: But I had determined, in Case there had appeared any Danger to the Service from such a Junction, as wou'd have interfered with the Rank and Command of the Provincial Officers, among their own Troops, to have march'd the Regulars, destined in my own Mind for the Expedition against Crown Point, in a separate Corps from the Provincials, and at so short a Distance from them, as to have been near enough to support them upon all Imergencies, in Case of Need; leaving a proper Number of the Provincials to Garrison Fort Edward and Fort Wm. Henry, and that at Sarahtoga, during the march to Ticonderoge etc. against your Lordships doing which, in Case Your Lordship is of Opinion to make an attempt against Crown Point this Year, and approve of such an Expedient under the present Circumstances of his Majestys Service, there does not appear the least Shadow of an Objection to be made on the Part of the Provincials.

This Shadow of an Objection to the Junction appears in Mr. Winslows Letter as follows — That it is declared in the *Grand debate.*

1st: That the General and Field Officers could not give up their rank and Command.

2dly: That being Executors in Trust to their respective Governments for the power committed to them, They could not resign it.

3dly: That it is not in the Power of Man, to remove the Opinion the privates hold, that the terms on which they are enlisted, are — That they are to be Commanded by their own Officers, in which Terms should any Alteration be made, it would end in the dissolution of the Army.

[10] I do say they are the Principal, and almost the only, and Mr. Gridley the foremost among them.

[11] I do say, that Mr. Shirley, first, by informing them falsely of my having charged them with Mutiny and disloyalty, and then Negotiating with them, as appears from the Papers he has sent me; obstructed our Accommodating matters sooner and better.

[12] I have found, by the Warrants granted, that this ought to be true, but in the proper Officers hands; I have found hardly any thing but

I take Notice, Your Lordship observes to me in your Letter of the 2d: Instant, that you are inform'd the Massachusets Officers are the Principal Opposers; All I can say, my Lord, in particular with Regard to them is, that the six Colonels, of whom I have the most knowledge, are the best Officers I cou'd find in the Province; and I have Reason to think, have as good a Disposition for his Majesty's Service as any among the Provincials; they may, for ought I know, be tenacious of Rank and Command, as their Countrymen generally are, But I hope your Lordship may have been misinform'd; and shall be very sorry to have them in particular give your Lordship Trouble. Nothing in my Power hath or shall be wanting for the Removal of that or any other Obstruction to the Service.

I have used my utmost endeavours to prepare every Thing in the best Manner I cou'd for your Lordship's Proceeding, upon your Arrival, in the Execution of your high Command, In which I most sincerely wish Your Lordship all imaginable Success, having the Honour to be with the greatest Respect,

My Lord,

Your Lordship's most Humble and most obedient Servant

W. SHIRLEY.

His Excy. The Rt. Honle. E. of Loudoun etc.

Provisions, great part of which, in Virginia Pork, which I am told, will mostly be condemned, when survey'd, which it was not in Mr. Shirleys time; and that a great part of it is spoilt, from Neglect; as to other things, they must be very well concealed in private Agents hands, for I have found very few.

I do own he has furnished me in this dispute with the Provincials, and by the State the Service is in, business sufficient to remedy the defects, and to avoid the dangers.

Endorsed:

Copy of M. G. Shirleys Letter to the E. of Loudoun

Boston 10th. August 1756. in the E. of Loudoun's Letter of Augt. 19th. 1756.

WILLIAM SHIRLEY TO JOHN WINSLOW[1]

Boston, August 10th, 1756.

Sir,

I am favour'd with your Letter of the 2d: instant (in Answer to mine of the 26th: of July) inclosing Copies of your Answer to the Question propos'd to you by Major General Abercromby at Albany, concerning the Effect of a Junction of the King's Regular Forces with the Provincial Troops in their March to Tionderoge, and of the Opinion of the Council of the Field Officers of the Provincials held at Fort Edward the 22d: of July upon the same Point; and I must own I wish they had been more to my satisfaction than I find them.

You say in your Letter that you found no one Member of the Council at Albany dissatisfied with your Answer; What satisfaction, the Gentlemen of that Council might have in your Answer, I know not; But the inclos'd Copy of a Paragraph of Lord Loudoun's Letter to me, will shew you that it is very dissatisfactory to him; as well as is the Opinion of

---

[1] P. R. O., C. O. 5, 46. Inclosed Shirley to Fox, Sept. 15. Another copy of this letter is in C. O. 5, 47, and transcripts are in the Library of Congress and in the Parkman Papers, Mass. Hist. Society.

the Council of the Field Officers of the Provincials, and I can't avoid saying both of them gives me great Surprize and Concern.

You acknowledge, Sir, in your Answer to the Council at Albany, that you look upon yourself to be under the Command of the King's General; I am perswaded, you must; the Terms of your Commissions expressly shew it, and if they did not, the nature of your Command would: Yet you proceed a few lines after to foorm an Argument from the Words of the Commission of the Provincial Officers under your Command, whereby you would exclude the King's General from a power to order His Majesty's Troops to join the Provincials, the force of the Argument, consists in this; that you are stil'd in those Commissions Commander in Chief of the Forces raised for the Services therein mentioned; and you say the Consequences of ordering such a Junction would be almost an universal Desertion, and that the four New England Colonies would not raise any more Men for any future Service.

To shew you, Sir, how much you misapprehend this Matter, I need only observe.

That when the Expedition against Crown Point was first set on foot the last Year, I appointed Sir William Johnson, then Colo: Johnson, Commander in Chief of it, and the Massachusetts Officers Commissions then ran in the like Terms with those of the present Officers; and Colonel William Johnson was therein named Commander in Chief of the Forces rais'd for the Expedition, as you are now: Yet so far was it from the intent of the Government of the Massachusetts Bay to exclude the late General Braddock from joining the King's Regular Forces with the Provincial Troops in that Expedition, if he had thought proper; that among the Resolves of the Massachusetts Assembly in raising Men for the said Service, this is one Vizt:

"That his Excellency be desired to endeavour that his own Regiment or Sir William Pepperrell's or both be employed in this service;" which was likewise very agreeable to the other New England Colonies.

This I promis'd the Assembly to do; and it would have been done if General Braddock had not employ'd both Regiments in the Expedition against Niagara.

There is still a stronger Reason why the New England Colonies should desire a Junction of the King's Regulars with the Provincials in the Expedition against Crown Point this Year, than there was the last; The Number of Troops determined by the Governments, as well as the Council of War held at New York to be requisite for the Reduction, of that and the neighbouring French Forts, are 10,000 Men of which there is rais'd as yet not more than 7000 inclusive of Officers.

This may suffice, Sir, to shew you how much you and the Field Officers under your Command mistake the Sense of the New England Colonies; for whom I dare be answerable, that they never entertain'd a thought of excluding the King from making Use of his Regular Troops jointly with the Provincial Forces in the Expedition against Crown Point.

Upon what Real foundation you assert that the Men were rais'd to serve solely under the Command of their own Officers, so as to exclude the King's Regular Troops from Acting in Conjunction with them I don't apprehend; If you would found it as you seem to do, upon the Terms of the Commissions of the Officers, there is no Colour for making such an Inference: The Reason of those Commissions being worded as they are was to make them as descriptive as may be of the particular Services to which the Assembly by their Resolves and Acts confin'd the Men which they did in order to hinder them from being employed in any other Service than that for which they are rais'd by them; but according to your reasoning, Sir, if I rightly comprehend it, the Soldiers enlisted for the Expedition against Crown Point would, in case you should cease to be Commander in Chief of it, be at liberty to quit the Service.

You come to the Root of the Matter, Sir, when you say in your Letter, " that the Grand Debate with the Officers in " regard to the Junction arises from the General and Field " Officers losing their Rank and Command," and in Defence of this you say "they were universally of Opinion that they "could not resign it up, as the Army was a proper Organiz'd "Body, and that they by the several Governments from "whom these Troops were rais'd, were Executors in Trust, "which was not in their power to resign; and even if they "should do it, it would end in a dissolution of the Army, as "the Privates universally hold it as one part of the Terms on "which they inlisted, that they were to be Commanded by "their own Officers; And that this is a principle so strongly "imbib'd, that it is not in the Power of Man to remove."

The Amount of this is that the Provincials will not Submit to the King's Regulation of Rank and Command between Regular and Provincial Troops; What you would infer in this Case when you say that the Army is a proper Organiz'd Body, I don't fully apprehend; and as to the Provincial Officers being Executors in Trust to the several Governments which rais'd the Troops, and therefore not having it in their power to give up their Rank; I think it clearly appears from what has been say'd before, that this is directly contrary to the declared sense of these Governments in the last Year; The Trust reposed in these Officers by the Governments which raised the Troops was the Defence of the Kings Territories and they refusing to execute it, if the King shall Order his Regular Troops to assist them in it, unless the General will give them Rank and Command contrary to the King's Regulation; The whole, Sir, centers in this Point, and I should think no Officer who hath had the honour to serve His Majesty in his Army and still belongs to it, could hesitate to pronounce this a most extraordinary Doctrine.

As to the Privates having universally imbib'd the principle you mention, it can't be, Sir, from the Terms of their Inlistment, and I can't But think it is in the power of their Officers to set them right in this Point.

The Earl of Loudoun justly observes that the Council of Officers at Fort Edward take upon them to direct the Motions of His Majesty's Troops with regard to carrying on an Expedition upon Lake Ontario this Year; This is still more surprizing as it was not a Matter in the least Pertinent to the Question put to them, and they must have known from yourself that one of the British Regiments was ordered to Oswego, which must prevent the French from drawing off any of their Forces from the Lake, to strengthen their Forces at Crown Point; which is what they appear to have been apprehensive of.

I am very sensible, Sir, of the difficult part you have had to Act with new rais'd Troops of several Governments, and put under different Regulations by the Governments which rais'd them, and I am fully satisfied of your good Conduct and Management of them, in which you have Shewn great Vigilance, Activity and Discretion, and I depend much upon your future Conduct and Behaviour in the prosecution of the Expedition : But you do not seem to me to have weighed the important Points I have been speaking of so thoroughly as I could wish, and hope you will yet do before it is too late.

Much will depend upon it. The security of these Colonies, the preservation of the King's Territories, and the honour of His Majesty's Arms are all deeply concerned in the Success of this Expedition. The Enemy we have reason to think are at least 3000, among which there is a Considerable Body of Regular Troops ; their Works are strong ; and you must expect to find them entrenched under Cover of their Cannon : Your Provincials consist, as you observe, of new rais'd Troops of different Governments, not well disciplin'd, and altogether unexperienced in every part of the Regular Service ; You can't reckon upon many more than 6000 Men fit for Duty among them, which without a Considerable Body of Regular Troops to support them, would not be equal to an Attack of the French Works defended with so strong a Body of Troops as they must have at Tionderoge ; and would, in my Opinion run a risque of being worsted if they should come to Action in their March, where the French Regulars can draw up in a Body and engage them.

The surest Path to honour, in this Case, lies through Victory ; and I hope you will not fail of arriving at it, if you pay a due Obedience to the Orders of the King's General, and are strengthened with a proper Body of Regular Troops, without both which I think Defeat and Ignominy are most likely to be your Lot.

I wish you and the Officers under your Command Success: and shall hope to hear from you by the Return of this Express; if not upon your March to Tionderoge, before this reaches Fort William Henry.

I am etca:

W. SHIRLEY.

Major General Winslow
  a true Copy
    JAMS BRADFORD Secy.

Endorsed:
    Copy
  Major General Shirley's Letter to
    Major General Winslow dated
      August 10th, 1756.
In Majr. Genl. Shirley's Letter of Septr. 15th, 1756.

WILLIAM SHIRLEY TO HENRY FOX [1]

Boston, August 13th, 1756.

SIR,

In my Letter of the 4th of July [2] I had the Honour to acquaint you, that " I had the Satisfaction to find at a Meet-
" ing between myself, Major General Abercromby, Colonel
" Webb, Major General Winslow, and the Commanding Officer
" of the provincial Artillery, held at my Lodgings the Day I
" left Albany, at General Abercromby's Request, that there
" was a very fair prospect of a right Understanding, good
" Agreement and Harmony's being maintain'd between the
" Regulars and Provincials."

Since then the Disposition of the Troops propos'd to Mr.

---

[1] P. R. O., C. O. 5, 46.   A transcript is in the Library of Congress.
[2] *Ante*, p. 478.

Winslow at that Meeting by General Abercromby; which was that the Provincials should march to Tionderoge and attempt the Reduction of that and Crown point, and the Regulars move to Fort Edward and Fort William Henry upon their quitting them, and be ready there to march, and join the Provincials, in case they should find, upon their coming before Tionderoge, that they wanted their Assistance (and which was perfectly agreeable to the provincials,) hath been alter'd; and upon the Question's being put by General Abercromby to Mr. Winslow, and by him afterwards to the Field Officers of the provincials, vizt. " what " Effect a Junction of the King's Forces with the provincial " Troops would have, if the former should be order'd to join " the latter;" which must be meant of a Junction between the Troops upon the *march* of the provincials to Tionderoge; the Officers of the Provincial Troops have express'd a general Dissatisfaction at it; as will appear from the several papers inclos'd, which it is necessary for me to trouble you with, Sir, in order to set this matter in a full light.

Upon this Turn, Sir, I thought it my Duty, tho' my Command is expir'd, to let Mr. Winslow, and thro' him the Field Officers of the provincials know my Opinion of their Behaviour; and have taken the liberty to offer my Sentiments upon this Emergency to the Earl of Loudoun.

Tho' I am sensible how delicate a Point Rank is with the New England Irregulars, yet as the Massachusetts Assembly had, in the last year, when the Provincial Troops were first rais'd for the Expedition against Crown point, made Application to me to use my Endeavours to have my own and Sir William Pepperrell's Regiments, or one of them at least, employ'd in it in conjunction with the Provincial Troops; which I found afterwards, was likewise the desire of the other New England Governments; and I found no Difficulties the last Campaigne from those two Regiments acting jointly with the New Jersey Regiment of Irregulars at Oswego; and the New England Officers were well appriz'd, at the time of their entering this Year into the Service for an Expedition against Crown point, of the King's Regulation of

Rank between the provincial and Regular Forces when acting jointly (which, notwithstanding other pretences, is their only real difficulty at Bottom) I had, Sir, so little Apprehension of the provincial Officers starting such Objections, as they have done, to a Junction of Regular Forces with them, that I had determin'd in my own mind, before I knew it was his Majesty's pleasure to alter the Chief Command this Year, to have join'd the 44th and 48th Regiments with the Provincial Troops in the Attempt for the Reduction of the Forts at Tionderoge and Crown point, without committing any Question upon it to a Council of *their* field Officers for their consideration.

As to the prejudices, they say the private Men have imbib'd against a Junction in this Case; provided the Officers had submitted to it, as it was their Duty to have done, I am perswaded, Sir, there is as little weight in that, as there is in the other Objection made by them, with regard to the several Governments where the Troops were rais'd, vizt: "that if such a Junction was to be made now, they would " never raise any more Men for future Service;" which I look upon as groundless.

However, as on the one hand, the Decision of the Question concerning the Junction of the Troops hath been so far committed to the Field Officers of the provincials, and they have given the Answer, they have done upon it, I think it would be running too great a risque to his Majesty's Service to have a Junction of the Troops order'd without a more favourable Answer from them upon this Point; And on the other, that if the Provincials should march without a Body of the Regulars ready at hand to support them, in case they should be attack'd by the French Regulars, where the Ground would admit of their forming in a Body to engage them, there might be danger of their being defeated; I have offer'd it to the Earl of Loudoun's Consideration, whether it might not be adviseable upon this Emergency, that a Body of the Regulars should march towards Tionderoge at the same time with the Provincials, in a separate Corps without interfering with the Field Officers in their Command, and at so short distances from those Troops, as to be ready to support them, if they should be attack'd by the French Regulars; in which Case the provincials would have, I am perswaded, no Scruple of admitting a Junction.

If his Lordship should approve of this Expedient, there does not appear the least Shadow of an Objection against it in the Provincials, and I should hope it might secure all Points.

Yesterday his Majesty's Frigate Mermaid arriv'd here from Halifax in order to carry me to England, and I shall embark, as soon as she is ready to receive me; before which time, I hope the Ship, which brings over the £120,000 Sterling for the Colonies will arrive, that I may see the £43,000 refunded, which I advanc'd to the Massachusetts, Connecticutt, and New Hampshire to enable them to raise Men in time for the Expedition against Crown point.

Captain Shirley, who commands the Mermaid, brings an Account of a late Engagement off Louisbourg between two French Ships of the line and two of their Frigates, one of the former of which is suppos'd to be the Soleil Royal of 84 Guns, the other a 70 Gun Ship; one of the Frigates to be mounted with 40 or 44 Guns, and the other with 30 or 36; and the Grafton, Captain Holmes, of 70 Guns, the Nottingham, Captn. Marshall, of 60, and the Jamaica Sloop, Captn. Hood; That the Engagement lasted seven hours, in which the French were worsted, the largest of the French Ships having been so shatter'd, that She was oblig'd to be tow'd into Louisbourg Harbour by the Frigates in the night; That the Grafton had not above 40 Men kill'd and wounded, and the Nottingham and Jamaica Sloop an inconsiderable Number; the French 84 Gun Ship is suppos'd to have lost a very large Number.

The two large French Ships were lately arriv'd from France with a Number of Soldiers, which they landed at Louisbourg, and soon after came out to attack the English Ships; and it is apprehended, that they may be forerunners of a French Squadron.

Captain Shirley likewise informs me, that it is suspected

at Halifax, that the French have 700 Men sculking on the Side of the peninsula next the Gulf of St. Lawrence with design to Attack our Fort at Gaspereau near Bay Verte. I have for some time look'd upon that End of the Isthmus as the most necessary for the English to fortify strongly, it lying expos'd to Attacks of the French from St. John's Island, Louisbourg and Quebec, thro' the Gulf of St. Lawrence, whereas we have little or nothing to fear from them on the Bay of Funda Side, where our own Strength lies; I observ'd it, Sir, to Governor Lawrence some Months ago for his Consideration, and that as Fort Lawrence seem'd to me, at present, to be of little or no Use, I thought the Expence of the Works, and the Garrison there might be spar'd towards strengthening Gaspereau, or erecting some proper Fort on a Spot near it.

This at least seems to have been the policy of the French; while they were in possession of the Isthmus; the side on which their Danger lay was the Bay of Funda, thro' which they were expos'd to sudden Attacks from New England; and therefore they guarded against them by building their strong Fort on the End of the Isthmus next that Bay; But looking upon themselves to be more secure at the End of it next Bay Verte, as they might be supported on that Side by the beforemention'd places, they thought one of less Force, and strong enough to secure their Magazines there for supplying their Fort at Beausejour from a Surprize was sufficient on that Side.

I have the honour to be with the Highest Respect,
Sir,
Your most Humble
and
Most Obedient Servant.
W. SHIRLEY.

Rt. Honble. Henry Fox, one of his ⎱
Majesty's principal Secretaries of State. ⎰

Endorsed:
Boston Augt. 13th, 1756. Majr. Genl. Shirley.
R Novr. 8th.

WILLIAM SHIRLEY TO THOMAS BOWEN [1]

Boston August 23, 1756.

SIR,

It has been represented to me that a number of the Men who were impressed for His Majesty's Service in the Expedition against Crown Point have paid the Fines required by Law to excuse them from the said Service, and that the same have not been applied towards providing able bodied Men in their Stead according to the intention of the Law in that case.

You are therefore hereby strictly required to render an accompt of all Fines that have been, or that hereafter shall be received by any Officer in your Regiment from any Person or Persons impressed for the said Expedition; and also of the application of the same, in all which I expect you will not fail at your peril.

I am Sir

Your assured Friend

and Servant

W. SHIRLEY.

Make Return of this

on the same day with

the Inclosed Warrant.

[Col. Thomas Bowen.]

---

[1] Shirley Manuscripts, No. 225, Boston Public Library. This is but a single example of the energy put forth by Shirley to raise forces for the Earl of Loudoun. See also Shirley to the General Court, Aug. 30 and Sept. 2, and to Israel Williams of Sept. 13, *post*, pp. 522, 527, and 560.

THE EARL OF LOUDOUN TO WILLIAM SHIRLEY[1]

Albany, August 29th, 1756.

SIR,

I had just now the honour of your Letter of the 26th.[2] to enquire the truth of the Report you had heard of the taking of Oswego; My publick letter to the Governor of Massachusetts will have inform'd you, long before this, of my opinion of that Affair; indeed after having seen Colonel Mercer's letter directed to you, which was plainly a series of correspondence on that subject, I never could doubt of the truth of it.

We have had ten people from thence, some of which being deserters from the French and enlisted since in your Regiment, and in Major General Pepperell's, came off as soon as the Garrison capitulated; others stay'd and surrendered their Arms with the rest of the troops there, and made their escapes afterwards, who all agree in Fort Ontario's being abandon'd after being fired on with small Arms for two days, without even having one Cannon brought up to it:[3] That night they raised a battery in the Front of Fort Ontario, and began to fire on the old Fort at five in the morning which surrendered about ten.

As to Mr. Saul's letter I know nothing of it; he was very idle if he writ any such; As to what you call Mr. Pownall's Message, it was in reality mine; for on the Post's calling on him to know if he knew any thing further about Oswego I bid him say, I saw no reason to doubt of the truth of the first Report; that really was my opinion then, and experience now shews I was right.

---

[1] P. R. O., C. O. 5, 46 and 47. Transcripts are in the Parkman Papers in the Mass. Hist. Society and in the Library of Congress.

[2] Shirley's letter of Aug. 26 is in P. R. O., C. O. 5, 47. It is of approximately 350 words, and consists mainly of an inquiry into the truth of the statement that Oswego had been captured by the French.

[3] See Shirley's comments upon these expressions in his letters to Loudoun of Sept. 4 (*post*, p. 538) and Sept. 5 (*post*, p. 542).

I sent off an Express from New York to Oswego the day after I arriv'd, which letters were return'd to me yesterday, the Messenger not being able to get into it for the Enemy's Partys, and the moment I knew the situation of the Garrison of Oswego from Mr. Mercer and of the defenseless Situation of the Fortifications of it from Mr. Mackellar, which you had never given me the least insinuation of, and had likewise conceal'd from Major General Abercromby,[1] I used the utmost Expedition, the situation you left things in would permit, to throw in succours to it, but never had it in my power, either to throw in a letter, or get up Succours in time to it.

I mean this as a publick Letter to your Government, to satisfy them as well as you, and do insist on your laying it before them,[2] in the whole and not by Extracts, otherwise I shall be obliged to send them a Copy of it.

I am etca.

LOUDOUN.

His Excellency Wm. Shirley Esqr.

Endorsed:
Copy of a Letter from his Excellency the Earl of Loudoun to Major Genl. Shirley dated Albany 29. August. 1756.

WILLIAM SHIRLEY TO THE GENERAL COURT OF MASSACHUSETTS [3]

GENTLEMEN OF THE COUNCIL AND HOUSE OF REPRESENTATIVES,

I have ordered the Secretary to lay before You a Copy of a Letter to me from His Excellency the Right Honble: the

---

[1] In view of this statement the letter of Shirley to Abercromby of June 27 (*ante*, p. 468) makes extremely interesting reading.

[2] See Shirley to the Earl of Loudoun, Sept. 3, *post*, p. 528, and Sept. 4, *post*, p. 536.

[3] Massachusetts Archives. A copy is in P. R. O., C. O. 5, 47, inclosed in Shirley to Loudoun, Aug. 30. A transcript is in the Library of Congress.

Earl of Loudoun, General, and Commander in Chief of all the Kings Forces in North America, by which You will perceive that His Lordship received "Accounts on the 19th: "Instant at Night, That His Majestys Fort and Garrison at "Oswego, together with the Naval Armament and Stores, are "fallen into the hands of the French; that from the Condition "and Number of the Troops, left with His Lordship when he "came to his Command, he can Scarce hope to do more, than "to resist the French power in that Quarter; and therefore "demands of me an Aid of as Considerable a Body of Men "with Arms, as I can send, to be raised in Companies, and "sent off as fast as raised; and also a Number of Carriages or "Ox Teams, wherewith his Lordship may be able to Transport "Provisions, as the province of New York alone, is not able "to Supply all." [1]

You are too sensible Gentlemen of the bad Consequences, which must arise to all His Majesty's Colonies upon this Continent, from the loss of Oswego to the French, to Stand in need of being urg'd to Comply with his Lordship's demands upon this Occasion.

[1] The letter of Aug. 20 from Loudoun follows: —

Albany, 20th August, 1756.

SIR,

As, by accounts I received last night, His Majesty's fort and garrison at Oswego, together with the naval armament and stores, have, by a series of bad circumstances, fallen into the hands of the French; and as, from the condition and number of the troops left to me, when I came to my command, I can scarce hope to do more than to resist the French power in that quarter, I must earnestly recommend to you to consider without delay, how far the provincials now in arms, are exposed to the weight of the French, in the parts towards Crown Point, and the dangerous events of any accident happening to them in consequence of these circumstances, and what forces you can immediately send to reinforce them, as it seems absolutely necessary to do, for the security and safety of the country.

Therefore, in consequence of the powers given to me, by His Majesty's commission under the great seal, and of his orders signified to you, by his secretary of state, I do demand of you an aid of as considerable a body of men, with arms, as you can send, to be raised in companies, and sent off as fast as raised; and also a

The French are, by this Acquisition, got into the possession of the Heart of the Country of the Six Nations of Indians; and if a very Vigorous Stand is not immediately made against their progress, there is the utmost danger that they will very soon make themselves Masters of the whole of it, from the Lower Castle of the Mohawk's, within 20 miles of Schenectady to the Castles of the Seneca's, in the Neighbourhood of Niagara, and Consequently have all those Indians entirely in their Interest.

You perceive likewise, Gentlemen, by his Lordships Letter, that his Misfortune at Oswego will require him to employ, all the Troops which were left with him, when he came to his Command, to resist the French power in that quarter; the Consequence of which is, that the Provincial Troops rais'd for the Expedition, against Crown point, will be expos'd alone to the whole weight of the French power there; which we know is already very great and it is much to be fear'd, may be suddenly encreased by the unfortunate Event at Oswego; and in case the Provincial Troops should receive a blow from the French on that Quarter (which from their present numbers unsupported by a Body of Regular Troops, there is reason to apprehend, especially, if they shou'd proceed to make an Attempt for the Reduction of the French Forts in those Parts) I need not Observe to You in how dangerous a Situation the whole Country must then be, on all sides.

The last Year, Gentlemen, this Government raised in the Whole for the Expedition then depending against Crown point 4200 Men; The Service now requires a greater Force, than it did then; It is therefore incumbent upon You to Augment Your number of Troops in proportion to the present Emergency; and it is the more incumbent upon You to number of carriages, or ox teams, wherewith I may be able to transport provisions, as this province alone is not able to supply all.

I am with great truth and regard, sir,
Your most humble servant,

LOUDOUN.

Shirley's reply of Aug. 30 is on p. 526.

do it, as the example of this province, will probably influence the Neighbouring Colonies upon this Occasion.

I can't therefore in the least doubt, Gentlemen, but that you will most readily Comply, with what his Lordship requires, by enabling me, in the most Expeditious manner, to send him an Aid, of as Considerable a Body of Men, with Arms, from this province, as Can be sent upon this Extraordinary Occasion; and I would recommend it to You, in the most Earnest manner, as a matter, which appears to me of the last importance, that the Service for which this Augmentation shall be made, be not Limited or Confin'd to any particular place, but that the Troops, should be employed, either towards Oswego, or Crown Point, as his Lordship shall Judge His Majesty's Service and the Security of the Colonies may require at this Critical Conjuncture.

His Lordship has likewise requir'd of me to send him a number of Carriages, or Ox Teams in order to Transport provisions. I know from Experience that the Country near Albany, can't furnish a Sufficient number; and I must therefore desire You to Consider and Advise me how they may be procur'd in the most expeditious and effectual manner in the parts of this Province nearest to Albany, and I will give immediate orders, that this part of his Lordship's desire may be Complied with.

GENTLEMEN OF THE HOUSE OF REPRESENTATIVES,

As the matters, I have now laid before this Court, are of very great importance, and this province is deeply interested in them, and as they will require the Court's most Speedy and Close Attention, I must desire you forthwith to send out Messengers to Call in your Absent Members, that there may be a full Court to Consult about them.

W. SHIRLEY.

Council Chamber August 30th, 1756.

WILLIAM SHIRLEY TO THE EARL OF LOUDOUN [1]

Boston, August 30th, 1756.

My Lord,

On Saturday the 28th Instant in the Afternoon, I had the honor of your Lordships Letter dated the 20th Instant, Acquainting me that your Lordship had received Accounts, that the Fort and Garrison, at Oswego, with the naval Armament and Stores are fallen into the hands of the French and demanding of me an aid from this province, of as Considerable a Body of Men with Arms, as I can send, to be rais'd in Companies, and sent off as Fast as rais'd.

The Governors of the Massachusetts Bay, My Lord, are prohibited by the Royal Charter to empress any of the Inhabitants to be transported out of the province, without the Consent of the Assembly; and it is by Virtue of an Act of Assembly, that I have Issued my Warrants, for empressing the Men, which I had the Honor to Acquaint your Lordship I was raising to Compleat the Quota of their Troops for the Expedition against Crown Point.

In order to Obtain such Consent, for raising an Additional number of Men for his Majesty's Service under your Lordships Command I have this day laid Your Lordships Letter before the General Assembly, and urg'd them in the Strongest manner to exert themselves to the utmost of their Abilities, at this Critical Juncture; a Copy of My Speech to them upon this Occasion I have enclosed; and I shall Continue to use my best endeavours to perswade them to Comply with your Lordships demand.

Yesterday afternoon I had the satisfaction to receive a Letter from Mr. Winslow, in answer to mine of the 10th Instant to him, a Copy of which I had the honor to send your Lordship, by which I perceive the provincial Officers were

[1] P. R. O., C. O. 5, 47. A transcript is in the Library of Congress. A copy of this letter was inclosed by Loudoun in his letter to Fox of Oct. 3, where the aid furnished by Shirley is acknowledged. See *post*, p. 577, note.

brought before his Receipt of that Letter, to a better sense of their duty, with respect to a Junction with his Majesty's Regular Troops, by Your Lordship's moderation and goodness towards them, than I thought appeared in their Answer, before given to the Question propos'd to them upon that point, which gave me great pleasure.

The late heavy blow received at Oswego, hath given me infinite Concern; whatever your Lordships Counsels shall be, for retrieving it as much as may be, I wish Your Lordship the utmost Success in them, and in every other part of His Majesty's Service under Your Lordships Command; Having the honour to be with very great Truth and Respect.

> My Lord,
> Your Lordship's
> most humble and
> most Obedient Servant
> W. SHIRLEY.

His Excellency the Rt: Honble: Earl of Loudoun etca.

Endorsed:
Copy of a Letter from
Majr. Genl: Shirley to
The Earl of Loudoun
August 30th: 1756
in the E. of Loudoun's Letter of Oct. 3d, 1756.

WILLIAM SHIRLEY TO THE GENERAL COURT OF MASSACHUSETTS [1]

GENTLEMEN OF THE COUNCIL AND HOUSE OF REPRESENTATIVES

I am sorry to Acquaint you, that I learn by the Return of an Express I sent to Albany last Friday Evening, that the

[1] Massachusetts Archives. A copy is in P. R. O., C. O. 5, 47, inclosed in Shirley to Loudoun of Sept. 3 and in Loudoun to Fox of Oct. 3, 1756. A transcript is in the Library of Congress. The Message of the Assembly in reply expressing concern at the loss of Oswego is in Mass. Arch. and in C. O. 5, 47. It covers about 400 words and is dated Sept. 8.

News of Oswego's being taken is Confirm'd ; and I must now press you in the most earnest manner, to lose no time for enabling me to send His Excellency the Right Honble. Earl of Loudoun the Aid of Men with Arms, which I recommended to you in my Speech of the 30th of August in Consequence of His Lordship's Letter to me of the 20th of August a Copy of which the Secretary deliver'd you ; As also to send His Lordship a Number of Carriages and Ox Teams.

The Motives, upon which I urg'd to do this in my Speech, are so Strong, that I think I need not add to them ; and shall only observe to you here, that it Appears by Governor Hopkins's Letter to me, which I sent yesterday to you, that your Example will in a great measure influence the other Governments concern'd, upon this extraordinary Emergency for His Majestys Service, and the Safety of these Colonies ; which I doubt not will have it's just Weight with you, in making you exert yourselves to the utmost upon this Occasion.

W. SHIRLEY.

Province House September 2d : 1756.
    Copy Attest
    THOS. CLARKE Depty Secry.

WILLIAM SHIRLEY TO THE EARL OF LOUDOUN [1]

Boston, Septr. 3d, 1756.

MY LORD,
    I have had the Honour of your Lordship's Letter of the 29th of August,[2] to which I shall very soon return a full Answer ; in the mean time I beg leave to remark upon the last paragraph of it, wherein your Lordship tells me, that you mean it as a publick Letter to my Government, and insist upon my laying it before them ; that otherwise you shall be

[1] P. R. O., C. O. 5, 46 ; 5, 47. Inclosed in Shirley to Fox, Sept. 15. Copies are in the Parkman transcripts in the Mass. Hist. Society and in the Library of Congress.
[2] *Ante*, p. 521.

oblig'd to send them a Copy of it; I should be extremely sorry, My Lord, to have this dispute between your Lordship and me, forc'd on before any of the Colonies; as it appears to me a very improper and unprecedented proceeding, which has not the least tendency to promote his Majesty's Service, but the direct Contrary, especially at this Juncture, by creating parties and Factions in the several Governments, at a time, when they ought to be the most closely united; It would besides, I apprehend be disapprov'd of by his Majesty for us to bring Affairs of this kind under the Examen of any of the Assemblies of the Colonies.

I think it therefore most adviseable to defer a Compliance with your Lordship's Command until I receive your Answer to this Letter; perhaps when your Lordship shall have employ'd a few cool and deliberate thoughts on the Subject you will be convinc'd of the great Impropriety of such a proceeding; It appears to me extremely irregular and ill tim'd; so that if it were not for the Measures, your Lordship seems determin'd to take to bring it before my Assembly, whether I will or not, I should decline a Compliance, even altho' your Lordship should repeat your Commands; Not that I am afraid that I shall not be able to vindicate myself from the Charge brought against me by your Lordship, or that any Impressions to my disadvantage will be left on the Minds of the People of my Government.

These are Matters of small Importance compar'd with that Harmony, which, in order to the promoting his Majesty's Service at this time more than ever, is necessary to be preserv'd thro' all the parts of it, and which, I am fully satisfy'd, a pursuit of your Lordship's Measure would interrupt and lessen; But as I am convinc'd that it will be in your Lordship's power to bring this Affair before my Assembly without my Consent and your Lordship has already furnish'd the Lt. Governor with a Copy of the Letter, I suppose for this purpose (for I can't suppose your Lordship to be so unacquainted with the Nature of Government and the Constitutions in the Colonies, as not to know that in case of my Absence your Letter directed to me would have come to the Hands of the Lt. Governor and Commander in chief) if your Lordship persist in your demand I will immediately, upon Advice of it, lay the Letter before the Assembly, if then sitting, if not, before the Council, one Branch of it, and I will take Care that it be communicated to the House of Representatives at their next meeting, but your Lordship must allow me, at the same time, to cause to be lay'd before them a full Answer to it, and you will likewise allow that I ought not to be answerable for the Consequences of a measure, which your Lordship has compell'd me to a Compliance with.

The Assembly have still under Consideration the augmenting their Troops in the manner, I recommended to them in my Speech, a Copy of which I sent your Lordship.

If the Information, that the French have quitted Oswego, after having burnt the Forts there, is true; there seems no room to doubt but that almost the whole Force, they had at Oswego, is gone to join their Troops at Crown-point and Tionderoge with a design to attack the provincial Troops at Lake George and Fort Edward; which may be very suddenly expected. If that should be the Case, and the French should prevail, it is difficult to say where their Incursions and Devastations would stop; And your Lordship is the best Judge how greatly the provincial Troops will be expos'd, if the Number of the French Forces are near equal to what they are reported to be, unless they are supported by a Body of his Majesty's British Troops.

Your Lordship is likewise the best Judge, whether it is adviseable with the whole Force, you can muster, of Regulars and provincials for that purpose to make an Attempt upon the French Forts at Tionderoge and Crown point this Year, and must be sensible of what infinite Advantage it would be to his Majesty's Service if a successful Stroke could be made upon them in that Quarter.

I presume only to mention these points for your Lordship's Consideration; being perfectly satisfy'd that your Lordship will pursue the most adviseable Measures at this critical Conjuncture, for the preservation of his Majesty's

Territories, and the Security of these Colonies; in which I wish your Lordship all possible Success.

I have the Honour to be,
My Lord etca.
W. SHIRLEY.

His Excellency the Rt. Honble. Earl of Loudoun etca.

A true Copy
JAMS BRADFORD Secy.

Endorsed:
Copy
Letter from Major General Shirley to His Excellency the Rt. Honble. Earl of Loudoun.
dated Septr. 3d, 1756.
in Majr. Genl. Shirley's Letter of Sepr. 15th, 1756.

WILLIAM SHIRLEY TO THE EARL OF HALIFAX [1]

(Triplicate)

Boston, September 4, 1756.

MY LORD,

It is with extreme Concern, I am to acquaint your Lordship, that the Earl of Loudoun in his Letter of the 20th of August [2] advises me, that by "Accounts he had received the Night before, the Fort and Garrison at Oswego together with the Naval Armament and Stores were fallen into the hands of the French," which Account his Lordship hath confirmed in his Letter of the 29th of the same Month, a Copy of which is inclosed in my other Pacquet.

As to the Particulars of this unfortunate Affair, further than what is contained in the Earl of Loudoun's last mentioned Letter, we are much in the Dark; some say the Enemy's Forces consisted of about 4000 Regulars and 3500 Canadeans and Indians; But I can scarcely Credit the Ac-

[1] Original, Massachusetts Manuscripts, Vol. 1, Library of Congress.   [2] *Ante*, p. 523, note.

count; The whole Garrison, I have very good Information, amounted on the 3d of July to about 1400 Troops. all, except five or six in good Health; and the Number of Carpenters and Workmen were about an hundred, and I suppose their Strength was about the same at the time of the Attack.

Since this we have had an Account that the Enemy had put the whole Garrison to the Sword except a few Officers, had carryed away the Seamen and Carpenters; burnt all the Works and carried off the Artillery, Stores, and Provisions, of which last there was a very large Quantity; I have Letters from Albany which inform me this Account is generally believ'd there; but a Courier from thence, who has been examined says, that two Indians and two White Men which were sent by Sir William Johnson and Colonel Webb to Oswego to discover the State of things there Report that all the Works are consumed to Ashes, that they saw no more than 400 or 500 dead Bodies in the whole, which lay in and about the old Fort, many with their Heads cut off; so that I hope there may be no more Slain, and that the rest are made Prisoners of War; All the Artillery Stores and Provisions they say were carried away, and the French with their Indians gone off.

If this is true, My Lord, it is highly probable that the Enemy have drawn off all their Forces from that part of the Country, in order to join those at Tionderoge and Crown Point, and to Attack our Forces at Lake George, where if they should prevail it is difficult to say where their Incursions will stop: If such a Blow should be struck there seems but one Way left of retrieving the Losses his Majesty will have sustain'd upon this Continent to the Westward of Nova Scotia, within these two last Years, and but the next Year to do it in. The Period seems now arriv'd for the grand Decision between us and the French concerning the Dominion of this Continent; and they pour their Regular Troops from old France by the Way of Quebec, and probably the Mississippi, so fast into it, that notwithstanding the Difficulties they may find to subsist a great Body of Troops upon it, they will soon in Conjunction with their Indians be too strong for us. His Majesty's Colonies those of New England at least, have still left among them a general Spirit (which will be much irritated by the Carnage the Enemy has made at Oswego) for attempting the Reduction of Canada, and if such an Expedition is prosecuted next Year, they would, I believe most chearfully and vigorously exert their united Strength, as one Man, but be difficultly brought to engage in any other, that does not strike at the Root of the French in North America.

In the mean time I shall use my best Endeavours, the few Days I shall stay here, to strengthen the Earl of Loudoun with more Provincial Troops; I did, soon after my Arrival at this place, issue a Warrant for impressing 600 Men out of this Government to compleat it's Quota; and have recommended it to the Assembly in the strongest Terms to augment their Troops; which they have now under Consideration; and I shall write to the other New England Governments upon the same Subject: I sent his Lordship two Companies of Rangers consisting of 60 Privates each, soon after my Return hither.

It is Reported from New York that about 900 Recruits (I suppose of Otways and the Highland Regiments) are arrived there lately; if that is so the Earl of Loudoun will have about 3500 British Troops between Lake George and the Great Carrying Place at Oneida inclusive. If it is true that the French have quitted the Country at Oswego a Body of 500 or 600 Troops seems sufficient to keep possession of the Country of the Indians of the Six Nations as far as the Great Carrying place, beyond which I suppose they will not attempt any thing in that Quarter this Year; and in such Case his Lordship will have a Body of about 2900 old Troops; which with the Provincials will make up 9, or 10,000 Men fit for Duty. Whether that Force would be sufficient for the Reduction of Crown Point, in case the French join their Forces, which they had at Oswego, with those they have at Tionderoge, etc. (which the Earl of Loudoun must best know from his Situation, and the Intelligence he may have) I won't take upon me to say, but if it is and his Lordship should employ the whole of that Force in an Attempt against Crown Point and succeed, that would go far towards immediately retrieving the Blow sustain'd at Oswego; at least such a Body of Troops would be sufficient to frustrate any Attempts, the Enemy might make in that Quarter.

It is unfortunate that the Provincials with such a Body of the Regulars as was determin'd upon in the Council of War held at Albany the 26th of May, did not March to Tionderoge; as I was in hopes they might have done before the end of July, in which Case they might not have found more than a third part of the Troops to oppose them which they now may.

I am informed from Albany by an Officer of my Regiment, that there are about 150 Soldiers of it with a proportionable Number of Officers posted at the several passes between Schenectada and Oswego. If there are any French Officers and Soldiers prisoners of War in Nova Scotia, I shall endeavour by that Means to get an Exchange of Officers and Soldiers of that and the other Regiments which were made prisoners of War, for them, as far as the Number of the French prisoners will go.

Upon my Return to Boston I found here Ninety Acadians which Governour Lawrence had sent to Georgia to be distributed in the Country there, from whence having obtain'd a let pass from the Governour, they coasted it in Boats to South Carolina, where they obtain'd another pass from Governour Glen, and with that they Coasted quite to New York, where Sir Charles Hardy gave them another, with which they Coasted it to this Province, where their progress is stopt and I have ordered them to be distributed in the Country Towns and provided for. The next Trip they had taken would have been to Nova Scotia, where they would have prov'd to that Government worse than Indians, and I suppose after this Voyage they must be exceeding good Pilots to every part of the English Coast for any French Ships of War. The Assembly is so sensible of the Mischiefs which must arise from this pernicious Practice, that three Days ago they sent me a Message to apprize me of another Company of Acadians, being upon a like Coasting Voyage from some Southern Government, and desireing I would write a Circular Letter to those Governments, pressing them to put an end to this practice; and they have promised me if this second Company should arrive here, they will keep them in the Province. I had before wrote to the Earl of Loudoun upon this Subject.

I had the satisfaction to hear that last Week his Majesty's Ship Stirling Castle arriv'd at New York with the £115,000, for the Colonies, and a Convoy of Transports having on Board Recruits and Stores for the Kings Troops: The £43,000 which I lent three of the New England Governments out of the Contingent Money to enable them to raise Men etc. for the Expedition against Crown Point is now replac'd in the hands of the Contractor's Agents here.

The Consequences of the Misfortune at Oswego will necessarily detain me here a very few Days, after which I shall embark for England on Board his Majesty's Ship the Mermaid.

I have the Honour to be with the highest Respect
My Lord
Your Lordships most Obliged
and most devoted humble Servant.
W. SHIRLEY.

The Rt: Honble: Earl of Hallifax.

Endorsed:
1756
Major Gl. Shirley
to
The Earl of Halifax.

WILLIAM SHIRLEY TO THE EARL OF LOUDOUN [1]

Boston, September 4, 1756.

My Lord,

By the Return of the Express, which carried my Letter of the 26th of August to your Lordship, I have, this Morning, the Honour of your Lordship's, dated the 29th of the same Month,[2] in Answer to it; in which your Lordship confirms the Advice you sent me in your Letter of the 20th of August, of the Surrender of Oswego to the French.

I am extreamly sorry that I have Occasion to have any Difference with your Lordship, especially upon so disagreeable a Subject as the Misfortune which hath lately befallen his Majesty's Service at Oswego; but as your Lordship hath endeavoured in your two Letters, especially that of the 29th of August, to fix the Blame of it upon my Conduct in my late Command, I am under an indispensable necessity of vindicating myself against that Charge.

Your Lordship, in your Letter of 29th August, imputes the Loss of this Important place to the Situation in which I left it; I suppose your Lordship means by that, the weak State of the Garrison and Works, at the Time when I was superseded in my Command. As to the Weakness of the Garrison, My Lord, it was reduced to that State, partly by great Desertions from the 50th and 51st Regiments, which continued ever since they have been raised, and partly by Fluxes upon their first arrival at Oswego, and a bad Scurvy, which prevail'd among the Soldiers from the Beginning of November to near the Middle of May; all which have made a great Havock among them, particularly the 50th Regiment; However, I am well informed that the whole Gar-

[1] Massachusetts Manuscripts, Vol. 1, Library of Congress, also P. R. O., C. O. 5, 46; 5, 47. Inclosed in Shirley to Fox, Sept. 5. Transcripts of this letter are in the Library of Congress and in the Parkman Papers in the Mass. Hist. Society.

[2] See Loudoun's letter of Aug. 29 on p. 521, *ante*, with note to same. Loudoun's letter of Aug. 20 is on p. 523.

rison consisted, at the time of making the Attack, of about 1400 Troops (besides Workmen) which is a larger Number, than was determined, by the Council of War held at Albany the 26th of May last, to be sufficient for putting it into a proper State of Defence; And, according to the Intelligence which we then had of the Strength of the French at Fort Frontenac and Niagara, might, together with his Majesty's Naval Force, which there was no Reason then to doubt would be upon the Lake Ontario by the latter End of July, be very justly deemed a sufficient Force for the Defence of Oswego.

As to the Fortifications, My Lord, I left them in as defensible a posture, as it was in my power to put them into; The short Time, I was at Oswego, which did not exceed two Months and three Days, would not allow me to have stronger erected, and there was, at the same time, an Hospital and Barracks to be built as soon as possible, one of the Vessels to finish, and new Carriages to be made for the Artillery. I stay'd till the 24th of October, to see them advanced, as far as was possible, before I left the fort; at my Departure I gave Orders for going forward with the Works as far as was practicable in the Winter; And I sent Mr. Mackellar and Mr. Hind, as early in the Spring as the Season would admit, to compleat and strengthen them. And, tho' they were far from being compleated, yet, at the Time of the Attack, the old Fort at Oswego was defended with a Ditch, Rampart, and strong Breast-work, which was carried on to the old Ravelin, and had 25 Cannon mounted, which made that Fort very defensible towards what they call the Street; And, tho' Fort Ontario was far from being finished according to my plan of it, yet, it was a strong Log-fort, was mounted with eight Cannon, and some Swivel Guns, and Garrison'd with about 300 Men, and was not to have been taken, without Cannon, Bombs, or scaling Ladders, by double the force that attacked it with Small Arms, which is said to have consisted of 4000 Regulars, besides upwards of 3000 Canadians and Indians, if the Garrison had done its Duty.

Your Lordship's Accounts say, that Fort Ontario was

abandoned, after being fired on for two Days, without even having one Cannon brought up to it. If these Accounts are just, the Behaviour is such as seems not to be accounted for, but by a Mutiny of the Men, which could not, I am satisfied, be for want of pay; but whatever was the Cause of such scandalous Behaviour, I hope, My Lord, I am not answerable for it.

What your Lordship intends by saying, in your last mentioned Letter, "that after having seen Colonel Mercer's Letter directed to me, you could never doubt of the Truth of Oswego's being taken" — and calling that Letter "*a Series of Correspondence upon that Subject*" — I am at a Loss to understand;[1] If your Lordship would insinuate anything by these Expressions to my prejudice, it would have been treating me with more Justice, if your Lordship had vouchsafed to have sent me a Copy at least of the Letter, especially as, you Say, it is directed to me. I doubt not whenever that is Done, to clear it from all Exceptions or Insinuations.

Your Lordship tells me in the same Letter — "that the Moment you knew the Situation of the Garrison of Oswego from Mr. Mercer, and of the defenceless Situation of the fortifications of it from Mr. Mackellar, which I had never given your Lordship the least Insinuation of, and had likewise concealed from Major General Abercromby, you used the utmost Expedition, the Situation I left things in could permit, to throw in Succours to it, but never had it in my power either to throw in a Letter, or get up Succours in time."

As to the former part of this Paragraph; I sent Major General Abercromby, before I left Albany, Colonel Mercer's and Colonel Littlehale's last Returns of the Strength of the 50th and 51st Regiments, and Copies of them to your Lordship at New York; If any thing further appears of the Weakness of those Regiments in Colonel Mercer's Letter which your Lordship speaks of, as I have never yet seen it, I can say nothing concerning it. I have full Information that on the 3d of July, the whole Garrison and the Workmen were

[1] The expressions to which Shirley refers are in the first paragraph of Loudoun's letter of August 29 (*ante*, p. 521).

in Good Health, and had not above seven or eight sick among them.

As to your Lordships Charge of my concealing the defenceless Situation of the fortifications from Major General Abercromby; Mr. Mackellar's Letter to Mr. Montresor, the Chief Engineer, which is what your Lordship refers to, was sent by me to Mr. Abercromby two or three Days after his Arrival at Albany, and if I mistake not, Mr. Montresor communicated to the General, the same Morning, the Letter which he had wrote to Mr. Mackellar by my Order, in answer to it.

And as to my not giving your Lordship the least Insinuation of it; I was so far from having any Reason to doubt of your being apprized of it by Major General Abercromby, that on the Contrary I had all imaginable Reason, from the Conversation I had with your Lordship, in the short Interviews at New York, to suppose you to have been as well informed of the State of these forts and the garrison, as of any part of the Service; Your Lordship must at least have known, from other papers I sent you at New York, that Fort Ontario was not defensible agains Cannon.

The use your Lordship would make of these parts of your Letter, seems clearly to be to excuse the Delay of sending Troops to strengthen Oswego before it was attacked, by endeavouring to shew that there was not time for doing it.

Upon this I beg Leave to observe to your Lordship, that it appearing from Colonel Webb's Letter to me, dated from New York the 9th of June, that Otway's and the Highland Regiments might be daily expected there, and being of Opinion that some British Troops might then be spared for strengthening Oswego, without interfering with the proposed attack of the French Forts at Ticonderoga and Crown point, I dispatch'd Orders, by Express, to Capt. Bradstreet, who was then upon his passage with Provisions and Stores to Oswego, to make the utmost Dispatch back with his Battoes to Schenactady, that he might be there in Time to carry a Body of those Troops with their provisions etc. to Oswego, in Case the Commander in Chief should be of such Sentiments. Capt. Bradstreet accordingly arrived at Schenactady the 10th or 11th of July; And it appears that about that time (at least before the 16th of July) it was determined by Major General Abercromby (your Lordship not being then arrived) that Colonel Webb should be sent with the 44th Regiment to Oswego; It was said on the 16th of that Month, that their Embarkation waited for a Sum of Money to pay the Battoe Men; On the 24th that it had been retarded several Days for want of having Provisions lay'd in for them at Schenactady; And it is publickly known, that either for these or other Reasons, the Embarkation of these Troops was delayed for about three Weeks, and that then they did embark for Oswego. What confirms me in this Matter is, that your Lordship told me, when I had the honour to wait on you, the Day you set out from New York for Albany, being the 26th of July, that the Garrison at Oswego was so weak, that the 44th Regiment was to be sent to strengthen it; and, at the same time, your Lordship mentioned, that you thought 900 Men, by which I suppose your Lordship meant Otway's and the Highland Regiments, were but a few to cover the Country.

Now, my Lord, it appears clearly from this Declaration of your Lordship's, at New York, that at the time of making it, which your Lordship seems to insinuate in your Letter, was before you knew of the defenceless Situation of the fortifications of Oswego *from Mr. Mackellar*, and the Situation of the Garrison of Oswego *from Mr. Mercer*, your Lordship so far knew of their State as to think they required being strengthened with another Regiment, and determined that the 44th should proceed to Oswego, according to the Destination made of it by Major General Abercromby; and consequently your Lordship's Determination to send another Regiment to Oswego, could not first arise from your seeing Mr. Mercer's Letter to me, and Mr. Mackellar's to Mr. Montresor, as your Lordship's Letter of the 29th of August, seems to imply.

Your Lordship's saying, therefore, in your Letter, that the Moment you knew of the Situation of the Garrison of Oswego from *Mr. Mercer*, and of the defenceless Situation of the fortifications from *Mr. Mackellar,* you used the utmost Expedition the situation I left things in would permit, to throw in Succours to it, but never had it in your power to get up any in time to it, does not seem to account why no Succours were sent to it in time; For as Capt. Bradstreet had been ready, at Schenactady, to transport the 44th Regiment, three Weeks before it embarked, tho' your Lordship should not have had it in your Power to get up Succours in time to Oswego, after you saw Mr. Mercer's Letter to me, and Mr. Mackellar's to Mr. Montresor, yet doubtless the 44th Regiment might have arrived in time, if it had embarked on the 16th of July, or even two or three Days later; and it seems highly probable, that, if that Regiment with the Battoemen, which would have made together about 1700 fighting Men, had arrived at Oswego before the French attacked it, (as they might certainly have done) that such a Reinforcement would have saved the place. I beg leave further to observe to your Lordship, that the 44th Regiment did not embark till five Days after your Arrival at Albany.

I would not be understood, my Lord, to tax your Lordship or any other person with Blame in this Matter, nor Shall I take upon me to determine whether it happened thro' Neglect or Misfortune; But let it have happened from what Cause it will, I can't but think, with many others, that the Loss of Oswego, may be much more justly imputed, to the Delay of sending the 44th Regiment thither, which, if it had been sent the 16th of July, or even two or three Days later, would have certainly preserved it, than to any part of my Conduct; which indeed I think is not, in the least chargeable with it.

I am, my Lord, etc.

W. SHIRLEY.

His Excellency the Rt. Honble. Earl of Loudoun etc.

Endorsed:

Copy of Major General Shirley's Letter to His Excellency the Rt. Honble. Earl of Loudoun. dated Septr. 4, 1756.

WILLIAM SHIRLEY TO HENRY FOX [1]

Boston, Septr. 5, 1756.

SIR,

I am extremely sorry to trouble you with the inclos'd Copy of the Earl of Loudoun's Letter of 29th of August to me, and my Answers to it,[2] but the extraordinary Attack his Lordship hath thought fit to make upon me lays me under an absolute Necessity of doing it for my own Vindication.

I beg leave, Sir, to refer to my Answers, and doubt not to support every fact that is asserted in them upon my Arrival in England: At present shall only add to the State of the Facts here, that one unhappy Consequence of the Delay of the Battoes, which waited for the 44th Regiment, was that some of the New Vessells, and of the greater Force, and which were much depended upon for the defence of Oswego, could not act upon Lake Ontario for want of Cannon; As also that the Want of provisions at Schenectada, on Acct. of which the Imbarcation of the 44th Regimt., was delay'd, happen'd, as I am inform'd, thus: Col. Webb, soon after his Arrival in New York forbid the former Agents to supply any more dry provisions, and the New Contractor's Agent failing to lay in a sufficient Quantity at Schenectada, the Imbarcation of the Regiment was delay'd by that Means. But the particular Circumstances of this Affair being of an uncommon Nature, I shall not go into, untill I know them with more Exactness than I do at present.

---

[1] P. R. O., C. O. 5, 46. A transcript is in the Library of Congress, as is the transcript of a like letter to the Earl of Halifax of same date. In a long letter to Fox of Sept. 4 (C. O. 5, 46) Shirley had already expressed his regret at the fall of Oswego and the capture of the garrison by the French. He had mentioned also the arrival of 90 Acadians at Boston, thus calling to mind the operations in the northeast where he had played a more glorious part earlier in his career. In this letter he endeavors to fix the responsibility for the Oswego disaster upon Webb, Abercromby, and Loudoun at least equally with himself. A copy of the letter of Sept. 4 is in the Library of Congress. See also Shirley to Loudoun of Sept. 4, preceding.　　　　[2] *Ante*, pp. 521 and 536, and *post*, p. 543.

Notwithstanding the Earl of Loudoun hath so peremptorily insisted upon my laying his Letter before the Assembly of this Government, yet as such a proceeding appears to me to be unprecedented and out of Character, and to have a direct tendency to hurt his Majesty's Service, especially at this Conjuncture, by creating factions and parties without any possibility of promoting it, I have suspended complying with his Demand for the present, and acquainted his Lordship with the Reasons; But if after a cooler Consideration he shall still persevere in his Demand, I shall then think myself under a Necessity of laying his Letter before the Court with my Answer to it; and if in such Case any Consequences should happen to the prejudice of the King's Service, I hope, Sir, the Blame will not be lay'd at my door.

I have the Honour to be with the Highest Respect.

Sir,

Your most Humble and
most Obedient Servant

W. SHIRLEY.

Rt. Honble. Henry Fox Esqr. one of his
Majesty's principal Secretaries of State.

Endorsed:

Boston, Septr. 5th, 1756.
    GOVR. SHIRLEY,
R Octr. 22d.

WILLIAM SHIRLEY TO THE EARL OF LOUDOUN [1]

Boston, Septr. 5, 1756.

MY LORD,

Since closing my Letter, of yesterday's Date, to your Lordship, I have had an Opportunity of Conversing with

[1] Massachusetts Manuscripts, Vol. I. Library of Congress, also P. R. O., C. O. 5, 46; 5, 47. Transcripts of this letter are in the Library of Congress and in the Parkman Papers in the Mass. Hist. Society.

Capt. Vickars, of my Regiment, a very intelligent, experienced Officer of 29 Years standing in the King's Army, and establish'd Character, who left Oswego, on Account of his extream low State of Health, the third of July; And he assures me, that, when he came away, Fort Ontario was mounted with eight Cannon, 6, and 9 pounders, and some Swivel Guns, and had some Cohorn Mortars in it; That it was Garrison'd with the whole of Pepperrell's Regiment, which was then at Oswego, and consisted, as he thinks, of about 400 Men; and that the Logs, with which it is picketed, are capable of resisting a small Cannon of 3 lb. if not 4lb. Ball (which I know was the general Opinion when I was at Oswego); and he is fully persuaded, that, in the Situation it was in when he left it, it could not be taken, with small Arms only, by 10,000. Men. I will venture to say, my Lord, that if the interior parts of the fort had been finished according to the plan given of it, the whole Force of Canada could not have taken it, with the Garrison it appears to have had in it at the time of the Attack, with Small Arms, and without the Enemy's bringing any Cannon or Mortars against it, as the Accounts mentioned in your Lordship's Letter of the 29th of August to be given you of it, seem to imply, it was.

That Account is thus express'd in your Lordship's Letter, "who" (meaning the French Deserters) "all agree in Fort Ontario's being abandoned, after being fired on with Small Arms for two Days, without even having one Cannon *brought up to it.*" That might possibly be, my Lord, and yet the Besiegers might have brought Cannon with them to attack it, and begun to raise a Battery against it; which, if the Account given of it in a Letter, which I have seen, from a person at Albany, to one at Boston, is true, was the Case.

That Letter says, that the Enemy "came with Small Arms and Attacked Fort Ontario; on the 13th, in the Night, they opened Trenches within Gun Shot, and the Fort," (meaning the Garrison within it) "withdrew to old Oswego; that the next Night the Enemy raised a Battery, from whence they played with five pieces of Cannon, 18, and 12, pounders, on the old Fort."

Now, I think, my Lord, it is clear, from this Account, that the Enemy brought Cannon with them to attack the forts of Oswego; and that, after firing upon Fort Ontario with their Small Arms (as your Lordships says they did for two Days) and finding they were not able to take it without using Cannon, they begun to raise a Battery against it, before the Garrison abandoned it; It is not indeed for the Honour of the Garrison, that they should quit it, before a Cannon was fired against it; But this Account effectually destroys, what I take to be the Drift of that part of your Lordship's Letter, vizt. to shew that the fort was not defensible against Small Arms.

That this is a just Account, is highly probable; since it would have been exceeding strange indeed, if the French had come without Cannon against Oswego: I should have observed that it likewise appears, that the Battering pieces the French mounted in the front of Fort Ontario, were heavier than any they found in that fort, and consequently must have been brought with them.

To this may be added, that Mr. Mackellar himself, in his Letter to Mr. Montresor, which is the piece your Lordship refers to, says in it, if I am not mistaken, that Fort Ontario was defensible against Small Arms, even, tho' thro' Mistake, he supposed it had but one tier of loop Holes, imagining the second Tier, (which he calls great part of its Defence) was taken away by the Situation of the Barracks.

As to an Engineer's critical Remarks upon an irregular wooden Fortification, as Fort Ontario was, and erected in so Short a time as not to allow its being made defensible against Cannon, except such very light pieces as I have mentioned, they are things to be expected, and of Course; especially what one Engineer writes to another; and, I think, not to be regarded in this Case; The only Question is, my Lord, Whether this fort was defensible or not against Small Arms.

The principal thing, for which I sent Mr. Mackellar to Oswego, was to strengthen Fort Ontario as much as he possibly could; and his Reasons for not doing anything to it, if scrutinized into, would not bear the Test.

I have likewise, since closing my Letter of yesterday, cast my Eye over the Letters which I have received from Colonel Mercer these last five or six Months, and from the Series of Correspondence contained in them, can't discover that he had the least Apprehensions of the Loss of Oswego; what the Contents of his Letter, which your Lordship hath in your Custody, discovers, I can't say; From what Capt. Vickars tells me, the Garrison, I find, was, during the whole Winter, and even till May, in a very weak State. Out of the eight Companies of my Regiment only, which wintered at Oswego, thirty nine Men of his Company dyed, several of the other Companies lost 35 by Deaths, and none of them under 30, besides the Loss of other Men, which were so reduced by Sickness as to be rendered intirely unfit for Service; And I suppose Pepperrell's Regiment lost in proportion. But, my Lord, the point is, what the Strength of the Garrison was, when it was attacked; and from the Information I have, there seems no Room to doubt, but that it then Consisted of about 1400 Troops, all in very good Health and Spirits, except five or six sick in the Hospital; and there were besides 100 Carpenters and Workmen there.

I am,
My Lord etc.
W. SHIRLEY.

His Excellency the Rt. Honble. Earl of Loudon etc.

Endorsed:
Copy
  Major General Shirley's Letter to
His Excy. the Rt. Honble. Earl of Loudoun
dated Septr. 5th 1756.

THE EARL OF LOUDOUN TO WILLIAM SHIRLEY [1]

Albany, Septr. 6th, 1756.

Sir,

The Night before last I receiv'd your Letter of the 30th of August, in answer to mine of the 20th, with a Copy of your Speech inclos'd.

You had, before my Arrival, receiv'd by Mr. Webb and Major General Abercromby two Letters from his Majesty's Secretary of State, commanding you to repair to England directly; and I myself did, on the 24th of July, deliver you a third Copy of the same; His Majesty's Ship, the Mermaid, appointed to carry you home, arriv'd at Boston the 13th of August; and as you have so far misunderstood those Orders, as to delay obeying them to this Day the 6th of September, and are still further delaying; I must by this acquaint you, as I am directed, that you are order'd to depart for England directly without Delay.

As for any Necessity for your personal Presence to carry on His Majesty's Service in the Government of Massachusetts Bay, I cannot but suppose, however you, Sir, may conceive it, that when his Majesty order'd you to England from thence, he did imagine his other Servants were able and proper to carry on his Service, 'till Mr. Pownall, whom his Majesty's Ministers have acquainted you, is destin'd to be your Successor, should be sent there; As Neither Mr. Webb, General Abercromby nor myself have recd. the least Aid or Assistance in the Service under my Command from your delaying, and as I am thoroughly convinc'd that no good can arise to the Civil Department of his Majesty's Service from your Endeavours to support and draw after you parties by misleading the People to expect that it is not certain that your political Connections with them will end, as you say in

[1] P. R. O., C. O. 5, 46; 5, 47. Inclosed in Shirley to Fox of Sept. 15, 1756. Transcripts of this letter are in the Library of Congress and in the Parkman Papers in the Mass. Hist. Society.

your publick Speech, at a time when you do know his Majesty's Ministers have signify'd to you, that it is the Intention of his Majesty's Orders, that you depart for England without Delay: A Copy of this Letter I shall send to his Majesty's Ministers, as a Justification of myself, that I have done my Duty.

I am,

Sir,

Your most Obedient Humble Servant.

LOUDOUN.

His Excellency William Shirley Esqr.
a true Copy,
JAMS BRADFORD Secy.

Endorsed:
Copy
    Letter from the Earl of Loudoun to
      Major General Shirley dated Septr. 6th, 1756.
In Majr. Genl. Shirley's Letter of Septr. 15th. 1756.

WILLIAM SHIRLEY TO THE GENERAL COURT OF MASSACHUSETTS [1]

GENTLEMEN OF THE COUNCIL AND HOUSE OF REPRESENTATIVES:

Your Committee deliver'd me this day your Message in answer to my speech to both Houses of the 30th: of August [2] upon the Subject of Augmenting the Troops of this Province, pursuant to the Right Honble: Earl of Loudoun's Demand in his Letter of 20th of the same Month, together with your Vote of the 7th: instant for making Provision for 1000 Men, to be drafted upon the Emergency therein mention'd out of Four of the Regiments in the Counties of Hampshire and Worcester, in order to be march'd as soon as they shall re-

---

[1] Mass. Archives. P. R. O., C. O. 5, 47; inclosed in Loudoun to Fox, Oct. 3, 1756. A transcript is in the Library of Congress.

[2] See Shirley's speech of Aug. 30, and note regarding message of General Court in answer to the same, *ante*, pp. 522 and 527.

ceive certain Intelligence from General Winslow of the Motions of the French army to Attack the Provincial Forces, that he Judges it Necessary for them to march to his Assistance, and to be sent home as soon as the Enemy may be withdrawn.

I could have wish'd, Gentlemen, you had made Provision for immediately sending this Reinforcement to Albany to be employed in such manner for his Majesty's service as the Earl of Loudoun should Judge proper, either towards Crown Point or Oswego, as I recommended to you in my Speech. Besides Gentlemen, this provision for 1000 Men's holding themselves in readiness, and not to march at present, seems not Calculated to guard against the instant sudden danger we are expos'd to from the Enemy, nor to answer the example which I recommended to you to set the other Colonies; some of which are so Situated as not to be Capable of sending timely Assistance after receiving intelligence of the motions of a French army to Attack the Forces at Lake George. I would also observe to you Gentlemen, that even if the 1000 mens holding themselves in readiness for marching upon the before mention'd Emergency was Sufficient Yet the Orders for their marching should have been left intirely to the Earl of Loudoun. The Kings General is Commander in Chief of that Expedition as well as others upon this Continent, and of the Forces employed in it and who is undoubtedly the best Judge of what his Majesty's Service requires upon this Occasion.[1]

I would further observe, Gentlemen, The reasons given in your message for not making an immediate Augmentation of Your Troops seem not Sufficient. I had Appriz'd the Earl of Loudoun of my issuing Warrants for Impressing 600 men to Compleat your Quota Voted in the beginning of

---

[1] It is interesting to note in the correspondence of Shirley his insistence on the precedence to be given to the commander in chief appointed by the king. He acts on the principle to which he had held fast in his controversy with Sir William Johnson, but which the latter, supported by the Government of New York, had refused to recognize. See Shirley to Hardy, Nov. 8, 1755, *ante*, p. 324.

this Campaigne, several days before I received his Lordships letter of the 20th August; also though you may have received information from your Committee at Albany of his Lordships orders to the Genls. of the Provincial Forces to proceed no further towards Crown point at present, yet those may arise from his Lordships thinking that those Troops are not of themselves sufficiently strong to make it adviseable for them to move towards the Enemy without a Body of British Troops to support them: which his Lordship seems in his Letter to think he cant at present spare for that purpose; so that those Orders seem rather to be an Argument for immediately Augmenting your Troops, which I think it would be adviseable for you to do considering our present danger even though the Provincial Troops should not march further this Campaigne.

I must therefore recommend it to you Gentlemen, to reconsider your Vote, and to make a more Suitable provision for the present Emergency of his Majestys service, and for the Security of these Colonies than that which you have made in your Vote appears to me to be.

I likewise in my Speech, Gentlemen, desired you to Consider and advise me how a Number of Carriages or Ox Teams for Transporting Provisions for the Forces under his Lordships Command may be procured in the most Expeditious and Effectual Manner in the parts of this Province nearest to Albany, which as you have Omitted to do either in your Vote or Message I would desire you to take under your immediate Consideration.

W. SHIRLEY.

Province House Sepr: 8th:

Copy Attest
Thos: Clarke Depty: Secry.

WILLIAM SHIRLEY TO THE EARL OF LOUDOUN [1]

Boston, September 13th, 1756.

MY LORD,

I have the Honor of Your Lordship's Letter of the 6th Instant; and must take the Liberty absolutely to deny Your Lordship's Charge of delaying to Obey His Majesty's Orders to me for going to England.

Paragraph 2d.

The Mermaid, has been on Service with Commodore Holmes, (all Summer,) who is certainly a Judge, when a Ship is proper for the Service he sends her on; If she really wanted Men to fit her for Service, there has come in and gone out, many a Merchant Ship since she came to Boston, as will appear by Mr: Shirley's Letters going home, whilst he delays the Man of War with my Packets at Boston.

2. Tho' the Mermaid arrived at Boston the 13th August, yet she is to this day, as Captain Shirley, who Commands her, Assures me, 40 men Short of Complement, which Deficiency, there is no other possible way, at this Juncture, of making up here, But by sending out a Schooner to Cruise between the two Capes, in order to impress Men out of Vessells, that she Shall find at Sea there, which is done.

Paragraph 3d.

The Plan for taking Crown Point was formed in December; the Act at Boston for raising the Troops etca. for that Service, past the Assembly, the Court, and had the Governors concurrence February 16h by the best

3. Your Lordship is pleased to tell me, that You have not received the least Aid or Assistance in the Service, under your Command, from my delaying; Your Lordship well knows, that since my being at Boston, I have Issued War-

[1] P. R. O., C. O. 5, 47. This copy contains the comments of Loudoun in the margin, and was inclosed by him in his letter of Oct. 3 to Fox. Shirley's copy lacks these comments, and was forwarded by him in his letter of Sept. 15, *post*, p. 563. A transcript of each copy is in the Library of Congress, and of the latter in the Parkman Papers, Mass. Hist. Society. See also Loudoun to Committee of War at Boston of Sept. 13, *post*, p. 561.

Information I can get, when the Troops from Massachusets Marched, they wanted of their Quota 1100 Men; they have since, lost many by Sickness, death etc. — On the 13th of September, Mr. Shirley is endeavouring to raise 600 Men, to make up part of those deficiencies, and to March them 250 Miles to serve this Campaign. I do not look on this as any Aid to the Service.

rants for raising 600 Men out of This province; the Carrying of which into Execution, hath, and will be Still attended with no small Difficulty and there is the utmost reason to think, would not have been in the least Effected, If I had not done it.

Paragraph 4th

The two Companies of Rangers here mentioned, were part of those provided by Mr: Shirley, to be raised at the King's Expence, to attend the Provincials, not the regular Troops; their Pay, by his Order, to commence from May 27h; the Officers to have English Pay, as that is higher than the Provinces give; the Men to be paid as the Men of Massachusetts Provincials, as that is more than the King gives; they were to consist of one Captain, one Lieutenant and one Ensign, three Serjeants and Sixty Privates — each Company: they arrived here, to be Armed and Cloathed, in order to begin the Campaign, on the 13h of September: the one Company consisting of 32 Privates, the other of 21 Privates; the best of their Men, Irish Roman Catholicks, the others mostly Sailors and Spaniards, in order to be rangers in the Woods; even in this Condition, I am forced to take them, but have made a saving

4. Your Lordship likewise well knows, that I have sent You, since my arrival here, two Companies of Rangers; what is it Your Lordship esteems to be an Aid or Assistance in the Service under your Command, if Augmenting the Forces under it is not?

5. I must further Observe to your Lordship, that in your Letter of the 20th August, which in that of the 29th of the same Month to me, Your Lordship calls Your publick Letter to the Government of the Massachusetts Bay, tho' specially directed to me at the Bottom of the first page, by the Appellation of His Excellency William Shirley Esqr:, without any other Addition, You demand of me, upon the loss of Oswego, " As Con-" siderable a Body of Men with Arms "as I can Send, etc."

on Mr. Shirley's bargain. You will Judge, what merit arises from this Aid.

Paragraphs 6, 7, 8, and 9

As to the words of my Letter, they were Copied from H. Ms: Instructions to me, which I thought, were the most proper for me to use on this urgent occasion; And I believe, no Man in America would have found the least fault with them, but Mr. Shirley, or by his Instigation.

I demanded an Aid of Men with Arms, and Carriages, to enable me to supply them with Provisions.

The reason of my demand, arose from the Situation of Affairs; which was, Oswego taken, and the only Accounts we then had, said by 4000 Men, against whom, Fort Ontario held out two days, against small Arms only; and Fort Oswego five hours, against a very small Battery.

Mr: Webb advanced to the great Carrying place, who had with him, and to guard the Posts West of Schenectady, the 44h Regiment, what he could collect of the 50h and 51st Regiments, what there were of three Independent Companies, what remain'd of Col: Schuylers New Jersey Regiment, and of the North Carolina Companies.

The Enemy at Oswego, supplyd with a very great quantity of Artillery and Ammunition; their own Fleet unhurt, and possessed of Ours; and

6. I did not receive this Letter, my Lord, till Saturday the 27th August, and took the first Opportunity, I had, of laying it before the Assembly, on the 30th of the same Month, in a Speech, pressing them to enable me to Comply with Your Lordship's Demand; Copy of which I sent You; and upon receiving your Lordships Letter of the 29th August I sent them on the 2d Instant a Message further Urging them to exert themselves upon this Occasion.[1]

7. Upon enquiring the reason of the Assembly's keeping this Matter longer under Consideration, than I expected, I understood by some of their Members, that a very great number of them, took unbrage at The Terms in which Your Lordship required an Aid of Men; which, though it ought not to have been An Obstacle with them, protracted the Affair some days before they got over their Difficulty; On the 8th Instant

[1] See this message, *ante*, p. 527.

above 400 boats belonging to Us; at liberty to chose, whether with those boats, they would advance to Attack Mr. Webb, and make their push that way, or Transport their People down to Montreal, and so round to Crown Point, which they could do in a fortnight, where our Situation stood thus;

At Fort William Henry and Fort Edward, the whole of the Provincial Troops; the whole of them fit for duty not above 4000 Men, the circumstances in which they were raised, you have seen in my former Letters, to which I shall only add, that on this occasion, in place of sending out the Inhabitants of the Country, which they always did before, Mr. Shirley gave leave to them, to hire any Man they could get, to go in their stead; and by this means, the New England Men, are almost all of those hirelings, who are dying daily, from a languishing to go home.

The 48th Regiment at Saratoga, in a fortified Camp, to secure that pass in the mean time, and to be at hand to Garrison the two Forts, as soon as they can be made defensible, or a possibility of lodging them in them.

I at Albany, with about 900 Men of Lt. Gl. Otways and the Highlanders, to secure the Magazines here; to secure the Communication with the two advanced posts of the Troops, and they came to the enclosed Vote, which they sent me with their Message of the same day, which is likewise enclosed; and as I dislik'd it, I sent them in the Afternoon another Message, copy of which your Lordship hath likewise enclos'd;[1] which produc'd their Vote and Message of the 11h Instant, by which Your Lordship will perceive that they have Voted 1000 Men to be fouthwith draughted out of Four of the Regiments in the two Counties, nearest to Albany, to hold themselves in Readiness to March, as soon as the Several Colonels, shall receive Certain Intelligence from your Lordship or Mr: Winslow of any Motions of the Enemy to Attack, the Provincial Forces; which is the utmost I cou'd obtain from them; And this day I shall dispatch the Necessary Orders for draughting the Men, and appoint the Officers, as also inform the several other New England Goverments; which wait to hear the Resolutions of the Massachusetts Assembly, of what they have done, and press them to exert themselves to the Utmost for His Majesty's Service.

[1] *Ante*, p. 548. The message of the General Court to Shirley is in Mass. Arch. and in P. R. O., C. O. 5, 47. The vote of Assembly is also in Mass. Arch.

to provide them with Provisions; No Magazines having been advanced, nor any means taken, to provide Waggons for that purpose; And an impossibility to get the number necessary; every one thing but Provisions still to provide; And the duty so hard for the Troops here, that neither Officers nor Men, had more than two Nights a bed.

And here I am at hand, to go to either of the Posts, where I may be most wanted; and if I were at either, and should be wanted at the other, it is impossible to get there in time.

At this time, I had not receiv'd the Accounts of the arrival of either the prest Men for Lt. Gl. Otways Regt., the Recruits for the Highland Regiment, the Artillery and Ammunition; and it was very long after, before I could get them here.

My Letters were wrote August 20th, this answer, which is the first Account I have receiv'd of any thing being done, arriv'd September 19h at Night; by the Papers Mr. Shirley transmits to me, with this Letter, you see he has brought his Assembly to vote, an Aid to the Provincials of 1000 Men, to be raised out of four Regts. of Militia, for which he is still to send Orders, and they are to Assemble their Men and March them, 200 Miles to Fort William Henry, on receiving from M. G. Winslow or me, an Account, that the Enemy, whose head quarters is

8. It is easy, My Lord, to Conjecture, if after receiving your Lordship's Letter of the 20th August, I had embarked, (in Case the Mermaid had been then ready to sail) and left the Care of this Affair with the Lieut: Governor, what Turn might have been given to it; and not without reason by others, as well as Your Lordship.

9. This, my Lord, is part of the Business, which hath employed my time ever since my Arrival here to this day, and which I apprehend is not foreign to the Service under your Lordship's Command.

but 35 Miles from them, and whose advanced Posts are much nearer, are advancing towards them; and to return as soon as they retire.

By those Orders, and the method of carrying on business, in this Country, I cannot have those Men, in less than a Month, from the time of giving the Orders.

I must further refer to Governor Hopkins's Letter to his Son, and Mr: Fitch's Letter from himself, at the desire of his Assembly, if I had not reason, to have expected an immediate Supply from those two Governments, if they had not been kept by Mr: Shirley's delays.

This I do not look on, as an Aid to the Service, but as a Cloak, to cover the Obstructions he gives, to every part of it.

Paragraph 10th

The Stirling Castle, with the Money, arrived at the Hook of New York, on the 17h of August; the Money was delivered to Sir Charles Hardy, to keep for the several Governments, till they sent for it;

And I am now forced to keep a Guard there, to secure it; and by my last Letters, none of the Governments had sent for it. — the Money to be repaid to the Contingencies, which he had lent, has been repaid long ago, or I could not have carried on the Service; So this furnishes no good Excuse for his Stay.

10. Another Material thing for me to take care of, if possible, before I left America, was the Replacing the £43,000, I had Advanced out of the Contingent Money, to The Massachusetts, Connecticut, and New Hampshire Governments, for enabling them to raise Men, and make other preparations for this Years Expedition against Crown Point with the like sum out of their Respective Quota's of the £115,000 granted by Parliament, to them, and the Other Colonies Concern'd: The effecting of this, Mr. Alexander informs me, your Lordship told him, You thought would be Attended with Difficulties, and bid him to Speak to me to take Care of: This, my Lord, could not be done before the arrival of the Stirling Castle, and I shall be able now to Compleat it.

Paragraph 11h

If Mr. Shirley has no plan for keeping up a party; for what purpose does he inform his Assembly, in his Speech, that he may come back? For what reason, does he abuse Mr. Pownall in the News Papers of every Colony on the Continent? For what reason, are his friends dispersed all over America, to give out, that he goes home to concert the plan for the next Campaign, and have the Sole Management of Affairs in America?

11. As to Your Lordship's Observation upon my Speech, to the Assembly, on my first Meeting them, after my Return to Boston; it was known at the time of my making it, to many of the Members, to whom I had declar'd it, and to some by a Sight of Mr. Fox's Letter, that it was his Majesty's Intention, as a mark of His Royal Favour, to Appoint me to be Governor of Jamaica; and that Mr. Pownall Had been thought of by His Majesty as a proper person to succeed me as Governor of the Massachusetts Bay; and I must further inform Your Lordship, that both I and Mr. Alexander understood from Mr. Pownall himself, that no new Commission would be made out for the Government of the Massachusetts Bay, 'till my arrival in England; all which is, I think a Sufficient Answer to Your Lordship's Observation on my Speech.

Paragraph 12h

I do think he is raising parties to support himself, and to convince You that no Man can serve the King in America but himself; and this he does by two methods, by enriching his friends, by lavishing the Publick Treasure, and by imposing on the People, that he is the only Man entrusted in American Affairs, by the King or his Servants.[1] As to his Services, you

12. The Inference, your Lordship would make from that Part of my Speech, is that I am endeavouring by it to Support and draw after me parties. — What parties, my Lord? Surely Your Lordship Can't mean parties to Obstruct His Majestys Service, either under Your Lordships Command, or in the Civil Department, within this Government, in the Hands of my Successor; A long Series of Faithfull Services to His Majesty, and my Establish'd Character

[1] See Shirley to Lords Commissioners of the Treasury, *post*, p. 581. The charge that the Massachusetts governor was reckless at the public expense is not borne out by the facts. See also Shirley to the Lord Bishop of Lincoln, Mar. 16, 1757, *post*, p. 584.

must know his former ones, better than I can; but when the Campaign is over, I hope to be able to shew you, in a clear light, what they have been here.

founded on 'em, will protect me, I doubt not from so injurious a Charge; let it come from what Quarter it will.

Paragraph 13h

All that passed between Mr. Alexander and me, in this Letter, was, that I thought it a very improper Letter for Mr. Shirley to write to me, and that it had cut off all personal correspondence between us; but that he might depend, on having an Answer to it, at a proper time.

13. I can't therefore but look upon this Letter as one of the Effects of the Resentment which Your Lordship sent me Word by Mr. Alexander, You was determin'd to Shew me, for writing You the Letter of the 10th August, in which I have been so unfortunate as to incur Your Lordship's Displeasure against my Intention.[1]

Paragraph 14h

I have enclosed a Copy of the Letter here mentioned, from whence you will be able to Judge, how far I was right in writing it.

My own Opinion was, that on the Information I send you, of his Management last year and this at Oswego, I am entitled to send him home Prisoner; but other People thought this would appear Violent; and I am always willing, to be advised to moderate measures.

14. After having given Your Lordship all the Satisfaction, I can, in answer to your Letter of the 6th Instant, I beg leave to say that Your Lordship seems to me, to have given Yourself a very needless trouble in sending me a Letter, to let me know that I am ordered directly to depart for England, by three Letters from His Majesty's Secretary of State, all which Your Lordship observes I have Received, and as they carry the Highest Authority in themselves, can't be suppos'd to receive any Additional Force from Your Lordships

[1] *Ante*, p. 501. A good discussion of this controversy between Shirley and Loudoun is given by Parkman in chapter 13 of his "Montcalm and Wolfe."

Letter; which I can't but think con-
cerns matters, which are entirely out of
Your Lordship's Department.
I have the Honor to be,
My Lord,
Your Lordship's
Most Humble and
Most Obedt: Servant
WM. SHIRLEY.

P.S. I have Issued a Warrant for empressing [25 ?] Ox Teams and Carriages,
for Your Lordship.[1]
His Excellency the Right Honble: the Earl of Loudoun etca.

Endorsed:
Copy
of a Letter from Gen: Shirley
To the Earl of Loudoun
Boston September 13th, 1756.
With His Lordships Remarks thereupon. —
in the E. of Loudoun's Letter of Octr. 3d, 1756.

WILLIAM SHIRLEY TO ISRAEL WILLIAMS[2]

[SEAL]

William Shirley Esqr. Captain General and
Governour in Chief in and over His Majestys
Province of the Massachusetts Bay in New
England &c.

To Israel Williams Esqr Greeting.
Whereas His Majestys Service does require a considerable
Number of Teams and Carriages for transporting Provisions

[1] See Shirley to Israel Williams of equal date, (*a*) warrant for
ox teams, etc., (*b*) warrant for raising troops, and (*c*) circular letter
to Colonial Governors urging the enlistment of additional troops,
following this letter.

[2] Original in Mass. Hist. Society, Col. Israel Williams Manuscripts, 71 D, 254.

for the Forces in the County of Albany within the Province of New York.

You are therefore hereby impowered and directed forthwith to issue your Warrants in His Majesty's Name to such Persons as you may judge will most effectually execute them, immediately to impress within the Limits of your Regiment Twenty five substantial Carts and Ox Teams with Drivers necessary and proper for transporting Provisions for the use of the said Forces, to proceed without delay to the said City of Albany there to be employed as His Excellency and the Right Honble Earl of Loudoun General and Commander in Chief of all His Majesty's Forces in North America shall direct; The Charge of which will be defrayed by the Publick, And make Return to me of your Doings hereon; Hereof fail not.

Given under my Hand and Seal at Arms at Boston the 13th day of Septr 1756 in the thirtieth Year of his Majestys Reign.

W. Shirley.

WILLIAM SHIRLEY TO ISRAEL WILLIAMS [1]

[Seal]   William Shirley Esqr. Captain General and Governour in Chief in and over His Majesty's Province of the Massachusetts Bay in New England &ca.

To Colonel Israel Williams,   Greeting.

I do hereby impower you and in his Majesty's Name require you forthwith to draw out or cause to be drawn out of the Regiment of Militia under your Command, either by Inlistment or Impressment as shall be found most proper and necessary Three hundred and fifty able bodied, effective Men, to be well armed and appointed, to be under the Command of such Officers as I shall commissionate; Who must hold themselves in readiness to march out upon any Emer-

---

[1] Original in Mass. Hist. Society, Col. Israel Williams Manuscripts, 71 D, 255.

gency for the Relief of the Provincial Troops under the Command of Major General Winslow, at what time you or in your Absence the Chief Commander over the Men so drafted out of your Regiment, shall call them out to this Service; Which you or the chief Commander of the Troops so to be drawn out of your Regiment are hereby ordered to do so soon as you or he shall receive certain Intelligence from the Right Honble. the Earl of Loudoun, or Major General Winslow of any Motions of the Enemy to attack the Provincial Forces; and for the Encouragement of the Soldiers so drawn out, that Provision is made for each Man so drawn out who shall furnish himself with a good Musket to carry with him, and shall actually proceed on the Service, that he shall receive Three Dollars Bounty Money at the Time when they shall receive their Wages, and to be added in the Muster Rolls accordingly; and that they shall be allowed the same Pay and Subsistence with the other Forces, in the Pay of this Province, and that they shall not be held to any further Duty of this kind, after the Enemy shall be withdrawn; for all which this shall be your Warrant. Given under my hand and Seal at Boston the 13th day of September 1756 in the 30th Year of his Majestys Reign.

W. SHIRLEY.

THE EARL OF LOUDOUN TO THE COMMITTEE OF WAR AT BOSTON

[Extract][1]

Mr. Shirley wrote to me on the 26th of August, to know the Truth or Falsehood of the Account of the Loss of Oswego, not only in his own Name, but in that of the Government. In Answer, I acquainted him therewith in a public Letter, and insisted "that he should lay it before the General Court not by Extracts, but in the Whole." This Desire of mine that you should be thus authentically informed of the facts, he calls, "a very improper and unprecedented proceed-

---

[1] P. R. O., C. O. 5, 46. Inclosed in Shirley to Fox, Sept. 15. A transcript is in the Library of Congress.

" ing, which has not the least Tendency to promote his Maj-
" esties Service, but the direct Contrary, especially at this
" Juncture, by creating parties and factions in the several
" Governments." In order to remove the Evils that this Aspersion may create, I herewith send you inclosed a Copy of
that Letter; which I cannot but think is a proper one for
me to write, in order to remove the Doubts, which had arisen
of the facts, and must consequently obstruct the necessary
Reinforcement, I had applied for.

a true Copy,
JAMS. BRADFORD Secy.

Endorsed:
Extract from the Earl of Loudoun's Letter to the Com-
mittee of War at Boston dated Septr. 13th: 1756.
In Majr. Genl. Shirley's Letter of Septr. 15th: 1756.

WILLIAM SHIRLEY TO STEPHEN HOPKINS[1]

Boston, September 13, 1756.
SIR,
I hereby acquaint Your Honour, that I have caused to be
raised within this Province, six hundred men, to make up
the deficiency that happens to be of the number of troops
this government had agreed to supply for the army of the
provincial forces, for His Majesty's service, against Crown
Point, which are now actually on their march; as also, that
I have issued orders for one thousand men to be drawn out
of the regiments of militia, in the western parts of this Province, to hold themselves in readiness to march forthwith to
the succor of the provincial forces, on any emergency, and
advices thereof received from the Right Honourable the Earl
of Loudoun, or Gen. Winslow, agreeably to the resolution of
our General Court, copy whereof, you have herewith.

[1] The letter here given was a circular one addressed to several
Colonial governors. This copy addressed to Governor Hopkins of
Rhode Island is printed R. I. Col. Records, 5, 533. See also letter
to Hopkins in Kimball, Corres. Col. Govs. of R. I. 2, 233.

And I would earnestly desire Your Honour to use your utmost endeavors, that your government might, in all proper ways, without delay, do every thing on their part to answer the present emergency of His Majesty's service, and the expectations of the Right Honourable the Earl of Loudoun, signified in the circular letters to the several governments herein concerned.

I am, with truth and Regard, Sir,
Your Honour's most Obedient humble Servant,
W. SHIRLEY.

To the Hon. Stephen Hopkins, Esq.

WILLIAM SHIRLEY TO HENRY FOX[1]

Boston, Septr. 15th, 1756.

SIR,

In the Letter, which I had the Honour to write you of the 5th Instant,[2] I inclosed a Copy of the Earl of Loudoun's Letter to me dated the 29th Augt., in a Postscript to which his Lordship tells me, " he had sent me a Message by Mr. Alexander, my Secretary."

The purport of this Message I could not learn, 'till Mr. Alexander's arrival; and he now informs me, it was, that his Lordship highly resented a Letter I had wrote to him (meaning one of the 10th Augt.) and that he was determined to shew me marks of it; His Lordship further signified to Mr. Alexander, that he thought I had used him ill in an appointment of an Ensign, concerning which Mr. Pownall wrote a Gentleman of this place by his Lordship's directions (as

---

[1] P. R. O., C. O. 5, 46. Transcripts of this letter are in the Library of Congress and in the Parkman Papers, Mass. Hist. Society. See also Shirley to Fox, Sept. 16, following. A careful reading of these two letters from Shirley to Fox will go far to convince the student that in the words of Parkman the change of command from Shirley to Webb, Abercromby, or Loudoun was a blunder. Certainly these letters lose nothing in dignity or patriotism by comparison with any of Loudoun's statements.

[2] *Ante*, p. 542. The letter of Aug. 29 is on p. 521, and Shirley's letters to Loudoun of Aug. 10 are on pp. 499 and 501.

he inform'd him) a Letter dated the 16th Augt., a Copy of which, and of my Answer are Inclos'd; and his Lordship added to Mr. Alexander, that if I did not very soon quit America, he should send me out of it; upon which subject his Lordship accordingly sent me a Letter, dated the 6th Instant, a Copy of which, and of my Answer is likewise Inclosed.[1]

These Letters, Sir, contain so evident marks of his Lordship's Acrimony against me, as will leave you no room to doubt of the strong Resentment he harbours; and as I should think myself blameable if I had given his Lordship (with whom his Majesty's Service made it my Duty to Cultivate the best Understanding I could) a just Cause for this displeasure; notwithstanding I have before transmitted you Copies of my Letter of the 10th Augt. to his Lordship, and of my Letter of the same date to Major General Winslow, which is referr'd to in it;[2] yet, as they seem to be the principal Sources of his Lordship's Quarrell with me, I have Inclosed other Copies of them herewith, as also one of my Letter of the 12th Septr.[3] to him, excusing those Letters, that you may judge, Sir, of my real Intention in writing them, and whether they contain any thing, which should provoke his Lordship's Resentment.

In my said Letter of the 5th Instant to you I mention'd, that the Earl of Loudoun had peremptorily insisted that I should lay his Letter to me of the 29th Aug. before the General Court of the Massachusetts Bay, and that I suspended doing it, 'till I should receive his Lordship's Answer to a Letter I had wrote him upon that Subject, wherein I

---

[1] Loudoun's letter of Sept. 6 is on p. 547, and Shirley's reply of Sept. 13 is on p. 550.

[2] See Shirley to Loudoun of Aug. 10, and to Winslow of the same date, *ante*, pp. 501 and 510.

[3] Shirley's letter of Sept. 12, here referred to, is of approximately 1000 words, and consists mainly of regrets for the appointment of an Ensign named Low, an appointment extremely distasteful to Loudoun. The letter is in P. R. O., C. O. 5, 46. Transcripts are in the Library of Congress and in the Parkman Papers in the Mass. Hist. Society.

had represented to him the Impropriety, as I conceiv'd, of such a proceeding. I now Send you, Sir, a Copy of that Letter, to which Lord Loudoun hath not vouchsaf'd to Send me any Answer, but hath chosen to publish his Letter of the 29th of Augt. to the Colonies, through a set of Gentlemen, who are appointed to act as a Standing Committee of War for this Province, and who could not avoid communicating it to the Council. A Copy of his Lordship's Letter to them, which accompanies a Copy of that of the 29th Augt. to me, is, so far as it concerns this matter, also Inclos'd.[1]

You will see, Sir, how unavoidable the publication of this dispute, and appeal upon it to the Massachusetts Assembly have been on my part; and I hope I shall not be condemn'd for refusing to acquiesce in giving up either to the Earl of Loudoun's Resentment, or to Screen the mistakes of others, not only the Reputation, which I have hitherto maintain'd in his Majesty's Service within the Colonies, but, what I have infinitely more at heart, his Majesty's Royal Approbation of them, which I have had the Honour to receive frequent marks of.

It is with extreme reluctance, Sir, that I trouble you with the foregoing Account, and the Inclos'd Packet of Letters relative to it; but as the detail of the former, and the perusal of the latter seem necessary to shew, how great a Degree of Personal Resentment Lord Loudoun hath mingled with his Representations concerning my Conduct, and how little (as I conceive) I have done to incur it; I hope, Sir, you will excuse it.

Having, Since my Letter of the 5th Septr. more fully inform'd myself of the Circumstances of the loss of Oswego I shall, in my next, lay before you in one view the Causes of that misfortune, and of the failure to prosecute this year to effect, the Expedition against Crown Point; and doubt not but it will appear from thence, that the loss of the former place to the French is wholly owing to measures, which have been taken Since the Expiration of my Command, and the failure in the reduction of the latter to the delays, which

[1] See Loudoun to the Committee of War, Sept. 13, *ante*, p. 561.

have likewise happen'd since that time; that Oswego would, in all human probability, have remain'd safe under the protection of the Land Forces and Naval Armament allotted by me for it's defence, without the Assistance of any further Reinforcement, if it had not been prevented from having the benefit of great part of them, at the time of it's being attack'd by the French; and the reduction of Crown Point been effected by the Troops destin'd by me for that Service, if their march to Ticonderoge had not been retarded by Delays.

> I have the honour to be with the highest Respect
> Sir,
> Your most Humble
> and
> most Obedient Servant,
> W. Shirley.

The Right Honble. Henry Fox Esqr.
One of His Majesty's principal secretaries of State.

Endorsed:
Boston Septr: 15th: 1756.
Majr. Genl. Shirley.
R Novr. 1st.

WILLIAM SHIRLEY TO HENRY FOX [1]

Boston, September 16th, 1756.

Sir,

Pursuant to the Letter, which I had the Honour to write you, dated the 15th instant, I shall now lay before you, in

[1] P. R. O., C. O. 5, 46. Transcripts of this letter are in the Library of Congress and in the Parkman Papers in the Mass. Hist. Society.

In this letter Shirley presents his defense against the charges of Loudoun for the loss of Oswego and shows the general hostility of Sir William Johnson and Gov. Charles Hardy of New York. Shirley does not clear himself of the responsibility for leaving Oswego with insufficient support during the spring of 1756, when the breaking up of the winter gave him the opportunity to act before

MEMOIRS

OF THE

Principal Transactions

OF THE

LAST WAR

BETWEEN THE

English and *French* in *North-America.*

FROM THE

Commencement of it in 1744, to the Conclusion of
the Treaty at *Aix la Chapelle.*

Containing in Particular

An ACCOUNT of the Importance of *Nova Scotia* or
Acadie, and the Island of Cape *Breton* to both
Nations.

The THIRD EDITION.

LONDON, Printed, 1757.

BOSTON, NEW-ENGLAND;

Re-printed and Sold by GREEN and RUSSELL, at
their Printing-Office in Queen-street.
MDCCLVIII.

WILLIAM SHIRLEY'S DEFENSE OF HIS MILITARY COMMAND IN AMERICA

one view, the several matters, which I apprehend will clearly determine to what Causes the loss of Oswego, and the failure to prosecute the Expedition against Crown Point this Year to Effect are to be imputed.

It appears from the Minutes of the Council of War held at Albany the 26th [25th ?] May last, and my Letter to Major General Abercromby dated the 27th June; Copies of both which I inclos'd in former Letters, particularly one dated the 4th July[1] from New York; that the Land and naval Forces, to which I had determin'd to trust the defence of Oswego, were to consist of a Garrison of 1300 Troops, 550 more to be posted at several passes between Oswego and Albany for Guarding the Magazines, and keeping open the Communication between those two places; two Vessels of ten Carriage Guns each, and two small Schooners (us'd as Row Gallies) of ten Swivels each, all built the last year; three Vessels built this Spring and Summer, mounting one of them 18 Cannon, one 16, and the other 12; which two last are in the Minutes of the Council of War held at Albany by mistake mentioned to carry only 10 and 8 Cannon; 250 Whaleboats capable of navigating the Lake Ontario, and holding 16 Men each; and 2000 Battoemen, which though

the French in the North could move effectively; yet he does show his appreciation of the strategic importance of the Great Lakes and the St. Lawrence as an effective line of defense and offense against the French. With them he would have secured the entrance to Lake Champlain, and thus have controlled the best route into Canada open to a land force. On Lake Ontario he planned to place vessels giving easy locomotion to the land forces, a line of action whose wisdom was proved by the combined British and American force two years later, but whose most pronounced justification came in the War of the American Revolution and in Perry's campaign on Lake Erie in 1813. This letter shows no less forcibly the difficulties faced by Shirley in 1756 and the policy of his superiors in command taking away the possibility of success for a really well-planned campaign. For a further statement in his own behalf, see Shirley to the Lords Commissioners of the Treasury, *post*, p. 581, and his petition to the Crown with accompanying papers, *post*, p. 587, Sept. 24, 1757.

[1] See Council Minutes of May 25, and letters of June 27 and July 4, *ante*, pp. 453, 468, and 478.

rais'd immediately for that Service, yet as they were arm'd
with Musquets and Hatchets and marshall'd in Companies
of 50 Men each, Commanded by two Officers, could be serviceable likewise for manning the Whaleboats or other Duty
at Land, as his Majesty's Service might require; And that,
besides this Force, I depended upon a large Body of the
Indians of the Six Nations, which Sir William Johnson was
to have assembled at Oswego this Summer, to be ready for
such Service as they should be order'd upon : to enable him
to do which, I had supplyed him with a large Sum of Money.

And with regard to the Expedition against Crown Point
it appears by the same Minutes of Council, that I had determin'd to have prosecuted it this Year (in case any Accident
should have prevented the timely arrival of the Earl of Loudoun, or the other General Officers sent by his Majesty, to
take upon them the Chief Command in North America, until
his Lordships arrival) with the Provincial Troops computed
to consist of 7000 Men (Officers included) one Company of
Rangers, 100 Indians, expected from Sir William Johnson,
and his Majesty's 44th and 48th Regiments computed at
1500 Men fit for Duty; and by my aforesaid Letter to Major
General Abercromby, that since the holding that Council,
I had rais'd a Company of Stockbridge or River Indians
consisting of 45 Men Commanded by Indian Officers, and
to be employed in this Expedition.

That the beforementioned Forces would have been sufficient for the Services, to which they were respectively destin'd, and most probably have effected them, if they had not
been prevented by Measures taken since the Expiration of
my Command, will appear from the following Observations.

The old Fort at Oswego was surrounded with a strong
Breastwork of Earth having a Ditch thrown up on the out-
side and mounted with 28 Cannon; and Fort Ontario
(though nothing had been done to strengthen it since my
departure from Oswego by the Engineers sent thither early
in the Spring, chiefly for that purpose) was picketted with
Logs from 3 to 4 feet thick, capable according to the General
Opinion, of resisting a 4 lb. Shott, was mounted with eight

pieces of Cannon besides Swivels, and had some Cohorns in it, and upon the whole was defensible against an Attack of almost any number of Men with Small Arms only.

The naval force design'd for the protection of Oswego was, according to all Accounts superior to that, which the French were preparing for Lake Ontario, (said to Consist at the most of no more than five Vessels mounted with Cannon, two of which were known to be of inferior force to any of the English Vessels which carry'd great Artillery) and consequently sufficient to have kept the Command of the Lake, and prevented the French from landing any large number of Men with Artillery and Stores near the Forts, particularly Artillery, without which Oswego was not to have been taken.

As to the Garrison, which was to consist of 1300 Troops, it might have been reinforc'd with such a number of the 2000 Battoemen, as any Emergency of the Service could, according to the best Accounts we have had of the Enemy's Strength in that Quarter, either before or since the loss of the place, be reasonably suppos'd to have requir'd; And if in addition to this force, a considerable Body of the Indians of the Six Nations had been assembled at Oswego, ready to act against the French in the defense of their own Country, as there ought to have been, it is not Credible that the French would have made any Attempt against Oswego this Year.[1]

And as to the sufficiency of the Forces destin'd for the Expedition against Crown Point; that seems to be put out of Question by the unanimous Opinion of the beforemention'd Council at Albany upon that point, and the Earl of Loudoun's continuing his Resolution to prosecute the Expedition with an equal, if not inferior force, and his not

[1] That Shirley could count on the coöperation of Sir William Johnson and the Six Nations might with reason be supposed from Johnson's letter to the Lords of Trade of July 17, 1756. In this the writer stated "the Six Nations appeared to me sincerely disposed to second any vigorous attempts which might be made on our side against the French." In the same letter Johnson mentions particularly that the Indians will aid in cutting a road through to Oswego and in building a fort at Oswego falls. (Doct. Hist. of New York, 2, 423.) See also notes on pp. 152 and 571.

Countermanding the Orders given for marching the Provincial Troops from Fort William Henry upon that Service, 'till the loss of Oswego occasion'd his Lordship's altering his Scheme.

With respect, Sir, to the state I left Oswego in and the Progress, which was made in the Expedition against Crown Point by the 26th June, the day on which my Command expired, they were as follows.

There were 1300 Troops in the Garrison at Oswego (which within seven days after was increas'd to 1400) with upwards of 250 Carpenters, Workmen and Sailors, all in good health, except 5 or 6; the old Fort was mounted with 28 Cannon and defended with the Works beforementioned; Fort Ontario was mounted with eight peices of Cannon, some Swivels and Cohorns; 550 Men [were] posted at the Passes between Albany and Oswego, and there were six Months Provisions in the Magazines at those places for 6000 Men.

The Oneida Carrying Place was reduc'd from eight to one mile Land Carriage; two small Forts were built upon it, and a third begun, and the Wood Creek was considerably clear'd of its Obstructions; both which render'd the Communication between Albany and Oswego more Convenient and Expeditious than it was the Year before.

The two Vessels built the last year, and one of the Row Gallies (the other having been taken by the French some time in June upon the Lake Ontario) were compleatly equipt for the Lake; two of the three new Vessels built this Year were launch'd on or about the 3d July, and the other on or about the 7th; All the naval Stores were arriv'd at Oswego by the 2d July, except 20 of the Cannon, which had waited at Connajoharie Falls and the Oneida Carrying Place ever since the 24th June for Capt. Bradstreet upon his third Passage from Schenectada to Oswego, without whose Convoy they would have been expos'd to the greatest risque, or rather certainty of being taken by the Enemy, before they had been landed at the last mention'd place.

The 250 Whaleboats design'd for the Lake Ontario were built, and the 2000 Battoemen rais'd by the first of April, and about 200 of the former arriv'd at Oswego by the middle of May, where they lay ready for Service on the Lake; and the latter, after having transported two Cargoes of Provisions and Stores to Oswego, had on their return defeated a considerable Body of the French, which attack'd them in the River Onondago, and arriv'd at Oswego by the 11th July, in order to transport Provisions and the remainder of the Stores with such Troops, as should embark on board the Battoes for Oswego; and might, if they had not been delay'd by waiting from the 11th of July to 12th August, for the Embarcation of the 44th Regiment, have returned thither with another Freight of Provisions, and the remaining Artillery for the Vessels before the end of July; which would have been 13 or 14 days before the French attack'd it; and in such case the whole naval Armament might have been out upon the Lake Ontario, in time to have prevented the French from landing their Men and Artillery near Oswego, or even from venturing to appear on the Lake, and the Garrison might have besides been reinforc'd with as many of the Battoemen, as the Service might have requir'd; all which collected force would, in all human probability have been sufficient to have protected the place, even without the Assistance of that Party of Indians, which Sir William Johnson had undertaken to have there by that time against any Attempt, which the French could have made against it this Year; but, if strengthen'd with those Indians could not have fail'd of doing it.[1]

As to the Preparations made for Carrying the Attempt against Crown Point into Execution, they were so far advanc'd, Sir, when I left the Command, that the Troops both British and Provincial destin'd to that Service, with their Provisions, Artillery and Stores and the Vessels and Battoes necessary for their transportation to the advanc'd Post of

[1] In his letter of July 26 to Fox (*ante*, p. 488), Shirley had mentioned the promise of Johnson to aid with the Indians of the Six Nations in the defense of Oswego. This aid had been promised by Johnson as a result of his meeting with the Indians at Onondaga, and even before the conference of July 7, 1756 (Johnson Manuscripts, 4, 70, 77; Docts. rel. Col. Hist. N. Y. 7, 146–160).

the French upon Lake George, (which is about five miles on this side of Tionderoge, and thirty beyond Fort William Henry,) were in such readiness, that the Provincial Troops might, as Major General Winslow inform'd me, have begun their march for that place by the end of the first Week in July; and before the 25th of June Provisions for 2500 Men for four Months were sent to Sarahtoga (which is within seven miles of Fort Edward) and there deposited for the use of his Majesty's Regular Troops, who also might have been ready to have march'd by the 7th of July; in which case, or even if the Troops had begun their march by the 20th of that Month, there seems to be no doubt, but that, according to the intelligence we had received, they might easily have made themselves Masters of that Post.

In the latter end of May we had undoubted Accounts that the number of the French Troops Regular and Irregular at Crown Point, Tionderoge and their advanc'd Post did not exceed 1100 in the whole besides Indians; that they were then at Work upon a new Road of Communication between the two last mention'd places; at the latter of which they had not then above 200 Men; and that Tionderoge was very accessible from thence by Land on the North west side to a Train of Artillery. In June we had certain intelligence, that they had demolish'd their Works at the advanc'd Post, abandon'd it, and drawn the Men lately posted there into their Garrison at Tionderoge; and, though since I left the Command, the French, according to the latest Accounts have return'd and taken possession of that Post, yet the Men posted there did not, on the 23d of July, exceed 400; the Works were then inconsiderable, and on the 2d September Major General Winslow attempted to make them a Visit there by Water with three Lighters, having two Cannon six Pounders, one seven Inch Mortar, and Swivels, accompanied with 7 Whaleboats, and in the whole 220 Men.

The making ourselves Masters of this Post would have secur'd a Communication by Water, as well as by Land, between that and Albany, and put it into our power to have transported Provisions, Stores and Artillery thither across

Lake George, from whence they might have been transported, and the Men march'd by Land, through a practicable Road of 5 miles to Tionderoge, without being expos'd to any of it's Batteries in their Passage; and in such case, with the Force, they had, they could not have fail'd in the reduction of that Fort, as the Army might, upon every occasion, have received fresh Supplies and Reinforcements from the Colonies, as well as British Troops, in time to have compass'd it this Year.

The Effect of the Reduction of Tionderoge, Sir, which is the place where the French seem clearly to have been for sometime collecting their main Strength between Montreal and Albany, and to design to make their stand in their dispute with us for the Command of the Lakes in that Quarter; would have been the putting Crown Point itself in our power, the distance of which from Tionderoge is not above 15 miles through a good Road for Wheel Carriages, and the same distance by Water, which is broad and navigable for Vessels of considerable Burthen; And in the mean time the compassing of all our points upon Lake George, as our possession of this Pass would effectually, of itself, have cover'd all the Country between Tionderoge and Albany against the Incursions of the French from Montreal into any part of it, either through the Lake, South Bay, or Wood Creek.

But, though the Provincial Forces did actually begin their Grand march from their Camp at Half Moon upon the Plan Settled with Major General Abercromby, yet so many Stops were from time to time put to their proceeding, that they advanc'd no further in it than Fort William Henry; where Major General Winslow receiv'd Orders from the Earl of Loudoun on the 22d of August "not to proceed to Crown "Point for the present, but to do the utmost in his power to "Guard against the Enemy's attacking them or getting into "the Country by slipping by South Bay, or Wood Creek."

His Lordship's apprehensions of the Enemy's slipping by South Bay or getting into the Country by Wood Creek, are founded I Suppose upon the Baron de Dieskau's making a march by the way of the former to attack Major General

Johnson last Year; but if it is consider'd that the Baron did that without either Artillery or even Baggage, and without expecting to be oppos'd with Cannon, how extremely difficult, if not altogether impracticable, it is for a large Body of Troops to march by South Bay with Artillery; or even by the way of Wood Creek without being discover'd. There seems no great reason to fear they will run the risque of exposing themselves to the resistance they must expect to meet with from so considerable a number of Regular Troops, as his Lordship now hath with him; supposing they could slip by the Provincials, and had Forces sufficient to leave behind them for the protection of their own Forts.

You now have the Account, Sir, of the failure in the Expedition against Crown Point. And, with regard to the misfortune at Oswego, I must proceed to observe that at the time of its being attack'd by the Enemy, it was depriv'd of the naval Armament design'd for its protection, by Capt. Bradstreet's being kept with the Battoes, and Battoemen at Schenectada from the 11th July to the 12th Augt. For if the 20 pieces of Cannon, which lay at the Carrying Place, and the Battoemen had been at Oswego by the 1st August, which would have been the case, had it not been for that delay, our whole naval Force might have been upon the Lake, and prevented the Embarcation, or at least the landing of the French with their Cannon and Stores near Oswego. Whereas for want of those 20 pieces of Cannon two of our best Vessels were without any, consequently could not appear on the Lake; and without their Assistance and that of our Whaleboats and Battoemen, or at least such a part of them as was necessary for manning the Whaleboats, our other Vessels were not strong enough for the Enemy.

Oswego was likewise, at the time of it's being attack'd, without any Assistance from the Indians of the Six Nations, which was occasion'd by Sir William Johnson's returning in July after the Council at Onondago to Albany, instead of carrying those Indians from thence to Oswego, agreeable to the appointment I made with them the year preceeding, and with the Messasagues and other Foreign Indians; which meeting Sir William Johnson, in some of his Letters to me observes, was of the greatest importance to his Majesty's Service.

This delay of the return of the Battoes to Oswego was occasion'd, Sir, by the following means.

Intelligence had been gain'd from a French Prisoner taken by Capt. Bradstreet on the 3d July,[1] that the French were forming a large Incampment at about 32 Miles distance from Oswego and design'd soon to attack the place; This Major General Abercromby was appriz'd of upon Capt. Bradstreet's arrival at Albany (being on the 10th or 11th July) and in one or two days after gave Orders for Colonel Webb and the 44th Regiment to hold themselves in readiness to march to Oswego; But their Embarcation was delay'd, and the Battoes detain'd, as is before observ'd, from the 11th July to the 12th August; which was thirteen days after the arrival of the Earl of Loudoun himself at Albany, though by mistake in my Letter of the 4th September to his Lordship,[2] I call'd it five days only; and this, according to the inclos'd Declaration and Extracts of two Letters relative to the same point (which I have good reason fully to Credit) and other Accounts, was owing to a dispute whether Colonel Webb should receive any Provisions for the transportation of those Troops, that were not supply'd by Mr. Kilby.

About the same time a great number of the Battoemen (800 as I am inform'd) whose usefulness not only by Water, but in an Action by Land, against the Enemy had been so lately experienc'd, were discharg'd.

To this delay therefore principally, the Discharge of so many Battoemen, and the failure of Sir William Johnson to assemble the Indians of the Six Nations at Oswego, whereby that place was depriv'd of so essential a part of the defence, which it ought to have had at the time of its being attack'd, and for want of which in all human probability it was lost, together with the Garrison and the Command of Lake On-

---

[1] See Bradstreet to Shirley, July 16, 1756, *ante*, p. 485, and July 24, 1756, *ante*, p. 487.

[2] See letter referred to, *ante*, p. 536.

tario, it seems evident, Sir, that the misfortune, which his Majesty's Service hath sustain'd there, is to be imputed.

If any other Endeavours have been used since the Expiration of my Command, either before or after the Earl of Loudouns arrival in America " to throw Succours into Oswego" (which his Lordship seems to allude to in his Letter of the 29th Augt. to me [1]) than those herein beforemention'd, which have most unhappily depriv'd it of that defence, it would otherwise have had; and which would have been sufficient for its protection, without any new Succours; I have not heard of them : Had indeed the 44th Regiment which Major General Abercromby at first, and the Earl of Loudoun afterwards order'd to proceed to Oswego, been, upon our receiving intelligence of the design of the French to attack it, embark'd in time for the Battoes to have arriv'd there before that Attack, which might easily have been done; such Endeavours would not only have sav'd the place; but might have strengthen'd the Forces there, so as possibly to have enabled them even to act offensively upon the Lake Ontario.

For a full Account of the beforemention'd Dispute concerning the Provisions, and the true Cause of the Delay in the Embarcation of the 44th Regiment, I beg leave to refer you, Sir, to the inclos'd State of it.[2]

I have the Honor to be with the Highest Respect,
Sir,
Your most Humble
and
most Obedient Servant
W. SHIRLEY.

[1] *Ante*, p. 521.

[2] The manuscript to which Shirley here refers is entitled: "State of the Dispute concerning the Provisions for transporting the 44th Regiment to Oswego, and the true Cause of the Delay of its Imbarcation." With it are four depositions, etc., tending to fortify the contention of Shirley. All are in P. R. O., C. O. 5, 46, inclosed in the letter here given. With this deposition of Shirley should be read the twenty-seven-page statement of Loudoun to Fox oi Oct. 3, inclosing his letter from Shirley of Sept. 13. The contrast

Right Honble. Henry Fox Esqr.
One of His Majesty's principal Secretaries of State.

Endorsed:
 Boston, Septr 16th, 1756.
  MAJR. GENL. SHIRLEY.
R Novr. 1st.

is illuminating so far as the characters of the two men are concerned. Shirley's letter is the sturdy honorable defense of an officer against what he considers unworthy attack. When Loudoun is compelled to admit a point in his predecessor's favor, he does it grudgingly. The Earl's letter may be judged by the following extracts: —

Albany 3d. October 1756.

*   *   *   *   *   *   *

From the time I received his Letter of August 10th, I resolved to drop all Correspondence with him, as Mr. Shirley; the governor I could not do that with: the only Letters I have writ him since, was the demand for Aid on the taking Oswego; the next was an Account of it's being certain that it was taken, in answer to one from him, in the name of his Assembly; the third was the Letter to Acquaint him, that it was expected, he should obey His Majestys Commands, in going home.

These are the only Letters I have wrote to him, for I have neither time nor Inclination, to enter into a Paper War with Mr. Shirley.

*   *   *   *   *   *   *

Since writing the above, I am informed, Mr. Shirley is endeavoring to lay the mismanagement at Oswego, on us; and says, that after he had forwarded Provisions to Schenectady, that we brought them back here; I was sure that had not happened after I arrived but must have been at the time he Commanded, if it was at all. And after examining into it, I have the State of that Case from the Commissary of Stores, who at that time, had the delivery of the whole Provisions, which I send enclosed.

I have said in my Observations on Mr. Shirley's last Letter, that I did not expect any of that Recruit to the Provincials of Six hundred Men, which he mentions or the Waggons, which there were no appearance of at that time; but that I may not do him any injustice I must now acknowledge, that there are arrived 320 Men, and Sixteen Ox Carts; and I hear, there are more Carts on the Road; they will be of great use, though they come very late, con-

WILLIAM SHIRLEY TO STEPHEN HOPKINS [1]

Boston, September 20, 1756.

SIR,

I have but a few moments time before the post will go out for the last time before I embark for England, to desire Your Honor to let me know by a letter to be transmitted to me, in England, under cover, to Messrs. Thomlinson and Trecothick, merchants, in London, how your Assembly and people would stand affected towards an expedition against Cape Breton, early in the spring, in case that should be proposed from England, with an assurance of the places being kept, and with proper arrangement.

I am, with great regard, &c., &c.

W. SHIRLEY.

To the Hon. Stephen Hopkins, Esq.

ROBERT HUNTER MORRIS TO HORATIO SHARPE [Extracts] [2]

Philad. Octor. 8th, 1756.

DEAR SIR,

Your favour I had the honor to receive a few days after I gave the Government into Mr. Denny's hands, to whom I

sidering I demanded them August 20th and they arrive October 2d.

* * * * * * *

The Right Honble.   ⎫   LOUDOUN.
  Henry Fox Esqr. ⎭

It should be remembered that between Aug. 20 and Oct. 2 the demand had to travel from Loudoun to Shirley, and the oxen had the return journey to take. See Morris to Sharpe of Oct. 8, following.

[1] R. I. Col. Rec. 5, 565. The letter is interesting as illustrating Shirley's activity and the eagerness with which he turned to a new field of effort.

[2] Original, Maryland Historical Society. Printed: Arch. of Maryland, 6, 492. These extracts are here given to show the view

wish a more agreeable, and advantageous administration, than fell to my share.

$$* \quad * \quad * \quad * \quad * \quad * \quad *$$

All designs of acting offensively seem to be laid aside for this year, and I do not know that we shall have as many men next summer as we had this, unless the New England governments are better pleased than I imagine they have had any reason of late to be. The Loss of Oswego I esteem a very fatal blow to the British Interest on this continent, and must be owing to the alterations made in the Plan of operations settled at New York which with great submission to better Judgements, I think could not be changed but for the worse. I find the N. York scheme is to lay the blame of that affair upon Genl. Shirley, but how just their censures are the following facts will show.

Genl. Webb arrived at New York . . .	June 7th	
Genl. Abercromby arrived	. . .	Do. 15
both arrived at Albany	. . .	Do. 25

taken of Shirley's campaign by the Governor of Pennsylvania. Franklin's view was equally favorable.

A different and less friendly opinion is that of Sir John St. Clair in his letter to Sharpe of Sept. 22: "What has happened to us by Mr. Shirley's conduct is enough to alter the nature of Man, nor do I find he has altered his way of thinking since he has been superceeded" [sic]. This was written before the aids raised by Shirley, after leaving New York, had been received and in the unfavorable atmosphere caused by the controversy regarding rank between the British and Colonial officers. Lt. Col. St. Clair served under Braddock at Fort Duquesne and saw in the failure of the New Nork campaign a disaster of almost equal weight. For this disaster he placed all blame upon Shirley, who appeared to be condemned already.

Judgments of the time favorable to Loudoun are liable to be influenced by the fact that the latter was the new Commander in Chief and representative of the Crown in America. An opinion of Governor Dinwiddie would be regarded as hardly impartial when we find him in a letter of Oct. 28 to Loudoun offering to pay that general from Mar. 8, 1756, the same amount that he had been paying Lord Albemarle for his commission as Governor of Virginia (Dinwiddie Papers, 2, 534); and judgments from other persons dependent upon the Earl would be little more trustworthy.

On the 26th of June Genl. Shirley acquainted Genl. Abercromby of the state of Oswego and advised the sending two Battalions there.

Bradstreet returned to Albany on the 12th of July having thrown into Oswego six months Provisions for five thousand men, and a great quantity of Ammunition and naval stores, and defeated a party of French and Indians on his way back; and on the same 12th of July informed Genl. Abercromby that he had intelligence from his Prisoners, that a french army was in motion and designed to attack Oswego; whereupon the 44th Regiment was ordered to hold itself in readyness to march to Oswego.

Lord Loudoun arrived at New York, . . . July 23
            Do   arrived at Albany   . . . Do 29

On the 12th of August the 44th Regiment moved towards Burnets field, with a number of Battoe men who had remained Idle at Schenectaday from the 11th of July and on the 19th of August Genl. Webb then at Burnets field, received the news of Oswego's being taken, upon which he marched to the Oneida carrying place and ordered the wood creek to be filld with trees, which was accordingly very effectually stopd.

I have mentioned these facts that you might be satisfied of the truth with respect to that important Loss.

* * * * * * *

I wish you much health and success in every affair you undertake and am with great truth,

Dr Sir
            Your Most obedt
            Humble servt
            ROBT H. MORRIS.

WILLIAM SHIRLEY TO THE LORDS COMMIS-
SIONERS OF THE TREASURY [1]

To the Rt. Honble. Lords Commissioners of his Majesty's Treasury.

> The Memorial of Major General William Shirley, late General and Commander in Chief of His Majesty's Forces in North America.

Humbly Sheweth,

That your Memorialist, pursuant to the Directions of His Majesty's late Secretary at War, reimburs'd himself in America for the Expences, he had been at, for Levy Money, and the incident Charges of inlisting the Soldiers of his late Regiment; which he did with all the Frugality in his power, the said Expences falling 10s. 3d. per man short of what was allow'd to him and Major General Sir William Pepperrell upon the Reduction of their former Regiment in 1749 for the like Charges; as also of what was allow'd by His Majesty for the like Expence of raising Levies in North America for the Royal American Regiment, since the Commencement of the present Warr.

That your Memorialist, in raising the beforementioned Levies, was oblig'd to employ Recruiting Parties in the four Colonies of New England, and the three Provinces of New Jersey, New York, and Pensilvania; from which three Provinces it was necessary to transport the Troops inlisted there (amounting to 426 Men) by Sea to Boston, chiefly in the Winter, which cost your Memorialist £575 : 1 : 6; and their Subsistence in the three beforementioned Provinces from the time of their being rais'd to their Imbarkation for Boston (which he likewise paid) cost him £148 : 8/, as will appear by the Accompt of those Expences herewith presented, and sworn to.

That he was likewise oblig'd to be at the Charge of £513 :

---

[1] *B. M., Additional Manuscript 33055, 240.* A transcript is in the Library of Congress.

6 : 7 in extraordinary Cloathing for the Levies and Recruits, which he rais'd for forming his Regiment (according to the annex'd Accompt, which is likewise duly sworn to) and for which the Service would not allow of any Stoppages to be made from the Men.

Your Memorialist further sheweth, that thro' Error, occasion'd by the great Variety of Business, he was engag'd in during his Command, he impress'd no more Money in America than £160 : 10s, towards reimbursing himself for the first mention'd Article of £575 : 1 : 6, and none for reimbursing him for the three last; So that there remains due to him from the Crown £1112 : 6 : 1 in the whole, on Account of all the aforesaid Articles; for which no Allowance has been hitherto made him in any shape; nor has he made any Charge of that Nature in his former Accompts; the Truth of which he has likewise attested by his Affidavit annex'd to his Accompt herewith presented.

Your Memorialist further sheweth, that whereas his Predecessor and Successor in his late Command receiv'd, each of them before they left England, from the Paymaster General by Virtue of a Warrant sign'd by the Lords of the Treasury, £2000 for Intelligence, Secret Services, and other Contingent Expences, and £1000 for Equipage Money, Your Memorialist being in America when he was appointed to the Command, had no Sum advanc'd to him, nor impress'd any in America on either of those Accounts. That with regard to the former of these Articles, your Memorialist lay'd out several considerable Sums, during his Command, in secret Services, wherein he employ'd Indians and others; the Benefit of which the Nation must soon have reap'd, if that had not been prevented by Misfortunes, which attended His Majesty's Service the Year following.

And with respect to the Article of Equipage, it costs more in America, where your Memorialist was oblig'd to purchase it, than when it is purchas'd in England; And he humbly hopes, that his being Governor of the Massachusetts Bay at the time of his being appointed to his late Military Command, will not be deem'd a reason for precluding him from the before mention'd Allowance of £1000 for Equipage Money, as the profits of that Government (which do not exceed £1100 per Annum) did not afford him more than what enabled him to live as a private Gentleman; And the Equipage necessary for him to purchase for his Outset in his Military Command from Boston was the same, that it would have been, if he had set out in it from England, and more expensive to him in America, than if he had furnish'd himself with it there.

That your Memorialist was not employ'd in his Military Command in America above ten Months, within which time he was at the Expence of a publick Table for two Campaigns; which, with the before mention'd Sums expended by him for the Transportation, Subsistence, and extraordinary Cloathing of his late Regiment, his Equipage and secret Services (for which last Article he makes no Charge in his Annex'd Accompt) exceed the pay, he receiv'd for his Service in the Command.

That your Memorialist humbly hopes, he has not forfeited his Pretensions to what his Majesty was graciously pleas'd to allow his immediate Predecessor and Successor in his Command by any Misconduct in his Military Operations; which, tho' of a short continuance, and without Regular Troops, except two new rais'd American Regiments, were attended with considerable publick Successes; particularly the saving of the province of Nova Scotia in 1755 by the Reduction of the French Forts there, owing principally to your Memorialist's timely raising a Body of 2000 New England Men, and fitting out the Armament, from Boston, which, in conjunction with 350 of his Majesty's regular troops posted in Schiegnecto, effected that service; and for which your Memorialist was honour'd with his Majesty's Royal Approbation signify'd to him by one of his principal Secretaries of State.

And with regard to his Management of the publick Money, he begs leave humbly to observe to your Lordships, that he executed that Trust with all the Frugality that was consistent with the good of his Majesty's Service; one Instance of which (among others) might be given in his obliging the Colonies to find Provisions at their own Expence for the troops, they rais'd for his Majesty's service in 1756 (amounting to about £80,000 sterling, which it appears, the Government thinks they ought to have been allow'd at the Expence of the Crown, and it has been lately pleas'd to reimburse them for; And it is well known that your Memorialist upon former Occasions, during the last Warr, sav'd the Nation about £60,000 by his Œconomy in the Execution of the publick Trusts, then repos'd in him.

Lastly, Your Memorialist begs leave to represent to your Lordships, that far from having acquir'd a Private Fortune in his Majesty's service, he shall be greatly distress'd in his circumstances unless the allowances, herein pray'd for, are granted him by your Lordships.

Your Memorialist therefore humbly prays, that your Lordships will be pleas'd to order him Payment of the several Sums of £414: 11: 6; £184: 8, and £513: 6: 7; for reimbursing him his Expences in his Accts. annex'd; as has been usual in like Cases; together with the further Sum of £1000, which was allow'd both to his Predecessor and Successor for their Equipage Money,

And Your Memorialist, etc.

W. SHIRLEY.

Endorsed:
Memorial of Major
General Shirley.

WILLIAM SHIRLEY TO THE LORD BISHOP OF LINCOLN [1]

St. James's place, March 16th, 1757.

MY LORD,
What your Lordship mention'd to me last night concerning my having furnish'd Mr. Charles Townshend with Evidence to attack the late Lords of the Treasury, which the Duke of Newcastle was at the head of, upon the present

---

[1] *B. M., Additional Manuscript 32877, 468.* A transcript is in the Library of Congress.

Contract made with Messrs. Baker and Kilby for supplying the King's Forces in North America with Provisions, hath dwelt so much upon my Mind, that I beg leave to trouble your Lordships with the following Acct. of that matter.

The inclos'd is an Extract of a private Letter from me to Lord Halifax dated from Boston 28th March 1756 in vindication of myself against some injurious Reports, which I had been inform'd were propagated in London concerning my management of the contingent money under my direction with regard to the purchasing provisions and stores, and which had reach'd his Lordship's Ears: And in order to contradict these Reports in the City, I transmitted in the same Vessell, which carry'd my Letter to Lord Halifax, the like Accts to my Correspondent there, and to Mr. Bollan, to be communicated as he should think proper for my Vindication about St. James's; I mention'd to him in particular Mr. West Secretary to the Treasury, thro' whom I was desirous the Duke of Newcastle and the late Lords of Treasury would be appriz'd of it; Mr. Calcraft, thro' whom I imagin'd Mr. Fox would be inform'd of it; the late Mr. John Sharpe, and Mr. Charles Townshend, all connected, as I then thought, with the Duke of Newcastle's Administration, and at a time when I had not the least Idea of the present Contract's being made with Messrs. Baker and Kilby by the Treasury.

Mr. Bollan, knowing at the time of his receiving my Letter to him with the inclos'd Acct. of my victualling the Troops after the Rate of $3\frac{1}{2}$ per man a Day, that I was sent for over to England, and should soon arrive there, determin'd not to deliver the papers inclos'd to him to any of the persons: But happening accidentally to mention them to Mr. Townshend, he desir'd one of the Accts. and had one of them deliver'd long before I arriv'd in England; and by that means became possess'd of my Rate of victualling the Army, and the 2000 New England Men sent to Nova Scotia.

The Minutes of the Treasury containing the Stipulation of Mr. Baker's Contract I was an utter stranger to, and were obtain'd from the Treasury; the second parcel of Papers he was furnish'd with from the Secretary of State's Office, were brought into the House at Mr. Baker's Motion, or that of one of his Friends, as I understand. Among these is contain'd the most material Evidence for shewing that the Crown was at the Expence of transporting provisions supply'd by Messrs. Baker and Kilby from Albany, arising from one of Lord Loudoun's Letters, which I knew nothing of before it was brought into the House: My Accts. he had of Course from the Treasury, which only tended to shew the Rate, at which the Troops were victual'd during my Command, and did not contain any thing relative to Mr. Baker's Contract; and as to Doctr. Kirkland's Evidence tending to shew that Lord Loudoun had paid out of the Crown's Money the Expences of transporting Mr. Baker's Provisions from Albany towards Fort William Henry, it was given Mr. Townshend before I knew Mr. Kirkland could give any Evidence of that kind; and Mr. Townshend has not been furnish'd by me with any papers whatever with the least View of putting it into his Power to attack the late Lords of the Treasury for making the present Contract relative to provisions; nor could I possibly help Mr. Townshend's making the Attack he did; which your Lordship, I believe, will recollect, put me under great Concern, when I first heard of it; and that I express'd great Uneasiness at it.

The great Obligations, I have to the Duke of Newcastle, my first Patron, I shall ever have the most grateful Sense of; And was it in my power to give the most solid proof of it, nothing would give me an higher pleasure, than to demonstrate thereby my unalterable Attachment to his Grace; And I should be highly oblig'd to your Lordship, for your good Offices in clearing up any Idea, that may be entertain'd to the contrary.

I am with the greatest Respect,
My Lord,
Your Lordship's most Oblig'd, and
most Obedient Servant.
W. SHIRLEY.

Rt. Revd. Lord Bishop of Lincoln.

WILLIAM SHIRLEY TO THE DUKE OF NEWCASTLE [1]

Upper Grosvenor Street, Septr. 24, 1757.

My Lord Duke,

I beg pardon for the repeated Trouble, I give your Grace, upon my Intended petition to his Majesty.

The Sollicitation now making, as I understand, My Lord, by a Gentleman for the Governmt. of Jamaica, which will appear, from the Inclos'd Extract of Mr. Fox's letter to me, it was H. My's Intention to confer upon me as a Mark of his Royal favour for my Services, has occasion'd an Alteration in my petition, which I think it my Duty to lay before your Grace, for your Grace's Approbation (as I did my first Draft of the petition) together with the Inclos'd Representation of some of my Services, which I intend shall accompany it.[2]

The first part of those Services, my Lord, your Grace is not unacquainted with, as they were done under your Grace's Immediate patronage and Support; which enabled me to execute them. And your Grace had then so favourable an Opinion of them as to Honour me with the highest Expressions of your Goodness and Regard for me. Some successfull Services have been done by me this War; and I am not conscious of having done any thing to forfeit his Majesty's Royal favour.

As to the Suggestions, my Lord, transmitted against me by my Successor, they are unsupported by proofs; and I hope, upon the Common presumption in favour of every Officer's having done his Duty, 'till the Contrary is prov'd, and the Credit of having faithfully done it in other well known Instances, I am intitl'd to be believ'd when I assert to your Grace, that they are intirely groundless and malig-

---

[1] *B. M., Additional Manuscript 32874, 276.* A transcript is in the Library of Congress.

[2] See Petitions of Shirley to the Crown with accompanying Representation, *post,* pp. 588 and 590.

nant; which I am ready to prove upon an Opportunity's being given me.

My present situation, my Lord, is thus; After spending many years of my life in faithfull Services to the Crown, most of them National, and successfull; in which I have acquired no private Fortune, and have had the unhappiness to lose my two Eldest Sons in one Campaign, I am now divested of my late Government and Regiment; both which marks of H. My's Royal favour your Grace procur'd for me, and am at present left without means of Support. And as I am not conscious, My Lord, of having fail'd in any one point of Duty, Gratitude or Attachment to your Grace or done anything to forfeit your Grace's favour and protection, I hope I shall be honour'd with them upon this Occasion, in the Support of my petition to his Majesty.

I am with the deepest sense of my Obligations to your Grace, and the most dutifull Respect,

My Lord,

Your Grace's most oblig'd and

most Devoted Servant,

W. SHIRLEY.

His Grace the Duke of Newcastle.

Endorsed:

  Upper Grosvenor Street

    Septr. 24th, 1757.

MR. SHIRLEY

R 25th.

WILLIAM SHIRLEY TO THE BRITISH CROWN [1]

To the King's most Excellent Majesty in Council.

The Petition of Major General William Shirley.

Most Humbly Sheweth,

  That your Majesty's Petitioner hath, by Virtue of divers

---

[1] *B. M.*, *Additional Manuscript 32874, 280.* Inclosed in Shirley to Newcastle of Sept. 24. A transcript is in the Library of Congress. This is apparently the first draft of the petition. The final copy is on p. 590.

Commissions and Authorities, which he hath had the Honour to receive from your Majesty, been engag'd in various parts of your Majesty's Service for the defence of your Majesty's just Rights in North America.

That he hath acted in the Execution of the Trusts repos'd in him by your Majesty with the utmost Fidelity and Zeal, and been at divers times honour'd with signal Marks of your Majesty's gracious Acceptance and Royal Approbation of several parts of his Service, as will appear by the Representation of them herewith presented.

That Suggestions against some parts of his Conduct in his late Command, as General of your Majesty's Forces in North America, having been transmitted in Letters from his Successors, your Majesty was pleas'd about six Months ago, to order an Inquiry to be made into his Conduct by a Board of General Officers.

That your Majesty's Petitioner conscious of his faithfull Regard for your Majesty's Service, and not doubting, that he is able to acquit himself upon an Inquiry into his Conduct, which he humbly conceives it was one part of your Majesty's gracious Intention, in case of his Innocence, to give him an Opportunity of doing, has solicited for several Months to have the Benefit of that Inquiry; But some Doubts having, as he understands, arisen concerning the Sufficiency of the Matter and Evidence transmitted from America for supporting a Charge of Misconduct against him, he finds no prospect of his obtaining it.

Wherefore your Majesty's Petitioner most Humbly prays as that Inquiry is not proceeded in, that your Majesty will be graciously pleas'd to order some other Inquiry to be made into his Conduct, in such manner, as your Majesty, in your Royal Wisdom and Goodness, shall think fit; whereby he may have an Opportunity (after laying so long under the Pressure of the Suggestions made against him) of justifying his Behaviour, vindicating his Honour from the Imputations cast upon it, and procuring the Continuance of your Majesty's Royal Favour, and which a long Series of faithfull Services had before advanc'd him.

And your Majesty's Petitioner, as in Duty bound, shall ever pray, etca.

WILLIAM SHIRLEY.

Endorsed:

Copy of the Intended Petition of Major General William Shirley to His Majesty in Council.

WILLIAM SHIRLEY TO THE BRITISH CROWN [1]

To the King's most Excellent Majesty.
The Petition of Major General William Shirley.

Most Humbly Sheweth,

That your Majesty's Petitioner hath had the Honour to be employ'd sixteen Years in various parts of your Majesty's Service, and to receive divers signal Marks of your Majesty's Royal Approbation of his Conduct; as will appear to your Majesty from the Representation of his Services herewith presented.

That in June 1756, He had the Honour to receive your Majesty's Orders to repair to England; in which Orders it was signify'd to him, that it was your Majesty's Intention, as a Mark of your Royal Favour, to appoint him to be Governor of Jamaica; And your Majesty was thereupon pleas'd to nominate Mr. Pownall to succeed him in his Government of the Massachusetts Bay.

That in Obedience to those Orders, your Majesty's Petitioner arriv'd in England in October last; since which your Majesty has been pleas'd to reduce the Regiment, which he had then the Honour to command.

That soon after his Arrival in England, Letters were transmitted thither from his Successors, as General of your Majesty's Forces in North America, containing Suggestions against his Military Conduct; and he was inform'd, that

[1] *B. M., Additional Manuscript 32874, 278.* Inclosed in Shirley to Newcastle of Sept. 24. A transcript is in the Library of Congress. This is the petition as presented.

your Majesty intended to order an Inquiry to be made into it.

That conscious of his Zeal and Fidelity in your Majesty's Service, and that these Suggestions were groundless, he has waited many Months in hopes and Expectation, that his Conduct would be inquir'd into; being satisfy'd that in such Case he could shew, that he had been instrumental in every part of your Majesty's Service in North America, which was attended with Success, and no ways accessory to any Misfortune, which had befall'n it during the War; and in particular, that neither the loss of Oswego, which happen'd fifty Days after the Expiration of his Command, nor the failure to prosecute the Expedition against Crown point to Effect could with Justice be imputed to him.

Wherefore as these Suggestions have so long continu'd unsupported by any proofs, your Majesty's Petitioner, who is divested of his late Government and Regiment (wherein his Support consisted) most Humbly begs leave to resort to your Majesty, praying That your Majesty will be graciously pleas'd to honour him with the Continuance of your Royal Favour, to which a long Series of faithfull Services, during the late and present War, had advanc'd him, by conferring upon him your Majesty's late intended Mark of it, or such other Mark, as your Majesty, in your Royal Goodness, shall think proper.

And your Majesty's Petitioner as in Duty bound shall ever pray, etc.

WILLIAM SHIRLEY.

Endorsed:
Copy Petition of Major General Shirley to His Majesty.

WILLIAM SHIRLEY TO THE BRITISH CROWN [1]

To the King's most Excellent Majesty
   The Representation of Major General William Shirley's
   Services in North America refer'd to in his Petition.

Most humbly sheweth,
   That the Governor of Cape Breton having immediately
after receiving notice from France of the Declaration of War
in 1744, fitted out an Armament from Louisbourg, which
burnt your Majesty's Fort at Canso, made the Garrison
prisoners of War, and destroyed the English Fishery there,
your Majesty's petitioner, then Governor of the Massachus-
setts Bay in New England, in order to prevent Annapolis
Royal (at that time the Capital of Nova Scotia) and the
whole province from undergoing the same Fate with Canso,
raised timely Succours for it's Relief, whereby they were
preserved twice that year, when upon the point of falling
into the Enemy's hands.
   That in 1745, upon gaining Intelligence that the French
Commander had, soon after the Defeat of his Attempt against
Annapolis Royal, embarked for France, in order to represent
there the weak State of Nova Scotia, and propose the sending
an Armament that year for the Reduction of it (in Consequence of which a Squadron of five Ships of War sailed from
France the succeeding Summer upon an Expedition against
it) Your Majesty's Petitioner, to counteract the Enemy's
Designs, and save your Majesty's American Dominions
from suffering so fatal a Loss, fitted out an Armament from
Boston early in the Spring upon an Expedition against Cape
Breton, in which an Acquisition was made of that Island to
your Majesty's Dominions, before the arrival of the French
squadron in America; And your Majesty's province of Nova
Scotia was thereby again preserved, the French fishery destroyed and the English fishery restored and enlarged.

   [1] *B. M.*, *Additional Manuscript 32874, 282.* Inclosed in Shirley
to Newcastle, Sept. 24, 1757. A transcript is in the Library of
Congress.

That in the year 1746, the French having fitted out a large Squadron under the Command of the Duke D'Anville upon an Expedition principally against Nova Scotia, and Mr. de la Corne having that Summer entered the Province with a Body of 1700 Canadeans and Indians, and advanced within About two Miles Distance of the Fort at Annapolis Royal, in Expectation of the Assistance of the French squadron, Your Majesty's Petitioner, before it's Arrival in America, sent to Annapolis Royal a considerable Reinforcement of the Massachusets Troops, raised that Year for the Reduction of Canada; which again saved that province from falling into the Hands of the French; and the Care of that Government being then committed to him, he afterwards prevented the Acadeans from a total Defection, and joining the French in attacking Annapolis Royal, which they were upon the point of doing, and the province was intirely cleared of the Enemy before the End of the War.

For the first of these Services done in 1744, your Majesty was pleased to honour your Majesty's Petitioner with declaring your Royal Approbation of them in your Majesty's Privy Council; for those done in 1745, with a Mark of your Royal Favour in giving him the Command of a Regiment to be forthwith raised by him in America; and as a proof of your Majesty's Intention to give him a further Mark of your Royal Favour for his Services done in 1746, it was signified to him by one of your Majesty's principal Secretaries of State, that your Majesty had thoughts of appointing him Governor of Nova Scotia, to hold it with the Government of the Massachusets Bay.

That in 1754, in order to put a Stop to the French extending their Settlements upon the River Chaudiere as far as the head of the River Kennebeck (which is within your Majesty's Territories) he induced the Assembly of the Province under his Government to raise 800 Men for an Expedition up the latter of those Rivers, and build a Fort upon it for it's protection against the Enemy, at the Province's Expence; which Service he personally attended, and, by renewing Treaties of peace with the Indians inhabiting those Parts, who were then upon the point of breaking out into Hostilities against the English, prevented the Designs of the French from taking Effect; for which Service your Majesty was likewise pleased to order your Royal Approbation of it to be signified to him.

That having, soon after, received your Majesty's Orders to concert Measures with Mr. Lawrence, then Lieutenant Governor of Nova Scotia, for attacking the French Forts in that Province, and dispossessing them of their Encroachments there, he raised 2000 New England Troops for that Service, provided them with Artillery, and dispatched them about the middle of May for Nova Scotia, where, in seventeen Days after their Arrival, in Conjunction with about 400 of your Majesty's Regular Forces of that Province, they attacked and reduced the French Forts upon the Isthmus, and cleared the Peninsula of those dangerous Encroachments; for which Service likewise he was honoured with your Majesty's Royal Approbation.

That in the same year, your Majesty's Petitioner having received Intelligence, that the French designed to strengthen and extend their Encroachments at Crown point, and judging that the Operations then carrying on against them, would afford a favourable Opportunity to the Colonies for the Reduction of that Fort, and at the same time cause a Diversion of the French Forces in favour of the English Operations, he engaged the four Colonies of New England in an Expedition against it (to which the Province of New York afterwards acceded) to be carried on at their own Expence; which was accordingly done.

That in April 1755, the late Major General Braddock, Commander in Chief of your Majesty's Forces in North America, ordered him to take upon him the Command of an Expedition against Niagara, with his own and Major General Sir William Pepperrell's Regiments then raising in America, which he did, and afterwards prevailed on the Province of New Jersey to strengthen it with a Regiment of 500 provincial Troops raised at that Government's Expence, and marched with them to Oswego, where he arrived the 18th of

August, and stayed 'till the 24th of October, and at his Return to Albany had the honour to receive your Majesty's Commission, appointing him, upon the Death of General Braddock, to be General and Commander in Chief of your Majesty's Forces in North America.

That in September 1755 he transmitted from Oswego to your Majesty's Ministers accounts of his whole proceedings there, containing the Reasons of his not going to Niagara that Year; and in December following from New York, the Plan of Operations, determined upon there, in a Council of War, consisting of Governors and Field Officers, for the Campaign in 1756, together with his whole proceedings to that time; All which as he was informed by a Letter, he received from one of your Majesty's principal Secretaries of State, were laid before your Majesty; and he had the honour to be therein acquainted, "that the new Disposition, your Majesty had thought proper to make of the Command of your Majesty's forces in North America, was not owing to any Dissatisfaction with his Services, but on the Contrary, it was your Majesty's Intention, as a Mark of your Royal Favour, to appoint him to be Governor of Jamaica."

That your Majesty's Petitioner afterwards, during the Continuance of his late Command, exerted his best Endeavours for making preparations to carry the Plan of Operations, concerted at New York, into Execution, by raising Troops, providing timely Magazines of provisions, and Stores, both for Oswego and Lake George, and building Vessels and Whale Boats for your Majesty's Service on Lake Ontario, and procured a Body of 8700 Troops to be voted by the Colonies of New England and Province of New York for prosecuting the Expedition against Crown Point, 7000 of which were assembled on the northern Frontier of the Province of New York, between Albany and Lake George, when he quitted the Command, and were ready, with about 2000 of your Majesty's Regular Troops, to march to Tionderoge or Crown Point by the Middle or latter End of July, which, if they had done, would, in all probability, have facilitated the Reduction of Crown Point that year; and if Oswego had been strengthened with the whole Force, which your Majesty's Petitioner had provided and destined for the protection of it, and it was prevented from having by the Measures taken by his Successors, that important Place would doubtless have been preserved from falling into the Enemy's Hands.

WILLIAM SHIRLEY TO THE DUKE OF NEWCASTLE [1]

Conduit Street, Feby. 2, 1758.

MY LORD DUKE,

The Appointment to the Government of Jamaica being now perfected, according to your Grace's pleasure, I propose to present the Inclos'd petition to the King,[2] provided it meets with your Grace's Approbation, upon which, and your Grace's Support of it, I place my whole Dependence for success.

As your Grace was pleas'd, when I had the honour of waiting upon you last Week to give me a permission to wait upon your Grace in this, for a short Audience, I beg your Grace to favour me with a very short one to morrow Morning as early, as would suit your Grace's Conveniency.

I have the honour to be with the most Gratefull sense of your Grace's favours, and the most Dutifull respect,

My Lord,
Your Grace's most Oblig'd,
and most Devoted Servant,
W. SHIRLEY.

His Grace the Duke of Newcastle etc.

---

[1] *B. M.*, *Additional Manuscript 32877, 315.* A transcript is in the Library of Congress.

[2] The petition was for the command of a regiment in the royal service, as the regiment formerly commanded by Shirley had been reduced. See Shirley to Newcastle, Feb. 10, opposite. Shirley was not a favorite with the Duke of Cumberland, who had been strongly prejudiced against him.

Endorsed:
  Febry. 2d, 1758.
    Mr. Gl. Shirley,
(with a Petition to the King.)

WILLIAM SHIRLEY TO THE DUKE OF NEWCASTLE [1]

Conduit Street, Feby. 10, 1758.

My Lord Duke,

As troubling your Grace with an account of my present Situation in a few lines may save your Grace time in the Audience, which I have requested your Grace to favour me with, I beg leave to do it.

My removal, my Lord, from the Chief Command of H. My's Forces in N. A., when I was entering upon Operations, in which I had conceiv'd hopes of Success, was a great Mortification to me; but allay'd by the Assurances, I had then given me, of H. My's Gracious acceptance of my Services, and intention to honour me with a further Mark of his Royal Favour.

Since that, my Lord, my late Government has been given to another, and my Regiment reduc'd.

The former of these, to which I was promoted by your Grace's favour, I influenc'd upon every Occasion to exert itself in a signal manner for his Majesty's service, and am not conscious of having incurr'd a forfeiture of it by any wrong Act of Civil Government during my Administration. The latter his Majesty was pleas'd to bestow upon me for some National Services done in the last War; and I am not conscious, My Lord, of having forfeited that mark of his Royal favour by any Demerit in the present War; On the contrary I have been principally instrumental in every part of it; which has been attended with Success in North America.

What makes me more sensible, my Lord, of the loss of my

---

[1] *B. M., Additional Manuscript 32877, 416.* A transcript is in the Library of Congress.

Posts is, that I have not acquir'd any fortune in them; so that upon being depriv'd of my Government and Regiment, and failing of the Post, which H. M. was pleas'd to design for me I am left without any Support, after having spent upwards of Sixteen Years in faithfull Services to the Crown; the Effects of some of which the Nation still feels.

I am therefore, my Lord, encourag'd to hope that upon my petition to His Majesty, he may be graciously pleas'd to take my case into his Royal Consideration, and replace me in the Command of one of his Regiments with some other mark of his Royal Favour; provided your Grace shall be pleas'd to favour me with your support of my Petition, when deliver'd; upon which I place my dependence for it's success.

The Expressions of Esteem, with which your Grace has been pleas'd to honour me upon former Occasions, together with Assurances of Protection upon future ones, encourage me to hope that your Grace will honour me with the continuance of your Support.

I have the honour to be with the Deepest Sense of your Grace's Favours, and most Dutifull Respect,
>My Lord,
>>Your Grace's most Oblig'd,
>>>and
>>>most Devoted Servant
>>>>>W. Shirley.

His Grace the Duke of Newcastle etc.

Endorsed:
Conduit Street Feb. 11th, 1758.
Mr. Shirley. R. 12th.

WILLIAM SHIRLEY TO THE DUKE OF NEWCASTLE [1]

Conduit Street, April 1, 1758.

My Lord Duke,

I beg leave to acquaint your Grace in this way, as I conceive it will least trespass upon your time, that having, with your Grace's leave, deliver'd my petition to the King (the prayer of which was for the Command of a Regiment, and some other mark of his Royal favour) his Majesty was pleas'd to direct Lord Ligonier to acquaint me, "that he did not design to employ me in *a Military way*."

The reason my Lord, as far as I can learn, of his Majesty's not being dispos'd to give me a Regiment is, that I was not bred a Soldier: But I don't apprehend, his Majesty is indispos'd to imploy me in some other way, especially as it was his Intention, when I was recall'd from the Command of his forces in North America, to give me a distinguishing mark of his Royal favour in consideration of my Services; and I can't but hope from his Majesty's wonted Goodness to his Old Servants, that upon your Grace's recommendation of me to his Royal favour, he will continue it to me; and not discard me after having spent so many Years in faithfull Services to the Crown, both in the last, and present Warr, without some provision for my comfortable Support, suitable to the Rank, and Character, in which I have had the honour to serve his Majesty.

The favour therefore, I would humbly beg of your Grace, is that your Grace will be pleas'd to recommend me to his Majesty for some such Mark of his Royal favour; and untill provision can be made for me in his Service, that he will be graciously pleas'd to allow me a Pension for my immediate Support.

My experience of your Grace's past Goodness, and the Assurances of it upon future Occasions, with which your

[1] *B. M., Additional Manuscript 32879, 15.* A transcript is in the Library of Congress.

Grace hath been pleas'd to favour me, encourage me to make this Application, and the need, I stand in, of Support, will I hope, plead my Excuse with your Grace.

I beg leave further to mention to your Grace, that both General Braddock, my predecessor, and the Earl of Loudoun my successor had, each of them, £1000 advanc'd to them by the Crown for the Expences of their Outset and £2000 for Contingent Occasions; but that being in America, when I was appointed I had no benefit of this kind, tho' my Extraordinary Expences requir'd the like Allowance, as much as either of theirs, and my Circumstances more, which Considerations, I hope, will have some weight.

I have the honour to be with the most Dutifull Respect,
My Lord,
Your Grace's most oblig'd,
and
most Devoted Servant,
W. SHIRLEY.

His Grace the Duke of Newcastle.

Endorsed:
Conduit Street Apl. 1st, 1758.
MR. SHIRLEY.

WILLIAM SHIRLEY TO THE DUKE OF NEWCASTLE [1]

Conduit Street, May 12, 1758.
MY LORD DUKE,

The Deep sense, I have of the late Assurances, which your Grace has been pleas'd to give me of your favour, and the perfect reliance, I have upon your Grace's Intention to conferr soon upon me the Mark of it, which your Grace designs me, would make me wait with pleasure your Grace's own time, without troubling your Grace with one word tending

[1] *B. M.*, *Additional Manuscript 32880, 48.* A transcript is in the Library of Congress.

to hasten it : But as I have not been able to save any thing out of my late Employments to support me out of his Majesty's Service, and am now divested of them, I hope, my Lord, the necessity of my Circumstances, and my faithful Services will plead my Excuse with your Grace for begging of you to take the first favourable Opportunity to bestow on me whatever mark of your favour, your Grace is pleas'd to intend for me.

I have the honour to be with the most Gratefull sense of your Grace's favours, and the most Dutifull Respect
My Lord,
Your Grace's most Oblig'd,
and
most Devoted Servant,
W. SHIRLEY.

His Grace the Duke of Newcastle.

Endorsed :
May 12th, **1758**
MR. GENL. SHIRLEY.

WILLIAM SHIRLEY TO THE DUKE OF NEWCASTLE [1]

Conduit Street, Jany. 13th, 1759.

MY LORD DUKE,

I beg your Grace's favourable Consideration of the inclos'd Memorial, and that your Grace will be pleas'd to order it to be read at the Board the next Treasury Day.

What incourages me to take the liberty of troubling your Grace with this request, is that I hope the Allowances pray'd for in the Memorial [2] will, for the reasons therein set forth, most clearly appear to your Grace to be just, and due

[1] *B. M., Additional Manuscript 32887, 145.* A transcript is in the Library of Congress.

[2] The memorial presented was for allowances for services in America and expenses attendant upon the same, but the editor has been unable to obtain a copy of the text of the application.

to me; and until they are granted, I shall be so greatly distress'd in my Circumstances as to be unable to proceed to the Government, his Majesty has been graciously pleas'd to give me as a mark of his Royal favour for my past services.[1]

This my Lord, will, I hope; plead my Excuse to your Grace for the Trouble, I give you; and induce your Grace to add this Instance to the former ones of your Goodness to me.

I am with the most Grateful sense of the protection, with which your Grace has ever honour'd me, and the most Dutiful Respect,

My Lord, Your Grace's most Oblig'd and most Devoted Servant

W. SHIRLEY.

His Grace the Duke of Newcastle.

Endorsed:
Conduit Street Janry. 13, 1759.
Genl. Shirley.
R 14th.

WILLIAM SHIRLEY TO THE DUKE OF NEWCASTLE [2]

Conduit Street, April 17th, 1759.

MY LORD DUKE,

Having this Afternoon been informed, that your Grace is perswaded, I had no Commission for the Chief Command of His Majesty's Forces in North America, as I represented in my late Memorial [3] to the Lords of Treasury, I had; the extreme Concern I am under that your Grace should continue in that mistake a minute longer than it is in my power

[1] The government granted Shirley was that of the Bahamas, a poor reward for this "strenuous champion of British interests" in America.

[2] *B. M., Additional Manuscript 32890, 120.* A transcript is in the Library of Congress.

[3] Probably the memorial mentioned in letter of Jan. 13, *ante,* 601, and again referred to in Shirley to Newcastle of June 6, 1759, *post,* p. 603.

to prevent it, makes me take the liberty to acquaint your Grace that I have produc'd my Commission for that Command in the Treasury Office to Mr. Martin, who, I doubt not, will make a satisfactory Report to your Grace upon that Point. That I have likewise produc'd it in the Secretary at War's Office, where the Deputy Secretary compar'd it with the Register of the Earl of Loudoun's Commission there, who was my immediate Successor in the Command, and found it of as large an Extent, as His Lordship's. That he has acquainted me since [that] Lord Barrington is fully satisfy'd of the same, And that the occasion of his representing to your Grace, that I had really no Commission for that Command from home, was owing to his not being Appriz'd that my Commission was register'd in his Office, as in fact it is.

I intreat your Grace to be perswaded, that I am incapable of abusing your Grace's Goodness to me by deceiving your Grace in any one point of his Majesty's Service, which I have had the Honour to be employ'd in; And that I shall ever be with the most gratefull Sense of all your favours to me, and the highest Respect,

My Lord Duke
Your Grace's most Oblig'd,
and most Devoted Servant.
W. SHIRLEY.

His Grace the Duke of Newcastle, etc.

Endorsed:
Conduit Str. Apl. 17, 1759.
MR. SHIRLEY.

WILLIAM SHIRLEY TO THE DUKE OF NEWCASTLE [1]

June 6, 1759.

MY LORD DUKE,

I beg leave to return your Grace thanks for obtaining his Majesty's Warrant for my Equipage money.

[1] *B. M., Additional Manuscript 32891, 455.* A transcript is in the Library of Congress.

When I troubled your Grace with my other Memorial praying for a reimbursment of £589, I was inform'd it would probably be referr'd, and if reported to be a debt due to me from the Crown, that my prayer for repayment in the Treasury would not be deem'd improper: But as I perceive, I have been too importunate in it, I shall not urge it further to your Grace, being perfectly sensible of the very great Obligations, I am already under to your Grace for the many signal marks of favour, you have been pleas'd to honour me with; and for which I shall ever remain with the most gratefull sense of them, and the most dutifull Respect

   My Lord,
     Your Grace's most Obliged
       and
      most Devoted Servant.

His Grace the Duke of Newcastle.   W. SHIRLEY.

Endorsed:
 June 6th, 1759. MR. SHIRLEY.
R 8th.

WILLIAM SHIRLEY TO THE DUKE OF NEWCASTLE [1]

June 8th, 1759.

MY LORD DUKE,

 I shall not trouble your Grace further about my last Memorial, being perfectly sensible of the very great Obligations, I am already under to your Grace, for the many signal marks of favour, which you have honour'd me with, and for which I shall ever remain with a most gratefull sense of them, and most Dutifull Respect,

   My Lord,
     Your Grace's most Oblig'd,
       and
      most Devoted Servant.
        W. SHIRLEY.

[1] *B. M., Additional Manuscript 32891, 504.* A transcript is in the Library of Congress.

P.S.   The Earl of Stirling being desirous to have the honour of being introduc'd to your Grace, I shall take the liberty of presenting him this morning.

Endorsed: June 8th. 1759.   MR. GL. SHIRLEY.

WILLIAM SHIRLEY TO THE DUKE OF NEWCASTLE [1]

New Providence, Bahama Islands.
May 19, 1760.

MY LORD DUKE,

The short Notice, I have of the Departure of this Vessell for Charleston, S. Carolina; thro' which lies the only Conveyance, we have from this place for Turtle by Ships bound directly for London, allows me no more time, than to have the honour of acquainting your Grace, that I have sent your Grace a Turtle, by this Opportunity: which is the first, that has offer'd for sending your Grace one since the season of the Year has been warm enough, and our Turtling Vessells have brought in any of a proper size for England, to this Port.

I hope it will get safe to England and have the honour of your Grace's kind Acceptance of it.

I am with the highest Respect,
My Lord,
Your Grace's most Oblig'd
and most Devoted Servant

W. SHIRLEY.

His Grace the Duke of Newcastle, etc.

Endorsed:
New Providence.
May 19th, 1760.   GOVR. SHIRLEY.
R Octr. 8th.

---

[1] *B. M., Additional Manuscript 33067, 138.*   A transcript is in the Library of Congress.

INDEX

INDEX

INDEX

Champlain (Lake), Crown Point, *and* Nova Scotia.

Campaign of 1755–1756, in general, II. 127–396. *See* Abercromby, Braddock, Crown Point, Champlain (Lake), Johnson, Loudoun, Niagara, Oswego, Shirley, Six Nations, Ticonderoga.

Canada, conquest of, suggested by Shirley (1746), I. 163, 203, 206, 220, 284; proclamation for conquest of, I. 323; plan of operations against, I. 329, 333; movement against, abandoned (1747), I. 386, 393; release of captives in, I. 506; plans against (1755), II. 128–129, 197, 238, 296, 305, 379, 426, 442; efforts of French to extend, II. 150, 240, 350, 380.

Canso (Canseau), women and children leave, I. 132, 137; terms of capitulation of, I. 147; importance of, I. 152, 191; resettled, I. 199, 208; stores sent to, I. 221. *See* Annapolis Royal, Cape Breton, Louisbourg.

Cape Breton Island, Shirley suggests neutrality of, in difficulties with France, I. 137; originally a part of Nova Scotia, I. 161; advance upon, urged, I. 159, 161, 167–169; importance of, to French, I. 177; movement against, I. 181, 193, 196; should not be abandoned, I. 339; Shirley requests coal lands in, I. 291. *See* Louisbourg.

Cape Sable Indians, I. 135, 139, 151, 157, 233, 258, 283, 348, 351.

Capitulation, of Louisbourg, I. 233, 234, 239. *See* Louisbourg. Of Oswego, II. 521. *See* Oswego.

Carrying Place, between Kennebec and Chaudiere rivers, II. 33, 53, 57, 73. *See* Great Carrying Place, Oneida Carrying Place.

Castle William, ordnance for, I. 93; II. 11, 24; Shirley appoints committee to supervise repairs on, I. 93n.; defense of, I. 100; deserters from, I. 152; to be fortified, I. 158.

Catawba Indians, efforts to secure friendship of, II. 390, 396, 398.

Cathcart, Charles, Baron, I. 17, 19n., 25.

Champlain, Samuel de, on the boundaries of Acadia, II. 55.

Champlain, Lake, campaign against fortresses on, suggested, I. 343; English fortress on, advised by Shirley, II. 67; importance of, emphasized, I. 297, 348; II. 181, 215, 239, 308; plan for campaign for control of, II. 424; company of rangers for, II. 436; naval forces on, II. 454, 471; victory of Capt. Rogers on, II. 491.

Chandler, John, Massachusetts commissioner at Albany, II. 60.

Chapin, Capt., II. 91.

Chapman, Major, II. 493.

Chappeaurous Bay. *See* Gabarus.

Charlemont, Mass., defense of, II. 87.

Charlestown, N. H. *See* Number 4.

Charter government for Nova Scotia. *See* Nova Scotia.

Chaudiere River, settlements on, II. 57; route to Canada, II. 33, 53, 329.

Chebucto, French withdrawal from, I. 360.

Cherokee Indians, importance in South, II. 355, 365; induced to take arms against the French, II. 390, 394, 396, 398, 416.

Choate, John, Massachusetts commissioner to Indian conference at Albany, I. 129, 429.

Clarke, Robert, fugitive from Massachusetts justice, I. 212.

Claus, Daniel, informs Johnson regarding Shirley's agents among the Indians, II. 244n.; familiar with conditions in Pennsylvania, 439, 441.

Clinton, Govr. George, letters of, I. 425, 449, 487; letters to, I. 392, 393, 398, 399, 426, 427, 441; promises to advance loyalty of Indians to Crown, I. 425; conditions of Indian and military affairs, I. 450–456; urges efforts to offset French work among the Canadian Indians, I. 487; mentioned, I. 203, 230, 286, 294; reclaims Six Nations from French sympathies, I. 298; I. 301, 302, 311, 345, 353; management of Six Nations committed to, I. 427; I. 429, 437, 451, 508; II. 183; notice of, I. 425n.

Coal land in Cape Breton, Shirley requests grant of, I. 291.

Colden, Cadwallader, informs Shirley as to conditions in New York, I. 441.

Cole, Lt. Col. Edward, II. 254.

Colonial union, for military purposes, suggested, II. 12n., 19; advocated by Shirley, I. xxvii, xxxiii; II. 26, 30, 43, 59, 95, 114, 138, 204; common fund suggested, II. 101, 204; Massachusetts Assembly on, II. 51; Franklin on, II. 103; Albany Congress on (1754), II. 111–118; Congress at New York proposed (1755), II. 251, 252; Provincial troops suggested, II. 225–226, 238.

Colrain, Mass., plans for defense of, II. 87.

INDEX

Commissioners for joint action against Indians (1748), I. 419.

Commissioners for Indian conference at Albany (1754), II. 60.

Committee of War (Massachusetts), Loudoun to, II. 561.

Congress, Provincial, at Albany (1747), I. 390; (1754), II. 111–118.

Connecticut, a refuge for fugitives from Massachusetts, I. 212, 230; commissioners for conference at Middletown, I. 419; expenses in King George's war, I. 460; quotas of troops (1754), II. 21; (1755), II. 238; attacked by Indians, II. 88. See Law, Jonathan.

Cook, Dr. (of Boston), I. 3; his memorial to the House of Commons, I. 4.

Coos, N.H., to be fortified, II. 141.

Cornwallis, Edward, I. 488; Shirley remonstrates against favors shown to, I. 503, 505.

Cosby, William, I. 442.

Council (British), Shirley to Lord President of, I. 93; approves conduct of Shirley, I. 142. See Crown, Lords Justices, Trade, Lords of, and individual ministers, members of the council.

Council of Massachusetts. See Massachusetts, General Court of.

Council of War at New York (1755), disposition of remnant of Braddock's army, II. 214; at Fort Edward, II. 499.

Counterfeiters from Massachusetts hiding in Connecticut, I. 212, 230.

Courcelle, Lt. Genl. Daniel de Rény Sieur de, erects Fort Frontenac, II. 351.

Court, Great and General. See Massachusetts.

Court martials, Shirley on the establishment of, I. 194, 195

Credit, Provincial. See Land banks, Paper currency.

Crown (British), right to forests in Massachusetts, I. 6; loyalty of New England to, I. 20; instructions to Gov. Shirley, I. 43, 73, 144; Gov. Belcher not always subservient to, I. 100; French declaration of war against (1744), I. 112; declares war against France (1744), I. 117; (1756), II. 450; approves conduct of Shirley, I. 142; Shirley outlines services rendered to, I. 505; II. 2, 587, 502; money granted Massachusetts by, I. 506; II. 7; Massachusetts to, II. 24; claim of, on Frontenac, II. 350; grant to colonies, II. 463; petitions of Shirley to, II. 588, 590, 592.

See Council (British), Lords Justices, Bedford, Holderness, Newcastle, and other ministers by name.

Crown Point, I. 297, 341, 349, 369; II. 134, 207; plans against, I. 302, 343n., 369, 392, 393, 403, 426; II. 120, 146, 162, 186n., 189, 272, 308, 424, 468, 471, 503; French plans against, I. 468; Sir William Johnson on, II. 152n., Braddock's plans against, II. 186n., 203; importance of, I. 478; II. 67, 137, 181, 189, 282n.; Sir William Johnson to attack, II. 136, 152–154, 158; refuses, II. 330n.; French at (1756), II. 456; forces available for campaign against (1755–1756), II. 219, 226, 372, 454, 469; Shirley urges movement against, I. xxviii; II. 530–532; conditions explained to Abercromby II. 471.

Cuba, troops sail for, I. 81.

Cumberland, Fort (Maryland), danger of attack upon (1756), II. 447.

Currency, Shirley on, I. xxiv. See Paper currency.

Cussenac (Cushenoc), English settlement on Kennebec River, II. 78.

Cutt, Richard, Jr., instructed by Shirley to enlist volunteers for Louisbourg expedition, I. 181.

Dagworthy, Capt. John, rank of, II. 372n.; compared with Washington, II. 412.

Danforth, Samuel, II. 72.

Declarations of war, French (1744), I. 112; British (1744), I. 117; (1756), II. 450.

De Lancey, Govr. James, at Shirley's conference with Indians, I. 429; arranges conference with Six Nations, II. 40; Shirley consults, regarding expedition against French and Indians under Sir William Johnson, II. 133; asked as to reluctance of New York to coöperate with Shirley, II. 182; mentioned, II. 96, 111, 153n., 167, 169, 174, 199, 251, 496; sides with Johnson against Shirley, II. 360.

De Lancey, Oliver, II. 169.

Delaware Indians, ravages in Pennsylvania, II. 439.

Delaware territories. See Pennsylvania.

Derby, Capt., in Boston riot, I. 192.

Deserters from Castle William, I. 152.

Detroit, Shirley's plans regarding, II. 228, 292.

De Young, John Batiste, states number of French troops at Quebec and in Canada (1745), I. 262.

INDEX

INDEX

INDEX

loaning Rhode Island vessels for Louisbourg expedition, I. 331; as to the Albany conference, I. 127n.; naval force requested from, I. 172; troops requested from, I. 319n.; as to commission for Edward Kinnicut, I. 360, 364; mentioned, II. 157.

Grenville, James, II. 14.

Gridley, Col. Richard, praised by Shirley for work on Louisbourg expedition, I. 288; commands Provincial artillery at Albany, II. 479; on service of Provincials, II. 502; decried by Loudoun, II. 509; notice of, II. 168n.

Gulston, Joseph, feeling toward Govr. Belcher, I. 16n.

"Gypsy," Mrs. (Govr. Belcher's name for Mrs. Shirley), I. 11n.

Hale, Robert, letters to, II. 131, 139; is to solicit aid for Crown Point expedition from Govr. Wentworth, II. 142.

Half Moon, II. 496.

Halifax, Earl of, approves conduct of Shirley, II. 5, 14, 110; plan for Indian settlements given to, II. 123; shown the importance to England and America of immediate action against the French, II. 531.

Halifax, Fort, II. 121n., 136.

Halifax, N.S., II. 24. See Chebucto.

Halkett, Sir Peter, II. 99, 120; ordered to Virginia, II. 134; notice of, II. 99n.

Halkett's regiment, ordered to New York, II. 216; at Albany, II. 296.

Hamilton, Govr. James, is informed by Shirley of French preparations to resist Colonial advance, I. 468; mentioned, II. 95, 110, 377, 385.

"Hard Money Colony," I. xxiv. See Massachusetts.

Hardy, Govr. Charles, on garrisons among Indians and provisions for raising troops, II. 325; Shirley to, II. 305, 324, 460; meeting with Shirley hoped for, II. 297; sides with Johnson against Shirley, II. 361; will act in harmony with Shirley, II. 380; mentioned, II. 432, 496, 505; notice of, II. 305n.

Hawke (Hawks), John, I. 437; II. 91.

Hawley, Major, II. 156.

Hector, British ship, I. 264.

Hendrick, Mohawk chief, at battle of Lake George, II. 256; Shirley's conference with, II. 355.

Herkimer, Col. Johan Jost, furnishes provisions for Shirley, II. 235.

Hoar, Major William, II. 335.

Holderness, Robert D'Arcy, Earl, orders Shirley to resist French, II. 12; Shirley to, on military matters and French encroachments in Maine, II. 18, 52; mentioned, II. 72, 100, 134; notice of, II. 12n.

Holmes, Capt. Charles, II. 518.

Hood, Capt. Samuel, II. 518.

Hooper, Samuel, of Marblehead, I. 174.

Hooper, Silas, I. 4.

Hoosack, Mass., defense of, II. 88.

Hopkins, Govr. Stephen, gives action of Rhode Island on Shirley's call for troops, II. 417; letters to, II. 385, 445, 483, 562, 578; mentioned, II. 282n., 429, 528, 556.

Howard, James, to Shirley, II. 143n.

Hubbard, Thomas, II. 25.

Hunter, Governor Robert, I. 442.

Hunt (Laforay), Capt., II. 426.

Huron Lake, Shirley plans to secure, II. 223, 228.

Hutchinson, Thomas, friendship with Shirley, I. iii, 129; as Speaker of Massachusetts House of Representatives, I. 350; at time of Boston riot, I. 407; Massachusetts Commissioner to Rhode Island, II. 140.

Impressment, in New Hampshire, I. 192n.; authorized by Shirley for Louisbourg expedition, I. 200; uprising at Boston regarding effort to obtain seamen for British ships (1747), I. 408–418; relief desired, I. 420; II. 287; for Crown Point expedition (1756), II. 434, 520; no impress to be made without consent of General Court, II. 526.

Indented servants, difficulties regarding enlistment of (in Maryland), II. 386 and note, 391 and note, 399n.; discussion of question with Govr. Morris of Pennsylvania, II. 405–411; Shirley refers question to Henry Fox, II. 413.

Indians (general), English relations with, I. 115, 493; in Maine, II. 33, 49, 52, 69, 71, 364; in New Hampshire, I. 248; French relations with, I. 150, 209, 247, 264, 392, 485, 487; II. 12, 34, 86, 133, 136, 368, 374; treaties with, I. 138, 399, 425, 429; II. 71, 74, 77; friendly relations urged, II. 123, 291n., 367; in Western Massachusetts, II. 84, 86, 285; in South and West, II. 364; effect of Braddock's defeat upon, II. 218; Shirley's efforts with, II. 355, 374; Indian situation explained by Shirley to Abercromby

INDEX

INDEX

INDEX

Monongahela, battle of, II. 208; Govr. Dinwiddie on, II. 211; effect of, II. 218–220; loss of arms at, II. 298; inquiry into behavior of troops at, II. 311, 316. *See* Braddock; Duquesne, Fort.

Montague, Capt., II. 7, 11.

Montreal, threatened, II. 135; possibility of capture of, II. 295, 308, 383.

Montresor, James, applied to for engineers, II. 423; at council of war, II. 453; consulted, II. 460, 473, 539.

Morpain (Morpang), Captain, port of Louisbourg, I. 274.

Morris, Lewis, II. 123n., 184, 482.

Morris, Govr. Robert Hunter, letters of, II. 12n., 130n., 330n., 333, 366, 388, 391, 399n., 431, 486, 578; letters to, II. 95, 110, 130, 133n., 232n., 248n., 249n., 326n., 327, 330, 393, 399, 405, 438, 481; states needs of Pennsylvania, II. 331; sympathy with Shirley, I. xxx; II. 431; proclamation regarding Delaware Indians, II. 478.

Morris, Roger, II. 131, 209, 369, 436; notice of, II. 369n.

Naval officer in New England, post sought for Shirley, I. xxii, 11; for his son, I. 37, 86.

Navy, importance of, I. xxv, 148, 173, 180, 196, 200, 205, 214, 224, 228, 334, 423; II. 149; on Lake Champlain, II. 168, 176; on Lake Ontario, II. 178, 187n., 200, 227, 298, 344; feeling of Shirley regarding, II. 202, 228, 249, 344, 537.

Necessity, Fort, Washington surrenders at, II. 82.

Neutrality of Cape Breton and New England proposed in 1744, I. 134; neutrality of Indians, II. 250n. *See* Indians.

Newcastle, Thomas Pelham, Duke of, letters of, I. 12, 17, 121, 155, 386, 401; letters to, I. 1, 2, 4, 5, 8, 10, 11, 13, 15, 20, 22, 38, 39, 79, 86, 89, 115, 116, 125, 131, 145, 153, 157, 159n., 161, 196, 221, 251, 254, 265, 273, 280, 287, 291, 293, 320n., 327, 332, 334, 336, 339, 395, 397, 404, 420, 424, 457, 493, 499, 505, 508; II. 1, 4, 7, 587, 596, 597, 599, 600, 601, 602, 603, 604, 605; quarrels with Duke of Bedford, I. xxvii; notice of, I. 12.

New England, attitude toward Govr. Belcher, I. 13, 17; loyalty to Crown, I. 20; neutrality of, proposed, I. 134; captures Louisbourg, I. xxv; paper currency in, I. 462. *See* Connecticut, Massachusetts, New Hampshire, *and* Rhode Island.

New Hampshire, appointment as governor sought by Shirley, I. 15; troops sought from (1744–1745), I. 154, 177, 190, 184, 187; (1755), II. 132; grant for Crown Point expedition, II. 426n. *See* Wentworth, Benning.

New York, commissioners from, I. 318, 419; Shirley requests post of governor of, I. 508; interest in Massachusetts Indian warfare, II. 91, 128; aid requested of, II. 138, 170n., 287; troops for Crown Point expedition, II. 156, 190n.; difficulties with Shirley, I. xxix; II. 324, 378. *See* Clinton, George; Hardy, Charles; Johnson, Sir William.

New York City, proceedings of council at, II. 214; Congress at, suggested, II. 252, 326n.; Council of War at, II. 371.

Niagara, plan for campaign against, II. 145, 146n., 164, 179, 184, 187, 189, 196, 215, 219, 249, 268n., 356, 457; Braddock's plans regarding, II. 147, 154n., 155, 203; danger from the French, II. 180, 214, 240, 261; importance of, II. 228, 393, 471; Shirley to command expedition of 1756 against, II. 404.

Nichols, Major Ebenezer, wounded at battle of Lake George, II. 258.

Norridgewalk (Norridgewock) Indians, Shirley to, I. 247; relations with the French, II. 33; mentioned, II. 69, 73, 74, 102.

Northampton, Mass., boundaries of, II. 90; Indian troubles near, II. 83–89, 102.

North Carolina, treatment of Indians by, II. 364; troops of, II. 457.

Northey, Sir Edward, I. 418.

Norris, Isaac, II. 171n.

Nottingham, British frigate, II. 518.

Nova Scotia, arms for, I. 456; boundaries of, II. 10, 55; plan of government for, I. 280, 291, 328, 336, 470, 472; need of troops for, I. 163, 402, 488; II. 347, 464; military operations in, I. 202, 210, 220, 222, 251, 351, 358, 386; II. 32, 119, 196, 225, I. 285; Shirley requests governorship of, I. 503; French encroachments upon, II. 62, 69, 128, 150, 450; settlement of English in, II. 63; French to be expelled from forts of, II. 128, 134, 145, 196, 206, 308; importance of, II. 148; Shirley explains situation in, to Abercromby (1756), II. 472.

Number 4 (Charlestown, N.H.), defense of, II. 89.

INDEX

INDEX

INDEX

INDEX

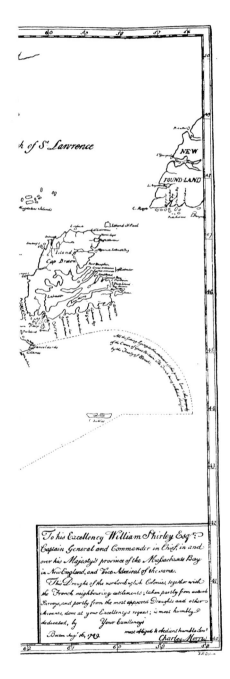

AND DEDICATED TO GOVERNOR WILLIAM SHIRLEY